Internet of Medicine for Smart Healthcare

Scrivener Publishing
100 Cummings Center, Suite 541J
Beverly, MA 01915-6106

Publishers at Scrivener
Martin Scrivener (martin@scrivenerpublishing.com)
Phillip Carmical (pcarmical@scrivenerpublishing.com)

Internet of Medicine for Smart Healthcare

Edited by

Abhishek Kumar

Narayan Vyas

Pramod Singh Rathore

Abhineet Anand

and

Pooja Dixit

Scrivener Publishing

WILEY

This edition first published 2025 by John Wiley & Sons, Inc., 111 River Street, Hoboken, NJ 07030, USA and Scrivener Publishing LLC, 100 Cummings Center, Suite 541J, Beverly, MA 01915, USA

For more information about Scrivener publications please visit www.scrivenerpublishing.com.

Wiley Global Headquarters
111 River Street, Hoboken, NJ 07030, USA

For details of our global editorial offices, customer services, and more information about Wiley products visit us at www.wiley.com.

Library of Congress Cataloging-in-Publication Data

ISBN 978-1-394-27223-5

Front cover images supplied by Pixabay.com
Cover design by Russell Richardson

Set in size of 11pt and Minion Pro by Manila Typesetting Company, Makati, Philippines

Printed in the USA

10 9 8 7 6 5 4 3 2 1

Contents

Preface

This book is organized into 22 chapters. In *Internet of Medicine (IOM) for Smart Healthcare*, we usher in a dialogue that melds the computational prowess of artificial intelligence (AI) with the nuanced realm of healthcare. Within 22 chapters, each is a beacon of innovation, exploring how AI is reshaping patient care, from diagnostics to treatment and beyond. As the editors, we have witnessed a tapestry of research that not only pushes the boundaries of technology but also tethers it closely to the human condition. From the micro-scale of genetic data to the macro-impact of wearable technology, the contributions herein address both the potential and the challenges of these converging worlds, underlining the importance of ethical considerations as we tread forward. This book stands as an invitation to embrace the future—a future where technology and healthcare converge to better human lives.

Delving into the intersection of omics data and AI, Chapter 1 illustrates how integrating vast biological datasets can refine neurodynamic exercises for PIVD patients, offering insights into personalized care strategies that yield both immediate and lasting therapeutic effects. Chapter 2, based on the exploration of graph-based methods in biological networks, reveals how AI can enhance the treatment of cervicogenic headache patients, optimizing reflex release techniques to reduce pain and disability more effectively than ever before. Focusing on the potent synergy of AI with primal reflex release techniques, Chapter 3 discusses the role of AI in quantifying the effects of such interventions on SI joint mobility, providing data-driven insights for clinicians. Next, Chapter 4 probes into the future of AI in bioinformatics, projecting its transformative impact on understanding and addressing neck pain and stiffness through innovative reflex release techniques. In Chapter 5, evolutionary computation underscores the value of bioinformatics in dissecting the effects of neurodynamic exercises, offering new avenues for treating pain and disability in carpal tunnel syndrome patients. In Chapter 6, AI and nanotechnology are presented as pivotal drivers for sustainable development in healthcare, with discussions centered on their imperative roles in ushering a new era of medical innovation. Chapter 7 basically synthesizes AI and yoga therapy as holistic approaches to sleep pattern enhancement, presenting a scientific approach that could redefine therapeutic strategies for better health. Next, Chapter 8 focused on ethical considerations in AI, and bioinformatics are dissected in the context of analyzing the rehabilitation effects of the SHAT device on stroke patients, underscoring the importance of ethical data handling. In Chapter 9, the AI's transformative impact on drug discovery and repurposing is discussed, with a focus on its potential to improve the long-term quality of life for patients with cervicogenic headaches. In Chapter 10, the antineoplastic potential of edible mushrooms is examined through the lens of AI, showcasing how advancements in AI can elucidate the polysaccharides' modes of action and their health benefits. Chapter 11 evaluates the role of AI in enhancing the bioremediation processes of dairy effluent using microalgae, highlighting the innovative use of resulting lipid byproducts. Chapter 12 focused on the smart collision recognition, and reporting system employing GPS and GSM technology is introduced, signifying how AI can leverage automation to enhance safety measures. In Chapter 13, the evolution and consequential impact of wearable devices in healthcare are chronicled, with particular attention to their anatomical integration and their expansive influence on medical science. In Chapter 14, the current overview of wearable healthcare technology delves into the physiological and biochemical intricacies of these devices, emphasizing their role in proactive health monitoring. In Chapter 15, techniques for real-time data acquisition and analysis are detailed, revealing their microbiological and immunological aspects and their revolutionary impact on health data collection. Chapter 16, based on real-time data applications in healthcare, discusses the groundbreaking implications for pharmacological interventions, heralding a new wave of data-informed treatment protocols. In Chapter 17, the strategies for the integration of wearable technology with healthcare systems are outlined, with a focus on the pathological considerations vital for successful device adoption. In Chapter 18, the challenges and solutions surrounding healthcare system integration are examined from a histological perspective, addressing the nuanced difficulties of incorporating wearable devices into medical routines. In Chapter 19, the wearable technology's role in mental health monitoring and management is dissected, providing psychiatric insights into the adoption and efficacy of these innovative tools. In Chapter 20, the ethical considerations in mental health data collection and analysis are scrutinized, discussing the delicate balance between technology's benefits and the privacy of the individuals. Next, Chapter 21 discusses the ethical challenges and guidelines necessary for the deployment of AI in healthcare, offering perspectives from urology and gastroenterology on how to navigate this complex landscape. Finally, Chapter 22 concludes the book, and a forward-looking perspective highlights the future directions and opportunities within AI-driven healthcare, inspiring family medicine and anaesthesiology to integrate AI in their practices.

To conclude, we extend heartfelt gratitude to all the authors who contributed their expertise to this volume. Their dedication to advancing our understanding and their commitment to ethical practice in Internet of Medicine and AI-driven healthcare sets the groundwork for the future of medicine. This book is dedicated to all those who stand at the forefront of technological innovation and healthcare, who seek to push the boundaries of what is possible for the benefit of patients worldwide.

Dr. Abhishek Kumar
Department of CSE, Chandigarh University, Mohali, India
Narayan Vyas
Department of Computer Science and Application, Vivekananda Global University, Jaipur, India
Dr. Pramod Singh Rathore
Department of Computer and Communication Engineering, Manipal University, Jaipur, India
Dr. Abhineed Anand
Professor & Dean Computer Science and Engineering, Bahara University, Waknaghat, Solan (HP), India
Pooja Dixit
Department of Computer Science, Sophia Girls' College (Autonomous), Ajmer, India

1

Omics Data Integration in AI System for Immediate and Carryover Effects of Neurodynamic Exercises on SLR Ranges Among Acute PIVD Patients

Durga Bahuguna, Vaibhav Agarwal* and Manish Kumar Jha

Department of Physiotherapy, Himalayan Institute of Medical Sciences, Swami Rama Himalayan University, Jolly Grant, Dehradun, India

Abstract

Prolapsed interverterbral disc (PIVD) is a disease that occurs when there is a rupture of annulus fibrosus, which further leads to an effusion of nucleus purposes. In order to obtain a more thorough knowledge of a biological system, data from several omics technologies—such as transcriptomics, proteomics, metabolomics, and genomics—are combined in a process known as "omics data integration." Thus, different medical data of each patient are collected, which makes easy for their treatment. The aim of this study is to analyze the immediate and carryover effects of neurodynamic exercises on straight leg raise test ranges among acute PIVD patients using omics data integration in artificial intelligence (AI) system. There is no evidence-based study on neurodynamic exercises including static opener and four levels of sliders and tensioners to decrease the mechanosensitivity and nerve root irritation among acute PIVD patients, to promote more tolerance to exercises with less pain experience, and to decrease more reliability over electrotherapy, using omics data integration in AI system. This study can be further carried by comparing the age and gender by giving two different interventions, and their effectiveness can be seen in longer period of time, which becomes easy due to AI.

Keywords: AI, data integration, SLR, neurodynamics, omics, PIVD

**Corresponding author*: VaibhavAgarwal79@outlook.com

Abhishek Kumar, Narayan Vyas, Pramod Singh Rathore, Abhineet Anand and Pooja Dixit (eds.) Internet of Medicine for Smart Healthcare, (1–22) © 2025 Scrivener Publishing LLC

1.1 Introduction

Prolapsed interverterbral disc (PIVD) is a disease that occurs when there is a rupture of annulus fibrosus, which further leads to an effusion of nucleus pulposus [1, 2]. Lumbar disc herniation is a frequent condition that affects 5% of individuals in adults [3]. In the world, the incidence of PIVD in males is from 1.9% to 7.6%, and, in females, it is between 2.2% and 5.0% [4]. It is one of the most common condition among low back ache (LBA) patients, which affects about 10% of the population [5, 6]. It consists of four stages that are nucleus degeneration, nucleus displacement, protusion, and extrusion [7, 8].

Studies have been conducted in usefulness of various physical examination results. They suggest that the straight leg raise (SLR) continues to remains the gold standard test for identifying the radicular symptoms [9]. Root irritation is typically thought to be present when the examiner elevates the affected limb and the pain reproduces or intensifies [10–15]. When the test reproduces pain in the gluteal or lower leg region as the examiner passively lifts the affected leg with the hip in flexion and knee in extension, it is said to be positive. The relevance given to the angle of elevation at which the pain is produced varies greatly. Brieg and Troups and others suggested that less than 70° is clinically relevant [16–19].

PIVD propulsion of disc leads to compression due to which there is compromised distal sliding of neural structures, which, in turn, possess challenges to physiotherapist in treatment of acute PIVD patients. There is no evidence-based study on neurodynamic exercises including static opener and four levels of sliders and tensioners to decrease the mechanosensitivity and nerve root irritation among acute PIVD patients. The purpose of this study was to analyze that neurodynamic exercise including static opener and four levels of sliders and tensioners can significantly alter neural mobility, SLR ranges, visual analog scale (VAS), and pain side code score [20–26].

The primary focus in gaining practical understanding of cellular processes is now on the examination of multi-omics data in conjunction with clinical informations. A methodical and thorough comprehension of complex biology seems to be possible through the integrations of multi-omics data relevant to biomolecule at several levels. They aid in evaluating the information transfer between omics levels and, hence, aid in closing the gap between genotype and phenotype. Integrative techniques can eventually contribute to better prevention and management because they can research biological phenomena holistically, which can enhance prognostics and the accuracy with which disease phenotypes are predicted [27–32].

The Omics Discovery Index (OmicsDI; https://www.omicsdi.org/) is a common data format that holds data sets from eleven repositories. Access, exploration, and integration of proteomics, transcriptomics, metabolomics, and genomics datasets are facilitated by this open-source platform. Human, model, and non-model organism datasets are all included. For each data collection that may be merged, OmicsDI includes an annotation as well as normalization stage in addition to indexing the data sets [33–36].

Numerous illnesses, including cancer, exhibit heterogeneity due to the notable variations in the extent of cancer growth across afflicted people. Furthermore, a variety of other variables, including lifestyle and environment, may contribute to illness heterogeneity. Therefore, in order to fully comprehend the etiology of the disorder and choose appropriate therapies for patient belonging to distinct subtype, it is essential to identify the underlying subcategories of diseases or categorize samples into recognized subgroups. A number of methods are available that use multi-omics data from sample to determine disease subtype or categorize different samples according to their omics profile. This section covers the instruments used to comprehend sample subgrouping according to underlying molecular patterns [35].

1.2 Literature Review

A systemic review to analyze the effectiveness of exercises program after lumbar discectomy surgery, by Nafsika Atsidakou *et al.*, in Journal of Clinical Orthopaedics and Trauma (2021): The current systemic review found that the included studies' methodologically quality, as measured by PEDro, is regarded moderate. Exercise programs are advised for patients who have undergone lumbar discectomy because the results indicated that they improved pain, disability, quality of life, muscle strength, and ability to return to work [1].

Prolapsed, herniated, or extruded intervertebral disc treatment by only stabilization, by Atul Goel *et al.*, in Journal of Craniovertebral Junction and Spine (2018): This study suggests that only fixation is also effective and safe in the management of lumbar herniated disc [2].

A case report and literature review: Spontaneous regression of a large sequestrated lumbar disc herniation, by Chengxiang Hu *et al.*, in Journal of International Medical Research, SAGE (2021): In this study, it was concluded, that compared to individuals with protruding or bulging disc, those with the disc herniation subtype known as sequestration are substantially more likely to experience spontaneous regression, and it also suggested that, in the absence of clear-cut surgical indication, conservative treatment is preferred for individuals with a large herniated lumbar discs, particularly if it is of the extrusions or sequestration subtype [3].

A case report: Prolapsed lumbar interverterbral disease treatment through acupuncture, by Dr. S. M. Shahidul Islam *et al.*, in Journal of Sports and Physical Education (2022): In this study, it was found that the patients having prolapsed lumbar intervertebral disc prolapse disease have significantly showed improvement in low back pain after doing exercises including lumbar mobilization, manipulation, isometric back muscle strengthening exercises, and acupuncture treatment in lumbar area [4].

A systemic "Review and meta-analysis: Efficacy of physiotherapy intervention in management of lumbar prolapsed intervertebral disc," by Varun Singh *et al.*, in International Journal of Health Sciences (2021): This study reveals that interventions in physiotherapy are successful in reducing pain and disability. Mechanisms involving physiology, biomechanics, and spinal mobility can be increased as a result of procedures including disc replacement foramina opening and intervertebral space expansion. This meta-analysis did not find any significant effects of physiotherapy on brain mobility [5].

A double blind randomized controlled trial: Effect of neurodynamic technique on radiating symptom and mechanosensitivity of neural tissue in subjects with lumbosacral radiculopathy, by Mohit Bipin *et al.*, in International Journal of Medical Science and Public Health (2021). This study revealed that patients with lumbosacral radiculopathy, neurodynamic treatments are useful in inducing centralization, lowering the mechanosensitivity of the neural tissues and decreasing the bothersomeness and frequency of radiating symptoms [6].

Randomized Control Trial: "Effect of Mckenzie approach and Mulligan's mobilization (SNAGS) in lumbar disc prolapse with unilateral radiculopathy," by Trupti Warude *et al.*, in International Journal of Science and Research (2014): In this study, the results showed that, in PIVD with unilateral radiculopathy, Mulligan's mobilization (SNAGS) technique showed more significant improvement than Mckenzie approach in response to relieve pain, improving ROM and reducing functional disability [7].

Straight leg raise test, by Camino-Willhuber *et al.* (2019); The interobserver reproducibility with low back pain in general practice, by Van den Hoogen *et al.*, in Journal Starpearls (1996): In this study, it was found that,

although the reproducibility of Lasegue's sign in ordinary general practices appears to be modest, it may be comparable to that seen in hospital setting in patient who is specifically chosen because they have high likelihood of experiencing low back pain as a result of a particular condition [8].
Dejong's The Neurologic examination, 7th edition, by William W. Campbell (ed.) South Asian edition, Chapter 47, page no 816: This book explains about the neurological examination, and one of its chapters explains about LBA examination [9].
"Passive straight leg raise test: Definition, interpretation, limitations and utilization spine health" (2014): According to this article, a true-positive SLR should replicate or worsen the pain/discomfort in the concerned limb at any level of passive elevation. False positives should be assumed to exist for those who only experience worsening back pain or any other leg pain outside the one that is the primary complaints [10].
Randomized Control Trial: "Difference between neurodynamic mobilization and streching exercises for chronic discogenic sciatica," by Haytham I. Morsi *et al.*, in Medical Journal of Cairo University (2021): This study reveals that, in the treatment of individuals with persistent discogenic sciatica, slider and tensioner neurodynamic mobilization techniques are more efficient than stretching exercise in decreasing pain intensity and enhancing functional impairment. Furthermore, there are no discernible differences between the two methods for increasing ankle dorsiflexion ROM [11].
"A prospective RCT: Effectiveness of nerve flossing technique in chronic lumbar radiculopathy," by Bhatia Sweta Satishkumar *et al.*, in Indian Journal of Physiotherapy and Occupational Therapy (2017): In this study, it was found that nerve flossing technique can be utilised as adjuvant therapy to help patients with chronic lumbar radiculopathy because of intervertebral disc prolapse to reduce pain, improve hip range of motion, and decrease functional impairment and fear avoidance beliefs (FABQ-G) [12].
A cross sectional study: The prevalence and correlates of low back pain in adults in Southern-Indian population, by Anil Chankaramangalam Mathew *et al.*, in International Journal of Medicine and Public Health (2013): According to this study, low back pain affects 40.7% of respondents who are years of age or older. In comparison to males (28.14%), women (52.9%) had a much greater prevalence, and this difference was statistically significant [13].
"A double-blind randomized controlled trial: The effect of spinal mobilization with leg movement in patients with lumbar radiculopathy," by Kiran Satpute *et al.*, in Journal Archives of Physical Medicine and Rehabilitation (2019): In this study, it was found that the addition of spinal mobilization

with leg movement to exercise and TENS dramatically increased benefits in leg and lower back ache, disability, SLR, and ROM, for patient with sub-acute lumbar radiculopathy in the short and long duration [14].
A randomized control trial: "Comparison of the effectiveness of core strengthening exercises and Mckenzie extension exercise on the pain functional disability in lumbar PIVD condition," by Jyoti Sharma *et al.*, in Physiotherapy and Occupational Therapy Journal (2018): This study demonstrated the great effectiveness of the Mckenzie extension exercise in term of reducing pain and improving functional disability in LBA patient having prolapsed lumbar intervertebral disc conditions. It also revealed that, while the Mckenzie exercise program assists to reduce disc prolapse, the core stabilization exercises assist in strengthening the surrounding muscles to provide stability [15].
A case report: "Otago home exercise program along with other physiotherapy interventions for the management of prolapsed intervertebral disc and associated symptoms in an elderly," by Sneha Chakraverty *et al.*, in Journal of Bulletin of Faculty of Physical Therapy (2023): This case study stated that the physical therapy and symptomatic management intervention had a positive effect on the patient, which led to decreased discomfort, increased muscle power and lower possibility of falling. The Otago home exercise program combined with physical therapy can be advantageous for old age cases to improve balance and possibility of falls and for the management of prolapsed intervertebral disc [16].
Cross-sectional study: "Demographic profile of the patients with lumbar disc herniation presented in a tertiary care centre," by Jungindro Singh Ningthoujam *et al.*, in Journal of Medical Society (2023): This study suggest that disc herniation is more prevalent in middle-aged group females. People with high BMI or overweight are more prone to disc prolapse, though it is not statistically significant. The levels of prolapse most frequently seen are L4-L5 and L5-S1. Left side and posterolateral disc prolapse is more frequent [17].
A randomized control trial: "Effect of neurodynamic mobilization on pain and function in subjects with lumbo-sacral radiculopathy," by Srishti Sanat Sharma *et al.*, in International Medical Journal (2018): This study suggest that neurodynamic treatment is advantageous for reducing pain (during activity not at rest) and improving function but hotpack, core and back isometric exercises only showed improvement in pain but not in function [18].

Indhupriya Subramanian *et al.* conducted a research, in which it is essential to use an integrative strategy that integrates multi-omics data to emphasize the links between the many biomolecule implicated and their roles in order to examine complicated biological processes coherently. The tools and techniques that use integrative approaches to evaluate numerous omics data were gathered for this study, and their capacity to handle applications such illness subtyping, biomarker prediction, and extracting insights from the data was summed up. They offer these tools' limits, use-cases, and approach; visualization portals; and the difficulties in integrating multi-omics data [35].

N. Shusharina *et al.* highlight the interesting directions in the study of machine learning application for the treatment and prevention of depression and neurodegenerative diseases. Finding novel method for diagnosing and treating depressive disorders and neurodegenerative illnesses continue to be a top focus for research in genetics, neurophysiology, psychology, and multidisciplinary medicine, even after decades of study. Before the improvements are extensively implemented in clinics, there is still work to be done to come to an agreement on how to apply the new machine learning techniques and integrate them with the present standards of care and assessments [36].

1.3 Methodology

1.3.1 Research Question

Are the neurodynamic exercises including static opener and four levels of neurodynamic can significantly alter neural mobility, SLR ranges, VAS, and pain site score (PSC) by using omics data integration?

1.3.2 Aim of the Study

The aim of this study is to analyze the immediate and carryover effect of neurodynamic exercises on SLR ranges among acute PIVD patients using omics data integration in artificial intelligence (AI) system [15].

1.3.3 Need of the Study

There is no evidence-based study on neurodynamic exercises including static opener and 4 levels of sliders and tensioners to decrease the mechanosensitivity and nerve root irritation among acute PIVD patients, to promote more tolerance to exercises with less pain experience, and to decrease more reliability over electrotherapy, using omics data integration in AI system; to gather research based evidences to neurodynamic approach using

AI in acute PIVD patients; and to explore rehabilitation options and strategies in managing acute PIVD patients using AI systems.

1.4 Hypothesis

1.4.1 Alternate Hypothesis

Neurodynamic treatment shows more significant improvement and SLR ranges among acute PIVD patients as compare to control group.

1.4.2 Null Hypothesis

Neurodynamic treatment may not show more significant improvement in SLR ranges among acute PIVD patients as compare to control group.

1.4.3 Study Design

The design of this study was double-blinded experimental study.

1.4.4 Study Center

The study was conducted in Neuromedicine Ward and Physiotherapy OPD, Himalayan Hospital Jolly Grant, Dehradun, Uttarakhand.

1.4.5 Study Population

All subjects were taken from Himalayan Hospital diagnosed with PIVD were considered as study population.

1.4.6 Sampling

Random sampling method

1.4.7 Study Duration

Nine months

1.4.8 Sample Size

Forty-four subjects are selected according to the inclusion and exclusion criteria.

1.4.9 Inclusion Criteria

- Acute PIVD patients (less than 3 months) with confirmed diagnosis with MRI.
- Unilateral radiculopathy
- SLR ranges less than 70°
- Age group between 20 and 60 years

1.4.10 Exclusion Criteria

- Myotomal involvement power less than 3
- Low back surgery in past 1 year
- Spondylolisthesis, spinal canal stenosis, SI joint pain, infection, tumor, and cauda equina syndrome

1.4.11 Outcome Variables

- Passive (SLR) test
- VAS score
- Pain site code (PSC)

1.4.12 Instrumentation

Universal goniometer, couch, pillow, and stopwatch. Figures 1.1 and 1.2 shows the Universal gonimeter and stopwatch respectively.

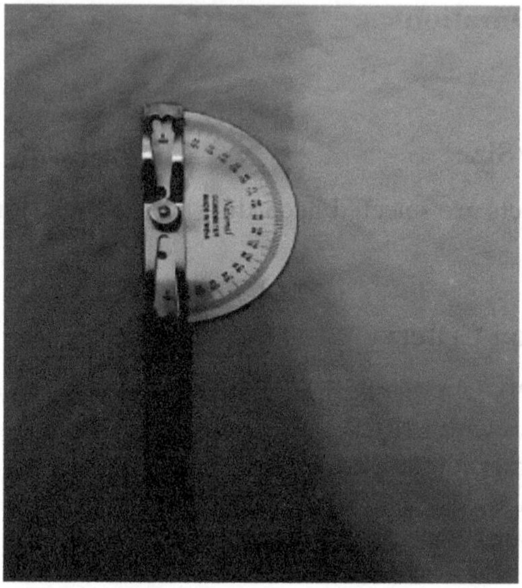

Figure 1.1 Universal goniometer.

Figure 1.2 Stopwatch.

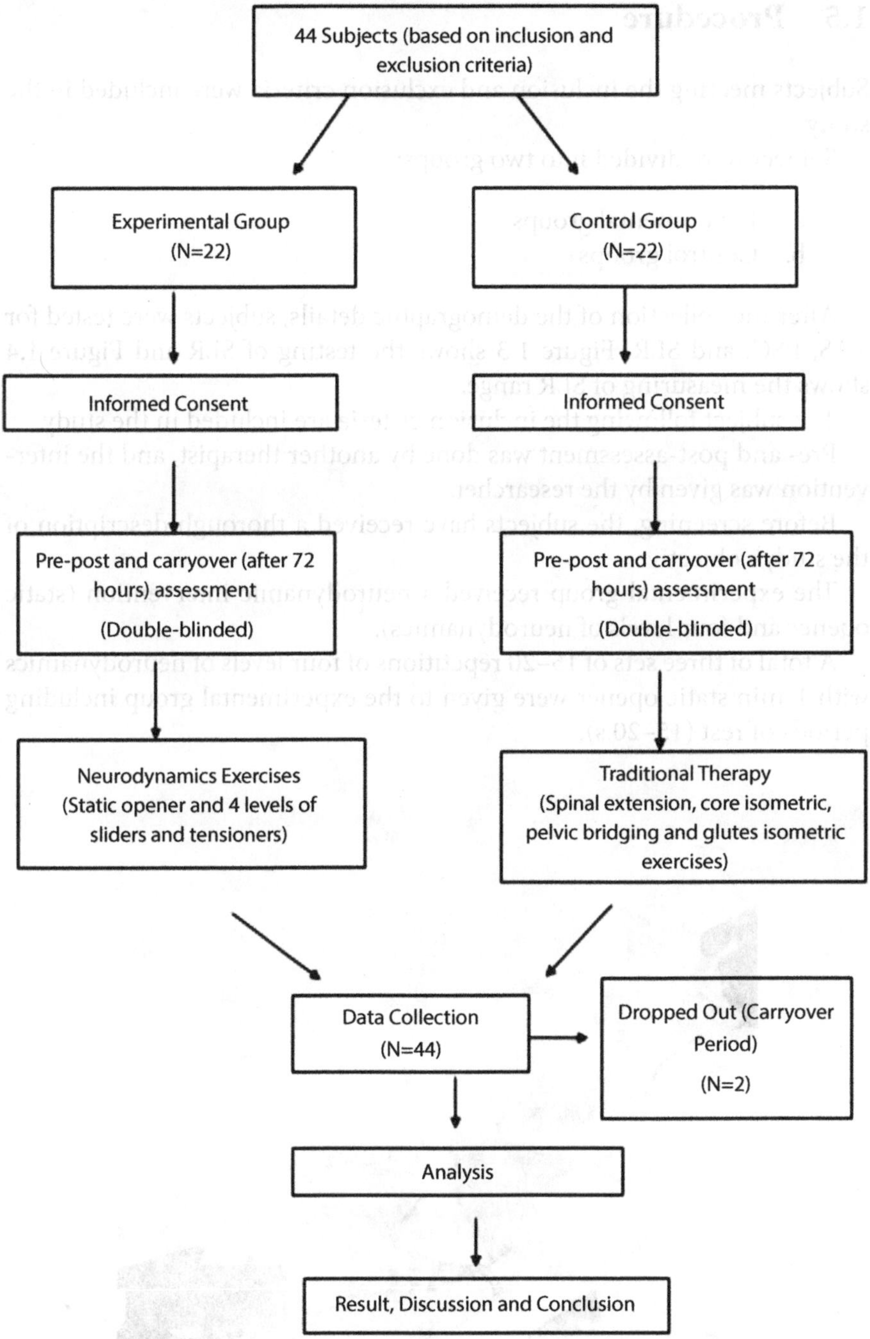
44 Subjects (based on inclusion and exclusion criteria)
Experimental Group (N=22)
Control Group (N=22)
Informed Consent
Informed Consent
Pre-post and carryover (after 72 hours) assessment (Double-blinded)
Pre-post and carryover (after 72 hours) assessment (Double-blinded)
Neurodynamics Exercises (Static opener and 4 levels of sliders and tensioners)
Traditional Therapy (Spinal extension, core isometric, pelvic bridging and glutes isometric exercises)
Data Collection (N=44)
Dropped Out (Carryover Period) (N=2)
Analysis
Result, Discussion and Conclusion

1.5 Procedure

Subjects meeting the inclusion and exclusion criteria were included in the study.

Subject were divided into two groups:

a. Experimental groups
b. Control groups

After the collection of the demographic details, subjects were tested for VAS, PSC, and SLR. Figure 1.3 shows the testing of SLR and Figure 1.4 shows the measuring of SLR range.

The subject following the inclusion criteria are included in the study.

Pre- and post-assessment was done by another therapist, and the intervention was given by the researcher.

Before screening, the subjects have received a thorough description of the study's objective.

The experimental group received a neurodynamic intervention (static opener and four levels of neurodynamics).

A total of three sets of 15–20 repetitions of four levels of neurodynamics with 1-min static opener were given to the experimental group including periods of rest (15–20 s).

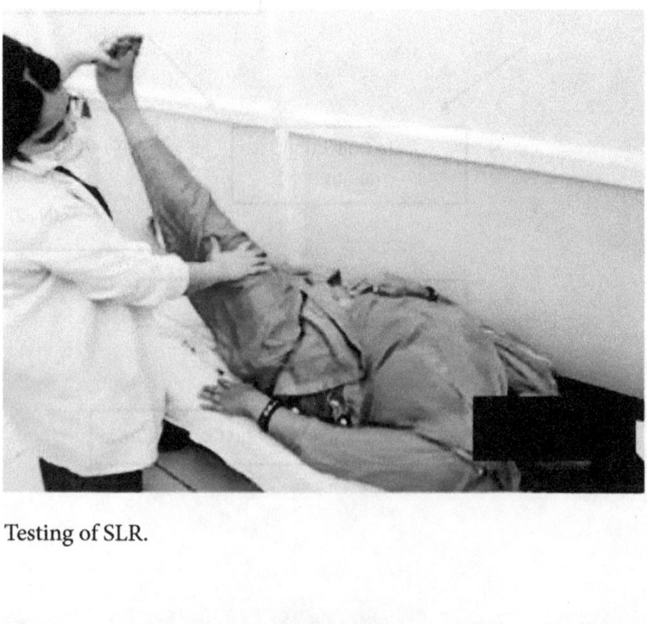

Figure 1.3 Testing of SLR.

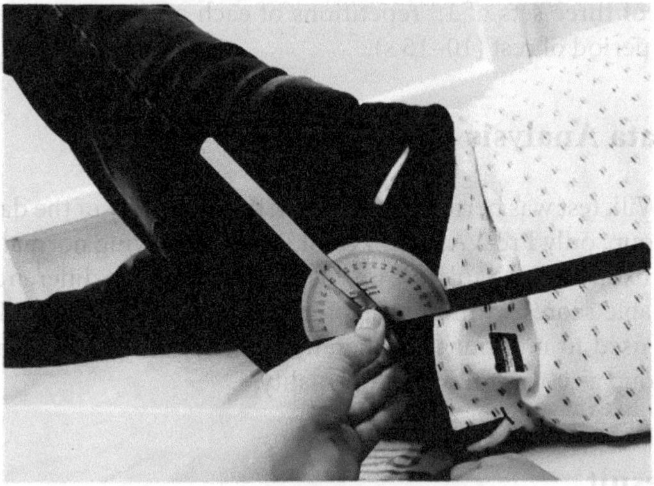

Figure 1.4 Measuring of SLR range.

1.6 Intervention

1.6.1 Four Levels of Neurodynamics

Position: Supine lying

Level 1: Position Away → Move Away
Passive Neck flexion along with hip and knee flexion

Level 2: Position Toward → Move Away
Neck extension along with hip and knee flexion

Level 3: Position Away → Move Toward
Neck flexion along with hip and knee extension followed by
C/L → SLR → B/L SLR → Affected SLR

Level 4: Position toward → Move Toward
Neck extension along with hip and knee extension followed by
C/L SLR → B/L SLR → Affected SLR.

1.6.2 Control Group Intervention

- Spinal extension exercise
- Core isometric exercise
- Glutes isometric exercise
- Pelvic bridging exercise

A total of three sets of 15 repetitions of each exercise were performed including period of rest (10–15 s).

1.7 Data Analysis

Shapiro–Wilk test was performed to check the normality of the data. In the control group, only Pre-VAS and Pre-SLR were following normality in the data. Wilcoxon signed-rank test was used to find out the difference of outcome variable scores within groups for VAS, PSC score, and SLR. Paired t-test was used to find out the difference of VAS and SLR variable in the control group as it was following normality.

1.8 Result

A total of 44 patients are included in the study. From this patient, 22 patients were enrolled in the experimental group and 22 in control group. Among them, 20 were male and 24 were female. Two patients were dropped out from the experimental group during carryover effect period. Table 1.1 and Figure 1.5 shows the mean and Standard deviation of Age, sex and side.

Table 1.1 Mean age, sex, and side.

Variable	N	Mean	Standard deviation
Age	44	39.14	9.833
Sex	44	1.55	0.510
Side	44	1.50	0.521

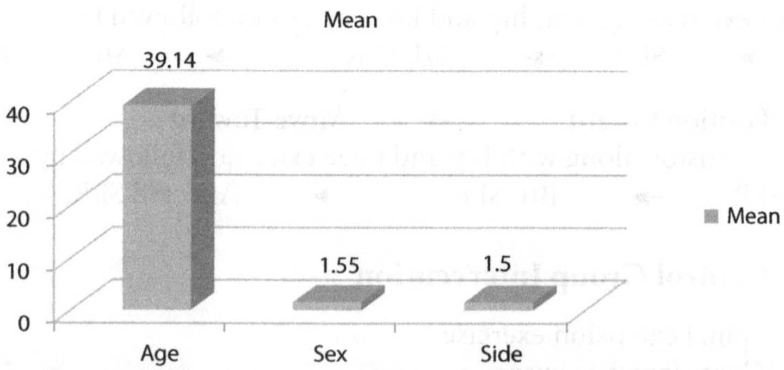

Figure 1.5 Mean age, sex, and side in both groups (baseline data for demographic details).

Table 1.2 Mean and standard deviation of age in both groups.

SN	Variable	N	Experimental group	Control group
1	Age	44	37.23 ± 9.783	41.05 ± 9.727

Mean age in the data was 39.14 ± 9.833.
Mean sex in the data was 1.55 ± 0.510.
Mean side in the data was 1.50 ± 0.521.

The percentage of males and females in the data was 45.5% and 54.5%, respectively.

Data are mean ± standard deviation (sd). In the experimental group, the mean age is 37.23 and sd is 9.783, and, in the control group, the mean age is 41.05 and sd is 9.727. Table 1.2 shows the mean ans standard deviation of age in both experimental and control group.

Wilcoxon signed-rank test was used to compare the outcome variable score in the experimental group. In the experimental group, the VAS score was reduced from 5.95 with standard deviation of 0.844 to post VAS score of 3.68 with standard deviation of 1.129, which was statistically significant (p-value < 0.001). The PSC score was reduced from 5.36 with standard deviation of 0.790 to post PSC score of 3.73 with standard deviation of 1.386, which was statistically significant (p value <0.001). The SLR score was increased from 49.45 with standard deviation of 9.635 to post SLR score of 58.18 with standard deviation of 14.608 which was statistically significant (p-value: 0.002). Table 1.3 and Figure 1.6 shows the pre and post data within the experimental group.

In the experimental group, the post VAS score was reduced from 3.68 with standard deviation of 1.129 to carry over VAS score of 2.60 with standard deviation of 1.465, which was statistically significant (p-value: 0.002). The post PSC score was reduced from 3.733 with standard deviation of

Table 1.3 Pre-post data within the experimental group.

SN no.	Variables	Pre Mean ± sd (Median)	Post Mean ± sd (Median)	P-Value
1	VAS	5.95 ± 0.844 (6.000)	3.68 ± 1.129 (4.000)	<0.001
2	PSC	5.36 ± 0.790 (5.500)	3.73 ± 1.386 (3.500)	<0.001
3	SLR	49.45 ± 9.635 (54.000)	58.18 ± 14.608 (63.000)	0.002

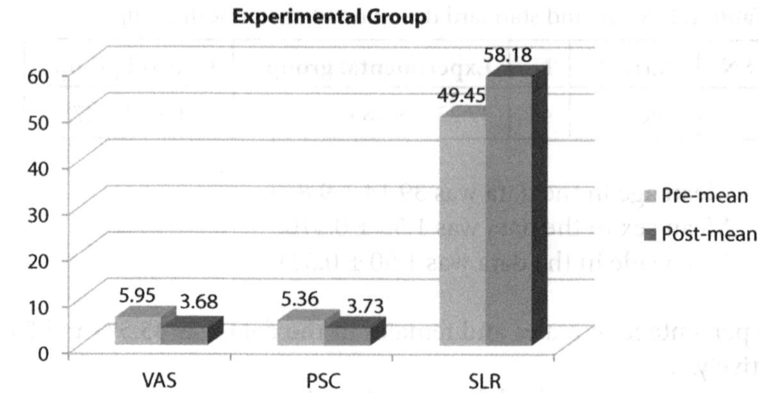

Figure 1.6 Pre-post data within the experimental group.

Table 1.4 Post and carryover data within the experimental group.

SN no.	Variables	Post mean ± sd (median)	Carryover mean ± sd (median)	P-Value
1	VAS	3.68 ± 1.129 (4.000)	2.60 ± 1.465 (2.500)	0.002
2	PSC	3.73 ± 1.386 (3.500)	3.05 ± 1.395 (2.500)	0.032
3	SLR	58.18 ± 14.608 (63.000)	70.70 ± 10.623 (72.000)	<0.001

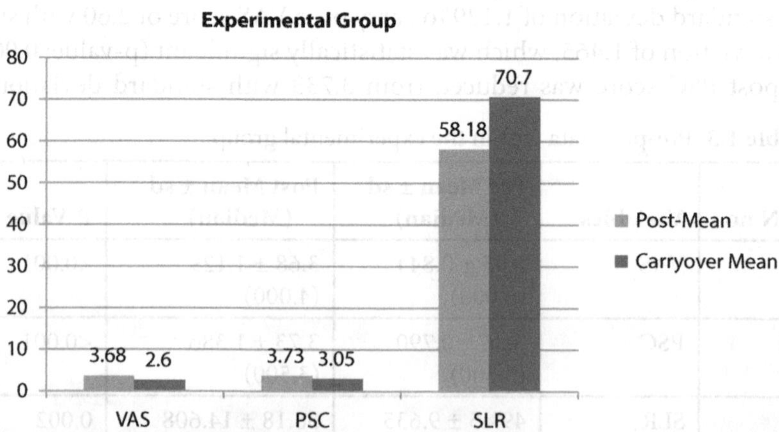

Figure 1.7 Post-carryover data within the experimental group.

Table 1.5 Pre-post data within the control group.

SN no.	Variables	Pre mean ± sd (Median)	Post mean ± sd (Median)	P-value
1	VAS	6.14 ± 1.283 (6.000)	4.73 ± 1.667 (5.000)	<0.001
2	PSC	5.32 ± 0.780 (5.500)	4.55 ± 1.335 (5.000)	0.007
3	SLR	48.73 ± 8.708 (49.000)	54.32 ± 11.623 (55.000)	0.007

1.386 to carry over PSC score of 3.05 with standard deviation of 1.395, which was statistically significant (p-value: 0.032). The post SLR score was increased from 58.18 with standard deviation of 14.608 to carry over SLR score from 70.70 with standard deviation of 10.623, which was statistically significant (p-value < 0.001). Table 1.4 and Figure 1.7 shows the post and carryover data withoion the experimental group.

In the control group, the VAS score was reduced from 6.14 with standard deviation of 1.283 to post VAS score of 4.73 with standard deviation of 1.667, which was statistically significant (p-value < 0.001). The PSC score was reduced from 5.32 with standard deviation of 0.780 to post PSC score of 4.55 with standard deviation of 1.335, which was statistically not significant (p-value: 0.007). The SLR score was increased from 48.73 with standard deviation of 8.708 to post SLR score of 54.32 with standard deviation of 11.623, which was statistically significant (p-value: 0.007). Table 1.5 shows the pre and post data within the control group.

1.9 Discussion

This study analyzed and compared the immediate and carryover effects of neurodynamics in SLR ranges among acute PIVD patients. The purpose of this study was to evaluate that neurodynamic exercises including static opener and four levels of sliders and tensioners can significantly alter neural mobility, SLR ranges, VAS, and PSC score using omics data.

Gaston Camino-Willhuber *et al.* (2019) suggested that neurodynamics helps in reducing pain by developing centralization [8]. Ali M. Alshami *et al.* (2021) conducted a study in which he found that patients receiving sliders and tensioners showed significant improvement in pain [31]. In a study, Dharti Hingarajia *et al.* (2019) found that sliders neural mobilization exercises are efficacious in reducing pain immediately [32]. The PSC score was statistically reduced when we compared the pre-post data (p-value < 0.001) and the post-carryover data (p-value: 0.032). Mohit Bipin Shah *et al.* (2021) conducted a research in which he found that the radiating symptoms may be centralized using neurodynamics [6]. In present study, the SLR range was increased when we compared the pre-post data (p-value: 0.002) and the post-carryover data, which was statistically significant (p-value < 0.001). Neha Tambekar *et al.* (2015) conducted a study in which the butler's neural mobilization showed significant improvement in SLR ranges immediately after the session, but it was not maintained for 24 h [21]. Muhammad Adnan *et al.* (2012) suggested that neurodynamic treatment is effective in improving SLR ranges in patients having radiating LBA [22].

When the data was analyzed in the control group, it was found that the VAS score was statistically reduced when the pre-post data was compared (p-value < 0.001), but it was not maintained for long time when we compared the post-carryover data (p-value: 0.424). Jyoti Sharma *et al.* (2018) advised that Mckenzie extension exercises were efficacious in decreasing lower back pain in patients with prolapsed intervertebral disc [16]. The PSC score was reduced when we compared the pre-post data (p-value < 0.007) but not in the post-carryover data (p-value: 0.0340). With the best of my knowledge, this might be because the VAS was reduced, which can alter the sensitivity of pain so the patient had experience the improvement in radiating pain. It was not maintained in carryover effect due to the reason that the intervention was given only for one session, but, if we will give the intervention in continuation for 1 week, then it might show improvement in PSC score. Jyoti Sharma *et al.* (2018) advised that Mckenzie extension exercises yield results in 3–4 days, whereas core strengthening exercises yield results in 10 days [16]. Deepak Anap *et al.* (2015) studied a case series in which they suggested that core strengthening exercises are useful in reducing nerve root irritation and decreasing the radiating pain [34]. In present study, the SLR range was increased when we compared the pre-post data (p-value < 0.007) but not in the post-carryover data (p-value: 0.388). This indicates that the core strengthening exercises can reduce the pain immediately due to which the patient will get relief in radiating pain as well as the SLR range will increase but effect will be for short period of time as compared AI-based devices.

In present study, when we compare the data between the groups, we came to know that there were significant immediate and carryover improvement in VAS score in the experimental group. Previous studies suggested that the neurodynamics has an efficacious effect in reducing pain in patients with lumbar radiculopathy [6, 8, 21, 32, 33]. The experimental and control groups have immediate effect in reducing PSC score, but, only in the experimental group, it was maintained for long period (p-value < 0.001). The SLR range was increased immediately in both the groups, but, only in the experimental group, it was maintained for long period (p-value < 0.001). From the previous studies, many authors suggested that the neurodynamics can alter the neural mobility, centralize the pain, increase SLR ranges, and improve functional ability by using omics data for study and treatment.

1.10 Conclusion

In the present study, it can be concluded that neurodynamics and omics data including static opener and four levels of sliders and tensioners showed significant immediate and carryover improvement in VAS, PSC score, and SLR ranges. Conventional treatment including spinal extension exercises, core isometric exercises, pelvic bridging, and glutes isometric exercises showed significant improvement immediately on VAS, PSC score, and SLR ranges, but it was not maintained in the carryover period. This study was conducted for short period of time on the collected genomic data.

However, the experimental group was better in improving pain, PSC score, and SLR ranges as compared to the control group. This research can be carried out on a larger sample size. This research can be conduct for longer duration. The study can be further carried out by combining neurodynamic exercises with Mckenzie and core isometric exercises along with different outcomes variables with different omics data integrated by AI system for the help of experts. This study can be further carried by comparing the age and gender by giving two different interventions, and their effectiveness can be seen in longer period of time. Thus, by collecting omics data, it becomes easy for examining the patients with different PIVD with different SLR ranges, which helps in curing the diseases from the roots due to omics data provided by AI.

References

1. Atsidakou, N., Matsi, A.E., Christakou, A., The effectiveness of exercise program after lumbar discectomy surgery. *J. Clin. Orthop. Trauma*, *16*, 99–105, 2021, https://doi.org/10.1016/j.jcot.2020.12.030.
2. Goel, A., Prolapsed, herniated, or extruded intervertebral disc-treatment by only stabilization. *J. Craniovertebr. Junction Spine*, 9, 3, 133–134, 2018, https://doi.org/10.4103/jcvjs.JCVJS_84_18.

3. Hu, C., Lin, B., Li, Z., Chen, X., Gao, K., Spontaneous regression of a large sequestered lumbar disc herniation: a case report and literature review. *J. Int. Med. Res.*, *49*, 11, 3000605211058987, 2021, https://doi.org/10.1177/03000605211058987.
4. Shahidul Islam, S.M., Li, H.H., Yasmin, S., Sheik, M.S., A case study on Prolapsed Lumbar Intervertebral Disease (PLID) acupuncture treatment in Bangladesh. *J. Adv. Med. Sci.*, *3*, 2, 01–03, 2023, Retrieved from https://dzarc.com/medical/article/view/306.
5. Singh, V., Malik, M., Kaur, J., Kulandaivelan, S., Punia, S., A systematic review and meta-analysis on the efficacy of physiotherapy intervention in management of lumbar prolapsed intervertebral disc. *Int. J. Health Sci.*, *15*, 2, 49–57, 2021.
6. Shah, M.B. and Soni, N., Effect Of Neurodynamic Techniques On Radiating Symptoms and Mechanosensitivity Of Neural Tissue In Subjects With Lumbosacral Radiculopathy: A Double-blind Randomized Controlled Trial. *Int. J. Med. Sci. Public Health*, 2, 10, 1, 2021, https://doi.org/10.5455/ijmsph.2021.07074202127082021.
7. Warude, T.A. and Shanmugam, S., The Effect of Mckenzie Approach and Mulligan's Mobilisation (SNAGS) in Lumbar Disc Prolapse with Unilateral Radiculopathy. *Int. J. Sci. Res.*, impact factor(2012), 3, 358, 2014, ISN(Online): 2319-7064.
8. Camino Willhuber, G.O. and Piuzzi, N.S., Straight Leg Raise Test, in: *StatPearls*, StatPearls Publishing, Treasure Island, Florida, USA, 2023.
9. Dejong's, *The Neurologic examination*, 7th edn, W.W. Campbell (Ed.), p. 816, south asian edition, Chapter 47, Philadelphia, Pennsylvania, USA, 2018.
10. McIntosh, G. and Hall, H., Passive Straight Leg Raise Test: Definition, Interpretation, Limitations and Utilization SPINE HEALTH. *J. Curr. Clin. Care*, 4, 25–32, 2014.
11. El Nahass, B.G.D., H.I.M.M., Ibrahim, M.M., Difference between Neurodynamic Mobilization and Stretching Exercises for 12. Chronic Discogenic Sciatica. *Med. J. Cairo Univ.*, *89*, September, 1869–1876, 2021, doi: 10.21608/mjcu.2021.203297.
12. Bhatia, S., Bid, D., Ramalingam, T., Effectiveness of Nerve Flossing Technique in Chronic Lumbar Radiculopathy. *IJPOT*, 11, 44–49, 2017, 10.5958/0973-5674.2017.00010.7.
13. Mathew, A., Safar, R., Anithadevi, T.S., Banu, M., Shankar, S., Rai, B., Chacko, T., The prevalence and correlates of low back pain in adults: A cross sectional study from Southern India. *Int. J. Med. Public Health*, 3, 14–17, 2010, 10.4103/2230-8598.123525.
14. Satpute, K., Hall, T., Bisen, R., Lokhande, P., The Effect of Spinal Mobilization With Leg Movement in Patients With Lumbar Radiculopathy-A Double-Blind Randomized Controlled Trial. *Arch. Phys. Med. Rehabil.*, *100*, 5, 828–836, 2019, https://doi.org/10.1016/j.apmr.2018.11.004\.

15. Pesonen, J., Shacklock, M., Rantanen, P. *et al.*, Extending the straight leg raise test for improved clinical evaluation of sciatica: reliability of hip internal rotation or ankle dorsiflexion. *BMC Musculoskelet. Disord.*, 22, 303, 2021, https://doi.org/10.1186/s12891-021-04159-y.
16. Sharma, J., Kumar, Kumar, S., Comparison of the Effectiveness of Core Strenghting Exercise and McKenzie Extension Exercise on the Pain Functional Disability in lumbar PIVD Condition. *Physiother. Occup. J.*, 11, 67–79, 2018, 10.21088/potj.0974.5777.11218.4.
17. Chakraverty, S., Jagtap, T., Mahapatra, C.O., Home Exercise Program along with other physiotherapy interventions for the management of prolapsed intervertebral disc and its associated symptoms in an elderly: a case report. *Bull. Fac. Phys. Ther.*, 28, 10, 2023, https://doi.org/10.1186/s43161-023-00121-22.
18. Ningthoujam, J.S., Naorem, A.S., Ningthoukhongjam, S.D., Demographic profile of the patients with lumbar disc herniation presented in a tertiary care center, Manipur. *J. Med. Soc.* [serial online], 35, 67–71, 2021 [cited 2023 Jun 18], Available from: https://www.jmedsoc.org/text.asp?2021/35/2/67/331336.
19. Sharma, S. and Sheth, M.S., Effect Of Neurodynamic Mobilization On Pain and Function In Subjects With Lumbo-sacral Radiculopathy. *Med.-Sci.*, 1, 23–30, 2017, https://doi.org/10.5455/medscience.2017.06.8664.
20. Bakhtiary, A., Safavi-Farokhi, Z., Rezasoltani, A., Lumbar stabilizing exercises improve activities of daily living in patients with lumbar disc herniation. *J. Back Musculoskelet. Rehabil.*, 18, 401–407, 2005, 10.3233/BMR-2005-183-401.
21. Tambekar, N., Sabnis, S., Phadke, A., Bedekar, N., Effect of Butler's neural tissue mobilization and Mulligan's bent leg raise on pain and straight leg raise in patients of low back ache. *J. Bodyw. Mov. Ther.*, *20*, 2, 280–285, 2016, https://doi.org/10.1016/j.jbmt.2015.08.003.
22. Rutuja, P., Neha, C., Mitushi, D., Arora, S.P., Waqar, M.N., Pratik, P., Comprehensive Physiotherapy Management in PIVD Patient: A case report. *J. Med. Pharm. Allied Sci.*, 10, 5, 1340, 3640–3642, 2021, doi: 10.22270/jmpas.V10I5.1340.
23. Danazumi, M., Bello, B., Yakasai, A., Kaka, B., Two manual therapy techniques for management of lumbar radiculopathy: a randomized clinical trial. *J. Osteopath. Med.*, 121, 2021.
24. Gohil, P., Baldha, G., Arunachalam, R., Current Trends Among Indian Physiotherapist About Lumbosacral Radiculopathy: A Cross Sectional Survey. *J. Sci. Res.*, 65, 84–88, 2021, 10.37398/JSR.2021.650311.
25. Patel, J., Effect of Mckenzie Method with tens on Lumbar Radiculopathy-A Randomized Controlled Trial. *Int. J. Physiother.*, 3, 30–37, 2016, 10.15621/ijphy/2016/v3i1/88919.
26. Chen, L., Liu, D., Zou, L., Huang, J., Chen, J., Zou, Y., Lai, J., Chen, J., Li, H., Liu, G., Efficacy of high intensity laser therapy in treatment of patients with

lumbar disc protrusion: A randomized controlled trial. *J. Back Musculoskelet. Rehabil.*, *31*, 1, 191–196, 2018, https://doi.org/10.3233/BMR-170793.
27. Thoomes, E., Falla, D., Cleland, J.A., Fernández-de-Las-Peñas, C., Gallina, A., de Graaf, M., Conservative management for lumbar radiculopathy based on the stage of the disorder: a Delphi study. *Disabil. Rehabil.*, 45, 21, 1–10, 2022, Advance online publication, https://doi.org/10.1080/09638288.2022.2130448.
28. Amjad, F., Mohseni-Bandpei, M.A., Gilani, S.A., Ahmad, A., Hanif, A., Effects of non-surgical decompression therapy in addition to routine physical therapy on pain, range of motion, endurance, functional disability and quality of life versus routine physical therapy alone in patients with lumbar radiculopathy; a randomized controlled trial. *BMC Musculoskelet. Disord.*, *23*, 1, 255, 2022, https://doi.org/10.1186/s12891-022-05196-x.
29. Gohil, P., Baldha, G., Arunachalam, R., Effectiveness of trigger pont dry needling on lumbosacral radiculopathy among Indian Homemakers: A Randomized Controlled Trial. *Ann. Natl. Acad. Med. Sci. (India)*, 57, 2021, https://doi.org/101.1055/s-0041-1739035. ISSN0379-038X.
30. Gupta, R., Sharma, S., Sharma, R., Sharma, S., Effect of Neurodynamic Mobilisation Plus Core Stability on Pain and Motor Nerve Conduction Velocity in Athletes with Lumbar Radiculopathy. *Pol. J. Sport Tour.*, 28, 3, 3–7, 2021, https://doi.org/10.2478/pjst-2021-0013.
31. Alshami, A.M., Alghamdi, M.A., Abdelsalam, M.S., Effect of Neural Mobilization Exercises in Patients With Low Back-Related Leg Pain With Peripheral Nerve Sensitization: A Prospective, Controlled Trial. *J. Chiropr. Med.*, *20*, 2, 59–69, 2021, https://doi.org/10.1016/j.jcm.2021.07.001.
32. Hingarajia, D. *et al.*, Comparative study on Immediate Effect of two Different Neural Mobilisation Techniques on Pain and Knee Extension range in Patients with Lumbosacral Radiculopathy. *Int. J. Recent Sci. Res.*, 10, 04, 31855–31861, 2019, DOI: http://dx.doi.org/10.24327/ijrsr.2019.1004.3352.
33. Adnan, M., Arsh, A., Ali, B., Ahmad, S., Effectiveness of bent leg raise technique and neurodynamics in patients with radiating low back pain. *Pak. J. Med. Sci.*, *38*, 1, 47–51, 2022, https://doi.org/10.12669/pjms.38.1.40101.
34. Roy, M.M.H. and Anap, D.D., Is McKenzie Method with Core Exercise Effective for patients with Disc Derangement? A Case Series. *VIMS Health Sci. J.*, *2*, 1, 26–31, 2015, https://vimshsj.edu.in/index.php/main/article/view/167.
35. Subramanian, I., Verma, S., Kumar, S., Jere, A., Anamika, K., Multi-omics Data Integration, Interpretation, and Its Application. *Bioinform. Biol. Insights*, 14, 1177932219899051, 2020 Jan 31, doi: 10.1177/1177932219899051. PMID: 32076369; PMCID: PMC7003173, https://www.ncbi.nlm.nih.gov/pmc/articles/PMC7003173/.
36. Shusharina, N., Yukhnenko, D., Botman, S., Sapunov, V., Savinov, V., Kamyshov, G., Sayapin, D., Voznyuk, I., Modern Methods of Diagnostics and Treatment of Neurodegenerative Diseases and Depression. *Diagnostics*, *13*, 573, 2023, https://doi.org/10.3390/diagnostics13030573.

2

Effectiveness of Graph-Based Methods for Biological Networks for Primal Reflex Release Techniques on Pain and Disability in Cervicogenic Headache Patient

Siddhartha Kuriyal, Manish Kumar Jha*, Vaibhav Agarwal and Amit Sharma

Department of Physiotherapy, Himalayan Institute of Medical Sciences, Swami Rama Himalayan University, Jolly Grant, Dehradun, India

Abstract
Cervicogenic headache (CGH), as the name implies, is a headache of cervical origin. Historically, severe headaches were difficult to identify and treat due to a lack of understanding of their genesis and pathophysiology. Even today, managing a CGH is difficult for sport rehabilitation professionals. The goal of this clinical recommendation is to do a literature evaluation on CGH and design an evidence-based method to CGH assessment and clinical therapy using graph-based analysis for identifying biological networks. An accurate diagnosis can only be made after a comprehensive history and clinical examination. A multimodal physical therapy solution, comprising modalities, manual therapy, and therapeutic exercise, is advised to treat specific deficits, much as with other musculoskeletal dysfunctions.

Keywords: CGH, graph, pain, primal reflex, PRRT

2.1 Introduction

The pain in a cervicogenic headache (CGH) starts in the soft tissues of the neck or cervical spine and radiates to the head. It is a chronic hemicranial pain syndrome. However, it can also happen without trauma if there has

**Corresponding author*: Manishjha1900@outlook.com

Abhishek Kumar, Narayan Vyas, Pramod Singh Rathore, Abhineet Anand and Pooja Dixit (eds.) Internet of Medicine for Smart Healthcare, (23–42) © 2025 Scrivener Publishing LLC

not been a head or neck injury. It can be challenging to discern between these types of headaches due to clinical features of CGH, such as tension type headache, migraine, or hemicranias continua. Shasta and colleagues coined the term "cervicogenic headache" in the 1980s and define it as a type of headache brought on by a condition affecting the cervical spines, its anatomical structure, and the components of bone, soft tissue, and circulatory system. The article "Cervicogenic headache: an update" by Bogduk (2014), which appeared in the current pain and headache report journal, examines the function of CGH [1].

A symptomatic headache may result from peripheral mechanism such as irritation of the excited cervical nerve roots or joints, which can generate nociceptive pain that is referred to the head. Sensitization of the central nervous system is a fundamental mechanism that can lead to hyperalgesia and enhance pain sensitivity. Another article "cervicogenic headache: diagnostic evaluation and treatment strategies" by Biondi (2005), which appeared reports magazine, explores the physiology of CGH. Previous studies and articles on CGH stated that there are numerous anatomical structures (muscles, fascia, etc.) in the body that can cause cervical stiffness and painful motion, including hypertonic and stiffness of both upper trapezius, sub-occipital muscles, cervical radiculopathy, secondary scapula winging, glenohumeral joint disorders, and bursitis (inhibited) week neck flexors and upper crossed syndrome [2].

The upper cervical spine has significant role in CGH, according to the author, who also says that this area is densely innervated by sensory nerve fibers that provide pain signals to the brainstem and trigeminal nucleus. This means that 92% of individuals had anesthesia in the dermatomes that the trigeminal nerve supplies. This appears to corroborate the idea that trigeminocervical nucleus, which descends in the neck to the level of the third cervical vertebra, is the mechanism by which pain is referred. In comparison to patients who had experienced trauma, those who had not experienced trauma tended to be hazier about the location of their headache. Identifying and addressing any underlying musculoskeletal or joint problems in cervical spine is crucial for managing CGH, according to Biondi. Numerous conditions, such as neck injuries, cervical arthritis, or tight muscle in the neck and shoulder area, can result CGH. Patients who have this kind of headache frequently describe pain that is confined to one side of the head and face and that is accompanied by stiffness and pain in the neck [3].

Cervicogenic headaches can send pain to other parts of the head, like the temples or forehead, which makes it difficult to differentiate then from other forms of headaches. Cervicogenic headache is frequently successfully treated with a mix of physical therapy treatment and the medication like painkillers. Headaches are a key signal of anatomical and physiological changes because of the pain and discomfort they cause. Dysfunction of the cervical spinal joint complex can cause headache. Cervicogenic headaches (CGHs) provide a difficulty for many sports physical therapists because the head discomfort originates elsewhere: the cervical spine. CGHs are, interestingly, one of the most prevalent forms of headache in weight-lifting athletes. Patients who have suffered whiplash or head injuries, resulting in neck discomfort, may develop CGH. In fact, headaches that appear 3 months or longer after a concussion are not usually caused by brain or head injury, indicating a probable cervical spine origin [4].

Because CGHs are a secondary kind of headache, it is critical to identify the underlying reasons by completing a complete musculoskeletal examination, particularly of the cervical spine. Dr. Vladimir Janda discovered distinct patterns of muscular imbalance in individuals suffering from cervical dysfunction, including those suffering from CGHs. This muscular stiffness and weakening patterns, termed as "upper crossed syndrome" (Figure 2.1), were further documented in various published CGH investigations [6]. Cervicogenic headache (CGH) is described by the International Headache Society as "a secondary type of headache caused by disorders of the cervical spine or any of its components." CGH is frequently accompanied by neck discomfort. CGH prevalence has been shown to range between 0.17%

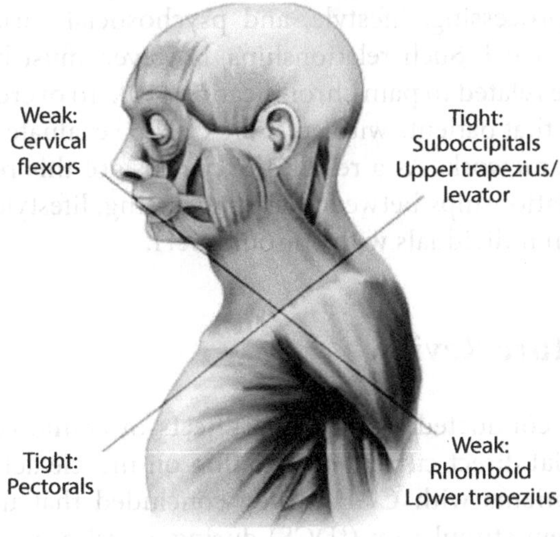

Figure 2.1 Janda's upper crossed syndrome (photo courtesy of Human Kinetics) [5].

and 2.5% [7] and may be as high as 26.73% for dentists [8] and 53% for whiplash victims. CGH is exacerbated by prolonged and/or atypical cervical spine motions. Problematically, no widely approved therapy plan for the management of CGH exists, especially when long-term patient outcomes are considered [9].

Headache accompanied with neck discomfort and stiffness is one of the diagnostic criteria for CGH. Cervicogenic headaches are unilateral, beginning on one side of the posterior head and neck and progressing to the front, and are occasionally accompanied by ipsilateral arm discomfort. Sjaastad *et al.* [8] discovered another kind of CGH characterized by bilateral head and neck discomfort exacerbated by neck postures and activities such as hairdressing, carpentry, and truck/tractor driving. The headache is preceded or coexisted by neck discomfort, which is increased by certain neck motions or prolonged postures. Vincent [9] identified numerous features that distinguish CGHs, including the following:

i. Unilateral discomfort emanating from the back of the head due to a facet "lock."
ii. Manual examination reveals evidence of cervical dysfunction.
iii. Trigger point palpation in the head or neck may occur.
iv. Exacerbated by prolonged neck postures.
v. Typical imaging.

To the best of our knowledge, research findings on the relationships between pain processing, lifestyle, and psychosocial variables are limited in episodic CeH. Such relationships, however, must be investigated because they are related to pain chronification [10]. To overcome this void, we recommend that patients with episodic CeH be evaluated within a biopsychosocial framework. As a result, the purpose of this research was to examine the relationships between pain processing, lifestyle, and psychosocial features in individuals with episodic CeH.

2.2 Literature Review

Kim *et al.* [11] conducted a study on "Effects of cranio-cervical flexion with trans cranial direct current stimulation on muscle activity and neck functions in patients with CGH." They concluded that using transcranial direct current stimulation (tDCS) during exercises involving craniocervical flexion reduces pain while boosting exercise, leading to functional improvement in CGHs. Cervicogenic headache patients would be more effectively managed and treated if exercise therapy was added to the treatment plan for both those with CGH and those with chronic cervical pain. In light of the positive effects that tDCS and manual therapy are having on CGH, it will be interesting to see whether electrotherapy and manual therapy will also have an impact. Therefore, let us examine how manual therapy, specifically a more recent method called primal reflex release technique (PRRT), affects CGH on its own [11].

Patil *et al.* [12] conducted a study on "Effectiveness of active release technique, positional release technique and myofascial release technique on pain, range of motion, functional disability as against conventional treatment in Patients with cervicogenic headache: Four arm parallel randomized study (2023)." This study findings, MFR, and exercise are efficient treatments for enhancing cervical muscle strength, particularly in those with CGH. An obstacle to a full muscle contribution in contraction can include pain and myofacial stiffness. The positional release technique is a successful strategy for reducing headache pain and impairment, which improve the patients physical functioning. It, therefore, appears that MFR and exercise are more effective together than either one alone. Patients with CGH can benefit from manual therapy, including myofacial releases techniques, as well as a combination of exercises, which can help them feel less discomfort and less disable [12].

Nowosilskyi *et al.* [13] conducted a study on "Evidence for the use of dry needling and physiotherapy in the management of cervicogenic or tension-type headache: A systematic review (2014)." They concluded that, because tension-type headache, CGH, and myofacial trigger point symptoms (like localized tenderness and referred pain) are similar, it seems plausible that management techniques that address myofascial trigger points may also lessen tension-type and CGH. There is evidence to support the idea that dry needling, when used in conjunction with other manual physiotherapy management, is successful in lowering the frequency and intensity of CGH [13].

Nykänen *et al.* [14] conducted a study on "Effect of neck exercises on Cervicogenic headache: A randomized controlled trial (2009)." It demonstrates that stretching exercise, along with strength and endurance training, is an efferent way to cure headache and arm discomfort brought on by neck pain. Strength training can, therefore, also be advised for individual who are having a strong headache coupled with neck pain because headache does not appear to be barrier to it. Regarding the pain and limitation, this manual therapy intervention for CGH may be useful treatment [14].

McDonnell *et al.* [15] conducted a study on "A specific exercise program and modification of postural alignment for treatment of cervicogenic headache." This study finds the cervical, scapulothoracic, and lumbar region alignments that were modified as part of the interventions, and the patient's function appeared to have improved. This study shown that variety of targeted exercise regimens and crucial manual therapy modification can help muscles regain their alignment and function. Following these precise changes, the primary focus will be treatment CGH and variables that contribute to their aggravation [15].

Park *et al.* [16] conducted a study on "Effects of cervical stretching and cranio-cervical flexion exercises on cervical muscle characteristics and posture of patients with cervicogenic headache." According to the results of this study, patients with CGH can change their posture and muscle properties by engaging in cranio-cervical exercise. Seung Kyu Park discovered that cranio-cervical flexion exercises can be used to cure headaches and their causes. Posterior muscle groups of the neck and shoulder are primarily to blame for the pain and headaches [16].

Lüdtke *et al.* [17] conducted a study on "Effect of treatment of tempromandibular disorders (TMD) in patients with cervicogenic headache: A single-blind, randomized controlled study." This study offers proof that conditions like tempromandibular joint dysfunction can impact the cervical spine and result in CGH. In comparison to other neuromusculoskeletal syndromes, patients having persistent neck discomfort, particularly headaches linked to neck dysfunction, require greater treatment; nevertheless, it is unclear how much TMD contributes to or is a cause of these patients' symptoms. The fact that the advantageous treatment effect in the group receiving experimental therapy is still present at 6 months follow-up or has improved, in contrast to the usual care group, where things either stay the same after treatment is over or get worse, adds to the theory that TMD may be a contributing or etiological factor in patients with persistent CGH. According to the criteria established by the researcher, we can state that there is no such short-term treatment that might alleviate CGH right away. The neuromuscular system is immediately downregulated, and the sympathetic nervous system activity is reduced by manual treatment procedure like PRRT [17].

Adams *et al.* [18] conducted a study on "A critical review of manual therapy use for headache disorders: prevalence, profiles, motivations, communication and self-reported effectiveness." Seeking pain relief was a popular justification for selecting this course of treatment. These 35 papers provided information on the prevalence, characteristics, motives, interpersonal interaction, and self-reported effectiveness of therapeutic manual use among people with headache disorders. The conclusion is that, even though there is a paucity of data and studies have serious methodological flaws, the findings suggest a potential benefit that warrants further investigation.

Mesa Jiménez *et al.* [19] conducted a study on "Efficacy of manual therapy in the treatment of tension-type headache: A systematic review from 2000 to 2013." In the line with our review, patients with TTH who receive manual therapy fare better than those who receive normal care or a placebo. Manual therapy did not result in a reduction in the usage of analgesic, but it does appear to lessen headache frequency and intensity as well as enhance patient's quality of life. However, because of the diversity in the study designs, measuring techniques, and therapeutic approaches, it is important to interpret our finding with care [19].

Chan *et al.* [20] conducted a study on "Efficacy of a C1-C2 self-sustained natural apophyseal glide (SNAG) in the management of cervicogenic headache." The goal of the study was to ascertain how a C1-C2 self-sustained natural apophyseal glide (SNAG) affected headaches caused by CGH factors. This difference persisted at the 1-year follow-up after being noticed four weeks after the start of the treatment. In addition, participants preferred the C1-C2 self-SNAG over the placebo treatment in terms of treatment benefits, according to their own report [20].

This report carefully examined "randomized clinical trials" (RCT) demonstrating the efficacy of manual treatments for "cervicogenic headache" (CEH), according to Aleksander Chaibi corresponding and Michael Bjrn Russell. Seven RCTs were identified, six of which employed cervical spinal manipulative treatment (SMT) and one of which utilized physiotherapy temporomandibular mobilization techniques. The RCTs suggest that PT and SMT could be useful therapies for CEH, although evaluating the findings is challenging, only one study had a control group, which did not get any medication. Moreover, there was an overrepresentation of individuals with intermittent CEH in the RCTs. Future CEH problems will be substantial in terms of treatment and diagnosis [21].

Aida Herranz-Gómez *et al.* used an umbrella review and mapping with meta-meta-analysis (MMA). Out of the eight papers that met the inclusion requirements, the quantitative analysis only included eight of them. For migraine, TTH, and CCH patients, the MMA produced positive results in terms of severity of pain and quality of life. In terms of TTH impairment and the frequency of migraine headache, the data similarly supported intervention. Conversely, TTH and CGH showed no discernible effects on the frequency of discomfort. The results showed some minor indications that aerobic exercise (AE) reduces migraineurs' pain severity [22].

According to the study by Pamela M. Rist *et al.*, spinal manipulation may lessen the frequency of migraines; however, the impact of multimodal chiropractic therapy on migraine frequency has not been assessed. EUC consisted of standard medical care as well as material on migraine education. Over the course of 14 weeks, MCC+ participants had 10 chiropractic appointments. Sixty-one of the 422 screened individuals underwent a 20-month randomization. Of the 29 individuals in MCC+, 24 (83%) attended more than 75% of the chiropractic sessions. Twenty-six individuals (43%) reported 88 non-serious adverse events, with 11 EUC participants reporting 39 events and 15 MCC+ participants reporting 59 incidents. While deficiencies were reversible, pre-established feasibility requirements were not fulfilled. Initial findings back up a conclusive MCC+ migraine study [23].

Pietro Bini and associates' comprehensive review and meta-analysis set out to evaluate the efficacy of various manual and exercise therapies for CGH patients in relation to other treatment, sham, or no treatment control. Included were randomized controlled studies that evaluated the impact of manual treatment or exercise therapy on individuals suffering from CGHs, with the key end measures being headache intensity or frequency. The study comprised 20 trials with 1,439 individuals in total. Metric analysis could only be performed on six manual treatment experiments using fictitious comparators. While the data indicates that manual and exercise treatment may help individuals with CGHs have shorter- and longer-term reductions in headache severity, frequency, and disability, the majority of the included trials had good overall return on investment. In contrast to other therapies, a sensitivity meta-analysis of low-RoB studies revealed moderately strong evidence in favor of spinal manipulation [24].

In their study, Christopher Kevin Wong *et al.* examined the clinical plus patient-reported results for individuals with post-concussion symptoms by looking at a regimen designed to tackle cervical dysfunction as well as paroxysms of positional vertigo during the first 3 weeks after injury, which included integrated visual and vestibular therapy. An analysis was conducted on the records of 38 patients (13 females and 25 males, ages 26.9 ± 19.7 years) who had suffered injuries from motor vehicle accidents, falls, sports, and assaults and had post-concussion symptoms [25].

2.3 Methodology

2.3.1 Need of the Study

Cervicogenic headache is very common in general population, and various research studies have been done on several intervention to treat CH, but none has done on PRRT. The objective is to gather research-based evidence related to the effectiveness of PRRTs in managing CGH.

2.3.2 Aim of the Study

The aim of this study is to determine the effects of PRRTs on the pain and disability in CGH.

2.3.3 Hypothesis

2.3.3.1 Experimental Hypothesis

E1. PRRT group may show more significant improvements in pain and disability score.
E2. Control group may show more significant improvements in pain and disability.
E3: Both groups may show similar significant improvement.

2.3.3.2 Null Hypothesis

There may be no significant difference between PRRT and control group.

Study setting: Swami Rama Himalayan Hospital, Jolly Grant.
Sample size: 56
Study design: Experimental study.
Study population: Students and staff in Himalayan Institute of Hospital Trust/Outpatient Department (HIHT/OPD)
Study duration: 1 year
Instrumentation:

- Pain visual analog scale, VAS neck disability index, NDI inclusion criteria
- Age (18–50) for both male and female
- Unilateral pain in neck and occipital region
- One-minute nociceptive examination test (£ 3) muscles involve in upper quadrant
- Multiple episodes of CGH

Exclusion criteria:

- Neck and cervical injury
- Bilateral headache in neck and occipital region
- Photophobia (eyes discomfort in bright light)
- Phonophobia (unwarranted fear of sound)

2.3.4 Protocol

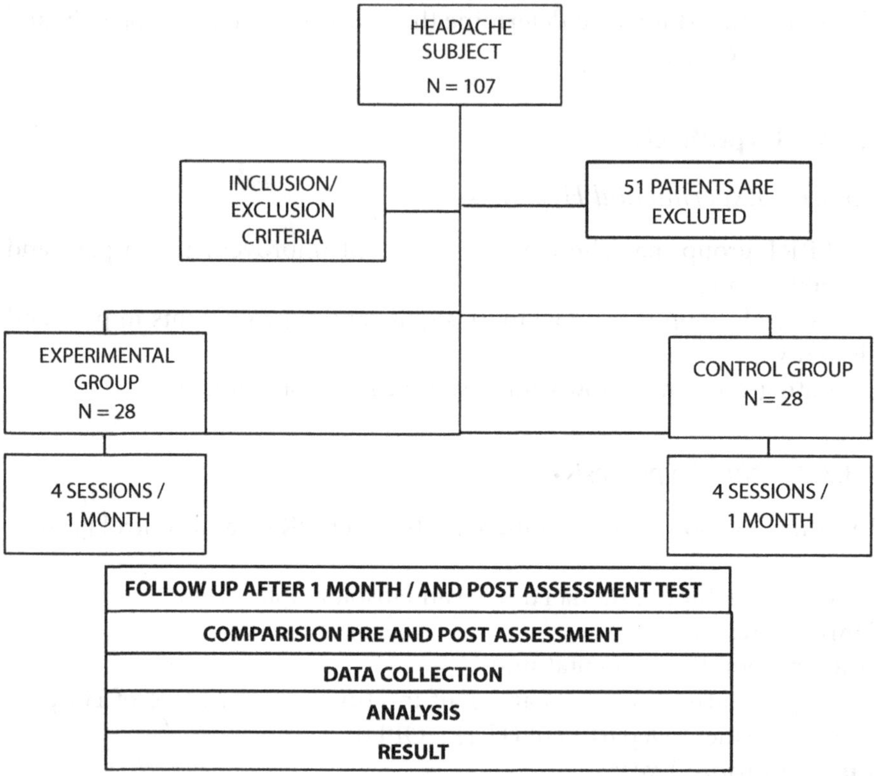

2.4 Procedure

After being found to meet the requirements for inclusion and exclusion, all CGH sufferers were assessed and asked to take part in the study.

2.4.1 Detailed Procedure

The objective of the research and the intervention were explained to the subjects who agreed to participate. They were informed about the study before their formal consent was obtained. Age, sex, and occupation-related information concerning demographics has been collected.

NDI (neck disability index) was performed both groups and evaluate each component of the scale.

For group A (experimental):
After obtaining the pre-treatment assessment, the researcher will perform a 1-minute nociceptive exam by palpating bilaterally. Each patient will be asked to use the Visual Analog Scale (VAS) to vocalize the pain they experience as each point is palpated. Researchers will look for the presence of hyperactive reflexes and unregulated autonomic nervous system (ANS) activity.

a. Barrier to entry (increased tone/tightness/stiffness)
b. NSRs (tenderness) causing grasp, grimace, or groan
c. Crepitus in muscles belly

Perform six primal techniques:

i. Duration of 1–1.5 min; for Group B (control)
ii. VAS assessment/1-min nociceptive examination/NDI was done and take pre assessment data
iii. Postural correction exercise and upper limb assessment and exercise
iv. Cervicogenic headache management
v. Strengthening exercises including deep neck flexors and thoracic muscles
vi. Home-based programs

Descriptive statistics was calculated for quantitative variable. Frequency along with percentage was calculated for qualitative variable. Shapiro–Wilk test was used to determine normality. To evaluate NDI outcome measure data within groups, a paired T-test was used. Analysis of the NDI outcome measure data between groups was done. When group A after treatment mean and standard deviation (3.21 ± 1.524) were compared to group A mean and standard deviation (7.57 ± 1.476) using VAS analysis, a significant difference was found.

The result of the VAS analysis showed a significant difference between group B's mean and standard deviation (4.54 ± 1.319) after treatment and group B's mean and deviation (6.50 ± 1.644) before treatment. Group A mean and SD (3.21 ± 1.524) and group B mean and SD (4.54 ± 1.319) of post-VAS analysis of both groups A and B. Both groups' post-data had a p-value of 0.001, which is less than 0.05 and indicates significance. This shows that there was no discernible difference between the two groups.

When group B's pre-treatment mean and standard error of mean (59.67 ± 2.376) were compared to group B's post-treatment mean and standard error of mean (37.33 ± 3.8808), there was a significant difference.

NDI post-data from group A and group A mean and SEM (3.71 ± 0.532) and group B mean and SEM (37.33 ± 0.8808) were investigated. Both groups' post-data had a p-value of 0.001, which is less than 0.05 and shows significance. This shows that there was no discernible difference between the two groups. Below are the tables having group comparison of group A and group B shown by Table 2.1 and Table 2.2. Table 2.3 are shown the outcome measure pre-post in group A and outcome measurement in grout A (mean and SEM) shown through Table 2.4. Table 2.5 shows the comparison outcome measure (VAS and NDI) in groups A and B. Table 2.6 describe the Cochran's Q-test for OMNE.

Table 2.1 Within-group comparison of outcome measure in group A (mean ± SD), P-value.

Outcome measure	Pre (mean±SD)	Post (mean±SD)	P value
VAS	7.57±1.476	3.21±1.524	0.001
NDI	54.43±14.487	3.71±2.816S	0.001

Table 2.2 Within-group comparison of outcome measure in group B (mean ± SD), P-value.

Outcome measure	Pre (mean±SD)	Post (mean±SD)	P value
VAS	6.50±1.644	4.54±1.319	0.001
NDI	59.82±20.690	37.29±14.909	0.001

Table 2.3 Within-group comparison of outcome measure pre-post in group A (mean ± SD), (mean ± SEM), P-value.

Outcome measure	Pre-post (mean ± SD)	Pre-post T (mean ± SEM)	P value
VAS	6.50±1.644	50.721±2.755	0.001
NDI	4.357±1.870	4.357±0.353	0.001

Table 2.4 Within-group comparison of outcome measure pre-post in group A (mean and SEM).

Outcome measure	Pre (mean±SEM	Post T (mean±SEM)
VAS	7.57±0.279	3.21±0.288
NDI	54.43±2.738	3.71±0.532

Table 2.5 Between group comparison outcome measure (VAS and NDI) in groups A and B.

Outcome measure	Group (A) post data (mean ± SEM)	Group (B) post data (mean ± SEM)	P value
VAS	3.21±1.524	4.54±1.319	0.001
NDI	3.71±2.816	37.29±14.909	0.001

Figure 2.2 shows the comparison of NDI-pre and NDI-post treatments, group A (mean and SD). Figure 2.3 shows the comparison of VAS-pre and VAS-post treatments, group A (mean and SD). Figure 2.4 shows the comparison of VAS-pre and VAS-post treatments, group B (mean and SD).

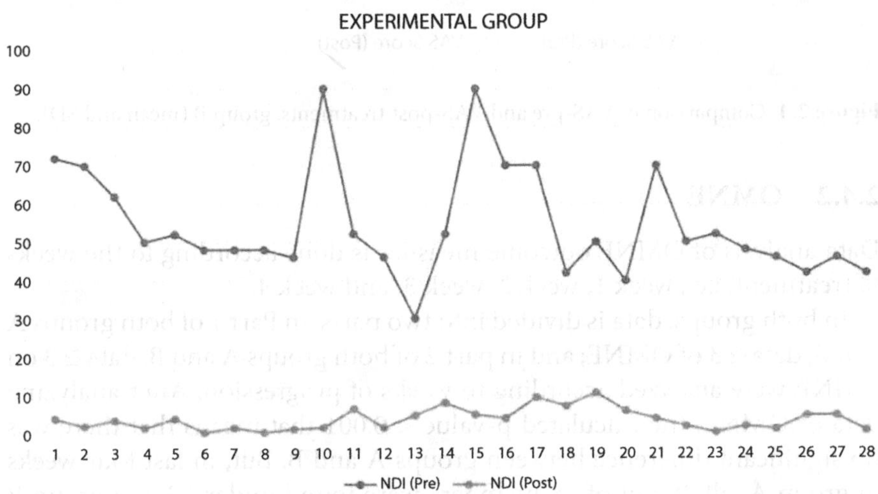

Figure 2.2 Comparison of NDI-pre and NDI-post treatments, group A (mean and SD).

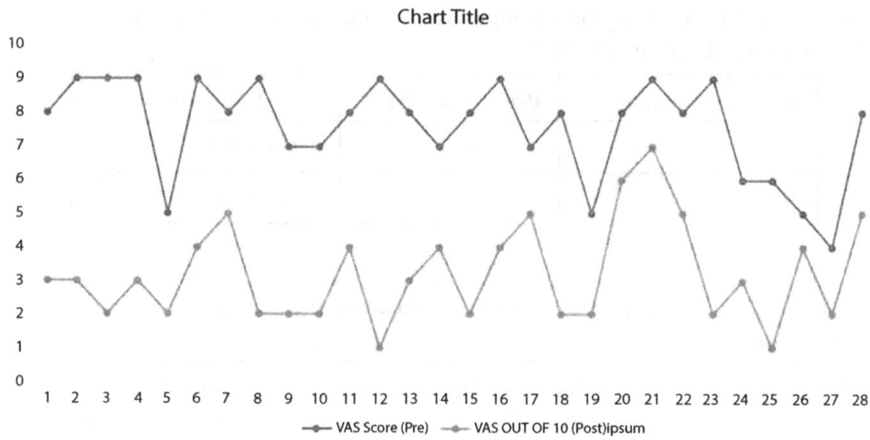

Figure 2.3 Comparison of VAS-pre and VAS-post treatments, group A (mean and SD).

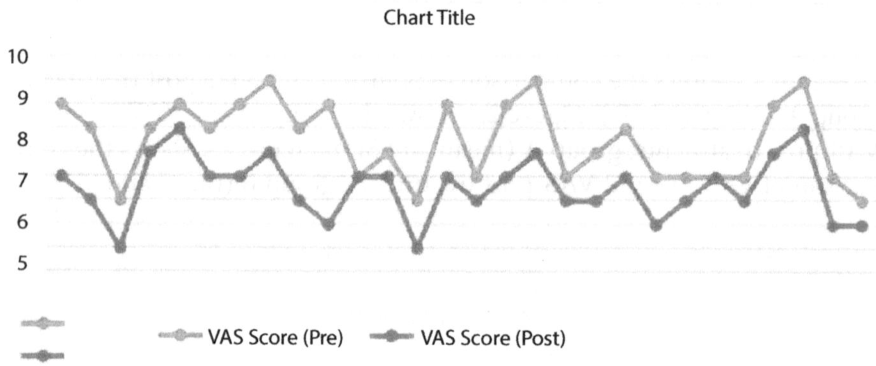

Figure 2.4 Comparison of VAS-pre and VAS-post treatments, group B (mean and SD).

2.4.2 OMNE

Data analysis of OMNE outcome measure is done according to the weeks of treatment, i.e., week 1, week 2, week 3, and week 4.

In both groups, data is divided into two parts: in Part 1 of both groups A and B, data ≥ 3 of OMNE; and in part 2 of both groups A and B, data ≥ 3 on OMNE were analyzed according to weeks of progression. After analyzing data of OMNE, the calculated p-value < 0.001 that means that there was no significant difference between groups A and B. But, in last four weeks in group A, all 28 out of 28 members were found under ≥ 3 and group B 20 out of 28 members were found ≥ 3. Figure 2.5 shows the comparison of NDI-pre and NDI-post treatments, group B (mean and SD).

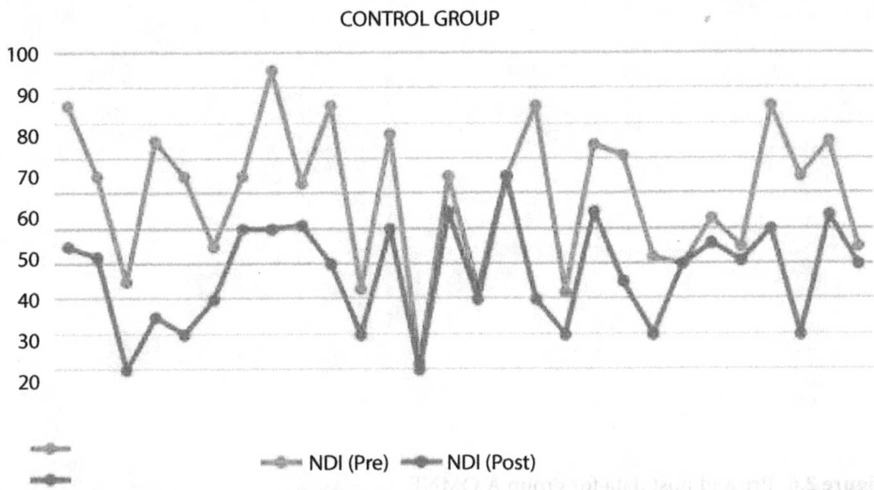

Figure 2.5 Comparison of NDI-pre and NDI-post treatments, group B (mean and SD).

Cochran's Q-test for OMNE:

Table 2.6 Cochran's Q-test for OMNE.

Groups	Muscle involved	Pre (%)	Week 1 (%)	Week 2 (%)	Week 3 (%)	Week 4 (%)	P value
Group 1	Part 1 ≤ 3	5 (17.9 %)	19 (67.9 %)	27 (96.4 %)	28 (96.4 %)	28 (96.4 %)	0.001
	Part 2 ≥ 3	23 (82.1 %)	9 (32.1 %)	1 (3.6 %)	0 (0 %)	0 (0 %)	
Group 2	Part 1 ≤ 3	2 (7.1 %)	7 (25.0 %)	13 (46.4 %)	17 (60.7 %)	20 (71.4 %)	0.001
	Part 2 ≥ 3	26 (92.9 %)	21 (75.0 %)	15 (53.6 %)	11 (39.3 %)	8 (28.6 %)	

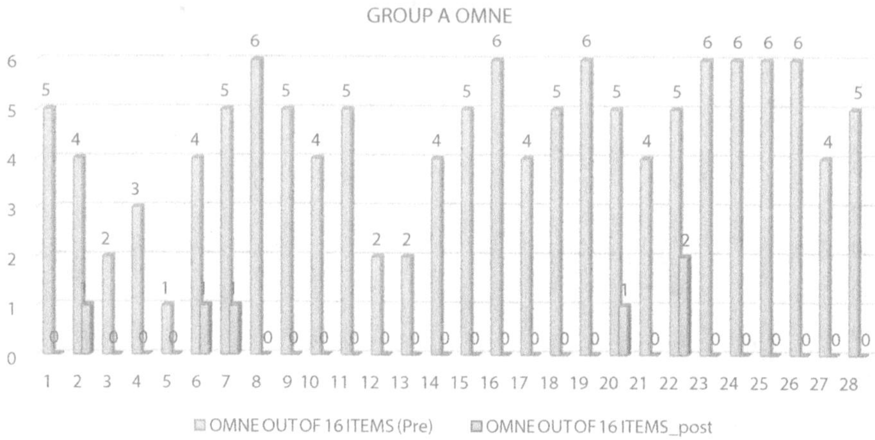

Figure 2.6 Pre and post data for group A OMNE.

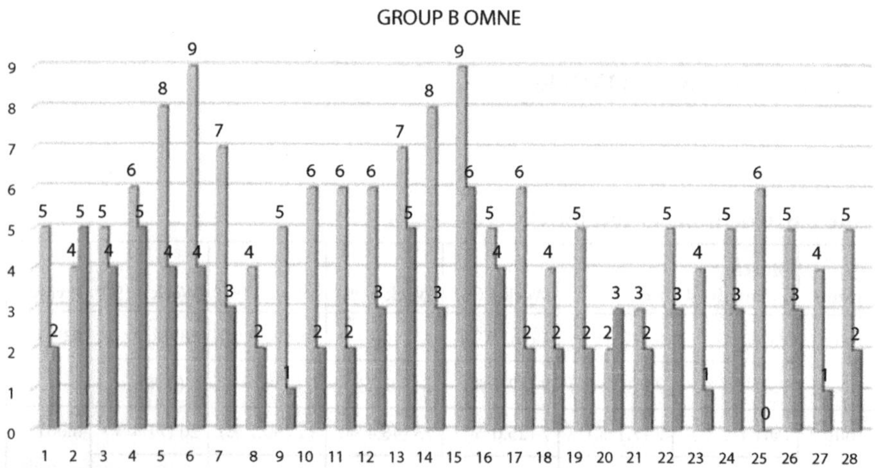

Figure 2.7 Pre and post data for group B OMNE.

Cervicogenic headaches are described, "Referred pain perceived in any region of the head caused by a primary nociceptive source in the musculoskeletal tissues innervated by cervical nerve." The cervical spine and its joint complex, not the head, is where pain starts to manifest. Cervicogenic headache is thought to affect between 0.4% and 2.5% of the population in general. The present study emphasizes on manual therapy intervention, namely, PRRT. In other groups, only conventional therapy is given to the patients suffer with CGH.

2.4.3 Clinical Relevance

Cervicogenic headaches, also known as chronic recurrent headaches, are a prevalent form of long-term and recurrent headache caused by muscular disorders of the cervical spine. Cervicogenic headache sufferers encounter significant functional limitations in daily life as well as social and emotional exclusion. As a first line of treatment for CGH, physical therapy is advised; however, it is unclear whether which kind of rehabilitation is most effective. According to this study, treating headaches with the PRRT is more successful. Therefore, they ought to be included in patients' treatment regimens to lessen the effects of CGH. Cervicogenic headaches are characterized by pain originating from the cervical spine and radiating to the head. Traditional treatment approaches often focus on symptomatic relief, but alternative therapies like PRRT, which target the underlying neurophysiological mechanisms, have gained attention.

The post-treatment analysis of pain and disability using the VAS and NDI revealed that both interventions show a significant improvement in CGH, but, on the basis of OMNE scales, it revealed significant improvements in CGH patients who underwent PRRT. These findings support the effectiveness of PRRT in alleviating symptoms and improving functional outcomes in this specific patient population. PRRT targets primal reflexes and associated muscle imbalances, addressing the root cause of the condition rather than providing symptomatic relief alone. The use of multiple outcome measures, including VAS, NDI, and OMNE, strengthens the validity of the findings. The consistent improvement across these measures suggests the broad impact of PRRT on both pain management and functional recovery. In conclusion, findings of this study suggest that PRRT shows promise as an effective treatment modality for CGH patients. The significant improvements in pain and disability support its potential to enhance the quality of life for individuals suffering from this condition.

2.4.4 Limitation of the Study

The study is done on a small sample sizes, and the study did not consider the long-term effects of the techniques on symptoms of CGH.

2.4.5 Scope of Future Research

Future research is necessary with a comparatively large sample size to determine if the improvement is permanent after the treatment session terminates. Also, the study can be limited to a particular age group. Long-term effects can be seen with proper follow-ups.

2.5 Conclusion

This study concluded that the PRRTs are more effective on the basis of the outcome measurement of the OMNE scale, as compared to the conventional therapy such as postural correction exercise, stretching, and other general exercises. Following a concussion, vestibular, musculoskeletal, and ocular impairment can all cause symptoms. Cervical restrictions can complicate symptoms in both vestibular and visual systems because cervical range of motion is important for both evaluation and therapy. Muscular imbalance and musculoskeletal dysfunction, characterized by recognizable patterns of muscular tension and weakness, are linked to CGHs. An accurate diagnosis can only be made after a comprehensive history and clinical examination. Sports physical therapists must diagnose athletes with CGHs accurately and offer the right treatments so that they may resume their sports activities as soon as feasible. These important discoveries close a vacuum in the body of knowledge about pertinent quality parameters for headache treatment so graphical analysis becomes necessary.

References

1. Adams, L. and Turk, D., Psychosocial factors and central sensitivity syndromes. *Curr. Rheumatol. Rev.*, 11, 2, 96–108, 2015.
2. Alburquerque-Sendín, F., Madeleine, P., Fernández-De-Las-Peñas, C., Camargo, P., Salvini, T., Spotlight on topographical pressure pain sensitivity maps: A review. *J. Pain Res.*, 11, 215–225, 2018.
3. Andrade, C., Author's response to: Multiple testing and protection against type I error using p value correction: Application in cross-sectional study designs. *Indian J. Psychol. Med.*, 41, 2, 198, 2019.
4. Stovner, L.J. *et al.*, Headache after concussion. *Eur. J. Neurol.*, 16, 1, 112–20, 2009.
5. Arendt-Nielsen, L., Morlion, B., Perrot, S., Dahan, A., Dickenson, A., Kress, H.G., Wells, C., Bouhassira, D., Mohr Drewes, A., Assessment and manifestation of central sensitisation across different chronic pain conditions. *Eur. J. Pain*, 22, 2, 216–241, 2018.
6. Zito, G., Jull, G., Story, I., Clinical tests of musculoskeletal dysfunction in the diagnosis of cervicogenic headache. *Man. Ther.*, 11, 2, 118–29, 2006.

7. Knackstedt, H., Bansevicius, D., Aaseth, K., BerlingGrande, R., Lundqvist, C., Russell, M.B., Cervicogenic headache in the general population: the Akershus study of chronic headache. *Cephalalgia*, 30, 1468–1476, 2010.
8. De Hertogh, W.J., Vaes, P.H., Devroey, D., Truijen, S., Duquet, W., Oostendorp, R., Management of headache disorders: design of a randomised clinical trial screening for prognostic patient characteristics. *BMC Musculoskelet. Disord.*, 8, 1-8, 2007.
9. View of prevalence of cervicogenic headache in Dentists.
10. Borsook, D., Youssef, A.M., Simons, L., Elman, I., Eccleston, C., When pain gets stuck: The evolution of pain chronification and treatment resistance. *Pain*, 159, 12, 2421–2436, 2018.
11. Park, S.K., Yang, D.J., Kim, J.H., Heo, J.W., Park, S.H., Uhm, Y.H., Yoon, J.H., Effects of cranio-cervical flexion with transcranial direct current stimulation on muscle activity and neck functions in patients with cervicogenic headache. *J. Phys. Ther. Sci.*, *31*, 1, 24–28, 2019, https://doi.org/10.1589/jpts.31.24.
12. Effectiveness of Active release technique, Positional release technique and Myofascial Release technique on Pain, Range of Motion, Functional Disability as against conventional treatment in Patients with Cervicogenic Headache: Four arm parallel randomized study, 2023.
13. France, S., Bown, J., Nowosilskyj, M., Mott, M., Rand, S., & Walters, J., Evidence for the use of dry needling and physiotherapy in the management of cervicogenic or tension-type headache: a systematic review. *Cephalalgia*, 34, 12, 994–1003, 2014.
14. Ylinen, J., Nikander, R., Nykänen, M., Kautiainen, H., & Häkkinen, A., Effect of neck exercises on cervicogenic headache: a randomized controlled trial. *J. Rehabil. Med.*, 42, 4, 344–349, 2010.
15. A Specific Exercise Program and Modification of Postural Alignment for Treatment of Cervicogenic Headache. *J. Orthop. Sports Phys. Ther.*
16. Park, S. K., Yang, D. J., Kim, J. H., Kang, D. H., Park, S. H., & Yoon, J. H., Effects of cervical stretching and cranio-cervical flexion exercises on cervical muscle characteristics and posture of patients with cervicogenic headache. *J. Phys. Ther. Sci.*, 29, 10, 1836–1840, 2017.
17. von Piekartz, H., & Lüdtke, K., Effect of treatment of temporomandibular disorders (TMD) in patients with cervicogenic headache: a single-blind, randomized controlled study. *Cranio®*, 29, 1, 43–56, 2011.
18. Moore, C. S., Sibbritt, D. W., & Adams, J., A critical review of manual therapy use for headache disorders: prevalence, profiles, motivations, communication and self-reported effectiveness. *BMC Neurol.*, 17, 1–11, 2017.
19. Bhargava, N., Rathore, P.S., Jha, M., and Goswami, A., Adaptive Clustering Algorithm for Big Health Data Classification. *2023 3rd Asian Conference on Innovation in Technology (ASIANCON)*, Ravet IN, India, pp. 1–4, 2023, doi: 10.1109/ASIANCON58793.2023.10270544.
20. Bhargava, N., Rathore, P. S., & Bhowmick, A., Study of X ray detection using CNN in machine learning, in: *International Conference on Advancements in*

Smart Computing and Information Security, pp. 295–303, Cham, Springer Nature, Switzerland, 2022, November.

21. Chaibi, A. and Russell, M.B., Manual therapies for cervicogenic headache: a systematic review. *J. Headache Pain*, 13, 5, 351–9, 2012 Jul, doi: 10.1007/s10194-012-0436-7. Epub 2012 Mar 30. PMID: 22460941; PMCID: PMC3381059.
22. Herranz-Gómez, A., García-Pascual, I., Montero-Iniesta, P., Touche, R.L., Paris-Alemany, A., Effectiveness of exercise and manual therapy as treatment for patients with migraine, tension-type headache or cervicogenic headache: an umbrella and mapping review with meta-meta-analysis. *Appl. Sci.*, 11, 15, 6856, 2021 Jul 26.
23. Rist, P.M., Bernstein, C., Kowalski, M., Osypiuk, K., Connor, J.P., Vining, R., Long, C.R., Macklin, E.A., Wayne, P.M., Multimodal chiropractic care for migraine: A pilot randomized controlled trial. *Cephalalgia*, 41, 3, 318–28, 2021 Mar.
24. Bini, P., Hohenschurz-Schmidt, D., Masullo, V., Pitt, D., Draper-Rodi, J., The effectiveness of manual and exercise therapy on headache intensity and frequency among patients with cervicogenic headache: a systematic review and meta-analysis. *Chiropr. Man. Ther.*, 30, 1, 49, 2022 Nov 23.
25. Wong, C.K., Ziaks, L., Vargas, S., DeMattos, T., Brown, C., Sequencing and integration of cervical manual therapy and vestibulo-oculomotor therapy for concussion symptoms: retrospective analysis. *Int. J. Sports Phys. Ther.*, 16, 1, 12, 2021.

3

Application of AI in Determining Immediate and Carryover Effects of Primal Reflex Release Technique Neural Reboot on SI Joint Mobility

Rakesh Chaudhary*, **Vaibhav Agarwal and Aashish Negi**

Department of Physiotherapy, Himalayan Institute of Medical Sciences, Swami Rama Himalayan University, Jolly Grant, Dehradun, India

Abstract

Many studies have identified that sacroiliac (SI) joint dysfunction is the major reason for lower back pain. It was estimated about 15%–30% of people with low back pain having SI joint as the origin but use of artificial intelligence (AI) is now making easy and accurate to cure and disease, and calculated P-value for outcome measures passive straight leg raise range (PSLR) and passive dorsiflexion range (PDFR) showed a significant difference, which means that one out of both groups reported positive changes due to AI. After comparing mean values of post data of both groups, the experimental group reported positive changes for outcome measures PSLR and PDFR. The results of this study showed that primal reflex release technique can be used to improve hamstring flexibility (passive straight leg raise range) and calf flexibility (passive dorsi-flexion range) using AI. But when mean of post data of both groups were compared, the calculated P-value showed no difference for outcome measures visual analog scale (VAS) and modified oswestry low back pain disability questionnaire (MOLBPDQ) in both groups A and B. This study should be performed on larger population with higher VAS values. The same study can be done comparing PRRT versus other intervention techniques. The long-term effect of PRRT can be analyzed.

Keywords: AI, SI, PRRT, PSLR, mobility

**Corresponding author*: RakeshChaudhary58@outlook.com

Abhishek Kumar, Narayan Vyas, Pramod Singh Rathore, Abhineet Anand and Pooja Dixit (eds.) Internet of Medicine for Smart Healthcare, (43–64) © 2025 Scrivener Publishing LLC

3.1 Introduction

Sedentary lifestyle is now prevalent throughout the world as more people spend a lot of time sitting down both at their work and at their home. Due to longer sitting times, low back pain (LBP) has also become more common among office workers. According to recent study, sitting for more than 7 h a day greatly raise the risk of LBP [1, 2]. The three hamstring muscles have a total of four heads that link to the tibia and fibula, two on each side. The gastrocnemius muscle, which makes up the lower half of the calf, has two heads that connect to the femur on either side. The three hamstring muscles have a total of four heads that link to the tibia and fibula, two on each side. The hamstring and the calf are joined together by facial [3–5].

In sacroiliac (SI) joint (SIJ) dysfunction (SIJD), physiotherapy interventions can help with pain management, disability management, and pelvic position restoration. Furthermore, it appears that manipulation is more efficient than therapeutic exercise, kinesiotaping, or non-interventional rest. According to Lee *et al.*, kinesio tape could successfully re-establish the correct pelvic posture [5]. Several interventions are being used, but no such study has been done on PRRT (primal reflex release technique) for treatment of SIJD [6].

A recent meta-analysis created highly generalizable brain–emotion correlations in an effort to explain the variability of reported findings, both in terms of research population and technique. Five fundamental emotions—happiness, fear, anger, disgust, and sadness—were shown to have distinct and archetypal patterns of activity (and connection) across several brain regions when new statistical learning approaches that look for tentative relationships—also known as machine learning—were applied.

The goal of PRRT, a therapy paradigm that is part of the regional interdependent methodology for patient care, is to lessen pain patterns by downregulating an overstimulated autonomic nerve system [7]. The idea behind the regional interdependence method is that perceived discomfort or deficit in one part of the body may be caused by malfunction in another system or area of the body. After an injury, reflexes can cause defensive muscle contractions during the fight-or-flight reaction. As long as the patient experiences pain, the autonomic nervous system (ANS) activates a release of messenger chemicals like acetylcholine and serotonin that maintain the protective spasm or trigger sites [8]. A cutaneous or nociceptive signal produced by the hyperactive neurons affects the muscle spindle, which, in turn, affects the length and tension of muscle [8–10].

3.2 Literature Review

Warneke Konstantin and Wohlann Tim (2023), "Acute effects of long-lasting stretching and strength training on maximal strength and flexibility in the calf muscle": The objectives of this study were to determine the long-lasting effect in three groups. Static stretching technique (SST) used a stretching orthosis for the calf muscle to execute a 1-h stretching intervention. To do this, the researcher placed the stretching orthosis on the subject's leg and secured the foot into the most dorsiflexed position possible. The calf muscles were stretched as a result. The strength training routine (STR) exercised their calf muscles by performing five sets of 12 calf lifts on a 45° leg press [11].

Kalita Abhijit *et al.* (2021), "The combined effectiveness of piriformis stretch and muscle activation exercises in patients with sacroiliac joint pain": The purpose of current study was to assess the combined impact of piriformis stretches and muscles activation activities in patient with sacroiliac joint pain. A total of 30 participant are divided into two groups, with primary diagnosis of sacroiliac joint pains from the consultant [12].

Bertoldo Dennis and Pirri Carmelo (2021): The goal of the current study is to assess the efficacy of using single sessions of the Stecco methods of facial manipulation to treat the muscular fascia away from the painful regions. The study is titled "Pilot study of sacroiliac joint dysfunction treated with a single session of fascial manipulation clinical objective implications for effective pain reduction." A quicker implementation of pain-free exercise programs can be made possible by the incorporation of this kind of approaches in SIJD. It can also improve patient management and tolerances for other therapies [13].

S. Kawishwar Shraddha and SamalSubrat (2020), "To study the effect of mulligan mobilization versus conventional therapy in sacroiliac joint pain": The purpose of this study was to determine the impact of mulligan mobilization against conventional therapy on pain on VAS, lumbar range of motion (ROM), and functional impairment in individuals with sacroiliac joint disturbance. The conclusion of this study is as follows: The Mulligan mobilization technique was found to be more beneficial than conventional therapy in the current investigation; however, both Mulligan mobilization and conventional therapy were found to be effective in participants with sacroiliac joint pain [14].

Erica S. Albertin *et al.* (2020), "An exploratory case series analysis of the use of PRRT to improve signs and symptoms of hamstring strain": The purpose of this case series was to investigate the immediate effects of PRRT for treating hamstring strains. In this case series, the application of PRRT led to the resolution of SIJD as well as improvement in function, ROM, and discomfort. Although the long-term consequences of the PRRT are still unknown, it may be helpful in temporarily reducing hamstring strain symptoms. When treating pain brought on by hamstring strain, doctors might think about adopting a therapy that concentrates on the autonomic nerve system [7].

Sarkar Manisha *et al.* (2019), "A non-blinded, 2 group, pre-test and post-test randomised clinical trial protocol comparing the effectiveness of the muscle energy technique and Kinesiotaping in Mechanical Sacroiliac Joint Dysfunction": This study compares the effects of muscle energy technique and kinesio taping in addition to conventional physiotherapy on improving pains and quality of life among patients with mechanical SIJD [15].

Laura López *et al.* (2019), "Effects of neurodynamic treatment on hamstrings flexibility: A systematic review and meta-analysis": This study's findings suggest that neurodynamic treatment is preferable to other approaches like stretching for enhancing the extensibility of the hamstring musculature and the passive knee extension ROM [16].

Parisa Nejati *et al.* (2018), "Effectiveness of exercise therapy and manipulation on sacroiliac joint dysfunction": The goal of a random controlled trial is to compare the efficacy of exercise therapy (ET), and manipulation therapy (MT), and pain and disability seem to be reduced with exercise and manipulation therapy. However, the results of these two therapies combined do not appear to be significantly superior to those of any strategy used alone [17].

Valerie F. Stevenson *et al.* (2018), "Treating groin and hip flexor pain using primal reflex release technique: A case series": In order to compares the effectiveness of ET, MT, and an EMT combination in the treatment of SIJD, a random controlled study was conducted. The study's findings with exercise and MT pain and disability appear to be lessened in people with SIJD. The combined effects of these two therapies, nevertheless, do not seem to be appreciably better than any single technique [18].

Erika K. Vichcales (2018) and Carnahan, "The psychological and physiological effect of performing the primal reflex release technique on female, division I collegiate athletes": The aim of the study is to analyze the effect of PRRTs (primal reflex release techniques) on anxiety in athletes and to conclude whether these techniques are effective. According to the analysis of the data from this exploratory trial, PRRT dynamic relaxation (dR) can help patients feel more relaxed by lowering their heart rate and offering instant relief from feelings of state anxiety. More athletes should be included in this study, especially those with anxiety disorders that have been recognized or who frequently report feelings of anxiety [19, 20].

Rajesh Sewani and Sandeep Shinde (2017), "Effect of hot moist pack and muscle energy technique in subjects with sacro-iliac joint dysfunction": This study ascertains the impact of hot moist packs (HMP) and muscle energy technique (MET) in SJD individuals and contrasts the impact of conventional therapy with HMP and MET in patients suffering from sacroiliac joint dysfunctions. In summary, the current study offered proof in favor of the application of muscle energy method and hot moist packs for SJD. MET improves muscular extensibility in addition to joint ROMs. In order to improve lumbar ROM, lessen disability, and relieve discomfort associated with sacroiliac joint dysfunction, hot moist packs and MET can be helpful [21].

Jena Hansen-Honeycutt *et al.* (2016), "A clinical guide to the assessment and treatment of breathing pattern disorders in the Physically active: A case series": In this case series, people who were physically active and had musculoskeletal discomfort, a BPD, as well as startle reflexes as their principal complaints were examined to see how well breathing exercises and PRRT worked. According to the present research, musculoskeletal discomfort and BPD may be related to the appearance of a startle reaction upon palpation. The "clamshell" exercise and/or PRRT helped individuals regain an ideal breathing pattern and, in theory, global motor control, which may have lessened their primary complaint of discomfort [23].

Erin B. Chapman *et al.* (2016), "A clinical guide to the assessment and treatment of breathing pattern disorders in the physically active: Part 1": This study concludes that all subjects display a change in their breathing pattern as well as a diminished or eliminated presence of a startle reflexes [22].

Tomasz Sipko *et al.* (2016), "Effect of sacroiliac joint mobilization on the level of soft tissue pain threshold in asymptomatic women": The purpose of this study was to assess how self-mobilization and/or SIJ mobilization affected the asymptomatic women in the age range of 21 to 23 who had a soft tissue pain threshold. In summary, in women without pain symptoms, there is evidence of both global and local short-term pain modulations in responses to oscillatory mobilization of the SIJ. The SIJ's ability to self-mobilize has limited analgesic effects [24].

Richard L. Smith *et al.* (2016), "Effect of sacroiliac joint mobilization on the standing position of the pelvis in healthy men": This study sought to ascertain how the standing posture of the pelvis was affected by unilateral posterior as well as unilateral anterior SIJ mobilization. The measurement methodologies exhibited a range of dependability from good to outstanding. The authors suggest doing more research with bigger samples of healthy participants and patients who have clinical issues that might alter their pelvic posture when standing [25].

Bharti Neha *et al.* (2016), "Effectiveness of therapeutic interventions in sacroiliac joint dysfunction: a systematic review": The purpose of the study is to identify gaps in the literature for further research on SJD and to present an overview of studies that have been conducted on the various treatment modalities. Therefore, it may be inferred that, in order to effectively treat the conditions of sacroiliac joints pain and dysfunctions, greater emphasis should be placed on alternative treatment modalities such as manual therapy and soft tissue release [26].

L. Mourot *et al.* (2022): In the creation of entertainment material, like as video game, virtual reality, or fiction film, human character animation is frequently essential. This introduces motion data formats first, along with the most popular datasets for human motions and how fundamental deep models may be improved to support the learning of temporal and spatial patterns in motion data. Second, this discusses cutting-edge methods for motion synthesis, character controls, and motion editing—three sizable families of functions used in human animation pipelines. Lastly, this talks about the shortcomings of the most advanced techniques now available for skeleton human character animations that rely on deep reinforcement learning or machine learning, as well as potential future research areas that might address these shortcomings and satisfy the demands of animators [27].

Erica S. Albertin *et al.* (2020): Treatment for hamstring strain (HS), a prevalent ailment among injured physically active people, generally consists of rest, stretches, and modalities. Manual treatment called PRRT is used to relieve pain resulting from overstimulation of the body's primitive reflexes. The treatment of six HS patients with PRRT was reported utilizing a multi-site case series methodology. Measurements of "range of motion (ROM)," the "patient specific functional scale (PSFS)," and the "numeric pain rating scale (NPRS)" were gathered. Additionally, the symmetry of the sacroiliac joints was assessed, which was classified as "sacroiliac joints dysfunction" (SJD). PRRT proved to be a successful therapy for HS patients. During the course of the therapy, subjects' average pain score on the NPRS decreased significantly, by five points (95% CI: 3.374, 6.626). Before therapy, SJD was noted in all participants, and, when the patients were reviewed following treatment, the condition was resolved in all subjects. The use of PRRT in this case series resolved SJD and led to improvements in function, ROM, and discomfort [7].

Yi Yang *et al.* (2023): The ability to emulate the sensory, cognitive, self-learning, and actuation characteristics of robots is greatly enhanced by neuromorphic electronics. Nonetheless, a thorough analysis of organic neuromorphic electronics' contribution to and function in robotic applications is still lacking. The paper emphasizes how neuromorphic circuits may be used in sophisticated robotic systems to sense, reason, and act. Robotics using organic, inorganic, along with hybrid materials for sensing, navigation, and control are described. The field's future research directions are delineated. By utilizing different neuromorphic circuits, intelligent robotic systems may be fully used for a wide range of applications [28].

3.3 Methodology

3.3.1 Aim of Study

The aim is to study the effectiveness of immediate and carryover effects on SIJ pain by neural reboot PRRT on SIJ mobility, hamstring, and calf flexibility in desk job workers.

3.3.2 Need of the Study

As we know that 80% to 90% of population sometime in their lifetime suffers from back pain and in that LBA, approximately 25% to 30% patients experience LBP due to SIJD. Although there are many interventions to treat SIJD, there has been no such study on PRRT, and, thus, it becomes important to check the effectiveness of PRRT on SIJD.

3.3.3 Hypothesis

3.3.3.1 Null Hypothesis

N1: There may not be any effectiveness of PRRT on SIJD.
N2: There may not be any effectiveness of Sham therapy on SIJD.

3.3.3.2 Alternate Hypothesis

A1: There might be effectiveness of PRRT on SIJD.
A2: There might be effectiveness of Sham therapy technique on SIJD.
A3: Both the technique may be equally effective.

3.3.4 Operational Definition

The PRRT is a therapeutic paradigm that aims to "downregulate" the ANS by identifying reflexes, resetting them, and employing reciprocal inhibition to reduce pain and muscular spasm.

3.3.4.1 Desk Job Worker

Office workers now spend between 65% and 75% of their waking hours sitting at their jobs or at home as a result of modernization and the computerization of labor that followed in recent years. Seventy-seven percent of the time that desk-based workers spend at work is spent sitting for more than 30 min. Sedentary behavior, such as prolonged sitting, is linked to a higher risk of cardiometabolic illness and a decline in an individual's cognitive function in office environments.

Study setting: Physiotherapy OPD, Himalayan Hospital, Swami Rama Himalayan University
Sample Size: 34
Type of Study: Experimental study
Study subjects: Desk job workers from various departments of Swami Rama Himalayan University
Sampling Techniques: Random Sampling Techniques
Study Duration: 1 year
Instrumentation: CorelDRAW software, screening form
Outcome measures: VAS, Modified Oswestry Low Back Pain Disability Questionnaire, Passive knee extension range, passive ankle dorsi-flexion range

Inclusion Criteria:

- Age Group: 18–50 years
- Sitting hours at work place: 5–8 h per day VAS: <5

Exclusion Criteria:

- Pain that needs medical attention
- Radicular pain with neurological (sensory or motor) deficits,
- History of spinal surgery
- History of spinal, pelvic, or lower extremity fracture
- History of hospitalization for trauma or motor vehicle accident,
- Hip or knee dysfunctions
- Pregnancy
- History of any systemic disease such as arthritis, tuberculosis, liver, or kidney failure
- Subjects with leg length discrepancies, because of its potential effect on hamstring muscle length, had been excluded.

3.3.5 Data Analysis

MS Excel 2010 was used to collect and input the data. Using the SPSS program version 20, several statistical analyses were carried out. With regard to the quantitative variables, descriptive statistics were computed. The proportion and frequency were computed for the qualitative factors. The "Shapiro–Wilk test," also known was used to determine normality. T-test in pairs and the Wilcoxon "signed-rank tests" were employed to compare the mean differences between groups A and B. The "Mann–Whitney test" and independent samples test were used to compares the mean differences between groups A and B.

3.3.6 Protocol

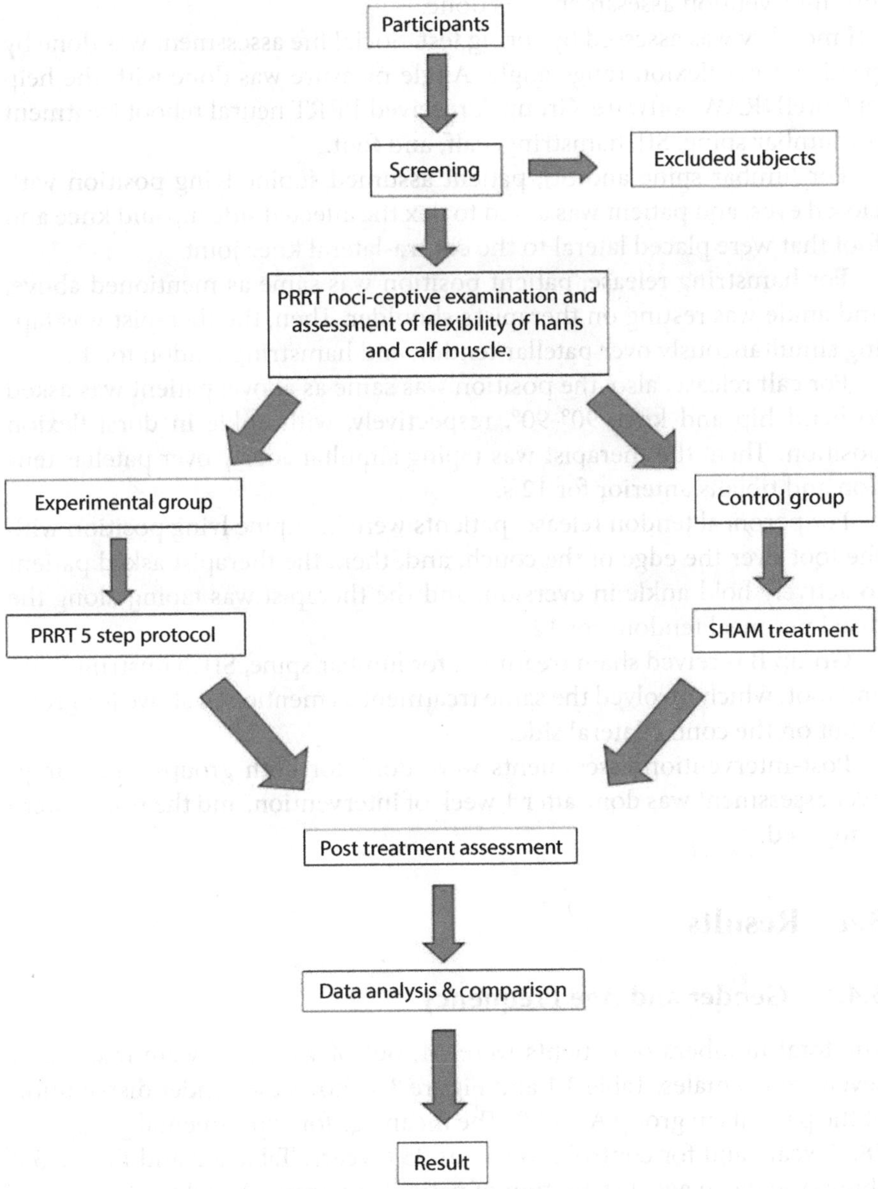

3.3.7 Procedure

Subjects were selected based on the inclusions and exclusions criteria.

After signing the informed consent forms, subjects are randomly divided into two groups; i.e., group A (experimental group) and group B (control group).

Pre-intervention assessment was done.

SIJ mobility was assessed by spring test. Social life assessment was done by passive dorsi-flexion range angle. Angle measure was done with the help of CorelDRAW software. Group A received PRRT neural reboot treatment for lumbar spine, SIJ, hamstring, calf, and foot.

For lumbar spine and SIJ, patient assumed supine lying position with closed eyes, and patient was asked to flex the affected side hip and knee and foot that were placed lateral to the contra-lateral knee joint.

For hamstring release, patient position was same as mentioned above, and ankle was resting on therapist's shoulder. Then, the therapist was taping simultaneously over patellar tendon and hamstring tendon for 12 s.

For calf release, also, the position was same as above; patient was asked to bend hip and knee 90°-90°, respectively, with ankle in dorsi-flexion position. Then, the therapist was taping simultaneously over patellar tendon and tibialis anterior for 12 s.

For peroneal tendon release, patients were in supine lying position with the foot over the edge of the couch, and, then, the therapist asked patient to actively hold ankle in eversion, and the therapist was taping along the distal peroneal tendons for 12 s.

Group B received sham treatment for lumbar spine, SIJ, hamstring, calf, and foot, which involved the same treatment as mentioned above for group A but on the contra-lateral side.

Post-intervention assessments were done for both groups, and carry-over assessment was done after 1 week of intervention, and the results were compared.

3.4 Results

3.4.1 Gender and Age Frequency

The total numbers of patients were 34, out of which 27 were males and seven were females. Table 3.1 and Figure 3.1 shows the gender distribution of the patients in group A and B. The mean age for experimental group was 38.17 years and for control group was 35.6 years. Table 3.2 and Figure 3.2 shows the mean age distribution of patients in group A and B.

Table 3.1 Gender distribution in groups A and B.

Group	Males	Females	Total
Group A	15	2	17
Group B	12	5	17
Total	27	7	34

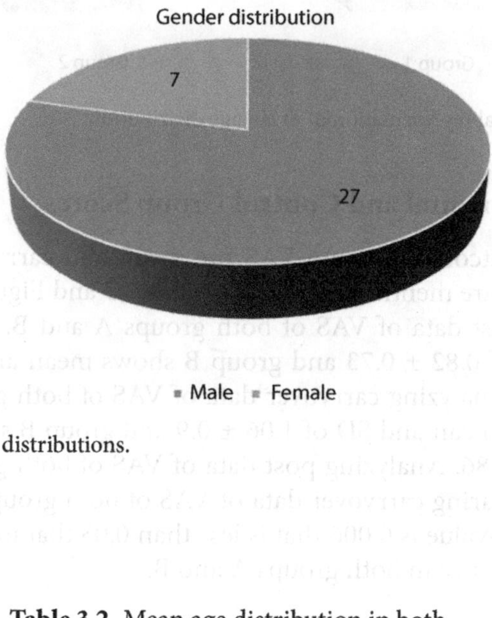

Figure 3.1 Gender distributions.

Table 3.2 Mean age distribution in both groups A and B.

Group	Total sample	Mean age
Group A	7	38.17
Group B	17	35.6

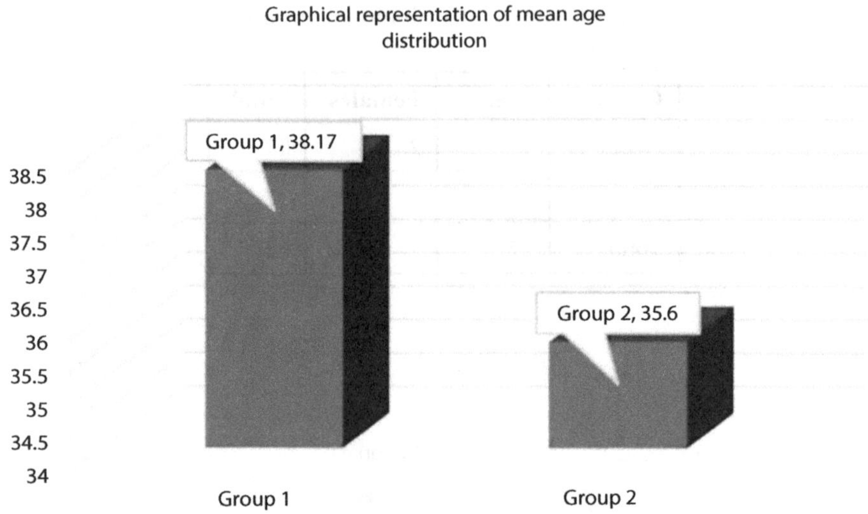

Figure 3.2 Graphical representation of mean age distribution.

3.4.2 Experimental and Control Group Scores

The mean of outcome measure VAS pre, post, and carryover scores for groups A and B are mentioned below in Table 3.3 and Figure 3.3.

Analyzing post data of VAS of both groups A and B, group A shows mean and SD of 0.82 ± 0.73 and group B shows mean and SD of 2.53 ± 1.546, whereas analyzing carryover data of VAS of both groups A and B, group A shows mean and SD of 1.06 ± 0.9 and group B shows mean and SD of 2.44 ± 1.586. Analyzing post data of VAS of both groups A and B, and while comparing carryover data of VAS of both groups A and B, and the calculated P-value is 0.006 that is less than 0.05 that means there is no significant difference in both groups A and B.

Table 3.3 Mean comparison of VAS pre, post, and carryover scores for groups A and B.

Outcome measure	Mean group A	Mean group B
VAS Pre	3.06	3.06
VAS Post	0.82	2.53
VAS Carryover	1.06	2.47

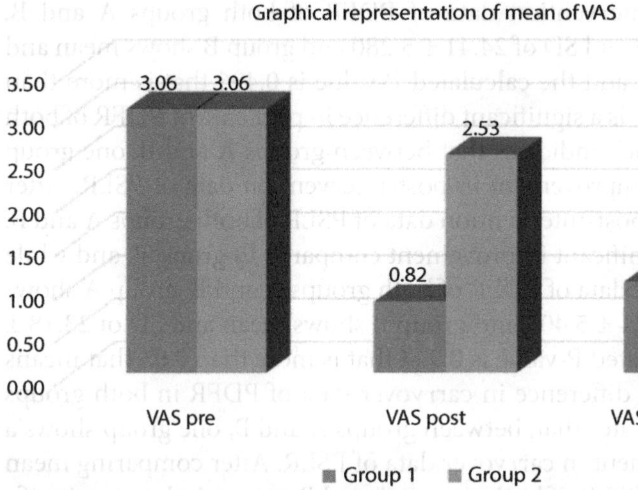

Figure 3.3 Graphical representation of VAS.

Analyzing carryover data of MOLBPDQ of both groups A and B, group A shows mean and SD of 25.18 ± 9.49 and group B shows mean and SD of 45.29 ± 10.048, and the calculated P-value is less than 0.001, which is less than 0.05 that means there is no significant difference in both groups A and B.

Analyzing post-intervention data of PSLR of both groups A and B, group A shows mean and SD of 80.35 ± 6.133 and group B shows mean and SD of 81.29 ± 7.904, and the calculated P-value is 0.628 that is more than 0.05 that means there is a significant difference in post-intervention data of PSLR of both groups A and B, which indicates that, between groups A and B, one group shows a significant improvement in post-intervention data of PSLR. After comparing mean of post-intervention data of PSLR of both groups A and B, group A shows a significant improvement as compared to group B. While comparing carryover data of PSLR of both groups A and B, group A shows mean and SD of 79.00 ± 6.083 and group B shows mean and SD of 81.65 ± 9.089, and the calculated P-value is 0.326 that is more than 0.05 that means there is a significant difference in carryover data of PSLR in both groups A and B, which indicates that, between groups A and B, one group shows a significant improvement in carryover data of PSLR. After comparing mean of carryover data of PSLR of both groups A and B, group A shows a significant improvement compared to group B.

Analyzing post-intervention data of PDFR of both groups A and B, group A shows mean and SD of 24.41 ± 5.280 and group B shows mean and SD of 23.29 ± 4.120, and the calculated P-value is 0.496 that is more than 0.05 that means there is a significant difference in post data of PDFR of both groups A and B, which indicates that between groups A and B, one group shows a significant improvement in post-intervention data of PSLR. After comparing mean of post-intervention data of PSLR of both groups A and B, group A shows a significant improvement compared to group B, and while comparing carryover data of PDFR of both groups A and B, group A shows mean and SD of 23.24 ± 5.403 and group B shows mean and SD of 23.18 ± 5.003, and the calculated P-value is 0.974 that is more than 0.05 that means there is a significant difference in carryover data of PDFR in both groups A and B, which indicates that, between groups A and B, one group shows a significant improvement in carryover data of PSLR. After comparing mean of carryover data of PSLR of both groups A and B, group A shows a significant improvement compared to group B illustrated in Table 3.4.

The post and carryover test comparison between both the groups VAS and MOLBPDQ showed no difference in P-value, which implies that both groups A and group B do improve VAS and MOLBPDQ after intervention. Other outcome measures PSLR and PDFR showed significant differences between groups A and B, which implies that one group showed a better improvement than other. There was a difference of mean values while analyzing the post and carryover mean values of PSLR and PDFR between groups A and group B, showing that group A has better improvement in PSLR and PDFR which is shown in Table 3.5.

Table 3.4 Within-group comparison of outcome measure from pre to post in group A (mean ± SD), (mean ± SEM), and P-value.

Outcome measure	Pre-post (mean ± SD)	Pre-post (mean ± SEM)	Pre-post (P-value)
VAS	-	-	-
MOLBPDQ	19.882 ± 10.331 (pre-carryover)	19.882 ± 2.506 (pre-carryover)	<0.001 (pre-carryover)
PSLR	−9.059 ± 3.750	−9.059 ± 0.909	<0.001
PDFR	−5.471 ± 1.807	−5.471 ± 0.438	<0.001

Table 3.5 Within-group comparisons of outcome measured from post to carryover in group A (mean ± SD), (mean ± SEM), and P-value.

Outcome measure	Post-carryover (mean ± SD)	Post-carryover (mean ± SEM)	(P-value)
VAS			
MOLBPDQ	19.882 ± 10.331 (pre-carryover)	19.882 ± 2.506 (pre-carryover)	<0.001 (pre-carryover)
PSLR	1.353 ± 2.668	1.353 ± 0.647	<0.053
PDFR	1.176 ± 1.879	1.176 ± 0.456	0.020

Table 3.6 Within-group comparison of outcome measure from pre to post in group B (mean ± SD), (mean ± SEM), and P-value.

Outcome measure	Pre-post (mean ± SD)	Pre-post (mean ± SEM)	Pre-post (P-value)
VAS	0.529 ± 0.624	0.529 ± 0.151	0.003
MOLBPDQ	0.706 ± 1.993 (pre-carryover)	0.706 ± 0.483 (pre-carryover)	0.163 (pre-carryover)
PSLR	−0.471 ± 1.125	−0.471 ± 0.273	0.104
PDFR	−0.235 ± 0.970	−0.235 ± 0.235	0.332

Table 3.7 Within-group comparison of outcomes measured from post to carryover in group B (mean ± SD), (mean ± SEM), and P-value.

Outcome measure	Post-carryover (mean ± SD)	Post-carryover (mean ± SEM)	(P-value)
VAS	0.059 ± 0.899	0.059 ± 0.218	0.791
MOLBPDQ	0.706 ± 1.993 (pre-carryover)	0.706 ± 0.483 (pre-carryover)	0.163 (pre-carryover)
PSLR	−0.353 ± 2.668	−0.353 ± 0.647	0.593
PDFR	0.118 ± 1.933	0.118 ± 0.469	0.805

This study was conducted to evaluate the impact of PRRT and Sham therapy on SIJD, hamstring, and calf flexibility in desk job workers. The results of this study suggest the rejection of the null hypothesis as both groups are showing positive changes on outcome measures. Analyzing the results suggested that the alternative hypothesis (A3: Both the groups may be equally effective) is accepted as both the groups are showing positive changes reported on outcome measures which is shown in Table 3.5.

A previous study for SIJD focuses on technique such as mobilization, manipulation, stretching exercises, and MET. Other studies for hamstring and calf flexibility such as neurodynamics, muscle energy technique, and stretching also showed effective results. Subjects of group A in this study received PRRT five-step protocol, which includes lumbar spine release, SIJ release, hamstring release, calf release, and peroneal release and plantar release. Subjects of group B in this study received Sham treatment, same as group A but on the contra-lateral side. When comparing the p-value of outcome measure VAS of both experimental and control groups, there was no significant difference, which means that both groups A and B were beneficial in treating pain which is illustrated in Table 3.7.

When comparing the p-value of outcome measure MOLBPDQ of both experimental and control groups, there was no significant difference, which means that both groups A and B were beneficial in treating pain and improving social life. When comparing the p-value of outcome measure PSLR of both experimental and control groups, there was a significant difference, which means that one group out of both showed a significant improvement as compared to other group. After comparing the mean of

Table 3.8 P-value of between-group comparison of post data of outcome measures.

Outcome measure (post group A–post group B)	P-value
VAS Post	<0.001
PSLR Post	0.628
PDFR Post	0.496

Table 3.9 P-value of between-group comparison of carryover data of outcome measures.

Outcome measure (carryover group A–carryover group B)	P-value
VAS Carryover	<0.006
MOLBPDQ Carryover	<0.001
PSLR Carryover	0.326
PDFR Carryover	0.974

post and carryover data of both groups A and B, group A showed a significant improvement as compared to group B which is demonstarted in Table 3.8.

When comparing the p-value of outcome measure PDFR of both experimental and control groups, there was a significant difference, which means that only one group was showing improvement. Analyzing the mean of post and carryover data of both groups A and B, group A showed a significant improvement as compared to group B which is clearly shown in Table 3.9.

Also, the results of this study suggested that both Sham therapy and PRRT showed a significant difference in VAS after intervention and are effective in reducing pain.

SIJD management with PRRT helps desk job workers in improving their professional life as well as social life and gives freedom from prolonged dull back pain.

3.4.3 Clinical Implication

The results of this study showed that PRRT can be used to improve hamstring flexibility (passive straight leg raise range) and calf flexibility (passive dorsi-flexion range). But when mean of post data of both groups were compared, the calculated P-value showed no difference for outcome measure VAS and MOLBPDQ in both groups A and B.

3.4.4 Future Research

i. This study should be performed on larger population with higher VAS values.
ii. The same study can be done comparing PRRT versus other intervention techniques.
iii. Long-term effect of PRRT can be analyzed.

3.4.5 Limitation

i. The number of sample size was less.
ii. Long-term effect was not analyzed.

3.5 Conclusion

The result of present study revealed that the use of PRRT in patient with SIJD showed positives change reported from pre to post and pre to carryover on outcome measures (VAS, MOLBPDQ, PSLR, and PDFR) in the experimental group using artificial intelligence (AI). But on the other end, while comparing mean values of post-post and carryover-carryover data of both experimental and control groups, there was no difference according to the p-value for outcome measures VAS and MOLBPDQ, which means that subjects of both groups reported positive changes for outcome measure VAS and MOLBPDQ with machine learning and AI, and the calculated P-value for outcome measures PSLR and PDFR showed a significant difference, which means that one out of both groups reported positive changes. After comparing mean values of post data of both groups, the experimental group reported positive changes for outcome measures PSLR and PDFR to get accuracy by the AI approach.

References

1. Bontrup, Taylor, W.R., Fliesser, Visscher, R., Green, T., Wippert, P.M., Zemp, R. *et al.*, LBP and its Relationship with Sitting Behaviour among Sedentary Office Workers. *Appl. Ergon.*, 81, 102894, 2019 Nov 1.

2. Sivakumar, Arun, Kamalakannan, Kalpana, A.P., Prakash, Pradeep, K.V., Prevalence of Sacroiliac Joint Dysfunction in College Students. *Biomedicine*, 41, 2, 293–6, 2021 Jul 7.
3. Dubey, N., Dubey, G., Tripathi, H., Naqvi, Z.A., Ergonomics for Desk Job Workers-An Overview. *Int. J. Health Sci. Res.*, 9, 7, 257–66, 2019.
4. Murakami, E., Aizawa, T., Kurosawa, D., Noguchi, K., Leg Symptoms Associated with SacroiliacJjoint Disorder and Related Pain. *Clin. Neurol. Neurosurg.*, 157, 55–8, 2017 Jun 1.
5. Al-Subahi, Alayat, M., Alshehri, M.A., Helal, O., Alhasan, H., Alalawi, Takrouni, Alfaqeh, *et al.*, The Effectiveness of Physiotherapy Interventions for Sacroiliac Joint Dysfunction: A Systematic Review. *J. Phys. Ther. Sci.*, 29, 9, 1689–94, 2017.
6. Hansberger, B.L., Baker, R.T., May, J., Nasypany, A., A novel approach to treating plantar fasciitis–effects of primal reflex release technique: a case series. *Int. J. Sports Phys. Ther.*, 10, 5, 690, 2015 Oct.
7. Albertin, E.S., Walters, M., May, J., Baker, R.T., Nasypany, A., Cheatham, S., An exploratory case series analysis of the use of Primal Reflex Release Technique™ to improve signs and symptoms of hamstring strain. *Int. J. Sports Phys. Ther.*, 15, 2, 263–273, 2020, doi: 10.26603/ijspt20200263.
8. Barros, G., McGrath, L., Gelfenbeyn, M., Sacroiliac joint dysfunction in patients with low back pain. *Fed. Pract.*, 36, 8, 370, 2019 Aug.
9. Chandrasekaran, B., Rao, C.R., Davis, F., Arumugam, A., SMART STEP-SMARTphone-driven exercise and pedometer-based STEP intervention to promote physical activity among desk-based employees: Study protocol for a three-arm cluster randomized controlled trial. *Work*, 69, 4, 1229–45, 2021 Jan 1.
10. Bennie, J.A., Pedisic, Z., Timperio, A., Crawford, D., Dunstan, D., Bauman, A., Van Uffelen, J., Salmon, J., Total and domain-specific sitting time among employees in desk-based work settings in Australia. *Aust. N. Z. J. Public Health*, 39, 3, 237–42, 2015 Jun.
11. Warneke, K., Wohlann, T., Lohmann, L.H., Wirth, K., Schiemann, S., Acute effects of long-lasting stretching and strength training on maximal strength and flexibility in the calf muscle. *Ger. J. Exercise Sport Res.*, 52, 1–7, 2022 Oct 26.
12. Karki, B., Kalita, A., Dutta, A., The Combined Effectiveness of Piriformis Stretch and Muscle Activation Exercises in Patients with Sacroiliac Joint Pain.(2021). *Int. J. Life Sci. Pharma Res.*, 11, 6, L77–87, 2021.
13. Bertoldo, D., Pirri, C., Roviaro, B., Stecco, L., Day, J.A., Fede, C., Guidolin, D., Stecco, C., Pilot study of sacroiliac joint dysfunction treated with a single session of fascial manipulation® method: clinical implications for effective pain reduction. *Medicina*, 57, 7, 691, 2021 Jul 6.

14. Kawishwar, S.S., Samal, S., Ramteke, S., To Study the Effect of Mulligan Mobilization Versus Conventional Therapy in Sacroiliac Joint Pain. *Indian J. Public Health Res. Dev.*, 11, 5, 444–9, 2020 May 18.
15. Miraj, M., Al Qahtani, M., Al Zhrani, M., Alanazi, A., Ahmad, F., Kashoo, F., Ahamed, R., Kumar, D., Comparative Study Between Muscle Energy Technique (Met) Versus Kinesiotaping (Kt) In Managing Work Related Low Back Pain (Wrlbp) Among Health Professionals: A Double Blinded Study. *Turk. J. Physiother. Rehabil.*, 32, 3, 2021.
16. López, L.L., Torres, J.R., Rubio, A.O., Sánchez, I.T., Martos, I.C., Valenza, M.C., Effects of neurodynamic treatment on hamstrings flexibility: A systematic review and meta-analysis. *Phys. Ther. Sport*, 40, 244–50, 2019 Nov 1.
17. Nejati, P., Safarcherati, A., Karimi, F., Effectiveness of exercise therapy and manipulation on sacroiliac joint dysfunction: a randomized controlled trial. *Pain Physician*, 22, 1, 53–61, 2019.
18. Stevenson, V.F., Baker, R.T., Nasypany, A., Treating Groin And Hip Flexor Pain Using Primal Reflex Release Technique™: A Case Series. *Int. J. Sports Phys. Ther.*, 13, 4, 715, 2018 Aug.
19. Vickcales, E., The Psychological and Physiological Effects of Performing the Primal Reflex Release Technique on Female, Division I Collegiate Athletes.
20. Carnahan, K., Inclusion of primal reflex release technique (PRRT) plan of care for shoulder pain: A case study, ND.
21. Sewani, R. and Shinde, S., Effect of Hot Moist Pack and Muscle Energy Technique in Subjects with Sacro-Iliac Joint Dysfunction. *Int. J. Sci. Res.*, 6, 2, 669–72, 2017 Feb.
22. Chapman, E.B., Hansen-Honeycutt, J., Nasypany, A., Baker, R.T., May, J., A clinical guide to the assessment and treatment of breathing pattern disorders in the physically active: Part 1. *Int. J. Sports Phys. Ther.*, 11, 5, 803, 2016 Oct.
23. Hansen-Honeycutt, J., Chapman, E.B., Nasypany, A., Baker, R.T., May, J., A clinical guide to the assessment and treatment of breathing pattern disorders in the physically active: part 2, a case series. *Int. J. Sports Phys. Ther.*, 11, 6, 971, 2016 Dec.
24. Sipko, T., Paluszak, A., Siudy, A., Effect of sacroiliac joint mobilization on the level of soft tissue pain threshold in asymptomatic women. *J. Manipulative Physiol. Ther.*, 41, 3, 258–64, 2018 Mar 1.
25. Smith, R.L., Sebastian, B.A., Gajdosik, R.L., Effect of sacroiliac joint mobilization on the standing position of the pelvis in healthy men. *J. Orthop. Sports Phys. Ther.*, 10, 3, 77–84, 1988 Sep.
26. Neha, B., Arunmozhi, R., Maneesh, A., Pooja, A., Effectiveness of therapeutic interventions in sacroiliac joint dysfunction: a systematic review. *Int. J. Physiother. Res.*, 4, 3, 1484–8, 2016.

27. Mourot, L., Hoyet, L., Le Clerc, F., Schnitzler, F., Hellier, P., A Survey on Deep Learning for Skeleton-Based Human Animation. *Comput. Graph. Forum*, 41, 1, 122–157, 2022, doi: 10.1111/cgf.14426.
28. Yang, Y., Bartolozzi, C., Zhang, H.H., Nawrocki, R.A., Neuromorphic electronics for robotic perception, navigation and control: A survey. *Eng. Appl. Artif. Intell.*, 126, 2023, doi: 10.1016/j.engappai.2023.106838.

4

Future Trends in Bioinformatics AI Integration for Analyzing Immediate Effect of Primal Reflex Release Technique in Neck Pain and Stiffness Patients

Aditya Sharma, Manish Kumar Jha*, Vaibhav Agarwal and Amit Sharma

Department of Physiotherapy, Himalayan Institute of Medical Sciences, Swami Rama Himalayan University, Jolly Grant, Dehradun, India

Abstract

Even while neck soreness may not be the most common musculoskeletal issue, it is a significant ailment. For mechanical neck pain (MNP), there are several therapy alternatives that have been demonstrated to be more effective than other treatment approaches using artificial intelligence (AI). An effective manual therapy method for treating musculoskeletal pain and dysfunction is primal reflex release technique (PRRT). PRRT includes applying light pressure to particular areas on the body to reduce tension, activate these reflexes, and return mobility and function to normal. To identify the clinically significant defences between two groups, the basis of pain was quantified on the NPRS scale on a single pre- and post-manifestation. This study used a total sample size of 40 male and female participants. The experimental and control groups were randomly assigned after consenting and fulfilling the inclusion criteria. Following the patient's evaluation by the therapist, the experimental group underwent PRRT downregulation therapy, which was completed by invoking certain reflexes, before and after the intervention of AI. The outcomes demonstrated a considerable decrease in pain and an increase in function in both groups.

Keywords: AI, neck pain, PRRT, stiffness

**Corresponding author*: Manishjha1900@outlook.com

Abhishek Kumar, Narayan Vyas, Pramod Singh Rathore, Abhineet Anand and Pooja Dixit (eds.) Internet of Medicine for Smart Healthcare, (65–88) © 2025 Scrivener Publishing LLC

4.1 Introduction

Mechanical neck pain is one of neuro musculoskeletal disorder; approximately two-thirds of the general population has neck pain, sometimes, in their whole lives. Mechanical neck pain is often caused by poor posture, repetitive strain, or injury to the neck muscles, ligaments, or joints. A very common condition is mechanical neck pain with a cervical etiology or contribution. Disrupted motor function, muscular weakness, and, most importantly, muscle stiffness are all possible motor features of muscle trigger sites. The movement and postural symmetries of people with chronic pain are typically stiff and guarded. It has been hypothesized that this conditioned adaptation of posture and movement impacts motor strategies, including muscle activation patterns. Studies on people with chronic neck pain from any previous trauma and repeated strain have found that the superficial cervical muscles are working more actively [1].

Neck pain, a complex condition, is a significant issue in contemporary life. Neck pain is a serious condition even if it may not be the most typical musculoskeletal problem. The significant financial impact of neck pain includes medical expenses, lost productivity, and work-related issues. So, here, we are attempting to determine how primal reflex release technique (PRRT) affects neck discomfort. One of the most common musculoskeletal conditions affecting adults is neck pain, with prevalence rates ranging from 16.7% to 75.1% globally [2]. Numerous factors contribute to the complex etiology of this condition: age, body mass index, genetics, history of musculoskeletal pain, level of physical activity and smoking, psychological variables (job satisfaction, levels of stress, nervousness, and depression), and ergonomic factors (strenuous physical activity, employing force and tremors, poor posture, and repetitive movement). In many countries, neck discomfort is a major cause of illness and disability in both the working and everyday worlds. It may have an impact on a person's physical, social, and mental health and well-being, increasing costs for businesses and society as a whole [3].

With an annual incidence rate of 37.2% (range, 16.7%–75.1%), neck discomfort is a significant global health issue. Even though neck discomfort is particularly common among healthcare workers as a result of their line of work, healthcare practitioners have created a variety of therapy and preventative strategies for this condition. It has been hypothesized, nevertheless, that neck discomfort among medical professionals begins even before they begin working. Neck discomfort has a complicated etiology and is thought to be a biopsychosocial issue. Previous research has identified a number of risk factors for neck discomfort, including gender, advanced age, greater BMI, smoking, excessive use of electronic devices, uncomfortable or prolonged postures, inactivity, negative emotions, and lack of social support [4].

The literature suggests a wide range of therapeutic modalities for non-specific neck pain (NS-NP). Because conclusive pathology cannot be established in most NS-NP patients, this medical model cannot guide treatment. Most patients undergo conservative care from a doctor or physiotherapist. Treatment options for MNP include manual therapy techniques, physiotherapy procedures, exercise, medicinal therapy, injection, and patient education. Mobilization strategies are used during MNP therapy, which has been shown to produce better outcomes than other treatment modalities. In cases of musculoskeletal disorders, the Mulligan mobilization technique has been shown to be helpful for correcting biomechanics and reducing discomfort during exercise [5].

A multidisciplinary approach is necessary for the challenging process of managing mechanical neck discomfort. One of the most often utilized methods for the treatment of mechanical neck discomfort is physiotherapy. Exercise treatment, manual therapy, electrotherapy, and education are examples of physiotherapy interventions. The solution of mechanical neck discomfort with physiotherapy must include exercise therapy. It involves a number of exercises designed to increase neck strength, endurance, and mobility. Exercise therapy may be customized to the individual's needs and can be carried out in a supervised or unsupervised setting. Another often utilized method in the treatment of mechanical neck discomfort is manual therapy. To lessen discomfort and increase mobility, it entails the use of hands-on treatments to the neck's muscles, ligaments, or joints. A physiotherapist or a chiropractor can administer manual treatment, which may use methods like mobilization, manipulation, or massage. Electrotherapy is a non-invasive intervention that involves the use of electrical currents to reduce pain and improve muscle function. Electrotherapy can be used in conjunction with exercise therapy and manual therapy to enhance the effects of these interventions [6].

Education is a critical component of physiotherapy management for mechanical neck pain. It involves teaching patients about their condition, its causes, and the various treatment options available. Education can help patients to better understand their condition, manage their symptoms, and prevent future episodes of mechanical neck pain. It is based on the principle that reflexes in the body can cause muscle tension and pain and that, by releasing these reflexes, pain and dysfunction can be reduced or eliminated.

PRRT involves the application of gentle pressure to specific points on the body to release these reflexes and restore normal movement and function [7].

As part of the regional interdependent approach to patient care, primal reflex release technique TM (PRRT) is a therapeutic paradigm that downregulates an overstimulated autonomic nerve system to lessen pain patterns. The paradigm works by resetting (recalibrating) the body's overly aroused primordial instincts in order to affect the neuronal system. During a 1-min nociceptive examination, sensitive regions are found utilizing bilateral palpation. However, if a particular ailment is the issue at hand, then the doctor can treat patients by using a particular PRRT. The procedure includes repeatedly inducing deep tendon reflexes, which tap or stimulate the skin for 12 s, to suppress painful regions. To avoid eliciting a pain response, these reflex stimulations are typically applied mildly and repeatedly. It is possible that the spinal cord and brain briefly "overload" and "reset" because of these recurrent reflex stimulations' high volume of impulses. The brain may then assess the scenario and ascertain the existing circumstances. The brain will correct the flawed pattern if there was merely a malfunctioning neurological circuit and no genuine sickness or illness. This process is comparable to what the gate theory of pain regulation postulates may be taking place [8].

In conclusion, mechanical neck pain is a common condition that can significantly impact a person's quality of life. Physiotherapy is a multidisciplinary approach that includes exercise therapy, manual therapy, electrotherapy, and education. These interventions can be used alone or in combination to manage mechanical neck pain effectively. PRRT is manual treatment approach that helps increase range of motion and relieve mechanical neck discomfort. PRRT is an effective strategy for individuals with acute or sub-acute neck discomfort because the recent studies have demonstrated that it can have an instantaneous effect on physical neck pain. To completely comprehend PRRT's mode of action and ascertain its long-term efficacy in the treatment of mechanical neck pain, more investigation is required [9].

Low back discomfort and musculoskeletal pains in the neck and shoulders are prevalent health issues among working people. The two most prevalent somatic complaints in Japan are low back discomfort and tight shoulders. For men, stiff shoulders are the most prevalent ailment, whereas low back discomfort is less common; however, in women, the order is different. Employee health issues have a significant financial impact on the expenses of medical treatment as well as low job productivity, which is shown by presenteeism and absenteeism [10]. Most musculoskeletal problems have uncleared etiology. On the other hand, poor posture and psychological stress are linked to nonspecific low back pain and main neck/shoulder pain/stiffness. There are two types of symptoms related to tight necks and shoulders: primary and secondary. Secondary disorders of the cervical spine, glenohumeral joints, heart problems, eye tiredness, and temporomandibular disorders can all contribute to neck and shoulder stiffness or discomfort. Primary discomfort or stiffness in the neck or shoulders is not fully understood. Nonetheless, it is anticipated that the trapezius muscle's hemodynamic will be implicated. In addition, head-down position, psychological variables, and inactivity are linked to persistent shoulder and neck discomfort [11].

The users were intended to get messages from the artificial intelligence (AI)–assisted chatbot with directions on how to exercise and other everyday life hacks to help alleviate such symptoms. Through LINE, the messages were sent daily at a certain time. Users have the option to modify the notification timing to a time that works best for them. Every day, the participants could complete their workout in 1 min. Participants in the interactive program may reply to messages via a straightforward option list, and the chatbot will provide them with customized responses based on their selections. Three elements made up the program's exercise: stretching, upholding proper posture, and mindfulness (see Figure 4.1). The chatbot encouraged the participants to keep working out even after they stopped. The software that we employed in this study was called secede Ver.0.9; it was developed and patented by Travoss Co., Ltd. and an orthopaedist with expertise in musculoskeletal problems since June 2017. This curriculum had not been utilized or assessed before to our interventional investigation.

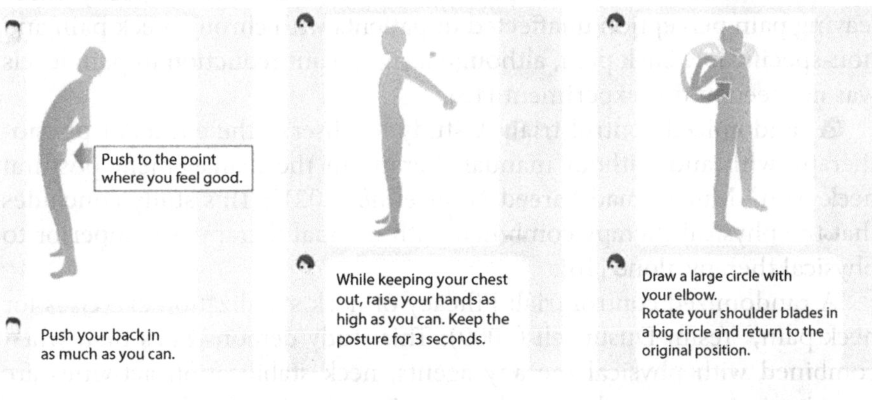

Figure 4.1 Illustrations of workouts using guidance from the AI-assisted health program [12].

Researchers informed participants during the intervention period that the company's occupational health staff would address any questions about changes in their physical conditions and that the program's provider would address technical inquiries about program access.

4.2 Literature Review

A randomized clinical trial published in the Journal of Clinical Medicine in 2021 by Belen-Diaz-Pulido *et al.* examined the effectiveness of electrical nerve stimulation through the skin and manual treatment in improving cervical movement and endurance in patients with subacute as well as chronic neck pain. According to this study, the only therapy that has been proven to be useful in improving the active cervical mobility with endurance in all three planes of individuals with neck discomfort is manual therapy. This therapy's adverse effects are almost nonexistent and have minimal therapeutic significance [13].

"A review study: Physiotherapy management for neck pain, Arianne P. Verhagen, in Journal of Physiotherapy" (2021): This study suggests that physiotherapy management choices may benefit from stratifying patients based on their prognosis or in subgroups. For most individuals with neck discomfort, manual therapy, exercise, and education, often in combination, seem to be preferred evidence-based physiotherapy treatment [14].

"A randomized control double blinded pilot trial: Effect of regular electrotherapy on spinal flexibility and pain sensitivity in patients with chronic non-specific neck pain and low back pain," Asami Naka *et al.* (2023): According to the current pilot study, consistent mid-frequency electrotherapy enhanced the lower spinal cord's range of motion greatly while leaving pain perception unaffected in patients with chronic neck pain and non-specific low back pain, although a significant reduction in pain levels was not seen in this experiment [15].

"A randomized control trial: A study to observe the effects of physiotherapy with and without manual therapy in the management postural neck pain," Muhammad Fareed Nasir *et al.* (2021): This study concludes that the physical therapy combined with manual therapy was superior to physical therapy alone [16].

"A randomized control trial: Efficacy of neck stabilization exercises for neck pain," Yesim Dusunceli (2009): This study demonstrates that, when combined with physical therapy agents, neck stabilization activities are superior to isometric along with stretching exercises for the treatment of neck anxiety, with some advantages in terms of pain and disability results [17].

Pakeeza seemal *et al.* conducted a comparative study between primal reflex release treatment and stretching exercise on pain and function in coccydynia: a randomized controlled trial: It showed that PRRT and stretching both interventions showed significant result in decreasing pain and function outcome measure, but PRRT is more effectful than stretching [18].

Peter kroeling *et al.* conducted a study on the use of electrotherapy for the neck pain patients: It was a randomized controlled trial. Four trials reported on additional outcomes, including function and overall perceived effects; however, none of the results were clinically significant [19].

Somaye kazeminasab *et al.* published an overview paper titled "Neck pain: Global epidemiology trends and risk factors" presents the findings of this investigation in a thorough and educational manner, which should be helpful in the prevention, diagnosis, and treatment of neck pain [20].

Another study done by Jena Hansen *et al.* in 2016: A clinical guide to the assessment and the treatment of breathing pattern disorder in physically active individual: This study concluded that it may be useful to assess for breathing pattern disorder and startle reflexes along with standard orthopeadic evaluation in the physically active individual active patients, and treatment of BDP may help in reducing in musculoskeletal pain [16].

Another study conducted by Cleland *et al.* (2005) investigated the immediate effects of PRRT on patients with mechanical neck pain. The study found that PRRT was effective in reducing pain and improving cervical range of motion immediately after treatment [21].

Tomomi Anan *et al.* examined in their study how an exercise-based interactive health promotion system aided by AI. A two-armed, randomized, controlled, and blinded experiment was carried out on workers who had low back discomfort, stiffness, or pain in their necks or shoulders, or both. The AI-assisted health program was given to the intervention group; for a period of 12 weeks, users of the smartphone talking app LINE got messages from the chatbot providing exercise instructions at a certain time each day. The software was entirely automated. This research demonstrates how, in just 12 weeks, the brief workouts offered by the AI-assisted health program reduced low back discomfort and relieved stiffness and pain in the neck, shoulders, and arms. To determine the factors influencing the AI-assisted health program's successful conclusion, more research is required [22].

According to study of Anna Marcuzzi *et al.*, among 294 persons with neck and possibly low back pain who were referred to specialized treatment, the personally designed app did not substantially enhance musculoskeletal health after 3 months compared to conventional care by itself or non-tailored web-based assistance. It was a clinical trial that was randomized. These findings indicate that further research is required to assess the efficacy of digitally assisted self-management procedures for patients referred to specialized care for neck as well as low back pain, as well as to develop instruments for measuring improvements in self-management behavior [23].

In the study of Wai Leung Ambrose Lo *et al.*, they talked about looking at how people view the advantages of using a smartphone app with AI integrated into it to self-manage chronic back and neck pain. A total of 161 people in all replied to the invitation. There was a daily rise in the amount of time spent engaging in therapeutic activity. It was also noted that adopting the AI-embedded mobile app reduced the need for further treatments. This study showed how utilizing the AI-integrated mobile app to deliver a customized therapeutic workout program had a good, self-perceived beneficial effect. The encouraging outcomes imply that more research is at least needed to determine how the AI-integrated smartphone app affects physiology and how it stacks up against standard medical treatment [24].

According to the findings of the study by Vikram Puri *et al.*, neck discomfort and cervical spondylosis issues are prevalent in both young and old patients, with medical professionals mostly focusing on the symptoms. A neckband is combined with an accelerometer and gyrometer-equipped sensor to track the position of the neck and transmit data for recording to a Google cloud server. Furthermore, when the user's neck is not in the proper posture, alarms are created and transmitted to them. To improve system accuracy, machine learning (ML) techniques are integrated with the suggested system [25].

In this study, Haytham Eloqayli *et al.* used artificial intelligence neural networks and slandered statistics to investigate whether vitamin D and ferritin are modifiable risk factors with persistent neck discomfort. Fifty-four patients receiving outpatient treatment or minor operations who were age-matched controls and 54 patients with persistent neck pain who were treated in King Abdullah University Hospital between February and August 2016 were recruited. Patients with persistent neck discomfort have significantly reduced blood levels of ferritin and vitamin D (p-value < 0.05), according to statistical analysis. Women made up 90% of patients with persistent neck discomfort. Ferritin and vitamin D were used as input variables, whereas chronic neck pain (CNP) was used as the output in the development and construction of the iron and vitamin D insufficiency, which are the two modifiable risk factors for persistent neck discomfort, even if they cannot be identified as the only risk factors. It is concerning that women had low ferritin, hypovitaminosis D, and a significant prevalence of persistent neck discomfort. Future categorization and prediction models for chronic neck pain may benefit from the application of artificial neural networks in bioinformatics predictions [26].

4.3 Methodology

4.3.1 Need of Study

Research-based evidence related to primal relax release techniques approach in managing mechanical neck pain patient needs to be gathered.

4.3.2 Aim of the Study

The aim of this study is to determine the effects of primal reflex release techniques on pain and stiffness in mechanical neck pain patients.

4.3.3 Experimental Hypothesis

E1: PRRT group may show more significant improvement in pain and stiffness as compared to control group.
E2: Control group may show more significant improvement in pain and stiffness as compared to control group.
E3: Both groups may show similar significant improvement.

4.3.3.1 Null Hypothesis

N1: PRRT group may not show significant improvement in pain and stiffness.
N2: Control group may not show significant improvement in pain and stiffness.

i. **Study setting:** Himalayan hospital, out patient department (OPD), neuro-surgery ward (NSW), neuro-medicine ward (NMW).
ii. **Sample size:** 40
iii. **Study design:** Experimental study
iv. **Study population:** OPD and WARD Patient
v. **Study duration:** 1 year

4.3.3.2 *Instrumentation*

- Goniometer
- Couch

4.3.4 Inclusion Criteria

Age: 18 to 65 years
Males and females both gender
Neck pain with stiffness
Neck pain with shoulder and upper back pain (without radiculopathy)
Tenderness in neck region and upper back region

4.3.5 Exclusion Criteria

Any serious cervical injury
Any degenerative cervical spine disease
Herniated disc
Spine fracture
Tumor

4.3.6 Protocol

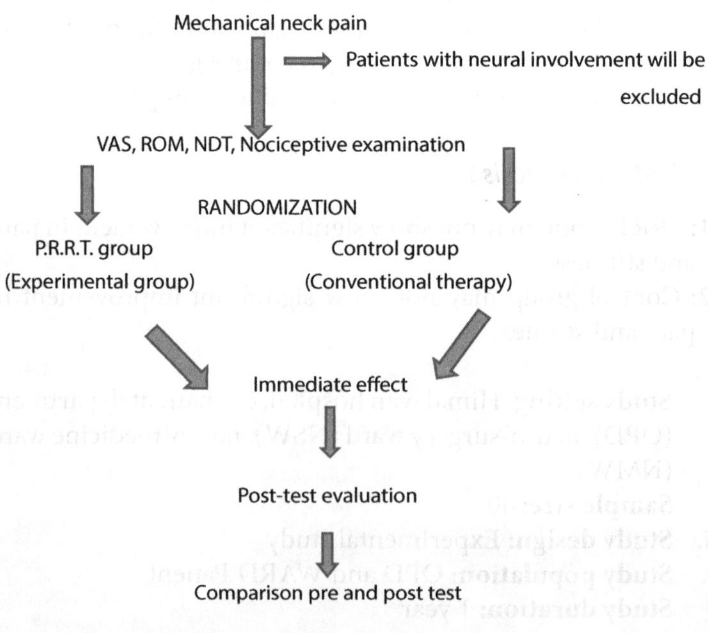

4.3.7 Procedure

This study was designed to see the effect of PPRT on neck pain. The basis of pain measured on NPRS scale on one-time pre and post manifestation to detect the clinical meaningful defences between two groups. A total sample size of 40 males and females was included in this study. During the initial appointment, participants were screened; the purpose and procedure of the study were explained to the patients; and each subject, after consenting and meeting inclusion criteria, was randomly divided into experimental and control groups. NPRS, 1-min nociceptive, and cervical ROM were performed before and after intervention after examination of the patient; the therapist performed the PRRT downregulation treatment of the experimental group completing by incanting certain reflexes in a specific order:

i. Process begins with
ii. Palmer release
iii. Epicranial release
iv. Frontalis release
v. Orbicularis oculi release
vi. Tricranial (TMJ, zygomatic arch)
vii. Tricranial frontal uplift release
viii. Rectus capitus posterior minor
ix. And all other hyper regulated or tender areas, which were found positive in the examination
x. Occipito: mastoid suture release
xi. Sphenoid release
xii. SCM release
xiii. Splenius capitus reflex release
xiv. C2–C3/levator scapulae release
xv. Omohyoid release
xvi. Masseter/TMJ reflex release technique
xvii. Turn and tap maneuverer
xviii. Shoulder, upper limb, thorax, and upper t spine
xix. Rotator cuff reflex release
xx. Rotator cuff positional release
xxi. First rib release
xxii. AC joint reflex release
xxiii. Cost- sternal reflex release
xxiv. Sternum reflex release
xxv. Hoffman reflex release

xxvi. C7–T1 reflex release
xxvii. Upper thoracic spine reflex release

For the control group, traditional therapy method was performed that included hot pack, interferential therapy (IFT), and stretching exercise for tight muscle group of the neck.

4.3.8 Statistical Analysis

The data was analyzed using IBM SPSS software version 20. Normality tests were performed, and, after that, paired and unpaired t-test was used in NPRS, cervical range of motions (flexion and extension). The chapter deals with result of the data analysis of the Analyzing immediate of primal reflex release technique in mechanical neck pain and stiffness patients between the experimental and control groups. Analyzing post data of NPRS of both groups A and B, group A mean = 4.35 and SD = 1.39 and group B mean = 4.35 and SD = 1.69, there was no significance difference, i.e., both groups show improvement, but, after analyzing, p-value was 0.5562, which is non-significant; thus, group A showed a slight significant result than group B which is demonstrated in Tables 4.1–4.3.

On comparison of pre and post reading of cervical range of motion flexion in the experimental group, it showed a significant improvement ($p = 0.031$), and, on comparison of pre and post reading of cervical range of motion flexion in the control group, it also showed a significant improvement ($p = 0.001$*). Analyzing post data of cervical range of motion of both groups A and B, group A mean = 80.50 and SD = 6.86 ($p = 0.32$) and group B mean = 77.65 and SD = 10.61 (p-value = 0.32), there was no significance difference, i.e., both groups show improvement, but, after analyzing, p-value was 0.32, which was non-significant; thus, group A showed a slight significant result than group B.

On comparison of pre and post reading of cervical range of motion extension in the control group, it also showed a significant improvement ($p \le 0.001$*). Analyzing post data of cervical range of motion of both groups A and B, group A mean = 68.45 and SD = 2.06 and group B mean = 67.60 and SD = 3.01 ($p = 0.32$), there was no significance difference, i.e., both groups show improvement, but, after analyzing, p-value was 0.30, which was non-significant which can be seen from Tables 4.4 and 4.5; thus, group A showed a very slight significant difference than group B. The comparison between pre and post reading of 1-min nociceptive examination in the experimental and control groups was shown in a graphical representation in Figures 4.2, 4.3, 4.4, 4.5 and 4.6. Tables 4.6 and 4.7 below show the cervical range motion of both group A and B.

4.3.9 Distribution of Study Subjects

The study interpretation with a total of 40 subjects both males and females [20 in the experimental group (11 females and nine males) and 20 in the control group (nine males and 11 females)]. Table 4.1 shows mean and standard deviation of age.

Table 4.1 Age mean and standard deviation.

			Age	
Group	**Minimum**	**Maximum**	**Mean**	**Standard deviation**
Experimental	27	65	41.4	12.146
Control	23	65	42.3	12.351

Table 4.2 Comparison of NPRS pre and post reading for the experimental and control groups.

	NPRS		
	Pre	**Post**	
Group	**Mean ± SD**	**Mean± SD**	**p-value**
Experimental	6.60 ± 1.09	4.35 ± 1.39	<0.001**
Control	5.75 ± 1.88	4.35 ± 1.69	<0.001**

Table 4.3 Post data of NPRS for control and experimental groups.

	NPRS	
	Pre	**Post**
D	**Mean ± SD**	**Mean ± SD**
Experimental	6.6 ± 1.09	4.35 ± 1.39
Control	5.75 ± 1.88	4.35 ± 1.69
P-value	0.09	0.5562

Table 4.4 Comparison of cervical extension range of motion for the experimental and control groups.

	ROM extension		
	Pre	Post	
Group	Mean ± SD	Mean ± SD	P-value
Experimental	63.95 ± 7.14	68.45 ± 2.06	<0.001**
Control	63.65 ± 4.73	67.60 ± 3.01	<0.001**

Table 4.5 Post data of ROM extension.

	ROM extension	
	Pre	Post
Group	Mean ± SD	Mean ± SD
Experimental	63.95 ± 7.14	68.45 ± 2.06
Control	63.65 ± 4.73	67.60 ± 3.01
P-value	0.87	0.3

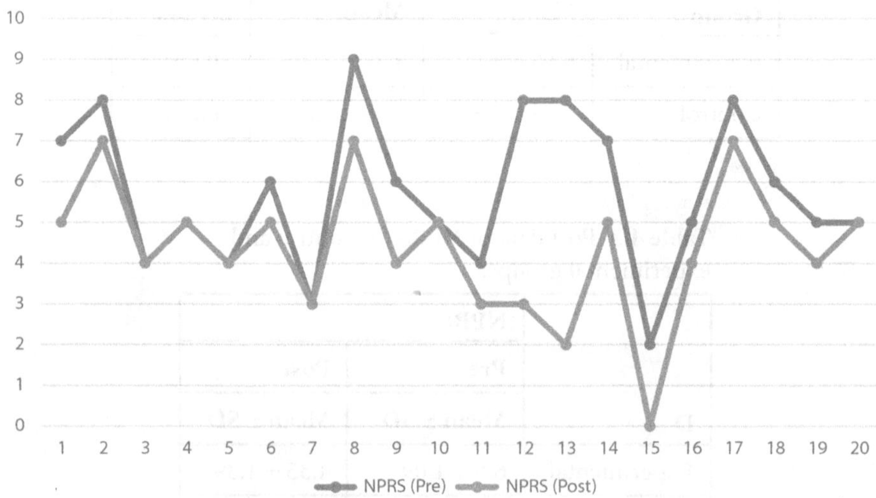

Figure 4.2 NPRS pre and post reading for the experimental group.

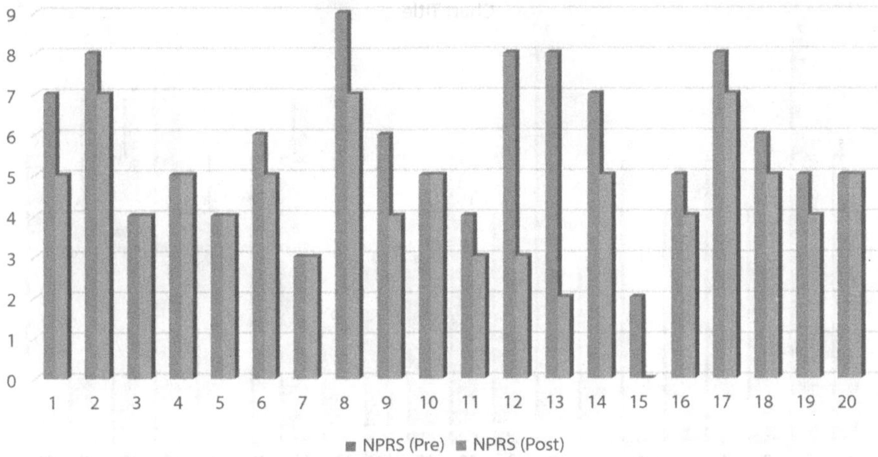

Figure 4.3 Pre and post data of NPRS.

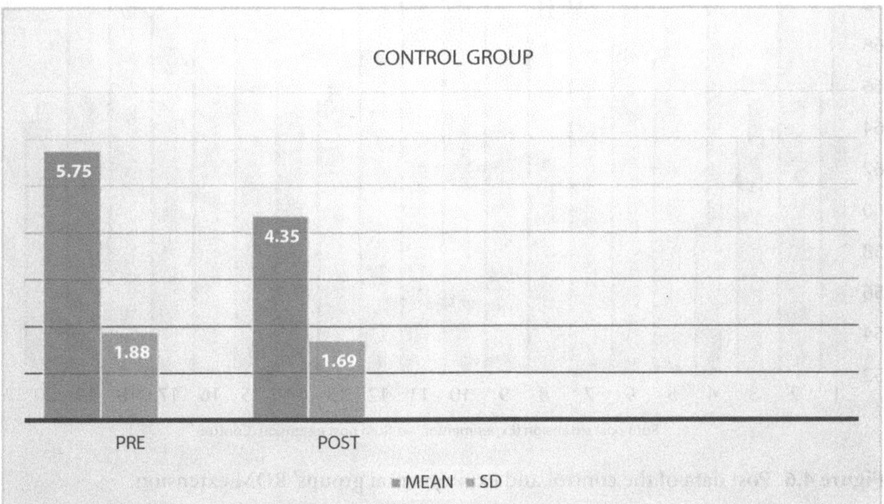

Figure 4.4 Pre and post mean and SD of the control group.

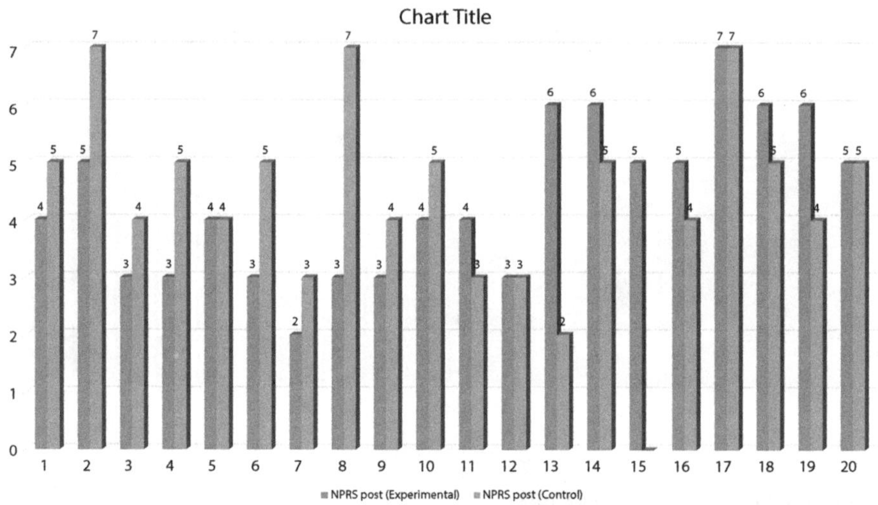

Figure 4.5 Post data of the experimental and control groups.

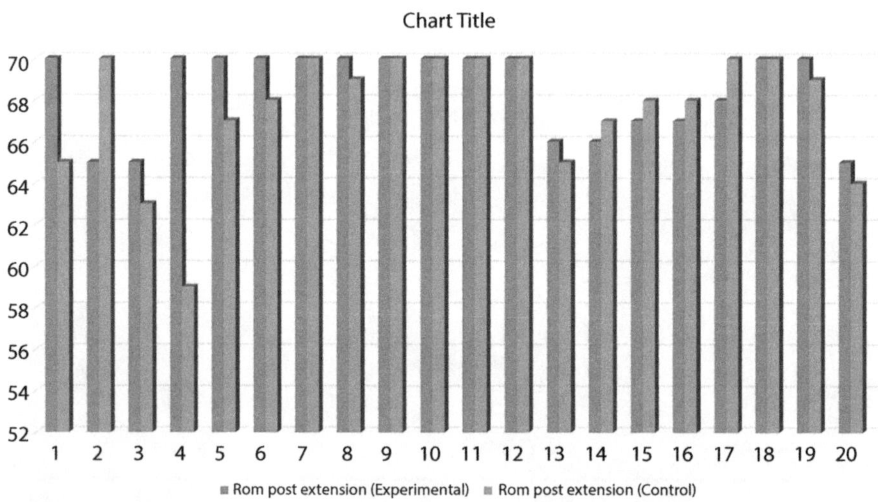

Figure 4.6 Post data of the control and experimental groups' ROM extension.

Table 4.6 Comparison of cervical flexion range motion between the experimental and control groups.

Group	ROM flexion		P-value
	Pre	**Post**	
Experimental	77.00 ± 10.56	80.50 ± 6.86	0.031
Control	74.55 ± 12.84	77.65 ± 10.61	0.001**

Table 4.7 Post data of ROM flexion.

Group	ROM flexion	
	Pre	**Post**
	Mean ± SD	**Mean ± SD**
Experimental	77 ± 10.56	80.50 ± 6.86
Control	74.55 ± 12.84	77.65 ± 10.61
P-value	0.5	0.32

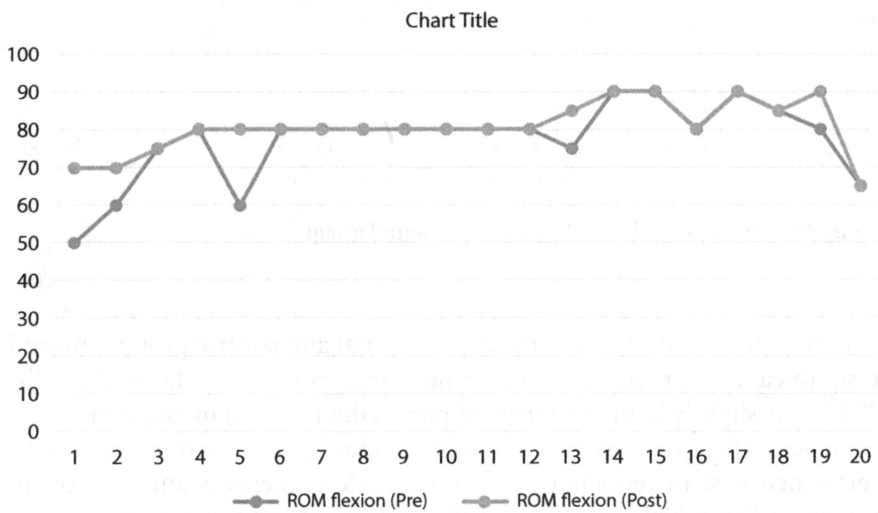

Figure 4.7 Pre and post data of ROM flexion.

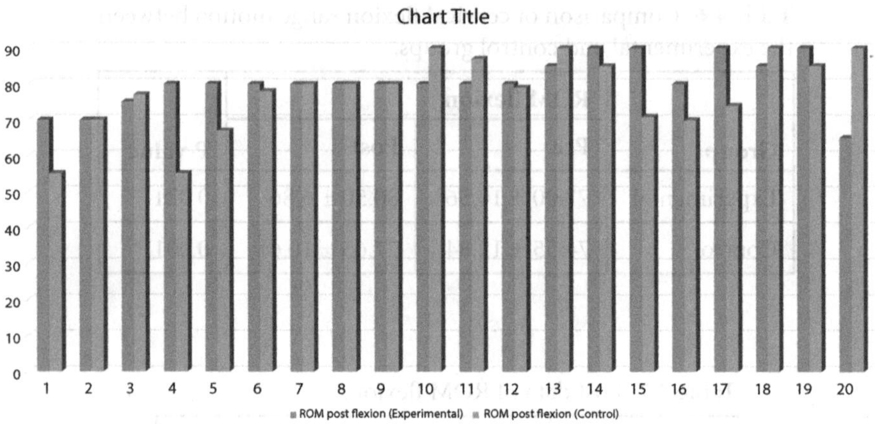

Figure 4.8 Post data of control and experimental groups.

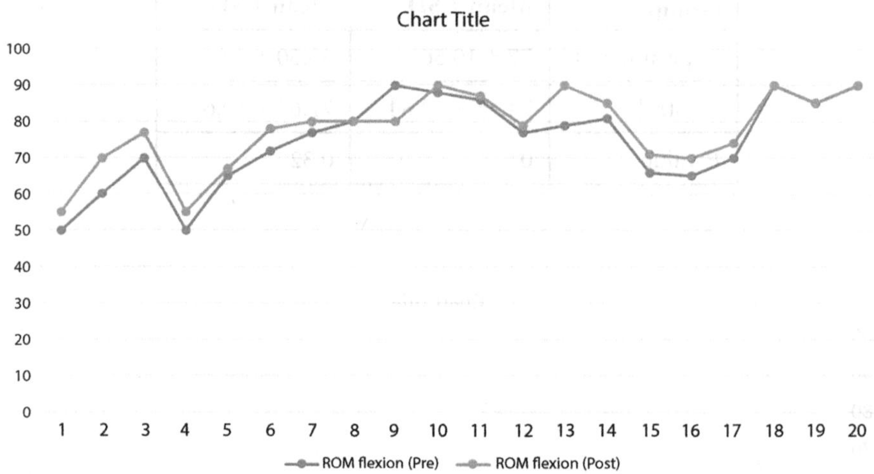

Figure 4.9 Pre and post data of ROM flexion control group.

In this present study, both the experimental and control groups showed a significant improvement, but, when analyzing the data statistically, PRRT was slightly better in terms of pain reduction and increase in ROM. However, when we assessed for 1-min nociceptive examination PRRT performed best in reducing NSR and muscle tenderness and improving quality of life, which we depicted through graphical representation as it could not be quantitatively measured. Immediate effects PRRT showed

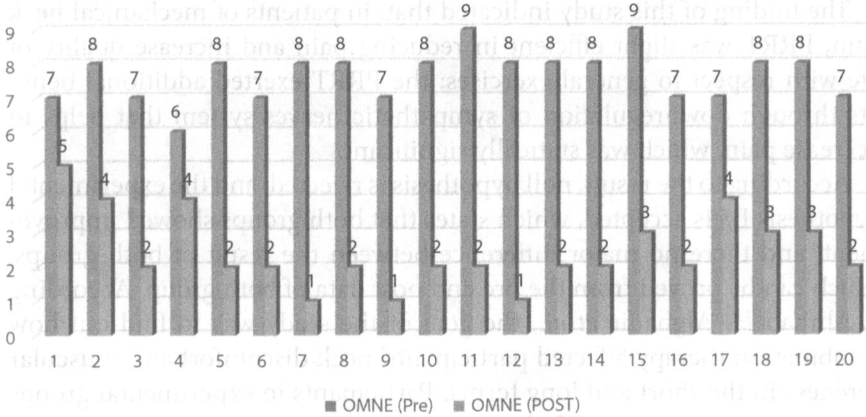

Figure 4.10 Pre and post data of the experimental group.

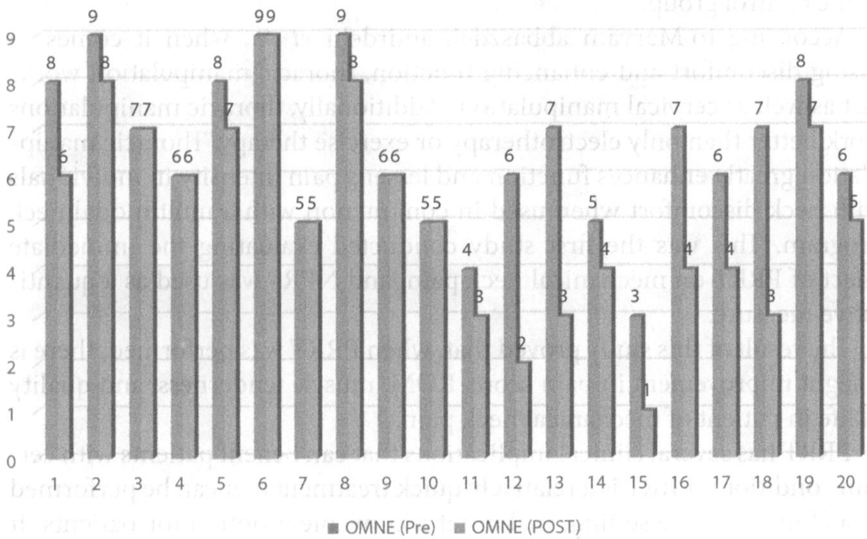

Figure 4.11 Pre and post data of the control group.

a slight significant result in NPRS, ROM, and significant improvement 1-min nociceptive examination in patients having mechanical neck pain. In current study, the pain score was measured through NPRS, and ROM was measured with the help of goniometer and muscle tenderness, barrier to entry, and three Gs, i.e., grimes-grasp-grown, which was assess through 1-min nociceptive examination; the outcome measure was taken pre and post of intervention and represented in Figures 4.7, 4.8, 4.9, 4.10 and 4.11.

The finding of this study indicated that, in patients of mechanical neck pain, PRRT was slight efficient in reducing pain and increase quality of life with respect to general exercises; the PRRT exerted additional benefits through downregulation of sympathetic nerves system that helps to decrease pain, which was statically significant.

According to the result, null hypothesis is rejected, and the experimental hypothesis E3 is accepted, which states that both groups showed improvement, and there no major difference between the result of both groups, which can be proved from the pre and post data of both group. According to Ahmad H. Alghadir *et al.*, the goal of the study was to find out how combination therapy affected participants' neck discomfort and muscular soreness in the short and long terms. Participants in experimental groups A and B received the specified interventions, while those in control group C got the prescribed intervention plan. The intergroup findings showed that the experimental groups had improved more significantly compared to the control group.

According to Maryam abbaszdeh-amirdehi *et al.*, when it comes to easing discomfort and enhancing function, thoracic manipulation works just as well as cervical manipulation. Additionally, thoracic manipulations work better than only electrotherapy or exercise therapy. Thoracic manipulation greatly enhances function and lessens pain intensity in individuals with neck discomfort when used in conjunction with a multimodal neck program. This was the first study conducted evaluating the immediate effect of PRRT on mechanical neck pain, and NPRS was used as a quantitative measure.

The result of this study proved that, when PRRT was performed, there is a slight improvement in pain score, ROM, muscle tenderness, and quality of life in patient of mechanical neck pain.

PRRT has several clinical implications that can benefit patients with certain conditions. PRRT is a relatively quick treatment that can be performed in a clinic or office setting, making it a convenient option for patients. It works by targeting the reflexes in the body that contribute to pain and tension and releasing them to promote healing and relaxation.

Another clinical implication of PRRT is that it can be used as a complementary treatment alongside other therapy. For example, PRRT can be used in combination with physical therapy, to provide a more comprehensive approach to pain management. PRRT can also be used to treat conditions that are related to stress or tension, such as anxiety and depression. By promoting relaxation and reducing tension in the body, PRRT can help to alleviate symptoms of these conditions and improve overall well-being.

Overall, PRRT has several clinical implications that make it a valuable treatment option for patients with certain conditions. Its non-invasive nature, quick treatment time, and ability to be used alongside other therapies make it a versatile option for pain management and stress reduction.

4.4 Conclusion

Primal reflex release therapy and conventional therapy both are effective in terms of NPRS and range of motion, but, in 1-min nociceptive examination, the PRRT group showed a significant effectiveness than the control group as shown in the graphical representation, as PRRT significantly decreases NSR of the body as compared to the control group. The study included participants with mechanical neck pain who were treated with PRRT. The results showed that there was a significant reduction in pain and improvement in function immediately after the treatment.

Without the need for regular and direct interaction with medical specialists, digital health initiatives might make it easier for busy workers to maintain their exercise regimens. To determine whether components of the AI-assisted health program were effective, more research is required. The present fervor surrounding ML and AI has to be balanced with a critical assessment of these techniques' drawbacks, some of which are outlined in this study. However, this is not exclusive to ML; proper application of appropriate methods to appropriate data is a general notion in science. Nevertheless, ML techniques are still in their infancy and are not as well-known as traditional statistics, which adds burdens to the process of reviewing scientific publications. There is a wider use of AI and ML that has bearing on pain. This covers their use in different pharmacological research domains as well as drug development and discovery. Furthermore, virtual reality approaches that have been launched recently in the scientific research of innovative ways to pain treatment are also using AI techniques.

Machine learning extends beyond developing and using classifiers as biomarkers or other diagnostic instruments. Finding patterns in the data that directly address complicated pain symptoms, the characteristics of these phenotypes, and the intricate mechanisms underlying them, including omics data, is an essential application. The current scientometric study was produced by human professionals with expertise in data science, biology, and medicine in addition to programmed information mining. One of the most promising methods for advancing pain research is likely to combine artificial and human intelligence.

References

1. Comprehensive survey of living condition in 2015, Ministry of Health, Labour and Welfare, Japan, 2021-01-16.
2. Ciallella, H.L. and Zhu, H., Advancing computational toxicology in the big data era by artificial intelligence: data-driven and mechanism-driven modeling for chemical toxicity. *Chem. Res. Toxicol.*, 32, 536–547, 2019.
3. Zhu, H., Big data and artificial intelligence modeling for drug discovery. *Annu. Rev. Pharmacol. Toxicol.*, 60, 573–589, 2020.
4. Baronzio, G., Overview of methods for overcoming hindrance to drug delivery to tumors, with special attention to tumor interstitial fluid. *Front. Oncol.*, 5, 165, 2015.
5. Duch, W., Artificial intelligence approaches for rational drug design and discovery. *Curr. Pharm. Des.*, 13, 1497–1508, 2007.
6. Medsker, L. and Jain, L.C., *Recurrent Neural Networks: Design and Applications*, CRC Press, Boca Raton, FL, 1999.
7. Kalyane, D., Artificial intelligence in the pharmaceutical sector: current scene and future prospect, in: *The Future of Pharmaceutical Product Development and Research*, K. Tekade Rakesh (Ed.), pp. 73–107, Elsevier, Amsterdam, Netherlands, 2020.
8. Bielecki, A. and Bielecki, A., Foundations of artificial neural networks, in: *Models of Neurons and Perceptrons: Selected Problems and Challenges*, K. Janusz (Ed.), pp. 15–28, Springer International Publishing, Cham, Switzerland, 2019.
9. Álvarez-Machancoses, O. and Fernández-Martínez, J.L., Using artificial intelligence methods to speed up drug discovery. *Expert Opin. Drug Discov.*, 14, 769–777, 2019.
10. I.S., A grand product design model for crystallization solvent design. *Comput. Chem. Eng.*, 135, 106764, 2020.
11. Elfering, A., Urs, M., Cornelia, R.S., Tamcan, O., Mannion, A.F., Pessimistic back beliefs and lack of exercise: a longitudinal risk study in relation to shoulder, neck, and back pain. *Psychol. Health Med.*, 20, 7, 767–80, 2015, doi: 10.1080/13548506.2015.1017824.
12. Fujii, T., Matsudaira, K., Yoshimura, N., Hirai, M., Tanaka, S., Associations between neck and shoulder discomfort (Katakori) and job demand, job control, and worksite support. *Mod. Rheumatol.*, 23, 6, 1198–1204, 2014 Jan 14, doi: 10.3109/s10165-012-0824-5.
13. Diaz-Pulido, B. *et al.*, Efficacy of manual therapy and Transcutaneous electrical nerve stimulation in cervical mobility and endurance in subacute and chronic neck pain. *J. Clin. Med.*, 10, 4243, 2021.
14. Verhagen, A.P. *et al.*, Physiotherapy management for neck pain. *J. Physiother.*, 61, 191–198, 2015.

15. Naka, A. *et al.*, Effects of regular electrotherapy on spinal flexibility and pain sensitivity in patients with chronic nonspecific neck pain. *J. Clin. Med.*, 12, 2431, 2023.
16. Nasir, M.F. *et al.*, A study to observe the effects of physiotherapy with and without manual therapy in the management of postural neck pain: randomized controlled trail. *J. Pak Med. Assoc.*, 71, 2851–2856, 2021.
17. Dusunceli, Y. *et al.*, Efficacy of neck stabilization j exercises for neck pain : randomized controlled trail. *J. Rehabil. Med.*, 41, 158–164, 2009.
18. Seemal, P. *et al.*, Comparing primal reflex release technique and stretching patient of coccydynia. *Iran. J. Rehabil.*, 22, 165–174, 2022.
19. Kroeling, P. *et al.*, A Cochrane review of electrotherapy for mechanical neck pain – a clinical trail. *Cochrane Database System. Rev.*, 2005, 2, Article ID - CD004249, Pubmed, 2005.
20. Kazeminasab, S. *et al.*, Neck pain: global epidemiology, trends and risk factors. *BMC Musculoskelet. Disord.*, 23, 450, 2022.
21. Clenand, J.A., Childs, J.D., Whiteman, J.M., Psychometric properties of the neck disability and numeric pain rating scale in patients with mechanical neck pain. *Physical Therapy*, 88, 11, 1244–1250, 2008.
22. Anan, T., Kajiki, S., Oka, H., Fujii, T., Kawamata, K., Mori, K., Matsudaira, K., Effects of an artificial intelligence–assisted health program on workers with neck/shoulder pain/stiffness and low back pain: randomized controlled trial. *JMIR mHealth uHealth*, 9, 9, e27535, 2021 Sep 24.
23. Marcuzzi, A., Nordstoga, A.L., Bach, K., Aasdahl, L., Nilsen, T.I., Bardal, E.M., Boldermo, NO., Bertheussen, G.F., Marchand, G.H., Gismervik, S., Mork, P.J., Effect of an Artificial Intelligence–Based Self-Management App on Musculoskeletal Health in Patients with Neck and/or Low Back Pain Referred to Specialist Care: A Randomized Clinical Trial. *JAMA Netw. Open*, 6, 6, e2320400, 2023 Jun 1.
24. Lo, W.L., Lei, D., Li, L., Huang, D.F., Tong, K.F., The perceived benefits of an artificial intelligence–embedded mobile app implementing evidence-based guidelines for the self-management of chronic neck and back pain: observational study. *JMIR Mhealth Uhealth*, 6, 11, e8127, 2018 Nov 26.
25. Puri, V., Van Le, C., Jagdev, S.S., Kim, L.C., Smart cervical band: an Internet of Things- and artificial intelligence-based neck pain and cervical spondylosis healing system, in: *An Industrial IoT Approach for Pharmaceutical Industry Growth*, pp. 289–304, Academic Press, Cambridge, MA, 2020 Jan 1.
26. Eloqayli, H., Al-Yousef, A., Jaradat, R., Vitamin D and ferritin correlation with chronic neck pain using standard statistics and a novel artificial neural network prediction model. *Br. J. Neurosurg.*, 32, 2, 172–6, 2018 Mar 4.

5

Evolutionary Computation in Bioinformatics Analyzing the Effects of Neurodynamic Exercises on Pain and Disability in Carpal Tunnel Syndrome Patients

Manish Pathak, Vaibhav Agarwal* and Manish Kumar Jha

Department of Physiotherapy, Himalayan Institute of Medical Sciences, Swami Rama Himalayan University, Jolly Grant, Dehradun, India

Abstract

Cervical radiculopathy (CR) is one of the most common health-related complaints. The most common cause of CR includes trauma, spondylosis, disk herniation, spinal instability, and osteophytosis, but rarely from oncogene-related diseases. Thus, the experimental study was carried out to reduce pain and increase range of motion with the help of neural tissue mobilization and stabilization exercises in unilateral CR subjects. To examine the combined effects of neural tissue mobilization and cervical stabilization exercises in unilateral CR subjects, researchers conducted a study focusing on the efficacy of these interventions in improving functional outcomes and reducing symptoms associated with the condition. Numerous geographical dimensions and diverse types of data that are saved and processed are covered by the databases and tools used in neuroinformatics. Innovative software tools and neuroinformatics databases are crucial for comprehending neurological illnesses, the nervous system in normal operation, and clinical applications. The bioinformatics community was introduced to intriguing examples of recent advancements through the succinctly described neuroinformatics initiatives.

Keywords: Bioinformatics, neurodynamics, neuroinformatics, CR, CTS, database

**Corresponding author*: VaibhavAgarwal79@outlook.com

Abhishek Kumar, Narayan Vyas, Pramod Singh Rathore, Abhineet Anand and Pooja Dixit (eds.) Internet of Medicine for Smart Healthcare, (89–110) © 2025 Scrivener Publishing LLC

5.1 Introduction

Cervical radiculopathy (CR) is a frequently occurring health concern. Disc herniations, spondylitic spur, and cervical osteophyte are examples of space-occupying lesions that can cause compression or inflammatory disease, which is why CR is a common clinical diagnostic that is categorized as a condition of a nerve root [1]. Infrequently, oncogene-related disorders are the cause of CR; instead, spondylosis, disk herniation, spinal instability, and trauma along with osteophytosis are the most frequent causes [2]. In addition to physically and functionally producing fibrosis, hypoxia, hypoxia, neural inflammation, edema, and ischemia, as well as reducing neural mobility, CR results in compressions and inflammations of nerve root.

Cervical radiculopathy having an average recurrence rate of 83 per 100,000 persons in the general population; however, a greater frequency of 203 per 100,000 persons occurs in the fifth decade of life. The C5 and C6 nerve root are most commonly affected, and this is usually due to spondylosis or a disc herniation between the C5-C6 or C6-C7 [3].

The most common symptoms that patients having CR seek medical attention for are neck discomfort, tingling, numbness, decreased grip strength, and generalized weakness in the upper extremities. Disability develops in the latter stages of the disease because the cervical muscles, which are responsible for 80% of the cervical region's mechanical stability, are impacted. Similar to this, upper extremity weakness resulting from the damaged nerve root level limits the functions of the upper extremities, and sensory complaints that usually follow a dermatomal pain pattern were more common at the C4 levels (60%) than at the C7 level (34%). A total of 51.6% of patients had scapular soreness. A physical examination usually indicates reduced deep tendon reflexes and uncomfortable range of motion in the cervical spine. Just 15% of instances feature weakness in the upper limb. Although less than 2% of patients show signs of muscular atrophy, reduced feeling is observed in one-third of cases. The nerve segments most commonly affected are C6 (17.6%–42.6%) and C7 (39.3%–46.3%). In 5–36% of instances, bilateral involvement is noted [4].

Patients suffering from cervical spine diseases benefit greatly from physical therapy programs in terms of treatment and symptom alleviation. For CR, nonsurgical therapy options include traction, medicine, and the temporary use of a soft cervical collar. Steroid injections, physical therapy, and manipulation are all incorporated in a gentle approach to treatment. Cervical traction is one of the preferred physical therapy procedures for individuals with CR. On the other hand, people with neck disorders often exhibit forward head position or postural distortion. Persistent forward head posture puts more strain on the posterior vertebral structures, which causes the deep cervical muscles to weaken. Forward head position has been linked to tighter and weaker anterior neck muscles as well as shorter posterior neck extensors, according to many studies. To improve cervical stabilization, one might perform safe workouts that promote cervical stabilization. Exercises like these can improve sensorimotor function, increase mobility, and align the vertebrae. The key muscles involved in stabilizing the cervical spine include the deep cervical extensors, semispinalis, and multifidus. Patients with neck discomfort are reported to be impaired by them [5].

Restoring the nervous system's plasticity—the capacity of the nerve and the tissues attached to it to change in response to one another's structures—is the aim of neural mobilization. Neural mobilization aims to improve the nerve's excursion or mobility in respect to its interface by increasing the collagen's pliability, which preserves the nerve's integrity. Neural tissue displacement has been used in a small number of trials with strict inclusion criteria, and the results have shown improved pain relief and improved functional outcomes. The main goal of this therapeutic strategy is to restore proper neuro-dynamics by passively mobilizing neural tissue structures that have been mechanically sensitized. The peripheral nervous system's neurophysiological and neuromechanical activities are enhanced by neural tissue mobility. Based on the sliding concept of neural tissue excursion, this technique modifies the combined actions of at least two joints. Compared to methods that only lengthen the nerve bed, this approach is supposed to cause a greater longitudinal excursion in order to mobilize a nerve with the least amount of tension rise [6]. In an effort to improve coordination among the superficial and deep cervical muscles and strengthen the deep muscles of the cervical spine, the use of cervical stability exercises has grown recently. Although no study has looked at the implications of cervical stabilization exercises in CR, these exercises need patient to maintain neutral spine alignments using stabilizer muscles activation in a variety of conditions, starting with cranio-cervical nodes and progressing through increased levels of extremity loading [7].

The neck disability index, a 10-item survey, is used to gauge a patient's self-reported neck pain-related handicap. In 2008, the same scholar assessed the NDI. Additionally, it has been demonstrated that the NDI is valid when compared to other pain and impairment measures [8]. Finding the right anticancer medication based on each patient's unique tumor genetic profile, clinical characteristics, and surrounding microenvironment is known as personalized or precision cancer therapy. Another goal of precision medicine is to treat cancer more successfully and with fewer side effects [9]. A prevalent medical condition affecting the general patient population is carpal tunnel syndrome (CTS). Roughly 90% of all focal entrapment neuropathies are caused by this most prevalent peripheral nerve (PN) entrapment illness. Compression of the median nerve during its passage through the wrist causes CTS, which manifests as pain, numbness, and paresthesia in these areas. Similarly, the dorsum of the distal halves of the same lateral three-and-a-half fingers, which is the dorsal distribution of the median nerve in the hand, experiences pain, numbness, and paresthesia [10]. Figure 5.1 illustrate the distribution of the median nerve in the palmar aspect of the right hand.

The condition may worsen and result in hand weakness, weak grip strength, poor fine motor coordination, and thenar muscle atrophy. At first, symptoms are more prevalent at night, but, as compression increases, they become more consistent. With annual healthcare expenses over $2 billion, CTS is the costliest upper extremity musculoskeletal condition in the US [12]. Most CTS patients who see doctors for the first time are elderly, female, and industrial workers. Therefore, it is critical that medical experts and other healthcare providers have a thorough understanding of the illness to identify CTS and prescribe appropriate treatment. Regarding the anatomy, epidemiology, pathophysiology, diagnosis, and treatment of CTS, this review outlines the state-of-the-art as well as the research and knowledge gaps. This study also emphasizes how the structural components that predispose an individual to CTS interact with biological, genetic, environmental, and occupational factors.

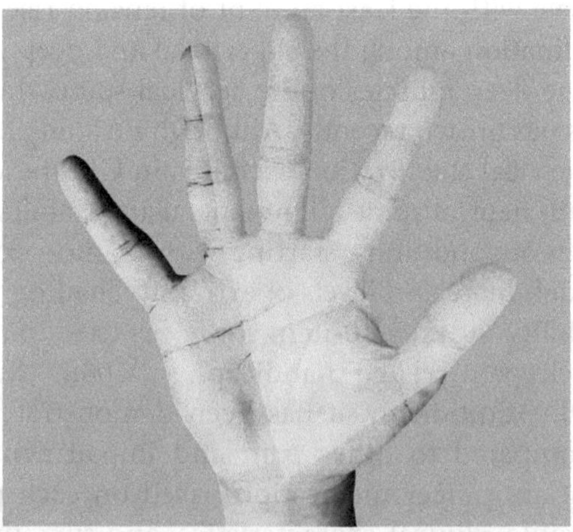

Figure 5.1 Distribution of the median nerve in the palmar aspect of the right hand [11].

5.2 Literature Review

Smati Sambyal and Sandeep Kumar: "Comparison between nerve mobilization and conventional physiotherapy in patient with cervical radiculopathy." According to the study's findings, individuals in Group A received better therapy than those in Group B; specifically, nerve mobilization helped those suffering from CR feel less discomfort [13].

Shin Ho Chung *et al.*: "The effect of neural mobilization on CR patients, pain, disability, ROM and deep flexor endurance." The findings of this study demonstrate that NMCT can help patients with CR with pain reduction, neck disability rehabilitation, range of motion, and deep flexor endurance [14].

Aniruddha Pradyuman Barot and Yagna Unmesh Shukla: "Effects of neural tissue mobilization versus intermittent cervical traction in unilateral cervical radiculopathy on pain, range of motion and quality of life—A comparative study." The findings of this study demonstrate that CR patients respond well to neural tissue mobilization in addition to traditional treatment [15].

Nihal Gelecek and Hakan Akkan: "The effect of stabilization exercise training on pain and functional status in patient with cervical radiculopathy." The study's findings indicate that cervical stability exercises might be quite beneficial for those with CR [16].

Robert J. Rodine and Howard Vernon: "Cervical radiculopathy a systemic review on treatment by spinal manipulation and measurement with the neck disability index." The findings of this study demonstrate that NDI is a suitable outcome measure [17].

Thavatchai Suvarnnat, Rungthip Puntumetakul *et al.*: "Effect of specific deep cervical muscle exercises on functional disability, pain intensity, craniovertebral angle, and neck-muscle strength in chronic mechanical neck pain: a randomized controlled trial." The results of this study indicate that after 6 weeks of training, the exercise groups' "neck disability index (NDI)" scores enhanced significantly more than those of the control group. The exercise groups' net promoter score (NPS) scores also improved substantially more than those of the control group, indicating that the 6 weeks of exercise produced a significant improvement in the exercise group [18].

According to research by Sun Woong Kim *et al.*, CTS is the most prevalent illness among focal neuropathies. Researchers' goal in this work was to confirm the usefulness of quantitative analysis of muscle ultrasonography in CTS with artificial intelligence (AI) assistance. One doctor did ultrasonography in the identical sonographic conditions. For comparison, machine learning (ML) and traditional quantitative grayscale analysis were also carried out. Analysis was done on 27 control hands and 47 hands with CTS. According to traditional quantitative analysis, the patient group's mean echo intensity (EI) ratio—that is, its mean thenar EI/mean hypothenar EI ratio—was considerably greater than the control groups, and the receiver operating characteristic (ROC) analysis area under the curve (AUC) was 0.76. The linear support vector classifier has the greatest AUC (AUC = 0.86) in the ML investigation. The classifier's AUC score increased to 0.89 when recursive feature removal was used. This study demonstrated that applying AI to the quantitative analysis of muscle ultrasound significantly improved diagnosis accuracy. Muscle ultrasound examinations can be used as a noninvasive and quick diagnostic auxiliary tool if a ML analysis procedure can be developed and installed on an ultrasound equipment [19].

Using the "Boston Carpal Tunnel Questionnaire (BCTQ)," Eleftherios Paraskevopoulos *et al.* examined how neuromobilization exercises (NE) affected individuals with CTS in terms of pain, grip along with pinch strength, two-point unfair treatment, motor and sensory distal latency, symptom severity, as well as functional status. The evidence quality was assessed using the GRADE approach, and the methodology was assessed using PEDro. Sixteen of the 25 included articles demonstrated good methodological quality. Most significantly, there was no proof of clinical efficacy for NE. There may not be any therapeutic advantages of NE for individuals with mild to moderate CTS, according to low- to very low-quality research [20].

CTS is a frequent peripheral canalicular nerve entrapment condition in the upper extremities, as Mahshid Malakootian *et al.* explained in their study. In addition to discussing the significance of genetic variables in CTS genesis, the current research analyzes the literature on the prevalence, pathophysiology, diagnosis, therapy, and risk factors of CTS. Although the diagnosis of CTS is mostly based on clinical symptoms, advanced methods like magnetic resonance imaging and ultrasonography make it easier to understand. Both conservative and surgical methods can reduce the symptoms of CTS. Variants within genes increase genetic predispositions to CTS; nonetheless, the etiology of CTS may involve wrist motions, injury, and certain situations. Due to the high frequency of CTS, which lowers patients' quality of life and places a financial burden on health systems, research and clinical trials are essential to understanding the pathophysiology of CTS and creating new targets for treatment [21].

Traditional Chinese remedies (TCM) represent a rich source of possible leads for medication development, as Yuan Quan *et al.* pointed out in their study. However, the current growth of TCM is severely impeded by fundamental contrasts between modern pharmacology and traditional Chinese medicinal beliefs. To tackle this obstacle, novel methodologies pertaining to genomes, transcriptomics, proteomics, metabolomics, and bioinformatics have been employed to analyze the pharmacological mechanisms of traditional Chinese medicine. This review article highlights the promise of omic and bioinformatic methodologies in TCM-based medication development and gives an outline of the state of the field's present research [22].

Teodoro Martín-Noguerol *et al.* conducted a review of the physical underpinnings of diffusion tensor imaging (DTI) and dynamic contrast-enhanced magnetic resonance imaging (DCE-MRI) applied to the evaluation of PNs to give readers an understanding of the key ideas and resources needed to get these kinds of sequences for PNs assessment. This study is on a pragmatic approach to these sophisticated sequences, offering practical advice on how to incorporate them into actual clinical settings. It focuses on imaging postprocessing and their present therapeutic use. There is also a synopsis of the possible uses of AI algorithms for PN evaluation. DTI may be used to evaluate PNs and has been effectively used to the central nervous system. Using DCE-MRI instead of the traditional gadolinium-enhanced MRI sequences method, one may assess the vascularization and integrity of the blood nerve barrier (Paterson). With encouraging first results, radiologists may find it easier to discover, segment, and characterize patient populations using AI algorithms. Tools like DTI and DCE-MRI are practical for evaluating PN lesions. The book focuses on the technological modifications required to get and process these photos. An additional viable option for PN assessment with encouraging outcomes is the use of AI algorithms [23].

5.3 Methodology

5.3.1 Objectives

The objectives of the study are as follows:

i. To measure range of motion of cervical spine using computational bioinformatics.
ii. To measure the pain of unilateral arm radiating pain.
iii. To measure the cranio-vertebral angle range.
iv. To determine whether CR pain is associated with forward head posture.

5.3.2 Hypothesis

5.3.2.1 Null Hypothesis

Null hypothesis combined the effects of neural tissue mobilization and cervical stabilization exercises, which will not show significant improvement in pain and range of motion in unilateral CR subjects.

5.3.2.2 Experimental Hypothesis

Experimental hypothesis combined the effects of neural tissue mobilization and cervical stabilization exercises, which will show significant improvement in pain and range of motion in unilateral CR subjects using computational bioinformatics.

5.3.3 Aim of Study

The aim of the study is to examine the combined effect of neural tissues mobilization and cervical stabilization exercises in unilateral CR subjects using computational bioinformatics.

5.3.3.1 Study Design

Experimental study

5.3.3.2 Study Center

Physiotherapy OPD, Neuro Medicine Ward Himalayan Hospital, Swami Rama Himalayan University Dehradun

5.3.3.3 Study Population

Subjects having unilateral CR were taken in this study

5.3.3.4 *Sample Method*

Random sampling method

5.3.3.5 *Sample Size*

Thirty CR subjects were recruited in the study followed the inclusion and exclusion criteria from the Neurology medicine ward and Neurophysiotherapy OPD of the Himalayan Hospital, Swami Rama Himalayan University Dehradun.

Inclusion criteria:
Individuals with a forward head posture (cranial-vertebral angle <45°) and an age range of 30 to 50 years.

- Upper limb unilateral radicular discomfort for less than three months.
- Range of motion of the cervical spine: less than 45° in extension, less than 25° in ipsilateral lateral flexion, and less than 60° in ipsilateral rotation.

Tests for distraction, median nerve tension, and Spurling's test should all be positive.

The following problems are excluded: neurological or orthopedic disorders affecting the shoulder and cervical spine.

- Heavy cervical spine motion
- Insufficiency of the vertebrae basilar, malignancy
- Those who have cervical surgery
- People with cervical radiculopathies on both sides
- Being pregnant

5.3.4 Procedure

5.3.4.1 Protocol

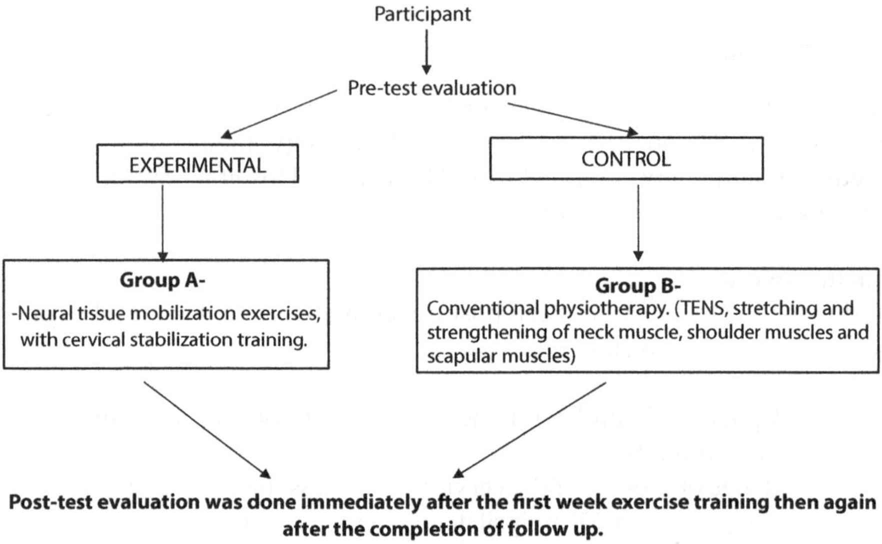

The subjects were given detailed explanation of the purpose of the study before screening. Based on the inclusion and exclusion criteria the subjects were divided into two group experimental group and control group. Neural mobilization along with cervical stabilization exercise was given to experimental group.

5.3.5 Experimental Group Intervention

5.3.5.1 Exercises

1) Neural mobilization exercise procedure:
A total of 15–20 repetitions in one session were done with 1 min of rest between the sets of neural mobilization with openers for 1 min of each level before treatment.

Cervical static and dynamic openers:

Technique 1: With the use of two cushions, the participant's neck was positioned in flexion and contralateral lateral flexion while supine for 1 to 2 min. This method's goal was to reduce distal symptoms like those in the hand and forearm.

Technique 2: The participant was lye on supine. Within the range that was available, the therapist conducted contralateral lateral flexion of the neck. Following the first strategy, this one seeks to further alleviate the symptoms.

Technique 3: The participant was lye on supine position, and the neck was slowly flexed to the ipsilateral side within the range that was possible. Because the nerve's physiological function should have improved by now and we are starting to repair the mechanical dysfunction, this change in direction of movement is necessary.

Neural mobilization treatment progression:

Progression 1: The subject lay in a supine posture with the afflicted arm flexed and the hand relaxed on the stomach. The opposing arm is extended into a horizontal abduction position.

Progression 2: The therapist put the participant's afflicted arm in the resting position as mentioned above and then moved the contralateral arm in a series of elbow flexion-wrist extensions and elbow extension-wrist flexions movements.

Progression 3: The afflicted arm was moved within the range of motions delineated in progression 2, whereas the contralateral arm of the participant was extended in a horizontal abduction.

Progression 4: The therapist proceeded to move the afflicted arm in the same sequences while keeping the contralateral arm of the person receiving treatment in line with the torso. Furthermore, the individual is requested to move their neck into an ipsilateral side flexor during elbow extension and a contralateral side flexion during elbow flexion.

2) Cervical stabilization exercises:
During exercises, all subjects were instructed to maintain their postural alignments.

These include cervical dynamic isometric, shoulder shrugs, shoulder roll, chest flies, and chin tuck exercises.

5.3.5.2 *Exercise Methods*

a) Shoulder shrugs (performed while standing): The participant raises their shoulders to their ears and then returns them to their natural posture.
b) Shoulder rolls: The person rolls their shoulders forward in a circle while standing. Next, make a circle with the shoulders rolled back.
c) Exercises for the chest fly (while standing): The person stood in the center of the thera-band, which was firmly fastened to a sturdy stand at shoulder height. One leg of the solid stand was positioned slightly ahead of the other behind the participants. Next, with their elbows straight, the participant grabs the bands at shoulder height, pulls them inward with their palms facing each other, and then gently moves back.
d) Cervical dynamic flexion, extension isometric exercise (in sitting position): The participant assumes an upright stance while the physiotherapist holds the other end of the thera-band looped over their hand and the subject's head. Throughout the exercise, the participants bend forward, backward, hold, and then gradually return to the starting position, maintaining an erect spine posture.
e) Chin tuck (in standing position): Participants had to get up and allowed their shoulders to drop. Look directly forward. Straighten your chin and slowly recline. It moves very little. Avoid bending your neck forward or tilting your head up or down.

The frequency of exercises was 10 repetitions per session for each exercise in cervical stabilization methods.

5.3.6 Data Analysis

Version 20 of the SPSS program was used to analyze the data. To determine the mean standard deviation (SD) for the demographic and outcome variables, descriptive statistics were used. Repeated action: The difference between the results for the VAS, NDI, and CROM (cranio-vertebral angle, cervical extension, cervical rotation, and cervical lateral flexion) within and between the groups was determined using the ANOVA test. Figure 5.2 illustrate the Pre and post mean and SD graph of VAS of both groups.

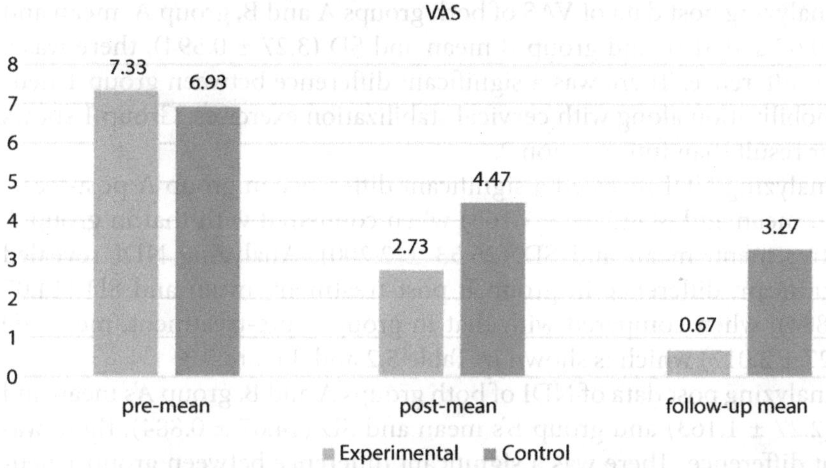

Figure 5.2 Pre and post mean and SD graph of VAS of both groups.

5.4 Result and Discussion

This chapter deals with the result of the data analysis of the three outcome measures: VAS, NDI, and CROM between group 1 (experimental) and group 2 (control). The scores were analyzed and interpreted to determine whether there is a significant/slight difference or not.

The normality of the data was determined using "Shapiro–Wilk test," and the data was found to be normally distributed. To assess the effectiveness of the intervention, repeated measures ANOVA was used.

Analyzing Visual Analog Scale (VAS) revealed a significant difference in experimental group post-treatment, mean and SD (0.67 ± 0.617), when compared with that in group A pre-treatment, mean and SD (7.33 ± 0.617).

Analyzing VAS revealed a slight difference in control group follow-up treatment, mean and SD (3.27 ± 0.594), when compared with that in group B pre-treatment, mean and SD (6.93 ± 0.704). Which is shown in Table 5.1.

Table 5.1 Mean and standard deviation of VAS score between both groups.

	VAS score			
Study group	**Pre (Mean ± Std. Deviation**	**Post (Mean ± Std. Deviation)**	**Follow-up (Mean ± Std. Deviation)**	**P-value**
Experimental	7.33 ± 0.617	2.73 ± 0.704	0.67 ± 0.617	<0.001
Control	6.93 ± 0.704	4.47 ± 0.915	3.27 ± 0.594	<0.001

Analyzing post data of VAS of both groups A and B, group A, mean and SD (0.67 ± 0.617), and group B mean and SD (3.27 ± 0.594), there was a slight difference. There was a significant difference between group 1 neural mobilization along with cervical stabilization exercises. Group 1 shows better result than intervention 2.

Analyzing NDI revealed a significant difference in group A post-treatment, mean and SD (2.27 ± 1.163) when compared with that in group A pre-treatment, mean and SD (26.53 ± 2.200). Analyzing NDI revealed a significant difference in group B post-treatment, mean and SD (14.07 ± 0.884), when compared with that in group B pre-treatment, mean SD (25.27 ± 2.017) which is shown in Table 5.2 and Figure 5.3.

Analyzing post data of NDI of both groups A and B, group A's mean and SD (2.27 ± 1.163) and group B's mean and SD (14.07 ± 0.884), there was slight difference. There was a significant difference between group 1 neural mobilization along with cervical stabilization exercises. Group 1 shows better result than intervention 2.

Analyzing CV angle revealed a significant difference in group A post-treatment, mean and SD (47.87 ± 1.356), when compared with that in

Table 5.2 Mean and standard deviation of NDI score between both groups.

	NDI			
Study group	**Pre (Mean ± Std. Deviation)**	**Post (Mean ± Std. Deviation)**	**Follow-up (Mean ± Std. Deviation)**	**P-value**
Experimental	26.53 ± 2.200	12.93 ± 1.486	2.27 ± 1.163	<0.001
Control	25.27 ± 2.017	18.13 ± 1.246	14.07 ± 0.884	<0.001

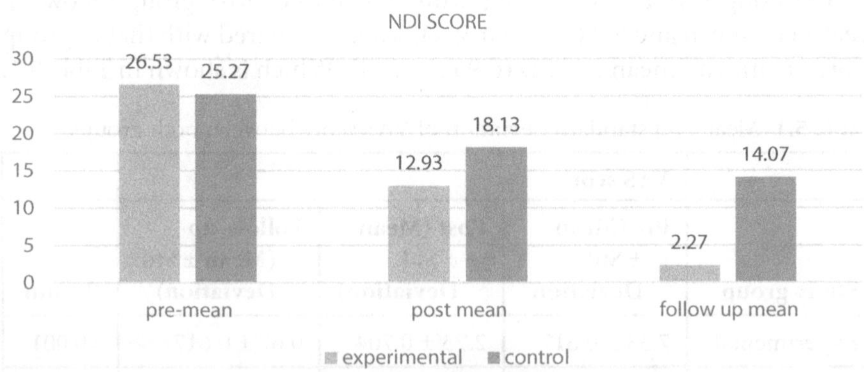

Figure 5.3 Pre and post mean and SD graph of NDI score of both groups.

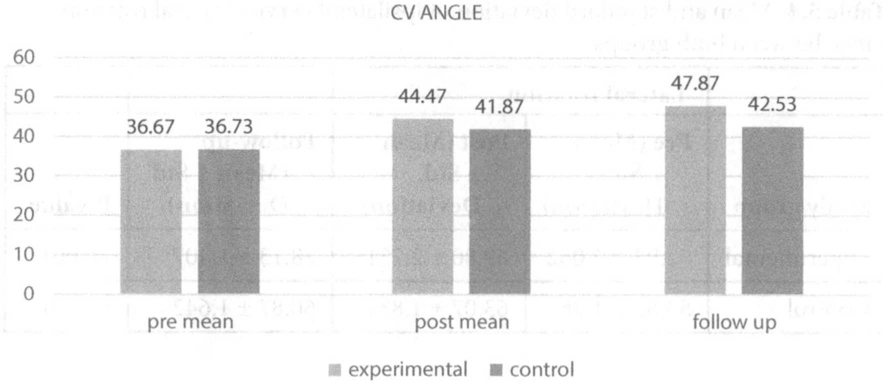

Figure 5.4 Pre and post mean and SD graph of CV angle of both groups.

Table 5.3 Mean and standard deviation of CV angle range between both groups.

	CV angle			
Study group	**Pre (Mean ± Std. Deviation)**	**Post (Mean ± Std. Deviation)**	**Follow-up (Mean ± Std. Deviation)**	**P-value**
Experimental	36.67 ± 2.127	44.47 ± 2.031	47.87 ± 1.356	<0.001
Control	36.73 ± 1.751	41.87 ± 0.951	42.53 ± 1.356	<0.001

group A pre-treatment, mean and SD (36.67 ± 2.127). Figure 5.4 and Table 5.3 illustrates Pre and post mean and SD graph of CV angle of both groups.

Analyzing CV angle revealed a slight difference in group B post-treatment, mean and SD (42.52 ± 1.356), when compared with that in group B pre-treatment, mean and SD (36.73 ± 1.751).

Analyzing post data of CV angle of both groups A and B, group A's mean and SD (47.87 ± 1.356) and group B's mean and SD (42.52 ± 1.356), there was a significant difference between group 1 neural mobilization along with cervical stabilization exercises. Group 1 shows better results than intervention 2.

Analyzing ipsilateral cervical lateral rotation angle revealed a significant difference in group A post-treatment, mean and SD (78.13± 1.407), when compared with that in group A pre-treatment, mean and SD (52.93 ± 2.052).

Analyzing ipsilateral cervical lateral rotation angle revealed a slight difference in group B post-treatment, mean and SD (60.87±1.642), when compared with that in group B pre-treatment, mean and SD (53.87 ± 1.767).

Table 5.4 Mean and standard deviation of ipsilateral cervical lateral rotation range between both groups.

	Lateral rotation			
Study group	Pre (Mean ± Std. Deviation)	Post (Mean ± Std. Deviation)	Follow-up (Mean ± Std. Deviation)	P-value
Experimental	52.93 ± 2.052	69.80 ± 2.731	78.13 ± 1.407	<0.001
Control	53.87 ± 1.767	63.07 ± 1.831	60.87 ± 1.642	<0.001

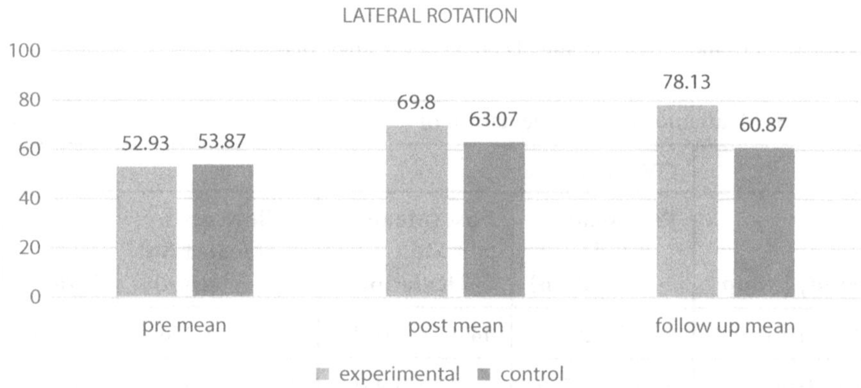

Figure 5.5 Pre and post mean and SD graph of ipsilateral cervical lateral rotation of both groups.

Analyzing post data of ipsilateral cervical lateral rotation angle of both groups A and B, group A's mean and SD (78.13 ± 1.407) and group B's mean and SD (60.87 ± 1.642), so there was a significant difference between group 1 neural mobilization along with cervical stabilization exercises. Group 1 shows better results than intervention 2 which can be clearly depicted from Table 5.4 and Figure 5.5.

Analyzing cervical extension angle revealed a significant difference in group A post-treatment, mean and SD (77.93 ± 2.052), when compared with that in group A pre-treatment, mean and SD (40.67 ± 2.870).

Analyzing cervical extension angle revealed a slight difference in group B post-treatment, mean and SD (67.33 ± 1.799), when compared with that in group B pre-treatment, mean and SD (41.40 ± 1.454) which can be clearly depicted from Table 5.5 and Figure 5.6.

Analyzing post data of cervical extension angle of both groups A and B, group A's mean and SEM (77.93 ± 2.052) and group B's mean and SEM

Table 5.5 Mean and standard deviation of cervical extension range between both groups.

	Cervical extension			
Study group	**Pre (Mean ± Std. Deviation)**	**Post (Mean ± Std. Deviation)**	**Follow-up (Mean ± Std. Deviation)**	**P-value**
Experimental	40.67 ± 2.870	68.27 ± 2.374	77.93 ± 2.052	<0.001
Control	41.40 ± 1.454	62.93 ± 1.486	67.33 ± 1.799	<0.001

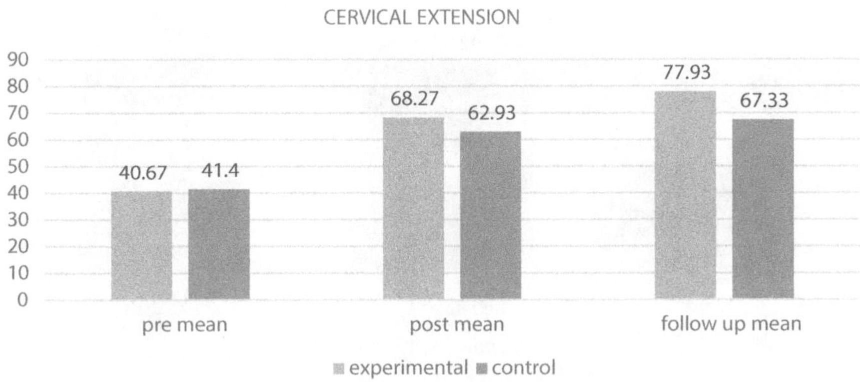

Figure 5.6 Pre and post mean and SD graph of cervical extension of both groups.

(67.33 ± 1.799), there was a significant difference between group 1 neural mobilization along with cervical stabilization exercises. Group 1 shows better results than intervention 2.

Analyzing cervical lateral flexion angle revealed a significant difference in group A post-treatment, mean and SD (43.93± 1.033), when compared with that in group A pre-treatment, mean and SD (21.93 ± 1.387).

Analyzing cervical lateral flexion angle revealed a slight difference in group B post-treatment, mean and SD (41.27 ± 0.704), when compared with that in group B pre-treatment, mean and SD (22.07 ± 1.335).

Analyzing post data of cervical lateral flexion angle of both groups A and B, group A's mean and SD (43.93 ± 1.033) and group B's mean and SD (41.27 ± 0.704), there was a significant difference between group 1 neural mobilization along with cervical stabilization exercises. Group 1 shows better results than intervention 2 which has been clearly illustrated in Table 5.6 and Figure 5.7.

Table 5.6 Mean and standard deviation of ipsilateral lateral flexion range between both groups.

	Lateral flexion range			
Study group	**Pre (Mean ± Std. Deviation)**	**Post (Mean ± Std. Deviation)**	**Follow-up (Mean ± Std. Deviation)**	**P-value**
Experimental	21.93 ± 1.387	42.07 ± 1.163	43.93 ± 1.033	<0.001
Control	22.07 ± 1.335	37.33 ± 2.127	41.27 ± 0.704	<0.001

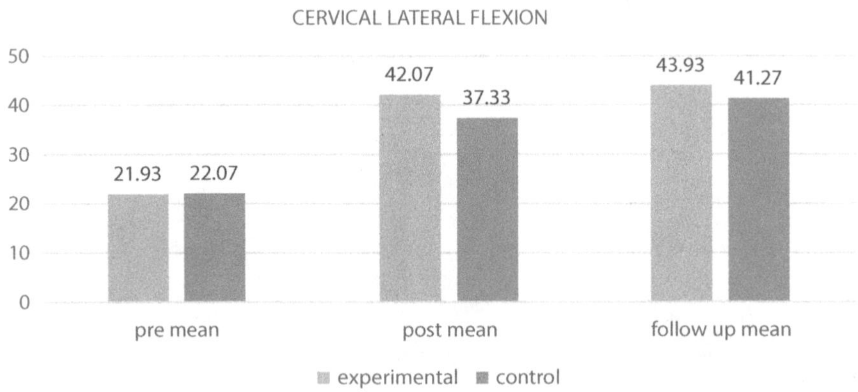

Figure 5.7 Pre and post mean and SD graph of ipsilateral cervical lateral flexion of both groups.

Analyzing both group data, although both groups show a significant difference, group A shows more a significant improvement, and, analyzing ALL the outcome measures, VAS, NDI, and CROM show a significant improvement in group 1.

In this study, we analyzed and compared the pre and follow-up effects of neural mobilization along with cervical stabilization exercise in VAS, NDI score, and CROM among CR subjects.

The present study finds the role of neural mobilization along with cervical stabilization exercises, which can be used as an adjunct with recent practices in treatment of patient with unilateral CR. In the present study, when we compared pre–follow-up mean score of VAS of group 1 to pre–follow-up mean score of VAS in group 2, it was found to be reduced, which was statistically significant (p-value < 0.001).

Young-ho (2020) found that neural mobilization with cervical traction was effective in improving VAS score in CR patients. Nishant H. Nar (2014) found that neural mobilization was effectively in improving VAS score in CR patient, and when we compared pre–follow-up mean score of NDI score of group 1 to pre–follow-up mean score of NDI score in group 2, it was found to be reduced which was statistically significant (p-value < 0.001). M. Srinivasulu *et al.* compare neural mobilization and mulligan mobilization, and they found that neural mobilization was effective in reducing the neck disability function. When we compared pre–follow-up mean score of all CROM of group 1 to pre–follow-up mean score of NDI in group 2, after analysis, all outcome measures show a significant difference in group 1, which was better than that in group 2. So, group 1 intervention was very effective in unilateral CR.

In a study conducted by Samati Sambyal and Sandeep Kumar in August 2013, they found that neural mobilizations significantly show an effective improvement in decreasing pain and disability in patients with CR. Unilateral CR subjects in a previous study conducted by Nihal Gelecek and Hakan Akan in 8 September 2013 found that stabilization exercise training shows an effective improvement in decreasing neck disability and improving quality of life and postures in patient with CR. So, here, also neural mobilization along with cervical stabilization exercises could be very effective intervention in decreasing pain, reducing cervical disability function, and improving cervical range of motion in unilateral CR patients.

Limitation: The limitation of this study is smaller size, which limits the generalization of the result.

In our study, only elderly age group people were included. Old elderly and young adults were not included. The patients with bilateral CR were not included.

Patients were not instructed on how to use a home exercise program. The outcome variables were not measured in between of the session.

5.5 Conclusion

This study was designed to improve cervical range of motion, decrease cervical disability function, and decrease the pain by addressing through neural mobilizations along with cervical stabilization exercises in unilateral CR patient. These exercises could be very effective intervention in reducing pain, improving cervical range of motions, increasing cranio-vertebral angle, and reducing neck function disability in unilateral CR subjects as compared to stretching and strengthening exercise of neck, shoulder, and scapular muscles. Patient with bilateral CR may be the subject of future research. Patient with acute CR can also be evaluated for the efficacy of neural tissue mobilization. To compare the sustainability of treatment, patients might be followed up with over an extended period of time using computational bioinformatics and AI. Different intervention should be developed to improvement in quality of life in CR subjects.

The most prevalent upper limb compressive neuropathy is CTS. Every year, it costs the US billions of dollars. Pain, numbness, and paresthesia along the median nerve's distribution are the hallmarks of typical CTS. For mild to severe instances of CTS, conservative treatment and restriction of repeated wrist motions are necessary. To identify this illness and provide appropriate therapy, primary care physicians need to be aware of it. Using AI to analyze the proteomics and metabolomics found in biofluids in RVO can help with clinical decision-making and pave the way for the future of RVO precision medicine through bioinformatics. Future research must address several limitations, including the straightforward application of AI, the small sample sizes, the uneven viability of office-based sampling, the absence of longitudinal follow-up, the absence of sampling prior to and following RVO, and the lack of healthy controls. One of the best examples of the present, fascinating, and rapidly increasing increase in bioinformatics knowledge and data is neuroinformatics. Numerous geographical dimensions and diverse types of data that are saved and processed are covered by the databases and tools used in neuroinformatics. Innovative software tools and neuroinformatics databases are crucial for comprehending neurological illnesses, the nervous system in normal operation, and clinical applications. The bioinformatics community was introduced to intriguing examples of recent advancements through the succinctly described neuroinformatics initiatives.

References

1. Newington, L., Harris, E.C., Walker-Bone, K., Carpal tunnel syndrome and work. *Best Pract. Res. Clin. Rheumatol.*, 29, 440–453, 2015.
2. Spagnoli, A.M., Fino, P., Fioramonti, P., Sanese, G., Scuderi, N., Bifid median nerve and carpal tunnel syndrome: an uncommon anatomical variation. *Ann. Ital. Chir.*, 88, 95–96, 2017, https://pubmed.ncbi.nlm.nih.gov/28447963/.
3. Lanz, U., Anatomical variations of the median nerve in the carpal tunnel. *J. Hand Surg. Am.*, 2, 44–53, 1977.
4. Garland, F.C., Garland, C.F., Doyle, E.J., Jr, Balazs, L.L., Levine, R., Pugh, W.M., Gorham, E.D., Carpal tunnel syndrome and occupation in US Navy enlisted personnel. *Arch. Environ. Health*, 51, 395–407, 1996.
5. Werner, R.A., Albers, J.W., Franzblau, A., Armstrong, T.J., The relationship between body mass index and the diagnosis of carpal tunnel syndrome. *Muscle Nerve*, 17, 632–636, 1994.

6. van Rijn, R.M., Huisstede, B.M., Koes, B.W., Burdorf, A., Associations between work-related factors and the carpal tunnel syndrome - a systematic review. *Scand. J. Work Environ. Health*, 35, 19–36, 2009.
7. Ganesh, S.B., Effectiveness of neural tissue mobilization in the management of cervico-brachial pain in subject between age group 25-40years. *Indian J. Physiother. Occup. Ther.*, 13, 1, 149–154, 2019.
8. Kuo, Y.-L., Lee, T.-H. *et al.*, Evaluation of a Cervical Stabilization Exercise Program for Pain, Disability, and Physical Impairments in university violinists with nonspecific neck pain. *Int. J. Environ. Res. Public Health*, 17, 5646, 15, Aug. 2020.
9. Massard, C., Michiels, S., Ferté, C. *et al.*, High-throughput genomics and clinical outcome in hard-to-treat advanced cancers: results of the MOSCATO 01 trial. *Cancer Discov.*, 7, 6, 586–595, 2017.
10. Rosario, N.B. and De Jesus, O., *Electrodiagnostic Evaluation of Carpal Tunnel Syndrome*, StatPearls Publishing, Treasure Island, FL, 2023.
11. Sevy, J.O. and Varacallo, M., *Carpal Tunnel Syndrome*, StatPearls Publishing, Treasure Island, FL, 2022.
12. Dale, A.M., Harris-Adamson, C., Rempel, D. *et al.*, Prevalence and incidence of carpal tunnel syndrome in US working populations: pooled analysis of six prospective studies. *Scand. J. Work Environ. Health*, 39, 495–505, 2013.
13. Sambyal, S. and Kumar, S., Comparison between nerve mobilization and conventional physiotherapy in patient with cervical radiculopathy. *Int. J. Innov. Res. Dev.*, 2, 8, 443–448, August 2013.
14. Kim, DG., Chung, S.H. *et al.*, the effect of neural mobilization on cervical radiculopathy patients, pain, disability, ROM and deep flexor endurance. *J. Back Musculoskelet. Rehabil.*, 1, 9, 951–959, 21 April 2017.
15. Kumar, S.A., Kumar, A., Dutt, V., Agrawal, R., Multi Model Implementation on General Medicine Prediction with Quantum Neural Networks, in: *2021 Third International Conference on Intelligent Communication Technologies and Virtual Mobile Networks (ICICV)*, Tirunelveli, India, pp. 1391–1395, 2021, doi: 10.1109/ICICV50876.2021.9388575.
16. Raj, P., Dubey, A.K., Kumar, A., Rathore, P.S., *Blockchain, Artificial Intelligence, and the Internet of Things*, Springer International Publishing, Cham, Switzerland, 2022.
17. Burri, S.R., Kumar, A., Baliyan, A., Kumar, T.A., Predictive Intelligence for Healthcare Outcomes: An AI Architecture Overview, in: *2023 2nd International Conference on Smart Technologies and Systems for Next Generation Computing (ICSTSN)*, Villupuram, India, pp. 1–6, 2023, doi: 10.1109/ICSTSN57873.2023.10151477.
18. Wani, S., Ahuja, S., Kumar, A., Application of Deep Neural Networks and Machine Learning algorithms for diagnosis of Brain tumour, in: *2023 International Conference on Computational Intelligence and Sustainable Engineering Solutions (CISES)*, Greater Noida, India, pp. 106–111, 2023, doi: 10.1109/CISES58720.2023.10183528.

19. Kour, S.P., Kumar, A., Ahuja, S., An Advance Approach for Diabetes Detection by Implementing Machine Learning Algorithms, in: *2023 IEEE World Conference on Applied Intelligence and Computing (AIC)*, Sonbhadra, India, pp. 136–141, 2023, doi: 10.1109/AIC57670.2023.10263919.
20. Raj, P., Kumar, A., Dubey, A.K., Bhatia, S., Oswalt, M.S., *Quantum Computing and Artificial Intelligence: Training Machine and Deep Learning Algorithms on Quantum Computers*, De Gruyter, Berlin, Boston, 2023, [Online]. Available: https://doi.org/10.1515/9783110791402.
21. Sasubilli, G. and Kumar, A., Machine Learning and Big Data Implementation on Health Care data, in: *2020 4th International Conference on Intelligent Computing and Control Systems (ICICCS)*, Madurai, India, pp. 859–864, 2020, doi: 10.1109/ICICCS48265.2020.9120906.
22. Swarna, S.R., Kumar, A., Dixit, P., Sairam, T.V.M., Parkinson's Disease Prediction using Adaptive Quantum Computing, in: *2021 Third International Conference on Intelligent Communication Technologies and Virtual Mobile Networks (ICICV)*, Tirunelveli, India, pp. 1396–1401, 2021, doi: 10.1109/ICICV50876.2021.9388628.
23. Burugadda, V.R., Pawar, P.S., Kumar, A., Bhati, N., Predicting Hospital Readmission Risk for Heart Failure Patients Using Machine Learning Techniques: A Comparative Study of Classification Algorithms, in: *2023 Second International Conference on Trends in Electrical, Electronics, and Computer Engineering (TEECCON)*, Bangalore, India, pp. 223–228, 2023, doi: 10.1109/TEECCON59234.2023.10335817.

6

Imperative Role of Artificial Intelligence and Nanotechnology in Healthcare Sector for Sustainable Development

Sheela Bijlwan

Himalayan Institute of Medical Sciences, Swami Rama Himalayan University, Jolly Grant, Dehradun, India

Abstract

There has been a continuous evolution in healthcare due to innovation in digital technologies. Regular technological innovation helps healthcare providers to deliver the quality services to the patients. The role of artificial intelligence (AI) in strengthening of healthcare sector is very encouraging as it helped in developing novel methods to deal with the challenges of healthcare industries. AI offers solutions to many issues, and "nanotechnology" is just one among them, which is widely used in a variety of fields, including pharmaceutical industry, cosmetics industry, and agriculture. AI plays a wide range of roles in healthcare, from skin examination to the detection of lung disease. By fusing AI with nanotechnology, this paper seeks to investigate potential applications of these technologies in healthcare. The ultimate objective of this study is to combine the applications and potential of these two technologies and revolutionize the healthcare industry. Moreover, nanotechnology has the crucial role in managing sustainability. With the integration of innovative technologies in every field we can support the United Nations' Sustainable Development Goals 3 by providing better health for every individual. Those involved in AI and medicine will gain from this research. Numerous conveniences are made possible by nanotechnology's integration of AI technology into the healthcare sector, including task automation and the analysis of vast volumes of patient data for better, quicker, and more inexpensive healthcare.

***Keywords*:** Artificial intelligence, nanotechnology, cost minimization, mental health, surgery

---

Email: sheelaBijlwan1@outlook.com

Abhishek Kumar, Narayan Vyas, Pramod Singh Rathore, Abhineet Anand and Pooja Dixit (eds.) Internet of Medicine for Smart Healthcare, (111–126) © 2025 Scrivener Publishing LLC

6.1 Introduction

By combining artificial intelligence (AI) and nanotechnology can act as best innovation in the field of healthcare. It can act as early detection tools for any disease and assist independent living elderly people to live without fear. This advancement of technologies can face many difficulties in terms of moral values and privacy of individual or institutions. Thus, the sole responsibilities lie on the shoulders of policymakers and technology developer to be careful and responsible while implementing these technologies in any sectors [1].

AI is leading the way in medical innovation. According to experts and AI developers, "trust" will be a key aspect in determining whether AI can be successfully implemented in medicines. Despite the crucial role that trust plays and the emergence of numerous expert-informed guideline on how to design and implement "trustworthy AI" in medicines, it is found that there was little consensus among these guideline on what precisely users' trust in AI entails [2].

Most studies are in favor of a conceptual framework of confidence in AI that is relevant to health that is grounded in strong empirical evidence, conceptual rigor, and not just expert opinion [3]. Healthcare systems are at danger of collapsing unless substantial structural and transformative reforms are adopted. Larger staffing is also required for health systems; however, there will still be a 9.9 million physicians, nurse, and midwife shortage, despite the creation of 40 million new employments in the field by the global economy (WHO, 2016). Not only do more healthcare workers need to be educated and hired, but it is also vital to ensure that they devote their time to patients, where it is most valuable [4, 5].

AI helps in the effective ways of diagnosis of patient's ailments without physical investigation. IT helps in providing better technological supports to the medical staff for the patient's treatments. IT also supports the whole medical industries in building the smart health care cities, which can further helps in cater the needs of patients by providing the technological supports to the medical staffs so that they can easily be able in dealing the critical patients cares. Figure 6.1 illustrates the role of AI in delivering efficient healthcare services to patients.

The main objective of this study is to focus on the factors that had the greatest bearing on the investigation into the moral implications of AI and nanotechnology in healthcare. For this, the cluster-based content analyses have been conducted on the reputed journal and determine the developing trends of research on this topic and to clarify the research underpinnings for moral AI and nanotechnology in healthcare [6].

Consumers in the digital age are demanding distinctive, personalized, and responsive services with secure flexibility as smart mobile apps and gadgets become more readily available. In this context, it is crucial to examine actual instances of AI use by healthcare organizations for managing operations and providing patient care, as well as to identify the requirements (like responsibility and regulation) and support needs (like ethics, training programmes, or consulting services) for sophisticated AI applications. Figure 6.2 provides a review of the database from the depository.

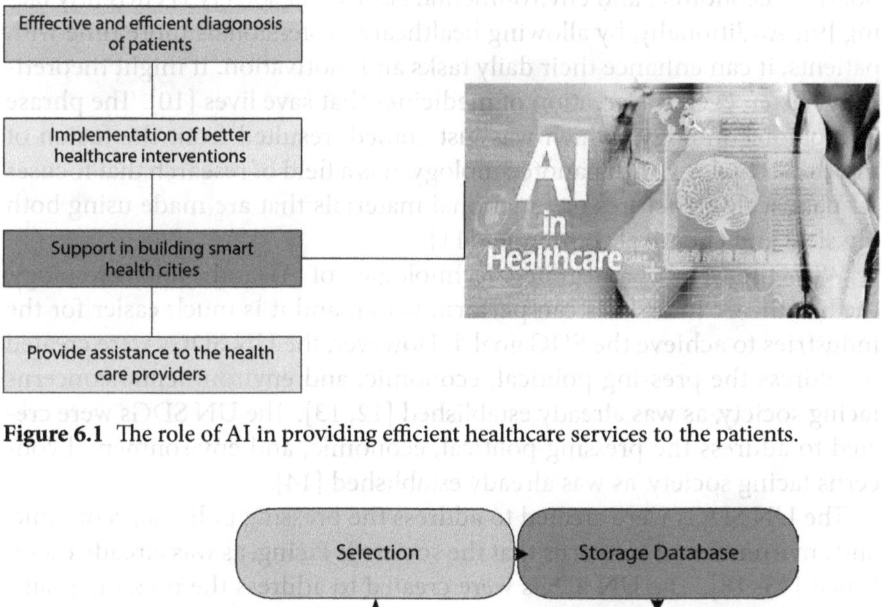

Figure 6.1 The role of AI in providing efficient healthcare services to the patients.

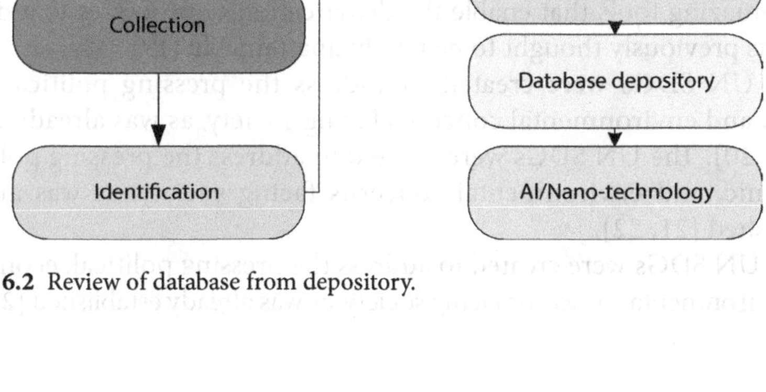

Figure 6.2 Review of database from depository.

6.2 Literature Review

The United Nations (UN) Sustainable Development Goals (SDGs) were created to address the pressing political, economic, and environmental concerns facing society, as was already established [7]. The healthcare industry has the potential to advance, and automation-based AI might be able to aid with improving patient care, enhancing diagnostic accuracy, and streamlining administrative processes. However, it was already said, the UN SDGs were created to address the pressing political, economic, and environmental issues that society is currently facing [8].

As was already said, the UN SDGs were created to address the pressing political, economic, and environmental issues that society is currently facing [9]. Additionally, by allowing healthcare professionals more time with patients, it can enhance their daily tasks and motivation. It might theoretically hasten even the creation of medicines that save lives [10]. The phrase "nanobiotechnology," which was just coined, resulted from the fusion of molecular biology with nanotechnology. It is a field of research that focuses on nanoscale structures or functional materials that are made using both physical and chemical techniques [11].

With the help of integrated technologies of AI and nanotechnology, the healthcare industries can perform better, and it is much easier for the industries to achieve the SDG goal 4. However, the UN SDGs were created to address the pressing political, economic, and environmental concerns facing society, as was already established [12, 13]. The UN SDGs were created to address the pressing political, economic, and environmental concerns facing society, as was already established [14].

The UN SDGs were created to address the pressing political, economic, and environmental concerns that the society is facing, as was already established [15–18]. The UN SDGs were created to address the pressing political, economic, and environmental concerns facing society, as was already established. The advancement of nanotechnology has given humanity some amazing tools that enable the demarcation of processes to a degree that was previously thought to be nearly unattainable [19].

The UN SDGs were created to address the pressing political, economic, and environmental concerns facing society, as was already established [20]. The UN SDGs were created to address the pressing political, economic, and environmental concerns facing society, as was already established [21, 22].

The UN SDGs were created to address the pressing political, economic, and environmental concerns facing society, as was already established [23, 24].

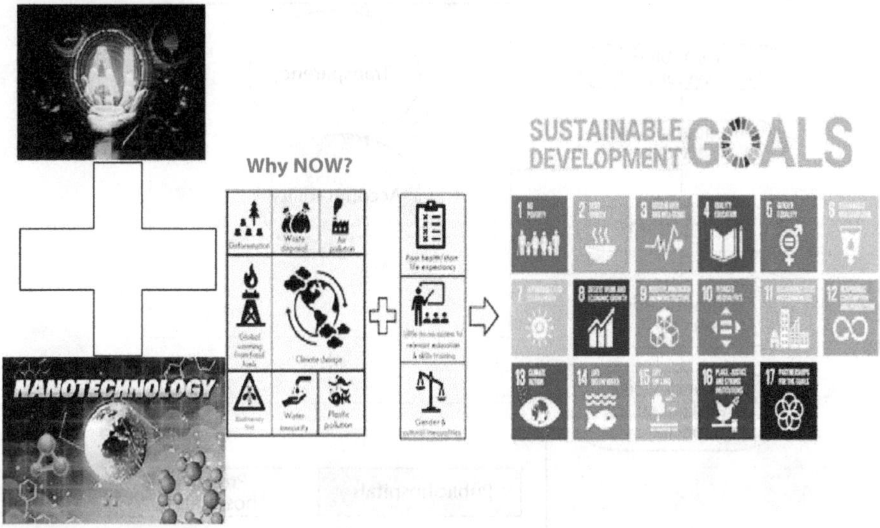

Figure 6.3 The achievement of SDG goals with integration of AI and nanotechnology.

Figure 6.3 illustrates the attainment of SDG goals through the integration of AI and nanotechnology. Due to the fact that the majority of biological systems are nanoscale, nanomaterials integrate well into biomedical equipment [25]. One of the top nanosystems currently being explored for targeted medication delivery is nanoliposomes [26].

Due to the limitations of the currently used approaches in terms of early diagnosis and treatments, advances in nanomedicine and nanodevice have motivated many researchers to hunt for alternative therapies [27]. The remarkable characteristics and uses of different nanomaterials and nanosystems have made them indispensable in the creation of future technologies. This review's objective is to compile information on the most recent uses of nanotechnology in the healthcare industry for readers. Additionally, we critically examine nanotechnology's drawbacks, difficulties, and potential applications in allied healthcare systems [28].

6.3 AI Applications in Healthcare Industries

According to the World Health Organization [36], 60% of the variables influencing a person's health and quality of life have to do with their way of life, including things like exercise, food, sleep, stress management, use of drugs and alcohol, and leisure activity. Figure 6.4 shows the application of AI in healthcare industries.

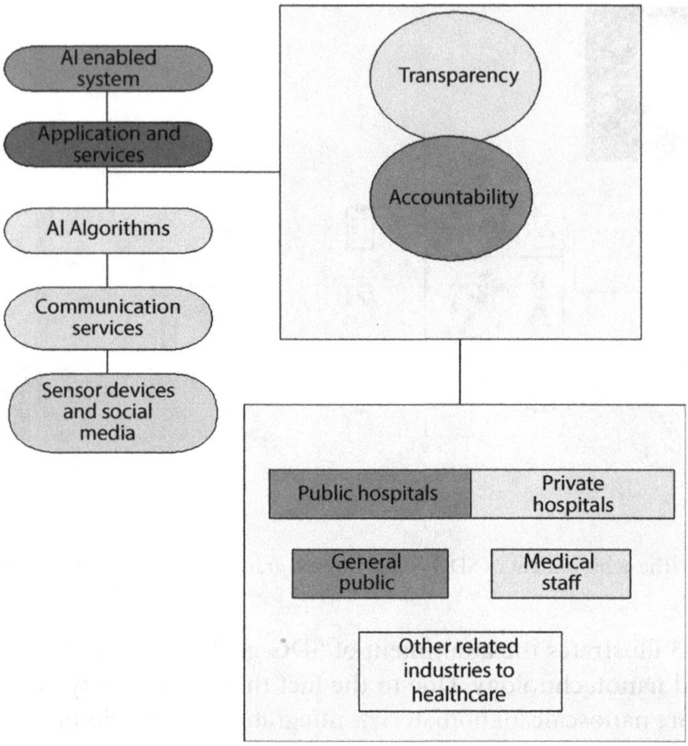

Figure 6.4 Application of AI in healthcare industries.

6.4 Application of AI and Nanotechnology in Medicine

In many transdisciplinary sectors of science and technology, nanotechnology is important. With the help of research and applications, therapeutic nanoparticles have played a significant role in medicine and healthcare. The field of oncological precision medicine has also adopted this idea [29]. A framework is provided by precision medicine for the development of a medical model that proposes data collecting, therapies, healthcare personalization, and practices for specific cancer patients [30, 31]. AI is now being used to design nano-encapsulated medications in order to maximize their unique features and validate the biological interactions and molecular pathways inside the cellular system. Effective deep learning techniques for comprehending the distinctive patterns of biological cells have gained a lot of recent interest in this area of AI. Table 6.1 outlines the role of artificial intelligence in medical practices. These works have demonstrated

Table 6.1 Intervention of artificial intelligence in medical practices.

Domain	Uses
Supporting in medicine and anesthesia delivery	1) AI helps in automatic delivery of medicine and anesthesia to the patients with the help of Bispectral Index (BIS) and Electroencephalogram (EEG) machines. 2) It helps in forecasting related to improvements needed in the drugs infusion processing. 3) It also helps in automation of mechanical ventilation for the proper curing of patients.
Event prediction	1) AI helps in the proper forecasting of future events.
	2) It helps in analyzing the difficulty of patients faced during anesthesia. 3) It supports the medical practitioner in taking right decision while curing patients of different ages.
Ultrasound guidance	AI helps in prediction of scanning of different ailments of the person.
Pain management	AI supports in prediction and assessment of patients pain and helps the doctors in providing right doses of medicines.
OT room assistance	AI supports in arranging the medical staff with proper medical equipment and guiding the doctors to take right decisions.

admirable fusion of AI and nanotechnology for curing the different ailments of the patients [32, 33].

6.5 AI and Nanotechnology in Anti-Aging Medicines

We are getting much better at slowing down the aging process. The average lifespan is also getting longer, which is progress [34]. The final outcome of decade-long processes is the primary causes of death (heart disease, cancer, lung disease, and diabetes). These diseases can be prevented or delayed using current understanding. Lifestyle decisions that include a healthy diet, exercise, stress reduction, and vitamin supplements can help with this. New genetic technology will enable people to create individualized plans, and cancer and heart disease early diagnosis will increase longevity [35, 36].

We are on the cusp of nanotechnology (NT) and AI. AI will make it possible to combine highly developed non-biological intellect with our biological thinking to greatly increase our capacity for thought, creation, and experience. The purpose of modern anti-aging medicine is to delay sickness and aging so that people can benefit from the potent biotechnology and nanotechnology remedies that will be created in the years to come. These upcoming treatments could significantly increase longevity [37, 38].

The application of both the technologies when combined together can develop the most effective drugs for curing different ailments. The use of

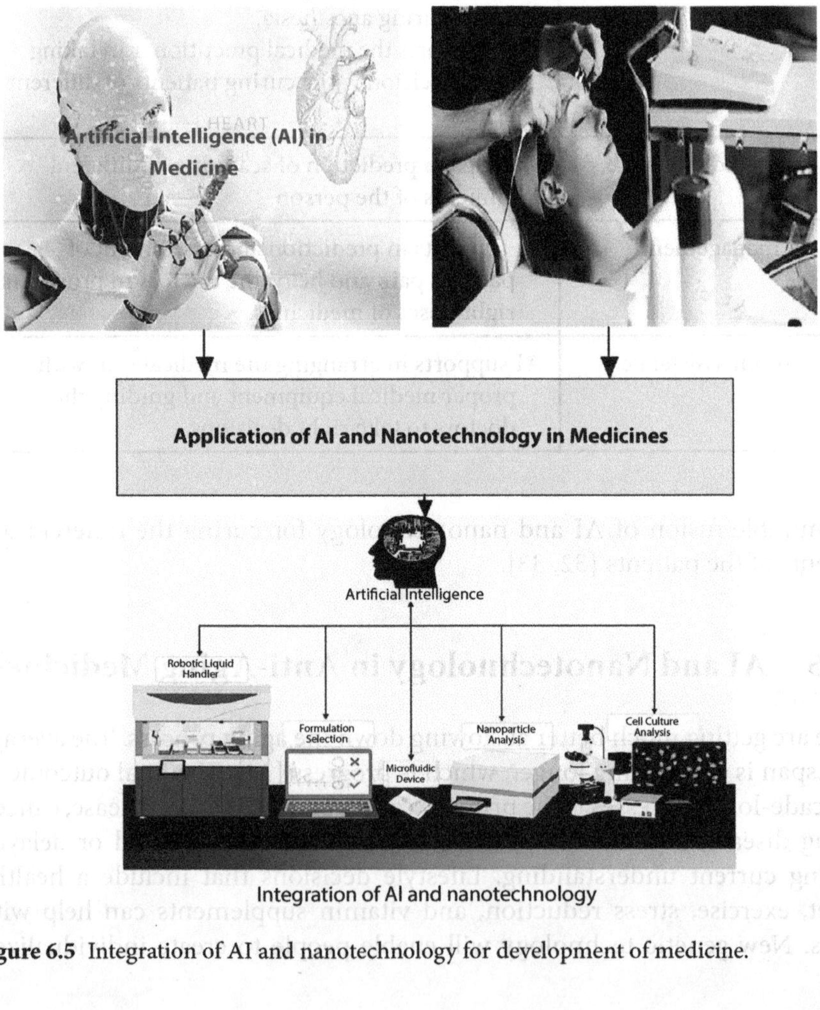

Figure 6.5 Integration of AI and nanotechnology for development of medicine.

nanotechnology in cosmetic industry, which is now the part of healthcare industry, is realized everyday with its amazing outcomes [39]. Figure 6.5 shows the integration of AI and nanotechnology for development of medicine.

6.6 Result

The negative impact of the global pandemic has transformed scientific experimentation and academic study across the board. For the first time, the inability to access laboratories resulted in a halt to practical experimental applications. Additionally, 1.3 billion college and high school students in 186 nations who are unable to attend classes are currently pursuing their education online [40]. Despite the global epidemic, the increasing demand for remote testing employing robotic devices may be able to provide a viable model for students and scientists [41].

6.7 Discussion

1) We are getting much better at slowing down the aging process. For many people, the later years of life are evolving into a time of continuous production, independence, and excellent health rather than a time of senility and deteriorating health. The average lifespan is also getting longer, which is a progress [42].
2) Utilization of AI and nanotechnology in the clinical diagnosis of critical patients helps in the effective management of disease without frequent personal visits to the hospitals. Moreover, virtual diagnosis and drug delivery to the patients is one of the best advantages of AI, in which the whole world realized during the recent COVID-19 pandemic [43]. Table 6.2 examines various studies conducted on AI and nanotechnology.
3) The final outcome of decade-long processes is the primary causes of death (heart disease, cancer, lung disease, and diabetes). These diseases can be prevented or delayed using current understanding. Lifestyle decisions that include a healthy diet, exercise, stress reduction, and vitamin supplements can help with this. New genetic technology will enable people

Table 6.2 Analysis of previous studies.

Reference	Objectives	Methodology	Findings
[1]	The objective of the study is to access the role of nanoparticles in medicines.	Exploratory research	The finding of study is to extensive use of nanotechnology in the development of nanoparticles helps in innovative drugs development.
[4]	To describe the novel methods to treat cancer disease with the help of bio-active nanoparticles.	Based on conceptual review of previous studies.	AI and nanotechnology have the vital role in curing the cancer disease, but still it faced lots of clinical challenges for its application in healthcare.
[11]	There are several prospects to diagnose, treat, and cure difficult diseases thanks to the development of nanoparticle-based medications.	Review article	Advancement in the diagnosis and treatment of disease have been made possible through nanotechnology, which uses nanostructures as a tool. Using this technology to treat diseases like AIDS, cancer, and many others has proven to be effective.
[8]	To study green nanotechnology which is based on plants.	Conceptual review	Nanotechnology and AI can play vital role in the development of herbal medicines.
[12]	To study the biotechnological therapies in treating the genetic dis-orders. The basic objective is to maximize the use of AI and NT.	Review	AI and nanotechnology when integrated together can play a vital role in drugs development.
[39]	To study the role of nanotechnology in medicine.	Exploratory research	Nanotechnology helps in treating the genetic disorder.

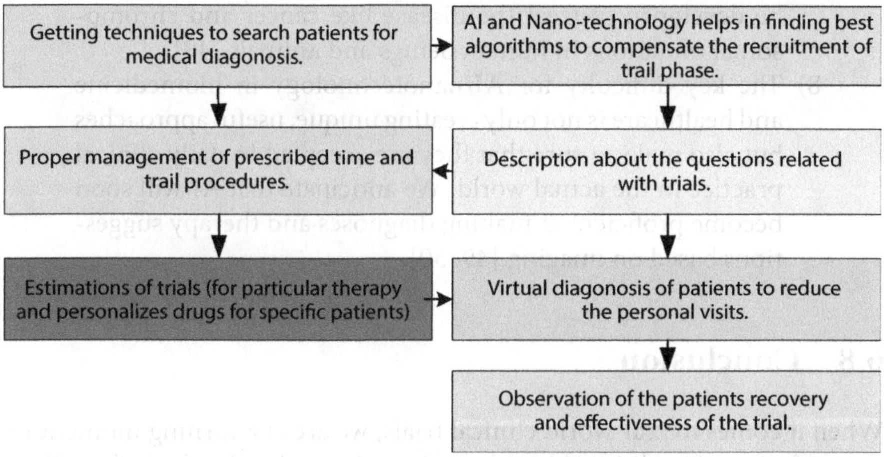

Figure 6.6 Utilizing AI and nanotechnology to improve clinical trials.

to create individualized plans, and cancer and heart disease early diagnosis will increase longevity [44].

4) Successful aging is anticipated to be significantly aided by biotechnological therapies incorporating stem cells, recombinant DNA, proteomics, therapeutic cloning, and gene-based therapeutics. We are on the cusp of AI and NT. AI will make it possible to combine our biological intelligence with sophisticated non-biological intelligence to greatly increase our capacity for thought, creation, and experience [45]. Figure 6.6 shows the utilizationof AI and nanotechnology to improve clinical trials.
5) Eventually, NT will enable us to create machines that can assemble molecules one atom at a time, much like our current cellular machinery. The purpose of modern anti-aging medicine is to delay sickness and aging so that people can benefit from the potent biotechnology and nanotechnology remedies that will be created in the years to come. These upcoming treatments could significantly increase longevity [46].
6) Moreover, the innovative green AI and green nanotechnology, which is totally based on the environmental friendly technology, is highly required [47].
7) There is future scope for the herbal medicines and ayurveda where AI and nanotechnology-based herbal medicines can

be developed to treat the disease like cancer and chromosomal mutations in human beings and animals [48].

8) The key difficulty for AI/nanotechnology in biomedicine and healthcare is not only creating unique, useful approaches but also making sure that they are accepted in daily clinical practice in the actual world. We anticipate that AI will soon become proficient at making diagnoses and therapy suggestions based on imaging [49, 50].

6.8 Conclusion

When it comes to real-world clinical trials, we are at a turning moment in the evolution of traditional healthcare practice and technological application. When it comes to successful planning and treatment, higher accuracy and shorter turnaround times are essential for diagnostic care. However, integration AI and nanotechnology has a vast and varied realm of data, analytics, neural networks, deep neural networks, and visualization methodologies that is constantly expanding and updating to meet the precise and accurate needs of the biomedical and health sectors. In addition, we need adequate funding and investment to educate healthcare professionals about the advantages and possibilities of the AI and nanotechnology-enabled healthcare system. AI has already begun to alter the patient experience, research on clinician medicine practice, and how the drug discovery company functions in the field of healthcare. Integration of AI and nanotechnology will have accessed numerous data sources by 2030 in order to better understand disease trends, anticipate diseases with more accuracy, and enhance treatment and care. Hence, it is anticipated that the next 10 years will lead to the development of outstanding data medical sets and cutting-edge AI and nanotechnologies that will benefit society by improving clinical outcomes and addressing its most pressing challenges.

References

1. Bogutska, K.I., Sklyarov, Y.P., Prylutskyy, Y., Zinc and zinc nanoparticles: biological role and application in biomedicine. *Ukr. Bioorg. Acta*, 1, 9–16, 2013.
2. El Shafey, A.M., Green synthesis of metal and metal oxide nanoparticles from plant leaf extracts and their applications: A review. *Green Process. Synth.*, 9, 1, 304–339, 2020.

3. Madamsetty, V.S., Mukherjee, A., Mukherjee, S., Recent trends of the bio-inspired nanoparticles in cancer theranostics. *Front. Pharmacol.*, 10, 1264, 2019.
4. Sahu, A.N., Nanotechnology in herbal medicines and cosmetics. *Int. J. Res. Ayurveda Pharm. (IJRAP)*, 4, 3, 472–474, 2013.
5. Roco, M.C., National nanotechnology initiative-past, present, future, in: *Handbook on nanoscience, engineering and technology*, 2, pp. 3–1, 2007.
6. Teleanu, D.M. *et al.*, Blood-brain delivery methods using nanotechnology. *Pharmaceutics*, 10, 4, 269, 2018.
7. Khan, A.U. *et al.*, Selected nanotechnologies and nanostructures for drug delivery, nanomedicine and cure. *Bioprocess. Biosyst. Eng.*, 43, 1339–1357, 2020.
8. Grossman, T., Latest advances in antiaging medicine. *Keio J. Med.*, 54, 2, 85–94, 2005.
9. Hobson, D.W., The commercialization of medical nanotechnology for medical applications, in: *Intracellular Delivery III: Market Entry Barriers of Nanomedicines*, pp. 405–449, 2016.
10. Moore, J.A. and Chow, J.C.L., Recent progress and applications of gold nano-technology in medical biophysics using artificial intelligence and mathematical modeling. *Nano Express*, 2, 2, 022001, 2021.
11. Olshansky, S.J., Carnes, B.A., Cassel, C., In search of Methuselah: estimating the upper limits to human longevity. *Science*, 250, 4981, 634–640, 1990.
12. Grossman, T., Latest advances in antiaging medicine. *Keio J. Med.*, 54, 2, 85–94, 2005.
13. Lewis, K., Human longevity: an evolutionary approach. *Mech. Ageing Dev.*, 109, 1, 43–51, 1999.
14. Fukuyama, F., *Our Posthuman Future: Consequences of the Biotechnology Revolution*, Farrar, Straus, and Giroux, New York, 2002; and Kass, L., *Life, Liberty, and the Defense of Dignity: The Challenge for Bioethics*, 2002.
15. Roy, S., Meena, T., Lim, S.-J., Demystifying supervised learning in healthcare 4.0: A new reality of transforming diagnostic medicine. *Diagnostics*, 12, 10, 2549, MDPI, Basel, Switzerland, 2022.
16. Mendosa, D., Revised international table of Glycemic Index (GI) and Glycemic Load (GL) values, Mendosa website http://www.mendosa.com/gilists. htm, Published December 2008.
17. Khor, G.L., Dietary fat quality: a nutritional epidemiologist's view. *Asia Pac. J. Clin. Nutr.*, 13, S22–S27, 2004.
18. Hu, F.B. and Willett, W.C., Optimal diets for prevention of coronary heart disease. *Jama*, 288, 20, 2569–2578, 2002.
19. Wollin, S.D. and Jones, P.J.H., Alcohol, red wine and cardiovascular disease. *J. Nutr.*, 131, 5, 1401–1404, American Society for Nutrition, Bethesda, Maryland, USA, 2001.
20. Wu, J.M. *et al.*, Mechanism of cardioprotection by resveratrol, a phenolic antioxidant present in red wine. *Int. J. Mol. Med.*, 8, 1, 3–17, 2001.

21. Li, D., Sun, F., Wang, K., Protein profile of aging and its retardation by caloric restriction in neural retina. *Biochem. Biophys. Res. Commun.*, 318, 1, 253–258, 2004.
22. Bergamini, E. *et al.*, The role of macroautophagy in the ageing process, anti-ageing intervention and age-associated diseases. *Int. J. Biochem. Cell Biol.*, 36, 12, 2392–2404, 2004.
23. Ingram, D.K. *et al.*, Development of calorie restriction mimetics as a prolongevity strategy. *Ann. N. Y. Acad. Sci.*, 1019, 1, 412–423, 2004.
24. Cohen, H.Y. *et al.*, Calorie restriction promotes mammalian cell survival by inducing the SIRT1 deacetylase. *Science*, 305, 5682, 390–392, 2004.
25. Weindruch, R. *et al.*, Microarray profiling of gene expression in aging and its alteration by caloric restriction in mice. *J. Nutr.*, 131, 3, 918S–923S, 2001.
26. Yamori, Y., Miura, A., Taira, K., Implications from and for food cultures for cardiovascular diseases: Japanese food, particularly Okinawan diets. *Asia Pac. J. Clin. Nutr.*, 10, 2, 144–145, 2001.
27. Willcox, B.J. *et al.*, How much should we eat? The association between energy intake and mortality in a 36-year follow-up study of Japanese-American men. *J. Gerontol. Ser. A: Biol. Sci. Med. Sci.*, 59, 8, B789–B795, 2004.
28. Mokdad, A.H. *et al.*, Actual causes of death in the United States, 2000. *JAMA*, 291, 10, 1238–1245, 2004.
29. Worthington, V., Effect of agricultural methods on nutritional quality: a comparison of organic with conventional crops. *Altern. Ther. Health Med.*, 4, 1, 58–69, 1998.
30. Fenech, M., Micronutrients and genomic stability: a new paradigm for recommended dietary allowances (RDAs). *Food Chem. Toxicol.*, 40, 8, 1113–1117, 2002.
31. Tworoger, S.S. *et al.*, Association of CYP17, CYP19, CYP1B1, and COMT polymorphisms with serum and urinary sex hormone concentrations in postmenopausal women. *Cancer Epidemiol. Biomarkers Prev.*, 13, 1, 94–101, 2004.
32. Somner, J. *et al.*, Polymorphisms in the P450 c17 (17-hydroxylase/17, 20-Lyase) and P450 c19 (aromatase) genes: association with serum sex steroid concentrations and bone mineral density in postmenopausal women. *J. Clin. Endocrinol. Metab.*, 89, 1, 344–351, 2004.
33. Villeneuve, J.-P. and Pichette, V., Cytochrome P450 and liver diseases. *Curr. Drug Metab.*, 5, 3, 273–282, 2004.
34. Kerber, A. *et al.*, The new DR-70 immunoassay detects cancer of the gastrointestinal tract: a validation study. *Aliment. Pharmacol. Ther.*, 20, 9, 983–987, 2004.
35. Fraschini, F. *et al.*, Melatonin involvement in immunity and cancer. *Neurosignals*, 7, 1, 61–72, 1998.
36. De Grey, A.D.N.J., The foreseeability of real anti-aging medicine: focusing the debate. *Exp. Gerontol.*, 38, 9, 927–934, 2003.

37. Hwang, W.S. *et al.*, Evidence of a pluripotent human embryonic stem cell line derived from a cloned blastocyst. *Science*, 303, 5664, 1669–1674, 2004.
38. Biroccio, A., Leonetti, C., Zupi, G., The future of antisense therapy: combination with anticancer treatments. *Oncogene*, 22, 42, 6579–6588, 2003.
39. Yang, L. *et al.*, *In vitro* trans-differentiation of adult hepatic stem cells into pancreatic endocrine hormone-producing cells. *Proc. Natl. Acad. Sci.*, 99, 12, 8078–8083, 2002.
40. Qu-Petersen, Z. *et al.*, Identification of a novel population of muscle stem cells in mice: potential for muscle regeneration. *J. Cell Biol.*, 157, 5, 851–864, 2002.
41. Phoenix, C. and Drexler, E., Safe exponential manufacturing. *Nanotechnology*, 15, 8, 869, 2004.
42. Kurzweil, R., *The singularity is near: when humans transcend biology*, Viking, New York, 2005.
43. Freitas, R.A., *Nanomedicine, volume IIA: biocompatibility*, CRC Press, is Boca Raton, Florida, 2023.
44. Freitas, R., Robots in the bloodstream: the promise of nanomedicine, 2001, www. kurzweilai. net/meme/frame. html? main=/articles/art0410. html.
45. Anjum, S. *et al.*, Emerging applications of nanotechnology in healthcare systems: Grand challenges and perspectives. *Pharmaceuticals*, 14, 8, 707, 2021.
46. Rizvi, S.A.A. and Saleh, A.M., Applications of nanoparticle systems in drug delivery technology. *Saudi Pharm. J.*, 26, 1, 64–70, 2018.
47. Santos, H.A. *et al.*, *In vitro* cytotoxicity of porous silicon microparticles: effect of the particle concentration, surface chemistry and size. *Acta Biomater.*, 6, 7, 2721–2731, 2010.
48. Bowles, E.J.A. *et al.*, Endocrine therapy initiation from 2001 to 2008 varies by age at breast cancer diagnosis and tumor size. *J. Oncol. Pract.*, 8, 2, 113–120, 2012.
49. Gennari, L., Nuti, R., Bilezikian, J.P., Aromatase activity and bone homeostasis in men. *J. Clin. Endocrinol. Metab.*, 89, 12, 5898–5907, 2004.
50. Pokrajac, L. *et al.*, Nanotechnology for a sustainable future: Addressing global challenges with the international network4sustainable nanotechnology. *Nat. Nanotechnol.*, 16, 18608–18623, 2021.

7

Holistic Approaches for Sleep Pattern Enhancement Using AI and Yoga Therapy: A Comprehensive Scientific Approach

Somlata Jha[1]* and Siddhant Rajhans[2]

[1]Himalayan School of Yoga Sciences, Swami Rama Himalayan University, Jolly Grant, Dehradun, India
[2]Department of Computer Science & Engineering, Swami Rama Himalayan University, Jolly Grant, Dehradun, India

Abstract
In today's fast-paced world, many people struggle with sleep-related issues. However, quality sleep is vital for physical, mental, and emotional well-being. An ancient practice of yoga and the power of AI (artificial intelligence) are used in this article to enhance sleep patterns through a comprehensive scientific approach. The role of AI and yoga in sleep improvement is discussed, as well as understanding sleep patterns, quality sleep, and the value of quality sleep. A holistic approach to sleep enhancement is offered, based on scientific research and the mind–body connection. AI-enabled sleep tracking devices, sleep plans tailored to individual needs, and lifestyle factors that impact sleep quality will also be discussed. Overall, this approach emphasizes the importance of quality sleep for a healthy and productive life, providing a scientifically sound solution to sleep-related issues.

***Keywords*:** REM sleep, sleep apnea, stress, physical comfort, screen time, therapy

7.1 Introduction

Human life begins with sleep, for it is when our bodies and minds rejuvenate, which makes us feel refreshed when we wake up in the morning. After sleeping, we can be ready to face the day with a fresh outlook on

**Corresponding author*: SomlataJha@outlook.com

Abhishek Kumar, Narayan Vyas, Pramod Singh Rathore, Abhineet Anand and Pooja Dixit (eds.) Internet of Medicine for Smart Healthcare, (127–138) © 2025 Scrivener Publishing LLC

it. Despite these challenges, more and more individuals find themselves struggling with sleep issues as a result of the demands of modern life. A comprehensive scientific approach integrating artificial intelligence (AI) with ancient yoga practices is the basis for this article, which examines the integration of AI to enhance sleep patterns [1, 2].

7.2 Understanding Sleep Patterns

During the course of a night's sleep, a series of sleep cycles will occur, initially light sleep, following by deep sleep, and finally REM (rapid eye movement) sleep. Each of these sleep stages plays an important role in ensuring a restful night's sleep [3].

It is important to understand sleep patterns so that you are able to get better sleep. Light sleep is when your mind and body are not completely relaxed yet, and deep sleep is when your body is still relatively alert. The REM sleep phase is when you have vivid dreams and consolidates memories. Deep sleep is when your body and mind are most refreshed [4].

7.3 The Importance of Quality Sleep

A quality night's sleep plays a crucial role in our physical, mental, and emotional well-being. Sleep has an impact on our cognitive abilities, memory, and overall health. Without adequate sleep, we become more susceptible to a number of health problems, such as obesity, heart disease, and mental health disorders [5].

While sleep duration is important, quality sleep is more important. Sleep-related health issues can still arise for people who get the recommended 7–9 h of sleep a night but have disruptions, like frequent awakenings. You need enough time in deep sleep, REM sleep, and uninterrupted sleep cycles if you want a good night's sleep [6, 7].

7.4 The Role of AI in Sleep Pattern Enhancement

With advanced AI algorithms, advanced sleep patterns can be analyzed, disturbances can be detected, and personalized insights into boosting sleep quality can be offered. AI has revolutionized a lot of industries, including healthcare. AI-powered sleep tracking devices are becoming increasingly sophisticated. These devices use sensors to monitor various parameters during sleep, including movement, heart rate, and even breathing patterns. They provide a wealth of data that can be analyzed to gain insights into an individual's sleep quality [8].

Using AI, we detect sleep patterns and disturbances. As a result, individuals and healthcare professionals can create targeted sleep strategies to improve sleep with this information, which can help them deal with sleep apnea, restless leg syndrome, or even stress-related sleep disruptions [9].

7.5 How AI Works to Enhance Sleep

AI focuses on several key aspects to enhance sleep patterns:

- **Sleep Cycles:** In order to ensure individuals are getting adequate restorative sleep, AI monitors sleep cycles, specifically deep sleep and REM sleep, in order to ensure that they are getting adequate sleep.
- **Sleep Disturbances:** Sleep disturbances like snoring, waking up, and irregular breathing patterns can be identified by AI.
- **Biometrics:** AI analyzes biometric data like heart rate variability during sleep, which can provide insights into sleep quality and potential issues.
- **Personalization:** AI tailors recommendations based on individual sleep patterns. If someone experiences frequent awakenings, then AI may suggest specific yoga poses or breathing exercises to address this issue.
- **Timing:** AI can provide insights into the best times for individuals to engage in yoga practices for optimal sleep benefits.

7.6 How Yoga Influences Sleep

Practicing yoga, an ancient practice with centuries of tradition, can help you sleep better. By relaxing the body and calming the mind, it helps you fall asleep.

Yoga promotes sleep in several ways:

- **Stress Reduction:** Stress is one of the biggest reasons people do not sleep well. Yoga, with its emphasis on deep breathing and relaxation, drastically lowers stress levels. As a result, it relaxes the body and prepares it for sleep by activating the parasympathetic nervous system.

- **Mental Calmness:** Taking part in yoga helps calm your mind. Racing thoughts and anxiety are common culprits in sleep disturbances. Mindfulness and presence allow the mind to be quiet and allow for better sleep.
- **Physical Comfort:** During yoga postures, we release tension in our bodies, especially in the neck, shoulders, and back. When the body is free of physical discomfort, it is easier to sleep.
- **Regulation of Breathing:** Breathing properly during sleep can prevent issues like snoring and sleep apnea since yoga focuses on deep, slow, and controlled breathing.

7.7 Combining AI and Yoga for Better Sleep

There is a synergy between AI and yoga that can lead to remarkable progress. AI-powered devices track your sleep cycles, and yoga addresses things like stress, anxiety, and physical discomfort. In order to improve the quality of sleep for individuals, AI can create insights about the patterns of their sleep, which can be used to develop tailored yoga practices. For instance, if an AI-generated insight indicates frequent disturbances during the night, then yoga poses and breathing exercises can be used to address the problem.

Furthermore, AI can give personalized recommendations about when to practice yoga to get the most sleep benefits. Some people do better in the evening, while other people do better in the morning or midday [10].

7.8 The Synergy of AI and Yoga

The combined efforts of AI and yoga can significantly enhance our sleep quality. AI-powered sleep tracking devices meticulously record data on our sleep cycles, whereas yoga offers practical techniques to tackle issues like stress, anxiety, and physical discomfort that can disrupt our sleep.

In order to improve our yoga routines, we can use AI to analyze our sleep patterns. For example, if the data show frequent disturbances during the night, then we can do specific yoga poses and breathing exercises. In addition, AI can suggest the best times to practice yoga so you get the most sleep-related benefits. Some people do best in the evening, whereas others do better in the morning or evening [11].

7.9 Scientific Research on Sleep Improvement

A combination of AI-assisted sleep tracking and yoga practices leads to significantly better sleep patterns and better well-being, according to solid scientific evidence. We need to do more research to confirm these results.

In 2019, sensors published a review called "Artificial Intelligence for Sleep Monitoring: A Review," which explores how AI can be used to sleep better. The researchers emphasize the potential of AI algorithms to analyze sleep data and offer personalized recommendations for improving sleep quality.

Likewise, a systematic review and meta-analysis published in the journal Depression and Anxiety in 2013, titled "Yoga for Depression," delved into the impact of yoga on mental health. The findings suggest that yoga can substantially alleviate symptoms of depression and anxiety, which are often linked to sleep disturbances.

Additionally, a study titled "Criterion Validity of the Pittsburgh Sleep Quality Index: Investigation in a Non-Clinical Sample," published in the journal Sleep and Biological Rhythms in 2006, examined the importance of accurately assessing sleep quality. This study underscores that evaluating sleep quality plays a crucial role in overall health and well-being.

7.10 The Mind–Body Connection

Understanding the deep connection between our mind and body is essential, as calming the mind during sleep greatly enhances sleep quality. A yoga practice teaches us to be mindful of our bodies and minds. This awareness extends to our sleep patterns and behaviors that might disrupt our sleep.

Yoga equips individuals with the tools to recognize and address these sleep-related issues through yoga practices and lifestyle adjustments, ultimately leading to improved sleep quality.

A high stress level can cause cortisol, a stress hormone, to be released, which can interfere with sleep patterns. Stress also exacerbates the mind–body connection. Yoga helps reduce cortisol levels and promote restful sleep by teaching relaxation and stress reduction techniques.

7.11 A Holistic Approach to Sleep

In order to improve your sleep patterns, it is important to think beyond just obtaining more sleep hours; it is important to consider the quality of sleep as well. A holistic approach is taken when it comes to sleep, considering the various factors that contribute to sleep patterns shown in Figure 7.1.

Several components contribute to a holistic approach to sleep:

- **Nutrition:** Diet plays a significant role in sleep. Avoiding heavy, rich, or spicy foods close to bedtime is recommended, as they can lead to indigestion and disrupt sleep. On the other hand, some foods, like cherries and almonds, contain natural sleep-promoting compounds and can be beneficial when consumed in moderation.
- **Exercise:** Regular physical activity can improve sleep. However, it is essential to time exercise correctly. Vigorous

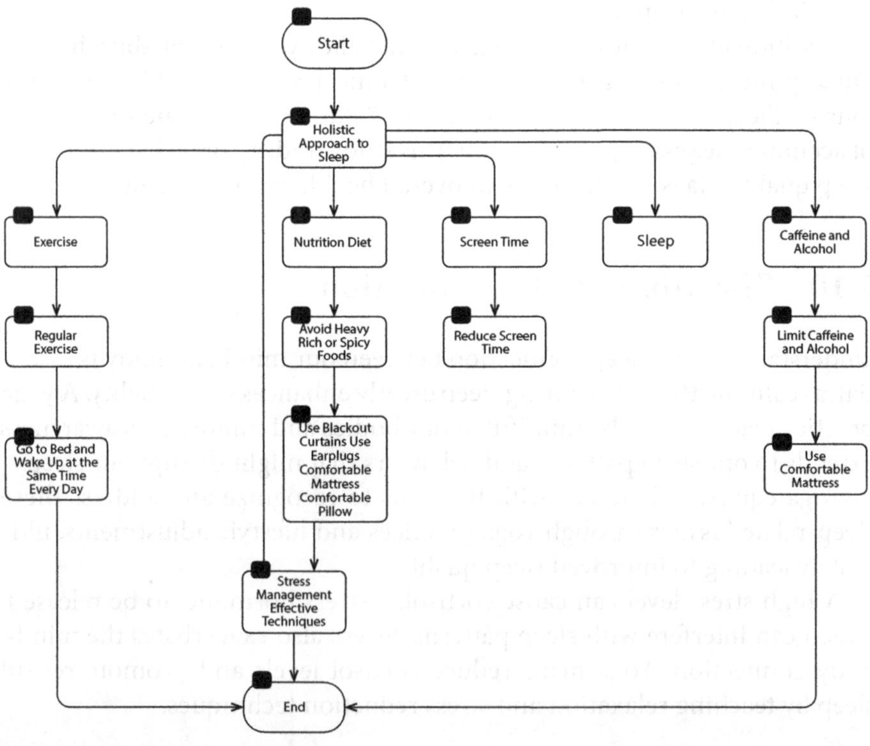

Figure 7.1 Holistic approach to sleep.

exercise close to bedtime may have an alerting effect, so it is better to exercise earlier in the day. Gentle yoga sessions can serve as an excellent pre-sleep routine.

- **Caffeine and Alcohol:** Both caffeine and alcohol can disrupt sleep patterns. It is advisable to limit their consumption, especially in the hours leading up to bedtime.
- **Screen Time:** Screens, such as phones, tablets, and computers, emit blue light, which can interfere with the production of melatonin, the hormone responsible for promoting sleep, which can interfere with sleep quality. You can promote better sleep by reducing the amount of time you spend watching screens before bed.
- **Sleep Environment:** A comfortable and dark sleep environment is essential for quality sleep. Consider using blackout curtains, earplugs, and a comfortable mattress and pillow.
- **Consistent Sleep Schedule:** A consistent sleep schedule can help improve sleep patterns and having the same wake-up and bedtime regulates the body's clock.
- **Stress Management:** Effective stress management techniques, including yoga and mindfulness, can significantly impact sleep quality.

7.12 Practicing Yoga for Better Sleep

There is no need to be a yoga expert to benefit from the sleep enhancing effects of yoga. Simple practices such as deep breathing and gentle stretching can make a big difference when it comes to improving your lifestyle.

- **Deep Breathing:** A fundamental part of yoga is controlled and deep breathing. Deep breathing exercises can relax your body and mind before bedtime. Using the 4-7-8 technique, for example, you breathe in for four, hold your breath for seven, and exhale for eight. It relaxes your mind and prepares you for sleep.
- **Yoga Poses:** A number of yoga poses have been found to be particularly useful for reducing sleeplessness, including Child's Pose, Legs-Up-the-Wall Pose, and Corpse Pose, which are examples of restorative poses that work to ease tension and promote relaxation.

- **Meditation:** Meditation is a powerful tool for quieting the mind and reducing stress. Guided meditation sessions or simply focusing on your breath for a few minutes can prepare you for a peaceful night's sleep.
- **Yoga Nidra:** It is a state of conscious relaxation, also referred to as yogic sleep in which you are guided through a body scan and visualizations while you are in a state of deep relaxation before sleeping. It is deeply relaxing and can be used as a practice before sleeping as well.

7.13 AI-Enabled Sleep Tracking Devices

Sleep trackers powered by AI are increasingly becoming affordable and accessible. These devices use sensors to monitor a variety of parameters during sleep such as movement, heart rate, and even breathing patterns.

There are all sorts of wearable and non-wearable trackers available today, from the wearable devices like smartwatches to the non-wearable sensors placed under the mattress.

These devices provide a lot of data that can be analyzed to get a better understanding of an individual's sleep shown in Figure 7.2.

The key components of AI-enabled sleep tracking devices are as follows:

- **Actigraphy:** The actigraphy method, which uses accelerometers to measure physical activity, can be used to estimate sleep patterns and identify waking periods [12].
- **Heart Rate Monitoring:** Some sleep trackers monitor heart rate variability during sleep. Changes in heart rate can provide insights into sleep quality and disturbances [13].

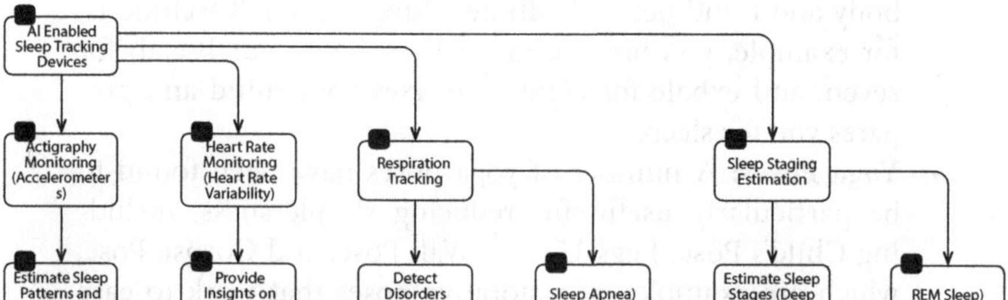

Figure 7.2 Sleep tracking device simulation.

- **Respiration Tracking:** Advanced sleep trackers can also monitor breathing patterns. Irregularities in respiration can be indicative of sleep apnea or other sleep-related disorders [14].
- **Sleep Staging:** The most advanced devices can estimate sleep stages, including deep sleep and REM sleep. This provides a comprehensive view of sleep quality [15].

7.14 Personalized Sleep Plans

With the data from sleep trackers, AI can generate personalized sleep plans. These plans may include yoga practices, breathing exercises, and lifestyle adjustments to help you achieve better sleep.

AI algorithms can identify patterns in your sleep data and recommend specific yoga poses or meditation techniques to address common sleep disruptions [16]. For instance, if you experience frequent awakenings during the night, then the AI might suggest deep breathing exercises or relaxation poses before bed.

The personalization aspect is crucial because everyone's sleep patterns and disturbances are unique. What works for one person may not work for another. AI takes the individual's data and tailors recommendations accordingly [17].

7.15 Lifestyle Factors and Sleep

Beyond AI and yoga, lifestyle factors such as diet, exercise, and screen time also play a role in sleep quality [18]. We will explore how these factors can be managed to promote better sleep.

- **Diet:** What you eat and when you eat can significantly impact your sleep. Avoiding large meals, caffeine, and alcohol close to bedtime is advisable [19]. Incorporating sleep-friendly foods like cherries, almonds, and herbal teas can be beneficial.
- **Exercise:** Regular physical activity can improve sleep, but the timing is crucial. Vigorous exercise close to bedtime may have an alerting effect. Gentle yoga sessions, on the other hand, can serve as an excellent pre-sleep routine.

- **Caffeine and Alcohol:** There is no doubt that caffeine and alcohol are capable of disrupting sleep patterns. If you limit your consumption, especially in the hours leading up to bedtime, then you can encourage better sleep patterns [20].
- **Screen Time:** The blue light that screens emit can interfere with sleep, so, if possible, it is helpful to limit the amount of time you spend on screens before bed and to use devices that contain blue light filters.
- **Sleep Environment:** A comfortable and dark sleep environment is essential for quality sleep. Consider using blackout curtains, earplugs, and a comfortable mattress and pillow.
- **Consistent Sleep Schedule:** In order for the body's internal clock to function correctly and for sleep patterns to improve, we need to commit to going to sleep and waking up at the same time each day.
- **Stress Management:** Effective stress management techniques, including yoga and mindfulness, can significantly impact sleep quality.

7.16 Conclusion

In conclusion, the fusion of AI and the ancient practice of yoga presents a scientifically grounded, holistic solution to the challenges of sleep-related issues. It is a profound acknowledgment of the intricate connection between the mind and the body, offering a path toward a life that is not just healthy but profoundly fulfilling.

Quality sleep is not a mere luxury; it is the cornerstone of a life filled with vitality and productivity. With the synergy of AI-powered sleep tracking, personally tailored yoga practices, and conscientious lifestyle adjustments, individuals have the potential to embark on a transformative journey toward improving their sleep quality.

As we venture further into the digital age, the scientific validation of this approach shines ever more brightly. The robust evidence supporting the harmonious marriage of AI and yoga underscores the vast potential for achieving not just better sleep, but a state of well-being that permeates every facet of life. It is a journey of self-discovery, rejuvenation, and a profound reconnection with one's inner self. In this quest for improved sleep, individuals can embark on a profound voyage toward a life that is truly worth living.

References

1. Zadeh, A., Izquierdo, A., Wong, K.J., Lee, J., Artificial Intelligence for Sleep Monitoring: A Review. *Sensors*, 19, 15, 3465, 2019.
2. Cramer, H., Lauche, R., Langhorst, J., Dobos, G., Yoga for depression: a systematic review and meta-analysis. *Depress. Anxiety*, 30, 11, 1068–1083, 2013.
3. Grandner, M.A., Kripke, D.F., Yoon, I.Y., Youngstedt, S.D., Criterion validity of the Pittsburgh Sleep Quality Index: Investigation in a non-clinical sample. *Sleep Biol. Rhythms*, 4, 2, 129–136, 2006.
4. Felder, J.N., Laraia, B.A., Coleman-Phox, K., Socioeconomic position, food insecurity, and sleep in U.S. adults: a complex relationship. *Sleep Health*, 4, 3, 282–288, 2018.
5. Khalsa, S.B.S., Treatment of chronic insomnia with yoga: A preliminary study with sleep-wake diaries. *Appl. Psychophysiol. Biofeedback*, 29, 4, 269–278, 2004.
6. Vallath, N., Perspectives on yoga inputs in the management of chronic pain. *Indian J. Palliat. Care*, 16, 1, 1–7, 2010.
7. Irwin, M.R., Olmstead, R., Motivala, S.J., Improving sleep quality in older adults with moderate sleep complaints: A randomized controlled trial of Tai Chi Chih. *Sleep*, 31, 7, 1001–1008, 2008.
8. Murali, R., Srinivasan, K., Thara, R., Yoga for persons with schizophrenia—A preliminary report. *Schizophr. Res.*, 18, 3, 285–287, 2002.
9. Musial, F., Spahn, G., Gerlach, A.L., Characteristics of yoga users: Results of a national survey. *J. Complement. Integr. Med.*, 8, 1, 1–10, 2011.
10. Neikrug, A.B. and Ancoli-Israel, S., Sleep disorders in the older adult—A mini-review. *Gerontology*, 56, 2, 181–189, 2010.
11. Sharma, M. and Haider, T., Tai Chi as an alternative and complementary therapy for patients with knee osteoarthritis: A systematic review. *J. Complement. Integr. Med.*, 9, 1, 1–12, 2012.
12. Kumar, S.A., Kumar, A., Dutt, V., Agrawal, R., Multi Model Implementation on General Medicine Prediction with Quantum Neural Networks, in: *2021 Third International Conference on Intelligent Communication Technologies and Virtual Mobile Networks (ICICV)*, Tirunelveli, India, pp. 1391–1395, 2021, doi: 10.1109/ICICV50876.2021.9388575.
13. Raj, P., Dubey, A.K., Kumar, A., Rathore, P.S., *Blockchain, Artificial Intelligence, and the Internet of Things*, Springer International Publishing, Cham, Switzerland, 2022.
14. Burri, S.R., Kumar, A., Baliyan, A., Kumar, T.A., Predictive Intelligence for Healthcare Outcomes: An AI Architecture Overview, in: *2023 2nd International Conference on Smart Technologies and Systems for Next Generation Computing (ICSTSN)*, Villupuram, India, pp. 1–6, 2023, doi: 10.1109/ICSTSN57873.2023.10151477.

15. Wani, S., Ahuja, S., Kumar, A., Application of Deep Neural Networks and Machine Learning algorithms for diagnosis of Brain tumour, in: *2023 International Conference on Computational Intelligence and Sustainable Engineering Solutions (CISES)*, Greater Noida, India, pp. 106–111, 2023, doi: 10.1109/CISES58720.2023.10183528.
16. Kour, S.P., Kumar, A., Ahuja, S., An Advance Approach for Diabetes Detection by Implementing Machine Learning Algorithms, in: *2023 IEEE World Conference on Applied Intelligence and Computing (AIC)*, Sonbhadra, India, pp. 136–141, 2023, doi: 10.1109/AIC57670.2023.10263919.
17. Raj, P., Kumar, A., Dubey, A.K., Bhatia, S., Oswalt, M.S., *Quantum Computing and Artificial Intelligence: Training Machine and Deep Learning Algorithms on Quantum Computers*, De Gruyter, Berlin, Boston, 2023, [Online]. Available: https://doi.org/10.1515/9783110791402.
18. Sasubilli, G. and Kumar, A., Machine Learning and Big Data Implementation on Health Care data, in: *2020 4th International Conference on Intelligent Computing and Control Systems (ICICCS)*, Madurai, India, pp. 859–864, 2020, doi: 10.1109/ICICCS48265.2020.9120906.
19. Swarna, S.R., Kumar, A., Dixit, P., Sairam, T.V.M., Parkinson's Disease Prediction using Adaptive Quantum Computing, in: *2021 Third International Conference on Intelligent Communication Technologies and Virtual Mobile Networks (ICICV)*, Tirunelveli, India, pp. 1396–1401, 2021, doi: 10.1109/ICICV50876.2021.9388628.
20. Burugadda, V.R., Pawar, P.S., Kumar, A., Bhati, N., Predicting Hospital Readmission Risk for Heart Failure Patients Using Machine Learning Techniques: A Comparative Study of Classification Algorithms, in: *2023 Second International Conference on Trends in Electrical, Electronics, and Computer Engineering (TEECCON)*, Bangalore, India, pp. 223–228, 2023, doi: 10.1109/TEECCON59234.2023.10335817.

8

Ethical Consideration in Bioinformatics in AI for Analyzing the Effects of Using SHAT Device on Upper Extremity Functions in Stroke Patients

Kapil Lakhwara, Vaibhav Agarwal* and Manish Kumar Jha

Department of Physiotherapy, Himalayan Institute of Medical Sciences, Swami Rama Himalayan University, Jolly Grant, Dehradun, India

Abstract

The study's objective was to assess how well the SHAT device helped stroke patients regain functional use of their upper limb using bioinformatics AI. Sample of convenience of 20 subjects of acute and sub-acute stroke patients was taken from Himalayan Hospital, Jolly Grant. The subjects belonged to the age group 30–65 years. All subjects were explained the procedure and were pre-assessed using Fugl–Meyer upper extremity assessment (FMA-UE) scale. The SHAT device, i.e., Synchronized Hand Arm Therapy device, was provided and implicated in upper limb functional training after stroke. The patients were re-assessed using FMA-UE scale. Highly significant changes were observed in the pre and post assessment scores. Changes were observed in both Fugl–Meyer Motor scores and Fugl–Meyer other components including sensation, joint range of motion (ROM), and joint pain. The findings of this study suggested that use of SHAT device from the early phase can prove to be beneficial to promote early recovery in patients with stroke. SHAT device is a cost-effective approach and can make easily available. It can provide an opportunity to the stroke patient to experience near normal movement patterns with the weaker arm, thereby facilitating neuroplasticity and cortical firing from the penumbra area. In this study, we also found that training caregivers for home exercise of patients with this device also became easy and risk free as the device is non mechanical and caregivers got familiar with it from the first day itself. Patient participation and interest also increased during the SHAT training

**Corresponding author*: vaibhavagarwal12@outlook.com

Abhishek Kumar, Narayan Vyas, Pramod Singh Rathore, Abhineet Anand and Pooja Dixit (eds.) Internet of Medicine for Smart Healthcare, (139–158) © 2025 Scrivener Publishing LLC

as they were able to get motivated by seeing the weaker arm in use from the first day of training itself, and there was prevention of common complications such as shoulder pain, subluxation, and hand pain using AI. This study demonstrated that both acute and sub-acute stroke patients improved in upper limb sensorimotor functioning while using the SHAT device with AI for upper limb.

Keywords: AI, SHAT, stroke, joints, limbs

8.1 Introduction

The abrupt loss of brain tissue due to oxygen deprivation brought on by an obstruction in blood flow or an artery burst in the brain, most commonly in the parietal lobe causing damage to the medial or lateral lemniscus systems. Each year, according to study, between 105 and 152/100,000 people get a stroke in India each year. Stroke leads to a number of disabilities. The most common typical stroke-related disabilities include slurred speech, limb weakness or paralysis on one side of the body, trouble gripping or holding objects, problems in walking and balancing, and a slowed capacity to speak [1]. It has also been seen that, compared to the lower extremity, the upper extremity recovers from a stroke less quickly and completely. People with lower extremity impairments may appear less impaired and be more functional than people with upper extremity abnormalities. The patient population needing rehabilitation for upper limb is constantly increasing, and daily living activities are significantly affected [2].

Therefore, the burden of upper limb impairments after stroke remains high and the recovery rate lags behind in upper limb as compared to that of lower limb. Current practices of rehabilitation for upper limb include constraint-induced movement therapy (CIMT), task specific training, virtual reality (VR), neurodevelopmental treatment (NDT) therapy, bilateral arm training, mirror therapy, orthotics, action observation, mental practice, electromyography (EMG) feedback, and music therapy. Robotic rehabilitation after a stroke offers the chance to boost and precisely regulate the quantity of therapy. However, very few studies have looked at robotic therapy in the initial weeks after a stroke, and these devices are broadly categorized into two: end-effector devices and exoskeletons. There availability is very limited in clinical and home settings along with the socio-economic factors, leaving plenty of room for improvement. It was seen that, in these devices, most of the hand devices works in one plane, unipolar, only flexion-extensions are the movements that these devices support. Exoskeleton machines might support multi-planer movements, but their availability is limited and are of high economy [3].

8.2 SHAT Device (Synchronized Hand Arm Training Device)

Considering all these points, the idea is to introduce a new concept of training upper limb functions in stroke patients, a method that is both efficient and affordable and easy to use device for caregivers and physiotherapist. The device allows the therapist to facilitate near normal movement sensations and motor patterns in the hemiplegic upper limb for performance of functional activities. SHAT device is made up of a customized cloth fabric that can be worn over the hemiplegic hand up to the distal elbow region. The device has elastic loops and Velcro's that allows the therapist's hand and forearm to get overlapped with the patient's hand and forearm [4]. The volar aspect of the cloth has cuts to expose areas of hemiplegic hand for sensory perception. Intensive exercises, task specific training, and strength training can be very effectively carried out with the help of SHAT device. It helps in matching the task demands by varying the assistance and resistance based on the level of motor recovery, i.e., from completely passive to active assisted to active and active resisted [5].

8.3 How to Perform SHAT Exercises

Depending on the chosen activity, the exercises can be performed in lying, sitting, and standing positions.

The therapist will position himself/herself beside or behind the hemiplegic side.

The same side hand of the therapist will be used to overlap with patient's hand (left on left and right or right).

The other hand of the therapist will provide support to the hemiplegic elbow joint.

Examples:

- i. Removing bedsheet
- ii. Scratching body parts (hair, forehead, cheeks, etc.)
- iii. Shaking hands
- iv. Listening to phone call
- v. Combing
- vi. Drinking glass of water
- vii. Removing medicine
- viii. Writing

ix. Operating doors and switches
x. Turning pages of books
xi. Working on computer/laptop
xii. Using cutlery
xiii. Brushing
xiv. Bathing
xv. Dancing
xvi. Playing and much more [6]

Training Progressions

Level 1: Patient feels the movement and mentally does it.
Level 2: Patient is asked to hold the end range of a movement (isometric-eccentric exercise) and let go.
Level 3: Patient performs movement in end range of function and control return.
Level 4: Patient performs movement from mid to end range and control return.
Level 5: Patient performs movement from start to end and control return.

Stroke is sixth in the US list of causes of mortality and is a major global contributor to severe disability. However, given the limited therapeutic window, identifying the indications of stroke in an acute situation remains difficult and results in missed opportunities to act. It is possible to develop a decision support system that will assist emergency department physicians in diagnosing strokes and reducing treatment delays by combining clinical data from electronic health records (EHRs), artificial intelligence (AI), and the symptoms that patients are presenting with [7]. Strokes, particularly those involving the posterior circulation, are linked to a substantial (>10%) diagnostic mistake rate. The latter may be caused by the following factors: stroke is frequently misdiagnosed in younger patients. To further increase the effectiveness and caliber of care, time-sensitive, intricate processes such as triage, consultations, admissions, discharges, and other procedures are part of emergency care [8].

A computational framework designed to mimic human intuition; AI is one of the most revolutionary technologies. The idea that intelligent algorithms may aid healthcare practitioners in diagnosis, treatment, and outcome prediction is what is driving the era of augmented intelligence in the field, particularly in light of the proliferation of digital and linked patient data as well as advancements in processing power [10]. Patients who prefer

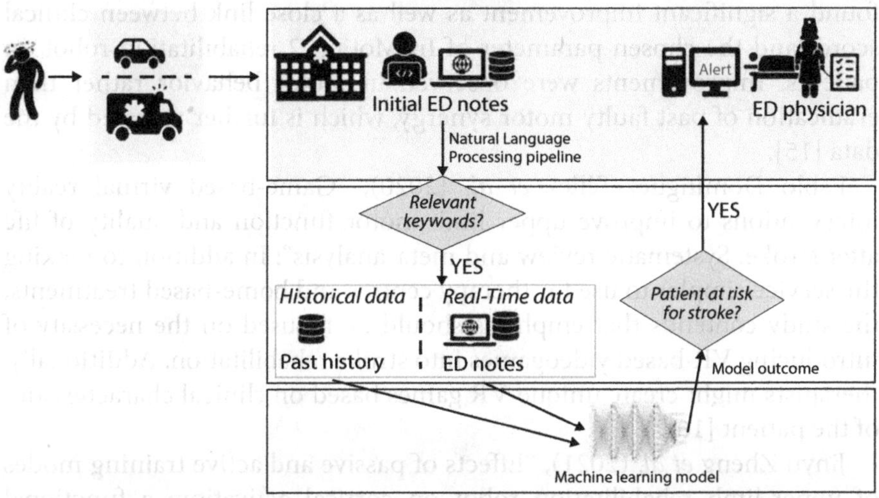

Figure 8.1 Important actions for an ED-based stroke machine learning decision support system [9].

to self-present to an emergency department (ED) will benefit from rapid diagnosis and access thanks to such a system. In this paper, we use data from EHRs in conjunction with the patient's presenting symptoms at the point of care to present a practical framework and outline the steps required to develop a clinical decision support system enabled by machine learning (ML) for the screening of stroke patients in EDs. At Geisinger, we have put together a group of specialists and are spearheading this initiative. A system like that has its main processes summarized in Figure 8.1 [11–13].

8.4 Literature Review

Ruth N. Barker *et al.* (2007), "Influential elements in upper limb recuperation following stroke: An investigation among Queensland, Australia stroke survivors": There was a correlation between their self-identified upper limb recovery and the kind and volume of exercise they did as well as their understanding of how to advance. "Use of the arm in everyday tasks" was the single most significant factor, accounting for approximately 12% of the difference in recovery on its own. "Insufficient range of motion" emerged as the second most significant factor, posing the biggest obstacle to rehabilitation [14].

Nurdiana Nordin *et al.* (2014), "Assessment of movement quality in robot-assisted upper limb rehabilitation after stroke: A review": This study found a significant improvement as well as a close link between clinical scores and the chosen parameter of In Motion 2 rehabilitation robot on patients. Improvements were observed in motor behavior rather than eradication of past faulty motor synergy, which is further revealed by the data [15].

Pablo Domínguez-Téllez *et al.* (2020), "Game-based virtual reality interventions to improve upper limb motor function and quality of life after stroke: Systematic review and meta-analysis": In addition to making the service simpler to use for therapy centres and home-based treatments, the study contends that emphasis should be focused on the necessity of introducing VR-based videogames into stroke rehabilitation. Additionally, therapists might create unique VR games based on clinical characteristics of the patient [16].

Jinyu Zheng *et al.* (2021), "Effects of passive and active training modes of upper-limb rehabilitation robot on cortical activation: a functional near-infrared spectroscopy study": This study focused primarily on the brain mechanisms of active and passive training modes at various speeds using an upper limb rehabilitation robot with an end-effector. Cortical activity related to cognitive and motor control was better enhanced by slow, active training [17].

Jeffery J. Summer *et al.* (2018), "Bilateral and unilateral movement training on upper limb function in chronic stroke patients: A TMS study": This study evaluated the neurophysiological and behavioral modifications brought on by unilateral and bilateral movement training, two such rehabilitation procedures with the use of activity-dependent therapies; chronic stroke patients have seen some improvement in their ability to utilize their upper limbs again [18].

Hwi-young Lee *et al.* (2012), "The mirror therapy program enhances upper-limb motor recovery and motor function in acute stroke patients": During upper-limb motor recovery, the experimental group outperformed the control group in terms of improvement in assessment scores with the upper limb and hand as well as Brannstrom stages for either upper limb and hand [19].

Chao Han *et al.* (2013), "Effects of intensity of arm training on hemiplegic upper extremity motor recovery in stroke patients: A randomized controlled trial": The motor function of the arm after a stroke might be improved by increasing the intensity of arm training. After 6 weeks of treatment, there was a substantial improvement in each group's Fugl-Meyer assessment, action research arm test, and Barthel index scores [20].

In their study, Nick M. Murray *et al.* described LVO detection software and provided a comprehensive evaluation of AI in acute large vessel occlusion (LVO) stroke recognition and triage. Using the keywords "artificial intelligence" or "machine learning or deep learning" and "ischemic stroke" or "large vessel occlusion," a systematic evaluation of acute stroke diagnostic-focused AI papers published in PubMed, Medline, and Embase between January 2014 and February 2019 was conducted. To identify LVO strokes, a variety of AI techniques are employed, such as ML techniques like convolutional neural networks (CNNs) and random forest learning (RFL). There are 20 research studies that make use of ML. RFL was frequently employed in the Alberta Stroke Program Early CT Score (ASPECTS), but CNNs were usually used for LVO identification. CNN outperformed RFL in image feature detection sensitivity, achieving 85% versus 68%. AI may enhance the quick triage required for accelerated treatment of LVO strokes. For next research, performance assessment has to be standardized [21].

Omid Shafaat and colleagues carried out a study showing the fundamentals of AI and ML are explained by researchers in this work. Their review, which targets doctors interested in stroke therapy but lack training in computers or mathematics, is devoid of coding and mathematical specifics. This article summarizes and categorizes the use of AI in ischemic stroke into three categories: prognosis prediction, patient selection for therapy, and stroke imaging (automatic brain infarction identification, automated ASPECT score computation, and infarction segmentation) [22].

In their study, Kiruba Nagaratnam *et al.* addressed the need for specialists to make fast judgments on therapy for acute stroke patients, including thrombolysis and referrals for mechanical thrombectomy. The COVID-19 epidemic is placing a great deal of strain on pathways intended to provide stroke victims with timely therapies. In this case study, we describe how, in collaboration with Brainomix, a UK-based software company, Royal Berkshire Hospital, embraced technological advancement and integrated it into the hyperacute stroke route. A case study is included to demonstrate how this breakthrough technology may enhance patient care and result in favorable patient outcomes. In order to deliver safe and efficient hyperacute stroke care, they believe that more hospitals and networks can adopt this model [23].

In their work, Chulho Kim *et al.* concluded that this study assessed the efficiency of natural language processing (NLP) and ML algorithms in categorizing brain MRI radiology reports into groups that correspond to acute ischemic stroke (AIS) and those that do not. For ML, all brain MRI results from a single educational institution were divided into two groups at random over a 2-year period: training (70%) and testing (30%). The "quanteda" NLP tool was used to convert the text data into tokens in order to create the data frequency matrix. Ten-fold cross-validations were applied for the bias correction of the training set. The clinical records for AIS were identified by manual labeling. Automated brain MRI report categorization is helpful in AIS patient identification using supervised ML-based NLP methods. The most effective classifier for identifying brain MRI reports with AIS was a single decision tree [24].

In their work, Urvish K. Patel *et al.* explored the unsupervised features of ML and how precision neurology may benefit from these components to enhance patient outcomes. Keeping in mind the existing burden of neurological illnesses, we have discussed the many kinds of available AI may help doctors handle vast amounts of data more accurately and efficiently. It can also be used to analyze medical data for illness prevention, diagnosis, patient monitoring, and the creation of new procedures [25].

8.5 Methodology

8.5.1 Need of the Study

Further exploring new evidence-based treatment protocols and technology for upper limb rehabilitation in stroke is needed.

8.5.2 Aim of the Study

The aim of this study is to determine the effectiveness of SHAT device on upper limb functional recovery in stroke patients.

8.5.3 Experimental Hypothesis

Use of SHAT device in performing intensive training for upper limb in stroke patients may be more effective as compared with training in the control group.

8.5.3.1 Null Hypothesis

Use of SHAT device in performing intensive training for upper limb in stroke patients may not be effective as compared with training in the control group.
Study Setting: Patients of Himalayan Hospital, Parent Hospital of Swami Rama Himalayan University, Dehradun.
Sample Size: 72

8.5.4 Study Design

8.5.4.1 Inclusion Criteria

1. Stroke patients with affected upper limb functions
2. Male and Female
3. Acute and sub-acute phase of stroke and disability

8.5.4.2 Exclusion Criteria

1. Patients with spasticity with (more than 2 score) of modified Ashworth scale
2. Patients with cognitive impairments or low GCS scores
3. Patients with CRPS upper limb, hand swelling/injury, or wound
4. Chronic patients with disability persisting since more than 9 months
5. Cerebellar strokes

Dependent Variables: Upper limb motor function
Independent Variables: SHAT device
Outcome Assessment Scale: Fugl–Meyer assessment scale (FMA)

8.6 Protocol

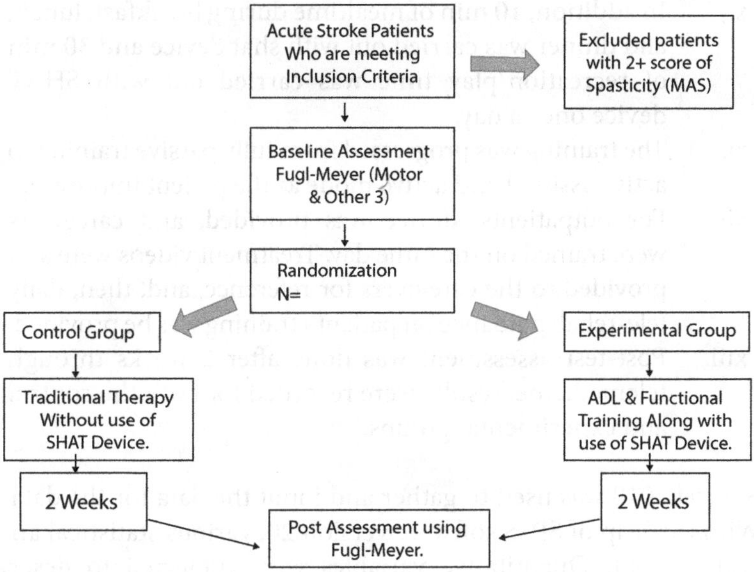

8.7 Procedure

i. Acute stroke patients with affected upper limb functions were taken as study population.
ii. Patients with 2+ score of spasticity (MAS), cognitive impairments, and low GCS scores were excluded from the study.
iii. Baseline assessment with Fugl–Meyer was done, and pre test scores were recorded.
iv. Randomization of samples was done into experimental or control group.
v. The control group population was on traditional therapy including Brunnstrom exercises, CIMT training, and NDT therapy.
vi. The experimental group patients were provided the SHAT device, daily task-specific training was performed by the therapist, and the caregivers were trained for the same.
vii. Daily training with a specific dosage was provided by the therapist until the date of discharge, and caregivers were simultaneously trained to perform activities for the rest of the day and for the home program.
viii. Ten tasks of patient's preference were chosen.
ix. Each task was performed for 20 repetition × three sets and three times a day.
x. In addition, 10 min of mealtime during breakfast, lunch, and dinner was carried out with shat device and 30 min of recreation/play time was carried out with SHAT device once a day.
xi. The training was progressed from fully passive training to active assisted and active mode as the patient improved.
xii. For outpatients, device was provided, and caregivers were trained on the same day. Treatment videos were and provided to the caregivers for reference, and, then, daily tele-rehab guidance on patient's training was be provided.
xiii. Post-test assessment was done after 2 weeks through telemedicine; results were recorded for both the control and experimental groups.

MS Excel 2018 was used to gather and input the data for the data analysis. With the help of SPSS software version 20, various statistical analyses were carried out. Quantitative variables were subjected to descriptive statistics calculations. For qualitative and categorical variables, frequency and percentage were determined. Comparison of difference of means was done using Wilcoxon signed-rank test for two groups, i.e., pre and post assessment as the data does not follow the normality or normal distribution.

8.8 Results

8.8.1 Gender and Age Frequency

The total number of patients was 72, out of which 50 were males and 22 were females. The mean age for the control group was 54 and for the experimental group was 49 years. Table 8.1 provide the information of gender and age frequency and Figure 8.2 shows the mean age in both groups.

Table 8.1 Gender and age frequency.

Gender percentage			Gender	
			Females	**Males**
Group	Females	Count	10	26
		% within Group	27.8%	72.2%
	Males	Count	12	24
		% within Group	33.3%	66.7%
Total		Count	22	50
		% within Group	30.6%	69.4%

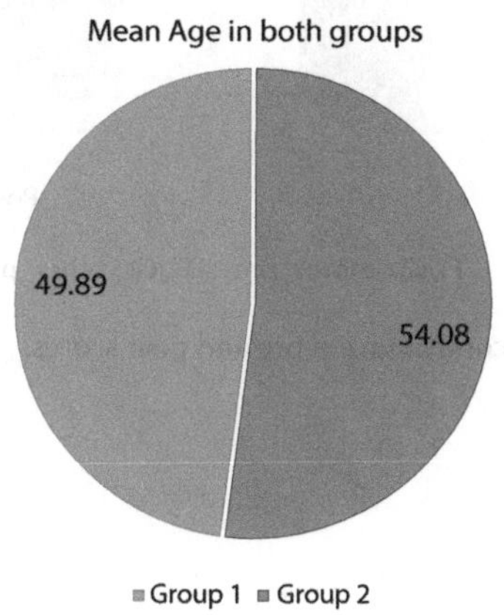

Figure 8.2 Mean age in both groups.

8.8.2 Control Group Scores

The mean and standard deviation of Fugl–Meyer pre and post assessment scores for the control group are mentioned in Table 8.2 and in Figure 8.3.

Table 8.2 Mean and SD of control group pre and post.

Outcome variables	N	Minimum	Maximum	Mean ± SD
FMA Motor PRE	36	10	23	15.13 ± 3.924
FMA Other PRE	36	48	57	52.55 ± 2.44
FMA Motor POST	36	10	28	17.63 ± 4.47
FMA Other POST	36	41	59	50.02 ± 4.35

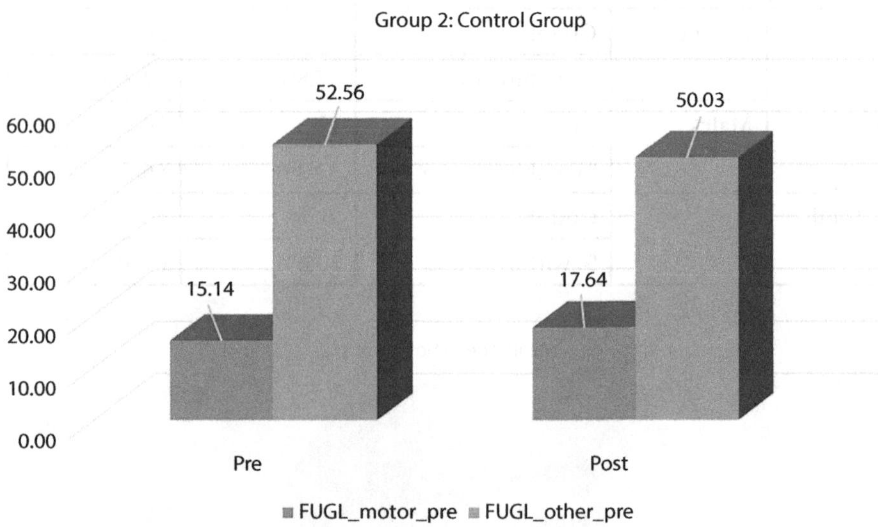

Figure 8.3 Comparison of control group pre and post scores.

8.8.3 Experimental Group Scores

The mean and standard deviation of Fugl–Meyer pre and post assessment scores for the experimental group are mentioned in Table 8.3 and Figure 8.4.

Table 8.3 Comparison of the experimental group pre and post.

Outcome variables	N	Minimum	Maximum	Mean ± SD
FMA Motor PRE	36	10	25	15.41 ± 3.94
FMA Other PRE	36	43	59	53.08 ± 3.14
FMA Motor POST	36	10	40	30.38 ± 6.41
FMA Other POST	36	51	59	55.63 ± 1.43

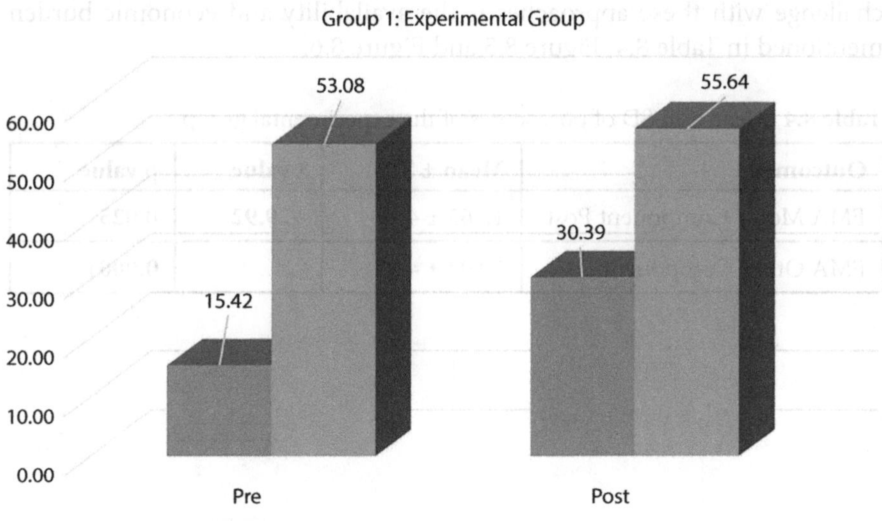

Figure 8.4 Comparison of experimental group pre and post scores.

8.8.4 Comparison of Means

The patients were pre-assessed using FMA (quantitative scale). After the protocol, the score was re-assessed, and a significant difference was found. The comparison was done using Wilcoxon signed-rank test as the data does not follow normality. The table below depicts the changes found in the FMA scale post assessment.

8.9 Discussion

This study looked at the impact of SHAT glove training on the sensorimotor functions of the upper extremities. The patients were assessed pre and post using the Fugl–Meyer assessment scale for upper extremity (FMA-UE). The results of this study revealed that using the SHAT device from the beginning may help promote an early recovery in stroke patients. Studies on upper limb rehabilitation typically concentrate on using high-technology machines and equipment such as robotics and VR machines. These ways may be effective and bring out remarkable improvements, but the main challenge with these approaches is the availability and economic burden mentioned in Table 8.4, Figure 8.5 and Figure 8.6.

Table 8.4 Mean and SD of post scores of the experimental group.

Outcomes	Mean ± SD	t value	p value
FMA Motor Component Post	17.63 ± 4.47	**–29.92**	**0.025**
FMA Other Component Post	50.02 ± 4.35		**0.0001**

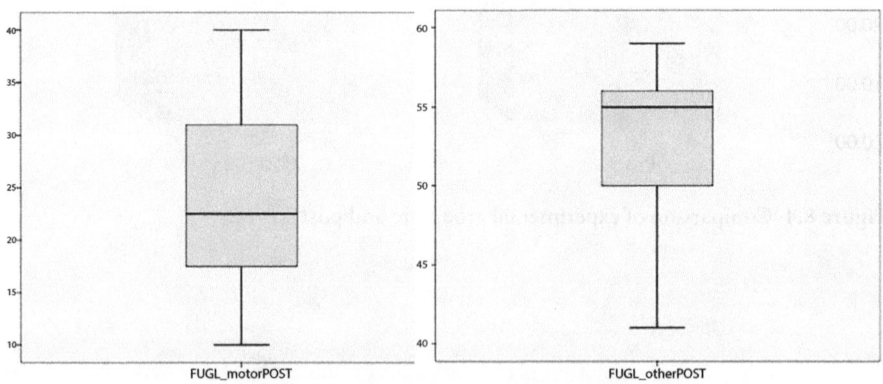

Figure 8.5 Comparison of post scores of the experimental groups.

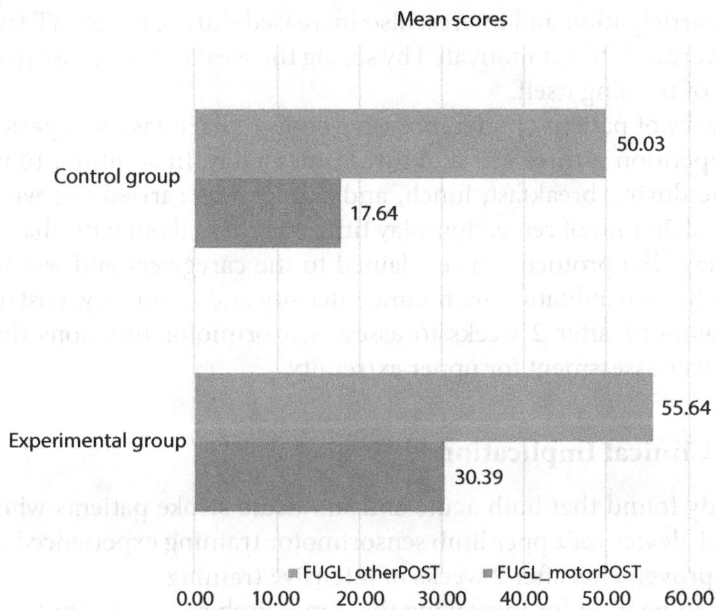

Figure 8.6 Comparison of post scores between the experimental and control groups.

SHAT device is a cost-effective approach and can made easily available. It can provide an opportunity to the stroke patient to experience near normal movement patterns with the weaker arm thereby facilitating neuroplasticity and cortical firing from the penumbra area. SHAT training can be provided from fully passive to active assisted and can be progressed to active phase as the patient improves. The goal is to make the patient experience and perform normal motor movement patterns such as combing, buttoning eating, brushing and other functional activities.

In this study, we found that SHAT device brought significant changes in the perception and pattern of firing in stroke patients. It also prevented development of abnormal tone and spasticity in the weaker arm following stroke. Patients who were flaccid in acute phase were improved from <20 to 40–45 scores out of 66 for upper extremity on Fugl–Meyer scale without development of abnormal tone. Other functions such as sensation, joint range of motion, coordination, and joint pain during passive range of motion were also significantly improved, and there was prevention of common complications such as shoulder pain, subluxation, and hand pain. In this study, we also found that training caregivers for home exercise of patients with this device also became easy and risk free as the device is nonmechanical and caregivers got familiar with it from the first day itself.

Patient participation and interest also increased during the SHAT training as they were able to get motivated by seeing the weaker arm in use from the first day of training itself.

Ten tasks of patient's preference were chosen. Each task was performed for 20 repetition × three sets and three times a day. In addition, 10 min of mealtime during breakfast, lunch, and dinner was carried out with shat device and 30 min of recreation/play time was carried out with shat device once a day. The protocol was explained to the caregivers and was told to perform the rehabilitation with same intensity and frequency. Post assessment was done after 2 weeks to assess sensorimotor functions through Fugl–Meyer assessment for upper extremity.

8.9.1 Clinical Implication

This study found that both acute and sub-acute stroke patients who used the SHAT device for upper limb sensorimotor training experienced significant improvements after 2 weeks of intensive training.

This can be used for improving the upper limb sensorimotor functions in the early phase itself.

8.9.2 Future Research

i. The study should be performed on larger population including the chronic stroke patients with predeveloped abnormal patterns.
ii. The same study can be combined with CIMT training protocols to observe the results.

8.9.3 Limitation

i. Follow up period was short, i.e., 2 weeks and carry over effects were not seen.
ii. The number of sample size was small.

8.10 Conclusion

This study showed that the use of SHAT device for upper limb sensorimotor training showed significant improvements in upper limb sensori-motor functions after 2 weeks of intensive training in acute and sub-acute stroke patients. The results proved to be highly significant for improvement in the upper limb sensorimotor functions in the early phase itself. Using smart devices to track tremors and identify their phenotypes to improve the results of deep brain stimulation; applications evaluating fine motor functions; AI-integrated electroencephalogram learning for recognizing epilepsy and psychological non-epileptic seizures; forecasting the outcome of seizure surgery; and identifying patterns of autonomic instability to prevent unexpected deaths in epilepsy (SUDEP) are just a few unusual examples of experimental use cases for AI in neurology. Additionally, smartwatches tracking atrial fibrillation to avoid strokes; prognostication in dementia; recognition of patterns in complicated algorithms in neuroimaging identifying cognitive impairment; and differentiation and categorization of concussion traits are part of this innovative approach.

It is rather subjective to define what an "ethical" AI system should be able to do in this situation, taking into account both our impression of the software's functionality and our experience working in the field. In general, ensuring equity, effectiveness, efficiency, and patient safety would be the main objectives. A system should ideally benefit all specified groups equally, but, in reality, this is frequently not feasible; hence, it will be important to establish what constitutes an acceptable bias. Strict regulatory bodies, like the US Food and Drug Administration (FDA), are beginning to provide guidelines for the creation and upkeep of AI systems to guarantee compliance and best practices for models that rely heavily on data. Defining the capabilities of an "ethical" AI system in this context is very subjective, based on our perception of the software's usability as well as our professional background. The primary goals would be to ensure patient safety, equity, efficacy, and efficiency. This is to ensure that models that extensively rely on data are compliant and follow best practices. The research that we have conducted indicates that AI models have a fair degree of accuracy in predicting the outcomes of ischemic stroke. It could be a useful tool for doctors to use when assessing stroke patients' prognoses. Updating AI algorithms and utilizing large data will improve the performance of subsequent AI prediction models.

References

1. Wang, H.L., Hsu, W.Y., Lee, M.H., Weng, H.H., Chang, S.W., Yang, J.T. *et al.*, Automatic machine-learning-based outcome prediction in patients with primary intracerebral hemorrhage. *Front. Neurol.*, 10, 910, 2019, doi: 10.3389/fneur.2019.00910.

2. Toyoda, K., Yoshimura, S., Nakai, M., Koga, M., Sasahara, Y., Sonoda, K. *et al.*, Twenty-year change in severity and outcome of ischemic and hemorrhagic strokes. *JAMA Neurol.*, 79, 61–69, 2022, doi: 10.1001/jamaneurol.2021.
3. Sung, S.M., Kang, Y.J., Cho, H.J., Kim, N.R., Lee, S.M., Choi, B.K. *et al.*, Prediction of early neurological deterioration in acute minor ischemic stroke by machine learning algorithms. *Clin. Neurol. Neurosurg.*, 195, 105892, 2020, doi: 10.1016/j.clineuro.2020.
4. Schwalbe, N. and Wahl, B., Artificial intelligence and the future of global health. *Lancet*, 395, 1579–1586, 2020, doi: 10.1016/S0140-6736(20)30226-9.
5. Roh, S.B., Oh, S.K., Pedrycz, W., Fu, Z., Dynamically generated hierarchical neural networks designed with the aid of multiple support vector regressors and pnn architecture with probabilistic selection. *IEEE Trans. Neural Netw. Learn. Syst.*, 33, 1385–1399, 2022, doi: 10.1109/TNNLS.2020.3041947.
6. Noble, W.S., What is a support vector machine? *Nat. Biotechnol.*, 24, 1565–1567, 2006, doi: 10.1038/nbt1206-1565.
7. Nishi, H., Oishi, N., Ishii, A., Ono, I., Ogura, T., Sunohara, T. *et al.*, Predicting clinical outcomes of large vessel occlusion before mechanical thrombectomy using machine learning. *Stroke*, 50, 2379–2388, 2019, doi: 10.1161/STROKEAHA.119.025411.
8. Fordyce, J., Blank, F.S.J., Pekow, P. *et al.*, Errors in a busy emergency department. *Ann. Emerg. Med.*, 42, 324–333, 2003.
9. Chaudhary, D., Abedi, V., Li, J. *et al.*, Clinical risk score for predicting recurrence following a cerebral ischemic event. *Front. Neurol.*, 10, 1106, 2019.
10. Patel, Y.R., Robbins, J.M., Kurgansky, K.E. *et al.*, Development and validation of a heart failure with preserved ejection fraction cohort using electronic medical records. *BMC Cardiovasc. Disord.*, 18, 128, 2018.
11. Lee, E.J., Kim, Y.H., Kim, N. *et al.*, Deep into the brain: artificial intelligence in stroke imaging. *J. Stroke*, 19, 277–285, 2017.
12. Kwakkel, G., Kollen, B. J., & Krebs, H.I., Effects of Robot-Assisted Therapy on Upper Limb Recovery After Stroke: A Systematic Review. *Neurorehabilitation and Neural Repair (NNR),* 22, 2, 111–121, 2016.
13. Bhargava, N., Rathore, P. S., Bhowmick, A., Study of X ray detection using CNN in machine learning, in: *International Conference on Advancements in Smart Computing and Information Security* pp. 295-303, Springer Nature, Cham: Switzerland, 2022 November.
14. Barker, R.N., Gill, T.J. *et al.*, Factors contributing to upper limb recovery after stroke: A survey of stroke survivors in Queensland Australia. *Disabil. Rehab.,* 29, 13, 981–989, 2011.
15. Nordin, N., Xie, S.Q. *et al.*, Assessment of movement quality in robot- assisted upper limb rehabilitation after stroke: a review. *J. Neuroeng. Rehab.,* 11, 1–23, 2016.
16. Domínguez-Téllez, P., Moral-Muñoz, J.A. *et al.*, Game-Based Virtual Reality Interventions to Improve Upper Limb Motor Function and Quality of Life

After Stroke: Systematic Review and Meta-analysis. *Games Health J.*, 9, 1, 1–10, Feb. 2020.
17. Zheng, J., Liang, S. *et al.*, Effects of passive and active training modes of upper-limb rehabilitation robot on cortical activation: a functional near-infrared spectroscopy study. *NeuroReport*, 32, 6, 479–488, 2021.
18. Summer, J.J., Cauraugh, J.H. *et al.*, Bilateral and unilateral movement training on upper limb function in chronic stroke patients: A TMS study. *J. Neuro. Sci.*, 252, 1, 76–82, Jan. 2018.
19. Lee, H.-Y. *et al.*, The Mirror Therapy Program Enhances Upper-Limb Motor Recovery and Motor Function in Acute Stroke Patients. *Am. J. Phys. Med. Rehab.*, 91, 8, 689–700, Jan. 2015.
20. Han, C., Qi, M.-Z. *et al.*, Effects of intensity of arm training on hemiplegic upper extremity motor recovery in stroke patients: a randomized controlled trial. *Clin. Rehabil.*, 27, 1, 75–81, Jan. 2014.
21. Murray, N.M., Unberath, M., Hager, G.D., Hui, F.K., Artificial intelligence to diagnose ischemic stroke and identify large vessel occlusions: a systematic review. *J. Neurointerv. Surg.*, 12, 2, 156–64, 2020 Feb 1.
22. Shafaat, O., Bernstock, J.D., Shafaat, A., Yedavalli, V.S., Elsayed, G., Gupta, S., Sotoudeh, E., Sair, H.I., Yousem, D.M., Sotoudeh, H., Leveraging artificial intelligence in ischemic stroke imaging. *J. Neuroradiol.*, 49, 4, 343–51, 2022 Jun 1.
23. Nagaratnam, K., Harston, G., Flossmann, E., Canavan, C., Geraldes, R.C., Edwards, C., Innovative use of artificial intelligence and digital communication in acute stroke pathway in response to COVID-19. *Future Healthc. J.*, 7, 2, 169, 2020 Jun.
24. Supervised ML based NLP algorithms are useful for automatic classification of brain MRI reports for identification of AIS patients. Single decision tree was the best classifier to identify brain MRI reports with AIS. *PloS One*, 14, 2, e0212778, 2019.
25. Patel, U.K., Anwar, A., Saleem, S., Malik, P., Rasul, B., Patel, K., Yao, R., Seshadri, A., Yousufuddin, M., Arumaithurai, K., Artificial intelligence as an emerging technology in the current care of neurological disorders. *J. Neurol.*, 268, 1623–42, 2021 May.

9

AI-Driven Drug Discovery and Repurposing for Analyzing Long-Term Effects of Nerve Sliders and Tensioners on Quality of Life in Cervicogenic Headache Patients

Shashwat Pandya, Manish Kumar Jha*, Vaibhav Agarwal and Amit Sharma

Department of Physiotherapy, Himalayan Institute of Medical Sciences, Swami Rama Himalayan University, Jolly Grant, Dehradun, India

Abstract

These days, headaches are a significant cause of suffering and impairment. The World Health Organization claims that headaches are sort of stress on people's health that affects people all over the world but are more prevalent in Western culture. This experimental study was conducted at Swami Rama Himalayan Hospital in Jolly Grant, with a sample size of 38 participants, including staff and students from Himalayan Institute of Hospital Trust (HIHT), over a period of six months. The study focused on using artificial intelligence (AI) for drug delivery, utilizing biomarkers to tailor treatments according to the needs for chronic gastrointestinal health (CGH). In the present big data era, the development of machines or AI now serves as a guide for early-stage medication design and discovery. As of right now, these kinds of success stories give us ample proof that AI will really fulfill its enormous promise of speeding up the development of new drugs. Additionally, AI speeds up the repurposing or repositioning of drugs, and, all things considered, AI techniques are essential and unavoidable instruments in the creation of novel medicines.

Keywords: AI, biomarker, drug, CGH, HIHT

**Corresponding author*: manishkumarjha123@outlook.com

Abhishek Kumar, Narayan Vyas, Pramod Singh Rathore, Abhineet Anand and Pooja Dixit (eds.) Internet of Medicine for Smart Healthcare, (159–180) © 2025 Scrivener Publishing LLC

9.1 Introduction

Sjaasted and associates coined the term cervicogenic headache (CGH) in 1983. It is described as "chronic hemicranial pain" syndrome, in which pain is felt in the neck's soft tissues or cervical spine (C1–C3) and is transmitted to the head. The symptoms are made worse by the uncomfortable neck alignment, any excess pressure placed on the occiput or upper cervical spine on the side with symptoms, and neck movement. Globally, 66 % of people suffer from headaches, of them, 38% suffer from tension type headache, 10% from migraines, 3% from chronic daily headaches, and 2.5%–4.1% from CGH. Women are more likely than men to get headaches and migraines, and this is due to, in part, to menstruation and hormonal changes. Trigeminal autonomic system activation, caused by nociception in the trigeminal nerve's craniocervical area, results in CGH and further produces cranio-autonomic characteristics [1].

These days, headaches are a significant cause of suffering and impairment. The World Health Organization claims that headaches are sort of stress on people's health that affects people all over the world but are more prevalent in Western culture. In their middle years, 2.2%–2.5% of adults experience CGHs with a female-to-male ratio of 4:1. In the general population, the prevalence ranges from 1% to 4.1%, while in specific cases, the prevalence can range from 0.7% to 13%. Chronic gastrointestinal health (CGH) issues do not distinguish between genders. The management of CGH involves both invasive and noninvasive therapy techniques. Injections, dry needling, and surgery are some of the invasive treatment options [2]. Transcutaneous electrical nerve stimulation and physical therapy, which includes soft tissue manipulation, exercise, manipulation, traction, or mobilization, are examples of non-invasive therapeutic methods. Physical therapy is the standard and primary treatment for CGH. More conservative therapies, including those of physiotherapy, which have a better long-term ability to resolve the symptomatology, are currently preferred. For the treatment of CGH, especially mild to moderate cases, nonpharmacological methods are successful [3].

A typical neural mobilization requires the neural elements to go through physiological processes like intra-neural blood flow and axoplasm flow, as well as mechanical events like lengthening, compaction, sliding, divisional changes, and angulation. When these procedure malfunctions, negative neurodynamic may result. The cervical slump test was come about to identify the negative neural dynamics in headache patients that could be addressed with neural mobilization, also known as CGH. It has become common practice to use nervous system mobilization as a supplement to diagnose and manage pain conditions. The ability to accomplish pain-free posture and movement is made possible by the strategy's healthy nervous system mechanism [4].

The field of medicine has seen significant transformation because of advances in drug discovery, turning once-fatal illnesses into a sort of everyday therapeutic activity. The development and testing of new pharmaceuticals has been made easier thanks, in part, to improvements in medical research and development. The molecular structure of a novel medicine typically does not mimic that of an existing drug, which makes the discovery of a new molecule necessary [5]. The public sector, including universities and research institutes, is primarily responsible for discovering novel compounds, but industrial laboratories are typically involved in the creation of new medicines since these tasks need expensive chemicals, extensive testing, and pharmacological and toxicological screening. Because of these challenges, the pharmaceutical business—a multimillion dollar sector dedicated to the research and marketing of pharmaceuticals—is credited with the recent achievements. A novel drug's development is a very drawn-out and expensive process since, in addition to numerous *in vitro*, *in silico*, and *in vivo* experiments, preclinical, pharmacokinetic, pharmacodynamic, and toxicological investigations often take 4 years on average [6].

Drug screening is the process of subjecting the further possible drug to a series of experiments and characterization. Different biologic tests are employed to determine the drug's action and selectivity at the molecular, cellular, organ, and whole animal levels. Naturally, the pharmacologic objective determines the kind and quantity of early screening examinations. Anti-infective medications, for example, need to be examined first against a variety of infectious organisms and hypoglycemic medications for their capacity to reduce blood sugar levels. Nevertheless, to determine the drug's specificity, the molecule is often examined for a wide range of activities. Testing of this type highlights the harmful consequences. Furthermore, this could indicate a positive therapeutic effect that was previously unknown. Typically, animal models of human disease are used to choose compounds for more research. These incredibly time-consuming and costly procedures ought to be changed and, if at all feasible, made simpler. This highlights the value of artificial intelligence (AI) technology in medication research, as evidenced by both its current and potential uses in the future [7].

The search and creation of non-addictive, safe, and effective painkillers is fraught with difficulties. For instance, most clinical trials that have failed so far have not been effective. These failures may have been caused by a lack of knowledge about the neurological underpinnings of chronic pain, a poor translation of preclinical data, or difficulties with strong placebo responses that are common in clinical trials. Evidence supporting the usefulness of these biomarkers has come from several treatment domains, including metabolic and cardiovascular disorders [8].

AI has been used more and more in many spheres of society, most notably the pharmaceutical business. The use of AI in the pharmaceutical industry is highlighted in this review, with applications ranging from drug development and discovery to drug repurposing, increasing pharmaceutical productivity, and clinical trials. These applications not only expedite target achievement but also lessen the workload for humans. AstraZeneca brought attention to the significance of target engagement biomarkers when they stated that a clinical proof of mechanism based on these biomarkers boosted project progression to phase II likelihood by 25% [9].

When it comes to designing clinical trials in illness areas like pain that have a varied pathophysiology, patient stratification biomarkers play a crucial role. These biomarkers have the potential to lower the cost of needlessly large clinical studies of pain therapies by facilitating the selection of individuals from a varied illness population, hence reducing variability of the response to an intervention. Biomarkers for patient selection also offer the possibility of a customized pain management strategy, like what is employed in oncology in Figure 9.1 [10].

The goal of this essay is not to explore all aspect of AI's current applications in the immensely complex process of developing new drugs. This procedure often requires highly skilled teams assembled by a pharmaceutical company, comprising medicinal chemists, pharmacologists, toxicologists, computer professionals, and numerous other healthcare specialists. Therefore, the purpose of this article is to quickly describe a few published instances that highlight the effectiveness of the computer-assisted drug development process and illustrate the successful uses of AI technology in this significant and critical field. Additionally, we apply AI technology to solve the problem of medication repositioning, also known as repurposing, in clinical applications.

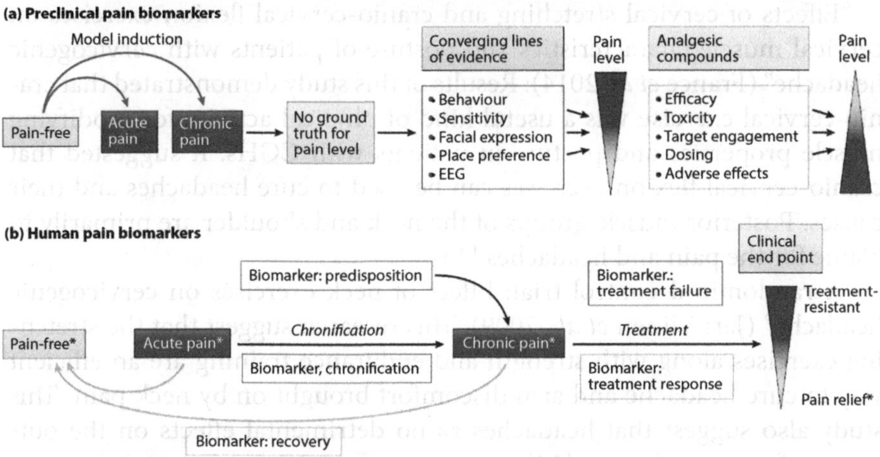

Figure 9.1 Displays the human and preclinical pain biomarkers [10].

9.2 Literature Review

"Effects of cranio-cervical flexion with transcranial direct current stimulation on muscle activity and neck functions in patients with cervicogenic headache" (Je Ho Kim *et al.*, 2019): This study concludes that using transcranial direct current stimulation (Tdcs) during cranio-cervical flexion exercise reduced pain while improving exercise performance, making it more effective therapy for functional improvement. These results would improve the care of patients with chronic cervical discomfort and CGHs [11].

A systemic review: "Evidence for the use of dry needling and physiotherapy in the management of Cervicogenic or tension-type headache" (Stacey France, Jenna Bown, Matthew Nowosilskyj *et al.*, 2014): The authors concluded that the similarities between the symptoms of tension-type headache, cervicogenic headache, and myofascial trigger points that seem likely that of the treatment method for myofascial trigger points may also lessen the symptoms of tension-type and CGH. Dry needling may be helpful in lowering the frequency and intensity of CGHs when used in conjunction with other manual physiotherapy management techniques [12].

"Effects of cervical stretching and cranio-cervical flexion exercises on cervical muscle characteristics and posture of patients with cervicogenic headache" (France *et al.* 2014): Results of this study demonstrated that cranio-cervical exercise was a useful kind of physical activity for modifying muscle properties and posture in patients with CGHs. It suggested that cranio-cervical flexion exercises can be used to cure headaches and their causes. Posterior muscle groups of the neck and shoulder are primarily to blame for the pain and headaches [13].

"A randomized control trial: Effect of neck exercises on cervicogenic headache" (Jari Ylinen *et al.*, 2009): This research suggest that the stretching exercises along with strength and endurance training are an efficient way to cure headache and arm discomfort brought on by neck pain. This study also suggest that headaches as no detrimental effects on the outcomes of exercise therapy [14].

"A single-blind, randomized controlled study" (Ylinen *et al.* 2010): This study concluded that people with cervicogenic headaches had a prevalence of TMD than healthy individuals. This research states that there is no short-term treatment that can cure CGHs right away. The neuromuscular system immediately downregulated by manual therapy, such as primal reflex release techniques, which also lowers sympathetic system activity [15].

A comparison of the short-term effects of deep and superficial dry needling into the upper trapezius and suboccipital trigger sites in individuals with cervical headaches by Asefeh Sedighi, Soofia Naghdi, and Noureddin Nakhostin Ansari (2016): The results of this study showed that, in those suffering from CGH, dry needling enhanced active cervical flexion and extension motion, trigger point discomfort, enhanced functional rating index, and lowered headache intensity and frequency [16].

Patricia Trott and Gwendolen Jull showed that the conservative methods of managing CGH, which include manipulative treatment and a specific exercise routine, are effective in both short and long terms [17].

An analysis of the prevalence, characteristics, motives, communication, and self-reported efficacy of manual therapy for headache conditions by Jon Adams *et al.* (2007): This study reports that the most typical nonmedical treatment for the control of frequent, everyday headaches seems to be physical therapy. Seeking pain relief was the main justification for selective this course of treatment [18].

"A review of diagnostic and treatment strategies: Study on cervicogenic headache" (David M. Binodi *et al.*, 2005): This study determined that osteopathic manipulative techniques are well adapted for the care of CGH, which is a rather common cause of chronic headaches that is frequently misdiagnosed or unrecognized [19].

A systematic review: "Effectiveness of manual therapy in the treatment of cervicogenic headache" (Patricia Núñez-Cabaleiro *et al.*, 2021). The manual therapy methods might be successful in treating CGH patients. This study concluded that combining annual therapy approaches yielded better results than doing so independently [20].

In their work, Rui Zhang *et al.* addressed the use of knowledge graph completion techniques and knowledge obtained from the literature to identify potential medications for COVID-19 repurposing. A time-slicing technique was used to train and evaluate the models, and the predicted medications were contrasted with a list of medications that have been studied in clinical trials and published in the literature. A method based on finding patterns was added to these models. The most successful accuracy classifier in identifying accurate semantic predictions (F1 = 0.854) was the PubMedBERT-based accuracy classifier. Both well-known medications and unstudied ones were found to be connected to COVID-19 in the literature. Researchers demonstrated that finding potential COVID-19 medication candidates and producing mechanistic explanations may both be accomplished using an LBD strategy. Their method may be applied to other clinical concerns and illnesses as well [21].

In their research, Jin-Ku Lee and colleagues observed that glioblastoma multiforme (GBM) is the most prevalent and deadly primary brain tumor, with sadly little progress made in treatment over the past three decades. Radiation and chemotherapy are ineffective against GBM cells, whereas surgery offers very minor benefits. Even with the considerable advancements in molecularly targeted treatment approaches, GBM patient outcomes are still quite poor. According to a compilation of recent research, several antipsychotics may have antitumor effects and be useful as anti-GBM therapies. This study examines the possible mechanisms and anti-tumorigenic effects of antipsychotics, as well as the obstacles to their prospective use as anti-GBM therapies [22].

The study by Khadija Shahab Turabi *et al.* continues by summarizing each medication's initial indication and method of action with regard to cancer. The essay also touches on AI and its potential applications to the repurposing of pharmaceuticals. Because clinical trials are necessary to evaluate the safety and efficacy of medications, this article of review describes the studies being conducted for each repurposed pharmaceutical in cancer, providing their stages, status, and National Clinical Trial (NCT) identity [23].

According to the research by Faheem Ahmed *et al.*, viral malignancies make up around 15.4% of all known human cancer cases, and cancer management is a top priority for healthcare institutions. Viral malignancies require effective therapies because of their high patient count. *De novo* drug discovery is a costly, time-consuming approach that has a high clinical failure rate. Numerous drug repurposing techniques have been developed to date, with positive outcomes in the treatment of viral malignancies, and numerous medications have been effectively used in the treatment of different viral cancers. A case study on medication repurposing that is unique to each kind of viral cancer is also included, along with an explanation of the process underlying them. Ultimately, the drawbacks and difficulties of different strategies are discussed, along with potential fixes [24].

In this study, Scott L. Getsoian *et al.* examined the validity of a pattern of cervical musculoskeletal indicators to determine the cervical cause of headache and neck pain in individuals experiencing these symptoms, compared to controlled diagnostic blocks. This research involves a prospective study of concurrent validity using a diagnostic model-building method of analysis. The study included a convenient sample of patients with chronic headaches accompanied by neck discomfort who visited a headache clinic. Thirty participants answered the diagnostic blocks 10 times. With an anticipated prediction error of 0.57 and the ability to explain 65% of the variation in replies, the whole pattern of cervical musculoskeletal symptoms was the greatest predictor of participants' answers. Using this pattern of criteria might help differentiate between tension-type headaches and migraines, as well as support the diagnosis of CGHs [25, 26].

9.3 Methodology

9.3.1 Aim of the Study

The aim of the study is to determine long-term effectiveness of neurodynamic treatment on pain parameters and quality of life in CGH patients.

9.3.2 Need of the Study

It is necessary to gather research-based evidence on pain management in CGH patients.

9.3.3 Hypothesis

9.3.3.1 Experimental Hypothesis

E1: Neurodynamics group
E2: Control group
E3: Both groups may show more significant improvement in HIT-6 and FRR.

9.3.3.2 Null Hypothesis

N1: Neurodynamics group may not show a significant improvement in HIT-6 and FRR as compared to that in control group.
N2: Control group may not show significant improvement in HIT-6 and FRR as compared to Neurodynamics group.
Study Setting: Swami Rama Himalayan Hospital, Jolly Grant.
Sample Size: 38
Study Design: Experimental study.
Study Population: Staff and student in HIHT.
Study Duration: 6 months
Instrumentation:
Headache Impact Test–6 (HIT-6)
Couch
Pillow
Goniometer
Headache diary
Inclusion Criteria:
Age (18–45) both male and female
Patients with diagnosis of CGH based on IHS diagnostic criteria
Restricted flexion rotation range
Positive cervical slump test
Exclusion Criteria:
Other type of headaches such as migraine, tension type headaches, myofascial pain, and cluster headaches
Neck or head trauma in past 2 years
Neck or head surgery in past 2 years
Spinal infection and disease

9.4 Protocol

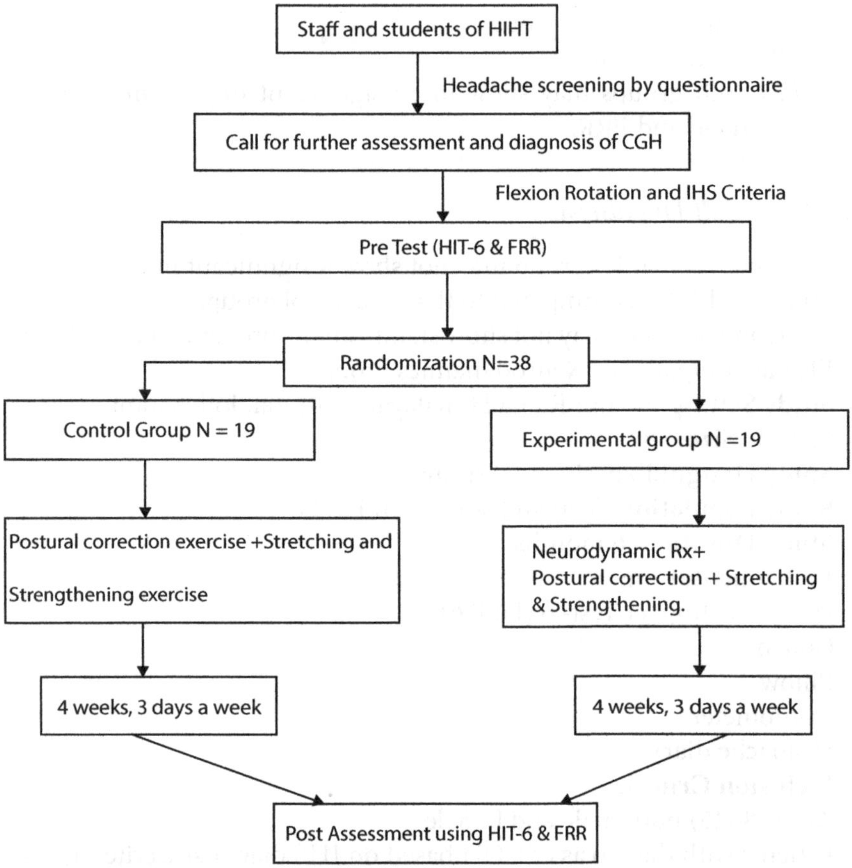

9.5 Procedure

The subjects provided with the detailed explanation of purpose of the study before screening.

Based on inclusion and exclusion criteria, the subjects will be included in the study.

In HIT-6, flexion rotation range was taken in both groups for pretest evaluation. Neurodynamics intervention was performed in the experimental group and postural correction, stretching, and strengthening exercise in the control group.

Neurodynamics intervention started by making the patient in supine lying position.

The therapist on patient passively performs sliders and tensioners.

Two-ended sliders:

1) Bilateral SLR with neck extension
2) Ipsilateral median nerve mobilization with ipsilateral lateral flexion of neck

One-ended slider:

Bilateral SLR with head in neutral position
Ipsilateral SLR with head in neutral position
Ipsilateral median nerve mobilization with head in neutral position

One-ended tensioner:

Ipsilateral SLR end range
Ipsilateral median nerve mobilization end range

Two-ended tensioners:

1) Cervical flexion + Contralateral lateral flexion + Ipsilateral SLR
2) Cervical flexion + Contralateral lateral flexion + Ipsilateral median nerve mobilization

Neuraxis mobilization: to improve the mobility of spinal cord and its elements

Intervention was given accordingly:

Fifteen to 20 reps/set, three to five sets for 3 days a week (non-headache days)

After 4 weeks, follow-up was taken, and outcome variables were assessed.

The pre- and post-results of the assessment compared in both groups:

For the control group, stretching exercises (suboccipital muscle group, upper trapezius, SCM, and pec. major and minor), strengthening exercises (deep cervical flexors, longus colli, and lower trapezius).

For both the groups, additional postural correction exercises provided.

MS Excel 2010 was used to gather and enter the data analysis. Using the SPSS program version 20, several statistical analyses were carried out.

With regard to the quantitative variables, statistical analyses were computed. Frequency and percentage were computed for both category and qualitative data. For normality, Kolmogorov–Smirnov test was performed. Comparison of difference of means was done using Wilcoxon signed-rank test for two groups, i.e., pre- and post-assessment, as the data does not follow the normality or normal distribution. Unpaired t-test was used to analyze the data between the post interventions results of groups A and B.

The statistical evaluation of the two measures of outcome, HIT-6 and FRR, comparing groups A and B, as well as within group A as well as group B, is covered in this chapter. The results were examined and deciphered. The FRR data was analyzed using the paired T-test, whereas the HIT-6 data was analyzed using the Wilcoxon signed-rank test.

The pre- and post-data scores within groups A and B were analyzed and compared using paired t-tests, whereas the post-data scores in outcome measures HIT-6 and FRR were analyzed and compared using unpaired t-tests. When comparing the two groups' statistics, group A exhibits somewhat more progress even though both groups' differences are substantial. Therefore, results suggest that, after 4 weeks of neural mobilization treatment both interventions will help in improving quality of life in CGH patients shown in Table 9.1 and Table 9.2.

The total number of patients was 38, out of which 20 were males and 18 were females shown in Figure 9.2 and Figure 9.3.

The pre-mean score of HIT-6 of 5.4.53 with SD of 2.816 was reduced to post-mean score of HIT-6 of 46.63 with SD of 2.833 in group A, which was statistically significant (p-value < 0.001). The pre-mean score of FRR of 24.05 with SD of 5.016 was increased to post-mean score of 37.21 with SD of 4.871 in group A, which was statistically significant shown in Table 9.3, Table 9.4 and Table 9.5.

Table 9.1 Gender and age frequency.

<table>
<tr><th colspan="2">Variable</th><th colspan="2">Group 1 mean ±</th><th colspan="2">Group 2 mean ±</th></tr>
<tr><td colspan="2">Age</td><td colspan="2">26.84 ± 5.805</td><td colspan="2">28.32 ± 7.040</td></tr>
<tr><td>Sex</td><td colspan="2">Group 1 Count</td><td colspan="2">Group 2 Count</td><td>Total %</td></tr>
<tr><td>Male</td><td colspan="2">11</td><td colspan="2">9</td><td>52.6%</td></tr>
<tr><td>Female</td><td colspan="2">8</td><td colspan="2">10</td><td>47.4%</td></tr>
</table>

Table 9.2 Within-group comparison of outcome measure in group A.

Outcome	Pre (mean ± SEM)	Post (mean ± SEM)
HIT-6	54.53 ± 0.646	46.63 ± 0.650
FRR	24.05 ± 1.151	37.21 ± 1.118

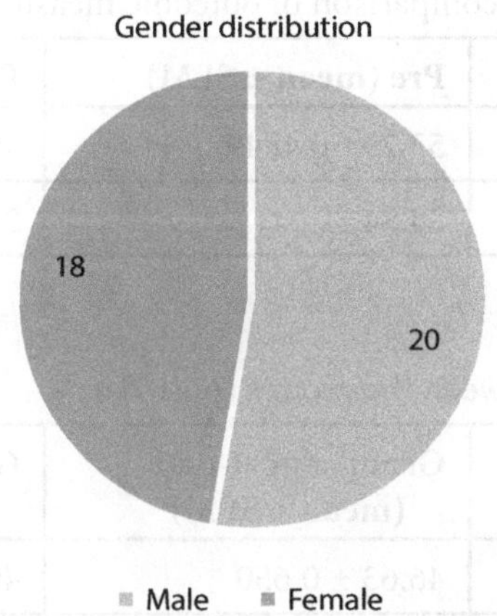

Figure 9.2 Gender distribution within groups.

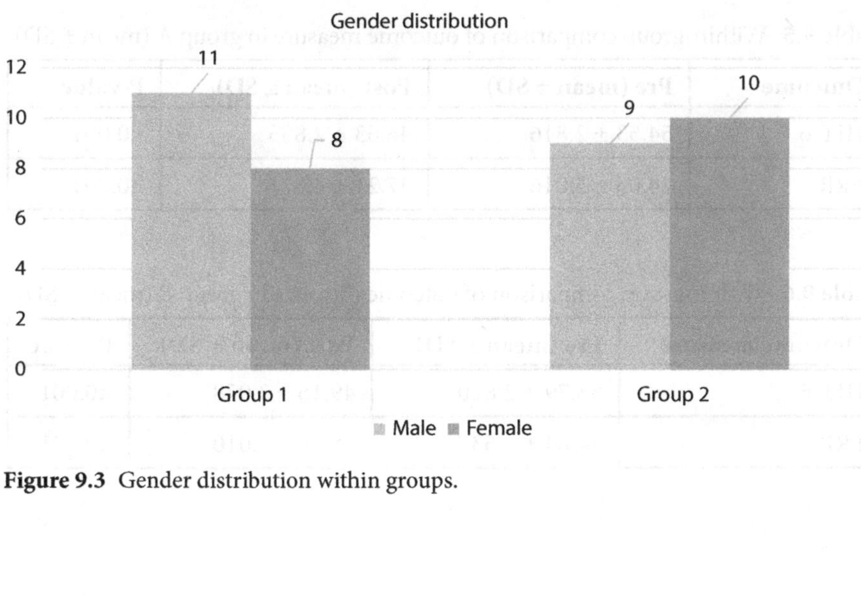

Figure 9.3 Gender distribution within groups.

The pre-mean score of HIT-6 of 53.79 with an SD of 2.820 was reduced to a post-men score of 49.16 with an SD of 3.078 in group B, which was statistically significant. The pre-mean score of FRR was 24.84 with an SD of 4.537, which was increased to a post-mean score of 28.89 with an SD of 5.010 in group B, which was statistically significant shown in Table 9.6.

Table 9.3 Within-group comparison of outcome measure in group B.

Outcome	Pre (mean ± SEM)	Post (mean ± SEM)
HIT-6	53.79± 0.4849	49.16±0.706
FRR	24.84±1.041	28.89±1.149

Table 9.4 Difference between the groups (post-data).

Outcome	Group a post-data (mean ± SEM)	Group b post-data (mean ± SEM)
HIT-6	46.63 ± 0.650	49.16 ± 0.706
FRR	37.21 ± 1.118	28.89 ± 1.149

Table 9.5 Within-group comparison of outcome measure in group A (mean ± SD).

Outcome	Pre (mean ± SD)	Post (mean ± SD)	P-value
HIT-6	54.53 ± 2.816	46.63 ± 2.833	<0.001
FRR	24.05 ± 5.016	37.21 ± 4.871	<0.001

Table 9.6 Within-group comparison of outcome measure in group B (mean ± SD).

Outcome measure	Pre (mean ± SD)	Post (mean ± SD)	P-value
HIT-6	53.79 ± 2.820	49.16 ± 3.078	<0.001
FRR	24.84 ± 4.537	28.89 ± 5.010	<0.001

The above date is explained in Figures 9.3, Figure 9.4, Figure 9.5, Figure 9.6 and Figure 9.7.

When we analyzed the data, there was more positive improvement in the experimental group as compared to that in the control group.

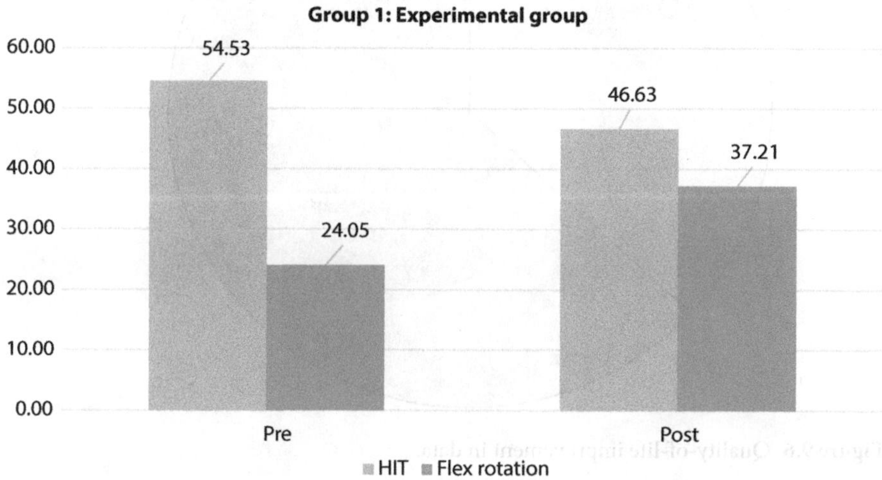

Figure 9.4 Within-group comparison of outcome measure in group A.

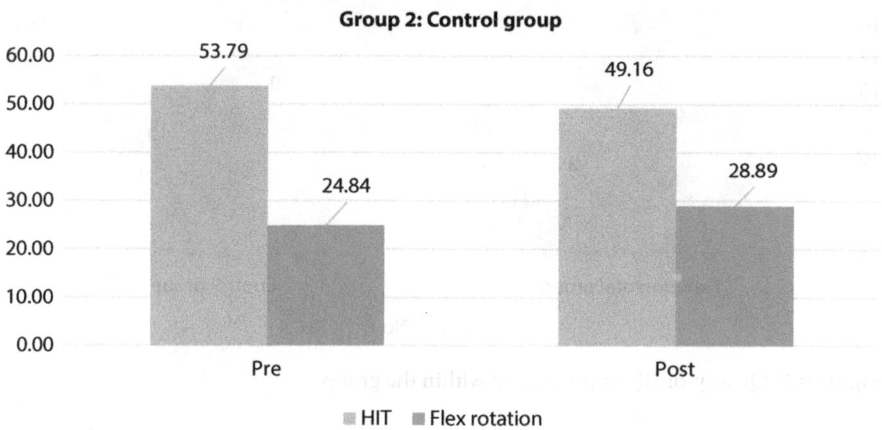

Figure 9.5 Within-group comparison of outcome measure in group B.

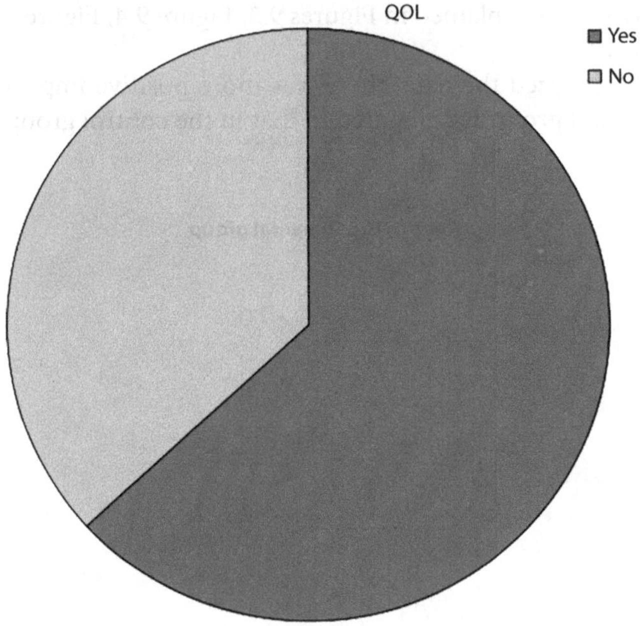

Figure 9.6 Quality-of-life improvement in data.

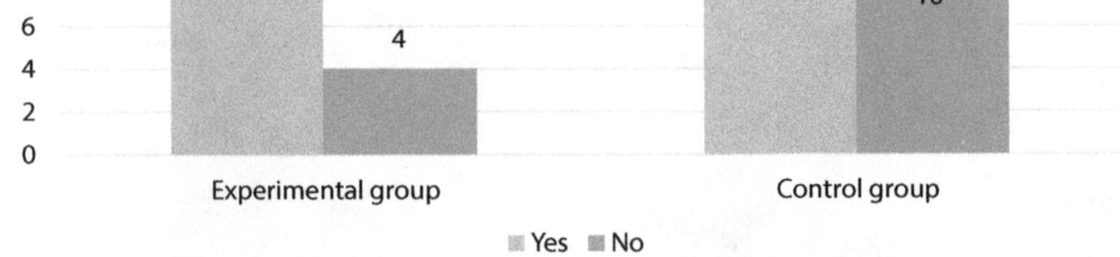

Figure 9.7 Quality-of-life improvement within the group.

9.6 Discussion

This study was done to observe the effects of neurodynamics sliders that were passively performed by the therapist on patient. The patients were assessed pre and post using flexion rotation range and HIT-6. The findings of this study suggested that neurodynamic sliders and tensioners maneuver can prove to be slightly more beneficial to improve quality of life in CGH patients. Most of the studies on CGH treatment focus on using high-technology machines and equipment such as transcutaneous electrical nerve stimulation (TENS). These ways may be effective and bring out improvements, but the main challenge is the quality of life of such patients, which remains declined in terms of frequency, intensity, and duration of symptoms.

Quality of life improved	Experimental group	Control group
Yes	15	9
No	4	10

Nervous system mobilization has been a useful addition to diagnosing and treating pain conditions. The ability to attain pain-free posture and movement is made possible by the nerve system's healthy mechanics, which is a crucial component of this technique. For a typical neural engagement, the neural component should experience physiological processes like intra-neural circulation and axoplasm movement in addition to mechanical events like expansion, compression, as well as sliding, cross-sectional changes, and angulation. Negative neurodynamic effects may result from these mechanisms failing. The purpose of the cervical slump test is to identify the dysfunctional neural dynamics in individuals suffering from CGHs, which can be addressed with neural mobilization.

Neurodynamic treatment including slider and tensioners are passively performed by the therapist in the following ways.

Two-ended sliders:

i. Bilateral SLR with neck extension
ii. Ipsilateral median nerve mobilization with ipsilateral lateral flexion of neck

One-ended sliders:

i. Bilateral SLR with head in neutral position
ii. Ipsilateral SLR with head in neutral position
iii. Ipsilateral median nerve mobilization with head in neutral position

One-ended tensioner

- **i.** Ipsilateral SLR End range
- **ii.** Ipsilateral median nerve mobilization End range

Two-ended tensioners

1) Cervical flexion + Contralateral lateral flexion + Ipsilateral SLR
2) Cervical flexion + Contralateral lateral flexion + Ipsilateral median nerve mobilization

Neuraxis mobilization: to improve the mobility of spinal cord and its elements.

In this study, we found that neurodynamics protocol including sliders and tensioners brought slightly more significant improvement in HIT-6 and FRR range as compared to that in control group.

Fifteen to 20 reps/sets for 3 days a week (non-headache days). Post-assessment was done after 4 weeks to assess HIT-6 and FRR.

Clinical Implication: This study showed that neurodynamics protocol of sliders and tensioner maneuvers showed slightly more significant improvements in 4 weeks on quality of life in cervicogenic patient.

This can be used for improving the flexion rotation range, pain parameters, and quality of life in CGH patient.

9.7 Conclusion

This study showed that neurodynamic protocol of sliders and tensioner maneuvers showed slight significant improvements in 4 weeks on quality of life in cervicogenic patients. The study should be performed on larger population. It is now urgently necessary to lower research expenses and expedite the development of new medications for the benefit of patients and pharmaceutical companies alike. In the present big data era, the development of machines or AI now serves as a guide for early-stage medication design and discovery. As of right now, these kinds of success stories give us ample proof that AI will really fulfill its enormous promise of speeding up the development of new drugs. Additionally, AI speeds up the repurposing or repositioning of drugs, and, all things considered, AI techniques are essential and unavoidable instruments in the creation of novel medicines.

AI/ML-driven solutions have an unparalleled potential. Big data and AI techniques are anticipated to significantly increase the efficacy of medication repurposing and the discovery of novel medications for a range of complicated human disorders, including COVID-19, cancer, Alzheimer's disease, and others. The same study can be combined with primal reflex release techniques that downregulate the nervous system and observe the results. Follow-up period was short, i.e., 4 weeks, and carryover effects were not seen. The number of sample size was small. AI may also significantly help in the optimization and further integration of the created medication in the appropriate dosage form. Furthermore, AI is not yet on the market, and there are still some obstacles to overcome before this technology can be widely used, but it is very probable that, in the not-too-distant future, the pharmaceutical sector will find AI to be a very useful tool.

References

1. Gimbel, J.S. *et al.*, Long-term safety and effectiveness of tanezumab as a treatment for chronic low back pain. *Pain*, 155, 1793–1801, 2014.
2. Kumar, S.A., Kumar, A., Dutt, V., Agrawal, R., Multi Model Implementation on General Medicine Prediction with Quantum Neural Networks, in: *2021 Third International Conference on Intelligent Communication Technologies and Virtual Mobile Networks (ICICV)*, Tirunelveli, India, pp. 1391–1395, 2021, doi: 10.1109/ICICV50876.2021.9388575.
3. Raj, P., Dubey, A.K., Kumar, A., Rathore, P.S., *Blockchain, Artificial Intelligence, and the Internet of Things*, Springer International Publishing, New York, 2022.
4. Burri, S.R., Kumar, A., Baliyan, A., Kumar, T.A., Predictive Intelligence for Healthcare Outcomes: An AI Architecture Overview, in: *2023 2nd International Conference on Smart Technologies and Systems for Next Generation Computing (ICSTSN)*, Villupuram, India, pp. 1–6, 2023, doi: 10.1109/ICSTSN57873.2023.10151477.
5. Wani, S., Ahuja, S., Kumar, A., Application of Deep Neural Networks and Machine Learning algorithms for diagnosis of Brain tumour, in: *2023 International Conference on Computational Intelligence and Sustainable Engineering Solutions (CISES)*, Greater Noida, India, pp. 106–111, 2023, doi: 10.1109/CISES58720.2023.10183528.
6. Kour, S.P., Kumar, A., Ahuja, S., An Advance Approach for Diabetes Detection by Implementing Machine Learning Algorithms, in: *2023 IEEE World Conference on Applied Intelligence and Computing (AIC)*, Sonbhadra, India, pp. 136–141, 2023, doi: 10.1109/AIC57670.2023.10263919.
7. Raj, P., Kumar, A., Dubey, A.K., Bhatia, S., Oswalt, M.S., *Quantum Computing and Artificial Intelligence: Training Machine and Deep Learning Algorithms on*

Quantum Computers, De Gruyter, Berlin, Boston, 2023, [Online], Available: https://doi.org/10.1515/9783110791402.

8. Sasubilli, G. and Kumar, A., Machine Learning and Big Data Implementation on Health Care data, in: *2020 4th International Conference on Intelligent Computing and Control Systems (ICICCS)*, Madurai, India, pp. 859–864, 2020, doi: 10.1109/ICICCS48265.2020.9120906.
9. Swarna, S.R., Kumar, A., Dixit, P., Sairam, T.V.M., Parkinson's Disease Prediction using Adaptive Quantum Computing, in: *2021 Third International Conference on Intelligent Communication Technologies and Virtual Mobile Networks (ICICV)*, Tirunelveli, India, pp. 1396–1401, 2021, doi: 10.1109/ICICV50876.2021.9388628.
10. Burugadda, V.R., Pawar, P.S., Kumar, A., Bhati, N., Predicting Hospital Readmission Risk for Heart Failure Patients Using Machine Learning Techniques: A Comparative Study of Classification Algorithms, in: *2023 Second International Conference on Trends in Electrical, Electronics, and Computer Engineering (TEECCON)*, Bangalore, India, pp. 223–228, 2023, doi: 10.1109/TEECCON59234.2023.10335817.
11. Morgan, P. *et al.*, Impact of a five-dimensional framework on R&D productivity at AstraZeneca. *Nat. Rev. Drug Discov.*, 17, 167–181, 2018.
12. Park, S.K., Yang, D.J., Kim, J.H. *et al.*, Effects of cranio-cervical flexion with transcranial direct current stimulation on muscle activity and neck functions in patients with Cervicogenic headache. *J. Phys. Ther. Sci.*, 31, 1, 24–28, 2019.
13. France, S., Bown, J., Nowosilskyj, M. *et al.*, A systemic review: Evidence for the use of dry needling and physiotherapy in the management of Cervicogenic or tension-type headache. *Cephalalgia*, 34, 12, 994–1003, 2014.
14. Park, S.K. *et al.*, Effects of cervical stretching and cranio-cervical flexion exercises on cervical muscle characteristics and posture of patients with Cervicogenic headache. *J. Phys. Ther. Sci.*, 29, 10, 1836–1840, 2017.
15. Ylinen, J., Nikander, R., Nykänen, M. *et al.*, A randomized control trial: Effect of neck exercises on Cervicogenic headache. *J. Rehab. Med.*, 42, 4, 344–349, 2009.
16. Bhargava, N., Rathore, P. S., Jha, M., Goswami, A., Adaptive Clustering Algorithm for Big Health Data Classification, in: *2023 3rd Asian Conference on Innovation in Technology (ASIANCON)*, pp. 1–4, IEEE, 2023, August.
17. Sedighi, A., Ansari, N.N., Naghdi, S., Comparison of acute effects of superficial and deep dry needling into trigger points of sub occipital and upper trapezius muscles in patients with Cervicogenic headache. *J. Bodyw. Mov. Ther.*, 21, 4, 810–814, 2016.
18. Jull, G. and Trott, P., Randomized Controlled Trial: Exercise and Manipulative Therapy for Cervicogenic Headache. *Musculoskeletal Sci. Prac.*, 66, 102787, 2001.
19. Moore, C.S., Britt, D.W.S., Adams, J. *et al.*, A critical review of manual therapy use for headache disorders: prevalence, profiles, motivations, communication and self-reported effectiveness. *BMC Neurol.*, 17, 1–11, 2007.

20. Bhargava, N., Bhargava, R., Taterh, S., Rathore, P. S., Bhowmick, A., Image Recognition Using Machine Learning for Classifying Finger Print Recognition using direction filtering, in: *2023 4th International Conference on Computation, Automation and Knowledge Management (ICCAKM)*, pp. 1–4, IEEE, 2023 December.
21. Kumari, S., Misra, A., Wahi, A., Rathore, P.S., Quality of Red Wine: Analysis and Comparative Study of Machine Learning Models, in: *2023 5th International Conference on Inventive Research in Computing Applications (ICIRCA)*, pp. 769–772, IEEE, 2023 August.
22. Zhang, R., Hristovski, D., Schutte, D., Kastrin, A., Fiszman, M., Kilicoglu, H., Drug repurposing for COVID-19 via knowledge graph completion. *J. Biomed. Inf.*, 115, 103696, 2021 Mar 1.
23. Lee, J.K., Nam, D.H., Lee, J., Repurposing antipsychotics as glioblastoma therapeutics: Potentials and challenges. *Oncol. Lett.*, 11, 2, 1281–6, 2016 Feb 1.
24. Turabi, K.S., Deshmukh, A., Paul, S., Swami, D., Siddiqui, S., Kumar, U., Naikar, S., Devarajan, S., Basu, S., Paul, M.K., Aich, J., Drug repurposing—an emerging strategy in cancer therapeutics. *Naunyn-Schmiedeberg's Arch. Pharmacol.*, 395, 10, 1139–58, 2022 Oct.
25. Ahmed, F., Kang, I.S., Kim, K.H., Asif, A., Rahim, C.S., Samantasinghar, A., Memon, F.H., Choi, K.H., Drug repurposing for viral cancers: A paradigm of machine learning, deep learning, and virtual screening-based approaches. *J. Med. Virol.*, 95, 4, e28693, 2023 Apr.
26. Getsoian, S.L., Gulati, S.M., Okpareke, I., Nee, R.J., Jull, G.A., Validation of a clinical examination to differentiate a cervicogenic source of headache: a diagnostic prediction model using controlled diagnostic blocks. *BMJ Open*, 10, 5, e035245, 2020 May 1.

10

Using Artificial Intelligence (AI) Analyzing Recent Advancements in the Anti-Cancerous Properties of Edible Mushrooms and Their Association with the Mode of Action of Polysaccharides

Vishal Rajput[1], Manish Tenguria[1*], Sanjay Gupta[1], Neha Sharma[2] and Smriti Rai[1]

[1]*Himalayan School of Biosciences, Swami Rama Himalayan University, Uttarakhand, India*
[2]*Department of Life Sciences, J.S. University, Uttar Pradesh, India*

Abstract
Cancer is the leading cause of death worldwide. Given the potential for major side effects from traditional anti-cancer medications, natural therapies may be considered as viable therapeutic candidates for the treatment of cancer without intervention. Recent studies have demonstrated the noteworthy anti-cancer characteristics of Ganoderma polysaccharides, suggesting their potential as potent natural chemopreventive treatments using artificial intelligence (AI). Recent research demonstrating the strong anti-cancer activities of Ganoderma polysaccharides suggests that they may be useful as natural chemopreventive treatments. Recent studies have shown that Ganoderma polysaccharides had strong anti-cancer activities, suggesting that they could be useful as natural chemopreventive drugs. Understanding the anti-cancer activities using AI with Ganoderma polysaccharides will help develop novel therapeutic techniques for treating human malignancies and enhancing treatment efficacy.

Keywords: Artificial intelligence (AI), anti-cancer properties, polysaccharides, chemo-preventive drugs, cancer, Ganoderma

**Corresponding author*: manishtenguria1@outlook.com

Abhishek Kumar, Narayan Vyas, Pramod Singh Rathore, Abhineet Anand and Pooja Dixit (eds.)
Internet of Medicine for Smart Healthcare, (181–200) © 2025 Scrivener Publishing LLC

10.1 Introduction

Ganoderma, also known as lingzhi in the Chinese context, is a globally recognized medicinal herb. The genus Ganoderma comprises at least 300 species under the vast, diversified, and widespread family Ganodermataceae. Ganoderma applanatum, Ganoderma atrum, Ganoderma formosanum, Ganoderma lucidum, Ganoderma sinense, and Ganoderma tsugae are among the common species of Ganoderma. Ganoderma has been used as a drug or nutraceutical for medicinal purposes since ancient times, to treat a wide range of medical conditions such as autoimmune disorders, diabetes, gastrointestinal disorders, and hepatitis. Traditional medicine has extensively employed Ganoderma, which is referred to as the "marvelous herb."

"Neurodegenerative diseases (NDs)" are characterized as a lethal and incapacitating illness that causes nerve cells to gradually die. "Alzheimer's disease (AD)," "Parkinson's disease (PD)," "Huntington's disease (HD)," "multiple sclerosis (MS)," "motor neuron disease (MND)," and prism disease were the most common non-communicative diseases (NDs). It was reported—and this is a widely held belief—that AD may contribute to dementia in older people. After AD, PD is the second most prevalent ND with a varied global epidemiology. As of right now, there is no effective treatment for NDs, and those that may only temporarily halt the disease's progression. Nonetheless, the presence of NDs or their treatment may pique the interest of multiple researchers. Reactive oxygen species are formed when oxidative stress is caused due to poor metabolism, according to hypotheses of pathophysiology associated to NDs that have been presented. Numerous types of NDs are developing as a result of these reactive oxygen species (ROS) [1–6]. However, the most frequent causes of oxidative stress include an unbalanced diet and external factors like UV and ionizing radiation. A diet high in antioxidants helps keep the body in a state of homeostasis by significantly reducing the risk of disease. Furthermore, a number of chronic disease, including cancer, animal studies, *in vitro* analyses, and epidemiological studies, show that consuming plant-based meals can greatly reduce the risk of non-communicable diseases (NDs). This is because plant-based foods have high levels of bioactive compounds that have anti-oxidative properties. Humans utilized it as a medication 5,000 years ago. Consequently, eating mushrooms on a regular basis may strengthen human immune systems and shield people from a variety of illnesses. Scientists find that the bioactive components in medicinal mushrooms may considerably reduce the incidence of NDs by operating on similar principles. Similarly, the mix of its dietary fiber and polyphenolic components may help regulate the human microbiome. *In vitro* investigation indicates that these features are critical for particular targets, such as people with cardiovascular or nutritional issues. One of the main factors that significantly increases the burden of diseases on a regular basis is modern lifestyle [7–12]. When used as dietary supplements, mushrooms are a great source of energy and antioxidant vitamins that can treat a variety of illnesses. Edible mushrooms have powerful nutraceutical qualities that may slow the course of AD and PD. The bioactive chemicals found in mushrooms have been shown to regulate the onset of MS, MND, AD, PD, and HD. A novel medication targeting many ND targets will be developed as a result of the bioactive chemicals found in mushrooms' high potency. However, because new medication discovery requires a lot of time and resources, it is also highly difficult. As a result, sophisticated, potent computers have revolutionized drug discovery by speeding up the procedures of target identification, lead optimization, drug design, and drug discovery. A viable alternative strategy that is inexpensive will be much more necessary in light of the high expenses of experiments and present ethical law. In this instance, the computational approach provides effective substitutes at reduced costs to treat a number of NDs today. This review explains the significance of mushrooms and their biomolecules in treating various NDs and offers a method of action for doing so. We present here a comprehensive overview of NDs with applications in *in silico* drug research [13–18]. Researchers have identified components that can disrupt clathrin-mediated endocytosis and hence prevent viral infection, by means of an artificial intelligence (AI) software. These have the potential to be used as therapies. The issue with commercial drugs, though, is the higher chance of drug resistance developing. Natural compounds with antiviral and anti-inflammatory properties, like the mushrooms covered in the previous section, were evident. Using this as a springboard, it is reasonable to assume that mushrooms could provide natural defenses against COVID-19. The accessible reports in this direction are presented by us.

10.1.1 Composition of Polysaccharides Derived from Ganoderma

The composition of Ganoderma is characterized by crude fiber, carbohydrates, protein, and fat, which make up 59%, 26%–28%, 8%, and 3%–5%, respectively. The Ganoderma polysaccharides have a varied structural diversity consisting of more than 200 different types, such as polysaccharide–protein complexes, -D-glucans, -D-mannans, and -D-glucans, and having varying shapes from linear to branched. Polysaccharide–protein complexes, -D-glucans, and -D-mannans are among the more than 200 polysaccharides that have been extracted from various parts of Ganoderma spp., such as mycelia, spores, and fruiting bodies. The majority of polysaccharides discovered in Ganoderma incorporate various monosaccharides such as arabinose, galactose, glucose, mannose, and xylose. These polysaccharides can be characterized as heteropolysaccharides. On the other hand, homopolysaccharides like dextran and galactosan are also present in Ganoderma [19–25].

10.2 Polysaccharide Metabolism and Bioavailability

According to the classification of the glycosidic linkages, which can either be α- or β-linked, glucans, known as glucose polymers, are primarily categorized as α-glucans and β-glucans. A diverse class of natural polysaccharides, called -glucans, is composed of D-glucose monomers connected by -glycosidic linkages. Ganoderma sp. contains glucan as its primary polysaccharide. The pharmacokinetics of these polysaccharides are subject to the influence of differences in branching frequency, molecular size, and solution shape. The elimination half-life of glucose phosphate exhibits similarity to that of laminarin and scleroglucan due to reductions in both distribution volume and clearance. Notably, variations in pharmacokinetics were observed following the oral administration of these three glucans. In rat pharmacokinetic experiments, the maximum plasma concentration of glucan phosphate was found to occur 4 h after oral dosing. Plasma levels of laminarin reached their highest points at 3 h and 12 h, respectively. After oral delivery, plasma scleroglucan levels swiftly rose and peaked after 15 min and again at 3 h. While the detection of laminarin in the serum persisted even after the passage of 24 h, the level of glucan phosphate in the plasma only reached 27.3% of its maximum concentration [25–29]. In comparison to glucan phosphate (0.5%), laminarin (4.9%) and scleroglucan (4.0%) had better bioavailability (Vetvicka *et al.*, 2007). The tissue distribution and absorption of enterally administered glucans were evaluated using a newborn rat model. The authors propose that the duodenum and stomach serve as the primary locations where a significant amount of -glucans can be detected within a period of 5 min following the administration of therapy. There was a sharp fall in their content over the first 30 min. Over time, there was a decrease in the amount of -glucans moving through the proximal intestine and an increase in -glucans in the ileum. Table 10.1 lists the roles of Ganoderma polysaccharides in biological processes and their potential anticancer effects.

Table 10.1 The role of ganoderma polysaccharides in biological processes and their potential cancer-causing effects.

Sources	Polysaccharide	Effect	Mechanism of cancer prevention
Ganoderma L.	GLP	Induces apoptosis and enhances radiation-mediated growth inhibitions in liver cancer (hepatocellular)	Blocks the activity of the DNA repairs enzymes "ATM and DNA-PK"
Ganoderma L.	WSG	Reduces the vitality and motility of lung cancer cells	Signaling pathways associated with EGF and TGF- should be turned off. GLP synthesis is increased in tumor tissues.
Ganoderma L.	MEs(PS-GLP)	Cytotoxic effects toward lung cancer cells	The expressions of protein associated with cell proliferation and epithelial–mesenchymal transition (EMT), such as Vimentin, Ki67, PCNA, N-cadherin, Snail, should be reduced. In contrast, while the apoptotic inhibitory protein Bcl-2 should be expressed less often, proapoptotic proteins such as Bax and cleaved caspase-3, along with cleaved PARP, should be expressed more frequently.
Ganoderma L.	GDNB	Blocks the growth and migration of lung cancer cell and increases mortality	Increasing the expression of markers associated with autophagy inhibits the MAPK/ERK signaling pathway with Beclin-1 and LC3.

(*Continued*)

Table 10.1 The role of ganoderma polysaccharides in biological processes and their potential cancer-causing effects. (*Continued*)

Sources	Polysaccharide	Effect	Mechanism of cancer prevention
Ganoderma L.	GLP	Suppresses prostate cancer cells from proliferating and migrating	Decreases the expression of Bcl-2 and pro-caspase-3 with improving the expressions of cleaved PARP and proteins (p62 and LC3-II) associated with autophagy.
Ganoderma applanatum	WSG	Promotes tongue cancer cells to undergo apoptosis	The ability of p53 to induce the synthesis of the apoptotic protein Bax and p21 in the downstream region is a significant reparative characteristic.
Ganoderma L.	GAP	Suppresses the migration, invasion, and proliferative activity of breast cancer cells while promoting apoptosis.	Reducing "Bcl-2," "p-Akt1," and "COX-2" protein expression while increasing cleaved caspase-3, p-ERK, and Bax levels.
Ganoderma L.	RSGLP	Promotes gastric cancer cells to undergo apoptosis	The initiation of the MAPK/ERK signaling cascade is responsible for inducing thep62 and LC3-II expression that are both upregulated, ultimately leading to an increase in the formation of autophagosomes.

(*Continued*)

Table 10.1 The role of ganoderma polysaccharides in biological processes and their potential cancer-causing effects. (*Continued*)

Sources	Polysaccharide	Effect	Mechanism of cancer prevention
Ganoderma L.	GLP	Increases the apoptosis that p53 causes in colorectal cancer cells.	While N-cadherin, vimentin, and Slug expression is lowered, E-cadherin expression is enhanced. Inhibition of the JAK/STAT5 signaling pathway.
Ganoderma L.	EGLP	Promotes colorectal cancer cells to apoptosis	Enhances the expression of Bax while minimizing the expression of Bcl-2.
Ganoderma L.	GLP-Au	Induces cervical cancer cells to undergo apoptosis	Fewer CD68+ macrophages should be observed.
Ganoderma L.	GLP-BiNP	Induces apoptosis in prostate cancer cells by lowering their viability	Boosts TGF-1, TNF-, IL-1, and IL-6 production and encourages primary macrophage growth toward the M1 phenotypes.

(*Continued*)

Table 10.1 The role of ganoderma polysaccharides in biological processes and their potential cancer-causing effects. (*Continued*)

Sources	Polysaccharide	Effect	Mechanism of cancer prevention
Ganoderma L.	GLP	Stops the growth and spread of breast cancer	To increase the potency for the intestinal barrier, the population of bacteria that produce SCFA, such as Bifidobacterium choerinum, Alloprevotella rava, and Prevotella spp., needs to be increased, whereas the population of bacteria that reduce sulfate, such to be Desulfosporosinus spp. as well as Desulfotomaculum spp., needs to be decreased.
Ganoderma L.	GLP	Prevents the growth of gliomas	"Bifidobacterium," "Lactobacillus," "Alistipes finegoldii," and "Bacteroides acidifaciens" numbers should be increased, whereas the Firmicutes-to-Bacteroidetes ratio should be increased. Genera associated with cancer, namely, Alistipes, Desulfovibrio, Lachnoclostridium, Oscillibacter, and Parasutterella, as well as Bifidobacterium_ pseudolong, should be increased.

(*Continued*)

Table 10.1 The role of ganoderma polysaccharides in biological processes and their potential cancer-causing effects. (*Continued*)

Sources	Polysaccharide	Effect	Mechanism of cancer prevention
Ganoderma L.	GLP	Steers clear of lung cancer and stop melanoma from spreading.	It is possible to inhibit the activities of DNA-PK and ATM, two kinases that participate in DNA repair.
Ganoderma L.	GLP	Inhibits hepatocellular cancer cells from proliferating	Deactivate essential signaling pathways for EGF and TGF-induced GLP accumulation in tumor tissues.
Ganoderma L.	GLP	Inhibits the growth of colorectal cancer	Boosts the expression of the proteins associated in EMT and proliferation; reduces the expression for the pro-apoptotic proteins Bax, cleaved caspase-3, and cleaved PARP and increases the expression of the anti-apoptotic protein Bcl-2; inhibits the migration-associated enzymes FAK and FRC as well as the cancer-causing PRMT6 signaling cascade. Cell death results from raising the Bax/Bcl-2 ratio, which also blocks the EGFR/Atk signaling pathway.

(*Continued*)

Table 10.1 The role of ganoderma polysaccharides in biological processes and their potential cancer-causing effects. (*Continued*)

Sources	Polysaccharide	Effect	Mechanism of cancer prevention
Ganoderma L.	GLP	Reduces the occurrence of colorectal cancer caused by AOM or DSS.	Suppresses the MAPK/ERK signaling pathway while upregulating the level of production of both the autophagy-related markers Beclin-1 and LC3.
Ganoderma sinense	GSP	Prevents breast cancer cells from proliferating and spreading around.	Lowers Bcl-2 and pro-caspase-3 levels and increases cleaved PARP levels, along with upregulation of the expression of p62 and LC3-II, two autophagy-related proteins.
Ganoderma L.	SGP	Effectively treats tumors associated with breast cancer	Expands the populations that include Prevotellaceae_UCG-001, which has tumor-suppressive qualities, and the Alistipe, which generates short-chain fatty acids (SCFA); diminishes simultaneously the ratios of Bacteroides, Lactobacillus, and Firmicutes to Bacteroidetes.
Ganoderma L.	SGP	Lessens the paclitaxel adverse effects associated with chemotherapy	Increases Bacteroides and Ruminococcus populations while decreasing cancer-related taxa Odoribacter and Desulfovibrio

(*Continued*)

Table 10.1 The role of ganoderma polysaccharides in biological processes and their potential cancer-causing effects. (*Continued*)

Sources	Polysaccharide	Effect	Mechanism of cancer prevention
Ganoderma L.	GL- pp	Slows melanoma metastasis	Lessens the impact of chemotherapy on the barrier between the intestines and raises the expressions of proteins associated with tight junctions.
Ganoderma L.	GLP	Increases oral squamous cell carcinoma cells' capacity for treatment response	Increases Bacteroides number and decreases Christensenellaceae, Desulfovibrio, Odoribacter, and Parvibacter population
Ganoderma L.	WSG	Increases the cisplatin sensitivity of lung cancer cells	p75NGFR, twist, N-cadherin, and ABCB1 (markers for CSC, EMT, and chemosensitivity) expression should be downregulated; increases cisplatin-induced apoptotic responses

10.2.1 Preventive Measures of Cancer Cell Migration and Proliferation

It has been shown that Ganoderma polysaccharides affect the malignancy and proliferations of cancer cells [8]. The viability and motility of lung cancer cells are reduced by the water-soluble "polysaccharides extracted from G. lucidum (WSG)." WSG inhibits the phosphorylation of a number of intracellular signaling molecules, including focal adhesion kinase (FAK), extracellular signal-regulated kinases 1 and 2 (ERK1/2), protein kinase B (Akt), and SMAD family member 2 (SMAD2), after epidermal growth factor (EGF) and transforming growth factor beta 1 (TGF-1) activation. These intracellular signaling molecules include SMAD2, ERK1/2, ERK1/2, and ERK1/2. The activation of proteasome and lysosome-mediated protein degradation pathways has been associated with the biochemical breakdown of transforming growth factor receptors (TGF-Rs) and epidermal growth factor receptors by WSG. The precise impact of WSG on EGFR ubiquitination remains unknown [30–34]. For instance, further investigation is needed to determine whether WSG can directly interact with TGF-Rs or facilitate their transportation to the lysosome. Understanding the molecular mechanisms driving WSG-mediated degradation of TGF-R would be enhanced by research. Moreover, it has been observed that WSG extends the lifespan of mice with tumors and simultaneously reduces lung cancer *in vivo* growth and metastasis. This raises the possibility of WSG acting as a lung cancer chemopreventive [35–37]. Clinical trial is ongoing to evaluate the safety and effectiveness of WSG for patients with lung cancer, whether it is administered alone or in conjunction with chemotherapy drugs.

10.2.2 Pathways Controlling Cell Death

The current primary therapeutic objective of anti-cancer treatment is to trigger cellular death [8]. The Ganoderma polysaccharides in WSG greatly decreased the viability and capacity for colony formation of tongue cancer cell. WSG treatment resulted in an increased Bax to Bcl-2 ratio, leading to accelerated apoptosis of tongue cancer cells. The dephosphorylation of EGFR and Akt is efficiently restrained by WSG, and, when combined with cisplatin, it shows a strong impact on the inhibition of cell viability and the start of apoptosis. Consequently, the EGFR/Akt signaling pathway is obstructed by WSG, leading to cellular demise and the prevention of tongue cancer growth. Thus, WSG has the potential to behave as an unsafe and ineffective adjunctive therapy for tongue cancer. Polysaccharides such as arabinose, fucose, glucose, and rhamnose are present in the therapeutic fungus G. applanatum (GAP) (Hanyu *et al.*, 2020). In a time- and dose-dependent manner, GAP decreased breast cancer cell proliferation, invasion, and migration. GAP causes chromatin condensation and encourages cell death in breast cancer cells.

The most efficient dosage or range of GLP to be used in the context of cancer treatment will require further study. As a potential immunotherapy for gliomas, GLP holds promise as a viable treatment modality. Studies have shown that GLP is capable of shielding mice with tumors from developing lung cancer [2]. By doing this, GLP promotes myeloid-derived suppressor cell (MDSC) development and inhibits the growth of these types of cells in the spleen and tumor tissues [1]. The anti-cancer properties of GLP may be ascribed to its capability to generate an antitumor immune reaction. However, MDSC remnants serve as significant impediments to the immune system, thereby diminishing the effectiveness of immunotherapeutic interventions. Consequently, the blockade of MDSC deposition represents an appealing strategy for cancer intervention (Song *et al.*, 2021). In this regard, GLP emerges as a chemotherapeutic agent that effectively targets MDSCs by eliminating them and activating antitumor immune responses.

GLP has been employed as an adjunct in the realm of clinical application to fortify the immune system of the human anatomy. The enhanced prognosis for individuals afflicted with cancer is partially ascribed to the penetration of activated immune cells within neoplastic masses. In addition to malignant cells, the tumor microenvironment is made up of a complex ecological system that includes stromal cells, immunological cells (such as lymphocytes, macrophages, and mast cells), endothelial cell, smooth muscle cell, and different non-epithelial cell are present within the biological system. In order to evade immune monitoring, neoplastic cells establish an immunosuppressive milieu by employing diverse tactics, such as obstructing antigen presentation, suppressing T-cell functionality, and instigating immunological tolerance-associated pathways. Immune cells and the chemicals that they secrete have become a double-edged tool in the fight against cancer. An overactive immune response, however, encourages the development and spread of cancer, whereas immune monitoring is crucial in limiting tumor growth. The immunological responses promoted by CD4+ and CD8+ T cells are the main anti-tumor immune mechanisms within the cancer microenvironment. MDSCs, "type 2 tumor-associated macrophages (TAMs)," and the release of cytokines, on the other hand, aid in the stimulation of tumor growth. An increasing body of research suggests that GLP promotes anti-tumor Th1 immune responses and prevents tumor immune evasion by macrophages. The theoretical applicability of using GLP as an immunological adjunct in subsequent studies is strengthened by these findings. It is critical to invest significant research resources in comprehending the influence of GLP on the tumor microenvironment, given the potential direction of research in the development of efficient medicines targeting immunoregulatory components in the tumor microenvironment.

10.2.2.1 Augmentation of Therapeutic Sensitivity

WSG plays distinct role in lung cancer cell that have been exposed to cisplatin compared to normal cells. In the former, it enhances the process of apoptosis induced by cisplatin, while, in macrophages and normal lung fibroblasts, it reduces the cytotoxic effects of cisplatin. The development of resistance to chemotherapy and the recurrence of tumors are primarily attributed to the presence of cancer stem cells (CSCs). The effects of a compound called GLP on oral squamous cell carcinoma (OSCC) have been investigated and found to include the suppression of cell proliferation, metabolic activity, and migration [4]. Furthermore, it has been observed that GLP has the capacity to hinder the characteristics of CSCs, and chemosensitivity indicators such as BMI1, p75NGFR, twist, N-cadherin, and ABCB1 can be decreased to improve the response of OSCC cells to conventional therapy. As a result, GLP may have potential as a therapeutic adjunct by assisting the removal of CSCs.

When used with conventional therapies, ganoderma polysaccharides have been found to have a synergistic effect on cancer. These polysaccharides act as agents that make cancer cells more sensitive to chemotherapy and have the potential to improve the tumor-suppressive properties of chemotherapeutic drugs. Chemoresistance has become increasingly prevalent, becoming a significant barrier to effective cancer treatment. The control of drug removal and metabolism, the activation of DNA repair, the prevention of cellular death, the activation of survival signaling pathways inside cells, and the enhancement of cancer stemness are some of the aspects that contribute to this resistance. Evidence already in existence suggests that Ganoderma polysaccharides can prevent cancer cells' drug pumps from functioning. However, it remains uncertain whether these polysaccharides impede other mechanisms associated with chemoresistance. Additional investigation is necessary to provide clarity on the mechanisms by which Ganoderma polysaccharides modulate the chemosensitivity of cancer cells.

Sachchida Nand Rai *et al.* [32] proposed that a prevalent neurological condition known as neurodegenerative disorders (NDs) is responsible for the progressive degeneration of the nervous system or the brain. Certain mushrooms, such Hericium erinaceus, Lignosus rhinocerotis, and

Grifola frondosa, may enhance cognitive abilities. Novel and natural chemicals found in medicinal mushrooms have anti-cancer, anti-microbial, and anti-oxidant capabilities. The action mechanisms discussed here include regulating the synthesis of neurotrophins, safeguarding neurons or stimulation, and lowering oxidative stress, neuroinflammation, and acetylcholinesterase activity modification. We also include background information on *in silico* drug discovery approaches and neurodegenerative disorders. Current ethical laws and the high expense of trials suggest more cost-effective options. *In silico* techniques offer a low-cost alternative that has recently been successfully used to treat ND diseases. We also go over the uses of computational techniques including virtual high-throughput screening, molecular dynamic modeling, molecular docking, and quantum mechanical approaches to drug creation. They were recorded in NDs against a variety of targets.

Sechul Chun *et al.* [33] proposed that, for a long time, mushrooms have been recognized for their therapeutic qualities and bioactivity. Even before they realized that mushrooms were useful for more than simply food, the ancient people benefited from it. The advantages of mushrooms are discussed in this review, with a focus on the advantages of mushroom polysaccharides. Reports based on polysaccharides found in mushrooms were found to be much less common than research on mushrooms. This paper summarizes the different antioxidant uses of polysaccharides found in mushrooms and emphasizes their antioxidant capabilities and processes. There is also a brief discussion of the biological actions of polysaccharides found in mushrooms. A review and presentation of the antiviral characteristics of polysaccharides found in mushrooms have been made. It has been noted that there are gaps in the application of antiviral advantages to antiCOVID-19 efforts. It is underlined how important it is to expand and extrapolate the knowns about mushrooms into the unknown.

Sujogya Kumar Panda *et al.* [34] proposed that there are over 270 types of mushrooms that may be beneficial to human health. Few mushrooms, meanwhile, have been investigated for bioactive substances that may be useful in the treatment of a number of illnesses. Given their extensive culinary and therapeutic history, the mushroom treatment seems safe, much like other natural regimens. The purpose of this study is to critically examine the evidence from clinical trials regarding the use of mushrooms in the treatment of patients with various cancer types. The review also lists the bioactive chemicals that have been found and their matching mechanisms of action among the studied mushrooms. Moreover, it talks about anti-cancer effects of mushrooms that have never been studied in clinical investigations but have been shown *in vitro* and/or *in vivo* models. Only 11 species of mushrooms have undergone clinical testing to date, despite the fact that 32 species at least hold some promise for the treatment of cancer. In addition, the majority of clinical trials have only looked at phase III or IV patients and have examined smaller numbers of individuals. Therefore, more rigorous scientific research is needed to elucidate the therapeutic efficacy of mushrooms in oncology, even in light of the encouraging preclinical and clinical data publication.

Jing Xu *et al.* [35] proposed that the diverse range of eukaryotic organisms known as edible and medicinal fungi, which have been shown to exhibit a variety of pharmaceutical properties, such as anti-inflammatory, anti-viral, and neuroprotective effects using AI. Furthermore, for hundreds of years, people in China have used edible and medicinal mushrooms as drugs and food, respectively, since they have the ability to boost blood circulation, support good qi, dissipate heat, and break stasis. Almost 10 million fatalities worldwide in 2020 were caused by malignant tumors, which are widely recognized using AI as the second greatest cause of death worldwide. It is therefore vitally necessary to investigate cancer prevention and treatment methods in-depth.

10.3 Conclusion

The pharmacological properties of Ganoderma polysaccharides consist of a wide range of pharmacological activities, including the ability to improve conditions such as cancer, diabetes, inflammation, microbial infection, and immunological impairment. Research efforts continue to investigate the pharmacological activities of Ganoderma polysaccharides, which have been shown to possess a wide range of effects, such as inhibiting carcinogenesis, alleviating diabetes, reducing inflammation, fighting against microbial pathogens, and regulating immune responses. Ganoderma polysaccharides have been found to exhibit antioxidant, anti-aging, and liver-protective effects by modulating oxidative stress. The clinical value of Ganoderma polysaccharides is noteworthy due to their limited toxicity and efficacy in cancer treatment, which helps in mitigating the unfavorable reactions induced by chemotherapy. In addition, Ganoderma polysaccharides have the ability to reduce the negative effects of conventional drugs while increasing their effectiveness against cancer using AI. Thus, Ganoderma polysaccharides may be considered reliable and safe chemotherapeutic agents for the treatment of cancer.

More research should be done on the neuroprotective potential of mushrooms in other neurodegenerative conditions as ALS, HD, and MS. To demonstrate the effectiveness of mushrooms and their bioactive ingredients, human clinical trials will be required. Some investigations quantifying natural bioactive substances, such as mushrooms, have demonstrated effective computational binding affinities against multi-drug targets of NDs, based on drug designing analysis. It has been discussed how mushroom polysaccharides have antioxidant qualities and how their antioxidant mechanisms work. It has been underlined that the advantageous characteristics of the present must be extended to the pandemic scenario. The use of mushrooms as a complementary therapy for COVID-19 is yet not well studied. This review addresses the gaps in this field of study and identifies issues that require more investigation and impact of AI for drug suggestion and properties. When the polysaccharide is applied *in vivo* to H22 malignant ascites tumor cells, it clearly causes cytokines to rise and pro-survival proteins to decrease in the tumor cells. This ultimately lengthens the mice's survival time. In conjunction with *in vivo* findings, the polysaccharide exhibits in cancer cell lines an upregulation of pro-apoptotic genes and a downregulation of anti-apoptotic proteins. Thus, our research suggests that Pleurotus ostreatus polysaccharide may be a great candidate for a more successful hepatocellular cancer treatment. Furthermore, employing current statistical and bioinformatics techniques, high-quality, long-term, randomized, double-blind, and placebo-controlled human clinical investigations are required, which is made possible by AI. These studies must have large sample numbers and adequate power. It would be ideal to conduct more research to determine using AI, which mushroom extracts or components work best for a given form of cancer.

References

1. Cao, Y., Xu, X., Liu, S., Huang, L., Gu, J., Ganoderma: A Cancer Immunotherapy Review. *Front. Pharmacol.*, 9, 1217, 2018, doi: 10.3389/fphar.2018. 01217.
2. Chen, X.J., Han, L.F., Wu, X.G., Wei, W.F., Wu, L.F., Yi, H.Y., Clinical Significance of CD163+ and CD68+ Tumor-Associated Macrophages in High-Risk HPV-Related Cervical Cancer. *J. Cancer*, 8, 18, 3868–3875, 2017, doi: 10.7150/jca.21444.
3. Das, S., Shukla, N., Singh, S.S., Kushwaha, S., Shrivastava, R., Mechanism of Interaction between Autophagy and Apoptosis in Cancer. *Apoptosis*, 26, 9-10, 512–533, 2021, doi: 10.1007/s10495-021-01687-9.
4. de Camargo, M.R., Frazon, T.F., Inacio, K.K., Smiderle, F.R., Amôr, N.G., Dionísio, T.J., Ganoderma Lucidum Polysaccharides Inhibit *In Vitro* Tumorigenesis, Cancer Stem Cell Properties and Epithelial-Mesenchymal Transition in Oral Squamous Cell Carcinoma. *J. Ethnopharmacol.*, 286, 114891, 2022, doi: 10.1016/j.jep.2021.114891.

5. Ferreira, I.C., Heleno, S.A., Reis, F.S., Stojkovic, D., Queiroz, M.J., Vasconcelos, M.H., Chemical Features of Ganoderma Polysaccharides with Antioxidant, Antitumor and Antimicrobial Activities. *Phytochemistry*, 114, 38–55, 2015, doi: 10.1016/j.phytochem.2014.10.011.
6. Guo, H., Deng, H., Liu, H., Jian, Z., Cui, H., Fang, J., Nickel Carcinogenesis Mechanism: Cell Cycle Dysregulation. *Environ. Sci. Pollut. Res. Int.*, 28, 5, 4893–4901, 2021b, doi: 10.1007/s11356-020-11764-2.
7. Hanyu, X., Lanyue, L., Miao, D., Wentao, F., Cangran, C., Hui, S., Effect of Ganoderma Applanatum Polysaccharides on MAPK/ERK Pathway Affecting Autophagy in Breast Cancer MCF-7 Cells. *Int. J. Biol. Macromol.*, 146, 353–362, 2020, doi: 10.1016/j.ijbiomac.2020.01.010.
8. Hsu, W.H., Hua, W.J., Qiu, W.L., Tseng, A.J., Cheng, H.C., Lin, T.Y., WSG, a Glucose-Enriched Polysaccharide from Ganoderma Lucidum, Suppresses Tongue Cancer Cells via Inhibition of EGFR-Mediated Signaling and Potentiates Cisplatin-Induced Apoptosis. *Int. J. Biol. Macromol.*, 193, Pt B, 1201–1208, 2021, doi: 10.1016/j.ijbiomac.2021.10.146.
9. Hu, S., Huang, J., Pei, S., Ouyang, Y., Ding, Y., Jiang, L., Ganoderma Lucidum Polysaccharide Inhibits UVB-Induced Melanogenesis by Antagonizing cAMP/PKA and ROS/MAPK Signaling Pathways. *J. Cell. Physiol.*, 234, 5, 7330–7340, 2019, doi: 10.1002/jcp.27492.
10. Kumar, S.A., Kumar, A., Dutt, V., Agrawal, R., Multi Model Implementation on General Medicine Prediction with Quantum Neural Networks, in: *2021 Third International Conference on Intelligent Communication Technologies and Virtual Mobile Networks (ICICV)*, Tirunelveli, India, pp. 1391–1395, 2021, doi: 10.1109/ICICV50876.2021.9388575.
11. Raj, P., Dubey, A.K., Kumar, A., Rathore, P.S., *Blockchain, Artificial Intelligence, and the Internet of Things*, Springer International Publishing, Springer International Publishing, Cham, Switzerland, 2022.
12. Burri, S.R., Kumar, A., Baliyan, A., Kumar, T.A., Predictive Intelligence for Healthcare Outcomes: An AI Architecture Overview, in: *2023 2nd International Conference on Smart Technologies and Systems for Next Generation Computing (ICSTSN)*, Villupuram, India, pp. 1–6, 2023, doi: 10.1109/ICSTSN57873.2023.10151477.
13. Wani, S., Ahuja, S., Kumar, A., Application of Deep Neural Networks and Machine Learning algorithms for diagnosis of Brain tumour, in: *2023 International Conference on Computational Intelligence and Sustainable Engineering Solutions (CISES)*, Greater Noida, India, pp. 106–111, 2023, doi: 10.1109/CISES58720.2023.10183528.
14. Kour, S.P., Kumar, A., Ahuja, S., An Advance Approach for Diabetes Detection by Implementing Machine Learning Algorithms, in: *2023 IEEE World Conference on Applied Intelligence and Computing (AIC)*, Sonbhadra, India, pp. 136–141, 2023, doi: 10.1109/AIC57670.2023.10263919.
15. Raj, P., Kumar, A., Dubey, A.K., Bhatia, S., Oswalt, M.S., *Quantum Computing and Artificial Intelligence: Training Machine and Deep Learning Algorithms on*

Quantum Computers, De Gruyter, Berlin, Boston, 2023, [Online], Available: https://doi.org/10.1515/9783110791402.

16. Sasubilli, G. and Kumar, A., Machine Learning and Big Data Implementation on Health Care data, in: *2020 4th International Conference on Intelligent Computing and Control Systems (ICICCS)*, Madurai, India, pp. 859–864, 2020, doi: 10.1109/ICICCS48265.2020.9120906.
17. Swarna, S.R., Kumar, A., Dixit, P., Sairam, T.V.M., Parkinson's Disease Prediction using Adaptive Quantum Computing, in: *2021 Third International Conference on Intelligent Communication Technologies and Virtual Mobile Networks (ICICV)*, Tirunelveli, India, pp. 1396–1401, 2021, doi: 10.1109/ICICV50876.2021.9388628.
18. Burugadda, V.R., Pawar, P.S., Kumar, A., Bhati, N., Predicting Hospital Readmission Risk for Heart Failure Patients Using Machine Learning Techniques: A Comparative Study of Classification Algorithms, in: *2023 Second International Conference on Trends in Electrical, Electronics, and Computer Engineering (TEECCON)*, Bangalore, India, pp. 223–228, 2023, doi: 10.1109/TEECCON59234.2023.10335817.
19. Rice, P.J., Lockhart, B.E., Barker, L.A., Adams, E.L., Ensley, H.E., Williams, D.L., Pharmacokinetics of Fungal (1-3)-Beta-D-Glucans Following Intravenous Administration in Rats. *Int. Immunopharmacol.*, 4, 9, 1209–1215, 2004, doi: 10.1016/j.intimp.2004.05.013.
20. Su, J., Li, D., Chen, Q., Li, M., Su, L., Luo, T., Anti-breast Cancer Enhancement of a Polysaccharide from Spore of Ganoderma Lucidum with Paclitaxel: Suppression on Tumor Metabolism with Gut Microbiota Reshaping. *Front. Microbiol.*, 9, 3099, 2018, doi: 10.3389/fmicb.2018.03099.
21. Vetvicka, V., Dvorak, B., Vetvickova, J., Richter, J., Krizan, J., Sima, P., Orally Administered Marine (1->3)Bbeta-DGglucan Phycarine Stimulates Both Humoral and Cellular Immunity. *Int. J. Biol. Macromol.*, 40, 4, 291–298, 2007, doi: 10.1016/j.ijbiomac.2006.08.009.
22. Vivarelli, S., Salemi, R., Candido, S., Falzone, L., Santagati, M., Stefani, S., Gut Microbiota and Cancer: From Pathogenesis to Therapy. *Cancers (Basel)*, 11, 1, 38, 2019, doi: 10.3390/cancers11010038.
23. Wang, J., Cao, B., Zhao, H., Feng, J., Emerging Roles of Ganoderma Lucidum in Anti-aging. *Aging Dis.*, 8, 6, 691–707, 2017a, doi: 10.14336/AD.2017.0410.
24. Wang, S., Awad, K.S., Elinoff, J.M., Dougherty, E.J., Ferreyra, G.A., Wang, J.Y., G Protein-Coupled Receptor 40 (GPR40) and Peroxisome Proliferator-Activated Receptor γ (PPARγ): AN INTEGRATED TWO- RECEPTOR SIGNALING PATHWAY. *J. Biol. Chem.*, 290, 32, 19544–19557, 2015, doi: 10.1074/jbc.M115.638924.
25. Wen, L., Sheng, Z., Wang, J., Jiang, Y., Yang, B., Structure of Water- Soluble Polysaccharides in Spore of Ganoderma Lucidum and Their Anti- inflammatory Activity. *Food Chem.*, 373, Pt A, 131374, 2022, doi: 10.1016/j.foodchem.2021.131374.

26. Wilson, I.D. and Nicholson, J.K., Gut Microbiome Interactions with Drug Metabolism, Efficacy, and Toxicity. *Transl. Res.*, 179, 204–222, 2017, doi: 10.1016/j.trsl. 2016.08.002.
27. Winska, K., Maczka, W., Gabryelska, K., Grabarczyk, M., Mushrooms of the Genus Ganoderma Used to Treat Diabetes and Insulin Resistance. *Molecules*, 24, 22, 4075, 2019, doi: 10.3390/molecules24224075.
28. Wu, A.H., Tseng, C., Vigen, C., Yu, Y., Cozen, W., Garcia, A.A., Gut Microbiome Associations with Breast Cancer Risk Factors and Tumor Characteristics: a Pilot Study. *Breast Cancer Res. Treat.*, 182, 2, 451–463, 2020, doi: 10.1007/s10549-020-05702-6.
29. Wu, K., Na, K., Chen, D., Wang, Y., Pan, H., Wang, X., Effects of Non-steroidal Anti-inflammatory Drug-Activated Gene-1 on Ganoderma Lucidum Polysaccharides-Induced Apoptosis of Human Prostate Cancer PC-3 Cells. *Int. J. Oncol.*, 53, 6, 2356–2368, 2018, doi: 10.3892/ijo.2018.4578.
30. Zeng, X., Li, P., Chen, X., Kang, Y., Xie, Y., Li, X., Effects of Deproteinization Methods on Primary Structure and Antioxidant Activity of Ganoderma Lucidum Polysaccharides. *Int. J. Biol. Macromol.*, 126, 867–876, 2019, doi: 10.1016/j.ijbiomac.2018.12.222.
31. Zhang, Y., Ding, C., Zhu, W., Li, X., Chen, T., Liu, Q., Chemotherapeutic Drugs Induce Oxidative Stress Associated with DNA Repair and Metabolism Modulation. *Life Sci.*, 289, 120242, 2022, doi: 10.1016/j.lfs.2021.120242.
32. Rai, S.N., Mishra, D., Singh, P., Vamanu, E., Singh, M.P., Therapeutic applications of mushrooms and their biomolecules along with a glimpse of in silico approach in neurodegenerative diseases. *Biomed. Pharmacother.*, 137, 111377, 2021, ISSN 0753-3322, https://doi.org/10.1016/j.biopha.2021.111377. (https://www.sciencedirect.com/science/article/pii/S0753332221001621).
33. Chun, S., Gopal, J., Muthu, M., Antioxidant Activity of Mushroom Extracts/ Polysaccharides—Their Antiviral Properties and Plausible AntiCOVID-19 Properties. *Antioxidants*, 10, 1899, 2021, https://doi.org/10.3390/antiox10121899.
34. Panda, S.K., Sahoo, G., Swain, S.S., Luyten, W., Anticancer Activities of Mushrooms: A Neglected Source for Drug Discovery. *Pharmaceuticals (Basel)*, 15, 2, 176, 2022 Jan 31, doi: 10.3390/ph15020176. PMID: 35215289; PMCID: PMC8876642.
35. Xu, J., Shen, R., Jiao, Z., Chen, W., Peng, D., Wang, L., Yu, N., Peng, C., Cai, B., Song, H., Chen, F., Liu, B., Current Advancements in Antitumor Properties and Mechanisms of Medicinal Components in Edible Mushrooms. *Nutrients*, 14, 1–23, 2022, 10.3390/nu14132622.
36. Alzorqi, I., Sudheer, S., Lu, T.J., Manickam, S., Ultrasonically extracted β-D-glucan from artificially cultivated mushroom, characteristic properties and antioxidant activity. *Ultrason. Sonochem.*, 35, 531–540, 2016.
37. Yang, F., Darsey, J.A., Ghosh, A., Li, H.-Y., Yang, M.Q., Wang, S., Artificial intelligence and cancer drug development. *Recent Pat. Anti-Cancer Drug Discov.*, 16, 471–485, 2021, doi: 10.2174/1574892816666210728123758.

11

Impact of Artificial Intelligence (AI) in Bioremediation of Dairy Effluent by Microalgae and the Potential Application of the Produced Lipid Byproducts

Nisha Dhillon, Vivek Kumar, Geeta Bhandari and Sanjay Gupta*

Himalayan School of Biosciences, Swami Rama Himalayan University, Jolly Grant, Dehradun, India

Abstract

In addition to being an excellent creator of numerous useful organic substances such as lipids, proteins, carbohydrates, pigments, antioxidants, and vitamins, microalgae also serve as bioremediators. Microalgal lipids are among these chemical molecules that have several uses in the fields of medicines, cosmetics, nutraceuticals, human health, and biofuel. The role of microalgae, which offer a promising source for treating dairy effluent and a nutrient supply for biomass production and accumulated lipids in the form of polyunsaturated fatty acids (PUFAs), carotenoids (pigments), oxylipins (oxygenated PUFAs), etc., is covered in this paper, so that the application of artificial intelligence in remediation and its impact for developing microalgae with bioreactors. As in the world of automation, it is necessary to use the technology for advancement of processes for better efficiency. There is a vast commercial application for these chemicals, so it is necessary to know all the factors which impacts dairy business.

Keywords: AI, microalgae, bioreactor, bioremediation, dairy effluent, lipid byproducts

**Corresponding author*: sanjaygupta3453@outlook.com

Abhishek Kumar, Narayan Vyas, Pramod Singh Rathore, Abhineet Anand and Pooja Dixit (eds.) Internet of Medicine for Smart Healthcare, (201–222) © 2025 Scrivener Publishing LLC

11.1 Introduction

In the present scenario, growing globalization causes industrialization to happen quickly in order to meet the need for food and feed. A variety of enterprises have recently grown, consumed large amounts of water, and produced harmful or life-threatening substances that were released into the environment and may have contributed to a number of dangerous diseases. Although industries play a vital role in the economy, the negative effects of growing industrialization on the environment have made them a major source of concern. Various businesses generate distinct kinds of wastewater; one such industry is the dairy sector, which generates copious amounts of waste water in the form of potent contaminants. The loss of dissolved oxygen in raw dairy wastewater that is discharged directly into the environment is one of the biggest issues. Due to the oil and fat molecules found in dairy effluents, a superficial layer is formed on the water's surface that obstructs oxygen transport and makes it harder for the local flora and fauna to survive. Safely disposing the wastewater generated by the dairy sector, which consumes a lot of water, becomes significant concern [1–5].

Making decisions using AI to enhance system performance can benefit from an understanding of how membrane photobioreactors (MPBRs) will behave in terms of fouling propensity and nutrient removal efficiency. For this, a methodical optimization and prediction tool is needed. Recently, numerous modeling scenarios under varied operating settings have been examined, and machine learning models have been employed to forecast the nutrient removal effectiveness of MBRs in treating waste water. Similarly, the quality of source water can be predicted, together with the efficiency of membrane filtration and membrane fouling, using artificial intelligence (AI) approaches that can model real-time concerns containing intricacies of puzzling situations [6–12].

11.1.1 Type of Wastes While Dairy Processing

The primary cause of the environmental hazards is the dairy wastewater. The most prevalent forms of effluents produced by dairy processors include organic waste and suspended particles, as well as high levels of nitrogen and phosphorus and molecules containing oil and fat, including grease. In addition, they could include cleaning product remnants from cleaning tools and utensils. According to their origin and composition, dairy effluents can be categorized into the following three types: a) "processing water," b) "cleaning wastewater," and c) "sanitary wastewater" [13–16].

A) **Processing water:** Dairy products can results in the form of wastes from milk fermentation processing, which may be applied to the creation of different dairy products, including cheese whey concentrations.
B) **Cleaning waste water:** This usually came from washed equipment such as tanker washing, refrigeration point, floor washing, and boiler house, which is in direct contact with milk or dairy products. It includes milk and whey spillage, operational errors, and equipment malfunction.
C) **Sanitary waste water:** It originates in shower rooms, labs, etc. Sanitary wastewater is often routed straight to sewage works and has a composition comparable to that of wastewater from cities. Dairy products processing result in huge amount of chemically modified liquid waste, which need a high consumption of water. These are highly polluted waste, thus requiring proper treatment before discharge. These leftovers can be efficiently used as raw materials to produce energy or other industrial goods [17–22].

The highest returns on investments for downstream processing will be ensured, regardless of the method of producing the biomass, if it can be carried out in integrated bio refineries that maximizes the numeral of product and co-product that can be extracted and produces the least amount of residues. Industry 4.0 is a cutting-edge manufacturing strategy built on machine-to-machine [or "Internet of Things" (IoT)] communication technologies. Automations, sensor, and machine learning combine to create self-adapting manufacturing processes that can instantly adapt to changes in the process. This implies that, in a microalgal biorefinery, the operator may led to monitors the production and evolution of the algae in real time by utilizing a network of plug-and-play IoT sensors, in addition to automating the algal cultivation and harvesting system to lower operating costs. By using sensor data to create a digital twin, or simulation, of the facility and the algae culture, Industry 4.0 takes its concept a step further. The simulation has the ability to predict future cellular yield in real time and modify operations to minimize waste and satisfy anticipated product demand [23–27].

11.1.2 Technologies Used for the Treatment of Dairy Effluent

Dairy waste can be treated using a variety of technologies before being released into the surrounding environment or natural habitat. Essentially, there are two methods for treating dairy waste:

- **(i) Physicochemical Treatment**
- **(ii) Biological Treatment**

Dairy wastewater is treated using a variety of physicochemical techniques, including membrane bioreactors, chemical precipitation, coagulation, coagulation/flocculation, adsorption, electrocoagulation, and electroflocculation. The use of physicochemical treatments has a number of drawbacks, including increased expense, the production of secondary pollutants, the use of chemical reagents that only provide partial treatment, and more [28–34].

11.2 Microalgae

Microalgae, which include diatoms, dinoflagellates, blue green algae, and green algae, are minute, unicellular, and eukaryotic microorganisms. They can live as a consortium as a group or as an autonomous colony. Microalgae are a diversified collection of aquatic organisms with a high productivity that may effectively remove pollutants and create lipids with a lot of potential [35].

11.3 Lipid-Producing Microalgal Strains

The fatty acid contents of numerous microalgal species—roughly 20%–50% of dry biomass, including lipid components—have been examined. Certain classes of polar and non-polar lipids have been found to be present in some microalgae, including species of Nannochloropsis, Neochloris, Chlorella, Dunaliella, Crypthecodinium, Chlamydomonas reinharditi, Cylindrotheca, Isochrysis, Nannochloris, Nitzschia, Schizochytrium, Phaeodactylum, Porphyridium, and Tetraselmis. Microalgae have been found to include polar lipids such as glycosylglycerides, phosphoglycerides, and sphingolipids, as well as nonpolar or neutral lipids such as sterols, free fatty acids, and acylglycerols. Table 11.1 shows the clssification of microalgar on the basics of theire pigment and reserve food and Table 11.2 shows the list of some lipid-containing microalgal species.

Table 11.1 Classification of microalgae based on their pigment and reserve food [3].

Class	Photosynthetic pigments	Reserve food material	Representative genera
Chlorophyceae (Green Algae)	Chlorophyll a and b and carotene	Starch	*Chlorella* sp., *Heamatococcuspluvialis*, and *Dunalialla salina*
Xanthophyceae (Heterokont or Yellow Green Algae)	Chlorophyll a and c, b- carotene, and xanthophylls	Fats and leucosin	*Chlorochromonas*, *Chlorosuccus*, *Vaucheria*, *Tribonema*, and *Botrydinum*
Chrysophyceae (Yellow-Brown Algae)	Chlorophyll a and b and carotenoids	Oils and leucosin	*Ochromonas*, *Dinobryon*, *Mallormonas*, *Synura*, and *Rhizochrysis*
Bacillariophyceae (Diatoms)	Cholorophyll a and c and carotenes	Leucosin and fats	*Cyclotella*, *Rutelaria*, *Corethron*, *Navicula*, and *Bacillaria*
Cryptophyceae	Chlorophyll a, b-carotenes, and xanthophylls	Starch	*Falcomonas*, *Rhinomonas*, *Plagioselis*, *Chilomonas*, and *Cryptomonas*
Dinophyceae (Dinoflagellates)	Chlorophyll a and c Carotenoids, and Xanthophylls	Starch and oil	*Dinophysis*, *Polykrikos*, *Gonyaulax*, and *Gymnodinium*

(Continued)

Table 11.1 Classification of microalgae based on their pigment and reserve food [3]. (*Continued*)

Class	Photosynthetic Pigments	Reserve Food Material	Representative Genera
Chloromonodiae (Raphidophytes)	Chlorophyll a, b-carotenes, and xanthophylls	Oils	*Vacuolaria*
Euglenophyceae (Phototrophic-Euglenids)	Chlorophyll a and b	Fats nd paramylon	*Euglena*
Phaeophyceae (Brown Algae)	Chlorophyll a and xanthophylls	Laminarin, mannitol, and fats	*Pelagophycus*, *Laminaria*, *Pelvetia*, and *Sargassum*
Rhodophyceae (Red Algae)	Chlorophyll a, phycocyanin, and phycoerythrin	Floridian starch	*Vacuolaria*, *Gomyostomum*, *Chattonella*, and *Psammamonas*
Myxophyceae (Blue-Green Algae)	Chlorophyll a, b- carotene, c-phycocyanin, and phycoerythrin	Glycoproteins and droplets of oil	*Chloroccus*, *Darmocarpa*, *Pleurocaspa*, *Oscillatoria*, and *Stigonema*

Table 11.2 Some lipid-containing microalgal species [7–18].

S. no.	Name of microalgae species	Lipid contents (% dry weight)	References
1.	*Botryococcusbraunii*	25%–45%	Lee *et al.* (2015)
2.	*Schizochytrium* sp.	30%–60%	Yokoyama and Honda (2007) [36]
3.	*Neochlorisoleoabundans*	25%–44%	Provost *et al.* (2009) and Breurer *et al.* (2012)
4.	*Nannochloropsis* sp.	31%–68%	Ma *et al.* (2016)
5.	*Nitzschia* sp.	45%–47%	Jiang *et al.* (2014)
6.	*Chlorella* sp.	35%–58%	Ghosh *et al.* (2017)
7.	*Scenedesmus* sp.	40%–68%	Kumar *et al.* (2021)
8.	*Chlococcum* sp.	40%–67%	Mahapatra and Ramachandra (2013)
9.	*Cylindrotheca* sp.	20%–35%	Demirel *et al.* (2015)
10.	*Dunaliella* sp.	36%–47%	Gharajeh *et al.* (2020)
11.	*Chlamydomonas reinharditi*	55%–65%	Xu *et al.* (2018)

11.4 Biosynthesis of Lipid in Microalgae

The presence of chlorophyll pigments and other metabolic processes for photosynthetic activity are characteristics of green microalgae that are similar to those of plant. They often synthesize triacylglycerols and free fatty acids, also known as neutral fatty acids. Whereas triacylgylcerols are produced in the smooth endoplasmic reticulum, neutral fatty acids are produced in the chloroplast. Fatty acid with 14–20 carbon chains are used to make biofuel, and long chains with 20 or more carbons are used in the food business (Jacob-Lopes *et al.*, 2015). Triacylglycerides, or oil droplets, are the kind of lipids that microalgae make and store in huge quantities within their many cell organelles. The way lipid content is converted and accumulates depends on the microalgal strains and cultural conditions (Radakovits *et al.*, 2010).

"ACCase, Acetyl-CoA carboxylase; ACP, acyl carrier protein; DHAP, dihydroxyacetone phosphate; ENR, enoyl-ACP reductase; FAT, fatty acyl transferase; G3PDH, gycerol-3-phosphate dehydrogenase; GPAT, glycerol-3-phosphate acyltransferase; HD, three-hydroxyacyl-ACP dehydratase; KAR, three-ketoacyl-ACP reductase; KAS, three-ketoacyl-ACP synthase; MAT, malonyl-CoA; ACP, transacylase; PDH, pyruvate dehydrogenase

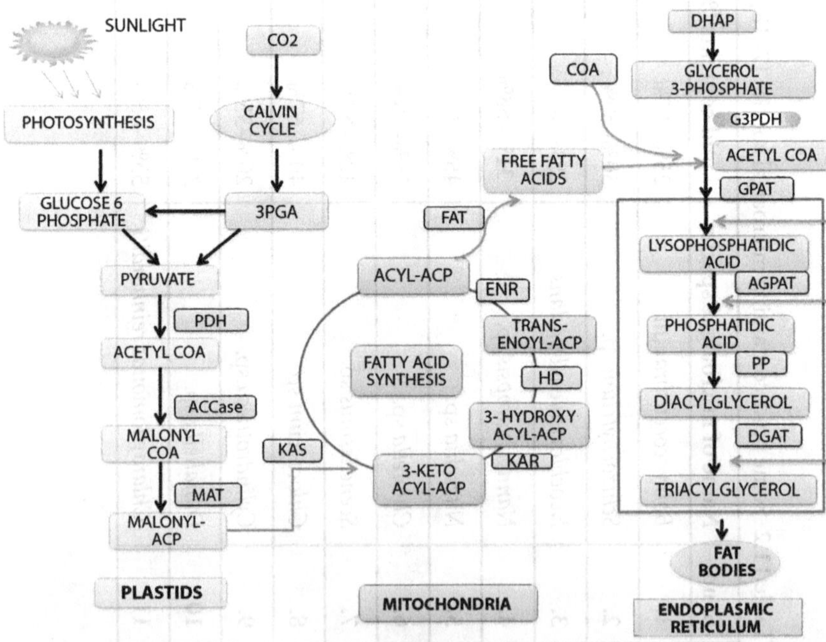

Figure 11.1 Biosynthesis of lipids in microalgae [20].

complex; PP, phosphatidic acid phosphatise; TAG, triacylglycerols." Figure 11.1 shows biosynthesis of lipids in microalgae.

In a different study, Chlorella sp. was identified and grown in dairy effluent, which led to increased production of algal biomass and a respectable amount of lipid. Because it had enough time to acclimate to the waste water, the microalga Chlorella sp. showed good growth on dairy waste water with high biochemical oxygen demand (BOD) and chemical oxygen demand (COD), trace elements, and other nutrients [3]. In a different study, the dairy effluent significantly increased the productivity of fat, carbs, and protein while also being effective in promoting the growth of Chlorella vulgaris and Anabaena ambigua. In BG11 media, both cultures were maximized. Compared to Anabaena ambigua, which has a high protein content, Chlorella vulgaris was shown to have a higher lipid and carbohydrate content. Both algae eliminated phosphates and ammonium nitrates nearly entirely. According to the present study, there was a noteworthy reduction in both COD and BOD, suggesting that algae are capable of eliminating contaminants [24]. According to Saud, Spirulina sp. is a promising biological treatment option because its results demonstrate a decrease in the amounts of nutrients including nitrate, phosphate, and sulfate found in wastewater. Alkalinity, chloride, COD, TDS, total hardness, and magnesium and calcium hardness are also decreased. The algae's documented capacity to eliminate 81% of nitrate, 72% of active phosphorus, and 61% of sulfate demonstrates its effectiveness in improving water quality and reducing pollutants.

Additionally, it was observed that Chlorococcum sp. RAP13 cultivated in dairy effluent produced a significant amount of lipids and biological mass, especially when grown in heterotrophic conditions with the addition of glycerol from the biodiesel industry waste. The microalgal cells displayed variations in lipid levels, fatty acid profiles, and growth properties. This discrepancy resulted from changes in the growing environment and carbon sources. Conditions of heterotrophic culture led to an expressive increase in biomass and lipid production. The microalga is a good contender for producing biodiesel because of its increased lipid synthesis. Furthermore, the quality of the dairy effluent was enhanced in terms of BOD and COD by the use of microalgae as the sources of carbon and energy [31].

Wastewater from dairy farms may be used as source of nutrient for the growth of algae. They found that, on the 10th and 15th days, respectively, there was a significant reduction in phosphate (96%) and nitrogen (90%) when Chlamydomonas polypyrenoideum was grown on dairy wastewater. They discovered that the main causes of eutrophications in any body of water were phosphate and nitrogen. Following treatment for 10 days, the microalgae biomass showed 42% (w/w) lipid contents; as a result, it was thought to be a likely biological oil source. This biomass was similar to the bio-oil derived from other natural resources, as the fourier transform infrared spectroscopy (FTIR) findings analysis made clear. These results suggested using microalgae to produce biodiesel and perform phyco-remediation on dairy effluent [11].

According to Msanne, when exposed to salt stress or nitrogen constraint, green alga Chlamydomonas reinhardtii gathers a notable amount of triacylglycerols in culture medium containing acetate. There was also a discernible decline in the amount of protein and chlorophyll, as well as reductions in ribosomal polypeptide and essential enzyme for the assimilations of carbon dioxide, including ribulose-1 and 5-bisphosphate carboxylase/oxygenase. These findings suggested that the production of triacylglycerols in nutritionally depleted cells could be facilitated by the throughput of N-rich complexes, such as proteins, which could provide both carbon and energy [19].

Pei Sean Goh *et al.* [37] proposed that the circular bioeconomy, which incorporates waste resource usage and ecosystem conservation, is addressed by the use of microalgae for wastewater remediations and nutrients recovery. One potential solution to the problems of water and energy source depletion is the combinations of microalgae farming with wastewater treatments. In particular, the treatment of wastewater with microalgae presents a chance to carry out wastewater cleanup and important biomass production at the same time. Membrane-based technologies are gaining popularity as a flexible solution for microalgae-based wastewater treatment integration. A study of the literature and a discussion of current developments and successes in the field of MPBR for the treatment of wastewater and the recovery of nutrients are provided in this review. The potential of treating wastewater utilizing microalgae as a fascinating solution to handle very nutrient-rich effluents is investigated. An assessment is conducted on the advancements in membrane photobioreactor design and performance.

Michele Fabris *et al.* [38] proposed that, for thousands of years, people have understood the importance of terrestrial plants as sustainable supplies of food, medicine, and building materials. Agricultural practices have undergone constant improvement and modification throughout human history to adapt to the shifting demands of civilization. Given the current industrial and agricultural techniques' practical constraints and grave environmental concerns, our fast expanding population demands even more innovation. A varied class of unicellular photosynthetic organisms known as microalgae are gaining traction as next-generation resources that could meet pressing needs in agriculture and industry. Algae possess a wide range of biological variability that can be utilized to generate a variety of useful bioproducts through natural processes or genetic modification. They talk about how cutting-edge technologies like synthetic biology, high-throughput phenomics, and the automation of the IoT can improve our knowledge of algal biology and eventually propel the development of an algal-based bioeconomy.

Ummalyma SB *et al.* [39] proposed that microalgae are known to be cell factories rich in biochemicals that can be used as feedstock for applications including medicines, nutraceuticals, food, feed, and bioenergy. Microalgae applications in industry face difficulties because of issues with bulk cultivation and biomass recovery. Given the anticipated rise in freshwater needs over the next several years, scaling up the production of microalgal biomass in freshwater is not a viable strategy. Recently, the growing of microalgae in wastewater has been promoted as a sustainable bioeconomy derived from biorefinery operations. It is well known that microalgae are cell factories rich in biochemicals that can be used as feedstock for applications including bioenergy, food, feed, pharmaceuticals, and nutraceuticals. The difficulties involved in bulk cultivation and biomass recovery make the industrial use of microalgae difficult. For the generation of microalgal biomass, food industry wastewater is a less harmful growing medium.

Asmaa Salah *et al.* [40] proposed that large volumes of liquid waste, with a high concentration of nutrients, are produced by agricultural companies. A sustainable solution for greener future is required in light of the significant population growth, pollution, and climate change that contribute to the loss of fresh water resources. By returning water for irrigating crops, wastewater treatment using microalgae can partially alleviate the issue. Algal cultures fed 15% cell wall (CW) enhanced with 50% Bold's Basal Medium (BBM) showed a strong reaction. Conversely, BBM had greater protein and photosynthetic pigment (carotenoids, chlorophyll a, and chlorophyll b) concentrations than any other treatment. The analysis of fatty acid composition revealed that the most abundant fatty acids were linoleic acid (13.22%), oleic acid (35.31%), and palmitic acid (25.86%). In conclusion, when grown on CW, Desmodesmus sp. can be a good option for phycoremediation, while it can cut the water and nutrition requirements of algal culture by 15% and 50%, respectively. As such, it might be a useful tactic for producing large amounts of algae in sustainable farming systems.

11.5 Applications of Microalgal Lipids

Lipids, high-density lipoproteins, oxylipins, carotenoids, proteins, carbohydrates, and other nutrients are abundant in microalgae. With yields

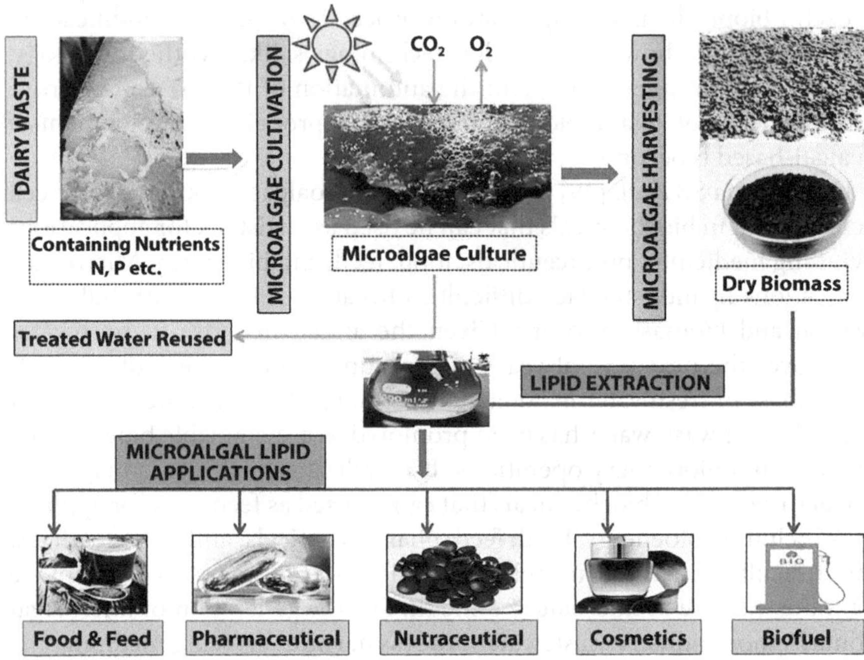

Figure 11.2 Production and applications of microalgal lipids [7].

ranging from 25% to 75% of their total lipids, many microalgal strains are capable of synthesizing long chain fatty acids. PUFAs are now produced using a variety of microalgae, including seawater microalgae like Thraustochytriacea sp. and Crythecodiniacea sp. and freshwater microalgae like Chlorella sp. and Scenedesmus sp. Figure 11.2 shows the production and applications of microalgal lipids.

Microalgae strains possess remarkable plasticity, enabling them to endure harsh environmental circumstances while yet harboring immense potential for yielding multiple beneficial outputs. Because they produce a wide range of lipids with remarkable applications in industries like food and feed manufacturing, biofuel production, cosmetics, and pharmaceuticals, microalgal species are now regarded as lipid biofactories.

11.5.1 In Food and Nutrition

The benefits of polyunsaturated fatty acids (PUFAs) on human health have long been recognized. Fish oil used to be the main source of PUFAs. However, given the present constraints (environmental dangers), the commercial production of PUFA from fish source is declining. Microalgae have recently

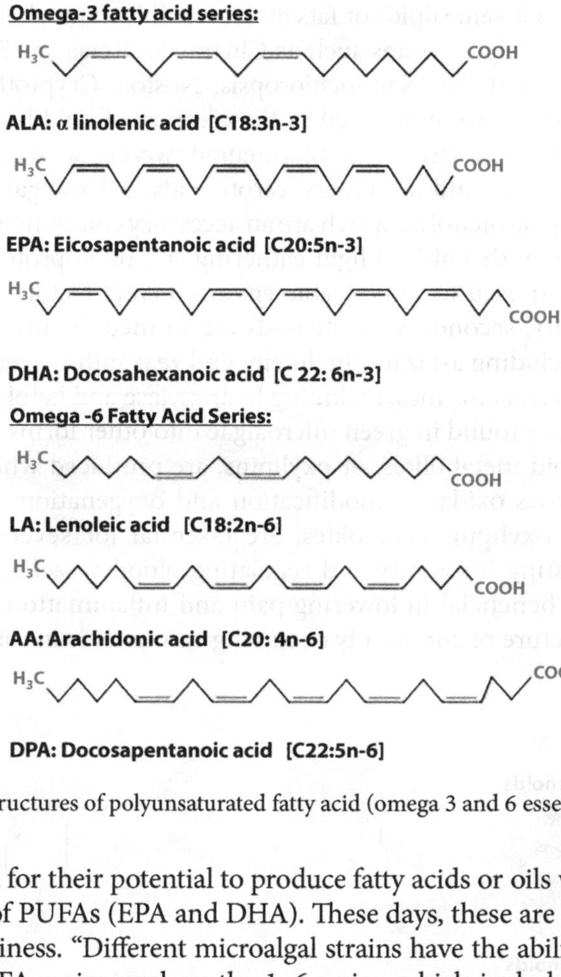

Figure 11.3 Structures of polyunsaturated fatty acid (omega 3 and 6 essential fatty acid).

been studied for their potential to produce fatty acids or oils with high concentrations of PUFAs (EPA and DHA). These days, these are widely used in the food business. "Different microalgal strains have the ability to combine different PUFA series, such as the 1–6 series, which includes linoleic acid (LA) and arachidonic acid (ARA), and the 1–3 series, which includes linolenic acid (ALA), eicosapentaenoic acid (EPA), and docosahexaenoic acid (DHA)." These fatty acids' carbon skeleton contains one or more double bonds. They are valuable components for food and feed additives and offer numerous health advantages. They are valuable components for food and feed additives and offer numerous health advantages. Figure 11.3 shows the structures of polyunsaturated fatty acid (omega 3 and 6 essential fatty acid).

11.5.2 In the Field of Pharmaceuticals

Numerous microalgal species produce high-value lipids that are used in pharmaceutical applications. It has been thought of as an emerging field to produce these high value lipids or fats molecules (bioactive chemicals) from microalgae. Microalgae strains such as Chlamydomonas sp., Spirulina sp., Chlorella sp., Dunaliella, Nannochloropsis, Nostoc, Cryptothecodinium, and Haematococcus were involved in the creation of lipid bioactive compounds or carotenoids. Two types of carotenoids were created by microalgae: primary carotenoids and secondary carotenoids. Microalgal membranes include primary carotenoids, which are an accessory component of the photosynthetic system that aids in light gathering and photoprotection. When algal cells are exposed to unfavorable environmental factors such intense light and salinity, secondary carotenoids are formed. Numerous types of carotenoids, including astazanthin, lutein, and zeaxanthin, were created by microalgae. Several enzymes, including hydroxylase and ketolase, can convert beta carotene found in green microalgae into other forms.

Oxidized lipid metabolites, or oxylipins, are produced when a class of PUFAs undergoes oxidative modification and oxygenation. Lipid mediators, such as oxylipin metabolites, are essential for several functions, including boosting immunity and regulating blood vessel vascular tone. These are also beneficial in lowering pain and inflammation. Figure 11.4 shows the structure of commonly occurring carotenoids in microalgae.

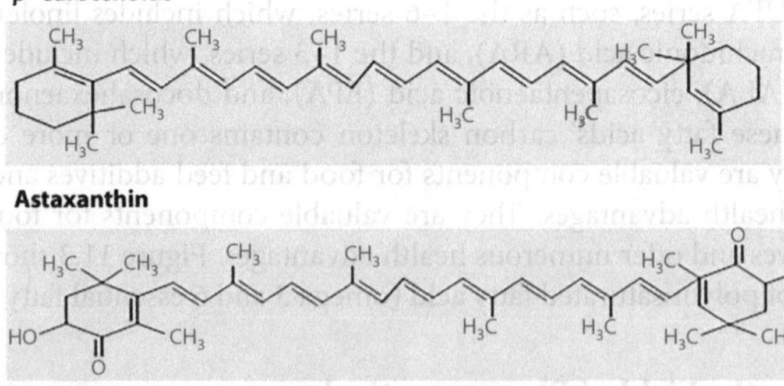

Figure 11.4 Structure of commonly occurring carotenoids in microalgae.

11.5.3 In the Field of Biofuel

The potential exists for the microalgal biomass to produce a variety of biofuels, including biodiesel through the transesterification of fatty acids, biogas through gasification or anaerobic digestion, bioethanol through the direct fermentation of the microalgae's carbohydrate fraction, and methane gas through the anaerobic fermentation of microalgal biomass.

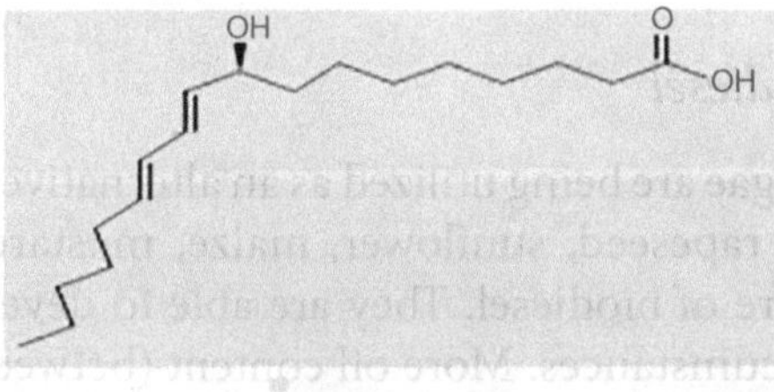

(a) (9-HODE)9-Hydroxyoctadecadienoic Acid(α-Linolenic acid) 18C Poly unsaturated fatty acids

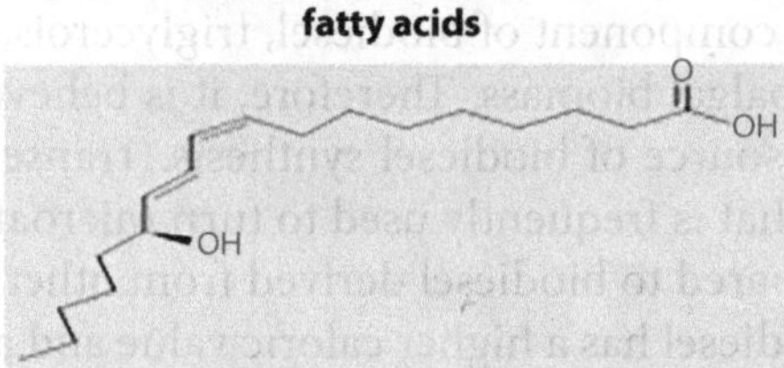

(b) (13-HODE) 13- Hydroxxoctadecadienoic Acid(Linoleic acid) 18CPoly unsaturated fatty acids

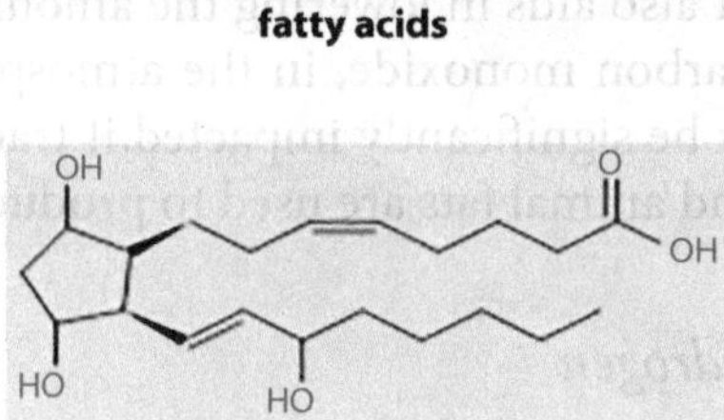

(c) prostaglandins (PGE2)

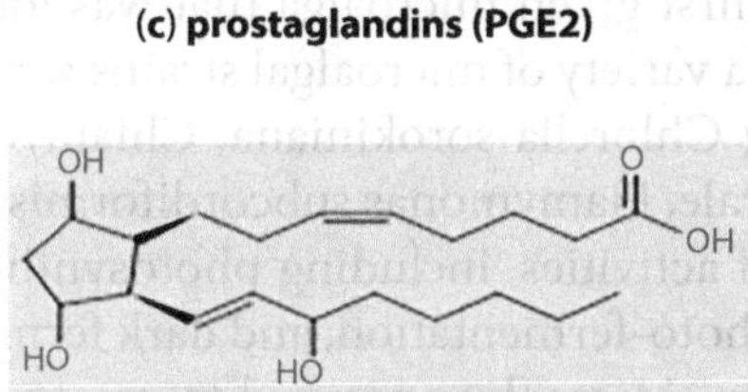

(d) Prostaglandins (PGF3α)

Figure 11.5 Structure of commonly occurring oxylipins (oxidized PUFA) in microalgae: (a) 9-hydroxyoctadecadienoic acid (linolenic acid) 18C; (b) 13- hydroxyoctadecadienoic acid (linoleic acid) 18C; (c) prostaglandins (PGE2); and (d) prostaglandins (PGF3α).

An alternative resource that is used to reduce the need of fossil fuels is microalgal lipids. Yields from microalgae farming are far higher than those from any other traditional bioenergy crop. Microalgal lipids can be used to make a wide range of fuels, including methane, biodiesel, biogas, bioethanol, biobutanol, and aircraft fuel (kerosene). Approximately 40%–60% of certain microalgal species, like Schizochytrium sp., Nitzschia sp., and Botyococcus braunii, have a greater lipid content. Figure 11.5 shows the structure of commonly occurring oxylipins (oxidized PUFA) in microalgae.

11.5.3.1 As Biodiesel

Currently, microalgae are being utilized as an alternative to traditional food crops like cotton, rapeseed, sunflower, maize, mustard, and palm seeds for the manufacture of biodiesel. They are able to develop in unfavorable environmental circumstances. More oil content (between 50% and 80% of their dry weight) can be produced by them than by any other conventional crop. The primary component of biodiesel, triglycerols, is present in good quantities in microalgal biomass. Therefore, it is believed that microalgae represent a major source of biodiesel synthesis. Transesterification is one of these methods that is frequently used to turn microalgal lipids into biodiesel. When compared to biodiesel derived from other feedstock sources, the microalgae biodiesel has a higher caloric value and a lower density and viscosity. Because microalgae biodiesel does not include aromatic hydrocarbons or sulfates, it also aids in lowering the amount of suspended contaminants, such as carbon monoxide, in the atmosphere when it ignites. The food supply may be significantly impacted if traditional food sources (oleaginous crops) and animal fats are used to produce biofuel.

11.5.3.2 As Biohydrogen

S. obliquus was the first green microalga that was found to create hydrogen. Following that, a variety of microalgal strains were employed to create hydrogen, including Chlorella sorokiniana, Chlamydomonas reinhardtii, Chlorococcum littorale, Plamymonas subcordiformis, and Chlorella fusca. Through a variety of activities, including photosynthesis, direct and indirect biophotolysis, photo-fermentation, and dark fermentation, microalgae generate biohydrogen. Microalgae are said to create a high concentration of hydrogen when exposed to sunshine, but a low concentration when exposed to darkness. The expression of the hydrogenase enzyme and the presence of components containing sulfur in the growing media are both necessary for microalgae to produce hydrogen. In comparison to other microalgal strains, Chlamydomonas reinhardtii was found to have a high concentration of hydrogenase enzyme—roughly 10 to 100 times higher. However, various technical difficulties prevented this strain's commercial production of biohydrogen from exceeding its capacity. Studies on the freshwater green microalga Chlorella sorokiniana and the marine alga Plasmodius subcordiformis showed that, when they were cultivated in a medium deficient on sulfur, they produced a significant amount of biohydrogen [27].

11.6 Challenges in the Field of Microalgal Biomass Productivity

Numerous obstacles face current research on the production of microalgal biomass. Here are some of these that are mentioned:

(i) To reduce the highest possible amount of organic and inorganic pollutant from wastewater and recycle waste water
(ii) To increase the productivity of outdoor microalgae
(iii) To create a photo reactor that is efficient in order to promote the growth of microalgae's and prevent pollution from the microalgal culture
(iv) To enhance the availability of light and carbon dioxide in dense cultures
(v) The process of choosing the ideal strain for culture and the actual circumstances of cultivation.
(vi) To create low-cost harvesting techniques and energy-efficient strategies for lipid and other useful co-product extraction

Converting solar energy into lipid and other organic molecules is the main objective of microalgal culture. The cultivation conditions themselves may be a part of the answer to overcoming these obstacles and achieving optimal lipid productivity in the microalgal cells. Other strategies to accomplish this goal include screening for novel species and genetic engineering of well-characterized strains [9]. A variety of methods are employed to increase the amount of light available, such as adjusting the reactor's architecture, using optics to direct light toward the reactor's center, creating flashes, and employing mixed species to use a range of light wavelengths that increase photosynthetic efficiency by collecting carbon dioxide. In order to increase productivity, the genes and key enzymes that control the metabolic pathways leading to lipid production are presently being studied and altered. On the other hand, controlling the nutrition supply can increase the lipid content of cells.

11.7 Conclusion

Few studies have provided a comprehensive characterization of the lipids in a given microalga. It is sometimes challenging to compare the results for an extensive biochemical profiling of biomolecules like lipid, protein, and carbohydrates, present in all microalgae species, due to the wide diversity among microalgae species and their growing circumstances. This means that further work is still required to completely define the different biomolecule components found in a single algal species, as well as to demonstrate the most suitable analytical technique for future application. For the synthesis of lipids to be used as biofuels and other high-value chemicals in the food and pharmaceutical industries, a thorough characterization of the lipid in microalgae is also necessary for the selection of suitable species. Microalgal cultivation has the potential to produce byproducts such PUFAs, omega-3 fatty acids, B-carotenoids, and others, as well as to aid in the bioremediation of the environment. It is also possible to modify microalgae to produce additional fuels, such as biohydrogen, bioethanol, and biobutanol. Numerous industries, including biofuel, pharmaceuticals, neutraceuticals, food and nutrition, cosmetics, aquafeed, and animal feed, can benefit greatly from these bioproducts. Thermal treatments have the potential to modify microalgae biomass into fuels that contain energy.

The creation of extremely effective algae biorefineries will enable the co-sourcing of various products, reducing waste and increasing productivity, and enhancing the economics of operations that would otherwise be inefficient. As a result, we believe that the advancement of algae biotechnology will upend the status quo in the industrial sector. This will be crucial in helping conventional agriculture overcome the obstacles and constraints it faces going forward. Focus has been placed on the advancements in photobioreactor and membrane design as well as parameter optimization to address current problems impeding deployment using AI. To address the technological issues and establish the microalgae-based MPBR as a viable and environmentally sustainable wastewater treatment option, more laboratory testing and pilot-scale validations are needed. This strategy will function as a robust and sustainable element in the water and wastewater treatment-related businesses, competing with more established methods of treating wastewater using AI-based bioreactors. A thorough discussion was also had regarding the process of gathering biomass and converting it into various bioproducts. Thus, choosing strong species may be essential for the treatment of wastewater, the ability to withstand unfavorable environmental conditions, self-flocculation, and the production of biomass in algal feeders for the production of products from several biorefineries with AI-based bioreactors. The production of microalgae biomass in conjunction with wastewater treatment yields renewable bioproducts and has several advantages for the energy and environmental sectors.

References

1. Chen, Z., Wang, L., Qiu, S., Ge, S., Determination of microalgal lipid content and fatty acid for biofuel production. *Biomed Res. Int.*, 2018, 1–17, 2018.
2. Kumar, S.A., Kumar, A., Dutt, V., Agrawal, R., Multi Model Implementation on General Medicine Prediction with Quantum Neural Networks, in: *2021 Third International Conference on Intelligent Communication Technologies and Virtual Mobile Networks (ICICV)*, Tirunelveli, India, pp. 1391–1395, 2021, doi: 10.1109/ICICV50876.2021.9388575.
3. Raj, P., Dubey, A.K., Kumar, A., Rathore, P.S., Blockchain-based IoT architecture for software-defined networking, in: *Blockchain, Artificial Intelligence, and the Internet of Things*, Springer International Publishing, Cham, Switzerland, 2022.
4. Burri, S.R., Kumar, A., Baliyan, A., Kumar, T.A., Predictive Intelligence for Healthcare Outcomes: An AI Architecture Overview, in: *2023 2nd International Conference on Smart Technologies and Systems for Next Generation Computing (ICSTSN)*, Villupuram, India, pp. 1–6, 2023, doi: 10.1109/ICSTSN57873.2023.10151477.
5. Wani, S., Ahuja, S., Kumar, A., Application of Deep Neural Networks and Machine Learning algorithms for diagnosis of Brain tumour, in: *2023 International Conference on Computational Intelligence and Sustainable Engineering Solutions (CISES)*, Greater Noida, India, pp. 106–111, 2023, doi: 10.1109/CISES58720.2023.10183528.
6. Kour, S.P., Kumar, A., Ahuja, S., An Advance Approach for Diabetes Detection by Implementing Machine Learning Algorithms, in: *2023 IEEE World Conference on Applied Intelligence and Computing (AIC)*, Sonbhadra, India, pp. 136–141, 2023, doi: 10.1109/AIC57670.2023.10263919.
7. Raj, P., Kumar, A., Dubey, A.K., Bhatia, S., Oswalt, M.S., *Quantum Computing and Artificial Intelligence: Training Machine and Deep Learning Algorithms on Quantum Computers*, De Gruyter, Berlin, Boston, 2023, [Online]. Available: https://doi.org/10.1515/9783110791402.

8. Sasubilli, G. and Kumar, A., Machine Learning and Big Data Implementation on Health Care data, in: *2020 4th International Conference on Intelligent Computing and Control Systems (ICICCS)*, Madurai, India, pp. 859–864, 2020, doi: 10.1109/ICICCS48265.2020.9120906.
9. Swarna, S.R., Kumar, A., Dixit, P., Sairam, T.V.M., Parkinson's Disease Prediction using Adaptive Quantum Computing, in: *2021 Third International Conference on Intelligent Communication Technologies and Virtual Mobile Networks (ICICV)*, Tirunelveli, India, pp. 1396–1401, 2021, doi: 10.1109/ICICV50876.2021.9388628.
10. Burugadda, V.R., Pawar, P.S., Kumar, A., Bhati, N., Predicting Hospital Readmission Risk for Heart Failure Patients Using Machine Learning Techniques: A Comparative Study of Classification Algorithms, in: *2023 Second International Conference on Trends in Electrical, Electronics, and Computer Engineering (TEECCON)*, Bangalore, India, pp. 223–228, 2023, doi: 10.1109/TEECCON59234.2023.10335817.
11. Kothari, R., Prasad, R., Kumar, V., Singh, D.P., Production of biodiesel from microalgae Chlamydomonas polypyrenoideum grown on dairy industry wastewater. *Bioresour. Technol.*, 144, 499–503, 2013 Sep 1.
12. Lee, C.H., Chae, H.S., Lee, S.H., Kim, H.S., Growth characteristics and lipid content of three Korean isolates of Botryococcusbraunii (Trebouxiophyceae). *J. Ecol. Environ.*, 38, 1, 67–74, 2015.
13. Liu, C., Huang, X., Wang, X., Zhang, X., Li, G., Phylogenetic studies on two strains of Antarctic ice algae based on morphological and molecular characteristics. *Phycologia*, 45, 2, 190–8, 2006 Mar 1.
14. Mata, M., Melo, A., Meireles, S., Mendes, A., Martins, A., Caetan, N., Potential of microalgae Scenedesmus obliquus grown in brewery wastewater for biodiesel production. *Chem. Eng. Trans.*, 32, 901–906, 2013.
15. Mata, T.M., Martins, A.A., Caetano, N.S., Microalgae for biodiesel production and other applications: a review. *Renew. Sustain. Energy Rev.*, 14, 1, 217–32, 2010 Jan 1.
16. Matos, J., Cardoso, C., Bandarra, N.M., Afonso, C., Bhalamurugan, G.L., Valerie, O., Mark, L., Valuable bioproducts obtained from microalgal biomass and their commercial applications: A review. *Environ. Eng. Res.*, 23, 3, 229–41, 2018.
17. Morando-Grijalva, C.A., Vázquez-Larios, A.L., Alcántara-Hernández, R.J., Ortega-Clemente, L.A., Robledo-Narváez, P.N., Isolation of a freshwater microalgae and its application for the treatment of wastewater and obtaining fatty acids from tilapia cultivation. *Environ. Sci. Pollut. Res.*, 27, 12, 14780–14789, 1–10, 2020 Mar 24.
18. Moser, B.R., Biodiesel production, properties, and feedstocks. *In Vitro Cell. Dev. Biol. Plant*, 45, 229–266, 2009.
19. Msanne, J., Xu, D., Konda, A.R., Casas-Mollano, J.A., Awada, T., Cahoon, E.B., Cerutti, H., Metabolic and gene expression changes triggered by nitrogen

deprivation in the photoautotrophically grown microalgae Chlamydomonas reinhardtii and Coccomyxa sp. C-169. *Phytochemistry*, 75, 50–9, 2012 Mar 1.
20. Patil, V., Källqvist, T., Olsen, E., Vogt, E., Gislerød, H.R., Fatty acid composition of 12 microalgae for possible use in aquaculture feed. *Aquacult. Int.*, 15, 1–9, 2007.
21. Pohl, C.H. and Kock, J.L., Oxidized fatty acids as inter-kingdom signaling molecules. *Molecules*, 19, 1, 1273–85, 2014 Jan.
22. Porwal, H.J., Mane, A.V., Velhal, S.G., Biodegradation of dairy effluent by using microbial isolates obtained from activated sludge. *Water Resour. Ind.*, 9, 1–5, 2015 Mar 1.
23. Radakovits, R., Jinkerson, R.E., Darzins, A., Posewitz, M.C., Genetic engineering of algae for enhanced biofuel production. *Eukaryot. Cell*, 9, 4, 486–501, 2010 Apr.
24. Rani, A.S., Rao, H.G., Kumar, A.B., Shruthi, M., Eco-Friendly Approach for Treating Dairy Effluent and Lipid Estimation Using Microalgae. *Biotechnol. J. Int.*, 11, 1, 33–39, 2015 Apr 1.
25. Renuka, N., Guldhe, A., Prasanna, R., Singh, P., Bux, F., Microalgae as multi-functional options in modern agriculture: current trends, prospects and challenges. *Biotechnol. Adv.*, 36, 4, 1255–73, 2018 Jul 1.
26. Rodolfi, L., ChiniZittelli, G., Bassi, N., Padovani, G., Biondi, N., Bonini, G., Tredici, M.R., Microalgae for oil: Strain selection, induction of lipid synthesis and outdoor mass cultivation in a low-cost photobioreactor. *Biotechnol. Bioeng.*, 102, 1, 100–12, 2009 Jan 1.
27. Siaut, M., Cuiné, S., Cagnon, C., Fessler, B., Nguyen, M., Carrier, P., Beyly, A., Beisson, F., Triantaphylidès, C., Li-Beisson, Y., Peltier, G., Oil accumulation in the model green alga Chlamydomonas reinhardtii: characterization, variability between common laboratory strains and relationship with starch reserves. *BMC Biotech.*, 11, 1, 1–5, 2011 Dec.
28. Skjånes, K., Rebours, C., Lindblad, P., Potential for green microalgae to produce hydrogen, pharmaceuticals and other high value products in a combined process. *Crit. Rev. Biotechnol.*, 33, 172–215, 2013.
29. Subashchandrabose, S.R., Ramakrishnan, B., Megharaj, M., Venkateswarlu, K., Naidu, R., Mixotrophic cyanobacteria and microalgae as distinctive biological agents for organic pollutant degradation. *Environ. Int.*, 51, 59–72, 2013 Jan 1.
30. Swain, P., Tiwari, A., Pandey, A., Enhanced lipid production in Tetraselmis sp. by two stage process optimization using simulated dairy wastewater as feedstock. *Biomass Bioenergy*, 139, 105643, 2020 Aug 1.
31. Ummalyma, S.B. and Sukumaran, R.K., Cultivation of microalgae in dairy effluent for oil production and removal of organic pollution load. *Bioresour. Technol.*, 165, 295–301, 2014 Aug 1.
32. Wang, B., Li, Y., Wu, N., Lan, C.Q., CO2 bio-mitigation using microalgae. *Appl. Microbiol. Biotechnol.*, 79, 707–718, 2008.

33. Wang, L., Li, Y., Chen, P., Min, M., Chen, Y., Zhu, J., Ruan, R.R., Anaerobic digested dairy manure as a nutrient supplement for cultivation of oil-rich green microalgae Chlorella sp. *Bioresour. Technol.*, 101, 8, 2623–8, 2010 Apr 1.
34. Xu, L., Cheng, X., Wang, Q., Enhanced lipid production in Chlamydomonas reinhardtii by co-culturing with Azotobacter chroococcum. *Front. Plant Sci.*, 9, 741, 2018 Jun 28.
35. Yan, N., Fan, C., Chen, Y., Hu, Z., The potential for microalgae as bioreactors to produce pharmaceuticals. *Int. J. Mol. Sci.*, 17, 1–24, 2016.
36. Yokoyama, R. and Honda, D., Taxonomic rearrangement of the genus Schizochytrium sensu lato based on morphology, chemotaxonomic characteristics, and 18S rRNA gene phylogeny (Thraustochytriaceae, Labyrinthulomycetes): emendation for Schizochytrium and erection of Aurantiochytrium and Oblongichytrium gen. nov. *Mycoscience*, 48, 4, 199–211, 2007.
37. Goh, P.S., Ahmad, N.A., Lim, J.W., Liang, Y.Y., Kang, H.S., Ismail, A.F., Arthanareeswaran, G., Microalgae-Enabled Wastewater Remediation and Nutrient Recovery through Membrane Photobioreactors: Recent Achievements and Future Perspective. *Membranes (Basel)*, 12, 11, 1094, 2022 Nov 3, doi: 10.3390/membranes12111094. PMID: 36363649; PMCID: PMC9699475.
38. Fabris, M., Abbriano Raffaela, M., Pernice, M., Sutherland, D.L., Commault Audrey, S., Hall Christopher, C., Labeeuw, L., McCauley Janice, I., Kuzhiuparambil, U., Ray, P., Kahlke, T., Ralph, P.J., emerging Technologies in Algal Biotechnology: Toward the Establishment of a Sustainable, Algae-Based Bioeconomy. *Front. Plant Sci.*, 11, 1–22, URL=https://www.frontiersin.org/articles/10.3389/fpls.2020.00279 DOI=10.3389/fpls.2020.00279.
39. Ummalyma, S.B., Sirohi, R., Udayan, A. *et al.*, Sustainable microalgal biomass production in food industry wastewater for low-cost biorefinery products: a review. *Phytochem. Rev. :Proc. Phytochem. Soc. Eur.*, 21, 2, 1–23, 2022 Apr, DOI: 10.1007/s11101-022-09814-3. PMID: 35431709; PMCID: PMC9006494.
40. Salah, A., Sany, H., El-Sayed, A.E.K.B. *et al.*, Growth Performance and Biochemical Composition of Desmodesmus sp. Green Alga Grown on Agricultural Industries Waste (Cheese Whey). *Water Air Soil Pollut.*, 234, 770, 2023, https://doi.org/10.1007/s11270-023-06780-0.

12

Smart Collision Recognition and Reporting System with GPS and GSM Integration

Gaurav Aggarwal*, Pooja Joshi and Ashutosh Bhatt

Department of Computer Science and Engineering, Himalayan School of Science and Technology, Swami Rama Himalayan University, Uttarakhand, India

Abstract

The progressive evolution of technology and infrastructure has streamlined our daily activities. However, vehicular collisions persist as a widespread challenge, highlighting the need for enhanced emergency response capabilities. Globally, automobile collisions continue to be a leading cause of fatalities and injuries. Swift recognition and reporting of these incidents can mitigate their impact on society and potentially save lives. In this investigation, we propose an Internet of Things–based system designed to detect and report automobile collisions, leveraging the capabilities of GPS (Global Positioning System) and GSM (Global System for Mobile Communication). Through an extensive review of existing literature, we elucidate the rationale behind our proposed methodology and present comprehensive performance data through visual aids. Our research demonstrates the system's efficacy in swiftly identifying collisions and promptly relaying this critical information, making it a valuable asset for enhancing overall traffic safety. Our work offers an optimal solution to address this critical challenge. Specifically, our project incorporates the use of an accelerometer to detect risky driving behavior, whereas GPS vehicle tracking technology allows for the continuous monitoring and positioning of the vehicle. The system proves to be a cost-effective asset for real-time vehicle tracking, serving as a valuable asset management tool and contributing to time and fuel savings through efficient route planning. A primary focus of this paper is the efficient localization of any vehicle collisions, followed by the dissemination of collision location details to pre-registered contacts, facilitating immediate assistance from emergency services or family members. The GSM

**Corresponding author*: gauravaggarwal3565@outlook.com

Abhishek Kumar, Narayan Vyas, Pramod Singh Rathore, Abhineet Anand and Pooja Dixit (eds.) Internet of Medicine for Smart Healthcare, (223–236) © 2025 Scrivener Publishing LLC

module plays a key role in transmitting the vehicle's precise coordinates, including longitude and latitude, through text messages. Moreover, the GPS enables the accurate tracking of the vehicle's location using a network of satellites. In the event of a collision, specialized sensors such as shock sensors and temperature sensors are triggered, promptly signaling the connected Arduino Uno for immediate action.

***Keywords*:** GPS, GSM, Arduino Uno, shock sensors, temperature sensor, IoT, vehicle collision recognition, emergency services

12.1 Introduction

In recent times, there has been a significant surge in vehicular usage, leading to escalating traffic congestion, a primary catalyst for road collisions. These collisions result in substantial loss of life and property due to inadequate post-collision signaling and difficulties in pinpointing the exact collision location. In today's modern world, transportation is indispensable, emphasizing the critical importance of ensuring the safety of drivers and passengers. Our primary goal in this project is to reduce the post-collision mortality rate by offering a solution that involves promptly reporting the collision location to nearby hospitals and relatives through GSM (Global System for Mobile Communication) and GPS (Global Positioning System) systems. Leveraging the GPS, our vehicle tracking system enhances safety measures. Given the frequency of collisions, swift notification of collision locations is essential for prompt first aid provision. Our system employs an accelerometer to detect collisions, triggering an alert message on an Android application. Additionally, a buzzer is integrated to sound an alarm upon collision recognition. Furthermore, temperature sensors are utilized to provide environmental temperature data. This study is Wi-Fi–based. The proliferation of vehicles, driven by the automobile industry's expansion, has contributed to a corresponding increase in collisions. The leading causes of road collisions include heterogeneous traffic and insufficient traffic separation measures. India, in particular, grapples with a high number of road collision fatalities, with 13 million deaths reported in 2014–2015. According to the WHO, traffic collisions claim over 1.3 million lives annually, with an estimated 50 million people sustaining injuries [1]. Collisions can be quickly identified and reported, saving lives and lessening their negative effects on society. In this article, we suggest an Internet of Things (IoT)–based system for detecting and reporting automobile collisions that makes use of GPS and GSM to do so. Collision victims will receive precise and prompt aid from the system, which is meant to automatically detect incidents and communicate real-time information to emergency personnel.

The remainder of the essay is structured as follows. We present a review of previous research in Section 12.2. In Section 12.3, we present the methods employed in our system. We show graphical representations of the system's performance in Section 12.4. Section 12.5 is where we offer our findings and talk about unfinished business.

12.2 Literature Review

In the current scenario, the challenge of accurately pinpointing collision locations poses a significant obstacle, resulting in the lack of timely alerts and, tragically, individual fatalities. Our project addresses this issue by employing a GPS module to precisely track the vehicle's location at the time of the collision, while a GSM module is utilized to transmit alerts to registered mobile numbers upon collision recognition. Aishwarya *et al.* [2] presented is an IoT-driven vehicle collision recognition and localization system integrating GPS technology. This paper elucidates the mechanism for swiftly detecting vehicular collisions and promptly relaying messages to registered mobile numbers. Hu *et al.* [3] propose an enhanced stolen vehicle security system: leveraging Arduino Uno and shock sensor technology for improved security and reliability. Utilizing GSM communication, the system provides regular updates on the vehicle's location in the event of a collision. Bhavthankar and Sayyed [4] overviewed the integrated vehicle collision recognition and reporting system utilizing shock sensor, GPS, and GSM wireless technology. This project employs various sensors including a shock sensor to detect car crashes and GPS for precise collision location tracking. Upon detecting a collision, the system automatically dispatches messages to registered mobile numbers such as family members, local authorities, or medical services. Kushwaha *et al.* [5] proposed a GPS- and GSM-based vehicle collision recognition system with the primary goal of accurately locating collisions and notifying relatives or nearby emergency services. Kushwaha *et al.* have implemented assembly programming to enhance accuracy alongside GPS and GSM technologies. Various other systems have been explored to address collision recognition. The system integrates two sensors, utilizing the adxl335 sensor for angle recognition and a shock sensor to identify vehicle collisions. Thakor *et al.* [6] opt for an automated vehicle collision recognition system utilizing shock or accelerometer sensors to detect collisions. Prabha *et al.* [7] selected automated vehicle collision recognition and notification system incorporating GSM and GPS. This study explores the utilization of a shock sensor within a vehicle alarm system for efficient collision recognition. Kishore *et al.* [8] introduced a cost-effective system leveraging modern internet connectivity for enhanced networking capabilities. Gujar and Itkikar [9] adopted cutting-edge embedded system for vehicle collision recognition and positioning. The primary objective is to pinpoint the precise collision location and dispatch messages to nearby emergency services. This system relies on GPS, GSM, and accelerometer sensors, enabling effective vehicle collision recognition [10]. Some other systematic reviews are as follows shown in Table 12.1.

12.3 Block Diagram

In this project, a schematic of the vehicle positioning system and collision recognition system is presented. The diagram (Figure 12.1) illustrates the conceptual framework for vehicle positioning and collision alerts, featuring connections between components such as the GPS module, GSM module, shock sensor, Arduino microcontroller, LM35 temperature sensor, and power supply.

12.4 Methodology

In this project, a diverse range of hardware components sourced from various manufacturers is utilized to construct a fully functional model. The following comprehensive list outlines all essential hardware devices required for this project, ensuring seamless operation and compatibility.

12.4.1 Arduino Uno

The Arduino Uno is a microcontroller board centered around the ATmega328P chip. Featuring 14 digital input/output pins, 6 analog inputs, and a 16-MHz quartz crystal oscillator, it also includes a USB connection, external power supply capabilities, and a reset button. As part of an open-source electronics platform, the Arduino Uno is accompanied by software code programmed using the Arduino IDE [22]. The name "Uno" derives from the Italian word for "one," chosen to signify the initial release of the Arduino Software. Its design aims to streamline electronics development for designers, artists, and enthusiasts interested in creating interactive objects or environments [23].

Table 12.1 Survey of some systematic study design vehicle safety [11–21].

Study title	Study design	Study objective	Key findings	Authors
A Comprehensive Survey on IoT Enabled Vehicle Collision Recognition and Reporting System	Review	To survey the current state-of-the-art in IoT-based vehicle collision recognition and reporting systems	IoT-based systems can provide accurate and timely information to emergency services, improving response times and potentially reducing fatalities	Mohammadi *et al.* (2018)
Smart Vehicle Collision Recognition and Alert System Utilizing IoT	Experimental	To develop and deploy a prototype IoT-enabled vehicle collision recognition and notification system	The system achieved high accuracy in detecting collisions and sending notifications to emergency services, minimizing emergency response duration and potentially preserving lives	Raja *et al.* (2019)

(Continued)

Table 12.1 Survey of some systematic study design vehicle safety [11–21]. (*Continued*)

Study title	Study design	Study objective	Key findings	Authors
Intelligent IoT-Driven Vehicle Collision Recognition and Alert System	Experimental	Developing and deploying an IoT-powered vehicle collision recognition and notification system	The system achieved high accuracy in detecting collisions and sending notifications to emergency services, potentially reducing response times and improving survival rates	Tripathi *et al.* (2020)
IoT-Integrated Intelligent Vehicle Collision Recognition and Notification System With Raspberry Pi	Experimental	Creating and deploying an IoT-driven vehicle collision recognition and notification system with Raspberry Pi	The system achieved high accuracy in detecting collisions and sending notifications to emergency services, potentially reducing response times and improving survival rates	Nirmala *et al.* (2021)

(*Continued*)

Table 12.1 Survey of some systematic study design vehicle safety [11–21]. (*Continued*)

Study title	Study design	Study objective	Key findings	Authors
Smart IoT-Powered Vehicle Collision Recognition and Notification System	Review	To assess the viability of IoT-enabled vehicle collision recognition and notification systems	IoT-based systems have the potential to reduce response times and save lives by providing accurate and timely information to emergency services	Ahmed *et al.* (2021)
IoT-Driven Vehicle Collision Recognition and Reporting System: An In-Depth Examination	Review	To provide a comprehensive review of IoT-powered vehicle collision recognition and reporting solutions	IoT-based systems have the potential to reduce response times and improve survival rates by accurately detecting and reporting collisions to emergency services	Sharma *et al.* (2021)
Development of an IoT-Driven Vehicle Collision Recognition and Notification System	Experimental	Developing and implementing an IoT-powered vehicle collision recognition and notification system	The system achieved high accuracy in detecting collisions and sending notifications to emergency services, potentially reducing response times and improving survival rates	Dar *et al.* (2019)

(*Continued*)

Table 12.1 Survey of some systematic study design vehicle safety [11–21]. (*Continued*)

Study title	Study design	Study objective	Key findings	Authors
Internet of Things (IoT) Enabled Vehicle Collision Recognition and Notification System	Experimental	Creating and deploying an IoT-driven vehicle collision recognition and notification system utilizing Raspberry Pi	The system achieved high accuracy in detecting collisions and sending notifications to emergency services, potentially reducing response times and improving survival rates	Swathi *et al.* (2019)
IoT-Powered Vehicle Collision Recognition and Notification Systems: A Comprehensive Survey	Review	Conducting an assessment of the latest developments in IoT-driven vehicle collision recognition and notification systems	IoT-based systems have the potential to reduce response times and improve survival rates by accurately detecting and reporting collisions to emergency services	Syed *et al.* (2021)

(*Continued*)

Table 12.1 Survey of some systematic study design vehicle safety [11–21]. (*Continued*)

Study title	Study design	Study objective	Key findings	Authors
IoT-Enabled Vehicle Collision Recognition and Notification System Enhanced with Machine Learning	Experimental	Creating and deploying an IoT-powered vehicle collision recognition and notification system integrated with machine learning algorithms	The system achieved high accuracy in detecting collisions and sending notifications to emergency services, potentially reducing response times and improving survival rates	Saifullah *et al.* (2021)
IoT-Enhanced Vehicle Collision Recognition and Notification System Leveraging Deep Learning	Experimental	Developing and deploying an IoT-powered vehicle collision recognition and notification system utilizing deep learning algorithms	The system achieved high accuracy in detecting collisions and sending notifications to emergency services, potentially reducing response times and improving survival rates	Abbhas *et al.* (2023)

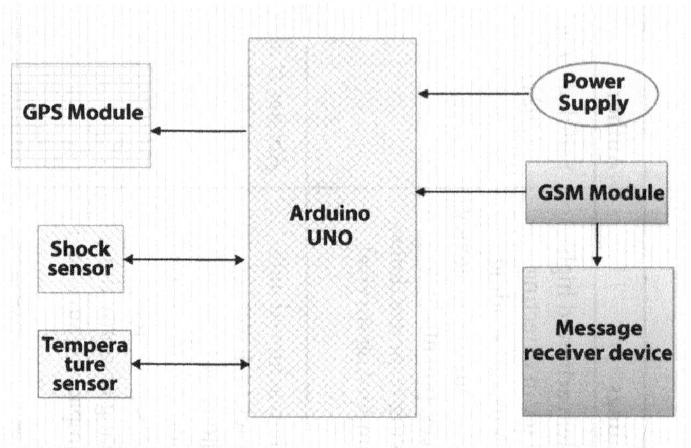

Figure 12.1 Schematic of vehicle collision recognition and alert system.

12.4.2 GSM Module

The GSM module, abbreviated from Global System for Mobile Communication, denotes a second-generation mobile network infrastructure [24]. It includes a SIM slot for inserting a SIM card, which contains a unique 15-digit serial number. In this project, the GSM module serves the purpose of transmitting data from the GPS in the event of vehicle collision recognition [25]. Additionally, the GSM module is utilized for contacting emergency services in case of a vehicle collision.

12.4.3 GPS Module

The GPS, known as the Global Positioning System, is a satellite-based navigation system. Through the transliteration process, GPS satellites emit signals received by ground receivers, which subsequently determine the receiver's position by analyzing the time that it takes for signals to reach from various satellites [26]. In this project, the GPS module is employed to receive precise location coordinates including longitude, latitude, and timestamp when a collision occurs. Moreover, within the vehicle monitoring system, the GPS module persistently traces and refreshes the precise whereabouts of the vehicle [27, 28].

12.4.4 Shock Sensor

Shock sensors, utilizing shockwave recognition technology, are designed to identify abrupt physical impacts or significant vibrations. Upon detecting a collision, they promptly trigger an alarm. The output of shock sensors is typically binary, indicating either the presence or absence of a shock event. These sensors play a critical role in collision recognition and enhancing vehicle safety.

12.4.5 Temperature Sensor

Temperature sensors are devices that convert analog signals into temperature readings, typically measured in Celsius. They produce output voltage proportional to the temperature, with voltage increasing as temperature rises [29]. These sensors operate autonomously, requiring no external devices for measurement. Known for their affordability and high accuracy, they offer advantages over linear temperature sensors, which are calibrated in Kelvin.

12.4.6 Automobile Collision Reporting System

An incident transpires when a vehicle collides with another vehicle, an animal, or an immobile object like a building or tree. In efforts to bolster safety, sensors are deployed, with shock or vibration sensors affixed to every door and window of the vehicle. These sensors are interconnected in an OR gate arrangement, guaranteeing that, upon collision detection, at least one of the shock sensors activates an alarm and generates an output signal. In this project, the shock sensor is linked to pin 12 of the Arduino board [30]. Upon detection of an impact by the shock sensor, triggering a signal to pin 12 and elevating its value, an alert message is dispatched to a control room or nearby hospital, signaling the occurrence of a collision and the need for assistance. GPS technology is utilized to relay these alert messages.

12.5 Conclusion

This investigation focuses on monitoring multiple vehicles traveling along various routes. It relies on GPS technology for vehicle tracking, which proves crucial for collision recognition and anti-theft purposes. Sensors are deployed for timely collision recognition, significantly aiding in saving lives. Leveraging GPS technology, the system offers real-time vehicle location updates to registered contact numbers, serving as a preventive measure against theft and facilitating prompt assistance. Additionally, the installation of dashcams, equipped with built-in GPS systems, can further enhance security by providing driver assistance and deterring theft.

References

1. World Health Organization Road Traffic Injuries Fact Sheet No 358, March 2013, Available from http://www.who.int/mediacentre/factsheets/fs358/en/ [Last accessed on 2017 Dec 16].
2. Aishwarya, S.R., Rai, A., Charitha, P.M.A., Savitha, S.C., An IoT based vehicle collision prevention and tracking system for night drivers. *Proc. IEEE*, 3, 4, 2320–9798, 2015.
3. Hu, J.-M., Li, J., Li, G.-H., Automobile Anti-theft System Based on GSM and GPS Module. *Intelligent Networks and Intelligent Systems (ICINIS), 2012 Fifth International Conferenceon*, 1-3 Nov. 2012, pp. 199–201.
4. Bhavthankar, S. and Sayyed, H.G., Wireless System for Vehicle Collision Recognition and Reporting using Accelerometer and GPS. *Proc. IEEE*, 6, 8, 2229–5518, 2015.
5. Kushwaha, A., Katiyar, G., Katiyar, H., Yadav, H., Saxena, GPS and GSM Based Collision Alarm System. *National Student Conference On "Advances in Electrical &Information Communication Technology" AEICT*, 2014.
6. Thakor, N., Vyas, T., Shah, D., Automatic Vehicle Collision Recognition System Based on ARM &GPS. *Int. J. Res. Technol. Stud.*, 1, 1, 17–19, Dec 2013, ISSN: - Applied (Online).
7. Prabha, C., Sunitha, R., Anitha, R., Automatic Vehicle Collision Recognition and Messaging System Using GSM and GPS Modem. *Int. J. Adv. Res. Electr. Electron. Instrum. Eng.*, 3, 7, 10723–10728, 2014.
8. Krishna Kishore, T., Sasi Vardhan, T., Lakshmi Narayana, N., Vehicle Tracking using A Reliable Embedded Data Acquisition System with GPS and GSM. *Int. J. Comput. Sci. Netw. Secur.*, 10, 2, 286–291, February 2010.
9. Gujar, S.R. and Itkikar, A.R., Advanced Embedded System of Vehicle Collision Recognition and Tracking System. *Proc. IEEE*, 5, 2, 2277 128X, 2015.
10. Varma, S.K.C., Poornesh, Varma, T., Harsha, Automatic Vehicle Collision Recognition And Messaging System Using GPS and GSM Modems. *Int. J. Sci. Eng. Res.*, 4, 8, 246–248, August-2013.
11. Mohammadi, M., Al-Fuqaha, A., Sorour, S., Guizani, M., Deep learning for IoT big data and streaming analytics: A survey. *IEEE Commun. Surv. Tutorials*, 20, 4, 2923–60, 2018 Jun 6.
12. Beckingsale, D.A., Burmark, J., Hornung, R., Jones, H., Killian, W., Kunen, A.J., Pearce, O., Robinson, P., Ryujin, B.S., Scogland, T.R., RAJA: Portable performance for large-scale scientific applications, in: *2019 ieee/acm international workshop on performance, portability and productivity in hpc (p3hpc)*, 2019 Nov 22, IEEE, pp. 71–81.
13. Emmert-Streib, F., Yang, Z., Feng, H., Tripathi, S., Dehmer, M., An introductory review of deep learning for prediction models with big data. *Front. Artif. Intell.*, 3, 4, 2020 Feb 28.

14. Nirmala, P., Ramesh, S., Tamilselvi, M., Ramkumar, G., Anitha, G., An artificial intelligence enabled smart industrial automation system based on internet of things assistance, in: *2022 International Conference on Advances in Computing, Communication and Applied Informatics (ACCAI)*, pp. 1–6, IEEE, 2022 Jan 28.
15. Abioye, S.O., Oyedele, L.O., Akanbi, L., Ajayi, A., Delgado, J.M., Bilal, M., Akinade, O.O., Ahmed, A., Artificial intelligence in the construction industry: A review of present status, opportunities and future challenges. *J. Build. Eng.*, 44, 103299, 2021 Dec 1.
16. Dwivedi, Y.K., Hughes, L., Ismagilova, E., Aarts, G., Coombs, C., Crick, T., Duan, Y., Dwivedi, R., Edwards, J., Eirug, A., Galanos, V., Artificial Intelligence (AI): Multidisciplinary perspectives on emerging challenges, opportunities, and agenda for research, practice and policy. *Int. J. Inf. Manage.*, 57, 101994, 2021 Apr 1.
17. Dar, B.K., Shah, M.A., Shahid, H., Naseem, A., Fog computing based automated collision recognition and emergency response system using android smartphone, in: *2018 14th International Conference on Emerging Technologies (ICET)*, pp. 1–6, IEEE, 2018 Nov 21.
18. Swathi, S.J., Raj, S., Devaraj, D., Microcontroller and sensor based smart biking system for driver's safety, in: *2019 IEEE International Conference on Intelligent Techniques in Control, Optimization and Signal Processing (INCOS)*, pp. 1–5, IEEE, 2019 Apr 11.
19. Syed, A.S., Sierra-Sosa, D., Kumar, A., Elmaghraby, A., IoT in smart cities: A survey of technologies, practices and challenges. *Smart Cities*, 4, 2, 429–75, 2021 Mar 30.
20. Saifullah, S., Fauziah, Y., Aribowo, A.S., Comparison of machine learning for sentiment analysis in detecting anxiety based on social media data. arXiv preprint arXiv:2101.06353, 2021 Jan 16.
21. Abbas, Q., Ahmad, G., Alyas, T., Alghamdi, T., Alsaawy, Y., Alzahrani, A., Revolutionizing Urban Mobility: IoT-Enhanced Autonomous Parking Solutions with Transfer Learning for Smart Cities. *Sensors*, 23, 21, 8753, 2023 Oct 27.
22. Kumar, A., Kumar, A., Dutt, V., Agrawal, R., Multi Model Implementation on General Medicine Prediction with Quantum Neural Networks, in: *2021 Third International Conference on Intelligent Communication Technologies and Virtual Mobile Networks (ICICV)*, Tirunelveli, India, pp. 1391–1395, 2021, doi: 10.1109/ICICV50876.2021.9388575.
23. Raj, P., Dubey, A.K., Kumar, A., Rathore, P.S., Blockchain-based IoT architecture for software-defined networking. *Blockchain, Artificial Intelligence, and the Internet of Things*, in: Springer International Publishing, Cham, Switzerland, 2022.
24. Burri, S.R., Kumar, A., Baliyan, A., Kumar, T.A., Predictive Intelligence for Healthcare Outcomes: An AI Architecture Overview, in: *2023 2nd International Conference on Smart Technologies and Systems for Next*

Generation Computing (ICSTSN), Villupuram, India, pp. 1–6, 2023, doi: 10.1109/ICSTSN57873.2023.10151477.

25. Wani, S., Ahuja, S., Kumar, A., Application of Deep Neural Networks and Machine Learning algorithms for diagnosis of Brain tumour, in: *2023 International Conference on Computational Intelligence and Sustainable Engineering Solutions (CISES)*, Greater Noida, India, pp. 106–111, 2023, doi: 10.1109/CISES58720.2023.10183528.
26. Kour, S.P., Kumar, A., Ahuja, S., An Advance Approach for Diabetes Detection by Implementing Machine Learning Algorithms, in: *2023 IEEE World Conference on Applied Intelligence and Computing (AIC)*, Sonbhadra, India, pp. 136–141, 2023, doi: 10.1109/AIC57670.2023.10263919.
27. Raj, P., Kumar, A., Dubey, A.K., Bhatia, S., Oswalt, M.S., *Quantum Computing and Artificial Intelligence: Training Machine and Deep Learning Algorithms on Quantum Computers*, De Gruyter, Berlin, Boston, 2023, [Online]. Available: https://doi.org/10.1515/9783110791402.
28. Sasubilli, G. and Kumar, A., Machine Learning and Big Data Implementation on Health Care data, in: *2020 4th International Conference on Intelligent Computing and Control Systems (ICICCS)*, Madurai, India, pp. 859–864, 2020, doi: 10.1109/ICICCS48265.2020.9120906.
29. Swarna, S.R., Kumar, A., Dixit, P., Sairam, T.V.M., Parkinson's Disease Prediction using Adaptive Quantum Computing, in: *2021 Third International Conference on Intelligent Communication Technologies and Virtual Mobile Networks (ICICV)*, Tirunelveli, India, pp. 1396–1401, 2021, doi: 10.1109/ICICV50876.2021.9388628.
30. Burugadda, V.R., Pawar, P.S., Kumar, A., Bhati, N., Predicting Hospital Readmission Risk for Heart Failure Patients Using Machine Learning Techniques: A Comparative Study of Classification Algorithms, in: *2023 Second International Conference on Trends in Electrical, Electronics, and Computer Engineering (TEECCON)*, Bangalore, India, pp. 223–228, 2023, doi: 10.1109/TEECCON59234.2023.10335817.

13

Evolution and Impact of Wearable Devices in Healthcare: Anatomy of Wearable Technology and its Influence on Medical Sciences

M. P. Ambali[1] and V. C. Patil[2*]

[1]*Department of Anatomy, Krishna Institute of Medical Sciences, Krishna Vishwa Vidyapeeth "Deemed To Be University", Karad, Maharashtra, India*

[2]*Department of General Medicine, Krishna Institute of Medical Sciences, Krishna Vishwa Vidyapeeth "Deemed To Be University", Karad, Maharashtra, India*

Abstract

Wearable technology has changed healthcare by letting doctors keep an eye on patients' vital signs all the time. This has increased patient participation and led to better clinical results. This essay gives an outline of how smart technology has changed and affected healthcare over time. Wearable electronics have come a long way since the first pedometers and heart rate monitors were made. But recent improvements in sensor technology, downsizing, and connection have made it possible for a lot of smart devices to track a lot of bodily factors, like heart rate, blood pressure, glucose levels, and physical exercise. Wearable technology has had a huge impact on medical science. These gadgets let us gather high-quality data in real time, which makes it possible for healthcare measures to be more personalized and effective. For instance, smart technology can keep an eye on a person's vital signs while they have a long-term illness like diabetes or heart disease, letting their healthcare workers know about any problems before they get worse. Also, smart technology has given people the power to take charge of their health and fitness. By letting users see their health data, these gadgets help people become more self-aware and support healthy living changes, like getting more exercise and sleeping better. Wearable technology has changed healthcare by making it possible to watch patients all the time, getting them more involved, and better treatment

**Corresponding author*: patilvirendra1250@gmail.com

Abhishek Kumar, Narayan Vyas, Pramod Singh Rathore, Abhineet Anand and Pooja Dixit (eds.) Internet of Medicine for Smart Healthcare, (237–262) © 2025 Scrivener Publishing LLC

results. But problems like data protection, following the rules, and being able to work with other systems still exist. To get the most out of smart technology in healthcare, future study should focus on finding solutions to these problems.

Keywords: Wearable technology, healthcare, physical exercise, ECG, CGM

13.1 Introduction

Wearable technology has become a major force in healthcare, providing never-before-seen chances for constant tracking, personalized treatments, and better results for patients. This chapter breaks down the structure of wearable technology and how it has changed medical studies to look at how wearable technology has changed over time and how it has affected healthcare. Wearable technology in healthcare has been around since the early 1900s, when simple devices like pedometers and heart rate monitors were making their debut. The first wearable technology was built on top of these early devices. Wearable technology has grown thanks to progress in sensor technology, downsizing, and connection. Wearable technology today can keep an eye on a lot of bodily factors in real time, like heart rate, blood pressure, glucose levels, and physical exercise. Wearable technology is made up of a few key parts that work together to make it work. To get bodily data, you need sensor systems like accelerometers, gyroscopes, and photoplethysmography (PPG) devices [1]. Connectivity choices, like Bluetooth and Wi-Fi, make it easy to send info to smartphones and other devices. Power control and battery life are very important for wearable technology because, most of the time, they are worn all the time and do not need to be charged or changed very often. Wearable technology is meant to be close to the body for long amounts of time, so design and usability are very important for making sure that people are comfortable and happy with it.

When used in healthcare, wearable technology includes a lot of different gadgets, each with its own uses and benefits. Fitbit and Garmin are two brands of fitness trackers that are made to keep an eye on your exercise level, sleep habits, and other health-related factors. Some smartwatches, like the Apple Watch and the Samsung Galaxy Watch, have extra features like apps, alerts, and even tracking for a heartbeat [electrocardiogram (ECG)]. Continuous glucose monitors (CGMs) and pulse oximeters are two examples of medical tracking devices that give doctors important information for controlling long-term illnesses. Wearable [2] drug delivery systems, like insulin pumps and transdermal patches, make it easy

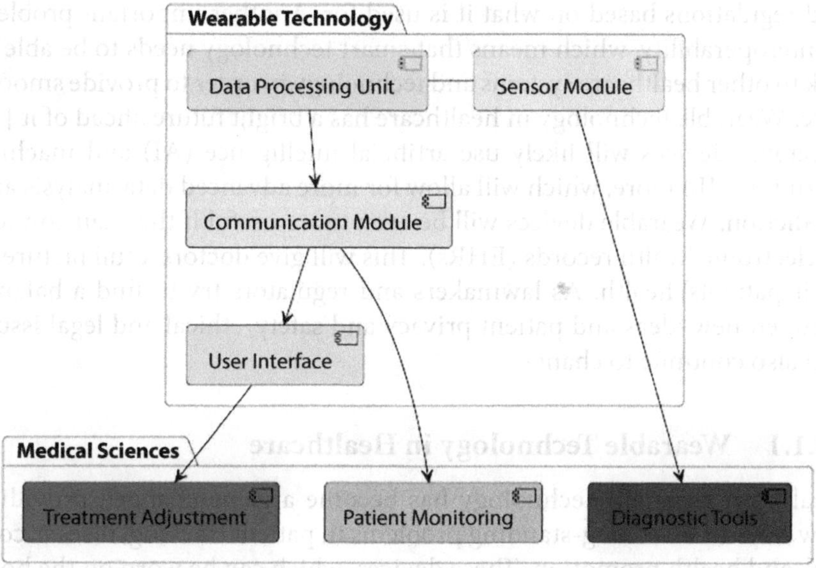

Figure 13.1 Overview of anatomy of wearable technology and its influence on medical sciences.

and accurate to give medications. Wearable technology can be used in a lot of different ways in medical science. Remote patient tracking is one of the biggest perks. It lets doctors check on patients' vital signs and health without them having to go to the office as often. This is especially helpful for people who have long-term diseases like heart disease, diabetes, or high blood pressure because it lets doctors find issues early and treat them quickly. Wearable technology is also very important for physical therapy and recovery because it gives patients and trainers real-time feedback and helps people stick to their treatment plans. Figure 13.1 gives an overview of anatomy of wearable technology and its influence on medical sciences.

Wearable technology [3] has had a huge effect on health care. Wearable technology has changed healthcare from being reactive to being proactive by allowing constant tracking and real-time data gathering. With access to their own health data and unique information, patients are able to take charge of their health and fitness. Healthcare workers can make better choices when they have more information, which improves patient results and lowers the cost of healthcare. Even with these pros, there are some problems with using smart technology in healthcare [4]. Wearable technology collects private health data that needs to be kept safe, so data privacy and security are big issues. Compliance with regulations is another problem because smart technology has to follow different rules and regulations based on what it is used for. Another important problem is interoperability, which means that smart technology needs to be able to talk to other healthcare systems and technology in order to provide smooth care. Wearable technology in healthcare has a bright future ahead of it [5]. Wearable devices will likely use artificial intelligence (AI) and machine learning (ML) more, which will allow for more advanced data analysis and prediction. Wearable devices will be even more useful if they can connect to electronic health records (EHRs). This will give doctors a full picture of their patients' health. As lawmakers and regulators try to find a balance between new ideas and patient privacy and safety, ethical and legal issues will also continue to change.

13.1.1 Wearable Technology in Healthcare

Healthcare wearable technology has become a game-changer, providing new ways to solve long-standing problems in patient tracking, disease control, and health promotion. These devices, which can be worn on the body or built into clothes or items, could change the way healthcare is provided by giving real-time data, making patients more involved, and allowing for more personalized care [6]. One of the best things about smart technology for healthcare is that it can continuously and non-invasively track vital data. Wearable technology with sensors can keep an eye on things like heart rate, blood pressure, oxygen levels, and even ECG readings. This lets doctors find problems early and fix them quickly [7]. This constant tracking is especially helpful for people with long-term conditions like heart disease, diabetes, or high blood pressure, as it can help keep problems from happening and improve their general health. Wearable technology in healthcare can keep track of more than just bodily measurements. It can also keep track of living factors that affect health, like stress levels, sleep habits, and physical exercise. This information can be collected and analyzed by smart devices, which can then give users specific health and wellness tips. An example of this is a fitness tracker can tell you how active you are each day and suggest ways to get more active or sleep better.

Patients are also [8] being given more control over their health by wearable technology in healthcare. Wearable technology helps people become more self-aware and change their behavior by giving them access to their own health info. For instance, a diabetic person can use a CGM to keep an eye on their blood sugar levels and change how much insulin they take as needed, which improves their glycemic control. Wearable technology is also leading to new ideas in medical study and the way healthcare is delivered. Wearable technology lets researchers get real-time data from big groups of people, which makes studies completer and more reliable. Wearable technology can help doctors keep an eye on patients from afar, so they do not have to see them in person as often and resources can be used more efficiently. Wearable [9] technology in healthcare is changing the way that we track, control, and improve health in a big way. These gadgets are helping to bring about a new age of personalized, preventative healthcare by keeping an eye on people all the time, encouraging them to learn more about themselves, and spurring new ideas. As technology keeps getting better, smart technology has the huge potential to change how healthcare is provided and make things better for patients.

13.1.2 Purpose and Objectives of the Chapter

This chapter's goal is to give a full picture of how wearable technology has changed and affected healthcare, with a focus on how wearable technology works and how it has affected medical studies. The goal of this chapter is to show how wearable technology has changed healthcare by looking at its history, main parts, different types, uses, and effects. Wearable technology has the potential to make healthcare better for patients, push medical research to new heights, and improve patient outcomes.

The following are the goals of this chapter:

- To show how wearable technology has changed over time in healthcare, from the first pedometers and heart rate monitors to more modern, multipurpose gadgets that can track many bodily functions.
- To look into the parts of wearable technology that make it work and be useful in healthcare settings, such as sensor technologies, connecting choices, power management, and design factors.
- To look at how smart technology has changed healthcare, including how it has improved patient results, contact between doctors and patients, cost-effectiveness, and the speed with which care is delivered, as well as any problems or restrictions that need to be fixed.

This chapter's main goals are to give readers a full picture of how wearable technology has changed over time, what it can be used for, how it has affected healthcare, and what the future holds for it. It also wants to show how it has the potential to completely change how healthcare is provided and make things better for patients.

13.2 Historical Development of Wearable Technology

The history of wearable technology in healthcare goes back more than 100 years, from simple devices to the high-technology ones we use today that can track a lot of different body functions. Wearable technology has changed over time thanks to improvements in sensor technology, downsizing, and connection, as well as rising customer desire for tools that track health and fitness [10]. The stethoscope, which was the first wearable medical gadget, was made in the early 1900s. This was the start of the idea of using wearable technology in healthcare. Since René Laennec invented it in 1816, the stethoscope has changed the way doctors listen to the heart and lungs. Though, wearable technology did not really start to take shape until the 1970s, when the first portable ECG machine was made. When digital technology came out in the 1980s, it made it possible for more advanced personal technology to be made. One important example is Zenith's creation of the first hearing aid that could be worn behind the ear in 1987. In order to improve the quality of life for people who have trouble hearing, this was the start of a new era in portable technology.

The 2000s saw the growth of sensor technology and internet connection, which made wearable technology even more useful [11]. One big step forward was the release of the Nike+ running tracker in 2006. This sensor, which runners put on their shoes, let them keep track of their route, pace, and calories burned. This was the first time that wearable technology was used for regular health and exercise tracking. Wearable technology in healthcare has grown over the years to include many different types of devices, such as fitness tracks, smartphones, medical tracking devices, and drug delivery systems that can be worn. Advanced sensors, like accelerometers, gyroscopes, and PPG sensors, are built into these devices. This lets them keep an eye on a number of bodily factors in real time. Figure 13.2 illustrates that how wearable device technology advanced in the future.

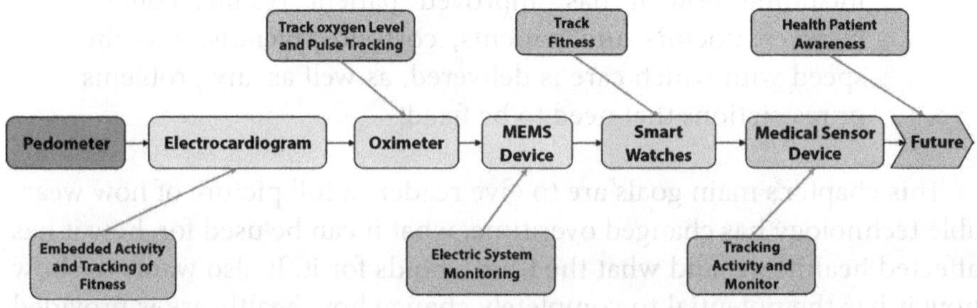

Figure 13.2 Wearable device technology in the future.

13.2.1 Early Wearable Devices in Healthcare

The first wearable medical gadgets paved the way for the revolutionary effects of today's wearable technology. These gadgets were pretty basic compared to what we have now, but they were big steps forward for their time and helped smart technology in healthcare grow. The pedometer, which was invented in the 1400s, is one of the first medical gadgets that could be worn. These tools, which were also called "step counters," were used to keep track of how many steps each person took. Early pedometers were mechanical and not very complicated, but they paved the way for more complex devices that could track a lot of different health measures.

After the Holter monitor was made in 1949, medical gadgets that could be worn started to appear in the 20th century. By letting patients wear a device that caught their heart beats for a long time, this portable ECG machine changed the way cardiac abnormalities were diagnosed and tracked. The Holter monitor showed that wearable technology could be used to continuously and non-invasively track vital data. The insulin pump, which came out in the 1970s, is another early example of personal technology in health care. People with diabetes wear these devices on their bodies, and they release insulin constantly throughout the day, acting like a healthy pancreas [12]. The invention of the insulin pump was a big step forward in managing diabetes. It gave people more freedom and control over their insulin therapy. In the 1980s, the first wearable hearing aids were made, which showed that wearable technology was still changing. Digital signal processing was used in these behind-the-ear gadgets to boost sounds and make life better for people who have trouble hearing. Wearable hearing aids were a big step forward in helpful technology because they are modest and work well to help people who are losing their hearing. In general, the first wearable medical devices paved the way for the creation of modern wearable technology by showing that they could be used to track health and manage long-term problems. Today's technology is much more advanced than these early devices, but they were the building blocks for more advanced personal devices that can track a wide range of bodily data in real time [13].

13.2.2 Technological Advancements Leading to Modern Wearable Devices

New technologies have been very important in the development of wearable technology, resulting in the creation of modern, multipurpose technology that can track a lot of different bodily factors. Sensor technology, downsizing, connection, and battery life improvements have made these steps forward possible. Together, they have turned wearable technology into powerful health tracking and management tools. The shrinking of parts is one of the most important technical advances that has led to the creation of modern smart technology. The first portable technology was big and heavy, so it was not useful for daily tasks [14]. Microelectronics and materials science, on the other hand, have made it possible to make parts that are smaller and lighter so that they can be easily put into wearable technology. Because of this shrinking, portable devices that are discrete, comfy, and able to track a wide range of bodily factors have been made possible. The creation of more powerful tracking systems is another important step forward. In the beginning, wearable technology could not do much to track bodily factors; they could only keep track of simple things like heart rate or steps taken. But, as sensor technology has improved, new devices have been made that can track a lot of different things, like heart rate variability, blood pressure, oxygen levels, and even ECG readings. With these monitors, people can get a fuller picture of their health, and doctors can make better decisions about their patients [15].

Another important improvement that has changed wearable technology is the ability to connect to the internet. In the beginning, wearable technology was usually stand-alone gadgets that did not have many ways to link. However, improvements in wireless technologies like Bluetooth and Wi-Fi have made it possible [16] for wearable technology to talk to smartphones, computers, and other gadgets, sending and analyzing data in real time. This connection has made wearable technology much more useful by letting us do things like remotely watch, share data, and store it in the cloud. Another important thing that has gotten a lot better with technology progress is battery life. In the beginning, batteries for smart technology often did not last long and had to be replaced or charged often. But, as battery technology has improved, more efficient batteries have been made that can last longer, so users can wear their devices for longer amounts of time without having to charge them.

13.3 Anatomy of Wearable Technology

There are several important parts that make portable technology work and allow it to be used in healthcare settings. Sensor technologies, connection choices, power management, and design factors are some of the things that make smart devices useful for keeping an eye on health and controlling long-term conditions [17]. At the heart of wearable technology are sensor technologies that let them track a lot of different bodily factors. Examples of these sensors are accelerometers, which measure speed and movement, gyroscopes, which measure rotation and direction, and PPG devices, which measure heart rate and blood flow. Together, these tools give people real-time information about their health, which lets problems be found early and treated quickly. Another important part of wearable technology is the ability to connect to other devices and send and receive data without any problems. Wearable technology often has connection choices like Bluetooth and Wi-Fi that let them talk to phones, computers, and other gadgets. This connection lets features like online tracking, data sharing, and cloud storing work, which makes smart technology more useful and functional. When it comes to wearable technology, power management is very important because these devices are worn all the time and do not need to be charged or changed very often. Better batteries with longer battery lives have been made possible by improvements in battery technology. This means that users can keep their devices for longer amounts of time without having to charge them. To get power from the surroundings, some wearable technology also has energy gathering technologies built in, like solar cells or motion energy harvesters. Design and comfort are very important when it comes to how well-worn technology is accepted and used. Because these gadgets are meant to be worn close to the body for long amounts of time, they need to be light, comfy, and unnoticeable. Water protection, longevity, and ease of use are also things that designers think about when making wearable technology. All of these things affect the general user experience and usefulness of the technology [18].

13.3.1 Sensor Technologies in Wearable Devices

Sensor technologies are important parts of personal technology because they let them track different body functions and external factors. These devices gather information about the wearer's health and actions in real time, which is very useful. These are some of the most important sensing systems used in personal technology:

- Accelerometers: These devices record acceleration forces, which lets them track movement, pick up on movements, and keep an eye on physical activity. A lot of fitness apps use them to keep track of how many steps you take, how far you walk, and how many calories you burn.

- Gyroscopes: These devices can tell when a gadget is moving or changing its position because they measure direction and spin. These are used with accelerometers to make motion tracking and gesture recognition more accurate.
- Heart Rate Monitors: People wear heart rate monitors, which measure their heart rate with visual sensors or wires. These monitors can pick up changes in heart rate, which tells you about the wearer's physical health and exercise level.
- Photoplethysmography (PPG) devices measure heart rate and blood flow with light. These sensors are often found in gadgets that you wear to check your blood pressure, heart rate, and oxygen levels in your blood.
- Temperature Sensors: Temperature sensors find out about a person's health and well-being by measuring their body temperature. They can also be used to keep an eye on the temperature of the area, which is helpful for sports and activities that take place outside.
- Electronic Dermal Activity (EDA) Sensors: These sensors check how well the skin conducts electricity and can tell when a person is feeling stressed or excited. Wearable gadgets that track stress often use these sensors.
- Global Positioning System (GPS): GPS systems use data from satellites to figure out where the user is. Fitness trackers and smartwatches often have GPS sensors that let them keep track of things you do outside and offer location-based services.
- Environmental Monitors: These monitors check things like the temperature, UV rays, and the cleanliness of the air. People who are sensitive to the climate or who like to do things outside can get useful information from these monitors.

13.3.2 Connectivity and Data Transmission

Wearable technology must be able to connect to other devices so it can talk to them and send info. The majority of wearable technology sends data to phones, computers, or cloud services through wireless networks like Bluetooth, Wi-Fi, and cellular networks. These technologies make it possible to send data in real time and watch devices from afar, which makes smart technology more useful and functional [19]. With its low power use and ability to work with many devices, Bluetooth is a popular way for smart technology to connect to the internet. Wearable technology can connect to phones, tablets, and computers via Bluetooth, letting users get alerts, keep an eye on their health, and change the settings of their devices. Another technology that is often found in wearable technology is Wi-Fi connection, which lets them connect to nearby Wi-Fi networks. Wi-Fi lets you send data more quickly and can be used to sync data with cloud sites or get to online material and services. Mobile communication lets wearable technology connect to cell networks, so users can talk on the phone, send messages, and browse the web without a smartphone. Smartwatches and other portable technology that works on their own often use cellular connection.

13.3.3 Power Management and Battery Life

Controlling power is an important part of wearable technology because these gadgets are worn all the time and need to work on small batteries. As battery technology has improved, more efficient cells with longer battery lives have been made [20]. This means that users can keep their devices for longer amounts of time without having to charge them. One way to make power control better in smart technology is to use parts and systems that use less energy. For instance, using sensors, computers, and displays that use less power can help cut down on power use and increase battery life. Moreover, making software and programs work better so they use less power when they are not needed can add to the battery's life.

Putting tools that collect energy into personal gadgets is another way to go. Energy harvesting technologies, like solar cells or motion energy harvesters, can get power from the surroundings, so they do not need to be charged from the outside. These technologies can be especially helpful for gadgets that are worn and are exposed to light or movement. Putting batteries in portable technology that can be taken out and charged or replaced can also help handle power better. Removable [21] batteries make it easy to switch out dead cells for fully charged ones, so the device can keep working. There are many ways to charge rechargeable batteries, including USB charging, wireless charging, and sun charging. This gives users a lot of options and makes things easier for them. Overall, smart power control is necessary to make sure that wearable technology can be used and does its job. Wearable devices are getting better at managing power thanks to advances in battery technology, energy-efficient parts, and energy harvesting technologies. This means that batteries last longer and users have a better experience.

13.3.4 Design and Ergonomics

Design and comfort are very important when it comes to how well-worn technology is accepted and used. Because these gadgets are meant to be worn close to the body for long amounts of time, they need to be light, comfy, and unnoticeable. When designing wearable technology, things like water proof, longevity, and ease of use are also taken into account. These all affect the total user experience and usefulness of the technology. The shape of personal technology is an important part of design [22]. It might be uncomfortable to wear devices that are too big or heavy for long periods of time. On the other hand, devices that are too small or light could be lost or broken easily. Making sure that wearing technology is both useful and practical means finding the best mix between size, weight, and comfort.

The materials that are used to make personal technology are another important thing to think about. If you wear something close to your skin, then materials that are soft, flexible, and transparent can help make you feel better and keep your skin from getting irritated [23]. Wearable technology can also stand up to the wear and tear of daily life if it is made of materials that are strong and do not get wet. Another important thing to think about when making smart technology is how easy it is to use. People are more likely to use devices that are simple and easy to understand. This includes things like screens that are easy to read, user interfaces that are simple, and buttons that are practical and easy to reach and use.

13.4 Types of Wearable Devices in Healthcare

Wearable medical devices are meant to keep an eye on different parts of your health and fitness, give you useful information about health measures, and help you better handle long-term problems. These gadgets come in different shapes and sizes and are used for different things, like keeping track

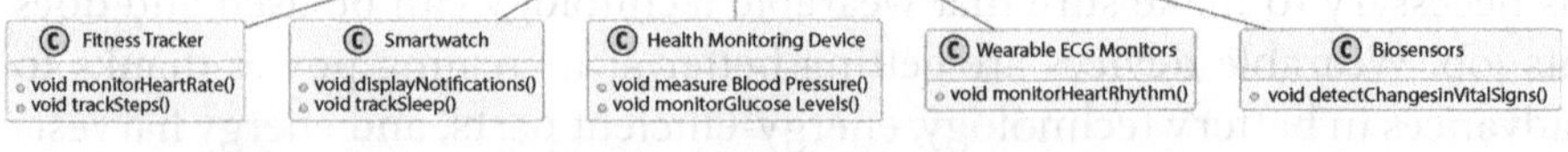

Figure 13.3 Different type of wearable device in healthcare.

of your health, medical monitoring, and drug delivery. People can make better choices about their health and happiness if they know about the different types of smart medical gadgets. In the medical field, fitness trackers, tablets, medical tracking devices, and personal drug delivery systems are some of the most popular types of wearable technology [24]. Figure 13.3 shows the different type of wearable device in healthcare.

13.4.1 Trackers for Fitness

It is possible that fitness trackers are the most well-known and widely used type of smart medical technology. These gadgets are made to keep track of your exercise, check your heart rate, and give you information about your general health and fitness. Fitness trackers usually have tools like accelerometers and heart rate monitors that keep track of how many steps you take, how far you walk, how many calories you burn, and your heart rate while you work out. Some fitness trackers have extra features like GPS tracking, sleep tracking, and practice coaching. One of the best things about fitness trackers is that they can encourage people to live better lives and be more active. Fitness trackers can help people stay inspired and see their progress over time by telling them in real time how active they are and how close they are to their fitness goals. Fitness trackers can also help people see trends in the way they move and sleep, which can help them make better choices about their health and happiness.

13.4.2 Wearable Technology

Another popular type of wearable technology used in healthcare is the smartwatch, which can do a lot more than just track your fitness. Like fitness trackers, smartwatches usually have a number of sensors and features built in, such as heart rate monitors, GPS tracking, and activity tracking. Smartwatches, on the other hand, have extra features like the ability to load apps and connect to the internet, as well as alerts for calls, texts, and planned events. Smartwatches are used in healthcare to check health measures like heart rate fluctuations, blood oxygen levels, and sleep habits, as well as to keep an eye on exercise levels. Some smartwatches also have tools that can help you deal with worry and be more aware, like guided breathing routines and relaxing methods. Smartwatches can also be used to keep track of medicine instructions and take care of long-term diseases like diabetes and high blood pressure.

13.4.3 Devices for Medical Monitoring

Medical tracking devices are wearable technology made to keep an eye on and help people with long-term diseases like heart disease, diabetes, and high blood pressure. These gadgets usually have sensors and functions that are designed to meet the unique needs of people who have these conditions. For example, CGMs are used to manage diabetes, and blood pressure monitors are used to manage high blood pressure. One of the best things about medical tracking devices is that they can keep an eye on health data all the time, in real time. This lets problems be found early and treated quickly. For example, CGMs can help diabetics keep an eye on their blood sugar levels all day long, which lowers the risk of both low and high blood sugar. In the same way, blood pressure monitors can help people with high blood pressure keep track of their readings and spot trends that might mean they need to change their medications or way of life.

13.4.4 Wearable Drug Delivery Systems

A newer type of worn medical gadget called a smart drug delivery system is made to make giving medicine easier and more managed. A patch, pump, or other worn part that gives medicine through the skin or a special delivery system is usually part of these devices. Wearable drug delivery

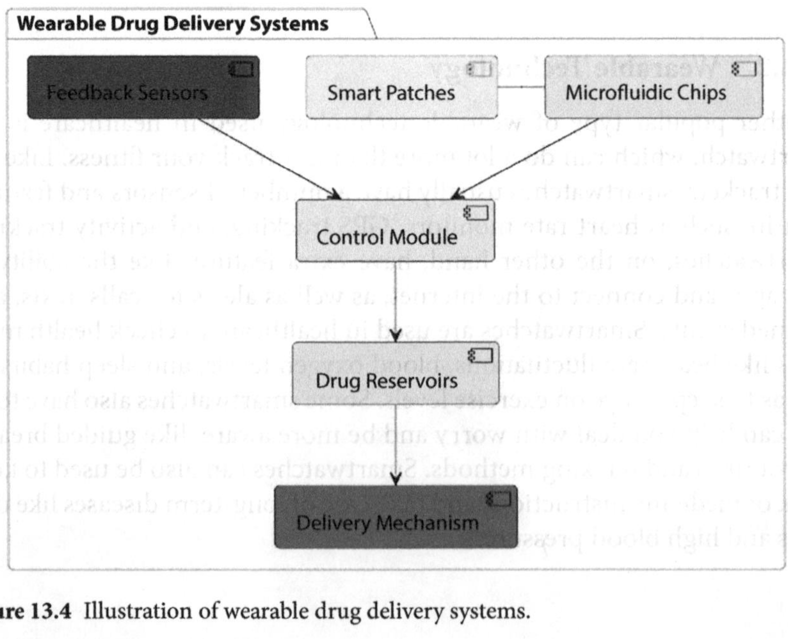

Figure 13.4 Illustration of wearable drug delivery systems.

systems are used for many things, such as giving diabetics insulin, helping people with chronic pain, and treating some medical conditions with hormone treatment. One great thing about wearing drug delivery systems is that they can give medicine precisely and safely, making sure that patients get the right amount at the right time. Wearable drug delivery systems can also help people take their medications as prescribed because they are simple to use and do not require much effort from the patient. Wearable drug delivery systems could help people with long-term diseases that need regular medicine live better lives and have better patient results. Figure 13.4 is the illustration of wearable drug delivery systems.

13.5 Applications of Wearable Technology in Medical Sciences

13.5.1 Remote Patient Monitoring

Remote patient monitoring (RPM) is a way to provide healthcare that uses smart technology to check on patients' health when they are not in a typical hospital or clinic. RPM lets doctors keep an eye on their patients' vital signs and other health information in real time, which lets them spot health problems early and treat them properly. This method works especially well for people with long-term illnesses who need to be watched over regularly but might not need to be treated. The ability to continuously and real-time watch patients' health data is one of the best things about RPM. This lets doctors notice changes in their patients' health early on, which could stop problems and keep them from having to stay in the hospital. RPM can also help patients better handle their conditions by keeping them informed about their health on a daily basis and pushing them to stick to their treatment plans. RPM is especially helpful for people who have long-term diseases like diabetes, high blood pressure, and heart disease. For instance, people with diabetes can use RPM to keep an eye on their blood sugar levels and change the amount of insulin they take as needed. In the same way, people with high blood pressure can use RPM to keep an eye on their numbers and get advice on how to change their habits and medications. Overall, RPM could lead to better results for patients, lower healthcare costs, and better care for people with long-term illnesses. RPM can help people stay healthy and avoid problems from their conditions by letting them be monitored remotely and getting help when it is needed. Table 13.1 gives the summary of different wearable devices.

Table 13.1 Summary of different wearable device.

Device type	Details	Advantage in healthcare	Application
Fitness Trackers	Track physical activity, heart rate, etc.	Motivate users to be more active, track progress, and identify patterns	Fitness monitoring and goal setting
Smartwatches	Include fitness tracking and notifications	Monitor health metrics, manage chronic conditions, and access to apps	Health monitoring, notifications, and apps access
Medical Monitoring Devices	Monitor chronic conditions	Provide continuous, real-time monitoring and early detection of complications	Diabetes management and hypertension monitoring
Wearable Drug Delivery Systems	Administer medication	Provide precise, controlled delivery and improve medication adherence	Insulin delivery, pain management, and hormone therapy
Sleep Trackers	Monitor sleep patterns, quality	Improve sleep quality and identify sleep disorders	Sleep monitoring and sleep disorder detection
Stress Trackers	Measure stress levels and provide feedback	Help manage stress and promote relaxation	Stress management and mindfulness
ECG Monitors	Monitor heart rhythm and function	Detect heart abnormalities and monitor cardiac health	Heart health monitoring and arrhythmia detection
Temperature Monitors	Measure body temperature	Monitor fever and detect infections	Fever monitoring and infection detection
Oxygen Monitors	Measure blood oxygen levels	Monitor respiratory health and detect hypoxemia	Respiratory health monitoring and hypoxemia detection
UV Monitors	Measure UV radiation exposure	Monitor sun exposure and prevent skin damage	Sun exposure monitoring and skin protection

13.5.2 Chronic Disease Management

Managing chronic diseases is another area where smart technology can make a big difference. People with chronic diseases like diabetes, high blood pressure, and heart disease need to be closely watched and managed over time to avoid problems and enhance their quality of life. Wearable technology can help people with health problems better handle their situations by giving them real-time information about their health and letting them make smart choices about their treatment plans. Wearable gadgets can keep an eye on a patient's health all the time, which is one of their best features for managing chronic diseases. This lets doctors keep track of their patients' growth over time and change their treatment plans as needed. People with diabetes, for example, can use smart technology to check their blood sugar levels on a daily basis and change how much insulin they take based on what they find.

Wearable technology can also help people with long-term illnesses stay encouraged and involved in their treatment plans. A lot of smart technology has features like setting goals, tracking progress, and award systems that can help people stay on track with their treatment plans and health goals. In general, smart technology could change the way chronic diseases are managed by giving people the tools they need to better handle their illnesses. Wearable technology can help people with chronic diseases live better, more active lives by letting them be monitored all the time, encouraging them to stick to their treatment plans, and giving them motivation and support.

13.5.3 Rehabilitation and Physical Therapy

Wearable technology is also used in physical treatment and recovery to keep an eye on patients' moves, see how they are doing, and give them feedback on how they are doing. By giving people specific, real-time feedback on their moves and workouts, these gadgets can help them get better faster after accidents or treatments.

One of the best things about smart technology for physical treatment and recovery is that it can give concrete, measurable information about how people are doing. This information can help doctors keep track of their patients' progress over time, see where they need to better, and make changes to their treatment plans as needed. For example, people who are healing from knee injuries can use smart technology to keep track of their strength and range of motion. They can also get feedback on their workouts to make sure they are doing them right. Patients can also stay inspired and involved in their recovery programs with the help of wearable technology. A lot of smart technology has features like setting goals, tracking progress, and award systems that can keep people encouraged to do their routines and reach their recovery goals. In general, portable technology could change recovery and physical therapy by giving patients specific feedback on their routines and moves in real time. Wearable technology can help people heal from accidents or treatments faster and better by letting them keep track of their progress, get feedback, and stay encouraged.

13.5.4 Health and Wellness Promotion

Wearable technology is being used more and more to promote health and happiness by getting people to change their habits to be better. These gadgets can keep track of a person's exercise levels, sleep habits, and general health and fitness, giving them information that can help them make smart choices about their health. One of the best things about smart technology for promoting health and happiness is that it can give people real-time feedback on their health data. This feedback can help people keep track of their progress toward their health goals, see where they need to improve, and change the way they live as a result. People who want to lose weight, for example, can use portable technology to keep track of how active they are and how many calories they eat every day. This helps them make smart choices about their food and exercise habits. People can also stay inspired and involved in their health and fitness goals with the help of wearable technology. A lot of smart technology has features like setting goals, tracking progress, and award systems that can help people stay inspired to live a better life. In general, wearable technology could give people the power to take charge of their health and fitness by giving them the tools they need to keep track of their progress, make smart choices, and stay inspired. Wearable technology can help people improve their health and well-being by encouraging them to live better lives.

13.6 Impact of Wearable Technology on Healthcare

13.6.1 Improved Patient Outcomes

Wearable technology has made a big difference in healthcare by making things better for patients in many ways. One important way that smart technology has done this is by letting doctors check on patients from afar. Wearable devices help doctors keep an eye on their patients' health in real time, which can help find health problems early and treat them quickly, which can improve patients' results. Wearable technology can be used to keep an eye on people who have long-term conditions like diabetes or high blood pressure, letting doctors check their blood sugar or blood pressure levels from afar. This constant tracking lets doctors find problems early and make changes to treatment plans, which helps people get a better handle on their situation and have better health results.

Wearable technology has also made a big difference in how well people who are in physical therapy or recovery do. Patients can get real-time feedback on their performance and growth from wearable gadgets that track their moves and workouts. This feedback helps patients do their workouts properly and effectively, which speeds up their healing and improves their results. Wearable technology has also been shown to help people take their medications as prescribed, especially those with long-term illnesses. Patients can be reminded to take their medicines on time and have their compliance tracked by wearable technology. This helps them stick to their treatment plans and have better health results. Overall, portable technology has the ability to make a big difference in how well patients do by letting doctors keep an eye on them from afar, making recovery and physical therapy better, and encouraging people to take their medications as prescribed. As smart technology keeps getting better and more integrated into healthcare, it will likely have a bigger effect on how well patients do, which will improve the health of people all over the world.

13.6.2 Enhanced Doctor–Patient Communication

Wearable technology has changed the way doctors and patients talk to each other by letting them talk more often, more personally, and more quickly. Patients can keep an eye on their health measures in real time and share this information with their doctors, which helps them have better conversations and make better choices about their care. One important way that smart technology improves contact between doctors and patients is by giving people more control over their health. Wearable technology lets people keep an eye on their health measures, like blood pressure, heart rate, and physical exercise, and share that information with their doctors. This real-time data gives doctors a fuller picture of their patients' health, which helps them make better decisions about how to care for them. Wearable technology also lets doctors and patients talk to each other more often. Wearable technology lets patients send texts, make appointments, and get notes about their appointments or medicines. More contact can help people stick to their treatment plans, which can lead to better health results.

In addition, portable technology can help people who do not see their doctors often between visits. Patients can keep track of their health measures between visits with smart technology and share this information with their doctors during virtual visits. This makes it easier to keep an eye on patients' health all the time and act quickly if any problems appear. The smart technology could improve contact between doctors and patients by letting them talk more often, in a more personalized way, and more quickly. Wearable technology can improve the quality of care and patient results by giving people more control over their health and making tracking and contact easier all the time.

13.6.3 Cost-Effectiveness and Efficiency in Healthcare Delivery

Wearable technology could make healthcare more cost-effective and efficient by allowing more preventative and personalized care, lowering the number of hospital visits and readmissions, and making it easier for people to stick to their treatment plans. One important way that smart technology can lower costs is by letting people get more preventative and individualized care. Wearable devices can help healthcare workers spot possible health problems early and take action before they get worse. This keeps patients from having to go through expensive procedures or stay in the hospital. Wearable technology can let doctors know when a patient's heart rate or blood pressure changes, which could mean there is a problem that needs to be looked at. Wearable technology can also help lower the number of hospital stays and readmissions by letting doctors keep a closer eye on patients' health when they are not in a professional setting. Patients with long-term illnesses can use smart technology to keep track of their health measures and share this information with their doctors. This lets doctors find problems early and take steps that can keep patients out of the hospital. Wearable technology can also help people stick to their treatment plans, which lowers the risk of problems that could need expensive fixes. Patients can use smart technology to keep track of how well they are taking their medicines, get alerts, and see how far they have come in reaching their health goals. This can lead to better attendance and better health outcomes. Overall, smart technology could make healthcare more cost-effective and efficient by allowing more preventative and personalized care, lowering the number of hospital stays and readmissions, and making it easier for people to stick to their treatment plans. As smart technology keeps getting better and more integrated into healthcare, it will likely have a bigger effect on how cost-effective and efficient healthcare is. This will be good for both individuals and healthcare systems.

13.6.4 Challenges and Limitations

Wearable technology has the ability to change the way healthcare is provided and make things better for patients, but it also has some problems that need to be fixed before it can be widely used and be effective.

- *Privacy and Security of Data:* One of the main worries about smart technology in healthcare is how to keep patient data private and safe. Wearable technology gathers a lot of private health information, like heart rate, blood pressure, and physical exercise. This information needs to be kept safe from people who should not have access to it. Making sure that data is private and safe is important for building trust between patients and healthcare workers and getting more people to use smart technology in healthcare.
- *Correctness and Dependability:* Another problem with smart technology is making sure that the data received is correct and reliable. Wearable technology can give you wrong or faulty information because of things like sensor mistakes, user error, or the surroundings. Making sure that smart technology is accurate and reliable is important for giving patients and doctors accurate information that they can use to make decisions about patient care.
- *Regulatory and Legal Problems:* Using wearable technology in healthcare comes with a number of regulatory and legal problems, such as making sure that data protection laws are followed, medical device rules are followed, and compensation issues are dealt with. For the safe and moral use of smart technology in healthcare, it is important to make sure that these rules and laws are followed.
- *Integration With Healthcare Systems:* It can be hard to connect smart technology to current healthcare systems and EHRs because of problems with data integration, portability, and compatibility. Making sure that smart technology works well with healthcare processes is important for getting the most out of it and making patient care better.
- *Acceptance and Adoption by Users:* It can be hard for users to accept and adopt smart technology in healthcare because of things like cost, ease of use, and how useful they think it is. To get more people to use and adopt smart technology in

healthcare, it is important to make sure that they are cheap, simple to use, and give users real benefits.
- *Moral and Social Effects:* Wearable technology in healthcare can cause moral and social effects, like worries about who owns data, getting permission, and being watched. To make sure that the use of smart technology in healthcare is moral and socially sound, these ethics and social issues must be dealt with.

Even with these problems and restrictions, smart technology has the ability to change the way healthcare is provided and make things better for patients. To make sure that smart technology is used safely, respectfully, and successfully in healthcare, everyone involved—including healthcare workers, technology creators, lawmakers, and policymakers—will need to work together to solve these problems.

13.7 Future Trends and Innovations in Wearable Technology

Because of improvements in technology and the need for more personalized and easy-to-reach health solutions, wearable technology is always changing. The future of smart technology in healthcare is being shaped by a number of new ideas and trends.

13.7.1 Artificial Intelligence and Machine Learning in Wearable Devices

Wearable technology is getting smarter with the help of AI and ML. These technologies let devices look at data and give you personalized advice and insights. Wearable devices collect a lot of data, like health measures and user behavior. AI and ML systems can look through this data to find patterns and trends that can help improve health. Predictive analytics is one of the most important uses of AI and ML in smart technology because it can help find and stop health problems before they happen. For instance, AI systems can look at data from smart technology to find early warning signs of diseases like diabetes and heart disease and suggest ways to change one's lifestyle or get help to stop these diseases from happening. Personalized health coaching is another way that AI and ML are used in smart technology. In this case, the gadgets give each person advice and comments based on their health data and goals. This can help people make better choices about their health and more closely follow their treatment plans.

13.7.2 Integrating Wearable Devices With Electronic Health Records

An important movement in wearable technology is connecting wearable devices to EHRs. This lets doctors view and look at data from wearable devices along with regular medical records. This combination can give a fuller picture of a patient's health and allow for more targeted and quick actions. By connecting personal technology to EHRs, doctors can keep an eye on their patients' health over time, spot patterns and trends, and make smart choices about their care. For instance, healthcare professionals can use data from smart technology to keep an eye on patients' progress after surgery or while they are in therapy. This makes care more personalized and effective.

13.7.3 Ethical and Legal Considerations in Wearable Technology

As smart technology keeps getting better, there are some moral and legal issues that need to be dealt with to make sure it is used properly in healthcare. Data privacy and security is one of the most important things to think about because wearable technology collects private health data that needs to be kept safe from hackers and other people who should not have access to it. Making sure that the data collected by smart technology is correct and reliable is another thing to think about. Data that is not correct or reliable can lead to wrong assessments or treatment suggestions. Wearable devices need to be validated and calibrated to make sure they give correct and reliable data. Concerns have also been raised about the moral issues that come up when AI and ML are used in smart technology, like how biased algorithms can be or how decisions are made without being clear. To deal with these moral issues, the creation and use of AI and ML systems in smart technology needs to be open, accountable, and supervised.

13.8 Conclusion

Wearable technology has had a big effect on healthcare, providing a new way to keep an eye on patients, control diseases, and promote general health.

Wearable technology, like sensor technologies, different ways to connect, power management systems, and comfortable designs, has made it possible for a lot of different medical uses. Not only have these gadgets changed how people take care of their health, but they have also changed the way doctors and patients interact, making care more specific and effective. The addition of AI and ML tools to wearable technology has made them even more useful by allowing for predictive analytics, personalized health advice, and early disease discovery. This merger could change the way healthcare is provided by making care more preventative and individualized, which would improve patient results and lower healthcare costs. However, there are some problems with the widespread use of smart technology in healthcare. To make wearable technology fully useful in healthcare, problems with data protection and security, accuracy and dependability, legal and regulatory issues, and user acceptance and usage need to be fixed. To get around these problems and make sure that smart technology is used in healthcare in a responsible and ethical way, everyone involved including healthcare workers, technology creators, lawmakers, and policymakers needs to work together. The future of wearable technology in healthcare looks bright, with new ideas like connecting wearable technology to electronic health data, making it easier for doctors and patients to talk to each other, and dealing with ethics and legal issues. Wearable technology could change the way healthcare is provided, help patients do better, and improve the general standard of care if it adopts these new ideas and trends.

References

1. Luo, N., Dai, W., Li, C., Zhou, Z., Lu, L., Poon, C.C., Chen, S.C., Zhang, Y., Zhao, N., Flexible piezoresistive sensor patch enabling ultralow power cuffless blood pressure measurement. *Adv. Funct. Mater.*, *26*, 8, 1178–1187, 2016.
2. Deng, Z., Guo, L., Chen, X., Wu, W., Smart wearable systems for health monitoring. *Sensors*, *23*, 5, 2479, 2023.
3. Wang, C., Li, X., Hu, H., Zhang, L., Huang, Z., Lin, M., Zhang, Z., Yin, Z., Huang, B., Gong, H., Bhaskaran, S., Monitoring of the central blood pressure waveform via a conformal ultrasonic device. *Nat. Biomed. Eng.*, *2*, 9, 687–695, 2018.
4. Yang, T., Jiang, X., Zhong, Y., Zhao, X., Lin, S., Li, J., Li, X., Xu, J., Li, Z., Zhu, H., A wearable and highly sensitive graphene strain sensor for precise home-based pulse wave monitoring. *ACS Sens.*, *2*, 7, 967–974, 2017.
5. Xin, Y., Liu, T., Sun, H., Xu, Y., Zhu, J., Qian, C., Lin, T., Recent progress on the wearable devices based on piezoelectric sensors. *Ferroelectrics*, *531*, 1, 102–113, 2018.

6. Park, D.Y., Joe, D.J., Kim, D.H., Park, H., Han, J.H., Jeong, C.K., Park, H., Park, J.G., Joung, B., Lee, K.J., Self-powered real-time arterial pulse monitoring using ultrathin epidermal piezoelectric sensors. *Adv. Mater.*, *29*, 37, 1702308, 2017.
7. Kim, J., Kim, N., Kwon, M., Lee, J., Attachable pulse sensors integrated with inorganic optoelectronic devices for monitoring heart rates at various body locations. *ACS Appl. Mater. Interfaces*, *9*, 31, 25700–25705, 2017.
8. Chen, L.Y., Tee, B.C.K., Chortos, A.L., Schwartz, G., Tse, V., J. Lipomi, D., Wong, H.S.P., McConnell, M.V., Bao, Z., Continuous wireless pressure monitoring and mapping with ultra-small passive sensors for health monitoring and critical care. *Nat. Commun.*, *5*, 1, 5028, 2014.
9. Zhang, J., Zhou, L.J., Zhang, H.M., Zhao, Z.X., Dong, S.L., Wei, S., Zhao, J., Wang, Z.L., Guo, B., Hu, P.A., Highly sensitive flexible three-axis tactile sensors based on the interface contact resistance of microstructured graphene. *Nanoscale*, *10*, 16, 7387–7395, 2018.
10. Ajani, S.N., Khobragade, P., Dhone, M., Ganguly, B., Shelke, N., Parati, N., Advancements in Computing: Emerging Trends in Computational Science with Next-Generation Computing. *Int. J. Intell. Syst. Appl. Eng.*, *12*, 7s, 546–559, 2024.
11. Sonner, Z., Wilder, E., Heikenfeld, J., Kasting, G., Beyette, F., Swaile, D., Sherman, F., Joyce, J., Hagen, J., Kelley-Loughnane, N., Naik, R., The microfluidics of the eccrine sweat gland, including biomarker partitioning, transport, and biosensing implications. *Biomicrofluidics*, *9*, 3, 031301, 2015.
12. Huang, X., Liu, Y., Chen, K., Shin, W.J., Lu, C.J., Kong, G.W., Patnaik, D., Lee, S.H., Cortes, J.F., Rogers, J.A., Stretchable, wireless sensors and functional substrates for epidermal characterization of sweat. *Small*, *10*, 15, 3083–3090, 2014.
13. Yatbaz, H.Y., Ever, E., Yazici, A., Activity recognition and anomaly detection in E-health applications using color-coded representation and lightweight CNN architectures. *IEEE Sens. J.*, *21*, 13, 14191–14202, 2021.
14. Al-Qaness, M.A., Dahou, A., Abd Elaziz, M., Helmi, A.M., Multi-ResAtt: Multilevel residual network with attention for human activity recognition using wearable sensors. *IEEE Trans. Ind. Inf.*, *19*, 1, 144–152, 2022.
15. Alsareii, S.A., Awais, M., Alamri, A.M., AlAsmari, M.Y., Irfan, M., Aslam, N., Raza, M., Physical activity monitoring and classification using machine learning techniques. *Life*, *12*, 8, 1103, 2022.
16. Kumar, S.A., Kumar, A., Dutt, V., Agrawal, R., Multi Model Implementation on General Medicine Prediction with Quantum Neural Networks, in: *2021 Third International Conference on Intelligent Communication Technologies and Virtual Mobile Networks (ICICV)*, Tirunelveli, India, pp. 1391–1395, 2021, doi: 10.1109/ICICV50876.2021.9388575.
17. Raj, P., Dubey, A.K., Kumar, A., Rathore, P.S., Blockchain-based IoT architecture for software-defined networking, in: *Blockchain, Artificial Intelligence, and the Internet of Things*, Springer International Publishing, 2022.

18. Burri, S.R., Kumar, A., Baliyan, A., Kumar, T.A., Predictive Intelligence for Healthcare Outcomes: An AI Architecture Overview, in: *2023 2nd International Conference on Smart Technologies and Systems for Next Generation Computing (ICSTSN)*, Villupuram, India, pp. 1–6, 2023, doi: 10.1109/ICSTSN57873.2023.10151477.
19. Wani, S., Ahuja, S., Kumar, A., Application of Deep Neural Networks and Machine Learning algorithms for diagnosis of Brain tumour, in: *2023 International Conference on Computational Intelligence and Sustainable Engineering Solutions (CISES)*, Greater Noida, India, pp. 106–111, 2023, doi: 10.1109/CISES58720.2023.10183528.
20. Kour, S.P., Kumar, A., Ahuja, S., An Advance Approach for Diabetes Detection by Implementing Machine Learning Algorithms, in: *2023 IEEE World Conference on Applied Intelligence and Computing (AIC)*, Sonbhadra, India, pp. 136–141, 2023, doi: 10.1109/AIC57670.2023.10263919.
21. Raj, P., Kumar, A., Dubey, A.K., Bhatia, S., Oswalt, M.S., *Quantum Computing and Artificial Intelligence: Training Machine and Deep Learning Algorithms on Quantum Computers*, De Gruyter, Berlin, Boston, 2023, [Online]. Available: https://doi.org/10.1515/9783110791402.
22. Sasubilli, G. and Kumar, A., Machine Learning and Big Data Implementation on Health Care data, in: *2020 4th International Conference on Intelligent Computing and Control Systems (ICICCS)*, Madurai, India, pp. 859–864, 2020, doi: 10.1109/ICICCS48265.2020.9120906.
23. Swarna, S.R., Kumar, A., Dixit, P., Sairam, T.V.M., Parkinson's Disease Prediction using Adaptive Quantum Computing, in: *2021 Third International Conference on Intelligent Communication Technologies and Virtual Mobile Networks (ICICV)*, Tirunelveli, India, pp. 1396–1401, 2021, doi: 10.1109/ICICV50876.2021.9388628.
24. Burugadda, V.R., Pawar, P.S., Kumar, A., Bhati, N., Predicting Hospital Readmission Risk for Heart Failure Patients Using Machine Learning Techniques: A Comparative Study of Classification Algorithms, in: *2023 Second International Conference on Trends in Electrical, Electronics, and Computer Engineering (TEECCON)*, Bangalore, India, pp. 223–228, 2023, doi: 10.1109/TEECCON59234.2023.10335817.

14

Current State of Wearable Healthcare Technology: Physiology and Biochemistry of Wearable Sensors and Devices

Jyotsna A. Patil[1]* and Shrirang N. Patil[2]

[1]*Department of Biochemistry, Krishna Institute of Medical Sciences, Krishna Vishwa Vidyapeeth "Deemed to be University", Karad, Maharashtra, India*
[2]*Department of Physiology, Krishna Institute of Medical Sciences, Krishna Vishwa Vidyapeeth "Deemed to be University", Karad, Maharashtra, India*

Abstract

Wearable medical technology has grown a lot and now offers useful ways to keep an eye on bodily and biological factors in real time. This essay gives an in-depth look at the present state of wearing electronics and sensors, with a focus on how they affect tracking in healthcare. Heart rate, body temperature, and blood pressure are all important physiological factors that show how healthy someone is. Sensors built into wearable technology can constantly check these factors, giving important information about a person's health. Adding biochemistry monitors to personal technology also makes it possible to keep an eye on biochemical signs like glucose, lactate, and cortisol. These signs are very important for controlling long-term conditions like diabetes, keeping track of how hard you are working out, and figuring out how stressed you are. As smart technology has improved, non-invasive and constant tracking solutions have been created. These make healthcare management easier and more efficient. Early discovery of health problems by these gadgets can help with quick treatment and personalized healthcare. The addition of data analytics and artificial intelligence to smart technology also makes them more useful by giving us more correct and useful information. Even with these improvements, there are still problems with getting smart health technology used by a lot of people. To make sure that smart devices can easily be added to healthcare systems, problems like data protection, dependability, and interoperability need to be fixed. In addition, healthcare workers, technology makers, and

**Corresponding author*: ja01patil@outlook.com

Abhishek Kumar, Narayan Vyas, Pramod Singh Rathore, Abhineet Anand and Pooja Dixit (eds.) Internet of Medicine for Smart Healthcare, (263–286) © 2025 Scrivener Publishing LLC

government bodies need to work together to make smart technology useful in clinical settings.

Keywords: Wearable devices, biochemical sensing, health monitoring, patient monitoring, wearable sensors

14.1 Introduction

Wearable monitors and gadgets have become very useful in healthcare because they let doctors keep an eye on bodily and biological factors all the time. These gadgets make it easy and painless to keep track of biomarkers and vital signs, which can tell you a lot about a person's health and well-being. There have been big steps forward in the last few years in making portable monitors, especially in the areas of biology and physiology [1]. Wearable technology with physiological sensors can keep an eye on many critical signs, like body temperature, heart rate, blood pressure, and breathing rate. Smartwatches, fitness bands, and patches often have these sensors built in, which lets doctors keep an eye on a person's health all the time. The information gathered by these sensors can be used to keep track of exercise levels, sleep habits, and any changes in vital signs that should not be there. This allows for early action and personalized healthcare [2].

Biochemical monitors, on the other hand, are made to find certain biomarkers in body fluids like tears, saliva, and sweat. These sensors can keep an eye on a person's glucose, lactate, electrolytes, and other substances, which tells us a lot about their metabolic health. Putting biochemical monitors into portable technology has changed the way that long-term conditions like diabetes, heart disease, and metabolic disorders are managed by making it possible to continuously track patients and create individual treatment plans [3]. One of the best things about personal sensors is that they can give you data in real time, so you can get feedback and help right away. For instance, a portable glucose monitor can let the person know if their blood sugar levels are too high or too low so they can take the right steps. This real-time tracking can be especially helpful for people with long-term conditions who need to have their health checked regularly. Wearable devices could also change the way healthcare is provided by making telemedicine and distant tracking possible. Patients can wear these gadgets at home, and they can send information to their doctors, which lets them do video consults and diagnose them from afar. This can be particularly helpful in rural or neglected places where it is hard to get medical care [4]. Wearable devices have many benefits, but they also have some problems that need to be fixed. Data safety and security is one of the biggest problems, because smart technology collects private health data that needs to be kept safe. Wearable medical gadgets must also be approved by regulators and standardized to make sure that they are safe and efficient.

14.1.1 Overview of Wearable Healthcare Technology

In the past few years, wearable healthcare technology has grown by leaps and bounds. This is due to improvements in sensor technology, downsizing, and data analytics. These gadgets are made to be put on the body, so they can constantly track different biological and bodily factors. They are used in many areas of healthcare, from keeping track of fitness to managing diseases and keeping an eye on patients [5]. One of the best things about personal health technology is that it can give you info in real time, so you can get feedback and help right away. For example, heart rate monitors built into smart technology can let users know when their heart beat is not normal, which can lead them to get medical help. People who have long-term diseases like heart disease, diabetes, or high blood pressure can benefit the most from this real-time tracking because it lets doctors find problems early and act on them quickly. Wearable technology also has the benefit of being easy to use and portable. Wearable medical devices are small and light, so you can wear them all day without any problems. This is different from traditional medical devices that are big and need special settings [6]. Because it is portable, it can be used for constant tracking outside of professional situations, giving a

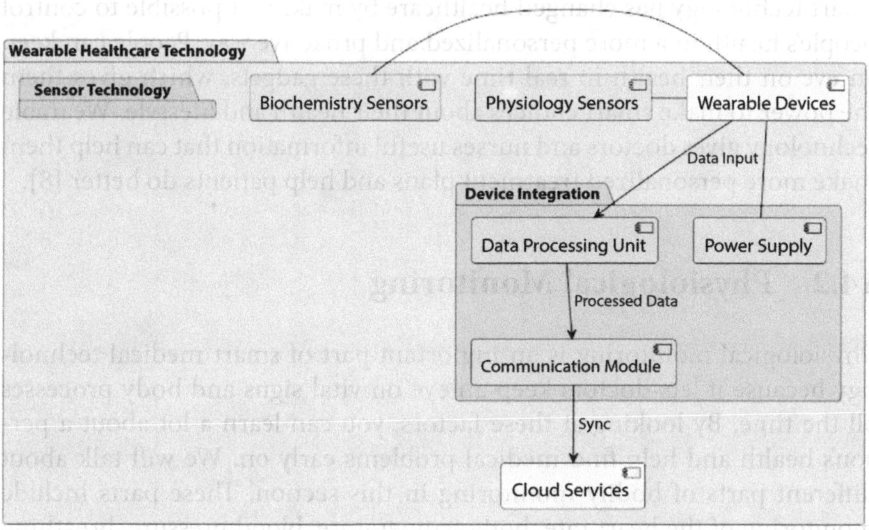

Figure 14.1 Overview of different parts of wearable healthcare technology.

fuller picture of a person's health. Wearable medical technology could also help patients get better care and lower the cost of that care. Wearable technology can help people better control their health and lower the need for expensive medical procedures by letting them find health problems earlier and encouraging preventive care. Also, online tracking lets doctors keep an eye on patients from afar, so they do not have to go to the hospital as often. This makes it easier for people to get care, especially in rural or poor areas. The entire process is illustrated in Figure 14.1.

14.1.2 Importance of Monitoring Physiology and Biochemistry

To figure out a person's health state and diagnose medical problems, it is important to keep an eye on their bodily and biological factors. Heart rate, blood pressure, breathing rate, and body temperature are all physiological factors that give us important information about how the body's critical processes work. If these factors change, then it could mean that you have a health problem like heart disease, breathing problems, or an illness. On the other hand, biochemical factors tell us about the body's internal processes and food amounts. Keeping an eye on biomarkers like glucose, lactate, electrolytes, and hormones can help find metabolic disorders, track the growth of long-term diseases like diabetes, and see how well treatment plans are working. For example, people with diabetes need to continuously check their glucose levels in order to keep their blood sugar levels under [7] control and avoid problems. Putting bodily and biological tracking into smart technology has changed healthcare by making it possible to control people's health in a more personalized and proactive way. People can keep an eye on their health in real time with these gadgets, which gives them the power to make smart choices about their health and lifestyle. Wearable technology gives doctors and nurses useful information that can help them make more personalized treatment plans and help patients do better [8].

14.2 Physiological Monitoring

Physiological monitoring is an important part of smart medical technology because it lets doctors keep an eye on vital signs and body processes all the time. By looking at these factors, you can learn a lot about a person's health and help find medical problems early on. We will talk about different parts of bodily monitoring in this section. These parts include monitoring of the heart rate, body temperature, blood pressure, breathing rate, exercise, and sleep.

14.2.1 Heart Rate Monitoring

Heart rate tracking is one of the most popular features of smart technology. It gives you information about your heart health and exercise level. Optical monitors [9] in wearable technology can measure heart rate by seeing changes in the amount of blood under the skin. This information can be used to track your heart rate at rest, during exercise, and after exercise, which gives you useful information about your general heart health. Continuous heart rate tracking can help people get the most out of their workouts, keep track of their fitness levels, and spot heart problems before they happen. For instance, a heart rate that is unusually high at rest could mean that you are stressed or tired, while a heart rate that changes a lot while you are exercising could mean that you have a heart problem. The entire flow diagram is illistrated in Figure 14.2.

14.2.2 Body Temperature Monitoring

Another important part of bodily tracking is keeping an eye on body temperature. Changes in body temperature can be a sign of an infection, inflammation, or other health problems. Wearable devices with temperature sensors can constantly check the skin's temperature, giving information about how the body controls its temperature. Monitoring body temperature is a great way to keep track of fevers, which are a typical sign of infections like the flu or COVID-19. People can find fevers early and take the right steps to stop the spread of dangerous diseases by keeping an eye on their body temperature all the time [11].

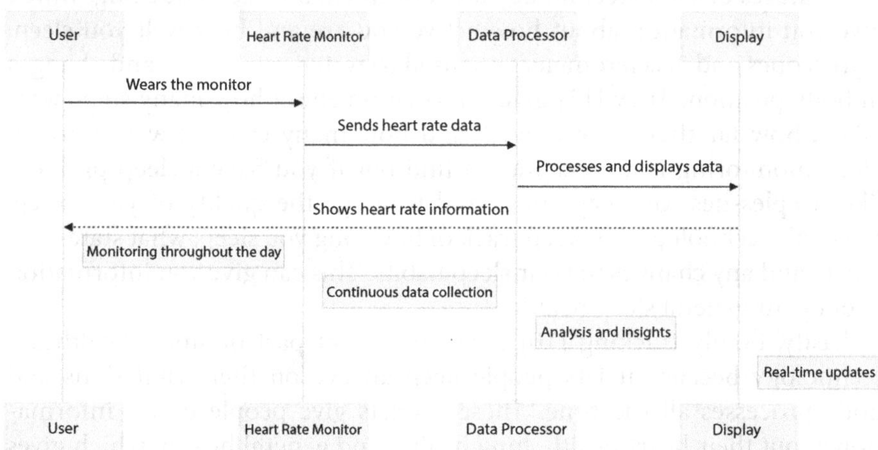

Figure 14.2 Illustration of the process of a heart rate monitoring system.

14.2.3 Blood Pressure Monitoring

Monitoring blood pressure is important for checking the health of your heart and finding hypertension, which is a big risk factor for heart disease and stroke. Blood pressure can be measured non-invasively with wearable gadgets that have blood pressure sensors. This gives important information about a person's heart health. Continuous blood pressure tracking can help people see how their blood pressure changes throughout the day and figure out what might be causing their high blood pressure. This information can help doctors diagnose and treat high blood pressure, as well as figure out how well treatment plans are working.

14.2.4 Respiratory Rate Monitoring

Monitoring the breathing rate is an important way to check how well the lungs are working and find breathing problems. Wearable technology can keep an eye on your breathing rate by tracking chest moves or airflow, giving you information about how you breathe and your lung health. Continuous respiratory [12] rate tracking can help people keep track of how they breathe while they work out, sleep, or do other daily tasks. If your breathing rate changes, then it could mean that your lungs are having trouble or that you have another health problem that needs to be looked into and fixed.

14.2.5 Activity and Sleep Monitoring

Key features of smart technology are movement and sleep tracking, which give you information about how active you are and how well you sleep. Gyroscopes and accelerometers are used to watch movement and changes in body position. They [13] give information about how many steps were taken, how far they were moved, and how many calories were burned. Sleep monitoring is a great way to find out if you have a sleep problem like sleeplessness or sleep apnea and to judge the quality of your sleep. Wearable technology can keep track of how long you sleep, what states you are in, and any changes to your sleep habits. This can give you information about your general sleep health.

Lastly, bodily tracking [10] is an important part of smart healthcare technology because it lets people keep an eye on their vital signs and body processes all the time. These gadgets give people useful information about their heart health, lung health, and general health, which gives them the power to take charge of their health and make their life better.

However, problems like accuracy, data protection, and user acceptance need to be fixed before bodily tracking in smart healthcare technology can fully reach its full potential.

14.3 Biochemical Monitoring

Biochemical monitoring is an [14] important part of smart medical technology because it lets biomarkers and metabolic factors be tracked all the time. These factors give us important information about a person's metabolic health and can help find and treat many medical problems early on. We will talk about different parts of biochemical monitoring in this section. These parts include glucose monitoring, lactate monitoring, cortisol monitoring, and other biochemical markers.

14.3.1 Glucose Monitoring

People with diabetes need to keep an eye on their glucose levels in order to control their blood sugar levels properly. Wearable technology with glucose sensors can constantly check blood sugar levels, giving important information about how glucose levels change and trend. A small sensor is put under the skin of a person using continuous glucose monitoring (CGM) equipment to check the amount of glucose in the interstitial fluid. The sensor sends glucose levels to a smart device that shows glucose data and trends in real time. People with diabetes can use CGM systems to keep track of their blood sugar levels throughout the day and make smart choices about how much insulin to take, what to eat, and how much to exercise. Technological progress in glucose tracking has led to the creation of non-invasive glucose monitoring devices that can check glucose levels without drawing blood from the finger. These devices use technologies like spectroscopy, impedance spectroscopy, and light sensors to check glucose levels through the skin. This is easier and does not hurt compared to other ways of checking glucose levels [15].

14.3.2 Lactate Monitoring

Athletes and fitness fans who want to find their lactate threshold and improve their workouts should keep an eye on their lactate levels. Muscles make lactate when they work out hard, and it can be used to measure how hard you worked out and how well you did.

Wearable systems with lactate sensors can measure lactate levels in real time, giving information about a person's physical health and lactate tolerance. By keeping an eye on their lactate levels while they work out, athletes can change how hard they work out and how long they work out for better results and to avoid overtraining [16].

People who have certain medical conditions, like sepsis or heart failure, can also benefit from continuous lactate tracking. This is because high lactate levels can be a sign of tissue hypoxia and metabolic dysfunction. By constantly checking lactate levels, doctors can figure out how bad the disease is and how well the treatment is working, which allows them to move quickly and improve the patient's result.

14.3.3 Cortisol Monitoring

The adrenal glands make cortisol when they are under a lot of stress. It is an important hormone for controlling metabolism, immunity function, and the stress reaction. Checking a person's cortisol levels can give you information about their stress and health in general. Wearable technology with cortisol sensors can check the amount of cortisol in your sweat, breath, or tears, giving you real-time information on your stress level. This information can help people who want to better control their stress and figure out what makes them stressed. Doctors can also use continuous cortisol tracking to check how well the adrenal glands are working and figure out if someone has Cushing's syndrome or adrenal insufficiency. By constantly checking cortisol levels, doctors can see trends of cortisol release and changes in hormone levels [17]. This helps them make more accurate diagnoses and more effective treatment plans for each patient.

14.3.4 Other Biochemical Markers

Wearable technology can check for many more biological factors besides glucose, lactate, and cortisol, such as electrolytes, hormones, and enzymes. These factors can tell you a lot about a person's health, like how well they are hydrated, how their hormones are balanced, and how well their liver is working. To avoid exhaustion and electrolyte issues, athletes and people who do a lot of hard physical activity should keep an eye on their electrolytes. Electrolyte sensors built into wearable technology can check the amounts of electrolytes in sweat, giving real-time information on water and electrolyte balance [18]. Women's health depends on keeping an eye on their hormones because changes in hormones can affect pregnancy, monthly patterns, and health in general. Hormone sensors built into wearable technology can check the amounts of hormones in saliva or blood, giving information about hormonal balance and sexual health.

14.4 Integration of Sensors and Devices

A key part of smart healthcare technology is combining sensors and gadgets so that data can be collected, sent, and analyzed without any problems. We will talk about the different sensor technologies used in wearable technology and how they can be used in healthcare in this part.

14.4.1 Wearable Sensor Technologies

Wearable gadgets apply a range of sensor technologies to measure bodily and chemistry data. These monitors need to be accurate, dependable, and easy to wear for long amounts of time. The following are some popular sensor methods found in wearable technology:

- *Optical Sensors:* These use light to find out things about the body like heart rate, blood oxygen levels, and glucose levels. Lasers are used to shine light through the skin and measure how much of it is received or reflected. Optical cameras are often used in smart technology because they do not get in the way and can give real-time info.
- *Electricity-Based Sensors:* These sensors measure things like glucose, lactate, and ions that are chemically related to living things. These sensors pick up changes in electrical signals that are made when the target sample reacts chemically with the sensor. Because electrochemical monitors are very selective and sensitive, they are perfect for keeping an eye on certain biomarkers.
- *Gyroscopes and Accelerometers:* Gyroscopes and accelerometers are used to find out how or where something is moving. These devices are widely used in fitness trackers and smartphones to track physical exercise, count steps, and record sleep habits. Accelerometers measure acceleration, whereas gyroscopes measure rotational motion.
- *Temperature Sensors:* Temperature sensors find out how hot or cold something is, both inside and outside. These sensors are important for tracking fever, spotting heat stress, and assessing weather conditions. Wearable technology can have

temperature monitors built in so that the temperature can be tracked in real time.

- *Electrocardiogram (ECG) Sensors:* ECG sensors check how the heart is beating electrically. These sensors are often found in portable technology that checks heart rate, finds irregular heartbeats, and evaluates general heart health. ECG sensors can tell us a lot about how the heart works and help us find heart problems early on.
- *Electromyography (EMG) Sensors:* EMG sensors measure how muscles are electrically active. You can use these devices to track muscle action while you work out, check how well your muscles are working, and find neuromuscular diseases. EMG monitors can tell you a lot about the health and function of your muscles.

14.4.2 Integration of Sensors into Wearable Devices

Putting sensors [19] into wearable technology is a complicated process that includes picking the right sensors, designing the tech, and adding sensor data to the software of the technology. This connection is very important for making sure that the smart gadget works correctly, is reliable, and can be used. In this part, we will talk about the most important things to think about and problems that can come up when adding sensors to wearable technology.

- *Selection of Sensors:* Picking the right sensors for the job is the first thing that needs to be done when adding sensors to smart technology. Some things to think about are the kind of data that needs to be received, how accurate and precise it needs to be, how much power the sensors will need, and their size and shape. An eye sensor could be used to track heart rate, while an electrochemical sensor could be used to track glucose.
- *Placement of Sensors:* Once the sensors have been chosen, the next step is to decide where on the smart gadget they will go. The placement of sensors is very important for getting accurate and reliable data. The physiological or physical position of the sensors, the user's comfort and ease of use, and the need to reduce influence from outside sources like motion effects or ambient light are some of the things that need to be thought about.

- *Integration With Device Hardware:* Once the sensors have been chosen and where they will be placed, they need to be built into the smart device's hardware. To do this, the electronics, connections, and power control systems that will support the sensors must be designed. Adding sensors to a device's hardware needs to be done carefully to get the best performance and the least amount of power use.
- *Calibration and Testing:* Once the sensors are built into the device, they need to be tested and adjusted to make sure that they work correctly and reliably. When sensors are calibrated, they are set up so that they give correct information in a range of situations. When sensors are being tested, their behavior is checked in the real world to make sure that they meet the needs and specs of the application.
- *Processing and Analysis of Data:* The sensor data needs to be processed and examined in order to get useful information from it. This could mean screening the data to get rid of noise, studying the data to find trends or outliers, and displaying the data so that the user can understand it. Processing and analyzing data are important steps for turning raw sensor data into information that can be used.
- *User Interface and Experience:* Finally, the user interface and experience must be thought about when sensors are added to smart technology. The data from the monitors needs to be shown to the user in a way that is clear and easy to understand so that they can quickly figure out what it all means. The user interface should also make it easy to use the device. For example, you could use voice prompts, touchscreens, or buttons to connect with the device.

In the end, adding sensors to wearable technology is a complicated process that involves picking the right sensors, putting them in the right places, and putting them together. It also involves testing, calibrating, data processing, and designing the user interface. Wearable devices can give people accurate, reliable, and useful data, giving them the power to take charge of their health and well-being, if these problems are fixed.

14.4.3 Data Transmission and Connectivity

Connectivity and data sharing are important parts of wearable healthcare technology because they make it easy for sensor data to be sent from the worn device to other devices, like smartphones, tablets, or cloud services. In this part, we will talk about the most important things to think about and problems that come up when it comes to connecting and sending data to smart technology.

- *Connection:* Most wearable technology sends data using Bluetooth, Wi-Fi, or cellphone networks, which are all types of wireless connection. Most of the time, Bluetooth is used for short-range communication between a worn device and a smartphone or computer. Wi-Fi or cellphone networks are used for longer-range communication or when you need to stay connected all the time.
- *Protocols for Data Transmission:* These protocols tell the smart device and other devices how to send data and what shape it should be in. Health Level Seven International (HL7) and Bluetooth Low Energy (BLE), which are both tuned for low power use, are common standards used in portable healthcare technology. HL7 is used for sharing health information between healthcare platforms.
- *Data Privacy and Security:* It is very important to protect the privacy and security of sensor data, especially when sending private health information. To keep data safe from people who should not be able to see or change it, encryption, identity, and access control should all be put in place. To protect patient information, it is also important to follow rules like the Health Insurance Portability and Accountability Act (HIPAA).
- *Data Synchronization and Storage:* Wearable technology must be able to share data with other devices and store data locally in case they cannot connect to the internet all the time. To do this, the portable gadget needs to have good data syncing methods and enough storing space. People can also put info in the cloud and get to it from anywhere.
- *Interoperability:* Wearable technology needs to be able to talk to a lot of different systems and gadgets, so interoperability is important. Standardized data forms and communication methods are needed for connectivity to work and for smart technology to be able to share data with healthcare apps, electronic health records (EHR) systems, and healthcare providers.

The data transmission and connection are important parts of wearable healthcare technology because they make it possible for sensor data to be easily sent from worn devices to other systems or devices [20]. Wearable devices can give people useful information about their health and well-being, giving them the power to make smart decisions about their health by solving problems like interoperability, security and privacy, wireless connectivity, and data transmission protocols.

14.5 Applications in Healthcare

Wearable health technology can be used for many things in healthcare, from managing chronic diseases to keeping track of exercise and stress. We will talk about some of the most important uses of smart healthcare technology and how it is changing the healthcare field in this part. Figure 14.3 show the applications of smart sensors in Healthcare.

14.5.1 Chronic Disease Management

One main way that smart medical technology is used is to help people with long-term illnesses like diabetes, high blood pressure, and heart disease. Wearable sensors can constantly check vital signs, glucose levels, and other

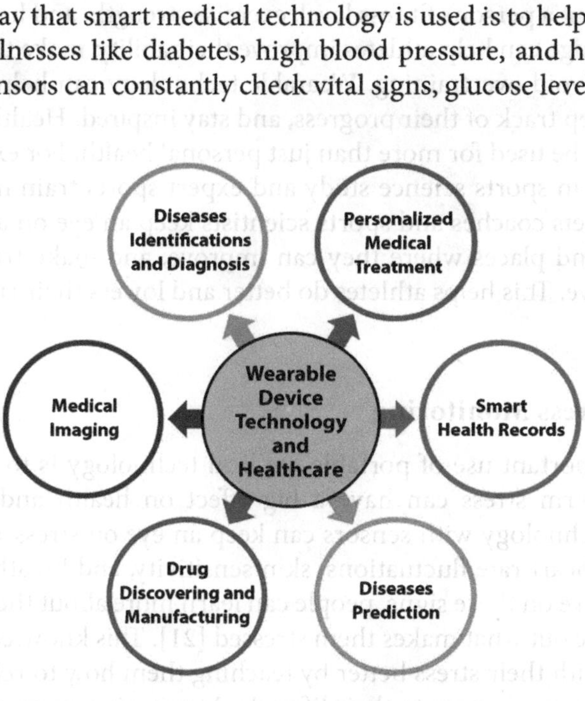

Figure 14.3 Overview of different applications in healthcare.

measures, giving us useful information about how diseases are progressing and how well treatments are working. For example, people with diabetes can use personal technology to constantly check their blood sugar levels, which helps them make smart choices about how much insulin to take, what to eat, and how much to exercise. People with high blood pressure can also use smart technology to keep an eye on their numbers and figure out what causes their high blood pressure. People with chronic diseases can better control their situation and avoid problems by keeping an eye on it all the time. It can also let doctors keep an eye on how a disease is progressing from afar and make changes to treatment plans as needed, which can help patients get better care and lower costs.

14.5.2 Monitoring for Fitness and Sports

Wearable medical technology is also used a lot in fitness and sports tracking, which lets players and fitness fans keep track of their workouts, performance, and healing. Wearable technology with accelerometers, gyroscopes, and heart rate monitors can keep track of your heart rate, steps, distance walked, and calories burned while you work out. This information can tell you a lot about a person's fitness level, exercise strength, and healing habits. This knowledge can help athletes improve their ability, make their training better, and avoid overtraining. Wearable technology can help fitness fans set goals, keep track of their progress, and stay inspired. Health and sports tracking can be used for more than just personal health. For example, they can be used in sports science study and expert sports training. Wearable technology lets coaches and sports scientists keep an eye on athletes' performance, find places where they can improve, and make training plans more effective. This helps athletes do better and lowers their risk of getting hurt.

14.5.3 Stress Monitoring

Another important use of portable medical technology is to track stress, since long-term stress can have a big effect on health and well-being. Wearable technology with sensors can keep an eye on stress-related body signals like heart rate fluctuations, skin sensitivity, and breathing rate. By keeping an eye on these signs, people can learn more about their stress levels and figure out what makes them stressed [21]. This knowledge can help them deal with their stress better by teaching them how to relax, be more aware, and make changes to their lifestyle. Monitoring stress can also help with health and safety at work, since too much stress can cause burnout, absences, and less work getting done. Wearable technology lets employers keep an eye on their workers' stress levels and take steps to lower it and improve health at work.

14.5.4 Remote Patient Monitoring

Wearable healthcare technology is being used more and more for remote patient monitoring (RPM), which lets doctors check on patients' health from afar and take action as needed. Wearable sensors can keep an eye on vital signs, how well people take their medications, and disease-specific factors, giving doctors useful information. RPM is especially helpful for taking care of people with chronic diseases, recovering from surgery, and the old. Wearable technology lets patients keep an eye on their health at home, so they do not have to go to the hospital as often and problems can be found early. This information can help doctors keep track of how the disease is getting worse, change treatment plans, and act quickly when needed, which will improve patient results and lower the cost of healthcare. Finally, smart healthcare technology can be used for many different things in healthcare, such as managing chronic diseases, keeping track of exercise, and dealing with stress. Wearable devices are changing the way healthcare is provided by letting doctors continuously check vital signs, biomarkers, and other health factors. This gives people more control over their health and lets doctors provide more personalized and effective care.

14.6 Advances in Data Analytics and Artificial Intelligence

Wearable healthcare technology is changing because of progress in data analytics and artificial intelligence (AI). This is making it possible to get more accurate, personalized, and up-to-date information about health and fitness. In this part, we will talk about some of the most important improvements in AI and data analytics that are making smart healthcare technology more innovative.

14.6.1 Machine Learning and Predictive Analytics

Machine learning algorithms are being used to look at the huge amounts of data that smart technology collects. This lets people make models that can predict what will happen with their health. These models can help find patterns and trends in data that could show when a disease starts or how well a treatment plan is working.

For instance, machine learning systems can look at data from smart technology to figure out how likely it is that a person will get a long-term illness like diabetes or heart disease. By finding people who are at a high risk, healthcare professionals can take early preventative steps, like making changes to a person's lifestyle or giving them medicine, to lower the chance that they will get sick.

14.6.2 Real-Time Health Monitoring and Alerts

Real-time health tracking and reports are made possible by AI systems. This means that help can be given right away in the event of a disaster or health problem. Wearable devices with AI algorithms can constantly check vital signs and other health factors, sending alerts to the user or their healthcare provider if something is wrong. AI systems can look at data from a smart device to find uneven heartbeats or signs of breathing problems, which can then cause the device to send a warning to the user or emergency services. In cases where medical help is needed right away, this real-time monitoring and warning can save lives. Figure 14.4 illustrates the real time heath monitoring system.

14.6.3 Personalized Healthcare and Treatment Planning

Based on each person's health data, AI systems are also being used to make healthcare and treatment plans more personalized. AI algorithms can find patterns and trends that are unique to each person by looking at data from wearable devices. This lets healthcare providers make treatment plans that are tailored to each person's needs. For instance, AI systems can look at data from a smart device to find things like worry or a lack of exercise that might be making a person's high blood pressure worse. Based on this analysis, doctors can make a unique treatment plan for each patient that may include medicine, changes to the patient's lifestyle, or other actions that are specific to their needs.

14.6.4 Data Security and Privacy

It is very important to protect data security and privacy because smart healthcare technology collects and analyzes private health data. New developments in data analytics and AI are being used to create strong privacy

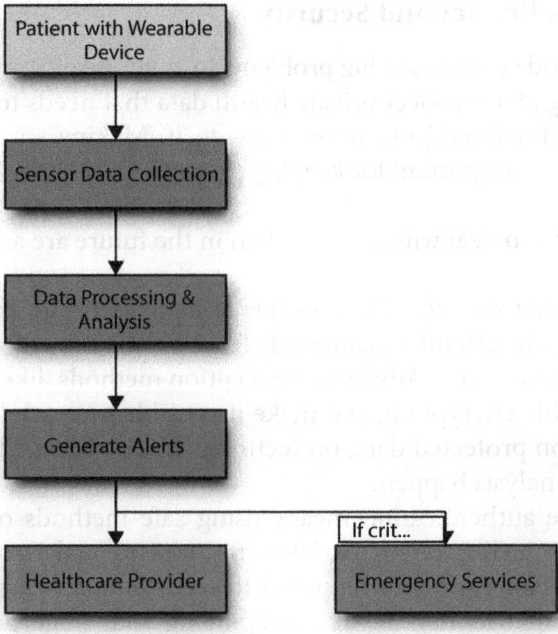

Figure 14.4 Illustration of health monitoring system.

and security measures, like encryption, identification, and access control, to keep health data safe from people who should not have access to it or from being hacked [22]. The progress in AI and data analytics is leading to new ideas in smart health technology, which gives us more accurate, personalized, and up-to-date information about our health and fitness. Wearable devices can give people and healthcare workers useful information by using these improvements, which can help them make smart choices about health and well-being.

14.7 Challenges and Future Directions

Wearable medical technology could change the way healthcare is provided by allowing for constant tracking and personalized care. But there are some problems that need to be fixed before this promise can be fully realized. We will talk about two major problems in wearable healthcare technology and how they might be solved in the future: data privacy and security, and the dependability and accuracy of wearable devices.

14.7.1 Data Privacy and Security

Data privacy and security are big problems in smart healthcare technology because these gadgets collect private health data that needs to be kept safe from people who should not have access to it. Making sure that data is private and safe is important for keeping patients' trust and following rules like HIPAA.

Possible ways to deal with this problem in the future are as follows:

- *Improved security:* The creation of better security methods to keep health information safe from people who should not have access to it. Advanced encryption methods, like homomorphic encryption, can make it possible to securely compute on protected data, protecting privacy while still letting data analysis happen.
- Secure authentication means using safe methods of identification, like biometric identification, to make sure that only people who are supposed to see health data can get to it. Biometric identity, like recognizing your fingerprints or face, can add another level of security.
- Access control means putting in place steps to limit who can see health data based on their jobs and rights. Role-based access control can make sure that only people who are allowed to see certain data can do so, based on their job in the healthcare system.
- *Blockchain Technology:* The use of blockchain technology to make a safe, open way to store and share health information. Blockchain technology can create an unchangeable and clear record of transactions, which can protect health data and keep it safe.
- Data reduction is the practice of only getting the data that is needed for a specific task and not collecting any private or useless data. Keeping data as small as possible can protect people's privacy and lower the risk of data leaks.

14.7.2 Reliability and Accuracy of Wearable Devices

The accuracy and dependability of the gadgets is another big problem with smart healthcare technology. For tracking and making decisions to work well, wearable gadgets need to give correct and reliable data. Wearable devices can be reliable and accurate, but things like sensor accuracy, signal noise, and human variability can make them less reliable or accurate.

Possible ways to deal with this problem in the future are as follows:

- *Advanced Sensor Technologies:* The creation of more advanced sensor technologies, like better biosensors and motion monitors, to make smart technology more accurate and dependable. Newer sensor technologies can give more accurate data and make it less likely that outside factors will change sensor results.
- *Calibration Techniques:* The process of coming up with ways to make sure that monitor results are accurate. When you calibrate a sensor, you compare its results to a known standard and make any necessary adjustments to make sure that the numbers are correct.
- Signal Processing Algorithms: Using signal processing algorithms to get rid of noise and make sensor data more accurate. Signal processing methods can improve the quality of sensor data by getting rid of signals and glitches that are not needed.
- Continuous Validation is the process of testing wearable technology all the time in real life to make sure that they work well and are reliable. Continuous validation means trying devices in a variety of settings and situations to find and fix any problems that might affect how reliable and accurate they are.
- *Training and Feedback for Users:* Giving users training and feedback on how to properly use smart devices to make sure that true data is collected. Training users can help make sensor data more reliable by lowering the amount of variation between users.

Finally, important problems in smart healthcare technology include keeping data safe and private, as well as making sure that gadgets work well and are accurate. Wearable healthcare technology can change the way healthcare is provided by allowing for constant tracking, personalized treatments, and preventive healthcare if it can deal with these problems and look to the future.

14.7.3 Interoperability with Healthcare Systems

Wearable healthcare technology faces a major challenge in interoperability with healthcare systems. This is because these devices need to be able to talk to and work with current healthcare systems so that data sharing and teamwork can happen easily. Interoperability is important to make sure that smart technology can give healthcare workers useful information and improve patient results. We will talk about the problems with connectivity in smart healthcare technology and where it might go in the future in this part.

Problems with being able to connect

- *Different Types of Data*: One of the biggest problems with sharing is that healthcare systems and smart technology use different types of data. Wearable technology might gather information in various forms, which makes it hard to connect to current healthcare systems.
- *Communication Protocols:* Another problem is that smart technology and healthcare systems do not have standard ways to talk to each other. Protocols can be different between devices, which can make it hard to communicate and share info without any problems.
- *Regulatory Compliance:* It can also be hard to make sure that rules like HIPAA in the US are followed. Data protection and security rules for wearable technology must be followed, and these rules can be different in different places.

Where interoperability is going in the future

- *Standardized Data Forms:* Creating standard data forms for smart technology can make it easier for them to work with each other. Standardized forms, like HL7's FHIR (Fast Healthcare Interoperability Resources), can make it easy to connect to other healthcare systems.
- *Unified Communication Protocols:* Healthcare systems and smart technology can talk to each other more easily if they use unified communication protocols like Bluetooth Low Energy (BLE) or Zigbee. Because these methods are made for short-range, low-power transmission, they work great with personal technology.

- *APIs and Integration Platforms:* Creating APIs (Application Programming Interfaces) and integration platforms can make it easier for smart technology to connect to care systems. APIs can let developers access and share data between healthcare systems and smart tech, making it easier for people to work together and share data.
- *Cloud-Based Solutions:* With cloud-based solutions, you can store and view info from smart devices from one central location. Cloud-based options can also let you analyze and make decisions about data in real time, which makes healthcare service more efficient and effective.

14.7.4 Future Trends in Wearable Healthcare Technology

Sensor technology, data analytics, and AI are all making progress that is speeding up the development of wearable healthcare technology. Wearable health technology will likely follow a number of trends in the years to come, such as:

- *Integration of AI and Machine Learning:* Putting AI and machine learning algorithms into smart technology will let us process and analyze data in more advanced ways, which will lead to personalized solutions and predictive analytics.
- *Wearable Technology for Mental Health:* More and more, wearable technology is being used to track and treat mental health problems like sadness, stress, and worry. These gadgets can keep an eye on physical and behavioral signs of mental health, which can help both individuals and healthcare professionals.
- *Wearable Technology for Seniors:* Wearable technology is also being used to care for seniors because it lets doctors keep an eye on their vital signs and exercise levels all the time. These gadgets can help older people stay independent and improve their quality of life, while also giving caregivers peace of mind.
- *Augmented Reality (AR) and Virtual Reality (VR) in Wearable Technology:* Putting AR and VR technologies into wearable technology can make the user experience better and offer more realistic healthcare uses, like virtual talks and medical training.

- *Smart Clothing and Textiles:* The development of smart clothing and textiles with sensors built in can make it possible to continuously track health factors without having to wear separate devices. Smart clothes can make tracking easier and more comfortable for people who wear it.

Interoperability with healthcare systems is a big problem for smart healthcare technology. However, progress in standardizing data forms, communication methods, and following the rules can help solve this problem. Wearable healthcare technology is expected to change the way healthcare is provided and improve patient results in the future. Some of the trends that will happen include the use of AI in wearable devices for mental health and care for the old, as well as smart clothes.

14.8 Conclusion

Wearable healthcare technology is an area that is changing quickly and has a lot of promise to change the way healthcare is delivered. Physiology and biochemistry are at the heart of developing personal sensors and devices that can continuously track vital signs and biomarkers to help people better control their health. Monitoring physiology and biochemistry is important because it can give you useful information about a person's health, which can help with early disease diagnosis, specific treatments, and preventive healthcare. Wearable monitors and devices could change healthcare by letting people be constantly monitored outside of regular healthcare situations. This could lead to more proactive and individualized healthcare actions. Wearable healthcare technology has come a long way, but there are still some problems that need to be fixed. Some of the most important problems that need to be fixed before smart healthcare technology can reach its full potential are data privacy and security, device dependability and accuracy, and the ability of devices to talk to other healthcare systems. These problems should be the focus of future study and development in order to move the field of smart healthcare technology forward. The future of smart healthcare technology looks bright, thanks to progress in sensor technology, data analytics, and AI. Wearable technology is going to be more and more important in healthcare because it will allow for personalized and proactive health management. Wearable healthcare technology could change the way healthcare is provided and improve patient results if people from different fields keep coming up with new ideas and working together.

References

1. Brophy, K., Davies, S., Olenik, S., Çotur, Y., Ming, D., Van Zalk, N., O'Hare, D., Guder, F., Yetisen, A.K., *The future of wearable technologies*, London, UK, Imperial College London, 2021.
2. Mavrogiorgou, A., Kiourtis, A., Touloupou, M., Kapassa, E., Kyriazis, D., Internet of medical things (IoMT): acquiring and transforming data into HL7 FHIR through 5G network slicing. *Emerg. Sci. J.*, *3*, 2, 64–77, 2019.
3. Teixeira, E., Fonseca, H., Diniz-Sousa, F., Veras, L., Boppre, G., Oliveira, J., Pinto, D., Alves, A.J., Barbosa, A., Mendes, R., Marques-Aleixo, I., Wearable devices for physical activity and healthcare monitoring in elderly people: A critical review. *Geriatrics*, *6*, 2, 38, 2021.
4. Mavrogiorgou, A., Kiourtis, A., Kyriazis, D., A pluggable IoT middleware for integrating data of wearable medical devices. *Smart Health*, 26, 100326, 2022.
5. Kim, D., Yang, Z., Cho, J., Park, D., Kim, D.H., Lee, J., Ryu, S., Kim, S.W., Kim, M., High-performance piezoelectric yarns for artificial intelligence-enabled wearable sensing and classification. *EcoMat*, *5*, 8, e12384, 2023.
6. Jeong, J.W., Yeo, W.H., Akhtar, A., Norton, J.J., Kwack, Y.J., Li, S., Jung, S.Y., Su, Y., Lee, W., Xia, J., Cheng, H., Materials and optimized designs for human-machine interfaces via epidermal electronics. *Adv. Mater.*, *25*, 47, 6839–6846, 2013.
7. Liu, H., Dong, W., Li, Y., Li, F., Geng, J., Zhu, M., Chen, T., Zhang, H., Sun, L., Lee, C., An epidermal sEMG tattoo-like patch as a new human–machine interface for patients with loss of voice. *Microsyst. Nanoeng.*, *6*, 1, 16, 2020.
8. Ileşan, R.R., Cordoş, C.G., Mihăilă, L.I., Fleşar, R., Popescu, A.S., Perju-Dumbravă, L., Faragó, P., Proof of concept in artificial-intelligence-based wearable gait monitoring for Parkinson's disease management optimization. *Biosensors*, *12*, 4, 189, 2022.
9. Ajani, S.N., Khobragade, P., Dhone, M., Ganguly, B., Shelke, N., Parati, N., Advancements in Computing: Emerging Trends in Computational Science with Next-Generation Computing. *Int. J. Intell. Syst. Appl. Eng.*, *12*, 7s, 546–559, 2024.
10. Zhang, S., Suresh, L., Yang, J., Zhang, X., Tan, S.C., Augmenting sensor performance with machine learning towards smart wearable sensing electronic systems. *Adv. Intell. Syst.*, *4*, 4, 2100194, 2022.
11. Xia, S., Song, S., Jia, F., Gao, G., A flexible, adhesive and self-healable hydrogel-based wearable strain sensor for human motion and physiological signal monitoring. *J. Mater. Chem. B*, *7*, 30, 4638–4648, 2019.
12. Liu, Z., Li, J., Li, J., Yang, T., Zhang, Z., Wu, H., Xu, H., Meng, J., Li, F., Explainable deep-learning-assisted sweat assessment via a programmable colorimetric chip. *Anal. Chem.*, *94*, 45, 15864–15872, 2022.
13. Wang, S., Lafaye, C., Saubade, M., Besson, C., Margarit-Taule, J.M., Gremeaux, V., Liu, S.C., Predicting hydration status using machine learning

models from physiological and sweat biomarkers during endurance exercise: a single case study. *IEEE J. Biomed. Health. Inf.*, *26*, 9, 4725–4732, 2022.

14. Kumar, S.A., Kumar, A., Dutt, V., Agrawal, R., Multi Model Implementation on General Medicine Prediction with Quantum Neural Networks, in: *2021 Third International Conference on Intelligent Communication Technologies and Virtual Mobile Networks (ICICV)*, Tirunelveli, India, pp. 1391–1395, 2021, doi: 10.1109/ICICV50876.2021.9388575.
15. Raj, P., Dubey, A.K., Kumar, A., Rathore, P.S., Blockchain-based iot architecture for software-defined networking. *Blockchain, Artificial Intelligence, and the Internet of Things*, Springer International Publishing, 2022.
16. Burri, S.R., Kumar, A., Baliyan, A., Kumar, T.A., Predictive Intelligence for Healthcare Outcomes: An AI Architecture Overview, in: *2023 2nd International Conference on Smart Technologies and Systems for Next Generation Computing (ICSTSN)*, Villupuram, India, pp. 1–6, 2023, doi: 10.1109/ICSTSN57873.2023.10151477.
17. Wani, S., Ahuja, S., Kumar, A., Application of Deep Neural Networks and Machine Learning algorithms for diagnosis of Brain tumour, in: *2023 International Conference on Computational Intelligence and Sustainable Engineering Solutions (CISES)*, Greater Noida, India, pp. 106–111, 2023, doi: 10.1109/CISES58720.2023.10183528.
18. Kour, S.P., Kumar, A., Ahuja, S., An Advance Approach for Diabetes Detection by Implementing Machine Learning Algorithms, in: *2023 IEEE World Conference on Applied Intelligence and Computing (AIC)*, Sonbhadra, India, pp. 136–141, 2023, doi: 10.1109/AIC57670.2023.10263919.
19. Raj, P., Kumar, A., Dubey, A.K., Bhatia, S., Oswalt, M.S., *Quantum Computing and Artificial Intelligence: Training Machine and Deep Learning Algorithms on Quantum Computers*, De Gruyter, Berlin, Boston, 2023, [Online]. Available: https://doi.org/10.1515/9783110791402.
20. Sasubilli, G. and Kumar, A., Machine Learning and Big Data Implementation on Health Care data, in: *2020 4th International Conference on Intelligent Computing and Control Systems (ICICCS)*, Madurai, India, pp. 859–864, 2020, doi: 10.1109/ICICCS48265.2020.9120906.
21. Swarna, S.R., Kumar, A., Dixit, P., Sairam, T.V.M., Parkinson's Disease Prediction using Adaptive Quantum Computing, in: *2021 Third International Conference on Intelligent Communication Technologies and Virtual Mobile Networks (ICICV)*, Tirunelveli, India, pp. 1396–1401, 2021, doi: 10.1109/ICICV50876.2021.9388628.
22. Burugadda, V.R., Pawar, P.S., Kumar, A., Bhati, N., Predicting Hospital Readmission Risk for Heart Failure Patients Using Machine Learning Techniques: A Comparative Study of Classification Algorithms, in: *2023 Second International Conference on Trends in Electrical, Electronics, and Computer Engineering (TEECCON)*, Bangalore, India, pp. 223–228, 2023, doi: 10.1109/TEECCON59234.2023.10335817.

15

Real-Time Data Acquisition and Analysis Techniques: Microbiological and Immunological Aspects of Real-Time Health Data Collection

Satish R. Patil[1] and Supriya S. Patil[2]*

[1]Department of Microbiology, Krishna Institute of Medical Sciences, Krishna Vishwa Vidyapeeth "Deemed to be University", Karad, Maharashtra, India
[2]Department of Community Medicine, Krishna Institute of Medical Sciences, Krishna Vishwa Vidyapeeth "Deemed to be University", Karad, Maharashtra, India

Abstract

Real-time data collection and analysis methods have changed the way healthcare is done by letting doctors keep an eye on patients' health all the time and quickly spot any problems that might arise. This essay looks at the bacterial and immunological parts of collecting real-time health data. It shows how important these methods are for better patient results and the ease of healthcare. Monitoring bacteria communities in different places, like the human body or healthcare buildings, is part of collecting microbiological data in real time. This information can tell us a lot about how infectious diseases spread, how antibiotic resistance trends change over time, and how well infection control methods work. Real-time microbiology tracking systems can quickly pick up on changes in microbial populations. This lets people take action quickly to stop breakouts and make patient care better. Real-time immunology data collection, on the other hand, looks at how people's immune systems react to pathogens and other things. This information can be used to judge how well vaccines work, track how infectious diseases spread, and find people who are likely to get immune-related illnesses. Real-time immune tracking tools can help doctors make better treatment decisions and get better results for their patients. The methods for collecting and analyzing data in real time are very important in modern medicine, especially in the areas of

**Corresponding author*: sspatilkvv@outlook.com

Abhishek Kumar, Narayan Vyas, Pramod Singh Rathore, Abhineet Anand and Pooja Dixit (eds.) Internet of Medicine for Smart Healthcare, (287–316) © 2025 Scrivener Publishing LLC

immunity and microbiology. These methods could change the way healthcare is provided and improve patient results by making it possible to continuously check on patients' health and quickly spot potential problems.

Keywords: Microbiome, immunological, data acquisition, health, monitoring

15.1 Introduction

The area of healthcare has changed a lot in the last few years thanks to improvements in technology. Real-time data collection and research methods are one of the main things that have changed the way healthcare is provided. These methods help doctors keep an eye on their patients' health all the time and act quickly when needed, which improves results and makes healthcare service more efficient. Microbiological and immunological statistics are very important for understanding and treating many health problems, like infectious diseases, immune-related illnesses, and how well medicines work [1]. Collecting real-time data in these areas could give doctors useful information about their patients' health and how their diseases are progressing. Monitoring bacteria communities in different places, like the human body or healthcare buildings, is part of collecting microbiological data in real time. This information can help find bacteria, keep track of trends of antibiotic resistance, and judge how well infection control methods are working. Real-time tracking tools can quickly pick up on changes in germ populations. This lets us respond quickly to possible breakouts and give better care to patients [2].

In the same way, real-time immunology data collection is all about keeping an eye on how people's immune systems react [3] to viruses and other things. This information can be used to judge how well vaccines work, track how infectious diseases spread, and find people who are likely to get immune-related illnesses. Real-time immune tracking tools can help doctors make better treatment decisions and get better results for their patients. Putting methods for collecting and analyzing data in real time into healthcare systems could change the way healthcare is provided. These methods [4] can help doctors give better, more personalized care by giving them real-time knowledge about their patients' health. This can lead to better results for patients. We will talk about the microbial and immune parts of collecting real-time health data in this chapter. We will talk about the technology and tools used for real-time data collection as well as how important these techniques are for better patient results and the ease of healthcare. We will also talk about the problems and possible solutions for getting and analyzing real-time data in healthcare.

15.1.1 Overview of Real-Time Data Acquisition and Analysis Techniques

Real-time data [5] collection and analysis methods have changed many fields, including healthcare, by making it possible to keep an eye on and analyze data all the time. These methods involve getting data from different sources, like monitors, devices, and other data sources, in real time and analyzing it right away to get useful information and make smart choices. When it comes to healthcare, real-time data collection and research methods could change how care is given, leading to better results for patients and more efficient care. One of the best things about real-time data collection and research methods is that they let you keep an eye on patients' health all the time. In the past, healthcare workers checked on patients' health by measuring and evaluating them on a regular basis. But [6] these ways are not very good at picking up changes in a patient's health that happen in real time. Real-time data collection methods, like wearing monitors and distant tracking devices, make it possible to keep an eye on a patient's heart rate, blood pressure, and glucose levels all the time. This constant tracking can give doctors a fuller picture of a patient's health and help them spot changes or problems early, so they can take action more quickly and get better results. Using real-time data collection and analysis tools also lets healthcare professionals tailor care to each patient. By keeping an eye on patient health data all the time, doctors can make sure that treatments and measures are tailored to each patient's needs and how they respond to treatment. For instance, checking glucose levels in diabetes patients in real time can help doctors change the amount of insulin they give them in real time, which improves glucose control and lowers the risk of problems [7].

Real-time data collection [8] and research methods not only can improve patient results but also can make healthcare more efficient. These methods can help cut down on the time and money doctors spend on tests and treatments that are not needed by giving them real-time information about their patients' health. Real-time monitoring of vital signs in admitted patients, for example, can help doctors spot patients whose health is getting worse quickly. This lets them do something about it before it gets worse, which saves money on expensive treatments like intensive care. Techniques for collecting and analyzing data in real time could also help improve healthcare in places with few resources [9]. In these places, it can be hard to get to medical tools like trained staff and medical equipment. Real-time tracking tools can help close this gap by letting healthcare workers keep an eye on patients from afar and get real-time feedback, which means that they can give fast, appropriate care even in places with few resources. The real-time data collection and analysis methods could change the way healthcare is provided by letting doctors keep an eye on each patient's health all the time, giving each patient more personalized care, and making healthcare more efficient. By using these methods, healthcare professionals can improve the level of care they give, lower costs, and improve patient results [10]. An overview of the structure for real-time data acquisition and analysis techniques is illustrated in Figure 15.1.

15.1.2 Importance of Microbiological and Immunological Data in Healthcare

Microbiological and immunological data are very important in healthcare because they give us important information about infectious diseases, immune system problems, and how well medicines work. This kind

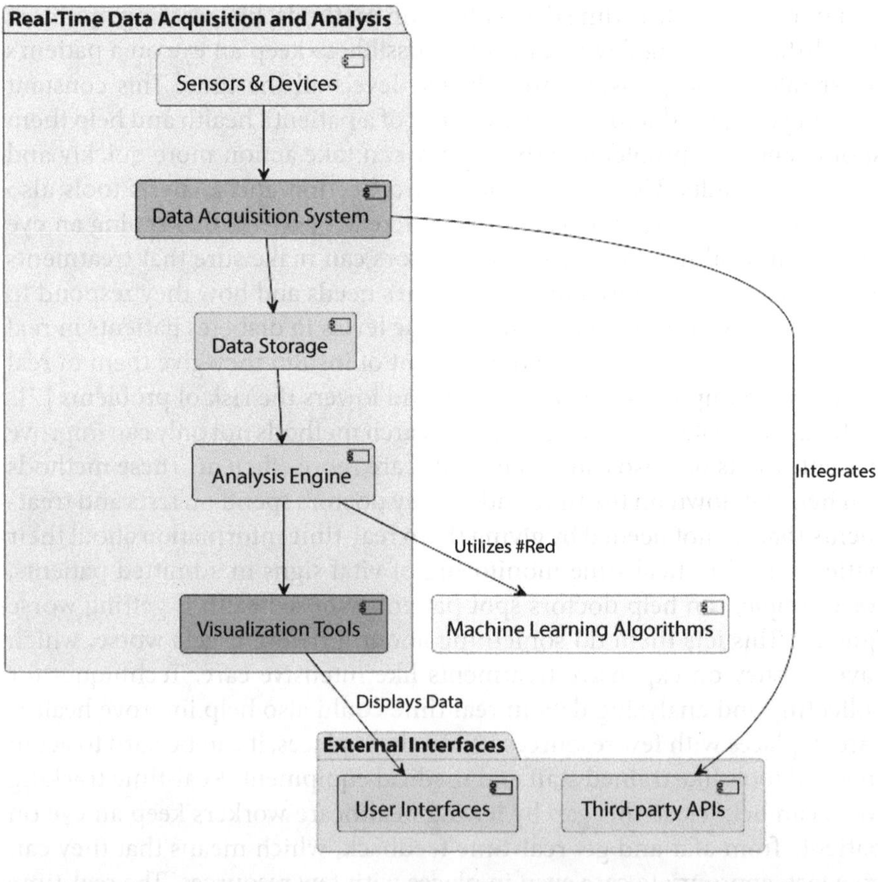

Figure 15.1 Overview of structure for real-time data acquisition and analysis techniques.

of information is very important for figuring out how diseases work and making good plans for protection and treatment. We will talk about how important bacterial and immune data are in healthcare in this part.

For finding and treating [11] infectious diseases, microbiological data is very important. This includes details about different types of microbes and how they interact with the host and their surroundings. By looking at microbial data, doctors can find the germs that cause infectious illnesses, like bacteria, viruses, fungi, and parasites, and figure out the best ways to treat them. Microbiological data are also needed to keep an eye on trends of antibiotic resistance, which is becoming a bigger problem around the world. Healthcare professionals can make smart choices about how to use antibiotics and other antimicrobials by keeping an eye on trends of resistance. This helps keep these drugs useful for future use [12].

However, immunological data give us information about how the immune system works and how it reacts to viruses and other things. Immunological data are needed to figure out how well vaccines work and to keep an eye on how people with immune-related diseases' immune systems react. Healthcare professionals can make sure that each patient has the best possible result by customizing treatment plans based on immune data. A better understanding of microbiology and immunology can help healthcare organizations give better, more personalized care to patients. As an example, healthcare professionals can find people who are likely to get illnesses or immune-related diseases by looking at their microbial and immunological data. They can then act quickly to stop or lessen these risks. In the same way, healthcare workers can change treatment plans to get the best results with the fewest side effects by keeping an eye on how a patient's immune system reacts to treatment [13].

Microbiological and immune data are also very important for keeping an eye on public health and stopping outbreaks [14]. By looking at information from many places, like labs, hospitals, and clinics, public health officials can find patterns and trends in contagious diseases and take specific steps to stop breakouts. For instance, public health officials can find germs in a community and take steps to stop the spread of disease by keeping an eye on microbial data from sewage systems. The microbial and immunological data are necessary to understand and treat infectious diseases and immune-related illnesses and to see how well medicines work. By looking at this kind of data, doctors can make sure that each patient gets the best treatment, which improves patient results and stops the spread of dangerous diseases in communities. Adding microbial and immune data to healthcare systems will become more important as technology improves. This will allow for more personalized and effective care for patients.

15.2 Real-Time Microbiological Data Collection

15.2.1 Monitoring Microbial Populations in Healthcare Settings

To stop and control the spread of infectious diseases, it is very important to keep an eye on bacteria communities in healthcare settings. Real-time microbiology data collection means keeping an eye on groups of microbes all the time in places like hospitals, clinics, and other healthcare centers [15]. This tracking helps healthcare professionals find possible infection sources, keep an eye on trends of antibiotic resistance, and put in place effective steps to stop infections. Environmental sampling is one of the most important ways that healthcare places keep an eye on bacteria communities. To find viruses, environmental sampling includes taking samples from surfaces, air, water, and other external sources. Then, molecular methods are used to find and count the bacteria communities in these samples. Real-time outdoor tracking tools can let healthcare professionals know right away if germs are present, so they can take action right away to stop the infection from spreading. One more important part of collecting real-time microbial data in healthcare situations is keeping an eye on diseases linked to healthcare (HAIs). HAIs [16] are diseases that people get while they are getting medical care. They are a major cause of illness and death around the world. In order to keep an eye on HAIs in real time, information about how often illnesses happen, what causes them, and how antibiotic resistance trends change must be gathered. This information can help healthcare professionals use focused measures to stop HAIs and make sure patients are safer. Summary fo real time data acquisation and analysis is illustrated in Table 15.1.

Collecting microbial [17] data in real time is also very important for finding and controlling outbreaks. By keeping an eye on microbial groups in healthcare settings all the time, doctors can quickly notice changes or rises in the number of cases, which could mean an outbreak is about to happen. Real-time data can help healthcare professionals take infection control steps, like isolating the patient and cleaning more thoroughly, to stop the disease from spreading further. Real-time microbiology data collection is used to keep an eye on food safety, the environment, and bacteria groups in hospital settings. For example, real-time tracking systems can find germs in places that process food, which helps keep people from getting sick from eating. Similarly, keeping an eye on samples of the environment in real time, like water and air, can help find places where diseases are

Table 15.1 Summary of real-time data acquisition and analysis.

Method	Key finding	Limitation	Scope	Application
Wearable Sensors	Continuous monitoring of physiological parameters such as heart rate, temperature, and activity level	Limited battery life, accuracy of sensors, and data privacy concerns	Monitoring of patients with chronic conditions and early detection of abnormalities	Remote patient monitoring and fitness tracking
Remote Monitoring	Remote collection of patient health data through devices connected to the internet	Dependence on internet connectivity and data security concerns	Monitoring of patients in remote or resource-limited settings	Telemedicine and rural healthcare
Real-time PCR	Rapid detection and quantification of microbial DNA or RNA in clinical samples	Expensive equipment, need for trained personnel, and limited multiplexing capability	Diagnosis of infectious diseases and monitoring of antimicrobial resistance	Clinical microbiology and infectious disease management
Flow Cytometry	Quantification of immune cells and their activation status in blood samples	Complexity of data analysis and need for specialized equipment and reagents	Monitoring of immune responses and identification of immune-related disorders	Immunology research and diagnosis of immune-related disorders
Next-generation Sequencing	Identification of microbial species and their genetic characteristics in clinical samples	High cost, long turnaround time, and data analysis challenges	Characterization of microbial communities and detection of novel pathogens	Microbiome research, infectious disease surveillance
ELISA	Quantification of specific proteins, antibodies, or antigens in clinical samples	Limited multiplexing capability and variability in results due to assay conditions	Diagnosis of infectious diseases and monitoring of immune responses	Clinical diagnostics and vaccine development
Microarray	Detection of multiple microbial species or genetic markers in a single assay	Limited sensitivity for low-abundance targets and data analysis complexity	Profiling of microbial communities and identification of genetic markers	Epidemiological studies and personalized medicine
Mass Spectrometry	Identification and quantification of proteins or metabolites in clinical samples	High cost of equipment, data analysis complexity, and limited sensitivity for low-abundance targets	Biomarker discovery, characterization of microbial communities, and metabolic profiling	Clinical diagnostics and personalized medicine

(Continued)

Table 15.1 Summary of real-time data acquisition and analysis. (*Continued*)

Method	Key finding	Limitation	Scope	Application
Biosensors	Detection of specific biomolecules or pathogens in clinical samples	Limited specificity and need for calibration and maintenance	Rapid diagnosis of infectious diseases and monitoring of biomarkers	Point-of-care testing and environmental monitoring
Artificial Intelligence	Analysis of large-scale microbiological and immunological data sets to identify patterns and predict outcomes	Data dependency, interpretability of results, and model generalizability	Prediction of disease outbreaks and personalized treatment strategies	Public health surveillance and precision medicine
Blockchain	Secure storage and sharing of microbiological and immuno-logical data	Scalability and regulatory concerns	Ensuring data integrity and facilitating data sharing and collaboration	Healthcare data management and clinical research
Telemedicine	Remote provision of healthcare services, including diagnosis and treatment	Dependence on technology and limited physical examination	Remote patient monitoring and consultation with specialists	Rural healthcare and chronic disease management

coming from and stop them from spreading. It can be hard to collect real-time microbial data in hospital situations because diagnostic tests need to be quick and effective [18]. Culture-based methods and other traditional bacterial methods can take a long time and might not give data fast enough for real-time tracking. But improvements in molecular tests, like polymerase chain reaction (PCR) and next-generation sequencing (NGS), have made it easier to watch in real time because bacteria can now be found more quickly and accurately.

Adding real-time microbial data to healthcare systems that are already in place is another problem. To support real-time tracking, healthcare workers may need to buy new tools and build new systems. They [19] may also need training on how to use and understand the data properly. Also, protecting the privacy and security of microbial data is very important because it contains private data that could be used in bad ways if it is not properly kept safe. Microbiological data collection in real time can give doctors and nurses useful information to make patients safer and stop outbreaks. But there are still problems with technology, infrastructure, and data security that need to be fixed before real-time microbial tracking in

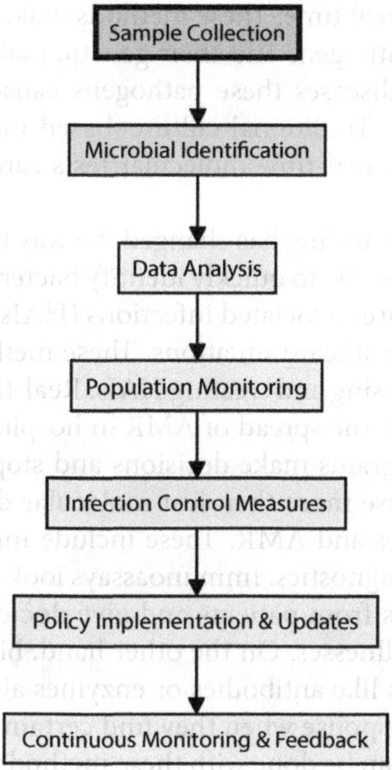

Figure 15.2 Illustration of the process of monitoring microbial populations in healthcare.

healthcare can reach its full potential. Process of monitoring microbial populations in healthcare is illustrated in Figure 15.2.

15.2.2 Detection of Infectious Diseases and Antimicrobial Resistance

A very important part of collecting real-time microbiology data in healthcare situations is finding infectious diseases and antibiotic resistance (AMR). Pathogenic germs, like bacteria, viruses, fungi, and parasites, cause infectious illnesses. These diseases can spread quickly in healthcare settings if they are not found and treated quickly. In the same way, AMR happens when bacteria develop ways to avoid being killed by antimicrobials, making illnesses hard to treat. Finding infectious diseases and AMR in real time is important for making decisions about treatment and putting in place infection control steps to stop the spread of illnesses. Molecular tests, like PCR and NGS, are one of the most important ways to find infectious illnesses and AMR in real time. These methods make it possible to quickly and accurately find pathogens and their genetic makeup. This helps doctors figure out what diseases these pathogens cause and how well they respond to antibiotics. Traditional culture–based methods can take days to produce results, but real-time molecular tests can give results in just a few hours [20].

Real-time molecular testing has changed the way infectious diseases are found by making it possible to quickly identify bacteria and keep an eye on AMR trends. Healthcare-associated infections (HAIs) are a major cause of illness and death in healthcare situations. These methods have been especially helpful in diagnosing and treating HAIs. Real-time genetic tests have also been used to track the spread of AMR in hospital settings. This helps antibiotic control programs make decisions and stop the development of resistance types. We use more than just molecular diagnostics to quickly find infectious diseases and AMR. These include immunoassays, biosensors, and molecular diagnostics. Immunoassays look for certain antibodies or antigens in samples from patients and give doctors a quick and accurate way to diagnose illnesses. On the other hand, biosensors use biological detection elements like antibodies or enzymes along with detectors to make a quantitative response when they find certain chemicals or viruses. Point-of-care testing can be done with these methods, which makes it possible to quickly diagnose and treat infectious diseases.

15.2.3 Applications in Infection Control and Outbreak Prevention

Collecting microbial data in real time can help avoid infections and outbreaks in healthcare situations in a number of ways. Healthcare professionals can stop the spread of illnesses and manage cases by keeping an eye on bacteria communities and trends of infectious diseases all the time. Some important ways that real-time microbial data collection is used to stop infections and outbreaks are as follows:

- Early discovery of outbreaks: Healthcare workers can find outbreaks early by keeping an eye on trends of infectious diseases in real time. This lets them act quickly to stop the disease from spreading further. When healthcare professionals look at microbial data in real time, they can find groups of cases and take infection control steps, like isolating patients and cleaning more thoroughly, to stop the spread.

- Antibiotic resistance surveillance: Keeping an eye on AMR patterns in real time can help doctors spot new resistance trends and plan antibiotic control programs. By looking at microbial data in real time, doctors can keep track of how common resistant types are and change treatment plans as needed to stop the spread of AMR.
- Watching of HAIs: Healthcare workers can find people who are likely to get infections and take steps to keep them from doing so by watching HAIs in real time. By looking at microbial data in real time, healthcare professionals can keep track of how often HAIs happen and find ways to make their infection control better.
- Review of steps to prevent infections: Collecting microbial data in real time can help healthcare professionals figure out how well infection control methods are working. Healthcare professionals can figure out how well interventions work at lowering the number of infections by comparing scientific data from before and after the interventions.
- Public health surveillance: Collecting microbial data in real time can help with public health surveillance by giving information on AMR patterns and trends in viral diseases. Healthcare workers can help find and stop infectious disease cases in their communities faster by sharing this information with public health officials.

15.3 Real-Time Immunological Data Collection

Real-time immunological data collection means keeping an eye on people's immune reactions all the time. This gives us useful information about how the immune system works and what role it plays in health and illness. This live tracking can help doctors figure out how well vaccines are working, see how infectious diseases are spreading, and find people who might be more likely to get immune-related illnesses. Flow cytometry is one of the most important tools used to collect real-time immunology data because it lets scientists count immune cells and see how activated they are in blood samples. Flow cytometry gives doctors a lot of information about the immune system's makeup and can help them find problems in immune cell groups that could mean there are deeper health problems. Keeping an eye on cytokines, which are messaging molecules made by immune cells, is another important part of collecting real-time immunology data. Cytokine levels can show how the immune system reacts to bacteria or other triggers, and they can also help doctors figure out how bad inflammation reactions are. Keeping an eye on cytokine levels in real time can help with treatment choices and see how patients are responding to medication.

Collecting real-time immunology data is also an important part of personalized medicine because it lets doctors change the way they treat each patient based on how their immune systems react. By keeping an eye on immune reactions all the time, doctors can find patients who might benefit from immunomodulatory medicines and make sure that their treatment plans work as well as they can. Overall, collecting real-time immunology data is a useful tool in medicine because it helps us understand how the immune system works and what part it plays in health and illness. Doctors can improve patient results and make treatment plans more effective by constantly tracking immunity reactions in real time. This makes healthcare more effective and personalized overall. Structure of a system for real-time immunological data collection is illuistrated in Figure 15.3.

15.3.1 Monitoring Immune Response to Pathogens and Vaccines

Monitoring the immune reaction to viruses and vaccines in real time is important for learning how the immune system responds to these things and figuring out how well medicines and vaccines work. The immune reaction is a complicated process that involves many types of cells and signaling molecules. Real-time monitoring lets us see how these interactions change over time. Biomarkers like cytokines, chemokines, and antibodies are measured all the time as a key way to keep an eye on the immune reaction. The immune system's activity and control can be understood better with these biomarkers, which can also help doctors figure out how well medicines and treatments are working. For instance, keeping an eye on the amounts of certain antibodies that a person makes after being vaccinated can show if they are immune to a certain disease.

When it comes to infectious diseases, keeping an eye on the immune response in real time is very important because the timing and strength of the immune response can affect how well the infection goes. By keeping an eye on people's immune responses all the time, doctors can find those who might be at risk of getting a serious illness and act quickly to stop problems from happening. To figure out how well vaccines work, it is also important to keep an eye on the immune reaction in real time. Vaccines work by telling the immune system to fight off certain germs. Keeping an eye on this

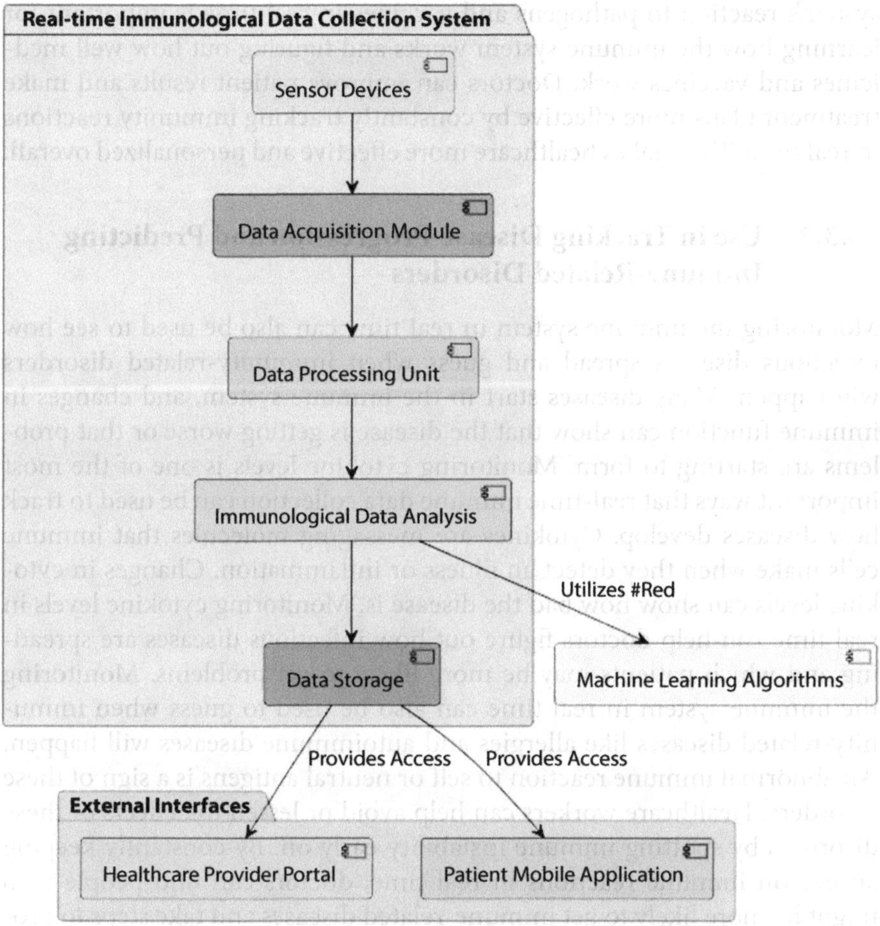

Figure 15.3 Illustration of the structure of a system for real-time immunological data collection.

reaction can help you figure out if the vaccine is causing the right immunity response. Real-time tracking can also help find people who might not be reacting to vaccinations and might need different ways to get vaccinated. Real-time monitoring of the immune system can be used to see how well immunomodulatory treatments work as well as to see how the immune system reacts to infections and vaccines. In order to treat immune-related illnesses like autoimmune diseases and allergies, these treatments change the way the immune system responds. Healthcare professionals can use real-time tracking to see if these treatments are having the desired effects and change treatment plans as needed. Keeping an eye on the immune system's reaction to pathogens and vaccines in real time is important for learning how the immune system works and figuring out how well medicines and vaccines work. Doctors can improve patient results and make treatment plans more effective by constantly tracking immunity reactions in real time. This makes healthcare more effective and personalized overall.

15.3.2 Use in Tracking Disease Progression and Predicting Immune-Related Disorders

Monitoring the immune system in real time can also be used to see how infectious diseases spread and guess when immunity-related disorders will happen. Many diseases start in the immune system, and changes in immune function can show that the disease is getting worse or that problems are starting to form. Monitoring cytokine levels is one of the most important ways that real-time immune data collection can be used to track how diseases develop. Cytokines are messaging molecules that immune cells make when they detect an illness or inflammation. Changes in cytokine levels can show how bad the disease is. Monitoring cytokine levels in real time can help doctors figure out how infectious diseases are spreading and which patients may be more likely to get problems. Monitoring the immune system in real time can also be used to guess when immunity-related diseases like allergies and autoimmune diseases will happen. An abnormal immune reaction to self or neutral antigens is a sign of these disorders. Healthcare workers can help avoid or lessen the effects of these disorders by spotting immune instability early on. By constantly keeping an eye on immune reactions in real time, doctors can find people who might be more likely to get immune-related diseases and take steps to protect them.

Real-time monitoring of the immune system can be used to see how well treatments for these disorders are working as well as to see how diseases are getting worse and to predict immune-related disorders. The immune reaction is changed by immunomodulatory treatments to treat immune-related diseases. Real-time tracking can help doctors see if these therapies are working as planned. By constantly tracking immunity reactions in real time, doctors can make treatment plans more effective and help patients do better. Keeping an eye on the immune system in real time is a useful way to see how diseases are getting worse and guess when immune-related disorders will happen. Doctors can improve patient results and make treatment plans more effective by constantly tracking immunity reactions in real time. This makes healthcare more effective and personalized overall.

15.3.3 Clinical Applications in Personalized Medicine and Patient Care

Collecting immune data in real time can be used in a number of ways to improve patient care and specialized medicine. To make healthcare more effective and specific, doctors can change treatment plans for each patient based on their immune state by constantly tracking immunity reactions in real time. Immunomodulatory treatments are one of the most important ways that real-time immune data collection is used in personalized medicine. This type of therapy changes the immune reaction to treat immune-related illnesses like autoimmune diseases and allergies. But not all patients react the same way to these treatments. Tracking the immune response in real time can help doctors figure out which patients are most likely to respond to certain treatments. Doctors can choose the best immunomodulatory medicine for each patient by constantly tracking their immune reactions in real time. This increases the chances that the treatment will work.

Collecting real-time immune data can also be used to keep an eye on how immunomodulatory treatments are working. The immune system can be affected in many different ways by these treatments. Real-time tracking can help doctors figure out if the therapies are having the desired effects. By keeping an eye on immune reactions all the time, doctors can change patients' treatment plans based on how they respond, which improves treatment results and reduces side effects. Predicting and stopping immune-related bad events is another important use of collecting real-time immunology data. Some treatments that change the immune system can cause bad immune-related events, like cytokine release syndrome or organ damage caused by the immune system. Healthcare workers can find patients who may be at risk of these bad outcomes and take steps to keep them from happening by constantly watching immune reactions in real time. One example is that if a patient is thought to be at risk of cytokine release syndrome, the immunomodulatory treatment amount or plan can be changed to lower the risk of side effects. Collecting real-time immunology data can also be used to keep an eye on how the immune system reacts to medicines. Vaccines work by activating the immune system to fight off certain pathogens. Real-time tracking can help doctors tell if a vaccine is causing the right immune reaction. By constantly tracking immunity reactions in real time, doctors can figure out which people may not be reacting to vaccinations and may need different ways to get vaccinated. In general, collecting real-time immune data can be used in a number of ways to improve personalized treatment and patient care. By keeping an eye on immune reactions all the time, doctors can make sure that each patient gets

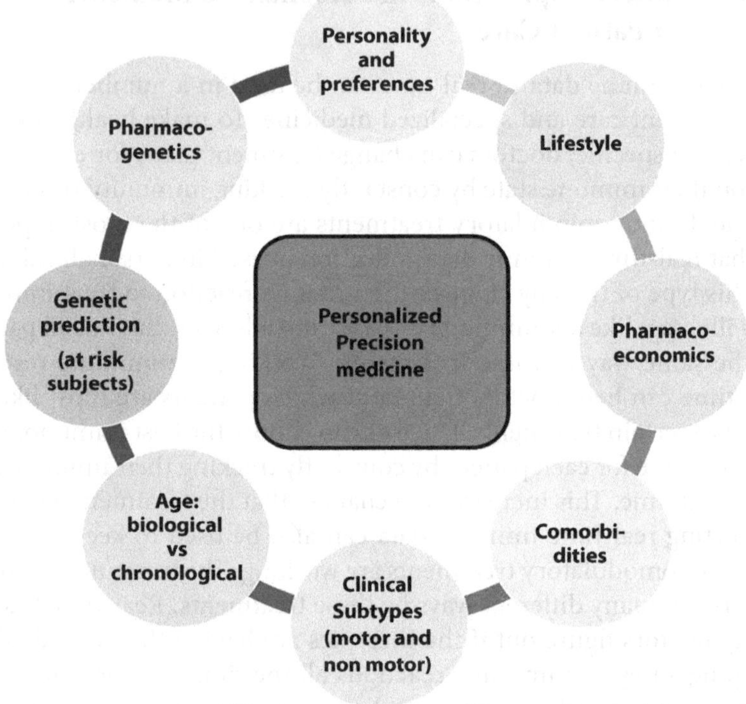

Figure 15.4 Representation of modern personalised medicine.

the best care, see how immunomodulatory medicines work, predict and stop immune-related side effects, and see how the immune system reacts to vaccines. These apps can help patients do better and make healthcare more successful and individualized. Modern personalised medicine system is represented in Figure 15.4.

15.4 Technology and Tools for Real-Time Data Collection

15.4.1 Sensors and Devices for Microbiological and Immunological Data

Sensors and other gadgets that can collect useful data are very important for real-time data collection in microbiology and immunology studies. These gadgets are very important for keeping an eye on bacteria populations, immune reactions, and other important factors in real time.

Wearable sensors are gadgets that people put on their bodies that can constantly check things like their heart rate, temperature, and level of exercise. Wearable devices let you keep track of a person's health in real time. They can also be used to track immunity reactions and find early signs of illness. Biosensors are instruments used in analysis that use biological molecules to find certain chemicals, like bacteria or signs of immune reaction. Biosensors are useful for real-time tracking because they can quickly and accurately pick up on bacteria and immune data.

- Remote tracking devices: These are used to get health information from people who are not in the same place as the healthcare worker. Remote tracking devices can gather information about a person's vital signs, symptoms, and how well they are taking their medications. This is useful for keeping an eye on bacteria and immune data in real time.
- Lab-on-a-chip devices: These tiny devices combine several lab functions onto a single chip, which lets biological materials be analyzed quickly and automatically. Lab-on-a-chip devices can be used at the point of care to keep an eye on bacteria and immune data in real time.
- Flow cytometers: These are tools used to look at the details of single cells, like their size, shape, and which proteins they produce. In real time, flow cytometers can help you keep an eye on immune reactions and give you useful information about how the immune system works.
- Next-generation sequencing (NGS) systems: NGS platforms are used to read DNA or RNA samples, which makes it possible to quickly identify and describe microbe species and their genetic traits. NGS systems are useful for keeping an eye on bacteria communities and trends of antibiotic resistance in real time.

The monitors and devices are very important for collecting real-time data in immunological and microbiological studies. They give us useful information about immune reactions, microbial populations, and other important factors.

15.4.2 Data Acquisition and Transmission Protocols

For bacterial and immune studies that need to collect data in real time, strong data capture and transfer procedures are needed to make sure that the data is collected correctly and sent safely. In this situation, a number of procedures are often used:

- Wireless communication protocols: Bluetooth and Wi-Fi are two examples of wireless communication protocols that are often used to send data from sensors and devices to data collection systems. Because they let data be sent in real time over short distances, these methods are great for use in healthcare settings.
- Internet protocols: transmission control protocol/internet protocol (TCP/IP) and other internet protocols are used to send messages over the internet. These procedures are necessary for remote tracking apps to work because they let doctors see real-time data from patients who are not in the same place.
- Data encryption protocols: To make sure that data is safe before it is sent, data encryption protocols like AES (Advanced Encryption Standard) are used to protect it. Encryption procedures are very important for keeping private health data safe from people who should not have access to it.
- Data storage protocols: To store and get data from databases, data storage protocols are used. As an example, SQL is a data storage protocol. For saving and handling huge amounts of real-time data from sensors and devices, these standards are a must.

The strong procedures for data capture and transfer are needed to make sure that real-time data collection in microbiology and immunology studies is accurate, safe, and reliable.

15.4.3 Integration with Existing Healthcare Systems

Integrating real-time data collection systems with current healthcare systems is important to make sure that healthcare workers can access the data and use it to make choices about how to care for patients. When adding real-time data collection tools to current healthcare systems, there are a few things that need to be thought about:

- Interoperability: Systems that receive real-time data should be able to share data with other healthcare systems that use standard forms and protocols. This makes sure that the data that is received can be easily added to current processes.

- Integration of data: Systems that receive data in real time should be able to combine data from different sources, like monitors, devices, and electronic health records (EHRs). With this connection, healthcare workers can see all of a patient's data at once and make smart choices.
- Data visualization: Systems that receive data in real time should include tools for showing data in a way that makes sense. Data visualization tools can help healthcare professionals make sense of large amounts of data and find patterns or trends that may be important for patient care.
- Data analytics: Systems that receive data in real time should have tools for data analytics that can look at large amounts of data and give information about a patient's health. These tools can help doctors figure out which patients are most likely to have problems and then make changes to their treatment plans to account for that.

Connecting real-time data collection systems to current healthcare systems is important to make sure that the data that is gathered can be accessed, understood, and used. Integration like this can help patients do better and make healthcare better overall.

15.5 Data Analysis Techniques

15.5.1 Statistical Analysis of Real-Time Microbiological and Immunological Data

Real-time statistical analysis of bacterial and immunology data is necessary to get useful information from the data and make smart healthcare decisions. Researchers and healthcare professionals can use statistical analysis to find patterns, trends, and connections in data. This lets them draw conclusions and make predictions based on the data. Describing statistics is an important part of using them to look at bacterial and immune data. Descriptive statistics, like mean, median, and standard deviation, are used to sum up and explain what the data means. These numbers give a short overview of the data, which helps experts figure out the data's central trend, range, and distribution. Inferential statistics are another important part of statistical study. Based on a small set of data, inferential statistics can be used to draw conclusions and make estimates about the whole community. When studying microbiology and immunology, inferential statistics are used to test theories and see if differences or patterns in the data are statistically meaningful. t-tests, ANOVA, chi-square tests, and regression analysis are all common inferential statistical tests used in microbiology and immunology research.

Statistical analysis is also very important in microbiology and immunology studies that use data mining and machine learning (ML). Clustering and classification are two data mining methods that are used to find trends and connections in the data that might not be obvious at first glance. Support vector machines and random forests are two examples of ML algorithms that are used to build predictive models from data. These models help researchers guess what will happen and make smart decisions based on the data.

15.5.2 Machine Learning and AI Approaches for Pattern Recognition and Prediction

More and more, ML and artificial intelligence (AI) methods are being used to look at real-time bacterial and immune data. Researchers and healthcare workers can use these methods to find complicated patterns in data and make guesses about what will happen in the future. They are especially useful for pattern recognition and prediction. Several ML and AI methods are often used in this situation: When you use labeled data to teach supervised learning algorithms how to find patterns and connections in the data, you can watch them work. These algorithms are used for tasks like identifying the presence of a certain disease based on data about microbes or the chance of getting an immune-related disorder based on data about the immune system. Decision trees, support vector machines, and neural networks are all supervised learning methods.

- Unsupervised learning: To find trends and connections in data that has not been identified, unsupervised learning methods are used. You can use these methods to find outliers in the data and group together data points that are similar. Some methods for unsupervised learning are principal component analysis, k-means clustering, and hierarchical clustering.
- Deep learning: This is a type of ML that uses neural networks with many layers to find complicated patterns in data. Deep learning methods are great for looking at big datasets with a lot of dimensions, like genetic data or image data. Tools for deep learning, like convolutional neural networks and recurrent neural networks, have been used in microbiology

and immunology studies to look at images, sequences, and do other tasks.

- Supportive learning: In this type of ML, an agent learns how to make choices by dealing with its surroundings and getting awards or punishments based on what it does. Using real-time bacterial and immunological data, reinforcement learning can be used to find the best way to treat patients. For example, it can be used to figure out the best amount of a drug based on how their immune system reacts to it.
- Transfer learning: In this method, a model that was learned on one task is used or changed to do a similar job. Transfer learning can help with microbiology and immunology studies that do not have a lot of data because it lets researchers use models that have already been taught to look at new data sets.
- Ensemble learning: This method uses more than one ML model to make predictions that are more accurate. Researchers in microbiology and immunology often use ensemble learning methods, like random forests and gradient boosting, to mix the results of several models and make the total performance better.

When used to find patterns and make predictions in real-time bacterial and immune data, ML and AI have a lot of benefits. With these methods, you can use big, complicated datasets to find small trends that people might miss, and use the data to make predictions. But they also have problems, like the fact that they need a lot of labeled data to be trained and could become too good at what they are doing if they are not checked properly. In general, ML and AI are useful ways to look at real-time data about microbiology and immunology. This helps us learn more about bacteria communities, immune reactions, and disease processes. Researchers and healthcare professionals can better understand bacterial and immune data and make better healthcare decisions by using these methods.

15.5.3 Visualization Techniques for Interpreting Complex Data

- Heatmaps: Heatmaps are graphical representations of data where values are represented as colors. Heatmaps are useful for visualizing large datasets, such as gene expression data or microbiome data, and for identifying clusters or patterns in the data.

- Scatter plots: Scatter plots are used to visualize the relationship between two variables. Scatter plots are useful for identifying correlations or trends in the data and for identifying outliers.
- Network diagrams: Network diagrams are used to visualize relationships between nodes in a network. In microbiological studies, network diagrams can be used to represent interactions between different microbial species or between microbes and host cells.
- Interactive visualizations: Interactive visualizations allow users to explore data dynamically by interacting with the visualization. These visualizations can be useful for exploring complex datasets and for gaining insights into the data.
- 3D visualizations: 3D visualizations are used to represent data in three dimensions. 3D visualizations can be useful for visualizing complex structures, such as protein structures or microbial communities, and for gaining a better understanding of spatial relationships in the data.

Visualization techniques are essential for interpreting complex data in microbiological and immunological studies. These techniques help researchers and healthcare providers identify patterns, trends, and relationships in the data, leading to a better understanding of microbial populations, immune responses, and disease processes. By using visualization techniques, researchers and healthcare providers can make more informed decisions and improve patient outcomes.

15.6 Case Studies and Applications

15.6.1 Real-World Examples of Real-Time Data Collection and Analysis in Healthcare

Real-time data collection and analysis have changed healthcare by letting decisions be made quickly, better patient results, and making healthcare more efficient. Several cases from real life show how well these tools work in different types of healthcare settings:

- Remote patient monitoring (RPM): Wearable technology and mobile apps let doctors check on their patients' health from afar with RPM. These gadgets send real-time information to healthcare workers about things like vital signs, exercise levels, and how well people are following their medications. During the COVID-19 pandemic, RPM has been especially helpful because it lets doctors keep an eye on patients with minor symptoms at home and act quickly if their condition gets worse.

- With telemedicine, doctors can diagnose and treat patients from afar using telecoms technology. Real-time data collection and analysis are very important to telemedicine because they let doctors check on patients' health from a distance and make choices about their care that are based on accurate information. Telemedicine is becoming more and more popular, especially in rural and underdeveloped places where it is hard to get medical care.
- Emergency response systems: In emergency response systems like medical services and hospital rooms, it is important to collect and analyze data in real time. In real time, these systems use information like a patient's vital signs, position, and medical background to sort and rank patients well. Real-time data collection and analysis help cut down on reaction times and improve the health of people who are in critical condition.
- Diabetes and high blood pressure are two examples of chronic diseases that are being managed in new ways thanks to real-time data collection and analysis. Wearable technology and mobile apps let people keep an eye on their health all the time and share information with their doctors. This real-time information helps doctors see how a disease is getting worse, change treatment plans, and step in early to avoid problems.
- Population health management: To improve the health of a group of people, real-time data collection and research are necessary for population health management. Healthcare professionals use real-time data to find groups of people who are at danger, put in place preventative measures, and keep an eye on how well these measures are working. Healthcare workers can better use their resources and improve the health of whole populations by collecting and analyzing data in real time.

15.6.2 Impact on Patient Outcomes and Healthcare Efficiency

Real-time data collection and analysis in healthcare has made a huge difference in how well patients do and how efficiently healthcare works. A number of studies have shown that these tools can help patients get better care and lower their costs:

- Better treatment choices: Healthcare workers can make decisions about patient care that are based on reliable and up-to-date information that they get from real-time data collection and analysis. Studies have shown that keeping an eye on a patient's vital signs and other health indicators in real time can help find problems early and improve the result of treatment.
- Less hospital readmissions: Collecting and analyzing data in real time can help find patients who are likely to need to go back to the hospital and act quickly to stop this from happening. Healthcare workers can lower the risk of return and improve patient results by keeping an eye on their patients' health from afar and acting quickly when needed.
- Better management of medications: Collecting and analyzing data in real time can help with better management of medications by making sure that people take their medicines as directed. Adhering to drug schedules is an important part of controlling chronic diseases. Real-time tracking can help doctors find patients who are not following their medication plans and help them start doing so sooner.
- More involved patients: Collecting and analyzing data in real time can give patients the power to take charge of their health by giving them feedback on their health in real time. Wearable technology and mobile apps that let patients actively track their health have been shown to make patients more involved in their care and more likely to stick to their treatment plans.
- Effective resource allocation: Healthcare workers can effectively distribute resources by finding the areas that need them the most through real-time data collection and analysis. By looking at real-time data on patients, healthcare workers can find patterns and trends that could mean they need more resources, like staff or tools, and change how they are allocated to meet those needs.

The collecting and analyzing data in real time has the ability to change healthcare by making it more efficient, lowering costs, and better patient results. When healthcare workers use real-time data, they can make better choices, give more personalized care, and eventually raise the level of healthcare throughout the world.

15.7 Future Directions and Challenges

15.7.1 Emerging Technologies and Trends in Real-Time Data Collection

Several emerging technologies and trends are shaping the future of real-time data collection in healthcare:

- Internet of Medical Things (IoMT): IoMT involves the use of connected devices, such as wearable sensors and medical devices, to collect and transmit health data in real time. IoMT is revolutionizing healthcare by enabling remote monitoring, personalized medicine, and early disease detection.
- Artificial intelligence (AI) and machine learning (ML): AI and ML are increasingly being used to analyze real-time health data and make predictions about patient outcomes. These technologies can identify patterns and trends in data that may not be apparent to human observers, leading to more personalized and effective care.
- Blockchain technology: Blockchain technology has the potential to revolutionize the way health data is stored and shared. By providing a secure and transparent way to store and access health data, blockchain technology can improve data security and interoperability in healthcare.
- Edge computing: Edge computing involves processing data closer to the source, reducing latency and enabling real-time data analysis. Edge computing is particularly valuable in healthcare settings where real-time decisions need to be made, such as in emergency response systems and telemedicine.
- Advanced sensors and wearables: Advances in sensor technology are enabling the development of more sophisticated wearable devices that can monitor a wide range of health parameters in real time. These devices are becoming smaller,

more affordable, and more accurate, making them ideal for continuous health monitoring.

15.7.2 Ethical and Regulatory Considerations

As real-time data collection technologies continue to advance, several ethical and regulatory considerations need to be addressed:

- Data privacy and security: Real-time health data is highly sensitive and must be protected from unauthorized access. Healthcare providers and technology companies must implement robust security measures to protect patient data.
- Informed consent: Patients must be informed about the types of data being collected, how it will be used, and who will have access to it. Informed consent is essential to ensure that patients are aware of and agree to the use of their data.
- Data ownership and sharing: There are complex issues surrounding the ownership and sharing of health data collected in real time. Clear guidelines and regulations are needed to govern the ownership and sharing of this data.
- Algorithm bias: AI and ML algorithms used to analyze real-time health data may be biased, leading to unfair or discriminatory outcomes. Healthcare providers must ensure that algorithms are fair and unbiased.

15.7.3 Challenges in Implementation and Adoption

Despite the potential benefits of real-time data collection in healthcare, several challenges remain in its implementation and adoption:

- Interoperability: Real-time data collection systems must be able to exchange data with existing healthcare systems and devices. Achieving interoperability is challenging due to the variety of data formats and standards used in healthcare.
- Cost: Implementing real-time data collection systems can be costly, especially for smaller healthcare providers and organizations. Cost-effective solutions are needed to ensure widespread adoption.
- Regulatory compliance: Healthcare providers must comply with a range of regulations and standards governing the

collection, storage, and use of health data. Ensuring compliance can be complex and time-consuming.

- Data integration and analysis: Real-time health data is often complex and heterogeneous, requiring sophisticated data integration and analysis techniques. Healthcare providers must have the necessary tools and expertise to analyze this data effectively.
- Patient acceptance: Patients may be hesitant to adopt real-time data collection technologies due to concerns about privacy and security. Educating patients about the benefits of these technologies and addressing their concerns is essential for widespread adoption.

15.8 Conclusion

Real-time data collection and analysis methods are changing the microbial and immune parts of health data gathering in ways that have never been seen before. This means that healthcare results can be improved in ways that have never been seen before. These methods let doctors keep an eye on bacteria populations, immune reactions, and other important factors all the time. This gives them accurate and up-to-date information to help them make decisions. Real-time data collection and analysis in healthcare has many benefits, such as better professional decision-making, fewer hospital readmissions, better drug control, more involved patients, and better use of resources. Health care workers can give more personalized and effective care by using real-time data. This improves patient results and lowers healthcare costs. However, using real-time data collection and analysis methods comes with some problems. For example, protecting data privacy and security, fixing algorithm bias, making sure systems can talk to each other, keeping costs down, and following rules are just a few of the issues that need to be solved. Getting past these problems is important if we want to use real-time data collection and processing in healthcare to its fullest.

In the future, new technologies like the IoMT, AI, ML, blockchain, and edge computing should make it easier for healthcare to gather and analyze data in real time. These technologies could completely change the way healthcare is provided by allowing for online tracking, personalized treatment, early disease spotting, and better healthcare systems. The methods for collecting and analyzing data in real time are changing healthcare by giving doctors and nurses the tools they need to give better, more personalized care. It is possible for healthcare workers to improve patient results, lower costs, and overall improve the standard of care by using real-time data.

References

1. Abuwarda, Z., Mostafa, K., Oetomo, A., Hegazy, T., Morita, P., Wearable devices: Cross benefits from healthcare to construction. *Autom. Constr., 142*, 104501, 2022.
2. Ghayvat, H., Awais, M., Pandya, S., Ren, H., Akbarzadeh, S., Chandra Mukhopadhyay, S., Chen, C., Gope, P., Chouhan, A., Chen, W., Smart aging system: uncovering the hidden wellness parameter for well-being monitoring and anomaly detection. *Sensors, 19*, 4, 766, 2019.
3. Marques, G. and Pitarma, R., Promoting health and well-being using wearable and smartphone technologies for ambient assisted living through internet of things, in: *Big Data and Networks Technologies*, vol. 3, pp. 12–22, Springer International Publishing, 2020.
4. Casaccia, S., Revel, G.M., Cosoli, G., Scalise, L., Assessment of domestic well-being: from perception to measurement. *IEEE Instrum. Meas. Mag., 24*, 6, 58–67, 2021.
5. Lou, Z., Wang, L., Jiang, K., Wei, Z., Shen, G., Reviews of wearable healthcare systems: Materials, devices and system integration. *Mater. Sci. Eng.: R: Rep., 140*, 100523, 2020.
6. Durán-Vega, L.A., Santana-Mancilla, P.C., Buenrostro-Mariscal, R., Contreras-Castillo, J., Anido-Rifón, L.E., García-Ruiz, M.A., Montesinos-López, O.A., Estrada-González, F., An IoT system for remote health monitoring in elderly adults through a wearable device and mobile application. *Geriatrics, 4*, 2, 34, 2019.
7. Santana-Mancilla, P.C., Anido-Rifón, L.E., Contreras-Castillo, J., Buenrostro-Mariscal, R., Heuristic evaluation of an IoMT system for remote health monitoring in senior care. *Int. J. Environ. Res. Public Health, 17*, 5, 1586, 2020.
8. Baker, S.B., Xiang, W., Atkinson, I., Internet of things for smart healthcare: Technologies, challenges, and opportunities. *IEEE Access, 5*, 26521–26544, 2017.
9. Ajani, S.N., Khobragade, P., Dhone, M., Ganguly, B., Shelke, N., Parati, N., Advancements in Computing: Emerging Trends in Computational Science with Next-Generation Computing. *Int. J. Intell. Syst. Appl. Eng., 12*, 7s, 546–559, 2024.

10. Gradim, L.C.C., José, M.A., da Cruz, D.M.C., de Deus Lopes, R., IoT services and applications in rehabilitation: An interdisciplinary and meta-analysis review. *IEEE Trans. Neural Syst. Rehabil. Eng.*, *28*, 9, 2043–2052, 2020.
11. Rodríguez-Rodríguez, I., Rodríguez, J.V., Chatzigiannakis, I., Zamora Izquierdo, M.A., On the possibility of predicting glycaemia 'on the fly'with constrained IoT devices in type 1 diabetes mellitus patients. *Sensors*, *19*, 20, 4538, 2019.
12. Kumar, S.A., Kumar, A., Dutt, V., Agrawal, R., Multi Model Implementation on General Medicine Prediction with Quantum Neural Networks, in: *2021 Third International Conference on Intelligent Communication Technologies and Virtual Mobile Networks (ICICV)*, Tirunelveli, India, pp. 1391–1395, 2021, doi: 10.1109/ICICV50876.2021.9388575.
13. Raj, P., Dubey, A.K., Kumar, A., Rathore, P.S., Blockchain-based IoT architecture for software-defined networking, in: *Blockchain, Artificial Intelligence, and the Internet of Things*, Springer International Publishing, 2022.
14. Burri, S.R., Kumar, A., Baliyan, A., Kumar, T.A., Predictive Intelligence for Healthcare Outcomes: An AI Architecture Overview, in: *2023 2nd International Conference on Smart Technologies and Systems for Next Generation Computing (ICSTSN)*, Villupuram, India, pp. 1–6, 2023, doi: 10.1109/ICSTSN57873.2023.10151477.
15. Wani, S., Ahuja, S., Kumar, A., Application of Deep Neural Networks and Machine Learning algorithms for diagnosis of Brain tumour, in: *2023 International Conference on Computational Intelligence and Sustainable Engineering Solutions (CISES)*, Greater Noida, India, pp. 106–111, 2023, doi: 10.1109/CISES58720.2023.10183528.
16. Kour, S.P., Kumar, A., Ahuja, S., An Advance Approach for Diabetes Detection by Implementing Machine Learning Algorithms, in: *2023 IEEE World Conference on Applied Intelligence and Computing (AIC)*, Sonbhadra, India, pp. 136–141, 2023, doi: 10.1109/AIC57670.2023.10263919.
17. Raj, P., Kumar, A., Dubey, A.K., Bhatia, S., Oswalt, M.S., *Quantum Computing and Artificial Intelligence: Training Machine and Deep Learning Algorithms on Quantum Computers*, De Gruyter, Berlin, Boston, 2023, [Online]. Available: https://doi.org/10.1515/9783110791402.
18. Sasubilli, G. and Kumar, A., Machine Learning and Big Data Implementation on Health Care data, in: *2020 4th International Conference on Intelligent Computing and Control Systems (ICICCS)*, Madurai, India, pp. 859–864, 2020, doi: 10.1109/ICICCS48265.2020.9120906.
19. Swarna, S.R., Kumar, A., Dixit, P., Sairam, T.V.M., Parkinson's Disease Prediction using Adaptive Quantum Computing, in: *2021 Third International Conference on Intelligent Communication Technologies and Virtual Mobile Networks (ICICV)*, Tirunelveli, India, pp. 1396–1401, 2021, doi: 10.1109/ICICV50876.2021.9388628.

20. Burugadda, V.R., Pawar, P.S., Kumar, A., Bhati, N., Predicting Hospital Readmission Risk for Heart Failure Patients Using Machine Learning Techniques: A Comparative Study of Classification Algorithms, in: *2023 Second International Conference on Trends in Electrical, Electronics, and Computer Engineering (TEECCON)*, Bangalore, India, pp. 223–228, 2023, doi: 10.1109/TEECCON59234.2023.10335817.

16

Applications of Real-Time Data in Healthcare Interventions: Pharmacological Interventions Based on Real-Time Data Analytics

V. M. Thorat[1]* and Satish V. Kakade[2]

[1]Department of Pharmacology, Krishna Institute of Medical Sciences, Krishna Vishwa Vidyapeeth "Deemed to be University", Karad, Maharashtra, India
[2]Department of Community Medicine, Krishna Institute of Medical Sciences, Krishna Vishwa Vidyapeeth "Deemed to be University", Karad, Maharashtra, India

Abstract

Real-time data analytics is changing how healthcare is provided, especially when it comes to drug treatments. This part talks about how real-time data is used to improve drug approaches, with a focus on personalized medicine and how well treatments work. Personalized health is one area where real-time data mining is very important. Healthcare professionals can make sure that each patient gets the right treatment by constantly checking data about them, like genetic information, biomarkers, and bodily factors. Real-time data analytics makes it easier to find the best medicine doses, treatment plans, and medications for each patient based on their individual needs. Real-time data analytics also improves the effectiveness of treatment by allowing early adjustments. For example, real-time tracking of blood glucose or blood pressure levels in people with long-term conditions like diabetes or high blood pressure can lead to quick changes in drug dose or treatment plans, which can prevent bad results and improve patient outcomes. Clinical studies are another important way that real-time data analytics is used in drug treatments. Researchers can learn more about how well drugs work, how safe they are, and how patients react by collecting and studying real-time data from users. This makes it possible for flexible trial designs, which can speed up the process of making new drugs. The real-time data analytics is a great way to improve the effectiveness of

**Corresponding author*: vmthoratkvv@outlook.com

Abhishek Kumar, Narayan Vyas, Pramod Singh Rathore, Abhineet Anand and Pooja Dixit (eds.) Internet of Medicine for Smart Healthcare, (317–346) © 2025 Scrivener Publishing LLC

pharmaceutical treatments in healthcare. With real-time patient data, doctors can tailor treatments to each patient, make treatments more effective, and speed up the development of new drugs. This chapter gives an in-depth look at these uses and shows how real-time data can completely change healthcare actions.

Keywords: Real-time applications, medication, precision medicine, drug therapy, healthcare interventions

16.1 Introduction

In the past few years, technology advances, especially in the area of data analytics, have caused the healthcare business to change quickly. One strong tool that has emerged to change healthcare treatments is real-time data analytics, especially in the field of drugs. This part talks about how real-time data can be used to improve drug approaches, with a focus on personalized medicine and the effectiveness of treatment. Real-time data analytics means gathering, processing, and analyzing data as it comes in, so that insights and actions can be taken right away [1]. Real-time data analytics has changed the way patients are cared for by giving doctors and nurses up-to-date information they can use to make smart choices. Real-time data analytics lets doctors take preventative steps and give more personalized care by constantly checking things like vital signs, lab results, and how well patients are taking their medications [2].

For pharmacological therapies to work and be safe, they need correct and up-to-date data all the time. In this case, real-time data analytics has a number of important benefits, including the following:

- Personalized medicine: Analyzing data in real time lets doctors change treatments based on how each patient is different. Healthcare professionals can make sure that each patient gets the best care by constantly checking things like genetic information, measurements, and bodily factors. This specific method makes medicine work better and lowers the risk of bad things happening [3].
- Treatment effectiveness: Real-time data analytics improves the effectiveness of treatment by letting professionals step in before problems happen. For example, people with long-term conditions like diabetes or high blood pressure can benefit from real-time tracking of their blood glucose or blood pressure levels, which can lead to changes in their drug dose or treatment plans that are more effective [4].

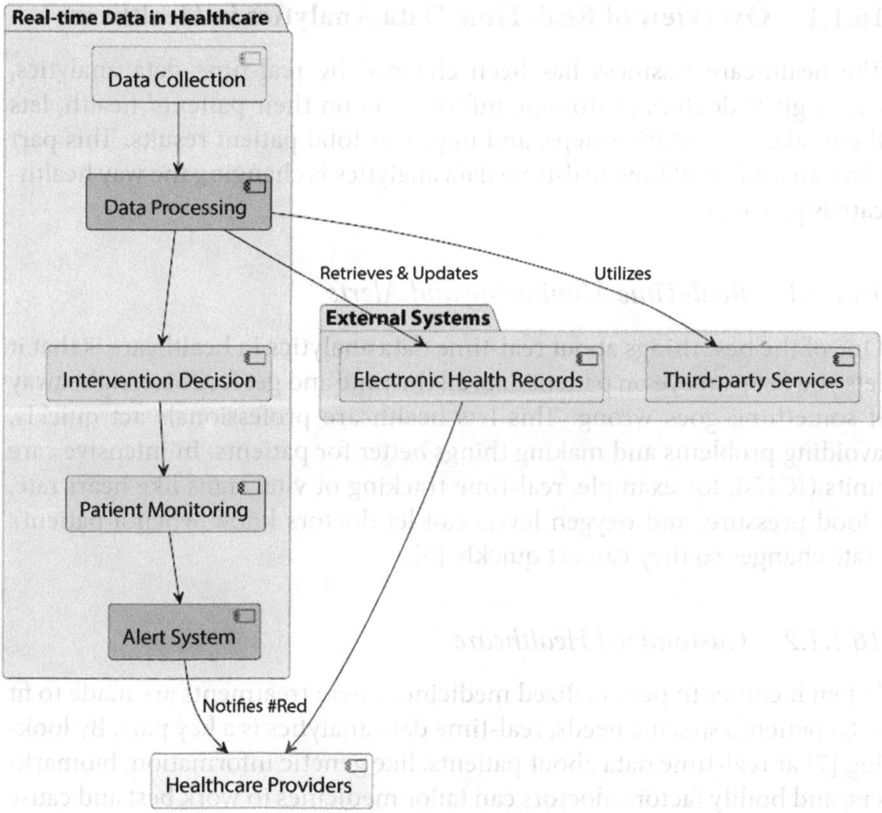

Figure 16.1 Overview of real-time data in healthcare interventions.

- Clinical studies: The way clinical studies are run is also changing because of real-time data analytics. Researchers can learn more about how well drugs work, how safe they are, and how patients react by collecting and studying real-time data from users. This makes it possible for flexible trial designs, which can speed up the process of making new drugs [5].

The goal of this chapter is to look at how real-time data can be used to improve pharmaceutical solutions in healthcare. It will talk about the part that real-time data plays in personalized medicine, the effectiveness of treatments, early intervention, and clinical studies. The part will also talk about the problems and possible solutions for using real-time data analytics in drug treatments in the future. Figure 16.1 gives the overview of the use of real time data in healthcare intervations.

16.1.1 Overview of Real-Time Data Analytics in Healthcare

The healthcare business has been changed by real-time data analytics, which gives doctors up-to-date information on their patients' health, lets them take preventative steps, and improves total patient results. This part gives an outline of how real-time data analytics is changing the way healthcare is provided.

16.1.1.1 Real-Time Monitoring and Alerts

One of the best things about real-time data analytics in healthcare is that it lets you keep an eye on patient data all the time and get feedback right away if something goes wrong. This lets healthcare professionals act quickly, avoiding problems and making things better for patients. In intensive care units (ICUs), for example, real-time tracking of vital signs like heart rate, blood pressure, and oxygen levels can let doctors know when a patient's state changes so they can act quickly [6].

16.1.1.2 Customized Healthcare

When it comes to personalized medicine, where treatments are made to fit each patient's specific needs, real-time data analytics is a key part. By looking [7] at real-time data about patients, like genetic information, biomarkers, and bodily factors, doctors can tailor medicines to work best and cause the fewest side effects. In cancer, for instance, real-time genetic analysis of tumors can help find specific treatments that work better and are safer than regular chemotherapy.

16.1.1.3 Analytics for Prediction

In healthcare, real-time [8] data analytics makes predictive analytics possible. In this type of analytics, computers use past and real-time data to guess what will happen in the future. Predictive analytics can help doctors figure out which people are most likely to get certain diseases so they can start treatment early and stop or slow the disease's development. For instance, prediction models can be used to find people who are likely to get sepsis based on real-time data like vital signs and lab results. This lets them get treatment sooner and improves their outcome [9].

16.1.1.4 Managing the Health of a Population

Real-time data analytics is also changing public health management by giving us new ways to look at the health of whole groups of people. Healthcare professionals can find patterns, trends, and differences in health results by looking at real-time data from smart technology, electronic health records (EHRs), and other sources. This data can be used to create focused policies and programs that will improve the health of the whole community.

16.1.2 Importance of Real-Time Data in Pharmacological Interventions

Real-time data is very important for pharmaceutical therapies because it makes treatments more effective, safe, and efficient. In pharmacy [10], one of the best things about real-time data is that it makes personalized medicine possible.

Healthcare professionals can make sure that each patient gets the best care by constantly checking things like genetic information, measurements, and bodily factors. This personalized method lets doctors find the best drug doses, treatment plans, and medications for each person based on their unique traits. This leads to better treatment results and a lower risk of side effects. Real-time data analytics also improves the effectiveness of treatment by allowing early adjustments. For example [11], real-time tracking of blood glucose or blood pressure levels in people with long-term conditions like diabetes or high blood pressure can lead to quick changes in drug dose or treatment plans, which can prevent bad results and improve patient outcomes. This cautious method not only makes patients healthier, but it also lowers the costs of healthcare that come with hospital stays and other problems. Real-time data is also [12] very helpful for making clinical studies for drug treatments more effective. Researchers can learn more about how well drugs work, how safe they are, and how patients react by collecting and studying real-time data from users. This makes it possible for flexible trial designs that can speed up the process of making new drugs, which means that new treatments can be approved and used more quickly. Real-time [13] data analytics in clinical studies also help researchers find and fix problems early on in the development process. This lowers the risk of mistakes in later stages and makes sure that only the most hopeful treatments make it to market. Real-time data is also useful for pharmacovigilance and post-marketing monitoring, which is another important part of pharmaceutical treatments. Watching patient data in real

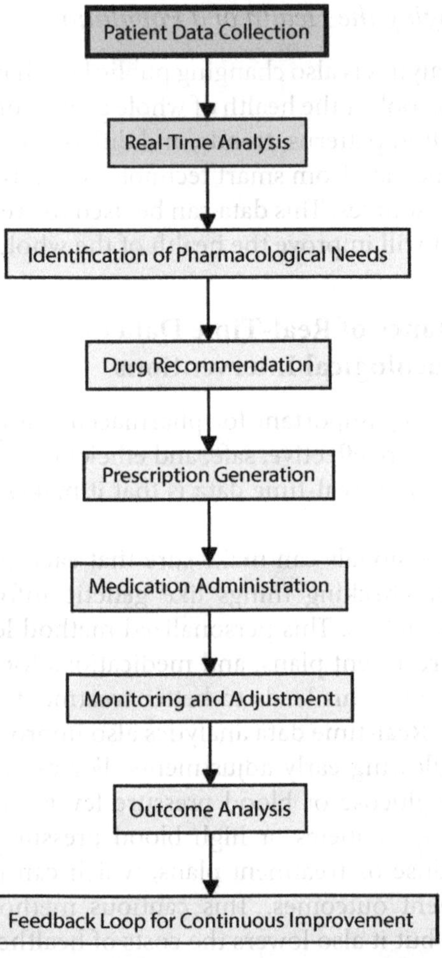

Figure 16.2 Illustration of the process steps involved in using real-time data in pharmacological interventions.

time can help find and test new medicines to make sure they are safe and work well once they are sold. This lets early discovery of possible safety issues or bad events happen, so actions can be taken quickly to improve patient safety. The real-time [14] data is very important for pharmaceutical therapies because it allows for personalized medicine, improves treatment effectiveness, makes clinical studies more efficient, and raises awareness about drug safety. Healthcare workers and academics can improve patient results, make medicines more effective, and move the field of pharmacology forward by using real-time patient data. Figure 16.2 illustrates the process involved in using real-time data in pharmacological interventions.

16.2 Personalized Medicine

16.2.1 Role of Real-Time Data in Personalized Medicine

Personalized medicine [15], which is also called precision medicine, is a way of providing healthcare that takes into account how genes, the environment, and culture can vary from person to person. This way of doing things lets doctors customize treatments to fit the unique needs of each patient, which increases the chances of therapy working and lowers the chance of side effects. Real-time data is an important part of personalized medicine because it gives doctors the up-to-date and useful information they need to make good choices about their patients' care. Figure 16.3 illustrates the system architecture for continuous monitoring for personalized treatments.

- Continuous Monitoring for Personalized Treatments
  One important part of personalized medicine [16] is being able to keep an eye on patient data all the time to help make decisions about care. Real-time data analytics lets doctors gather and look at information like genetics, biomarkers, and bodily factors right away, which helps them figure out the best ways to treat patients. In cancer, for instance, real-time genetic analysis of tumors can help find specific treatments that work better and are safer than regular chemotherapy. Real-time data processing also makes it possible to change drug doses based on the unique features of each patient. By constantly keeping an eye on patient data, doctors can change drug doses in real time to get the best treatment results. For example, real-time tracking of kidney function can help change medicine doses in people with kidney disease to keep them from becoming harmful and to make sure they work.
- **Selection of the Most Suitable Medication**
  Analytics of real-time [17] data can also help doctors choose the best medicine for each patient. Looking at real-time data on patients helps doctors figure out which medicines are most likely to work for each patient based on their specific needs. This specific method can make medicine work better and lower the risk of side effects.
- **Benefits of Real-Time Data in Personalized Medicine**
  When used in [18] personalized treatment, real-time data has a number of important advantages. First, it lets treatment plans be optimized based on the unique needs of each

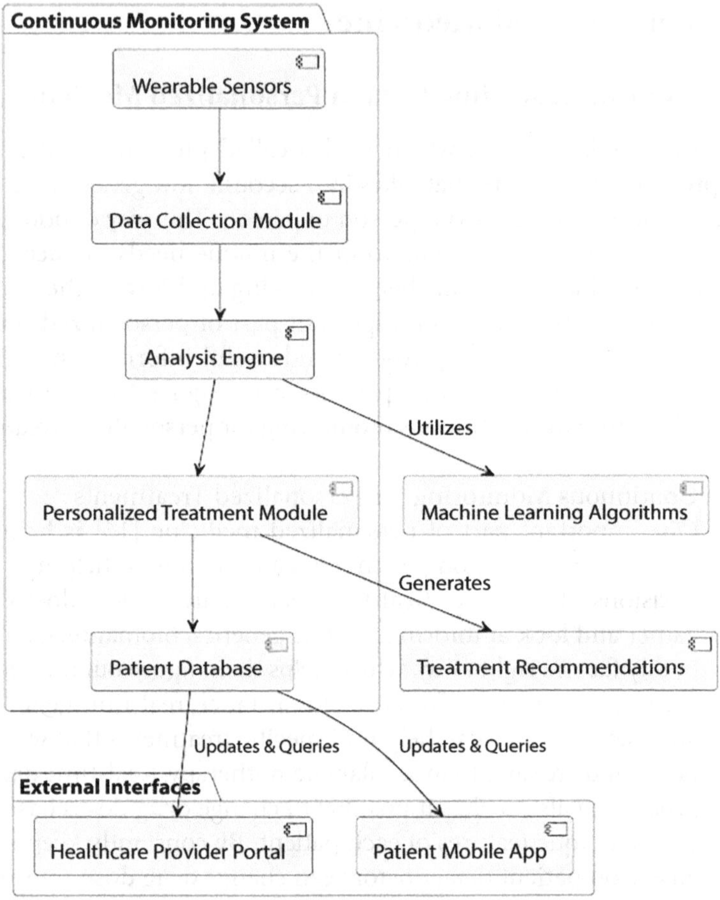

Figure 16.3 Illustration of the system architecture for continuous monitoring for personalized treatments.

patient, which leads to better therapy results. Second, real-time data analytics lets doctors see how patients are responding to treatment right away, which lets them make changes to treatment plans quickly. Lastly, real-time data analytics can help find people who are likely to have bad results or whose treatments would not work, so that steps can be taken ahead of time to avoid these problems. There are a lot of good things about real-time data analytics for personalized health, but there are also some problems and things to think about. Concerns about data protection and privacy, the need for different healthcare systems to be able to talk to each other, and the need for healthcare workers to be taught how to use real-time data analytics tools are some of these. Strong data control systems are also needed to make sure that real-time data is used in an honest and responsible way.

16.2.2 Examples of Personalized Medicine in Pharmacological Interventions

Personalized medicine has changed the way drugs are used by making treatments more effective by adjusting them to each patient's specific needs. For personalized medicine to work, real-time data is very important because it gives doctors the right knowledge at the right time to make good treatment choices [19]. Here are some examples of personalized medicine used in drug treatments:

- *Genetic Testing in Oncology*: Genetic testing is used to find specific genetic changes in cancers that can help doctors decide how to treat them. For instance, people with non-small-cell lung cancer (NSCLC) who have a change in the epidermal growth factor receptor (EGFR) gene may do better with EGFR drugs like erlotinib or gefitinib. Healthcare professionals can do genetic tests and get answers quickly thanks to real-time data analytics. This lets them start focused treatments on time.
- *Dosing for Warfarin*: Warfarin is a popular blood thinner that needs to be carefully dosed to avoid problems with bleeding. Differences in the CYP2C9 and VKORC1 genes can impact how people break down warfarin, which can cause a range of responses to treatment. Real-time data analytics can help doctors figure out the best amount of warfarin for each patient based on their genetics. This lowers the risk of blood problems [20].
- *Clopidogrel Response Testing*: Clopidogrel is an antiplatelet drug that people with coronary artery disease take to keep their blood from clotting. However, some people have a natural difference in the CYP2C19 gene that makes it harder for them to process clopidogrel, which means that it does not work as well for them. Real-time data analytics can help doctors figure out which people do not properly break down clopidogrel and make treatment choices, like switching them to a different blood-thinning drug [21].

Immune checkpoint inhibitors (ICIs) are a type of cancer treatment that works by letting the body's immune system go after cancer cells. Real-time data analytics can help find patients who are likely to react to ICIs based on the features of their tumors and immune systems. This lets doctors choose the patients who will gain the most from this treatment.

16.2.3 Benefits and Challenges of Personalized Medicine

Personalized medicine has a number of important advantages that can help patients get better care at lower costs. One [22] of the biggest benefits is that treatments can be tailored to each patient's unique needs. This makes it more likely that the therapy will work and lowers the risk of side effects. This personalized method can help patients get better results from their treatment, be happier with their care, and be more likely to stick to their goals. One more benefit of personalized medicine is that it might lower the cost of healthcare by preventing treatments and measures that are not needed. Healthcare workers can avoid expensive trial-and-error methods and lower the risk of bad events that may require more medical care by figuring out the best medicine for each patient.

By making it [23] easier to decide what treatment to give, personalized medicine could also make healthcare delivery more efficient. When healthcare professionals have access to real-time data analytics, they can quickly look at patient data and make smart choices about treatment options. This means that patients can start treatment faster and have better results. Personalized medicine has a lot of benefits, but it also has some problems that need to be fixed. To help receive, store, and analyze patient data, one of the biggest problems is that there needs to be a strong data infrastructure and communication standards. To do real-time data analytics, you need to be able to access a lot of data from different places, like genetic databases, smart technology, and EHRs. This data can be hard to combine and analyze correctly. Another problem is that healthcare professionals need to be taught how to use real-time data mining tools and have access to the tools they need to use personalized medicine. This might need money to be spent on training programs, changes to equipment, and the ability to analyze data, all of which can be expensive and take a lot of time [24].

Personalized medicine also comes with social and legal problems. For example, protecting patients' privacy and security, getting their permission for genetic tests and data sharing, and making sure everyone has equal access to personalized treatments are all things that need to be thought about.

To make sure that personalized medicine is used in an ethical and responsible way, healthcare workers, lawmakers, and regulatory bodies need to carefully think about these issues and work together.

16.3 Treatment Efficacy

16.3.1 Enhancing Treatment Efficacy Through Real-Time Data Analytics

Real-time data analytics has the ability to make a lot of different types of healthcare treatments much more effective. Real-time data analytics helps doctors make choices that can improve treatment results by giving them up-to-date and useful information in real time. This part talks about the different ways that real-time data analytics can improve the effectiveness of treatment.

- **Continuous Monitoring for Timely Interventions**
  One of the best things about real-time data analytics for improving treatment effectiveness is that it lets you keep an eye on patient data all the time. By constantly checking things like vital signs, lab results, and how well patients take their medications, doctors can spot changes in their patients' situations early and act quickly to avoid problems. For example, keeping an eye on a person's weight, blood pressure, and other factors in real time can help doctors spot signs of worsening in people with long-term conditions like heart failure and act quickly to change things, like drug doses or lifestyle choices.
- **Optimization of Treatment Regimens**
  Real-time data analytics can also help improve treatment plans by giving doctors information about how patients are reacting to treatment. By looking at real-time data on how patients are doing and how they are responding to treatment, doctors can change treatment plans to work better. For instance, when people are getting chemotherapy, real-time tracking of side effects and blood counts can help doctors change doses and plans to keep side effects to a minimum and treatment effectiveness high.

- **Personalized Treatment Plans**
  With real-time data processing, care plans can be made that are specific to each patient. Healthcare professionals can tailor treatments to each patient's specific needs by keeping an eye on data like genetic information, biomarkers, and bodily factors all the time. This personalized method can help treatment work better by making sure that patients get the best medicines for them based on their unique traits.
- **Predictive Analytics for Early Detection of Complications**
  Predictive analytics can also be used with real-time data analytics to find problems early on. Healthcare workers can find patients who are likely to have problems and take action early to stop them by looking at real-time data on patient

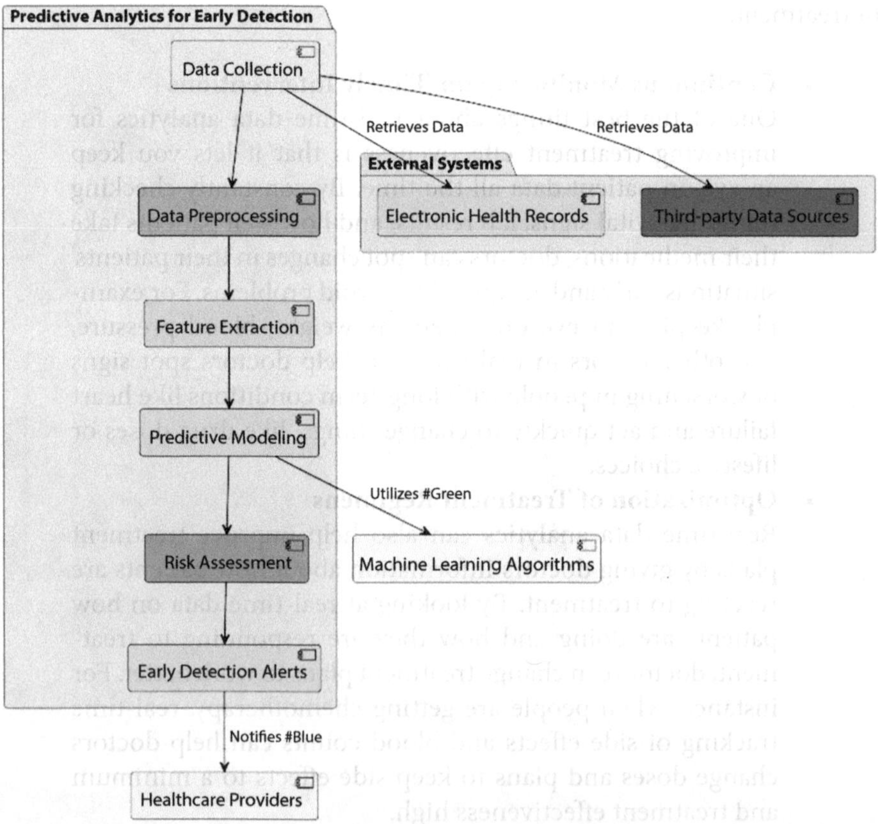

Figure 16.4 Illustration of the architecture of predictive analytics for early detection.

results and trends. Real-time tracking of vital signs and blood numbers can help doctors figure out which patients are most likely to have problems after surgery, so they can take steps right away to improve results. Figure 16.4 illustrates the architecture of predictive analytics for early detection.

- **Clinical Decision Support Systems**
  Real-time data analytics can also be used to create clinical decision support tools that give doctors and nurses advice and suggestions in real time based on the most up-to-date research and standards. These methods can help doctors make smart choices about treatments, doses, and ways to keep an eye on patients. This can lead to more successful treatments and better results for patients.
- **Problems and Things to Think About**
  There are many good things about using real-time data analytics to improve treatment effectiveness, but there are also some problems and things to think about. Concerns about data protection and privacy, the need for different healthcare systems to be able to talk to each other, and the need for healthcare workers to be taught how to use real-time data analytics tools are some of these. Strong data control systems are also needed to make sure that real-time data is used in an honest and responsible way.

16.3.2 Case Studies Demonstrating Improved Treatment Outcomes

Real-time data analytics has been a key part of improving the results of many types of healthcare measures. Several case studies show that real-time data analytics can help make treatment plans more effective, patients better monitored, and healthcare decisions better. The following are some examples:

1. Cancer care:
   Researchers used real-time data analytics to find the best way to give treatment to people with colon cancer in a study published in the Journal of Clinical Oncology. Researchers were able to lower the number of serious side effects like neutropenia and improve overall treatment results by keeping an eye on patients' blood counts all the time and changing the doses of chemotherapy in real time.

2. Heart disease:
   In a different study, real-time data analytics were used to keep an eye on people with heart failure and spot early signs of getting worse. Researchers were able to predict heart failure flare-ups and act quickly to keep patients out of the hospital and improve their results by looking at real-time data on patients' weight, blood pressure, and other factors.
3. Diabetes Management:
   Analytics of real-time data have also been used to help people with diabetes do better. In a study that was released in the Journal of Diabetes Science and Technology, insulin doses were changed in real time by keeping an eye on blood glucose levels. Researchers were able to improve glycemic control and lower the risk of hypoglycemia by constantly checking the blood glucose levels of their patients and making changes to their insulin doses as needed.
4. ICUs (Intensive Care Units):
   Real-time data mining has been especially helpful for better the health of people in critical care units (ICUs). Researchers in a study published in Critical Care Medicine used to keep an eye on patients' vital signs and lab results in real time to find early signs of sepsis and other problems. By stepping in early, researchers were able to lower the length of ICU stays and increase the number of people who survived.
5. Diseases that spread:
   Real-time data analytics has also been used to help people with infectious diseases do better. In a study that was published in The Lancet Infectious Diseases, researchers tracked patients' symptoms and lab results in real time to find early signs of infection and start the right treatment. Researchers were able to lower the chance of problems and improve results by stepping in early.

16.3.3 Strategies for Optimizing Treatment Efficacy Using Real-Time Data

Using real-time data to improve treatment effectiveness needs a comprehensive method that includes gathering, analyzing, and using the data. There are a number of effective ways to use real-time data in healthcare measures to make treatments more successful. Here are some important plans:

1. Continuous Monitoring and Feedback:

    - Monitor patient data all the time, such as vital signs, lab results, and how well they are taking their medications.
    - Use tools that give healthcare workers feedback in real time to let them know when a patient's state or reaction to treatment changes.

2. Personalized Treatment Plans:

    - Based on real-time data like DNA information, hormones, and bodily factors, make treatment plans that are specific to each patient.
    - Use real-time data analytics to find the best treatment plans for each patient, which will be the most effective and have the fewest side effects.

3. Analytics for Prediction:

    - Using real-time data and predictive analytics, you can guess how a patient will do. This lets you act quickly to avoid problems or make treatment plans work better.
    - Use machine learning techniques to look at real-time data and guess how patients will react to treatment. This will help doctors make decisions.

4. Systems that help doctors make decisions (CDSS):

    - Create and use CDSS that give real-time advice and suggestions based on the newest research and standards.
    - Providers can use CDSS to help them make smart choices about treatment options, doses, and tracking plans.

5. Getting patients involved and teaching them:

    - Patients should be involved in their own care by giving them access to real-time data and teaching them about their illness and treatment choices.
    - Give people real-time data to help them make smart choices about their health and care, which will increase loyalty and improve results.

6. Working together and talking to each other:
   - Encourage healthcare professionals, patients, and other interested parties to work together and talk to each other so that real-time data can be used successfully in planning treatments and making decisions.
   - Real-time data can help people from different fields work together and talk to each other, which will improve the organization of care and the health of the patients.
7. Security and privacy of data:
   - Protect patient data and make sure you are following the rules by putting in place strong data protection and security measures.
   - To send real-time data safely, use encryption and secure communication methods. This will lower the risk of data leaks and illegal access.
8. Evaluation and improvement all the time:
   - Always check how well real-time data analytics are working to improve the success of treatment and make changes as required.
   - Make sure that treatments are safe and successful by keeping an eye on and evaluating the effects of actions on patient results in real time.

16.4 Proactive Interventions

16.4.1 Real-Time Monitoring for Proactive Interventions

Monitoring in real time is a key part of being able to take preventative steps in healthcare. By keeping an eye on things like vital signs, lab results, and how well patients take their medications, healthcare professionals can spot early signs of worsening and act quickly to avoid problems. Real-time tracking lets treatment plans, drug doses, and lifestyle changes be changed quickly, which improves patient results and lowers healthcare costs. One of the best things about real-time tracking is that it can find changes in patients' situations that might not be seen with older methods. Real-time tracking of weight, blood pressure, and other factors can help find signs of decompensation before symptoms get worse in people with long-term conditions like heart failure. This lets early steps happen, like changing the amount of medicine a person takes or what they eat, which can keep them out of the hospital and improve their health. Real-time tracking also lets doctors see how a patient is doing over time and change their treatment plans as needed. Healthcare professionals can find patterns and make smart choices about treatment by looking at trends in patient data. Real-time tracking of blood glucose levels can help doctors make changes to insulin doses and food plans for people with diabetes so that they have the best glycemic control.

16.4.2 Examples of Proactive Interventions in Chronic Disease Management

Real-time tracking lets people in a variety of healthcare situations take proactive steps to handle chronic diseases. The following are some examples:

Heart Failure Management:

- Weight, blood pressure, and other factors should be tracked in real time to spot signs of decompensation.
- Proactive actions, like changing the amount of medicine someone takes or what they eat, can help keep people out of the hospital and improve their results.

Diabetes Management:

- Monitoring blood sugar levels in real time so that insulin doses and food plans can be changed.
- Active measures, like changing your habits and medications, are needed to get the best glucose control.

Chronic Obstructive Pulmonary Disease (COPD) Management:

- Monitoring oxygen levels and lung function in real time to find flare-ups early.
- Proactive actions, like changing the doses of medications or starting lung therapy, to stop flare-ups and make things better.

Hypertension Management:

- Monitoring blood pressure in real time so that drug doses and lifestyle changes can be made.
- Proactive measures, like making changes to your food and learning how to deal with stress, are needed to get the best blood pressure control.

16.4.3 Impact on Patient Outcomes and Healthcare Costs

Real-time tracking makes it possible for proactive actions that have a big effect on how well patients do and how much healthcare costs. Healthcare workers can avoid problems, cut down on hospital stays, and improve patients' quality of life by spotting early signs of decline and acting quickly. This preventive method also saves money because it lowers the number of times people need medical care and makes healthcare service more efficient.

Several studies have shown that proactive measures can improve patient results and lower the cost of healthcare. For instance, a study in the Journal of the American College of Cardiology found that using remote tracking to take charge of heart failure led to 36% fewer stays and 45% fewer deaths compared to normal care. A study in the New England Journal of Medicine found that using real-time tracking to take charge of diabetes management led to better control of blood sugar levels and a lower chance of problems. Real-time tracking makes proactive actions possible, which not only improves patient results and lowers healthcare costs but also has a good effect on healthcare workers. As problems happen, real-time tracking lets doctors and nurses know right away and take action, which makes their jobs easier and helps them give better care.

16.5 Clinical Trials

16.5.1 Real-Time Data Analytics in Clinical Trial Design

To check if new treatments and approaches are safe and effective, they need to be put through clinical studies. Real-time data analytics can be very helpful for making sure that patients are safe, that clinical trials are well planned, and that the whole process runs more smoothly. This part talks about the different ways that real-time data analytics can be used in planning clinical trials.

Optimization of Trial Protocols:

- Real-time data analytics can help improve study methods by looking at information about the patients, how the disease is progressing, and how well the treatments are working.
- Researchers can find the best doses, treatment plans, and patient groups for the study by keeping an eye on patient data all the time and making real-time changes to trial methods.

Adaptive Trial Designs:

- Adaptive trial designs are possible with real-time data analytics. In these designs, trial methods are changed as more data is collected.
- Researchers can change study methods to be more efficient and lower the risk of late-stage fails by looking at real-time data on how treatments are working and how patients are doing.

Patient Recruitment and Retention:

- Real-time data analytics can help find and keep qualified patients in a study, which can lead to more patients being recruited and kept.
- Researchers can find ways to get more people to join and keep them in a trial by looking at real-time data on patient traits and study participation.

Watching for Safety:

- Real-time data tools make it possible to keep an eye on the safety of the patients throughout the study.
- Researchers can find safety issues early and take action quickly to protect patient safety by looking at real-time data on bad events and treatment reactions.

Quickly Gathering and Analyzing Data:

- Real-time data analytics speeds up the processes of gathering and analyzing data, which cuts down on the time and resources needed for the trial.

- Researchers can focus on figuring out what the results mean and making smart choices about the trial by automating the collection and analysis of data.

Adaptive Trial Design in Oncology: A Case Study

- For people with advanced NSCLC, a study in the New England Journal of Medicine used real-time data analytics to plan an adaptable clinical trial.
- Biomarkers were used in the study to find patients who were most likely to react to a certain tailored treatment.
- Researchers were able to find the best doses and treatment plans for the focused therapy by keeping an eye on patient data all the time and changing the study protocol based on how the treatment was working.

16.5.2 Adaptive Trial Designs Enabled by Real-Time Data

Adaptive trial designs are a type of clinical trial design that lets the trial procedure be changed as more data comes in. Real-time data analytics is a key part of adaptive trial designs because it gives researchers the right information at the right time to make decisions about the trial. This part talks about the different ways that real-time data analytics make flexible trial designs possible.

Continuous Monitoring and Interim Analysis:

- Real-time data processing lets the trial's researchers keep an eye on patient data all the time.
- By looking at the data in chunks, researchers can find patterns and trends early on and change the study strategy to fit them.

Changes to the Treatment Arms:

- Real-time data processing lets treatment tools be changed based on how well they work.
- Researchers can change treatment plans and doses to make them more effective and safe by looking at real-time data on how treatments work and how patients do.

Size of Sample Estimation Again:

- Real-time data analytics lets you re-estimate the sample size based on new data.
- Researchers can change the sample size to make sure the study has enough power to find treatment benefits by looking at real-time data on how many patients signed up and how they did.

Analysis of Patient Subgroups:

- Real-time data processing makes it easier to look at subgroups of patients based on their traits and how well they respond to treatment.
- Researchers can find groups of patients who might gain more from the treatment by looking at real-time data on their demographics, biomarkers, and other factors. They can then change the study procedure to include these groups.

Case Study: Adaptive Trial Design in Immunotherapy for Cancer

- Real-time data analytics were used in a study released in the Journal of Clinical Oncology to create an adaptable clinical trial for people with advanced melanoma.
- Biomarkers were used in the study to find people who were most likely to react to a certain treatment.
- Researchers were able to improve patient results and make the treatment plan better by constantly checking patient data and changing the study process based on how the treatment was working.

16.5.3 Accelerating Drug Development with Real-Time Data Analytics

Real-time data analytics could speed up drug development by making it easier to find new drugs, making clinical trials better designed, and getting more patients to sign up and keep them on board. This part talks about the different ways that real-time data analytics speeds up the development of drugs.

Early Identification of Possible Drugs:

- Real-time data analytics quickly finds good drug options by looking at huge sets of chemical compounds and guessing how well they might work and how safe they might be.
- Researchers can choose which drug options to try further based on how likely they are to work by using real-time data analytics.

Improving the Design of Clinical Trials:

- Real-time data analytics helps improve the design of clinical trials by giving experts up-to-date, useful data that they can use to make smart choices about the trials.
- Researchers can make more efficient and effective clinical trials by keeping an eye on patient data all the time and changing the trial procedure as more data comes in.

Getting More Patients and Keeping Them:

- Real-time data analytics aids in finding and keeping patients by spotting those who are qualified and keeping an eye on their involvement in the study.
- Researchers can find ways to get more people to join and keep them in a trial by looking at real-time data on patient traits and study participation.

Case Study: Speeding Up the Creation of Alzheimer's Drugs

- A study in the Journal of Alzheimer's Disease used real-time data analytics to speed up the process of making Alzheimer's disease drugs.
- Genetic data, biomarkers, and clinical data were all used together in the study to find possible drug targets and come up with new ways to treat the condition.
- Researchers were able to speed up the drug creation process and find potential new Alzheimer's disease treatments by using real-time data analytics.

16.6 Challenges and Future Directions

16.6.1 Ethical Considerations in Real-Time Data Analytics

When used in healthcare, real-time data analytics brings up a number of ethics issues that need to be carefully thought through to protect patients' rights and liberty. Some of these social concerns are as follows:

1. *Privacy and Confidentiality:* Sensitive patient data, like medical records, genetic data, and treatment results, is often collected and analyzed in real time. This information needs to be kept private and anonymous so that it cannot be accessed by people who should not be able to or for privacy reasons.
2. *Informed Consent:* When real-time data analytics are used in healthcare, informed consent is a must. Patients should be told how their information will be used and be able to choose not to take part if they do not want to. But in real-time data analytics, where data is gathered and studied quickly, it can be hard to get educated permission.
3. *Data Security:* Strong data security measures are needed for real-time data analytics to keep patient data safe from hackers and other people who should not have access to it. To make sure that data is safe, this includes encryption, safe data keeping, and regular security checks.
4. *Bias and Fairness:* When real-time data analytics tools are used, they can be biased, which means that some patient groups may not get fair care. It is important to keep an eye on algorithms for bias on a daily basis and fix any flaws that are found.
5. *Accountability and Transparency:* Real-time data analytics should be open and clear about how data is gathered, processed, and used. Also, there should be ways for people to see their information and ask for changes if they need that.
6. *Data Ownership:* People who are patients should own and be in charge of their data and be able to choose how it is used. This includes the right to at any time stop giving permission for data use.

7. *Regulatory Compliance:* Real-time data analytics needs to follow the rules and laws that apply, like the Health Insurance Portability and Accountability Act (HIPAA) in the US. This means protecting patients' rights and making sure that data is used and kept safely.

16.6.2 Addressing Data Privacy and Security Concerns

In healthcare, real-time data analytics has a huge potential to improve patient results and make healthcare service better. But it also makes me very worried about the protection and safety of my info. It is very important to address these worries so that patients' private health information is kept safe and they can trust the healthcare system to use their information in a good way. Concerns about data protection and security can be dealt with in real-time data analytics in a number of ways:

1. *Encrypting Data:* Encrypting data while it is being sent or stored can help keep it safe from people who should not have access to it. It is important to use strong encryption methods to keep private health information private.
2. *Safe Data Storage:* Using firewalls, access controls, and regular security checks are some safe ways to store data that can help keep it safe from online dangers.
3. *Anonymization and Pseudonymization:* Making patient data anonymous or pseudonymous can protect their privacy and lower the chance that they will be re-identified. But care must be taken to make sure the data can still be used for research.
4. *Access Controls:* Strict access controls can help keep medical info from getting into the wrong hands. Sensitive health information should only be seen by people who are allowed to see it, and they should only see it if they need to.
5. *Data Minimization:* The risk of data breaches can be lowered by only collecting the data that is needed for a certain task. It is best to only gather, handle, and keep data for as long as it is needed.
6. *Transparency and Accountability:* Patients will trust you more if you are clear about how you collect and use their data. Healthcare organizations should take responsibility for how they handle data and have ways to deal with security events and data leaks.

7. *Following the Rules:* To keep patient data safe, it is important to make sure that you follow the rules and laws that apply, like HIPAA in the US and GDPR in the EU. To make sure they are following the rules, healthcare groups should review and change their data security policies on a regular basis.
8. *Teaching the Patient:* Teaching the patient about data privacy and security can help them understand how important it is to keep their health information safe. Patients should be told what rights they have when their data is used and how it is being used.
9. *Data Governance:* Setting up a strong system for data governance can help make sure that data is used in an honest and responsible way. Setting clear rules and guidelines for gathering, handling, and sharing data is part of this.
10. *Working With Cybersecurity Experts:* Healthcare groups can find and reduce possible security risks by working with cybersecurity experts. Security checks and reviews should be done on a regular basis to find holes and keep data safe.

16.6.3 Future Trends and Innovations in Real-Time Data Analytics for Pharmacological Interventions

Real-time data analytics is about to change the way drugs are used by making treatments more specific and efficient. Real-time data analytics for drug treatments is likely to be shaped by a number of new ideas and trends in the coming years:

1. *Precision Medicine:* The goal of precision medicine is to make sure that each patient gets the best care possible by taking into account their genes, habits, and surroundings. Real-time data analytics is an important part of precision medicine because it looks at real-time patient data to find the best treatment plans for each person.
2. *Identifying Biomarkers:* Biomarkers are biological signs that can be used to guess how a disease will get worse and how well a treatment will work. Real-time data analytics can help find new biomarkers and keep an eye on their amounts in real time, which lets diseases be found early and treatments be tailored to each person.

3. *Adaptive Trial Designs:* Analyzing data in real time lets you make adaptive trial designs, in which trial methods are changed as more data comes in. This method makes clinical studies more efficient and effective, which speeds up the process of making drugs and getting them approved.
4. *Reusing Drugs:* Real-time data analytics can help find new uses for old drugs by looking at real-time patient data and finding possible treatment options. This method can speed up the process of making new drugs and lower the costs of doing so.
5. *Pharmacovigilance:* Real-time data analytics can help with pharmacovigilance by constantly checking patient data for any bad drug responses or other safety issues. This method can help find safety problems early on, which can make patients safer.
6. *Artificial Intelligence (AI) and Machine Learning (ML):* AI and ML systems can look at big sets of patient data to find trends and guess how they will respond to treatment. These tools can help doctors and nurses make better choices about which treatments to use and how much to give.
7. *Wearable Devices and IoT:* Vital signs and exercise levels can be collected in real time by wearable devices and the Internet of Things (IoT). This information can be looked at in real time to keep an eye on patients' health and make changes to their treatment plans as needed.
8. *Data Integration and Interoperability:* Putting together data from different sources, like smart technology, genetic data, and EHRs, can give a fuller picture of a patient's health. Using real-time data analytics to combine and look at all of this information can help make treatment work better.

The real-time data analytics has the ability to completely change drug therapies by making treatments more personalized, efficient, and effective. In this area, new ideas and trends for the future are likely to come from things like personalized medicine, finding biomarkers, adaptable trial designs, reusing drugs, pharmacovigilance, AI and ML, smart technology and the IoT, and combining and sharing data. Healthcare professionals can improve patient results and change the field of drug treatments by adopting these new ideas and trends.

16.7 Conclusion

A big step forward in healthcare is the use of real-time data analytics in drug treatments. By using real-time data, healthcare professionals can tailor treatments to each patient, improve their results, and make healthcare service better overall. One of the best things about real-time data processing is that it makes precision care possible. Healthcare professionals can make treatments more effective and less harmful to each patient by looking at real-time patient data such as genetic information, biomarkers, and treatment reactions. This personalized method to drug interventions could change the way healthcare is provided by making treatments more effective and patients happier. Real-time data analytics is also very important for making sure that clinical study designs and drug creation processes work as well as they can. Researchers can make clinical trials more efficient and effective by keeping an eye on patient data all the time and changing trial methods as more data comes in. This means that new drugs can be approved faster and more people can get these treatments. Real-time data analytics can also help with pharmacovigilance by constantly checking patient data for bad drug responses and other safety issues. When it comes to drug safety, this proactive method can help find problems early on and make patients safer. With using real-time data analytics in pharmaceutical treatments has a huge amount of potential to make things better for patients, speed up drug development, and make healthcare better all around. With technology always changing, it is important for academics and healthcare professionals to keep looking for new ways to use real-time data to improve patient care and lead to new drug treatments.

References

1. Faisal, S., Ivo, J., Lee, C., Carter, C., Patel, T., The usability, acceptability, and functionality of smart oral multidose dispensing systems for medication adherence: a scoping review. *J. Pharm. Pract.*, *35*, 3, 455–468, 2022.
2. Steinkamp, J.M., Goldblatt, N., Borodovsky, J.T., LaVertu, A., Kronish, I.M., Marsch, L.A., Schuman-Olivier, Z., Technological interventions for medication adherence in adult mental health and substance use disorders: a systematic review. *JMIR Ment. Health*, 6, 3, e12493, 2019.
3. Faisal, S., Ivo, J., Tennant, R., Prior, K.A., Grindrod, K., McMillan, C., Patel, T., Integration of a smart multidose blister package for medication intake: A mixed method ethnographic informed study of older adults with chronic diseases. *PLoS One*, *17*, 1, e0262012, 2022.

4. Patel, T., Ivo, J., Faisal, S., McDougall, A., Carducci, J., Pritchard, S., Chang, F., A prospective study of usability and workload of electronic medication adherence products by older adults, caregivers, and health care providers. *J. Med. Internet Res.*, *22*, 6, e18073, 2020.
5. Baumgartner, S.L., Buffkin Jr., D.E., Rukavina, E., Jones, J., Weiler, E., Carnes, T.C., A novel digital pill system for medication adherence measurement and reporting: Usability validation study. *JMIR Hum. Factors*, *8*, 4, e30786, 2021.
6. Musiimenta, A., Tumuhimbise, W., Mugaba, A.T., Muzoora, C., Armstrong-Hough, M., Bangsberg, D., Davis, J.L., Haberer, J.E., Digital monitoring technologies could enhance tuberculosis medication adherence in Uganda: Mixed methods study. *J. Clin. Tuberc. Other Mycobact. Dis.*, *17*, 100119, 2019.
7. Faisal, S., Ivo, J., McDougall, A., Patel, T., Stakeholder feedback of electronic medication adherence products: qualitative analysis. *J. Med. Internet Res.*, *22*, 12, e18074, 2020.
8. Faisal, S., Ivo, J., Tennant, R., Prior, K.A., Grindrod, K., McMillan, C., Patel, T., Implementation of a real-time medication intake monitoring technology intervention in community pharmacy settings: A mixed-method pilot study. *Pharmacy*, *9*, 2, 105, 2021.
9. Ajani, S.N., Khobragade, P., Dhone, M., Ganguly, B., Shelke, N., Parati, N., Advancements in Computing: Emerging Trends in Computational Science with Next-Generation Computing. *Int. J. Intell. Syst. Appl. Eng.*, *12*, 7s, 546–559, 2024.
10. Hill, L.M., Golin, C.E., Pack, A., Carda-Auten, J., Wallace, D.D., Cherkur, S., Farel, C.E., Rosen, E.P., Gandhi, M., Prince, H.M.A., Kashuba, A.D., Using real-time adherence feedback to enhance communication about adherence to antiretroviral therapy: patient and clinician perspectives. *J. Assoc. Nurses AIDS Care*, *31*, 1, 25–34, 2020.
11. Kumar, S.A., Kumar, A., Dutt, V., Agrawal, R., Multi Model Implementation on General Medicine Prediction with Quantum Neural Networks, in: *2021 Third International Conference on Intelligent Communication Technologies and Virtual Mobile Networks (ICICV)*, Tirunelveli, India, pp. 1391–1395, 2021, doi: 10.1109/ICICV50876.2021.9388575.
12. Raj, P., Dubey, A.K., Kumar, A., Rathore, P.S., Blockchain-based IoT architecture for software-defined networking, in: *Blockchain, Artificial Intelligence, and the Internet of Things*, Springer International Publishing, 2022.
13. Burri, S.R., Kumar, A., Baliyan, A., Kumar, T.A., Predictive Intelligence for Healthcare Outcomes: An AI Architecture Overview, in: *2023 2nd International Conference on Smart Technologies and Systems for Next Generation Computing (ICSTSN)*, Villupuram, India, pp. 1–6, 2023, doi: 10.1109/ICSTSN57873.2023.10151477.
14. Wani, S., Ahuja, S., Kumar, A., Application of Deep Neural Networks and Machine Learning algorithms for diagnosis of Brain tumour, in: *2023 International Conference on Computational Intelligence and Sustainable*

Engineering Solutions (CISES), Greater Noida, India, pp. 106–111, 2023, doi: 10.1109/CISES58720.2023.10183528.
15. Kour, S.P., Kumar, A., Ahuja, S., An Advance Approach for Diabetes Detection by Implementing Machine Learning Algorithms, in: *2023 IEEE World Conference on Applied Intelligence and Computing (AIC)*, Sonbhadra, India, pp. 136–141, 2023, doi: 10.1109/AIC57670.2023.10263919.
16. Raj, P., Kumar, A., Dubey, A.K., Bhatia, S., Oswalt, M.S., *Quantum Computing and Artificial Intelligence: Training Machine and Deep Learning Algorithms on Quantum Computers*, De Gruyter, Berlin, Boston, 2023, [Online]. Available: https://doi.org/10.1515/9783110791402.
17. Sasubilli, G. and Kumar, A., Machine Learning and Big Data Implementation on Health Care data, in: *2020 4th International Conference on Intelligent Computing and Control Systems (ICICCS)*, Madurai, India, pp. 859–864, 2020, doi: 10.1109/ICICCS48265.2020.9120906.
18. Swarna, S.R., Kumar, A., Dixit, P., Sairam, T.V.M., Parkinson's Disease Prediction using Adaptive Quantum Computing, in: *2021 Third International Conference on Intelligent Communication Technologies and Virtual Mobile Networks (ICICV)*, Tirunelveli, India, pp. 1396–1401, 2021, doi: 10.1109/ICICV50876.2021.9388628.
19. Burugadda, V.R., Pawar, P.S., Kumar, A., Bhati, N., Predicting Hospital Readmission Risk for Heart Failure Patients Using Machine Learning Techniques: A Comparative Study of Classification Algorithms, in: *2023 Second International Conference on Trends in Electrical, Electronics, and Computer Engineering (TEECCON)*, Bangalore, India, pp. 223–228, 2023, doi: 10.1109/TEECCON59234.2023.10335817.
20. Shete, D. and Khobragade, P., An empirical analysis of different data visualization techniques from statistical perspective. *AIP Conf. Proc.*, 2839, 1, 040016-1–040016-8, 2023, September, AIP Publishing.
21. Mohsen, F., Al-Saadi, B., Abdi, N., Khan, S., Shah, Z., Artificial Intelligence-Based Methods for Precision Cardiovascular Medicine. *J. Pers. Med.*, 13, 8, 1268, 2023.
22. da Silva, N.C., Albertini, M.K., Backes, A.R., das Graças Pena, G., Machine learning for hospital readmission prediction in pediatric population. *Comput. Methods Programs Biomed.*, 244, 107980, 2024.
23. Abraham, A., Jose, R., Ahmad, J., Joshi, J., Jacob, T., Khalid, A.U.R., Ali, H., Patel, P., Singh, J., Toma, M., Comparative Analysis of Machine Learning Models for Image Detection of Colonic Polyps vs. Resected Polyps. *J. Imaging*, 9, 10, 215, 2023.
24. Fuhrman, J.D., Gorre, N., Hu, Q., Li, H., El Naqa, I., Giger, M.L., A review of explainable and interpretable AI with applications in COVID-19 imaging. *Med. Phys.*, *49*, 1, 1–14, 2022.

17

Strategies for Integrating Wearable Technology with Healthcare Systems: Pathological Considerations in Wearable Device Integration

Sujata Raghunath Kanetkar[1]* and Vaishali V. Raje[2]

[1]Department of Pathology, Krishna Institute of Medical Sciences, Krishna Vishwa Vidyapeeth "Deemed to be University", Karad, Maharashtra, India
[2]Department of Community Medicine, Krishna Institute of Medical Sciences, Krishna Vishwa Vidyapeeth "Deemed to be University", Karad, Maharashtra, India

Abstract

Wearable technology has become an interesting way to keep an eye on health factors and make personalized healthcare easier to get. There are some problems with putting smart technology into healthcare systems, especially when it comes to managing and figuring out what abnormal data means. This paper talks about ways to successfully combine smart technology with healthcare systems, focusing on issues related to illness. The first problem is getting reliable data from smart gadgets about health problems and figuring out what it means. Wearable technology must be able to collect data that is important to certain diseases, like changes in the heart rate for heart conditions or blood sugar levels for diabetes. As part of integration strategies, the creation of special devices and algorithms that can correctly find and understand abnormal data should be encouraged. Second, when smart technology is added, it should be thought about how well it will work with other healthcare systems. Electronic health records and other healthcare systems should be able to easily share data from smart devices with them so that all of the patient's health information is available at once. To do this, rules need to be made so that smart technology and healthcare systems can share data and work together. The use of smart technology should also protect the safety and protection of patient data. Because medical data is private, strong security measures must be

**Corresponding author*: sujatakanetkarkvv@outlook.com

Abhishek Kumar, Narayan Vyas, Pramod Singh Rathore, Abhineet Anand and Pooja Dixit (eds.) Internet of Medicine for Smart Healthcare, (347–372) © 2025 Scrivener Publishing LLC

put in place to protect patient privacy and stop people from getting in without permission. Connecting smart technology to healthcare systems opens up huge chances to make care and results better for patients. But good integration plans need to deal with the problems that come with abnormal data, like making sure that the data is collected and interpreted correctly, that it can work with other systems, and that patient data is kept private and safe.

***Keywords*:** Wearable technology, HER, CDSS, healthcare, chronic diseases

17.1 Introduction

Wearable technology has changed healthcare by making it possible to continuously track bodily factors and make it easier to tailor health treatments to each person's needs. These gadgets, like biosensors and trackers, collect a lot of information that can tell you a lot about a person's health and behavior. Wearable technology [1] that is connected to healthcare systems could change the way healthcare is provided by better prevention care, finding diseases early, and making it easier to handle long-term conditions. But this combination comes with some problems, especially when it comes to managing and making sense of abnormal data. The ideas in this chapter are about how to effectively combine smart technology with healthcare systems, focusing on issues related to illness. Due to [2] its complexity and variety, pathological data, which includes signs of sickness or bodily situations that are not working normally, presents its own set of problems. For wearable technology to really change healthcare, it needs to be able to gather and understand medical data correctly, work with current healthcare systems without any problems, and keep patient information private and safe. One of the biggest problems with combining smart technology with healthcare systems is getting correct data on diseases and figuring out what it means. A lot of different factors are included in pathological data, like blood glucose levels, heart rate fluctuations, and biomarker amounts. These are very important for keeping an eye on and controlling many different illnesses. Specialized sensors and algorithms must be built into wearable technology so that it can correctly find and understand these signs of disease. For instance [3], a smart device meant to check on heart health should be able to correctly measure changes in the heart rate and spot any issues that could point to a heart problem. Interoperability is another important thing to think about when combining smart technology with healthcare systems. Electronic health records (EHRs) and other healthcare systems must be able to easily share data from smart devices in order to give a full picture of a patient's health. To do this, rules need to be made so that smart technology and healthcare systems can share data and work together. Without connectivity, smart technology in healthcare may not be able to reach its full potential because doctors may not have a full picture of a patient's health [4].

When you connect smart technology to healthcare systems, privacy and security are also important things to think about, especially when it comes to disease data. Pathological data is naturally private because it can show private information about a person's health. Strong security means must be put in place to keep this info safe from people who should not be able to see or view it. Patients also need to know that their information is being used in a way that is responsible and follows all privacy laws and rules [5]. Even with these problems, combining smart technology with healthcare systems has a lot of potential to make care and results better for patients. Wearable technology can let doctors keep an eye on patients all the time, so problems can be found early and treated quickly. By giving patients real-time feedback and specific suggestions, they can also give patients the power to take charge of their own health. Wearable technology can also help lower healthcare costs by letting doctors keep an eye on patients from afar and cutting down on the number of times people have to go to the hospital. The combining [6] smart technology with healthcare systems could completely change the way healthcare is provided by giving people constant, individualized care. You should be careful when integrating abnormal data, though, because it comes with its own set of problems. Wearable technology can become an important part of modern healthcare by creating specific devices and algorithms, making sure they can work with other systems, and putting in place strong security measures.

17.1.1 Overview of Wearable Technology in Healthcare

In recent years, wearable technology has become an important and innovative tool in healthcare. It has many uses that can have a big effect on patient care and results. These devices, which can be worn on the body [7] or built into clothes, can track exercise levels, measure different bodily factors, and give users and healthcare workers feedback in real time. Addition of smart technology to healthcare systems could change the way healthcare is provided, providing benefits like constant tracking, early discovery of health problems, and individual treatments. When it comes to healthcare, one of the best things about smart technology is that it can constantly track bodily factors. In traditional healthcare methods, measures are only taken at doctor visits, which might not show the whole picture of a patient's health. On the [8] other hand, wearable technology can give you real-time information about things like blood sugar, heart rate, and blood pressure, which lets you take more thorough and quick actions. This constant monitoring can be especially helpful for people who have long-term conditions like diabetes or high blood pressure, which need regular tracking to be managed.

The field of [9] preventive care is another important area where smart technology is used in healthcare. Wearable technology can keep track of how active you are, how much sleep you get, and other aspects of your lifestyle, giving you information about how you are taking care of your health. With this knowledge, possible health risks can be found early on, and people can be encouraged to start living in a healthy way. For example, a portable gadget that tracks movement can encourage people to work out more often, which lower their risk of health problems linked to being overweight. Wearable technology could also make it easier to take care of people with long-term illnesses. Wearable technology can help doctors keep an eye on patients from afar and make changes to their treatment plans as needed by giving them real-time information on bodily factors. This [10] can help people with chronic conditions live better by reducing the number of times they need to go to the doctor or hospital. Wearable technology can do more than just track bodily data. It can also make it easier for patients and healthcare workers to talk to each other. Some smart technology comes with communication features like texting or video talking that make it easy for patients to get help or advice from their healthcare providers. This [11] can help patients be more involved in their care and follow their treatment plans more closely, which can improve their health. The smart technology could change the way healthcare is provided by allowing for constant tracking, early discovery of health problems, and individual treatments. Healthcare workers can improve patient care and results, lower costs, and give people more control over their health by incorporating smart devices into their systems.

17.1.2 Importance of Integrating Wearable Devices with Healthcare Systems

Incorporating smart technology with healthcare systems is very important for modern healthcare because it offers many benefits that can greatly enhance patient care and results. By bringing smart technology into healthcare systems in a smooth way, healthcare professionals can use real-time data to improve preventive care, find diseases early, and tailor treatments to each person's needs. This part talks about why combining smart technology with healthcare systems is important and what the main benefits are. One [12] of the best things about connecting smart technology to healthcare systems is that it lets bodily factors be tracked all the time. Wearable gadgets can keep track of many things, like blood sugar, heart rate, and blood pressure, so doctors can check on a patient's health at any time. This constant monitoring is especially helpful for people who have long-term conditions like diabetes or high blood pressure, which need regular tracking to be managed. Wearable gadgets let doctors make quick changes that can stop problems and improve patient results by giving them real-time data. One of the best things about connecting smart technology to healthcare systems is that it can help find health problems early on. Wearable technology can keep an eye on small changes in body functions that could mean a health problem is starting. For instance, changes in the unpredictability of the heart rate may show the early stages of cardiac arrhythmia, whereas changes in blood glucose levels may show the start of diabetes. Wearable [13] technology can help doctors catch these changes early, so they can take action quickly to stop the disease from getting worse and improve the patient's health.

When smart technology is connected to healthcare systems, it also makes it possible for personalized solutions. Wearable devices can give patients specific advice on how to eat, exercise, and take their medications because they

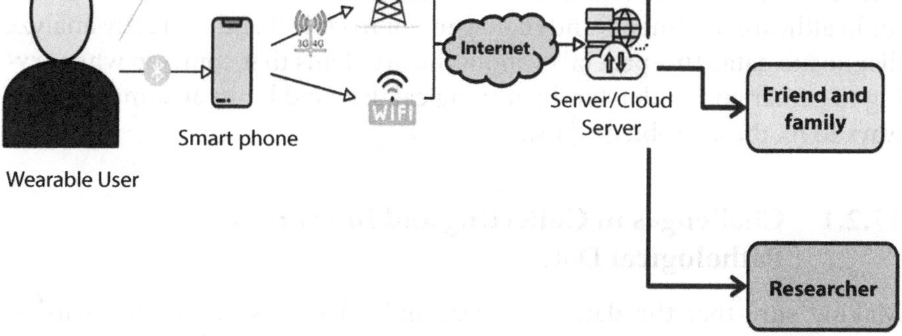

Figure 17.1 Overview of wearable devices with healthcare systems.

can track their health in real time. For instance, a smart gadget that tracks how active a person is can give them specific exercise suggestions based on their health goals and level of fitness. In the same way, a portable gadget that checks blood sugar levels can give a patient specific food suggestions based on their glucose levels and caloric needs. With these specific treatments, patients may be able to better take care of their health and enjoy life more generally [14]. Combining smart technology with healthcare systems not only can improve care and results for patients but also can save money. Wearable technology can lower the need for costly medical procedures like hospital stays and treatments by finding health problems early and stopping consequences before they happen. Wearable technology can also help patients avoid going to the clinic as often by letting doctors check on them from afar, which saves time and money for both patients and doctors [15]. Overall, putting smart technology into healthcare processes is very important for how healthcare is given today. Wearable gadgets can make a big difference in patient care and results by watching patients all the time, finding health problems early, and letting patients choose how to be helped. Wearable technology can also help healthcare systems give better care to more people by lowering costs and making things run more smoothly. Figure 17.1 presents an overview of wearable devices integrated with healthcare systems.

17.2 Pathological Considerations in Wearable Device Integration

Adding smart technology to healthcare systems to track abnormal data comes with a number of problems when it comes to gathering and analyzing the data. Pathological data includes signs of disease or bodily problems, like blood glucose levels for diabetes, heart rate variability for heart conditions, or biomarker amounts for different diseases. It is very important for healthcare treatments and management to collect and correctly analyze diagnostic data. This part talks about the problems that come up when trying to gather and understand pathological data and looks at some possible ways to fix these problems [18].

17.2.1 Challenges in Collecting and Interpreting Pathological Data

Making sure that the data is correct and reliable is one of the hardest parts of getting clinical data with smart devices. Sensors that can correctly measure bodily factors related to certain diseases must be built into wearable technology. For instance, a smart gadget meant to track diabetes must correctly record blood glucose levels, which can change a lot during the day. Making sure that these numbers are correct is important for giving healthcare workers accurate information and making sure that patients get the right care [20]. The fact that the data is not always the same is another problem with getting abnormal data. It is possible for pathological statistics to be very different from one person to the next or even from one person to the next over time. Pathological statistics can be affected by things like age, gender, and way of life, which makes it hard to set global rules or limits for these factors. Wearable technology needs to be able to handle this range of differences and give each person specific health-related information [16].

It can also be hard to figure out what clinical data from smart devices means, especially when trying to tell the difference between usual changes and signs of disease or other problems. Changes in heart rate, for instance, may be common when you are working out but could be a sign of a cardiac arrhythmia in other situations. Wearable [17] technology must be able to look at data in real time and give healthcare professionals useful information that helps them make decisions about how to care for patients. One way to deal with the problems that come up when trying to collect and understand pathological data is to create monitors and algorithms that are specifically designed for each pathology. For example, researchers have made portable devices with slightly invasive monitors that can constantly check blood glucose levels. These gadgets can show glucose levels in real time, which makes diabetes control more accurate. Another way is to use machine learning techniques to look at bad data and find trends or outliers that might point to disease or other problems. Large sets of clinical data can be used to teach machine learning algorithms how to spot trends that point to certain illnesses or conditions. Then, these algorithms can be used to look at data from smart technology and give healthcare professionals new ideas. For bringing clinical data into patient care, it is also important to make sure that smart devices can communicate with current healthcare systems. To get a full picture of a patient's health, wearable technology needs to be able to connect easily to EHRs and other healthcare systems [19]. To do this, rules need to be made so that smart technology and healthcare systems can share data and work together.

Adding smart technology to healthcare systems to track abnormal data comes with a number of problems when it comes to gathering and analyzing this data. Making sure the data is correct and reliable, taking into account how the data can vary, and understanding the data in a useful way are all important for managing and intervening in healthcare effectively.

These problems can be fixed by creating special devices and algorithms, using machine learning to look at data, and making sure that new and old healthcare systems can talk to each other. This will allow abnormal data to be effectively used in patient care.

17.2.2 Specialized Sensors and Algorithms for Pathological Data

Specialized sensors and algorithms are very important for getting abnormal data from smart technology and figuring out what it means. These devices and algorithms are made to find and study certain bodily factors that are linked to different diseases, like blood glucose levels for people with diabetes or heart rate variability for people with heart conditions. This part talks about why it is important to use specific sensors and algorithms to gather and understand abnormal data. It also looks at some personal devices that use these technologies [21].

One of the best things about specialized monitors is that they can give you correct data you can trust. For instance, monitors that check blood glucose levels must be able to measure glucose levels correctly, because even small mistakes can have big effects on how diabetes is managed. Specialized devices are made to measure certain bodily factors accurately [22]. This makes sure that the data gathered is accurate and can be used to make clinical decisions. Specialized monitors are also made to be as painless as possible, so they can be worn by anyone and be monitored all the time. For example, monitors that check blood sugar levels can be built into smartphones, patches, and other gadgets that you put on your body. These scanners can constantly check glucose levels through the skin, so you do not have to stick your finger in your arm to get real-time information. In addition to specialized sensors, algorithms are used to make sense of the data that these devices receive and give healthcare workers useful information. A lot of sick data is used to teach these algorithms how to find trends or outliers that could mean there is a disease or something is wrong. For instance, machine learning techniques can be used to look at data about heart rate fluctuations and find trends that point to heart rhythms.

Specialized sensors and algorithms are used in smart technology to keep an eye on heart problems, for example. Wearable technology with special sensors can keep an eye on heart rate variability all the time, which is a key sign of heart health. This data is looked at in real time by algorithms that look for trends that could mean someone has a cardiac arrhythmia or another heart disease. This information can then be used to let the person wearing it or their healthcare providers know about possible health problems so that they can be treated quickly. One more example is keeping an eye on people with diabetes. Wearable technology with special sensors can keep an eye on blood sugar levels all day, giving you real-time information about your glucose levels. Algorithms are used to look at this information and make specific suggestions for how to eat, exercise, and take medications. This might help people with diabetes handle their situation better and make their life better in general. The specific sensors and algorithms are very important for getting abnormal data from personal technology and figuring out what it means. These technologies allow for accurate and reliable tracking of certain bodily factors, which gives the user useful information about their health. By putting special sensors and algorithms into wearable technology, doctors can better treat a wide range of illnesses and improve care and results for patients.

17.2.3 Interoperability with Existing Healthcare Systems

Concerns about privacy and security, as well as the ability to work with current healthcare systems, are important parts of incorporating personal devices into healthcare for tracking abnormal data. For smart technology to be used effectively and ethically in healthcare, it needs to work well with existing systems and protect patients' privacy and safety. This part talks about why connectivity is important and how privacy and security issues can arise when abnormal data is taken from smart devices. For diagnostic data from smart devices to be used in patient care, they need to be able to communicate with other healthcare systems. Electronic health records (EHRs), clinical decision support systems (CDSSs), and other platforms that store patient data are common parts of healthcare systems. Wearable technology needs to be able to talk to and share info with these systems in order to work well together [23].

One problem with compatibility is that there are not any standard data forms or transmission methods for gadgets that you wear. It can be hard to connect wearable technology to current healthcare systems because they often use their own data forms and contact methods. Standardizing the forms and methods for wearable technology can make it easier for devices to talk to each other and work with healthcare systems. The fact that info from smart gadgets is not always consistent is another problem. Wearable devices can collect pathological data that can be very different from one person to the next or even from one person to the next over time. Healthcare systems need to be able to deal with this range of conditions and the different types of data that smart technology generates. To do this, you need data models and storage systems that are flexible enough to handle the different types of data forms and patterns. Another important part of putting smart technology into healthcare is addressing privacy and security issues. The pathological data that is collected from smart devices is naturally private because it can show private information about a person's health. It is very important to keep this information safe from people who should not have access to it or from being stolen. Figure 17.2 illustrates the earlier system in healthcare.

Making sure that smart technology follows privacy rules and laws, like the Health Insurance Portability and Accountability Act (HIPAA) in the US, is one problem. These rules make it very hard to get health information, even abnormal data, store it, or share it with other people. To protect patients' privacy, companies that make wearable technology must make sure that their products follow these rules. Another problem is making sure that the ways that smart technology and healthcare systems talk to each other are safe. Pathological data from wearable technology must be sent safely so that it cannot be hacked or intercepted. To do this, strong encryption and verification tools must be used to keep the data in transit safe. Also, healthcare systems need to set up strict access rules to make sure that only allowed people can see the disease data that smart devices receive. This includes setting up role-based access controls, checking access logs for errors, and reviewing and changing access rules on a regular basis. Despite these problems, ensuring sharing and handling privacy and security issues are very important for bringing smart technology into healthcare to track medical data that is not working right. Healthcare workers can safely use smart technology in their patients' care while protecting their privacy and data security by creating standard forms and protocols, setting up flexible data models and storage systems, and making sure they follow privacy laws.

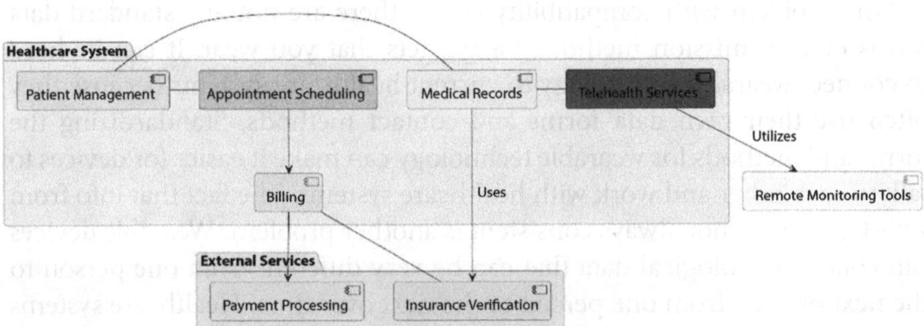

Figure 17.2 Illustration of earlier system in healthcare.

17.3 Strategies for Effective Integration

To successfully add wearable technology to healthcare systems for tracking abnormal data, strategies must be carefully planned and put into action that take into account the unique problems these techs cause. This part talks about some important ways to make integration work well, such as creating standards for exchanging data, putting in place strong security measures, making sure that integration with EHRs works smoothly, and getting users more involved and following the rules. Making sure that smart technology and healthcare systems can talk to each other requires setting rules for how data should be exchanged. Standards set up common ways for devices and systems to talk to each other and share data. They do this by defining common data forms and communication methods. By accepting and using these guidelines, healthcare workers can make sure that wearable technology works well with current healthcare systems, letting abnormal data be shared and analyzed. Strong security means must be put in place to protect the privacy and safety of medical data gathered from smart technology. This means encoding data while it is being sent and while it is being stored, using strong security methods, and only letting allowed people view the data. Healthcare workers must also make sure they follow privacy rules and laws, like HIPAA, to keep patient information safe from people who should not have access to it or from being stolen. Another important thing to do for successful integration is to make sure that the merger with EHRs goes smoothly. EHRs have useful details about a patient's medical background, medications, and treatment plans that can be added to the data gathered from smart technology. When smart devices are connected to EHRs, healthcare workers can see a full picture of a patient's health. This lets them make better decisions and give more personalized care.

Improving user involvement and cooperation is also important for making smart technology work well in healthcare. To make sure that accurate and dependable data is collected, patients must be encouraged to regularly wear gadgets and follow tracking routines. Healthcare workers can get people more involved by teaching patients how important it is to keep an eye on their health and giving them personalized comments and suggestions based on data from smart devices. The methods that deal with the problems that smart devices cause are needed to make the merging of these devices into healthcare systems for watching abnormal data work well. Healthcare workers can successfully use smart devices to improve patient care and health results by creating guidelines for data sharing, putting in place strong security measures, making sure that smooth interaction with EHRs is achieved, and increasing user engagement and compliance.

17.3.1 Developing Standards for Data Exchange

Making sure that smart technology and healthcare systems can talk to each other requires setting rules for how data should be exchanged. Standards set the rules for how devices and systems can talk to each other and share data. They do this by defining standard data forms, communication methods, and other technical details. When it comes to personal devices that track clinical data, making rules for data sharing is important so that healthcare workers can use these devices to really help patients. One of the best things about making guidelines for data sharing is that it lets different healthcare systems and smart technology work together. Standards make it easy for data from different devices to be shared and added to healthcare systems by setting up standard data forms and communication methods. This gives doctors and nurses a full picture of a patient's health, which can help them make better decisions and give better care.

Creating guidelines for data sharing also makes it easier to make products and systems that work with each other. Wearable technology and healthcare systems can be made that meet these standards, so they can talk to each other and share info without any problems. This makes sure that products and systems from different makers can work well together and lowers the chance of connection problems. Making guidelines for exchanging data can also help make data more accurate and of higher quality. Standards can make sure that data from smart technology is uniform and accurate by setting up standard data forms and communication methods. This is very important to make sure that healthcare professionals can trust the data that these gadgets receive and use it to make smart choices about how to care for their patients. The making rules for exchanging data is very important to make sure that smart technology and healthcare systems can work together. Standards make it possible for healthcare workers to use smart technology in a way that improves patient care and results by setting common data forms, communication methods, and other technical requirements. Figure 17.3 illustrates the integration process with electronic health records.

17.3.2 Implementing Robust Security Measures

Strong security means must be put in place to protect the privacy and safety of medical data gathered from smart technology. Pathological data is naturally private because it can show private information about a person's health. Healthcare companies must put in place strong security means to keep this information safe from people who should not have access to it or from being stolen. Encryption is one of the most important security steps

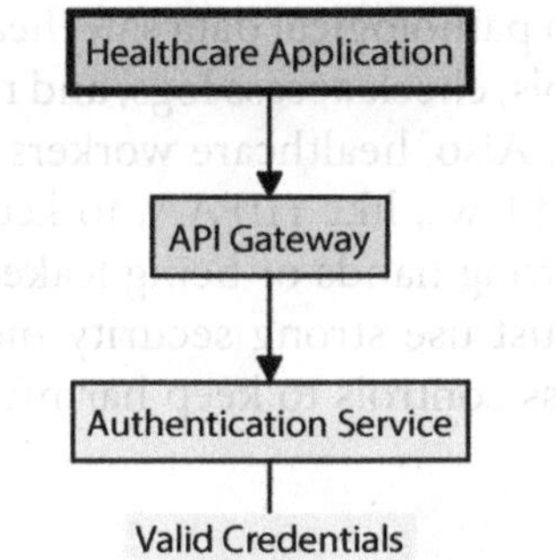

Figure 17.3 Illustration of the integration process with electronic health records.

that healthcare workers can use. The process of encrypting data means that only people who are allowed to can read it. Pathological data gathered from smart devices can be encrypted by healthcare providers while it is at rest or in motion. This keeps the data safe from people who are not supposed to see it or steal it.

An important extra safety step is identification. Before letting a person or gadget access data, authentication makes sure that they are who they say they are. Strong authentication methods, like passwords, facial authentication, or two-factor authentication, can be used by healthcare workers to make sure that only authorized staff can access the medical data received by smart devices. Healthcare providers must use more than just security and identification to keep abnormal data from getting into the wrong hands. Access limits make sure that only approved people can see the data that smart technology collects. This lowers the risk of data leaks or illegal access. To keep pathological data safe, healthcare workers can use role-based access controls, check access logs, and review and update access rules on a regular basis. Also, healthcare workers need to make sure they follow privacy rules and laws, like HIPAA, to keep sensitive information from getting into the wrong hands or being leaked. To follow these rules, healthcare providers must use strong security measures like encryption, identification, and access controls to keep harmful data safe and patients' privacy protected.

17.3.3 Ensuring Seamless Integration with Electronic Health Records (EHRs)

Electronic health records (EHRs) must be easily connected to personal devices in order for them to be used in healthcare systems to track abnormal data. EHRs have useful details about a patient's medical background, medications, and treatment plans that can be added to the data gathered from smart technology. Making sure that smart devices and EHRs work together without any problems gives doctors a full picture of a patient's health, which helps them make better decisions and give more personalized care. The fact that data from smart devices can be different makes it hard to make sure that they work well with EHRs. Wearable devices can collect pathological data that can be very different from one person to the next or even from one person to the next over time. Healthcare systems need to be able to deal with this range of conditions and the different types of data that smart technology generates. To do this, you need data models and storage systems that are flexible enough to handle the different types of data forms and patterns. One more problem is that there are not any standard platforms for connecting smart technology to EHRs. It can be hard to connect wearable technology to current healthcare systems because they often use their own data forms and contact methods. Standardized platforms for data exchange between smart devices and EHRs can make merging easier and allow abnormal data to be shared and analyzed.

For smooth interaction with EHRs, it is also important to make sure that the data is correct and reliable. For smart devices to collect true pathological data that can be used to make treatment decisions, the data must be correct and reliable. Healthcare providers need to set up quality assurance procedures to check the accuracy of data gathered from smart technology and make sure it matches data kept in EHRs. To deal with these problems, healthcare workers can use a number of methods to make sure that EHRs work well with their other systems. One plan is to create standard platforms so that smart technology and EHRs can share info. These interfaces should set standard data forms, connection methods, and other technical details that let different systems and gadgets work together without any problems. One more idea is to use adaptable data models and storage systems that can handle the different kinds of data that smart technology can collect. Healthcare professionals can use data modeling to create flexible data models that can change to fit the different data patterns and forms that smart technology creates. These changes make it possible for clinical data to be easily added to EHRs, giving doctors a full picture of a patient's health. Overall, making sure that smooth interaction with EHRs is important for putting smart technology into healthcare systems that track abnormal data so that they work well. Healthcare workers can make sure that smart devices can be easily connected to EHRs by creating standard interfaces, putting in place flexible data models, and checking the correctness and dependability of the data. This will allow for better decision-making and more personalized care.

17.3.4 Enhancing User Engagement and Compliance

For smart devices to be used effectively for watching abnormal data, users must be more engaged and follow the rules. Compliance means that users follow the monitoring plans and protocols that have been set. User involvement is how involved users are in using smart devices and following the monitoring protocols. Improving health results and making sure that correct data is collected by increasing user involvement and cooperation. One important way to get people to be more involved and follow through is to give them specific comments and suggestions based on the information gathered from smart technology. Machine learning algorithms can be used by healthcare professionals to look at abnormal data and give people personalized insights and suggestions. For instance, a smart gadget that tracks how active a person is can give them specific exercise suggestions based on their health goals and level of fitness. Users should also be taught why it is important to keep an eye on their health and how smart technology can help them reach their health goals. Healthcare workers can help users understand the benefits of using smart devices to track disease data and how it can improve their health by giving them information and tools.

Additionally, adding game-like features to smart technology can help increase user interest and compliance. Gamification is the process of adding game-like elements to wearable technology, like tasks, prizes, and leaderboards, to get people to interact with the technology and follow the rules for tracking. For instance, a smart gadget that tracks how active a person is can give them badges or other prizes when they meet their daily exercise goals.

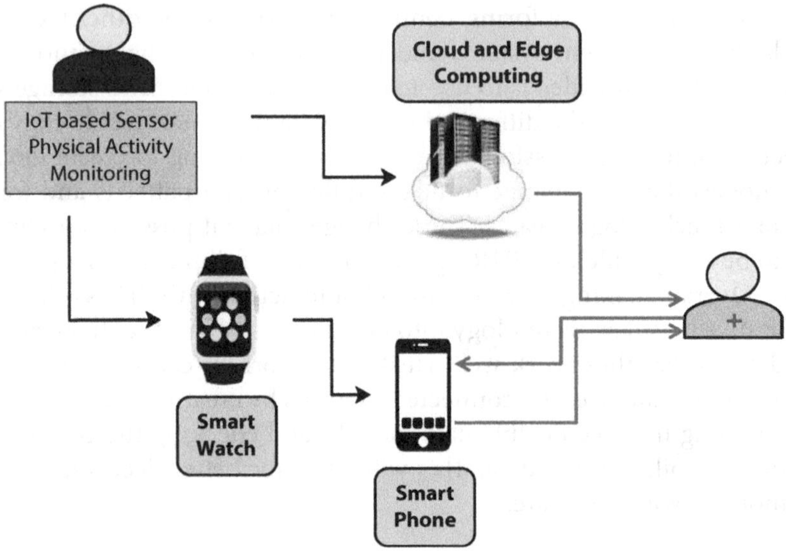

Figure 17.4 Detection of user data and health monitoring.

Involving users in the creation and development of smart technology can also help keep users interested and compliant. Healthcare workers can make sure that smart devices meet the needs and wishes of users by asking for feedback and using that feedback in the planning process. This will lead to more engagement and compliance. Overall, getting people to be more involved and follow the rules is very important for making personal devices for tracking clinical data work well. Healthcare providers can improve user engagement and compliance by giving users personalized feedback and suggestions, teaching users about the benefits of monitoring their health, adding game-like elements, and involving users in the design process. This will lead to more accurate and reliable data collection and better health outcomes. Figure 17.4 depicts the detection of user data and health monitoring.

17.4 Case Studies and Examples

17.4.1 Successful Integration of Wearable Technology in Pathological Monitoring

There are several examples of how wearable technology can be used effectively in disease tracking. These examples show how these devices can improve patient care and results. One example is how portable technology is used to check the blood sugar levels of people with diabetes. Continuous glucose monitoring (CGM) systems, like those made by Dexcom and Medtronic, use sensors that people with diabetes wear to keep an eye on their blood sugar levels all the time. These devices are put under the skin and talk to a receiver worn on the body or a smartphone app to give real-time glucose levels. By connecting CGM systems to EHRs, doctors can see glucose data in real time and use it to make decisions about how to care for patients. Wearable gadgets for tracking heart problems are another example of a good use case. Wearable devices with sensors that track changes in the heart rate and other heart-related factors can tell a lot about a person's heart health. For instance, the Apple Watch has a tool that can spot odd heart beats like atrial fibrillation and let users know they need to see a doctor. In both of these cases, a number of important factors have made it possible for smart technology to be successfully used in clinical tracking. One reason is the creation of special devices and computer programs that can precisely record and understand data about diseases. For instance, CGM systems use monitors that can precisely measure the amount of glucose in interstitial fluid. Algorithms then look at this data and give glucose readings in real time. Table 17.1 presents statistical data on the integration of wearable devices in healthcare.

Another issue is how well wearable technology works with current healthcare systems, like EHRs. By creating standard data sharing platforms and protocols, healthcare workers can quickly add smart devices to their patients' care processes. This lets them make better decisions and give more personalized care. Also, getting people to use and follow the technology has been very important for making it work well in abnormal tracking. Healthcare providers can improve user engagement and compliance, which will lead to more accurate and reliable data collection, by giving users personalized feedback and suggestions, teaching them about the benefits of monitoring their health, and adding game-like elements to wearable devices. Figure 17.5 shows the distribution of diseases among patient groups.

17.4.2 Lessons Learned and Best Practices

Healthcare professionals who want to use wearable technology in their work can learn a lot from the mistakes and best practices that have been made when these devices were used in clinical tracking. Wearable technology has been used successfully in clinical tracking, which has taught us a few important lessons and best practices:

- *Focus on User-Centric Design:* When making wearable technology, keep the person who will be using it in mind by

Table 17.1 Statistical data showing for integration of wearable device in healthcare.

Group	No of patients	Type of disease	Finding	Type of device	Disease identification	Disease name
Group A	50	Diabetes	Continuous glucose monitoring	Wearable sensor	Glucose levels monitoring	Diabetes Mellitus
Group B	30	Cardiovascular	Irregular heart rhythms detection	Smartwatch	ECG monitoring	Atrial Fibrillation
Group C	40	Respiratory	Environmental factors affecting respiratory conditions	Wearable sensor	Air quality monitoring	Asthma
Group D	25	Neurological	Early detection of neurological disorders	Head-mounted device	Brain activity monitoring	Parkinson's Disease
Group E	35	Dermatological	Skin condition monitoring	Wearable patch	Skin health monitoring	Psoriasis

thinking about things like comfort, ease of use, and looks. During the planning process, talk to users to make sure that the gadgets meet their wants and needs.

- *Make Sure the Data Is Correct and Reliable:* Make sure the data you get from smart technology is correct and reliable by using special sensors and software. Set up quality assurance procedures to check that the data is correct and that it matches the data in EHRs.
- *Make Sure That the New System Works Well With the Old Ones:* Standardize the platforms and methods that smart devices and EHRs use to share data so that the two can work together without any problems. Make sure that smart technology can talk to and share data with current healthcare systems without any problems.
- *Improve User Engagement and Compliance:* Use the data from smart devices to give users specific comments and suggestions. Inform users about the advantages of keeping an eye on their health, and add game-like features to smart technology to make them more interested and likely to follow through.

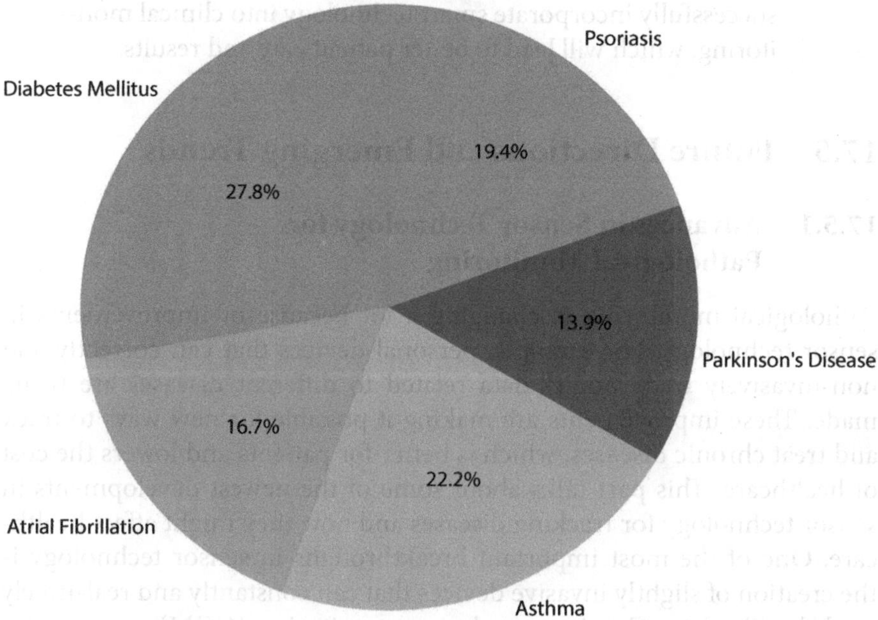

Figure 17.5 Distribution of diseases in patient groups.

- *Take Care of Privacy and Safety Issues:* Protect the harmful data gathered from smart technology with strong security measures like encryption, identification, and access controls. Make sure you follow privacy rules and laws, like HIPAA, to keep patient information safe from people who should not have access to it or from being stolen.
- *Monitor and Evaluate Performance:* In clinical tracking, personal devices should always be watched and their performance should be evaluated. Get comments from users and healthcare workers to find ways to make the systems and products better, and then keep making small changes to them over time.
- *Collaborate With Stakeholders:* To make sure that the successful integration of smart technology in disease tracking, collaborate with stakeholders such as patients, healthcare providers, gadget makers, and regulatory bodies. Talk to these people to get their ideas, address their worries, and encourage the use of smart technology in healthcare. Healthcare workers can use these best practices and lessons learned to

successfully incorporate smart technology into clinical monitoring, which will lead to better patient care and results.

17.5 Future Directions and Emerging Trends

17.5.1 Advances in Sensor Technology for Pathological Monitoring

Pathological monitoring is changing a lot because of improvements in sensor technology. For example, personal devices that can correctly and non-invasively track bodily data related to different diseases are being made. These improvements are making it possible for new ways to track and treat chronic diseases, which is better for patients and lowers the cost of healthcare. This part talks about some of the newest developments in sensor technology for tracking diseases and how they might affect healthcare. One of the most important breakthroughs in sensor technology is the creation of slightly invasive devices that can constantly and real-timely track bodily data. Continuous glucose monitoring (CGM) systems, for instance, use sensors that are barely noticeable when they are put under the skin to keep an eye on glucose levels all the time. These monitors can give glucose readings in real time, which makes managing diabetes more accurate and lowers the risk of both low and high blood sugar. Wearable devices that can check multiple bodily factors at the same time are another step forward. Some smart technology can check a person's heart rate, blood pressure, and oxygen intake levels, giving doctors a full picture of their health. These multi-parameter sensors let doctors keep a closer eye on patients all around, and they can help find and treat complicated diseases more effectively. Sensors that can track biomarkers and other signs of sickness have also been made possible by progress in sensor technology. For instance, external monitors that can pick up signs for heart diseases like troponin and B-type natriuretic peptide (BNP) can help find people who are at risk of heart failure or myocardial infarction so that they can get help right away.

Also, improvements in sensor technology have led to the creation of sensors that can track external factors that have an impact on health. For example, wearing monitors that can check the temperature, humidity, and quality of the air can help people with asthma or chronic obstructive lung disease figure out what in their surroundings might make their conditions worse so they can take steps to avoid them. One of the most important trends in sensor technology for tracking diseases is putting sensors into comfy, easy-to-use, and nice-looking gadgets that people can wear. Wearable technology that looks like watches or jewelry, for example, is becoming more and more popular among patients because it is easy to hide and comfortable to wear all day. Another trend is the use of sensors that are bendable and can be stretched to fit the shape of the body. This makes tracking more comfortable and reliable. These sensors can be built into clothing or put on with sticky tape, so they can be used for constant tracking without having to carry around big, uncomfortable gadgets. Also, improvements in sensor technology are making it possible to make monitors that can talk to smartphones or other devices wirelessly. This lets data be shared and monitored from afar. For example, wearable technology with Bluetooth or Wi-Fi can send data to a smartphone app. This lets patients and healthcare workers see data in real time and make choices about care that are best for the patient.

17.5.2 Integration with Artificial Intelligence and Machine Learning

A major trend in the growth of smart technology for tracking diseases is the integration of artificial intelligence (AI) and machine learning (ML). More and more, AI and ML algorithms are being used to look at the huge amounts of data that smart technology collects. This makes it possible for healthcare treatments to be more personalized and proactive. In this part, we talk about how combining smart technology with AI and ML might change the way we watch people with diseases.

One of the best things about combining smart technology with AI and ML is that it lets you look at complicated data trends and find useful information. Wearable technology gathers a lot of information about your body and surroundings, like your heart rate, blood pressure, and level of movement, which can be hard to understand by hand. AI and machine learning systems can look at this data and find trends or outliers that could mean there is a disease or other health problem. AI and ML systems can, for instance, look at data from smart technology to find early signs of diseases like diabetes and cardiac fibrillation. By looking for trends in things like blood glucose levels or changes in heart rate, these programs can let users or healthcare workers know about possible health problems so that they can be treated quickly. When you combine smart technology with AI and ML, you can also tailor healthcare treatments to each person. AI and ML systems can look at data from smart technology to make users' unique health profiles, which include things like their age, gender, and medical background. Individual users' wants can be taken into account when making healthcare decisions, like how much medicine to take or how often to exercise.

Also, combining smart technology with AI and ML can make it possible to predict how health results will turn out. By looking at old data from smart technology, AI and ML systems can guess how people's health will be in the future and find out what makes them more likely to get certain diseases. With this information, people can come up with ways to avoid getting certain diseases and help those who already have them. One of the biggest problems with combining smart technology with AI and ML is that data needs to be kept safe and private. Wearable technology gathers private health information, and it is important to keep this information safe from people who should not have access to it. To keep the data gathered from smart technology safe, healthcare workers need to use encryption, identification, and access controls. Another problem is that AI and ML systems and smart gadgets need to be able to talk to each other. It can be hard to connect wearable technology to other AI and ML systems because they often use their own data forms and communication methods. Creating standard data sharing platforms and protocols can help solve this problem and make merging go more smoothly.

The combining smart technology with AI and ML could change the way disease tracking is done by making healthcare treatments more personalized, proactive, and effective. AI and ML systems can help improve patient outcomes and quality of life by looking at complicated data patterns, tailoring healthcare treatments to each patient, and letting us predict how health results will turn out. To get the most out of this combination, though, problems like data privacy and security, as well as connectivity, need to be fixed.

17.5.3 Regulatory Considerations and Policy Implications

Wearable technology for tracking diseases is developed and used with a lot of thought given to regulatory issues and policy impacts. Some of these things to think about are the approval processes for regulators, rules about data protection and security, compensation policies, and moral concerns. This part talks about the policy and regulation issues that come up when using smart technology for tracking diseases.

- *Regulatory Approval Processes:* In many countries, wearable gadgets for monitoring diseases must go through regulatory approval processes to make sure they are safe and effective.

In the US, the Food and Drug Administration (FDA) oversees medical equipment, such as smart technology. Before selling their products, makers must get FDA approval or clearance. Other countries also have similar groups that make sure medical gadgets are safe.

- *Data Privacy and Security Regulations:* Data received from personal devices for watching people with mental illnesses is often private and needs to be kept safe from people who should not have access to it or who break the security. The General Data Protection Regulation (GDPR) in the EU and the Health Insurance Portability and Accountability Act (HIPAA) in the US set rules for how health data can be collected, stored, and shared. These rules are meant to protect patients' privacy.
- *Reimbursement Policies:* The use of smart technology for disease monitoring can be affected by reimbursement policies. If healthcare workers get paid for using smart technology to help patients, then they might be more likely to start using them. In many countries, payment policies depend on proof that wearable technology is clinically useful and cost-effective, which can affect how many people use them.

There are some ethical issues that need to be thought about when developing and using smart technology for disease tracking. These include informed permission, data ownership, and equal access to healthcare. Healthcare professionals need to make sure that patients know the pros and cons of wearing gadgets and that their information is used in an honest and responsible way.

- *Standards and Interoperability:* Regulatory bodies and lawmakers care a lot about how smart devices can work together and with each other. Standardized interfaces and standards can make it easier for smart technology and healthcare systems to share data, which makes integration and communication possible.
- *Post-Market Surveillance:* One important rule for wearable devices used for disease monitoring is that they must be supervised after they have been sold. Once their products are on the market, manufacturers have to keep an eye on how safe and well they work and report any problems to the officials in charge.

- *International Collaboration:* It is important to work together with people from other countries to solve the legal and policy problems that come up with using smart technology for medical tracking. Regulatory groups and lawmakers need to work together to make sure that all laws and standards are the same. This will make it easier for smart devices to be used all over the world.

The regulation issues and policy impacts are very important in the creation and use of smart technology for tracking diseases. Healthcare workers, gadget makers, and lawmakers can make sure that wearable technology is safe, effective, and morally good by thinking about these things. This will eventually improve patient results and quality of life.

17.6 Conclusion

Putting smart technology into healthcare systems for tracking diseases has a huge potential to change the way healthcare is provided. Wearable devices with advanced sensors and AI systems can give real-time, specific information about a patient's health, which can help find and treat many diseases early on. But there are a few important things that need to be thought about to make sure that smart technology works well in healthcare settings. For starters, creating standard interfaces and methods is important so that smart technology can easily share data with current healthcare systems. This will enable sharing and ensure that data gathered from smart devices can be quickly combined into EHRs and other healthcare platforms. A strong data protection and security means must be put in place to keep the private health data that smart technology collects safe. To protect patient privacy and make sure that data is used properly, it is important to follow rules like GDPR and HIPAA. The healthcare workers need to focus on getting users more involved and making sure they follow the rules so that smart devices can be used effectively for disease tracking. Giving users specific feedback, teaching them about the benefits of watching their health, and adding game-like features can help encourage them to regularly use smart devices and follow tracking routines. The successful inclusion of smart technology into healthcare systems for disease monitoring needs a joint effort between healthcare workers, gadget developers, regulators, and lawmakers. By taking these things into account and following best practices, healthcare workers can use smart technology to its fullest to improve patient results and change the way healthcare is delivered.

References

1. Kim, J.J., Wang, Y., Wang, H., Lee, S., Yokota, T., Someya, T., Skin Electronics: Next-Generation Device Platform for Virtual and Augmented Reality. *Adv. Funct. Mater.*, *31*, 39, 2170286, 2021.
2. Matsuhisa, N., Chen, X., Bao, Z., Someya, T., Materials and structural designs of stretchable conductors. *Chem. Soc. Rev.*, *48*, 11, 2946–2966, 2019.
3. Ray, T., Choi, J., Reeder, J., Lee, S.P., Aranyosi, A.J., Ghaffari, R., Rogers, J.A., Soft, skin-interfaced wearable systems for sports science and analytics. *Curr. Opin. Biomed. Eng.*, 9, 47–56, 2019.
4. Wang, Y., Haick, H., Guo, S., Wang, C., Lee, S., Yokota, T., Someya, T., Skin bioelectronics towards long-term, continuous health monitoring. *Chem. Soc. Rev.*, *51*, 9, 3759–3793, 2022.
5. Kumar, S.A., Kumar, A., Dutt, V., Agrawal, R., Multi Model Implementation on General Medicine Prediction with Quantum Neural Networks, in: *2021 Third International Conference on Intelligent Communication Technologies and Virtual Mobile Networks (ICICV)*, Tirunelveli, India, pp. 1391–1395, 2021, doi: 10.1109/ICICV50876.2021.9388575.
6. Raj, P., Dubey, A.K., Kumar, A., Rathore, P.S., Blockchain-based IoT architecture for software-defined networking, in: *Blockchain, Artificial Intelligence, and the Internet of Things*, Springer International Publishing, 2022.
7. Burri, S.R., Kumar, A., Baliyan, A., Kumar, T.A., Predictive Intelligence for Healthcare Outcomes: An AI Architecture Overview, in: *2023 2nd International Conference on Smart Technologies and Systems for Next Generation Computing (ICSTSN)*, Villupuram, India, pp. 1–6, 2023, doi: 10.1109/ICSTSN57873.2023.10151477.
8. Wani, S., Ahuja, S., Kumar, A., Application of Deep Neural Networks and Machine Learning algorithms for diagnosis of Brain tumour, in: *2023 International Conference on Computational Intelligence and Sustainable Engineering Solutions (CISES)*, Greater Noida, India, pp. 106–111, 2023, doi: 10.1109/CISES58720.2023.10183528.
9. Kour, S.P., Kumar, A., Ahuja, S., An Advance Approach for Diabetes Detection by Implementing Machine Learning Algorithms, in: *2023 IEEE World Conference on Applied Intelligence and Computing (AIC)*, Sonbhadra, India, pp. 136–141, 2023, doi: 10.1109/AIC57670.2023.10263919.
10. Raj, P., Kumar, A., Dubey, A.K., Bhatia, S., Oswalt, M.S., *Quantum Computing and Artificial Intelligence: Training Machine and Deep Learning Algorithms on Quantum Computers*, De Gruyter, Berlin, Boston, 2023, [Online]. Available: https://doi.org/10.1515/9783110791402.
11. Sasubilli, G. and Kumar, A., Machine Learning and Big Data Implementation on Health Care data, in: *2020 4th International Conference on Intelligent Computing and Control Systems (ICICCS)*, Madurai, India, pp. 859–864, 2020, doi: 10.1109/ICICCS48265.2020.9120906.

12. Swarna, S.R., Kumar, A., Dixit, P., Sairam, T.V.M., Parkinson's Disease Prediction using Adaptive Quantum Computing, in: *2021 Third International Conference on Intelligent Communication Technologies and Virtual Mobile Networks (ICICV)*, Tirunelveli, India, pp. 1396–1401, 2021, doi: 10.1109/ICICV50876.2021.9388628.
13. Burugadda, V.R., Pawar, P.S., Kumar, A., Bhati, N., Predicting Hospital Readmission Risk for Heart Failure Patients Using Machine Learning Techniques: A Comparative Study of Classification Algorithms, in: *2023 Second International Conference on Trends in Electrical, Electronics, and Computer Engineering (TEECCON)*, Bangalore, India, pp. 223–228, 2023, doi: 10.1109/TEECCON59234.2023.10335817.
14. Gambhir, S.S., Ge, T.J., Vermesh, O., Spitler, R., Gold, G.E., Continuous health monitoring: An opportunity for precision health. *Sci. Transl. Med.*, 13, 597, eabe5383, 2021.
15. Liu, H. and Zhao, C., Wearable electrochemical sensors for noninvasive monitoring of health—a perspective. *Curr. Opin. Electrochem.*, 23, 42–46, 2020.
16. Rohmetra, H., Raghunath, N., Narang, P., Chamola, V., Guizani, M., Lakkaniga, N.R., AI-enabled remote monitoring of vital signs for COVID-19: methods, prospects and challenges. *Computing*, 105, 1–27, 2023.
17. Pace, P., Aloi, G., Gravina, R., Caliciuri, G., Fortino, G., Liotta, A., An edge-based architecture to support efficient applications for healthcare industry 4.0. *IEEE Trans. Ind. Inf.*, *15*, 1, 481–489, 2018.
18. Shukla, A., Chaturvedi, S., Simmhan, Y., Riotbench: An iot benchmark for distributed stream processing systems. *Concurrency Comput. Pract. Exper.*, *29*, 21, e4257, 2017.
19. Lu, Z.X., Qian, P., Bi, D., Ye, Z.W., He, X., Zhao, Y.H., Su, L., Li, S.L., Zhu, Z.L., Application of AI and IoT in clinical medicine: summary and challenges. *Curr. Med. Sci.*, *41*, 6, 1134–1150, 2021.
20. Henderson, J., Condell, J., Connolly, J., Kelly, D., Curran, K., Review of wearable sensor-based health monitoring glove devices for rheumatoid arthritis. *Sensors*, *21*, 5, 1576, 2021.
21. Pasquale, G. and Mastrototaro, L., Glove-based systems for medical applications: Review of recent advancements. *J. Text. Eng. Fash. Technol.*, *4*, 3, 253–262, 2018.
22. Djurić-Jovičić, M., Jovičić, N.S., Roby-Brami, A., Popović, M.B., Kostić, V.S., Djordjević, A.R., Quantification of finger-tapping angle based on wearable sensors. *Sensors*, *17*, 2, 203, 2017.
23. Shyr, T.W., Shie, J.W., Jiang, C.H., Li, J.J., A textile-based wearable sensing device designed for monitoring the flexion angle of elbow and knee movements. *Sensors*, *14*, 3, 4050–4059, 2014.

18

Challenges and Solutions in Healthcare System Integration: Histological Perspectives on Wearable Device Integration Challenges

Yugantara R. Kadam[1] and Sujata Raghunath Kanetkar[2]*

[1]Department of Community Medicine, Krishna Institute of Medical Sciences, Krishna Vishwa Vidyapeeth "Deemed To Be University", Karad, Maharashtra, India
[2]Department of Pathology, Krishna Institute of Medical Sciences, Krishna Vishwa Vidyapeeth "Deemed To Be University", Karad, Maharashtra, India

Abstract

Wearable devices must be integrated into healthcare systems, but there are some problems that need to be fixed before they can fully improve patient results and healthcare service. This essay looks at the problems and possible answers for putting wearable technology together, focused on tissue points of view. One of the biggest problems is making sure that smart technology can work with current healthcare systems. It can be hard to easily add data from wearable devices to electronic health records and other healthcare systems because they often use different data types and communication methods. Another problem is making sure that data from smart devices is safe and private. Healthcare data is very private, so it is important to keep data on smart devices safe from hackers and other people who should not be able to see it. There are also problems with how accurate and reliable the data from smart devices is. The accuracy of sensors, the way data is calibrated, and how well users follow the instructions can all change the quality of the data that smart devices produce, which can make them less useful for making healthcare decisions. There are also problems with how personal devices can be added on a large scale and in the long term. As the number of smart devices used in healthcare grows, healthcare systems need to be able to expand their infrastructure to handle the extra data that these devices create. Several ideas are put

**Corresponding author*: sujatakanetkarkvv@outlook.com

Abhishek Kumar, Narayan Vyas, Pramod Singh Rathore, Abhineet Anand and Pooja Dixit (eds.) Internet of Medicine for Smart Healthcare, (373–404) © 2025 Scrivener Publishing LLC

forward for how to deal with these problems. Wearable device data can be more accurate and reliable if the sensors are better, the data is checked more thoroughly, and users are taught how to use the devices. There are ways to deal with scalability and sustainability that use cloud-based storage and processing options.

Keywords: Histological perspectives, health system, clinical barriers, wearable devices integration, electronic health records

18.1 Introduction

Wearable gadgets could change the way healthcare is provided and handled if they are added to healthcare platforms. These gadgets, which include fitness trackers and medical-grade sensors, constantly check a patient's vital signs, exercise levels, and other health-related information, giving doctors useful information about the patient's health. Some problems have been found with adding smart technology to healthcare systems, though. This chapter focuses on histology views to look at the problems and possible answers that come up when smart devices are used together [1]. In recent years, wearable gadgets have become more common because they can give real-time information about different health factors. Wearable technology can keep an eye on things like blood sugar levels, heart rate, and even falls or strange moves. It is possible that this constant tracking will help find health problems earlier, allow for proactive measures, and improve total patient care. There are some problems with adding smart technology to healthcare systems, even though they could be helpful. Interoperability is one of the main problems. It can be hard to easily add data from wearable devices to electronic health records (EHRs) and other healthcare systems because they often use different data types and communication methods. This problem with compatibility can make it harder for healthcare workers to get to and use the data that smart devices produce [2].

Another problem is making sure that data from smart devices is safe and private. Healthcare data is very private, so it is important to keep data on smart devices safe from hackers and other people who should not be able to see it. To lower these risks, encryption and other security measures can be used. However [3], healthcare organizations must also follow rules like the Health Insurance Portability and Accountability Act (HIPAA) to protect patient information. There are also problems with how accurate and reliable the data from smart devices is. The accuracy of sensors, the way data is calibrated, and how well users follow the instructions can all change the quality of the data that smart devices produce, which can make them less useful for making healthcare decisions. To make good choices about how to care for patients, healthcare professionals need to be able to trust the data that smart technology collects. There are also problems with how personal devices can be added on a large scale and in the long term. As [4] the number of smart devices used in healthcare grows, healthcare systems need to be able to expand their infrastructure to handle the extra data that these devices create. This includes making sure there is enough space for storage and processing to handle the data and fixing any problems that might come up with data delays and network connections. Several methods can be used to deal with these problems. Creating and using guidelines for data forms and communication methods can help make things work better together. Wearable device data can be more accurate and reliable if the sensors are better, the data is checked more thoroughly, and users are taught how to use the devices. There are ways to deal with scalability and sustainability that use cloud-based storage and processing options.

18.1.1 Overview of Wearable Devices in Healthcare

Wearable technology has changed quickly from simple fitness apps to complex health tracking tools that can keep track of many biometrics. These gadgets are meant to be worn on the body, usually as clothes or ornaments. They have sensors that gather different kinds of information. Wearable technology is very important in healthcare because it lets doctors keep an eye on patients' health all the time. They [5] can keep an eye on things like oxygen levels, heart rate, blood pressure, and other vital signs. They can also keep an eye on things like exercise levels, sleep habits, and even temperature and humidity in the air. Wearable devices collect data that can be used for many healthcare purposes, such as finding health problems early, keeping an eye on long-term conditions, and managing your health in a way that is unique to you. For instance, smart technology can let doctors know when a patient's vital signs are not working right, so they can act quickly. They can also help people keep track of their own health data and make smart choices about their care and way of life [6].

Wearable technology is not just used to keep an eye on patients in healthcare. These gadgets can also be used for telemedicine, which lets doctors check on patients from afar and have video talks. Wearable technology can also help with clinical studies by giving experts real-time information about the health and treatment results of trial subjects. Overall [7], wearable technology could change healthcare by making it possible to keep an eye on patients' health in a proactive, specialized, and faraway way. But for

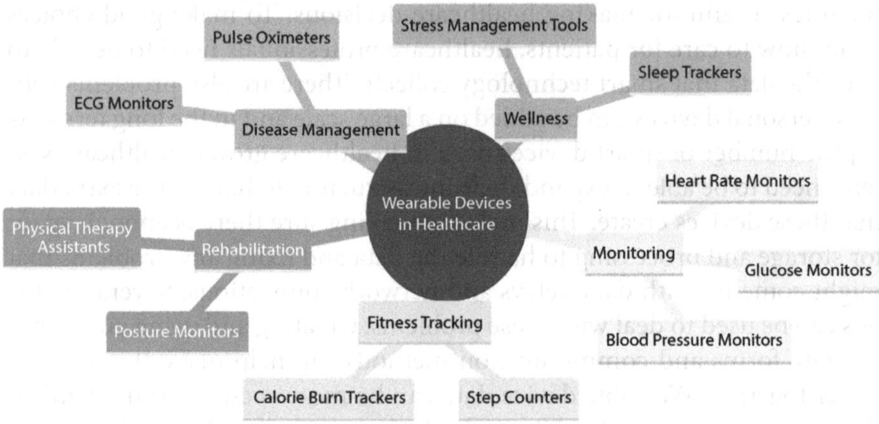

Figure 18.1 Illustration of wearable devices in healthcare and their applications.

this potential to be fully realized, these gadgets need to be built into healthcare systems in a way that makes it easy to gather, analyze, and understand data. Figure 18.1 demonstrates the use of wearable devices in healthcare.

18.1.2 Importance of Integration in Healthcare Systems

For smart technology to have the most effect on patient care and healthcare services, they need to be fully integrated into healthcare systems. Integrated smart devices can give doctors a full picture of a patient's health, which helps them make better decisions and create more personalized treatment plans. One [8] of the best things about adding smart technology to healthcare systems is that it makes it possible to keep an eye on patients' health all the time. This constant tracking can help find health problems early, before they get worse, and it can also help see how long-term conditions get worse over time. Another good thing about integration is that it lets you give each patient individualized care. Healthcare professionals can learn more about a patient's health and behavior trends by looking at the data collected by smart devices. This lets them make more personalized treatment plans and actions. Adding smart technology could also make healthcare service more efficient. Wearable [9] devices can cut down on the number of in-person visits needed by healthcare professionals by giving them real-time access to patient data. This can lead to more quick actions. Adding smart technology can also make patients more involved and give them more power. Wearable technology can help people stick to their treatment plans and make good lifestyle changes by letting them keep track of their own health data and be involved in their own care.

18.2 Challenges in Integrating Wearable Devices

Adding smart technology to healthcare systems comes with some problems that need to be fixed before they can be used safely and effectively to help patients. Some of these problems are connectivity issues, as well as security and privacy issues, which will be talked about in more depth below.

18.2.1 Interoperability Issues

Interoperability is one of the main problems that come up when trying to add smart technology to healthcare systems. It can be hard to easily add data from wearable devices to EHRs and other healthcare systems because they often use different data types and communication methods. Because these devices do not talk to each other, it can be hard for healthcare professionals to get to and use the data that smart devices produce [10]. To fix problems with compatibility, work is being done to create and accept guidelines for communication methods and data forms. For instance, the Continua Health Alliance has created a set of rules and guidelines for healthcare devices, such as smart ones, to be able to talk to each other. The goal [11] of these guidelines is to make sure that gadgets from different makers can share data and talk to each other properly, no matter what technology they use. Application programming interfaces (APIs) let smart technology connect to current healthcare systems, which is another way to make interoperability better. APIs give gadgets and healthcare companies a standard way to talk to each other and share data. This makes data sharing and interaction easy. Interoperability is still a big problem when it comes to putting smart technology into hospital systems, despite these attempts. To make sure that smart devices can work well with current healthcare systems, healthcare groups need to keep working on standards and collaboration.

18.2.2 Security and Privacy Concerns

Another big problem with adding smart technology to healthcare systems is that people are worried about security and privacy. Healthcare data is very private, so it is important to keep data on smart devices safe from hackers and other people who should not be able to see it. Data protection is one of the main security issues with smart technology. Wearable technology often gathers and sends private health information [12]. To keep this information safe from people who should not have access to it, it needs to be protected. When data is encrypted, it cannot be

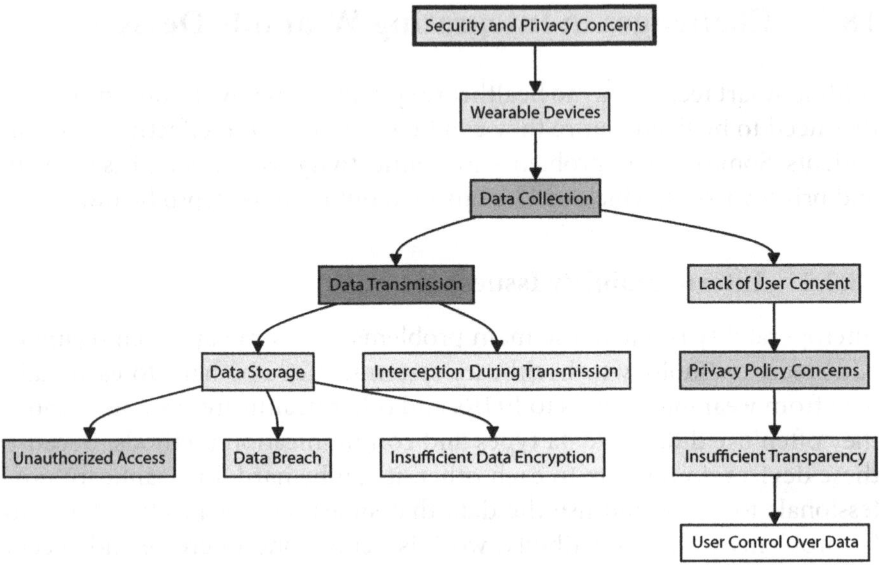

Figure 18.2 Security and privacy concern in healthcare systems.

read or changed without the encryption key, even if it is stolen. Controlling who can see and do things is another security issue. Healthcare companies need to make sure that only approved people can see the data from smart devices. A strong security method, like fingerprint authentication or two-factor authentication, can be used to make this happen. Aside from security issues, privacy is another big problem when it comes to adding smart technology to healthcare systems. The HIPAA and other privacy laws must be followed so that patients can trust that their health information is being treated properly. Healthcare companies need to take strong security steps, like data protection, identification, and access control, to deal with security and privacy issues. In addition, they need to make sure they follow privacy laws and tell people exactly how their data is being used and kept safe [13]. Figure 18.2 highlights the security and privacy concerns associated with wearable devices in healthcare systems.

18.2.3 Accuracy and Reliability of Data

Making sure that [14] the data that smart devices produce is correct and reliable is important for making sure that they work well with healthcare systems. The accuracy of sensors, the way data is calibrated, and how well users follow the instructions can all change the quality of the data that smart devices produce, which can make them less useful for making healthcare decisions. Sensor precision is one of the most difficult things to make sure is correct. Wearable technology uses many kinds of sensors to gather information. For example, accelerometers track movement and heart rate monitors keep an eye on heart rate [15]. The accuracy of these sensors can change, though, based on things like how the gadget is built, where the sensors are placed, and the weather. To get accurate data, it is important to make sure that monitors are set and checked for correctness.

Calibration of the data [16] is another problem. A lot of the time, wearable technology needs to be calibrated to make sure the data it collects is correct and reliable. Heart rate monitors, for instance, might need to be adjusted to take into account the fact that everyone's heart rate is different. Devices that are not properly calibrated can give wrong data and results that cannot be trusted. The correctness and dependability of data created by smart devices are also affected by how well users follow the instructions. To make sure correct data collection, users must wear the devices as directed and follow any other instructions given by healthcare providers [17]. If users do not follow the rules, then data can be missing or wrong, which makes the collected data less reliable. Healthcare groups can deal with these problems by putting in place plans to make data more accurate and reliable. This includes teaching people how to use smart technology correctly and making sure that the technology is set and checked to make sure it works right. Healthcare workers can also use methods for data checking to find and fix any mistakes or problems with the data they receive.

18.2.4 Scalability and Sustainability

Adding smart technology to healthcare systems can be hard because they need to be scalable and last a long time. As the number of smart devices used in healthcare grows, healthcare systems need to be able to expand their infrastructure to handle the extra data that these devices create. Storing and handling information is one of the biggest problems with growth. Wearable technology creates a lot of data that needs to be saved and handled quickly so that it can be analyzed and accessed when needed. To handle this data, healthcare groups need to have enough storing and processing power, which can be hard to expand as the amount of data grows [18].

Scalability problems can be solved with cloud-based storage and processing options, which offer an open and scalable way to store and process data.

Cloud computing lets healthcare companies change the size of their equipment as needed, so they can handle the growing amount of data that smart technology creates [19]. Another problem with putting smart technology into healthcare systems is that they need to be long-lasting. Healthcare groups need to make sure that the long-term viability of the infrastructure that supports smart technology. This means thinking about things like how much energy is used, how it affects the world, and how much it costs. Healthcare groups can deal with these problems by using tactics that make them more scalable and long-lasting. Adopting cloud-based storage and processing solutions and using energy-efficient technologies to lower energy use are two ways to do this. When planning their infrastructure,

Table 18.1 Summary of different security and privacy concerns.

Parameter	Description
Data Security	Ensuring the protection of sensitive patient data from unauthorized access or breaches.
Data Privacy	Protecting patient information from being accessed or used without their consent.
Regulatory Compliance	Ensuring that healthcare systems comply with relevant regulations and standards, such as HIPAA.
Identity Management	Managing and securing the identities of users accessing the healthcare system.
Access Control	Implementing measures to control who can access certain information or functions within the system.
Data Encryption	Encrypting sensitive data to protect it from being intercepted or accessed by unauthorized parties.
Secure Communication	Ensuring that data transmitted between devices and systems is done so securely to prevent interception.
Vulnerability Management	Identifying and mitigating vulnerabilities in the system that could be exploited by attackers.
Security Monitoring	Monitoring the system for any suspicious activity or breaches in real time.
Data Retention Policies	Establishing policies for how long data is retained and how it is securely disposed of when no longer needed.

healthcare groups can also think about how smart gadgets will affect the environment and how much they will cost in the long run. Table 18.1 presents the list of security and privacy concerns.

18.3 Interoperability Challenges

When you add smart technology to healthcare systems, you need to make sure that data can be shared and understood between devices and systems. This is called interoperability. Interoperability is hard to achieve, though, because different data forms and standards must be used.

18.3.1 Different Data Formats and Standards

Different data forms and standards are one of the main problems that make it hard for smart devices to work with healthcare systems. Wearable devices often have their own data forms that are unique to their maker. This makes [20] it hard to send data from one device to another. Some wearable technology may use a certain data format for heart rate data, whereas other wearable technology may use a different format for the same kind of data. Because of this lack of standards, it is hard to combine and examine data from many devices, which makes it harder for healthcare workers to get a full picture of a patient's health. In order to deal with this problem, work is being done to create and accept guidelines for communication methods and data forms. One group, Health Level Seven International (HL7), has created rules for exchanging healthcare data. One of these rules is the Fast Healthcare Interoperability Resources standard, which tries to make healthcare data sharing data forms more consistent.

Healthcare companies [21] can make sure that data from smart technology can be shared and understood across different systems and devices by following these guidelines. This compatibility is necessary for data to be easily shared and integrated, so healthcare professionals can get to and use data from smart technology devices correctly. Application programming interfaces (APIs) let smart devices connect to current healthcare systems. This is another way to solve the problem of communication. APIs give gadgets and healthcare companies a standard way to talk to each other and share data. This makes data sharing and interaction easy. Even with all of these attempts, there are still problems with sharing when it comes to adding smart technology to healthcare systems. To make sure that smart devices can work well with current healthcare systems, healthcare groups need to keep working on standards and collaboration.

18.3.2 Integration with Electronic Health Records (EHRs)

It is very important to connect wearable technology to EHRs so that the information gathered by these technology gadgets can be easily added to patients' medical records and used to help doctors make decisions. But connecting data from smart devices to EHRs is not always easy. EHR in healthcare sytem is illustrated in Figure 18.3.

There are issues with data structure, data protection, and merging workflows. One big problem with connecting smart technology to EHRs is that data needs to be formatted in a certain way. There are a lot of private data forms used by wearable technology that are hard to convert to EHR standards [22]. This can make it hard to move data from smart technology to EHRs in a way that keeps the data safe and makes it easy for healthcare workers to access. Healthcare companies can deal with this problem by using data normalization methods to turn data from smart technology into a standard code that EHRs can read. This can include connecting data elements from smart devices to their related elements in the EHR data model. This makes sure that the data is sent correctly and can be easily understood by healthcare professionals. Data protection is also a problem. Wearable technology gathers private health information that needs to be kept safe

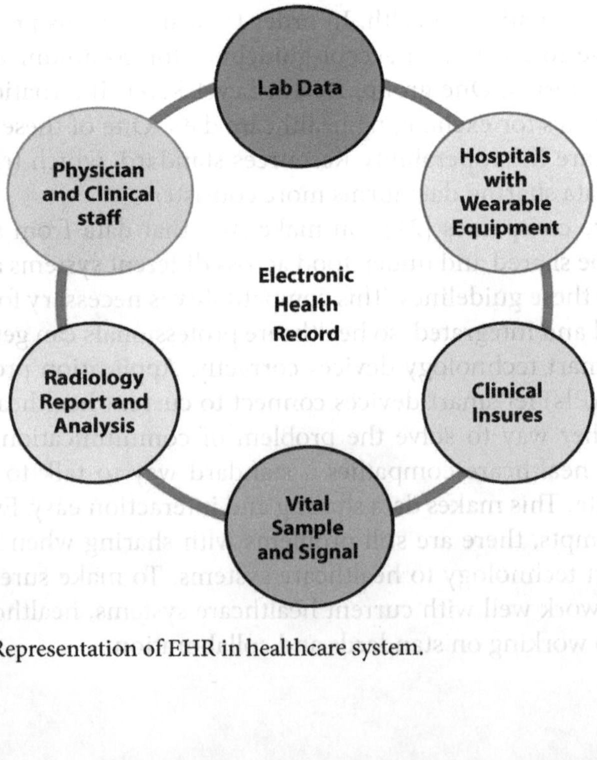

Figure 18.3 Representation of EHR in healthcare system.

from hackers and other people who should not have access to it. When you connect data from smart devices to EHRs, you need to use strong security measures, like encryption and access rules, to keep the data safe during the transfer process. Healthcare companies should also think about how to add data from smart devices to their EHRs without changing the way work is done. Doctors and nurses need to be able to access and look over data from smart devices in the setting of a patient's medical record without stopping what they are doing. To do this, data from smart devices needs to be smoothly added to the EHR screen so that it is easy to find and can be analyzed along with other health data [23].

Healthcare groups can deal with these problems in a number of ways. First, they can work with companies that make wearable technology to make sure that the devices are made so that they can work with each other by using standard data forms and communication methods. This could make it easy to integrate smart technology with EHRs and move data between the two. Second, healthcare groups can protect the data on smart devices with strong security methods. This can be done by securing data while it is being sent and while it is being stored, setting up access controls to make sure that only allowed people can access the data, and checking security practices on a regular basis to find and fix holes. Third [24], healthcare groups can create EHR platforms that are simple and easy to use, which makes it simple for healthcare workers to get to and understand data from smart devices. This could mean adding data from smart devices to current EHR processes and making sure it is shown in a way that healthcare workers can understand and use. In combining smart technology with EHRs comes with a number of problems, such as how to organize data, keep data safe, and make sure that workflows work together. But healthcare groups can get around these problems by using standard data forms, strong security measures, and easy-to-use tools to make sure that data from smart devices can be properly added to EHRs. This will improve the level of care for patients.

18.4 Security and Privacy Concerns

There are a lot of security and privacy worries about adding smart devices to healthcare systems because the data that these devices receive is very private. There are strict rules about healthcare data, like the HIPAA, which say that healthcare organizations must keep patient information private and safe. Data protection is one of the main security issues with smart technology. Wearable technology records and sends private health information, like heart rate, exercise levels, and sleep habits. This information needs to be protected so that it cannot be viewed by people who are not supposed to. When data is encrypted, it cannot be read or changed without the encryption key, even if it is stolen [25].

Controlling who can see and do things is another security issue. Healthcare companies need to make sure that only approved people can see the data from smart devices. Strong security methods, like fingerprint authentication or two-factor authentication, can be used to keep private data from getting into the wrong hands. When smart technology is added to healthcare systems, data security is also a worry. Healthcare groups need to make sure that the data that smart technology collects has not been changed or messed with in any way. Using data checking methods can help make sure that the data is correct and find any strange or inconsistent data that has been collected. When it comes to personal technology, privacy is another big issue. Patients need to know that their health information is being treated properly and in line with privacy laws. Healthcare groups must make sure that data from smart devices is saved safely and that only allowed people can access this data. Healthcare groups can take a number of steps to handle these security and privacy issues. First, they can make sure that wearable technology uses strong security to keep data safe while it is being sent and while it is being stored. Second, they can set up access rules so that only approved people can see the data on smart devices. Third, they can check their security measures on a daily basis to find and fix any holes [26].

18.4.1 Data Encryption

Encrypting data is a very important safety step for healthcare systems that use smart technology. Wearable devices collect private health data that cannot be read or changed by people who are not supposed to see it. Encryption protects this data from people who are not supposed to see it. The way encryption works is by changing data into a form that cannot be read without the right encryption key. This makes sure that data cannot be read or viewed without the encryption key, even if it is stolen while being sent or saved on a device. Several types of encryption can be used to keep the information that smart technology collects safe. The same key is used for both encryption and decoding, which is called symmetric encryption. This method works quickly and well, but both the author and the user need to know the encryption key. Some people use asymmetric encryption, which has two keys: a public key for encryption and a secret key for decoding. Because the private key is kept hidden and not given to anyone else, this method is safer than symmetric encryption. Asymmetric encryption, on the other hand, is slower and needs more computing power than symmetric encryption.

Healthcare groups can use encryption to keep smart technology data safe while it is being sent and while it is being stored. Safe communication methods, like Transport Layer Security, can be used by healthcare groups to protect data as it is sent over the internet or other networks. This makes sure that information cannot be accessed by people who are not supposed to. Healthcare groups can secure data that is not being used. This can be done on computers or smart technology. So, even if you lose or steal a device, the information on it will still be safe. Encryption can also be used to protect data saved in the cloud by healthcare organizations. This way, data is safe even when it is on computers far away. Healthcare groups need to do more than just secure data; they also need to make sure that only allowed people can view private data. As part of access limits, users may have to prove who they are before they can access data. This can be done through physical authentication or two-factor identification. Healthcare groups can protect data even more from people who should not have access to it by using access limits. To make sure that encryption works, healthcare organizations must also check their encryption methods on a daily basis to find and fix any problems. As part of this, you may need to make sure that encryption keys are kept safely and that encryption methods are up to date and meet industry standards.

18.4.2 Authorization and Access Control

Controlling who can see and access the data that smart medical devices receive is a key part of keeping that data safe and private. Authorization is the process of letting users access data based on who they are and what rights they have. Access control is the set of tools used to make sure that authorization rules are followed. Making sure that only approved people can see private health data received by smart technology is one of the hardest parts of authorization and access control. Healthcare organizations need to make sure people are who they say they are before letting them access data by using strong security methods. To prove who they are, users may have to enter a username and password, use biometric security like palm or face recognition, or use two-factor authentication. Healthcare organizations must set up access control systems to make sure that users have the right permissions to access data once a user's name has been verified. This can include limiting a user's access to certain types of data based on their job or role in the company. As an example, healthcare workers may be able to see health records of patients, whereas office staff may be able to see information about bills.

For permission and access control to work well, healthcare organizations need to set clear rules and guidelines for controlling who can see what data. This includes checking and changing access permissions on a daily basis when user jobs or responsibilities change, as well as checking access logs to make sure the right people are given and taken away access. Making sure that data is safe from unwanted access both while it is being sent and while it is being stored is another problem in authorization and access control. Encryption can help healthcare groups keep data safe while it is being sent over networks, so that it cannot be read by people who are not supposed to. In the same way, data saved on computers or wearable technology should be protected so that it cannot be accessed by people who should not be able to if the technology is lost or stolen. In addition to encryption, healthcare groups can protect data from people who should not have access to it by using firewalls, attack detection systems, and data loss prevention tools. By taking these steps, healthcare groups can keep the private health information that smart technology collects safe and out of the hands of people who should not have access to it.

18.4.3 Compliance with Regulations (e.g., HIPAA)

Another important part of putting smart technology into healthcare systems is making sure they follow rules like the HIPAA. HIPAA sets rules for how to keep health information safe and requires healthcare organizations to put in place measures to keep this information private and safe. Making sure that personal gadgets meet the rules set out in HIPAA is one of the hardest parts of following the law. This includes putting in place the right security and protection measures for health data received by smart technology, like encryption, access controls, and audit tracks. Also, healthcare groups need to make sure that the data gathered by smart technology is used and shared in a way that follows HIPAA rules. This means getting permission from patients before using or sharing their health information and making sure that any data shared with third parties is done safely and in line with HIPAA rules. In addition to HIPAA, healthcare groups must also follow other rules and laws that cover the use of smart technology in healthcare. There are rules for medical equipment set by the Food and Drug Administration, and there are rules for data security and privacy set by groups like the International Organization for Standardization. In order to follow these rules, healthcare groups need to set up rules and instructions for handling smart technology that protect data, keep personal information safe, and meet the rules. This includes taking steps to keep data safe from people who should not have access to it, making sure that data is kept safely, and regularly checking that rules are being followed. The permission and access control are very important for keeping the data received by smart technology in healthcare systems safe and private. To keep data safe from people who should not have access to it, healthcare organizations need to set up strong security and access control systems. It is also important for smart devices to follow rules like HIPAA to make sure they meet the standards for keeping health information safe. Businesses in the healthcare field can make sure that smart technology is safely and legally integrated into their systems by taking these steps.

18.5 Accuracy and Reliability of Data

Making sure that the data that smart technology collects is correct and reliable is important for making sure that they work well with healthcare systems. Sensor technology, data checking methods, and user behavior are some of the things that can affect how accurate and reliable data from smart devices is.

18.5.1 Sensor Technology

When it comes to how accurate and reliable the data that smart devices receive is, sensor technology is very important. Wearable technology uses different monitors to gather information about your health, like your heart rate, how active you are, and how you sleep. The quality of these sensors can change based on things like how the gadget is built, where the sensors are placed, and the weather. Making sure that sensors work correctly on all kinds of gadgets and with all kinds of people is one of the hardest parts of sensor technology. If sensors are not always accurate, then the data they collect might not be consistent, which would make it less useful for making healthcare decisions. To deal with this problem, companies that make smart technology need to adjust sensors to make sure they give correct and regular readings.

Making sure that devices are delicate enough to pick up on small changes in health data is another problem. Heart rate monitors, for instance, need to be able to correctly pick up changes in heart rate, even when people are under a lot of stress or physical action. In the same way, activity trackers need to be able to correctly measure how active someone is, even in tough conditions like water or very hot or cold temps. Wearable device makers can deal with these issues by using cutting edge sensor technologies, like photoplethysmography (PPG) to track movement and heart rate and PPG to measure heart rate. Because these technologies are more delicate and exact than older monitors, you can trust the data that smart technology collects. Along with sensor technology, data validation methods can also help make the data from smart devices more accurate and reliable. As a way to make sure the data is correct and reliable, data validation approaches compare data from smart devices with data from gold standard methods, like clinical measurements. An electrocardiogram (ECG) and a wireless device that measures heart rate can be put next to each other to make sure the worn device is accurate. In the same way, you can check the accuracy of a smart device by comparing its movement data with data from a tracker. Another thing that can affect how accurate and reliable data from smart devices is how well users follow the instructions. To make sure correct data collection, users must wear the devices as directed and follow any other instructions given by healthcare providers. If users do not follow the rules, then data can be missing or wrong, which makes the collected data less reliable.

18.5.2 Data Calibration

Data calibration is an important step in making sure that the data that smart devices receive is correct and reliable. Sensor results must be adjusted and checked to make sure they properly reflect the actual numbers being recorded. It is important to calibrate smart devices correctly so that the data they collect is correct and can be used effectively in healthcare settings. Making sure that sensors are calibrated properly so that they give accurate and reliable readings is one of the hardest parts of data calibration. Over time, sensors can move around, which can make the data they receive less accurate. Sensor readings are calibrated by comparing them to a known standard and making changes to make sure they are correct. For instance, to make sure that it gives correct heart rate readings, a heart rate tracker might need to be set against a reference heart rate monitor. In the same way, an activity tracker might need to be compared to a Fitbit to make sure it is recording movement levels correctly.

For medical reasons, like keeping an eye on people with long-term illnesses or following the spread of a disease, calibration is very important for personal medical devices. Incorrect data from sensors can lead to wrong evaluations or treatment choices, which shows how important it is to calibrate properly. Manufacturers of smart technology can use calibration methods to fix sensor readings based on known standards. This helps with the problems that come with data calibration. These methods can be made to take into account things like sensor drift, human unpredictability, and changes in the environment. This makes sure that sensor data are correct and reliable. Making sure that calibration processes are done properly and regularly is another difficult part of data calibration. Wearable technology might need to be calibrated on a regular basis to make sure that sensor readings stay correct over time. Healthcare professionals can help users make sure that the right steps are taken for calibration and that sensor numbers are checked against known standards. Data calibration includes both sensor calibration and algorithm calibration to make sure that the data processing methods are giving correct and reliable results. To make sure they are correct, data processing programs might need to be checked against clinical measurements or other gold standard methods. Healthcare professionals can also use methods for data checking to make sure that the data received by smart technology is correct and reliable. To make sure the data is correct and reliable, data collected by smart devices is compared to data collected by gold standard methods. To prove that a smart device is accurate, heart rate data from it can be compared to heart rate data from an ECG. Data calibration [27] is a very important step in making sure that the data that smart devices receive is correct and reliable. Wearable device makers can make sure that sensor readings are correct and reliable by using calibration methods, doing regular calibration processes, and checking sensor readings against known standards. This is very important to make sure that smart technology can be used correctly in healthcare, giving doctors useful information about patients' health and letting them give better, more personalized care.

18.5.3 User Compliance and Education

Compliance and teaching of users are important factors that can affect how accurate and reliable the data received by smart devices is. The level of user obedience is how well people follow the directions for wearing and using wearable technology. On the other hand, education is the process of giving people knowledge and direction on how to use the technology correctly. One of the hardest parts of user obedience is making sure that people wear the devices as prescribed and follow any other instructions that healthcare workers give them. For instance, people may have to wear the devices all the time for a certain amount of time in order to get correct data, or they may have to wear the devices in a certain place on their bodies for the sensors to work best.

To solve this problem, healthcare professionals can teach people why it is important to wear the gadgets properly and show them how to do it. This can include giving people information on the possible benefits of wearing the gadgets correctly as well as directions on how to do it right. Making sure that people know how to use the gadgets well is another problem. Wearable technology often has complicated features and functions that people may not know how to use, which can lead to wrong data collection and incorrect use. Providers of health care can deal with this problem by teaching people how to use technologies properly. Users can also learn how important it is for data to be correct and reliable by being taught about it. Healthcare workers can get people to follow the rules for wearing and using smart devices by telling them how their data is used and how wrong data can affect healthcare decisions. In addition to educating and making sure users follow instructions, healthcare workers can also use feedback systems to keep an eye on things and make sure users are following them better. For instance, wearable technology can give users real-time feedback on their data collection efforts, like alerts when they forget to wear the technology or prompts when they are using it wrong. Education and user cooperation are very important factors that can affect how accurate and trustworthy the data received by smart devices is. Healthcare providers can improve data quality and make sure that wearable devices are used to their full potential in healthcare uses by teaching users how to use the devices properly and teaching them why it is important to wear the devices correctly.

18.6 Scalability and Sustainability

When adding smart technology to healthcare systems, scalability and long-term viability are very important things to think about. In computing, scalability means that a system can handle more data or people as they come in, whereas sustainability means that a system can keep working overtime. It is important for smart devices to be scalable and long-lasting so that they can work well in healthcare systems and provide long-term benefits. One of the hardest parts of growth is keeping up with the growing amount of data that smart technology creates. As the number of smart devices used in healthcare grows, healthcare systems need to be able to expand their systems to handle the data that these devices create. This includes making sure that the storing and processing of data are up to the task of handling the growing amount of data. Scalability problems can be solved with cloud computing, which offers an open and scalable way to store and process data. Cloud-based solutions let healthcare companies change the size of their equipment as needed, so they can handle the growing amount of data that smart technology creates. Additionally, cloud-based solutions can offer storing and processing services at low costs, which makes them a good choice for healthcare groups that want to expand their infrastructure. Ensuring that personal devices can talk to other systems and devices well is another problem in scale. Interoperability is important to make sure that smart technology can share data with other technology and systems, so that healthcare professionals can get to and use data correctly. Standardized data forms and communication methods can help healthcare groups deal with interoperability issues by making sure that smart devices can talk to other systems and devices. Another important thing to think about when putting smart technology into healthcare systems is how long the gadgets will last. Sustainability means making sure that wearable technology keeps working over time. This means making sure that they stay safe, effective, and backed by the companies that make them. Making sure that personal technology stays safe over time is one of the challenges of sustainability. Attackers are more likely to go after smart technology as they become more common in healthcare systems. Healthcare groups need to put in place strong security means to keep portable technology safe from hackers and other people who should not be able to get to it. This will keep the technology safe over time. Making sure that smart technology stays effective and is backed by manufacturers is another issue in sustainability. Wearable technology might need to be updated and fixed on a regular basis to keep working and working with other technology and gadgets. Healthcare groups need to work closely with makers to make sure that smart technology is always supported and that regular upkeep and changes are done. When adding smart technology to healthcare systems, it is important to think about how to make them scalable and long-lasting. Healthcare organizations can make sure that wearable devices can be effectively integrated into healthcare systems and provide long-term benefits for patient care. They can do this by addressing scalability issues through cloud computing and interoperability standards and addressing sustainability issues through strong security measures and working together with manufacturers.

18.6.1 Cloud-Based Solutions

Adding smart technology to healthcare systems is easier and more scalable with cloud-based options. These solutions give healthcare groups a central place to store and process data from wearable technology, so they can change their infrastructure as needed to handle the growing amount of data that these technology-enabled gadgets produce. One great thing about cloud-based options is that they can grow as needed. Some of the services that cloud companies offer are data storage, processing, and analytics. These services can be scaled up or down depending on what customers need. This makes it easy for healthcare groups to add to their systems to handle the growing amount of data that smart technology creates, making sure they can keep up with the work. Another good thing about cloud-based options is that they are adaptable. Public, private, and mixed clouds are just some of the services and operation types that cloud companies offer. This means that healthcare businesses can pick the one that best fits their needs. This gives healthcare groups the freedom to change their infrastructure to meet the needs of adding smart technology to their systems.

It is also cheaper to store and handle data with cloud-based options. Most cloud service companies charge by the use, so healthcare groups only pay for the tools they actually use. This could save you a lot of money compared to standard on-premises infrastructure, which needs to be set up and maintained with gear that you buy up front. But there are also problems that come with cloud-based options. One problem is keeping information safe.

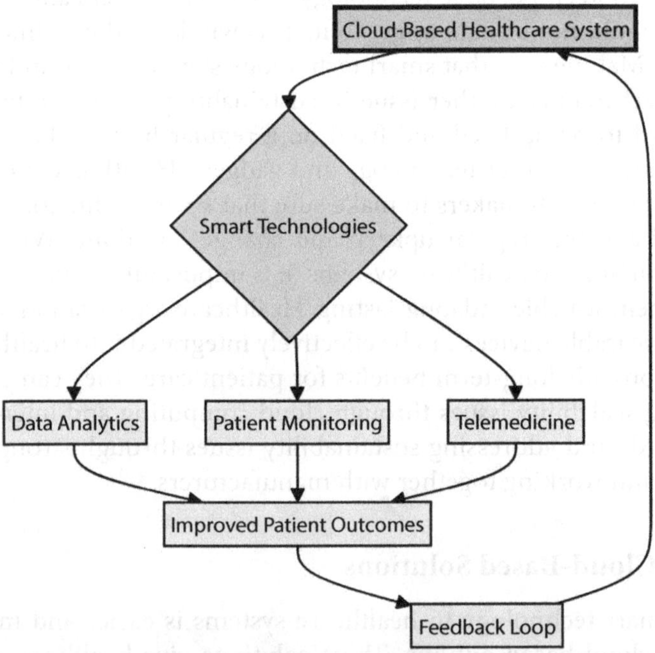

Figure 18.4 Overview of cloud-based solution for healthcare systems.

Healthcare companies need to make sure that smart devices that collect personal health data are safe from leaks and illegal access. To help with these worries, cloud service providers offer many safety features, such as encryption, access controls, and regular checks. Data protection is also a problem. Healthcare organizations have to follow rules, like the HIPAA, that say they have to keep patient information private. Cloud service companies can help healthcare groups follow these rules by providing services that are made to meet the needs of HIPAA and other privacy rules. For putting smart technology into healthcare systems, cloud-based options let you store and handle data in a way that is flexible, scalable, and cost-effective. Healthcare companies can use cloud-based solutions to successfully add smart devices to their healthcare systems and improve patient care by dealing with issues like data security and privacy. Figure 18.4 provides an overview of the cloud-based solution for healthcare systems.

18.6.2 Needs for Infrastructure

To connect smart technology to healthcare systems, you need a strong network that can store, process, and analyze data. Healthcare companies need to make sure their system can handle the growing amount of data that smart technology creates and meets the requirements for adding these devices. Data storage is one of the most important building needs for putting smart technology together. A lot of data is created by wearable technology, like health measures like heart rate, exercise levels, and sleep habits. This data needs to be kept safely and quickly. Cloud-based storage options can help healthcare groups store their data, and they can change how much space they have as needed. Data handling is another need for infrastructure. To get useful information, healthcare groups need to be able to quickly and efficiently handle data from smart devices. Strong data processing skills are needed for this, such as the ability to use real-time analytics and machine learning (ML) techniques to look at data from smart technology. It is also important for healthcare groups to make sure that their infrastructure can support adding smart technology to their current systems. This includes making sure that wearable technology can talk to other technology and processes correctly so that healthcare professionals can get to and use data from wearable technology in their daily work. To meet these infrastructure needs, healthcare groups can use cloud-based options that let them store and handle data on an as-needed basis. Cloud service providers offer many services, such as data storage, processing, and analytics, that can help healthcare groups set up the right foundation for adding smart technology to their systems. Overall, healthcare organizations need to make sure that their infrastructure is scalable, flexible, and safe in order to meet the infrastructure needs for adding smart devices into healthcare systems. It is possible for healthcare companies to successfully add smart devices to their systems and improve patient care by using cloud-based solutions and solving key infrastructure issues.

18.6.3 Cost Considerations

Adding wearable technology to healthcare systems comes with a number of costs, such as the gadgets themselves, the costs of setting up the technology, and the ongoing costs of running the technology. For healthcare companies to successfully pay for and handle the addition of smart devices to their healthcare systems, they need to know what these costs are. The cost of the smart technology is one of the main things to think about when it comes to costs. The price of wearable technology varies based on things like the brand, functions, and how well they work. Healthcare groups need to think about how much it costs to buy smart technology for patients and how much it costs to keep and replace technology over time. Infrastructure prices are another cost to think about. To connect smart technology to healthcare systems, you need a strong network that can store, process, and analyze data. Healthcare businesses need to think about how much it will cost to set up and manage this infrastructure. This includes the cost of cloud-based services, data storage, and the ability to handle data.

The costs of running the business are also important to think about. There are ongoing costs associated with incorporating wearable technology into healthcare systems. These include teaching healthcare professionals and staff how to use the technology as well as the cost of keeping the technology and infrastructure up to date. To make sure they can handle the addition of smart devices to their healthcare systems well, healthcare groups need to plan for these routine costs. Using cloud-based tools is one way to keep costs down. Cloud companies provide flexible and inexpensive ways for healthcare groups to store and process data from smart technology, so they only have to pay for the resources they actually use. This could help healthcare groups save money on building costs and better control their budgets. The total cost of ownership (TCO) of smart technology is another way to keep costs down. TCO covers not only the price of buying the gadgets but also the price of fixing, replacing, and helping with them over the course of their life. Healthcare organizations can make better choices about which smart technology to buy and how to pay for adding them to their systems when they think about the TCO. Overall, adding smart technology to healthcare systems comes with a number of cost issues. Healthcare organizations can successfully add smart devices to their systems and improve patient care by knowing these costs and putting plans in place to handle them.

18.7 Solutions to Integration Challenges

Adding smart technology to healthcare systems can be hard for a number of reasons, such as problems with data accuracy and reliability, security and privacy, and being able to talk to other devices. To deal with these problems, healthcare groups can use a variety of methods, such as creating and using standards. Standards can help make sure that wearable technology is safe, effective, and able to work with other devices. This makes it easier to add them to healthcare systems and better for patients.

18.7.1 Development and Adoption of Standards

Creating and using guidelines for smart technology is one of the best ways to solve interaction problems. Standards make sure that all wearable devices are designed, built, and used in the same way. They also make sure that the devices can work with other devices and are safe and reliable. The Continua Health Alliance is an example of a standard for smart devices. It gives instructions for the design and development of healthcare systems and devices that can talk to each other. The Continua Health Alliance makes sure that smart devices can talk to other systems and devices by standardizing data forms, communication methods, and security measures. The HL7 standard is another example of a standard for smart devices. It sets rules for how electronic health information can be shared, exchanged, integrated, and retrieved. The HL7 standardizes data forms and communication methods so that smart technology can share data with other healthcare systems and EHR systems.

Healthcare groups can make sure that smart devices work with other systems and devices by creating and accepting standards for them. This makes it easier to add them to healthcare systems. Standards also help make sure that smart technology meets certain safety and dependability requirements, which makes them better for patient care. Standards for data protection and privacy can also help healthcare groups, along with standards for smart technology. In order to protect the safety and security of patient information, rules like the Health Insurance Portability and Accountability Act (HIPAA) make sure that smart devices follow these rules. Overall, making and using standards is very important for solving the problems that come up with integrating smart technology. Healthcare groups can make sure that smart devices are easier to add to healthcare systems and better for patient care by setting guidelines for communication, security, and dependability.

18.7.2 Enhanced Security Measures

To handle the security and privacy issues that come up when smart technology is used in healthcare settings, we need to put in place stronger security measures. These steps help keep sensitive health data collected by smart technology safe from hackers and other people who should not have access to it. This keeps patient data safe and private. Data protection is one of the most important safety features for smart technology. By changing the data collected by wearable technology into a code that can only be read with the right decoding key, encryption keeps it safe from people who should not have access to it. Encryption can protect healthcare organizations' data while it is being sent and while it is being stored. This way, even if a device is lost or stolen, the data will still be safe. Controlling who can get in is another important security step. Wearable devices collect sensitive health data. Access control methods help make sure that only approved people can see this data. Healthcare organizations can use access controls like identification and authorization to make sure that only authorized users can get to data. They can also use audit trails to keep an eye on access and find any attempts to get in without permission. Data safety methods are also very important for making sure that the data that smart technology collects is safe. Data security methods help make sure that data has not been changed or messed with in any way. Digital fingerprints and checksums can be used by healthcare groups to make sure that data received by smart devices is correct and has not been changed while it was being sent or stored. In addition to these steps, healthcare groups can also take steps to keep smart technology from being stolen or tampered with. For example, tamper-evident seals and physical locks can be used to keep devices safe from people who should not have access to them, and remote wipe can be used to delete data from a lost or stolen device. Overall, stronger security steps are needed to make sure that the data collected by smart technology in healthcare systems is safe and private. Healthcare companies can keep personal health data safe from people who should not have access to it by using data protection, access control, and data security. This way, patient information stays private and secure.

18.7.3 Improvements in Sensor Technology

Improvements in sensor technology have helped a lot with the problems that come up when you try to add smart technology to healthcare systems. Because of these changes, data quality, dependability, and usefulness have all gotten better. This means that smart devices are now better tools for keeping an eye on and controlling patients' health. Improved devices that measure health factors like heart rate, exercise levels, and sleep habits are one of the most important things that sensor technology has done to get better. These sensors use cutting edge technologies like PPG to track movement and heart rate and PPG to track heart rate. They give more accurate and reliable data than older sensors. As sensor technology gets better, sensors that are smaller, lighter, and easier for people to wear are also being made. These improvements have made wearable technology easier to use, which means that people are more likely to keep wearing them and give healthcare workers more accurate data.

Sensor technology has also led to longer battery lives, which means that smart technology can collect data for longer amounts of time without having to be charged. This is especially important for wearing devices that are used for constant tracking, like those that are used to keep an eye on people who have long-term illnesses. As sensor technology has gotten better, so have data processing methods. Both of these changes have made personal healthcare gadgets more useful. These programs use ML and artificial intelligence (AI) to look at data from smart technology. This gives doctors important information about their patients' health and makes care more personalized and effective. Overall, progress in sensor technology has been very helpful in solving problems that come up when smart technology is used in healthcare systems. These improvements have made

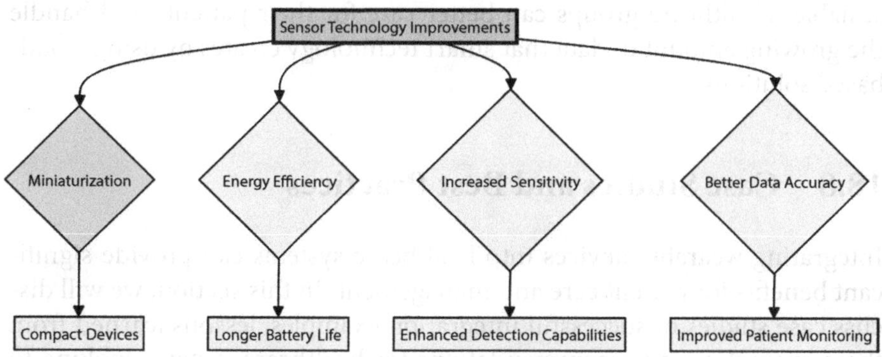

Figure 18.5 Overview of sensor technology improvement in healthcare.

portable devices better tools for controlling and keeping an eye on patients' health, leading to better results and lower healthcare costs by making sensors more accurate, reliable, and easy to use. Figure 18.5 illustrates that how sensor technology can be improved in healthcare.

18.7.4 Cloud-Based Storage and Processing Solutions

Cloud-based storage and processing solutions have become an important way to deal with the problems of data management and scaling that come up when smart devices are added to healthcare systems. These solutions give healthcare organizations a tool that can be changed and expanded to store, process, and analyze data from smart devices. This lets them handle the growing amount of data that these devices produce in a useful way. One great thing about cloud-based storage and processing is that they can grow as needed. Some of the services that cloud companies offer are data storage, processing, and analytics. These services can be scaled up or down depending on what customers need. This makes it easy for healthcare groups to add to their systems to handle the growing amount of data that smart technology creates, making sure they can keep up with the work. It is also cheaper to store and handle data with cloud-based options. Most cloud service companies charge by the use, so healthcare groups only pay for the tools they actually use. One more good thing about cloud-based storage and processing is that they are adaptable. Public, private, and mixed clouds are just some of the services and operation types that cloud companies offer. This means that healthcare businesses can pick the one that best fits their needs. This gives healthcare groups the freedom to change their infrastructure to meet the needs of adding smart technology to their systems. In general, cloud-based storage and processing options let healthcare companies add smart technology to their systems in a way that is open and scalable. Healthcare groups can better care for their patients and handle the growing amount of data that smart technology creates by using cloud-based solutions.

18.8 Case Studies and Best Practices

Integrating wearable devices into healthcare systems can provide significant benefits for patient care and management. In this section, we will discuss case studies of successful integration examples, lessons learned from these examples, and recommendations for healthcare systems looking to integrate wearable devices.

18.8.1 Successful Integration Examples

One successful integration example is the use of wearable devices for remote patient monitoring. In this case, healthcare providers use wearable devices to monitor patients with chronic conditions, such as diabetes or hypertension, from a distance. The devices collect data on the patient's health metrics, such as blood glucose levels or blood pressure, and transmit this data to healthcare providers for analysis. This allows healthcare providers to monitor patients' health in real time and intervene if necessary, leading to improved patient outcomes and reduced healthcare costs. Another successful integration example is the use of wearable devices for post-operative care. In this case, patients wear wearable devices after surgery to monitor their recovery progress. The devices collect data on the patient's vital signs, activity levels, and pain levels, and transmit this data to healthcare providers for analysis. This allows healthcare providers to monitor patients' recovery progress remotely and intervene if necessary, leading to faster recovery times and reduced hospital readmissions.

18.8.2 Lessons Learned

One of the key lessons learned from successful integration examples is the importance of stakeholder engagement. Healthcare organizations must engage with patients, healthcare providers, and other stakeholders early and often to ensure that the integration of wearable devices meets their needs and expectations. This can help ensure that the integration is successful and that the devices are used effectively. Another lesson learned is the importance of data integration and interoperability. Healthcare organizations must ensure that wearable devices can integrate seamlessly with existing healthcare systems, such as EHR systems, to ensure that data can be shared and accessed effectively. This can help ensure that wearable devices provide valuable insights into patient health and improve patient care.

18.8.3 Recommendations for Healthcare Systems

Based on successful integration examples and lessons learned, here are some recommendations for healthcare systems looking to integrate wearable devices:

- Define clear objectives: Define clear objectives for integrating wearable devices into healthcare systems, such as

improving patient outcomes or reducing healthcare costs. This can help focus efforts and ensure that the integration is successful.
- Engage stakeholders: Engage with patients, healthcare providers, and other stakeholders early and often to ensure that the integration meets their needs and expectations.
- Ensure data integration and interoperability: Ensure that wearable devices can integrate seamlessly with existing healthcare systems, such as EHR systems, to ensure that data can be shared and accessed effectively.
- Provide training and support: Provide training and support to patients and healthcare providers on how to use wearable devices effectively. This can help ensure that the devices are used correctly and that data collection is accurate.
- Monitor and evaluate: Monitor and evaluate the integration of wearable devices to ensure that it is meeting its objectives and making a positive impact on patient care.

By following these recommendations, healthcare systems can effectively integrate wearable devices into their healthcare systems and improve patient care and management.

18.9 Future Trends and Outlook

Wearable technology is getting better, more people are using online patient tracking, and people want more personalized and preventive healthcare. These factors are likely to keep driving the growth of wearable technology in healthcare systems over the next few years. We will talk about future trends and predictions for how smart technology will be used in healthcare systems in this part.

18.9.1 Advancements in Wearable Technology

Significant changes in the features and functions of wearable devices are likely to come from progress in wearable technology. Wearable technology of the future is likely to be smaller, lighter, and more comfy to wear. This will make them easier to use and more likely to be worn all the time. Also, improvements in sensor technology should lead to more accurate and reliable devices that can track health measures like heart rate, exercise levels, and sleep habits. There is a chance that these monitors can also measure other health factors, like blood sugar or water levels, giving doctors more complete information. Adding AI and ML tools to smart technology is another step forward in the field. These programs can look at data from smart technology in real time, giving doctors important information about their patients' health and making care more personalized and effective.

18.9.2 Integration Challenges and Opportunities

Wearable technology is getting better, which could lead to better care and control of patients, but it is also getting harder to integrate these devices into healthcare systems. One issue is making sure that smart technology can work with current health care systems, like EHR systems, so that information can be shared and viewed easily. Making sure that the data that smart devices receive is safe and private is another problem. Healthcare organizations need to put in place strong security measures to keep sensitive health data safe from hackers and other people who should not have access to it. This will keep patient information safe and private. Even with these problems, adding smart technology to healthcare systems opens up a lot of great chances to improve care and control for patients. Wearable technology can give doctors useful information about their patients' health, so they can keep an eye on them in real time and help if they need to. This could help patients get better care and lower the cost of healthcare.

18.9.3 Implications for Healthcare Delivery

Wearable gadgets being added to healthcare systems is likely to have big effects on how healthcare is provided. Wearable technology can allow for online patient tracking, which lets doctors check on patients' health from afar and take action if needed. This can cut down on the need for in-person trips and stays in the hospital, making healthcare service more efficient and cost-effective. Wearable technology can also help with more personalized and preventative health care. Wearable technology can help find health problems early and stop them from getting worse by giving doctors real-time information about their patients' health. This could help people have better results and a better quality of life. The use of wearable technology in healthcare systems is going to keep growing over the next few years. This is because wearable technology is getting better and more people want personalized and protective healthcare. Healthcare companies can improve patient care and management, as well as make healthcare more efficient and cost-effective, by figuring out how to integrate smart devices and taking advantage of the possibilities they offer.

18.10 Conclusion

Wearable technology in healthcare systems can help improve care and control of patients, but it also comes with some difficulties. Wearable technology is getting better, which means more personalized and preventive healthcare. However, adding these devices to healthcare systems is hard because of problems with connectivity, security and privacy, and the accuracy and dependability of data. Healthcare groups can deal with these problems in a number of ways, such as by creating and using standards, stepping up security, making monitoring technology better, and using cloud-based storage and processing. These solutions can help make sure that smart technology is safe, secure, and dependable. This makes it easier to add them to healthcare systems and better for patients. Looking ahead, it looks like adding smart technology to healthcare systems will continue to grow and improve. Wearable technology is likely to make a big difference in the features and functions of wearable devices, making them easier to use and better at keeping an eye on and controlling patients' health. Wearable devices are also expected to have big effects on healthcare delivery, making it possible to watch patients from afar, provide more personalized and preventative care, and make healthcare delivery more efficient and cost-effective. Healthcare groups can improve patient care and management by solving these issues and taking advantage of the possibilities that smart devices offer. This will lead to better patient results and a higher quality of life for patients.

References

1. Rajan Jeyaraj, P. and Nadar, E.R.S., Smart-monitor: patient monitoring system for IoT-based healthcare system using deep learning. *IETE J. Res., 68*, 2, 1435–1442, 2022.
2. Shu, Y., Li, C., Wang, Z., Mi, W., Li, Y., Ren, T.L., A pressure sensing system for heart rate monitoring with polymer-based pressure sensors and an anti-interference post processing circuit. *Sensors, 15*, 2, 3224–3235, 2015.
3. Singh, P.D., Dhiman, G., Sharma, R., Internet of things for sustaining a smart and secure healthcare system. *Sustain. Comput.: Inform. Syst., 33*, 100622, 2022.
4. Zhang, Y., Berthelot, M., Lo, B., Wireless wearable photoplethysmography sensors for continuous blood pressure monitoring, in: *2016 IEEE Wireless Health (WH)*, IEEE, pp. 1–8, 2016, October.

5. Alhayani, B., Kwekha-Rashid, A.S., Mahajan, H.B., Ilhan, H., Uke, N., Alkhayyat, A., Mohammed, H.J., RETRACTED ARTICLE: 5G standards for the Industry 4.0 enabled communication systems using artificial intelligence: perspective of smart healthcare system. *Appl. Nanosci.*, *13*, 3, 1807–1817, 2023.
6. Griggs, D., Sharma, M., Naghibi, A., Wallin, C., Ho, V., Barbosa, K., Ghirmai, T., Cao, H., Krishnan, S.K., Design and development of continuous cuff-less blood pressure monitoring devices, in: *2016 IEEE sensors*, IEEE, pp. 1–3, 2016, October.
7. Lin, H., Xu, W., Guan, N., Ji, D., Wei, Y., Yi, W., Noninvasive and continuous blood pressure monitoring using wearable body sensor networks. *IEEE Intell. Syst.*, *30*, 6, 38–48, 2015.
8. Chang, S.H., Chiang, R.D., Wu, S.J., Chang, W.T., A context-aware, interactive M-health system for diabetics. *IT Prof.*, *18*, 3, 14–22, 2016.
9. Alasmari, S. and Anwar, M., Security & privacy challenges in IoT-based health cloud, in: *2016 International Conference on Computational Science and Computational Intelligence (CSCI)*, IEEE, pp. 198–201, 2016, December.
10. Cook, A., Robinson, M., Ferrag, M.A., Maglaras, L.A., He, Y., Jones, K., Janicke, H., Internet of cloud: Security and privacy issues, in: *Cloud Computing for Optimization: Foundations, Applications, and Challenges*, pp. 271–301, 2018.
11. Kumar, S.A., Kumar, A., Dutt, V., Agrawal, R., Multi Model Implementation on General Medicine Prediction with Quantum Neural Networks, in: *2021 Third International Conference on Intelligent Communication Technologies and Virtual Mobile Networks (ICICV)*, Tirunelveli, India, pp. 1391–1395, 2021, doi: 10.1109/ICICV50876.2021.9388575.
12. Raj, P., Dubey, A.K., Kumar, A., Rathore, P.S., *Blockchain, Artificial Intelligence, and the Internet of Things*, Springer International Publishing, Cham, 2022.
13. Burri, S.R., Kumar, A., Baliyan, A., Kumar, T.A., Predictive Intelligence for Healthcare Outcomes: An AI Architecture Overview, in: *2023 2nd International Conference on Smart Technologies and Systems for Next Generation Computing (ICSTSN)*, Villupuram, India, pp. 1–6, 2023, doi: 10.1109/ICSTSN57873.2023.10151477.
14. Wani, S., Ahuja, S., Kumar, A., Application of Deep Neural Networks and Machine Learning algorithms for diagnosis of Brain tumour, in: *2023 International Conference on Computational Intelligence and Sustainable Engineering Solutions (CISES)*, Greater Noida, India, pp. 106–111, 2023, doi: 10.1109/CISES58720.2023.10183528.
15. Kour, S.P., Kumar, A., Ahuja, S., An Advance Approach for Diabetes Detection by Implementing Machine Learning Algorithms, in: *2023 IEEE World Conference on Applied Intelligence and Computing (AIC)*, Sonbhadra, India, pp. 136–141, 2023, doi: 10.1109/AIC57670.2023.10263919.

16. Raj, P., Kumar, A., Dubey, A.K., Bhatia, S., Oswalt, M.S., *Quantum Computing and Artificial Intelligence: Training Machine and Deep Learning Algorithms on Quantum Computers*, De Gruyter, Berlin, Boston, 2023, [Online]. Available: https://doi.org/10.1515/9783110791402.
17. Sasubilli, G. and Kumar, A., Machine Learning and Big Data Implementation on Health Care data, in: *2020 4th International Conference on Intelligent Computing and Control Systems (ICICCS)*, Madurai, India, pp. 859–864, 2020, doi: 10.1109/ICICCS48265.2020.9120906.
18. Swarna, S.R., Kumar, A., Dixit, P., Sairam, T.V.M., Parkinson's Disease Prediction using Adaptive Quantum Computing, in: *2021 Third International Conference on Intelligent Communication Technologies and Virtual Mobile Networks (ICICV)*, Tirunelveli, India, pp. 1396–1401, 2021, doi: 10.1109/ICICV50876.2021.9388628.
19. Burugadda, V.R., Pawar, P.S., Kumar, A., Bhati, N., Predicting Hospital Readmission Risk for Heart Failure Patients Using Machine Learning Techniques: A Comparative Study of Classification Algorithms, in: *2023 Second International Conference on Trends in Electrical, Electronics, and Computer Engineering (TEECCON)*, Bangalore, India, pp. 223–228, 2023, doi: 10.1109/TEECCON59234.2023.10335817.
20. Díaz, M., Martín, C., Rubio, B., State-of-the-art, challenges, and open issues in the integration of Internet of things and cloud computing. *J. Network Comput. Appl.*, *67*, 99–117, 2016.
21. Dizdarević, J., Carpio, F., Jukan, A., Masip-Bruin, X., A survey of communication protocols for internet of things and related challenges of fog and cloud computing integration. *ACM Comput. Surv. (CSUR)*, *51*, 6, 1–29, 2019.
22. Ali, A., Pasha, M.F., Ali, J., Fang, O.H., Masud, M., Jurcut, A.D., Alzain, M.A., Deep learning based homomorphic secure search-able encryption for keyword search in blockchain healthcare system: A novel approach to cryptography. *Sensors*, *22*, 2, 528, 2022.
23. Kumar, A., A cloud-based buyer-seller watermarking protocol (CB-BSWP) using semi-trusted third party for copy deterrence and privacy preserving. *Multimedia Tools Appl.*, *81*, 15, 21417–21448, 2022.
24. Puttagunta, M. and Ravi, S., Medical image analysis based on deep learning approach. *Multimedia Tools Appl.*, *80*, 16, 24365–24398, 2021.
25. Guo, Y., Gao, Y., Shen, D., Deformable MR prostate segmentation via deep feature learning and sparse patch matching. *IEEE Trans. Med. Imaging*, *35*, 4, 1077–1089, 2015.
26. Zhao, X., Wu, Y., Song, G., Li, Z., Zhang, Y., Fan, Y., A deep learning model integrating FCNNs and CRFs for brain tumor segmentation. *Med. Image Anal.*, *43*, 98–111, 2018.
27. Mohsen, H., El-Dahshan, E.S.A., El-Horbaty, E.S.M., Salem, A.B.M., Classification using deep learning neural networks for brain tumors. *Future Comput. Inf. J.*, *3*, 1, 68–71, 2018.

19

Role of Wearable Technology in Mental Health Monitoring and Management: Psychiatric Insights into Wearable Technology Adoption

Sharad V. Kshirsagar[1] and V. C. Patil[2*]

[1]Department of Psychiatry, Krishna Institute of Medical Sciences, Krishna Vishwa Vidyapeeth "Deemed To Be University", Karad, Maharashtra, India
[2]Department of General Medicine, Krishna Institute of Medical Sciences, Krishna Vishwa Vidyapeeth "Deemed To Be University", Karad, Maharashtra, India

Abstract

Wearable technology is becoming an interesting tool for managing and keeping an eye on mental health because it can collect data continuously and without being annoying. Through the view of psychiatry, this paper looks at the role of wearable technology in mental healthcare, focusing on how it is used, the problems it faces, and the effects it might have. Wearable technology's use in mental healthcare depends on a number of things, such as how well users accept it, how secure the data is, and how well it meets legal requirements. Psychiatrists' knowledge of these factors can help people come up with useful solutions. Acceptance by users is very important because people with mental health problems may have unique needs and tastes that need to be met. Figuring out how people think and what they like can help designers make smart technology that is easy for people to use. When it comes to mental healthcare, data safety and security are very important because private information is used. Psychiatric knowledge can help create safe data management systems that protect users' privacy and make sure that healthcare workers can access and use correct data. Another important factor is regulatory compliance. Wearable technology used in mental healthcare needs to follow the right laws and standards to be safe and successful. Wearable technology has the ability to make a big difference in mental healthcare. Real-time data collection

**Corresponding author*: patilvirendra1250@gmail.com

Abhishek Kumar, Narayan Vyas, Pramod Singh Rathore, Abhineet Anand and Pooja Dixit (eds.) Internet of Medicine for Smart Healthcare, (405–428) © 2025 Scrivener Publishing LLC

makes it possible to find signs early and tailor treatments to each person, which improves the results of treatment. Wearable technology can also help patients be more involved and take charge of their own care, giving them more power over their mental health.

Keywords: Wearable technology, mental health monitoring, psychiatric insights, remote monitoring, neurological disorders

19.1 Introduction

Wearable technology is being used in mental healthcare, which is a huge change in how we track and handle mental health. Now that there are more advanced monitors and gadgets, people can keep an eye on their mental health in real time. This [1] gives them useful information about their feelings, actions, and body reactions. This part talks about the role of wearable technology in managing and tracking mental health, focusing on how psychology brings a unique point of view to the use of these technologies. Wearable technology has changed quickly from simple fitness trackers to complex gadgets that can keep an eye on many mental and physical factors. These [2] gadgets can keep track of changes in a person's skin conductance, sleep habits, exercise levels, and even changes in their heart rate variability. This gives a full picture of their mental and physical health. In mental healthcare, smart technology has a lot of benefits over old-fashioned ways of keeping an eye on things, like having people self-report and getting regular checks ups. Wearable devices can pick up on small changes in a person's mood or behavior that they or their healthcare provider might miss. This is because they collect data all the time. Psychiatric knowledge is very important for knowing how smart technology is being used in mental healthcare. Psychologists are the only ones who can really understand how mental illnesses and technology affect each other, as well as the specific needs and wants of people who have these illnesses. When mental health professionals are involved in the planning and creation of smart technology, it helps designers make better, easier-to-use gadgets that meet the special needs of people with mental health problems [3].

User satisfaction is one of the most important things that affects how smart technology is used in mental healthcare. People with mental health problems may have different needs and concerns when it comes to wearing technology, such as worries about privacy, social shame, and how easy it is to use. To help [4] solve these problems, psychiatric knowledge can be used to make gadgets that are simple to use and private and do not invade people's privacy. To make sure that people with mental health problems can successfully use smart technology, it is important to understand their specific needs and interests. When it comes to using smart technology in mental healthcare, data safety and security are also very important. It is very important to make sure that this information is kept safe and used properly because these devices record private information about a person's mental health. Expertise from the field of psychiatry can help create safe data management tools that respect users' privacy and make good use of data in professional decision-making. Developers can make more reliable and strong smart devices for mental health monitoring by taking psychiatric views into account when designing data privacy and security measures [5].

Another important thing that affects the use of smart technology in mental healthcare is how well it meets regulatory requirements. There are rules about medical equipment and data security that apply to wearable gadgets used to track mental health. Psychiatrists can help make sure that personal gadgets follow the laws and standards that apply by giving useful advice on these matters. Developers can get around the complicated rules for bringing safe and useful wearable technology to market by working closely with psychologists and other mental health workers. Wearable technology has the ability to make a big difference in mental healthcare. Wearable devices can help find signs early, personalize care, and improve treatment results by giving real-time information about a person's mental health. These gadgets can also improve patient participation and self-management, giving people more control over their mental healthcare. We can use the full power of smart technology to improve mental healthcare by adding psychological ideas into its creation and widespread use.

19.1.1 Overview of Wearable Technology in Mental Health Monitoring and Management

Wearable technology has changed the way mental health is monitored and managed, providing new ways to solve problems that have been around for a long time in diagnosing and treating mental illnesses. These technologies [6], which include things like smartphones, fitness trackers, and biosensors, can collect real-time data on a person's bodily and behavioral factors. This gives doctors useful information about the person's mental health. One of the best things about smart technology for mental healthcare is that it lets doctors keep an eye on patients even when they are not in a professional setting. This is especially helpful for people with conditions like bipolar disorder, sadness, or anxiety, whose symptoms can change throughout the day and might not be picked up on during regular checks [7].

Patients can give doctors a more complete picture of their mental health by carrying a gadget that constantly records their bodily and behavioral data. This helps doctors make more accurate diagnoses and create more personalized treatment plans. It is also helpful to find mental health problems early on with wearable technology. Through tracking changes in a person's heart rate, sleep habits, and level of exercise, smart technology can find early warning signs of mental illness that may not show up as clearly in later stages. This early spotting can help doctors step in and help patients, which could stop mental health problems from getting worse and improve their results [8].

Wearable technology can help people with mental health issues take care of themselves, as well as track and find problems early. Many smart technology gadgets have features like mood tracking, guided meditation, and stress management tools that let people keep an eye on their symptoms and take care of themselves. This can give people the tools they need to take charge of their mental health, giving them more freedom and a better quality of life. Wearable technology could also make standard forms of therapy more effective. For instance, doctors can use information gathered from smart technology to make treatment plans that are unique for each patient. This way, they [9, 10] can make sure that solutions are personalized and meet the needs of each person. Wearable technology can also give doctors objective information about how well a treatment is working, which helps them decide what kind of care to give next. There are some problems with using smart technology in mental healthcare, even though it has some benefits. Being sure that the data these gadgets gather is correct and reliable is one of the main worries. A lot of smart technology can gather a lot of information about your body and behavior, but how accurate that information is can change based on things like the sensors' quality and the methods used to process it. Clinicians need to be careful when figuring out what data from smart technology means because these technologies have their limits. The privacy and safety of the data that smart technology collects is another problem [10]. Because these devices record private data about a person's mental health, it is very important to keep this data safe from people who should not have access to it and from being misused. It is very important for clinicians and academics to follow strict ethical and legal rules when they receive, store, and use data from smart devices. This is to protect patients' privacy at all times. Wearable technology has a lot of promise to help mental healthcare, even with these problems. Wearable devices have the ability to change the way we diagnose and treat mental illnesses by offering constant tracking, early identification, and help for self-management. Wearable technology could become an important part of mental healthcare if more research and development is done on it. This would give people who are dealing with these difficult situations new hope. Figure 19.1 gives an overview of mental healthcare system.

19.1.2 Importance of Psychiatric Insights in Wearable Technology Adoption

The use of smart technology in mental healthcare is greatly affected by what psychiatrists know. Because they know so much about mental illnesses and how they affect people, psychiatrists are very important in making sure that smart technology is used properly in professional settings. When designers [11], implementers, and testers of wearable technology include psychological viewpoints, they can make gadgets that meet the specific needs of people with mental health problems and improve the general quality of care. One of the most important things that psychiatric insights can help you do is figure out what people with mental health problems want and need. As part of their training, psychiatrists are taught to evaluate mental health in three areas: cognitive, social, and behavioral. This lets [12] them figure out which traits and functions are most important to their patients. Developers can make sure that wearable technology is sensitive to the needs of people with mental health problems by working closely with

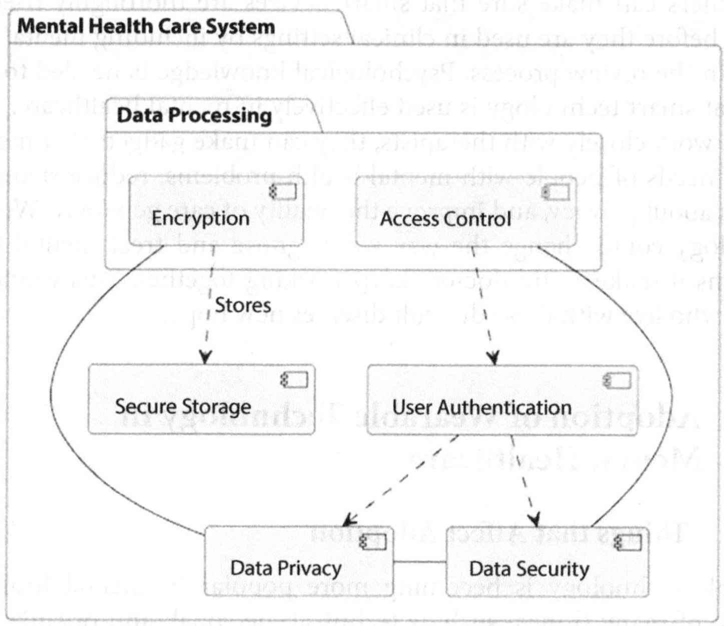

Figure 19.1 Overview of mental healthcare system.

therapists. This makes it more likely that the technology will be accepted and used. Psychiatric views are also very important for getting rid of the shame that surrounds mental health problems. People with mental health problems may not want to use wearable technology because they are worried about privacy, confidentiality, and the social stigma of being called "mentally ill." Psychiatrists can help developers address these concerns by making technology that is discreet, easy to use, and respects patient privacy. By taking psychological views into account during the planning process, engineers can make gadgets that people with mental health problems are more likely to accept and use. Also, psychological knowledge is needed to make sure that smart technology is used in professional settings in a way that improves the quality of care generally. Psychiatrists can give helpful advice on how smart technology can be used to add to current assessment and treatment methods instead of removing them. By adding smart technology to current care paths, psychologists can make sure that these technology tools do not get in the way of the therapy relationship between patients and doctors [13].

Psychiatric knowledge is also very important for figuring out how well smart technology works in mental healthcare. Psychiatrists are taught to figure out how new technologies can help patients. This means that they can figure out the pros and cons of smart technology in real-life situations. Researchers can make sure that smart devices are thoroughly tried and proven before they are used in clinical settings by including mental viewpoints in the review process. Psychological knowledge is needed to make sure that smart technology is used effectively in mental healthcare. When makers work closely with therapists, they can make gadgets that meet the unique needs of people with mental health problems, reduce shame and worries about privacy, and improve the quality of care generally. Wearable technology could change the way we diagnose and treat mental health problems if makers and doctors keep working together. This would give people who live with these difficult diseases new hope.

19.2 Adoption of Wearable Technology in Mental Healthcare

19.2.1 Things that Affect Adoption

Wearable technology is becoming more popular in mental healthcare because of many things, such as technical, personal, and organizational factors. It is important to understand these factors in order to successfully use smart technology in healthcare settings and get the most out of its benefits for both patients and caregivers.

- *Things related to technology*:
  The usefulness and ease of use of the gadgets is one of the most important technical factors affecting the use of smart technology in mental healthcare [14]. It is important that wearable technology is simple to use, comfortable to wear, and able to gather correct data. Patients and doctors are not likely to use devices that are big, hard to use, or prone to technology problems. Because of this, developers must make sure that their gadgets are easy to use and effective, and they should include comments from users, such as people with mental health problems and healthcare workers, all the way through the development process. Interoperability with other systems and devices is another technology factor that affects usage. A lot of different digital health tools are used in mental healthcare, and wearable technology needs to be able to work with all of them without any problems. Interoperability is important to make sure that doctors can quickly access and use the data received by smart devices to make decisions about care.
- *Personality traits*:
  Wearable technology's use in [15] mental healthcare is also affected by things that are personal, like how well the user accepts it and how useful they think it is. For personal gadgets to become popular, patients must think they are helpful and simple to use. This means that makers need to make sure that patients understand the possible benefits of smart technology and are involved in the decision-making process about how to use it. Psychiatric views are especially helpful for figuring out and fixing the personal issues that affect adoption. Psychiatrists can help figure out which groups of patients are most likely to benefit from smart technology and then personalize treatments to meet those patients' needs. By taking psychiatric views into account when designing and making smart technology, makers can make it more likely that people with mental health problems will use it [16].

- *Things about the organization*:
  The use of smart technology in mental healthcare is also affected by things that happen within the organization, like its rules and procedures. For smart technology to be used in hospital settings, healthcare groups need to make sure they have the right equipment and tools in place. This includes making sure that doctors know how to use smart technology and that there are clear rules for how the data that these technologies collect will be used and handled [17]. Adoption is also affected by the culture of the company. Wearable technology is more likely to be used to improve patient care by healthcare groups that value new ideas and technology. On the other hand, groups that do not like change might not want to use smart technology, even if it has worked well in other places. Wearable technology is becoming more popular in mental healthcare because of many things, such as technical, personal, and organizational factors. Developers and healthcare workers can make it more likely that wearable technology will be adopted and used in clinical practice by knowing and solving these factors. To make matters better, this could lead to better results for people with mental health problems and better mental healthcare generally. Figure 19.2 shows adoption of wearable healthcare technology by consumers.

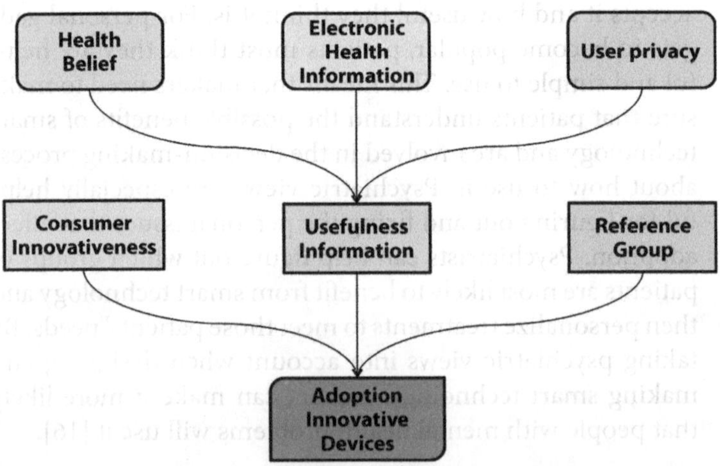

Figure 19.2 Adoption of wearable healthcare technology by consumers.

19.2.2 Psychiatric Perspectives on User Acceptance

Acceptance by users is a key part of putting smart technology to use in mental healthcare. People who have mental health problems may have specific needs and tastes that need to be taken into account when smart technology is designed and put into use. Psychiatric views can help makers make gadgets that users are more likely to accept and enjoy by giving them useful information about these issues. The shame that comes with having a mental health problem is an important thing to think about when it comes to user acceptance. A lot of people with mental health problems might not want to use smart technology that looks too medical or like something that would make them look bad. Psychiatric insights can help designers make gadgets that are small, stylish, and not bothersome. This [21] lowers the risk of stigma and raises the chance of acceptance. The mental and emotional state of people is another thing to think about. People who have mental health problems may have trouble thinking or feeling, which can make it harder for them to use and connect with technology. Researchers in the field of psychology can help engineers make gadgets that are smart, simple, and aware of people's mental and emotional needs.

In addition, mental points of view can help figure out which features and functions are most important to users. For example, people with depression might benefit from devices that track their mood and give them feedback on how to deal with problems. People with anxiety might benefit from devices that track their stress levels and give them feedback on how to relax. When makers make wearable technology, they can make things that are more likely to meet users' wants and tastes if they use these ideas.

Along with these things, psychological views can also help find things that make it hard for users to accept something and come up with ways to get around them. For instance, people with mental health problems might worry about their privacy and data protection when they use smart technology. Psychiatric insights can help developers deal with these worries by putting in place strong data protection measures and being clear about how the data collected by the devices will be used and handled. Finally, psychiatry points of view are necessary to understand how people will accept smart technology in mental healthcare. When designers and makers of wearable technology take these points of view into account, they can make gadgets that people are more likely to accept and love. This can lead to better results for people with mental health problems.

19.2.3 Design Considerations for User-Friendly Wearable Devices

Wearable mental health gadgets that are easy for people to use need to be carefully designed with a number of things in mind, such as usefulness, comfort, and looks. For people to accept and use these gadgets, they need to be simple to use, comfortable to wear, and nice to look at. Usability is an important thing to think about when making smart technology that is easy for people to use. Devices need to be simple and easy to use, even for people who are cognitively impaired or do not have much experience with technology. Because of this, developers have to make sure that user experiences are as simple and clear as possible, so that users do not have to know a lot about technology or how to use them [22].

Another important thing that goes into making smart technology is comfort. It is important that people can wear the gadgets for long amounts of time without any pain or soreness. This means that the people who make the gadgets have to pay attention to the materials they are made of as well as their size and weight. When making portable technology that is easy to use, looks are also important. People are more likely to use and accept devices that look good and are stylish, especially those who are worried about the social shame that comes with mental health problems. Because of this, developers need to pay attention to how their gadgets look and style to make sure they appeal to a wide range of users [23]. In addition to these things, coders also need to think about what people with mental health problems want and need. For instance, people with anxiety might like devices that are small and do not get in the way, whereas people with sadness might do better with devices that are bright and interesting. Researchers can make portable technology that people are more likely to accept and love by taking these things into account when designing it. This can lead to better results for people with mental health problems.

19.3 Data Privacy and Security in Mental Healthcare

19.3.1 Importance of Data Privacy in Mental Health Monitoring

When using smart technology to track mental health, data safety is very important to think about. There must be strong steps in place to protect the privacy and security of people's mental health data because it is important. Not doing so could lead to major problems, such as breaks of trust, damage to people's identities, and legal problems. One of the main reasons data privacy is important in mental health tracking is that the data being gathered is private. A lot of the time, mental health data includes very private and sensitive information about how someone thinks, feels, and acts. A lot of people think this information is more private than other kinds of health data, like medical background or physical health state, so it needs to be kept safer. Along with this, mental health statistics is often met with prejudice and shame. People who have mental health problems may not want to get help or talk about their problems because they are afraid of being judged or discriminated against. Unauthorized sharing of mental health information can make these worries worse, which can lead to more abuse and stigma against people with mental health problems.

Mental health data is important, and there are also legal and moral issues that need to be thought about when it is used. In many places, laws and rules protect mental health data by controlling how it is collected, used, and shared. The goal of these laws and rules is to protect people's privacy and make sure that their mental health information is used in a responsible way. The possible effects of data breaches make the need for data protection in mental health monitoring even clearer. People can suffer a lot from a data breach that involves their mental health information, such as damage to their image, loss of trust in the healthcare system, and mental suffering. The group that caused the breach could also face fines, lawsuits, and damage to their image in the legal system. Strong data privacy and security means should be put in place to protect the privacy of mental health data. These steps should include encrypting data while it is being sent or stored, controlling access so that only approved people can see the data, and regular checks and reports to find and stop leaks or illegal access. Data protection is very important when tracking mental health. Due to the private nature of mental health data and the bad things that could happen if it gets stolen, strong data privacy and security means are needed to protect people's privacy and make sure that their mental health data is used in a responsible way. Following these steps will help protect the safety and security of people's information while also making sure that smart technology stays a useful tool in mental healthcare.

19.3.2 Psychiatric Insights into Secure Data Management Systems

To keep patients' information private and safe, secure data management tools are very important in mental healthcare. Psychiatric views are very helpful for understanding the special problems and things to think about when handling mental health data safely. One important thing to think about is how sensitive mental health data is. Psychiatric insights help us understand the type of information that is mental health knowledge, which usually includes data about how people feel, what they do, and their own experiences. This is very private information that needs to be treated carefully so that it does not get into the wrong hands or get shared without permission. Psychiatric knowledge also helps us figure out what risks might come with using technology in mental healthcare. Developers and healthcare workers can get help from psychiatrists to understand these risks and take steps to reduce them, like using encryption, controlling who can access what, and doing regular security checks. The effect of data breaches on patients' mental health is another important thing to think about. Psychiatric thoughts help us understand the mental effects of a data breach, like how it might make people feel violated, lose trust, or have more worry or grief. By knowing about these risks, developers and healthcare workers can take steps to make breaches less likely and lessen their effects if they do happen.

Psychiatric thoughts can also help you figure out what your patients want and need when it comes to data protection. People with certain mental illnesses may have special worries about privacy and secrecy that need to be taken into account. Developers and healthcare workers can make data management systems that respect patients' privacy and take into account their wishes if they know what those needs are. Psychiatry views are necessary to make sure that mental health data is managed safely. Developers and healthcare providers can make data management systems that protect patients' privacy and confidentiality while meeting their mental healthcare needs by understanding how sensitive mental health information is, figuring out what risks might be involved, and taking into account the unique needs of each patient. Figure 19.3 gives an overview of psychiatric insights into secure data management systems.

19.3.3 Regulatory Compliance in Wearable Technology Adoption

Regulatory compliance is one of the most important things to think about when using smart technology in mental healthcare. There are many laws and rules that developers and healthcare providers must follow when they gather, use, and share mental health data. This is to protect the rights and security of patients. The Health Insurance Portability and Accountability Act (HIPAA) in the US is a major law that controls the use of smart technology in mental healthcare. HIPAA has strict rules about how to keep patients' health information, including mental health information and safe.

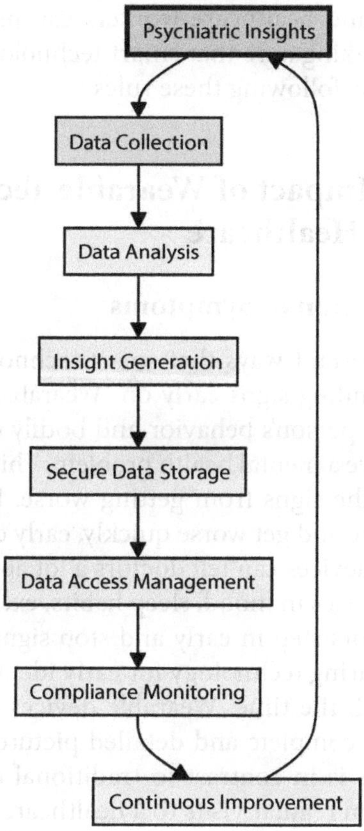

Figure 19.3 Overview of psychiatric insights into secure data management systems.

Healthcare workers and developers must make sure that their use of smart technology is in line with HIPAA rules. This includes putting in place security measures like encryption, access controls, and regular checks.

Aside from HIPAA, developers and healthcare companies must also follow other laws and rules that apply, like the General Data Protection Regulation (GDPR) in the EU. The GDPR has strict rules for protecting personal data, which includes mental health information. Before companies and healthcare providers can collect or use a patient's data, they must get clear permission from the patient. When using smart technology in mental healthcare, it is very important to follow these laws and rules to protect patients' privacy and secrecy. If you do not follow these rules, then you could face legal problems like fines, lawsuits, and damage to the organization's image that caused the breach. There are many laws and rules that developers and healthcare providers must follow when they gather, use, and share mental health data. This is to protect the rights and security of patients. Developers and healthcare workers can protect patients' rights and interests while making sure that smart technology stays a useful tool in mental healthcare by following these rules.

19.4 Potential Impact of Wearable Technology in Mental Healthcare

19.4.1 Early Detection of Symptoms

One of the most important ways that smart technology could help with mental health is by finding signs early on. Wearable devices can pick up on small changes in a person's behavior and bodily data that could mean they are starting to have a mental health problem. This lets them start treatment early and stop the signs from getting worse. In mental healthcare, where signs can change and get worse quickly, early discovery is especially important. Wearable devices can tell doctors a lot about a patient's mental health by tracking changes in mood, sleep habits, exercise levels, and other factors. This lets doctors step in early and stop signs from getting worse. One big benefit of wearing technology for early identification is that it can keep an eye on you all the time. Wearable devices can collect data constantly, giving a more complete and detailed picture of a person's mental health over time. This is in contrast to traditional methods of measurement, which depend on regular visits to a healthcare provider.

Heart rate variability (HRV), which has been linked to worry, anxiety, and sadness, can be tracked by wearable technology. Wearable technology can find trends that could mean the start of a mental health problem by looking at changes in HRV over time. This lets help start sooner. In the same way, smart technology can keep track of changes in sleep habits, which can be hard for people with mental health problems. By tracking sleep habits, smart technology can spot changes that could mean someone has a mental health problem, like sleeplessness or hypersomnia, so help can be given right away. Wearable technology can keep an eye on more than just your body's health. It can also see how your behavior changes over time, like how much you move and talk to other people. If these factors change, then it could mean the start of a mental health problem, like withdrawing from society or losing drive, so help and guidance can be given early on. That signs are arbitrary is one of the main problems with finding mental health problems early on. Mood, behavior, and thought changes that are not always obvious to the person or their healthcare provider can be signs of many mental health conditions. Wearable technology can help doctors find early signs of a mental health problem that might not have been seen otherwise by giving them concrete data on these factors.

Wearable technology can also help find mental health problems earlier by letting people be monitored from afar. This is especially helpful for people who might not be able to get regular mental healthcare or who might be afraid to ask for help because of shame or other issues. Wearable technology can make sure that people get the help and solutions they need at the right time, no matter where they are or what their situation is. Smart technology could have a big effect on mental healthcare by making it easier to spot signs early on. Wearable devices can pick up on small changes in a person's behavior and bodily data that could mean they are starting to have a mental health problem. This lets them start treatment early and stop the signs from getting worse. As more study and development is done, portable technology could become an extremely useful tool for quickly identifying and treating mental health problems, which would greatly improve the lives of people who have them. Figure 19.4 illustrates the process flow for wearable technology in mental healthcare early detection system.

19.4.2 Personalized Interventions

One important way that smart technology can change mental healthcare is by making it possible for more personalized approaches. By constantly collecting information about a person's bodily and behavioral states, wearable technology can help doctors understand each patient's specific needs and tastes, which can then be used to create custom treatment plans that meet those needs. When it comes to mental healthcare, where treatment can be very different from person to person, personalized approaches are very important. Clinicians can find patterns and trends that may be unique to each patient by using data from smart devices in the planning of treatment. This lets them come up with solutions that are more likely to work. One great thing about personalized treatments is that they can focus on particular habits or symptoms. Wearable technology can keep track of changes in mood, sleep patterns, and exercise levels, for instance. This lets doctors find trends that might be causing a patient's complaints. Therapists can make treatment more successful and lower the risk of return by coming up with strategies that focus on these specific signs or behaviors. Personalized treatments can also make patients more interested and motivated. Therapists can give patients the power to be involved in their own care by including them in the creation of their treatment plans and making sure that approaches are tailored to their specific needs. This can make people more interested in and committed to care, which can lead to better results in the long run.

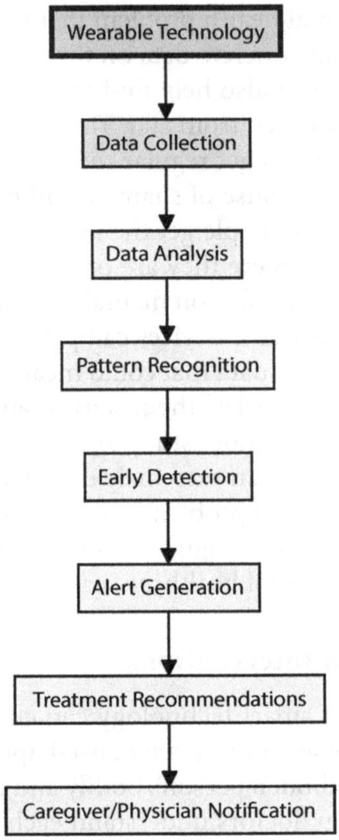

Figure 19.4 Illustration of process flow for wearable technology in mental healthcare early detection system.

One more thing is that individual treatments can make mental healthcare more effective. Clinicians can cut down on the need for trial-and-error in treatment by focusing on specific symptoms or habits. This makes results faster and more effective. This can also make things easier for healthcare workers and resources, so they can be used more efficiently and people can get care more quickly. One of the best things about smart technology in mental healthcare is that it lets people get personalized help. By constantly collecting information about a person's bodily and behavioral states, wearable technology can help doctors understand each patient's specific needs and tastes, which can then be used to create custom treatment plans that meet those needs. Personalized treatments could change the way we treat mental health problems and make things better for people with mental health problems if more study and development goes into them [22].

19.4.3 Patient Engagement and Self-Management

Engaging patients and helping them take care of themselves are important parts of mental healthcare that can be greatly improved by smart technology. Wearable gadgets that give people real-time information about their mental health can give patients the tools they need to take an active part in controlling their conditions, which can lead to better results and quality of life. One important way that smart technology can get patients more involved is by giving them feedback on their symptoms and habits in real time. Wearable technology can, for instance, keep track of changes in mood, sleep habits, and exercise levels. This lets people know right away how their actions are affecting their mental health. This can help people figure out what sets off their symptoms or trends that may be causing them, giving them the power to make smart choices about their care. Wearable technology can also get patients more involved by giving them information and tools for self-management. For instance, smart technology can offer guided breathing routines, ways to deal with stress, and other self-care tools that people can use to handle their conditions. Because they make these tools easy to find and use, smart technology can help people improve their mental health on their own. Wearable technology can also improve patient involvement by making it easier for patients and doctors to talk to each other. Wearable technology can let patients share information with their doctors, so doctors can check on their progress and make changes to treatment plans as required. This can help improve the consistency of care and make sure that people get the help they need when they need it.

19.5 Case Studies and Examples

19.5.1 Successful Implementation of Wearable Technology in Mental Healthcare

Wearable technology has been used successfully in a number of mental healthcare situations, showing that it has the ability to make things better for people with mental health problems. Several case studies and examples show how smart technology has been used successfully in mental healthcare and how it has improved the results for patients. Wearable gadgets that track and help with worry and depression signs are an example of a good application. A study [17] showed that smart technology could correctly track changes in bipolar disorder patients' moods, levels of exercise, and sleep habits. Wearable devices gave doctors real-time information on these factors, which helped them spot changes in mood early and act on them quickly. This led to better treatment of symptoms and fewer stays.

One more example is how smart technology can help with cognitive behavioral therapy (CBT) for worry conditions. Swarna *et al.* [18] study showed that smart technology could be used to give CBT treatments in real time, giving people the chance to practice coping skills and deal with anxiety feelings in their everyday lives. Wearable gadgets made CBT more successful and helped people with anxiety problems do better by giving them instant feedback and support. Wearable technology has been used to improve conversation and participation in mental healthcare, as well as for tracking and assistance. For instance, using smart technology to keep track of social relationships and speech habits has been shown to help people with schizophrenia [19]. Wearable technology can help people improve their social skills and feel less alone by giving them real-time feedback on their social contacts. This can lead to a higher quality of life. Wearable technology has also been used to help people with mental health problems take their medications as prescribed. Choi *et al.* [20] did a study that showed smart technology could be used to track people's obedience to their medicine plans and tell them to take them. Wearable gadgets helped people with schizophrenia take their medications as prescribed and lower the number of relapses by sending them notes and reports on how well they were doing.

All together, these case studies and examples show how smart technology can be used successfully in mental healthcare and how it can help people with mental health problems. Wearable technology has the ability to change the way we provide mental healthcare, which will lead to better results for people with mental health problems. It can do this by giving therapists real-time data, improving the delivery of treatments, and supporting conversation and engagement.

19.5.2 Lessons Learned and Best Practices

The successful use of wearable technology in mental healthcare has taught us important lessons and best practices that can help us when we try to use wearable technology in clinical practice again. The creation and use of smart technology in mental healthcare can be guided by a few important lessons learned from past attempts:

- Design With the User in Mind: One of the most important things that we learned is how important it is to design with the user in mind. It is important that wearable technology is simple to use, comfy, and aware of what users want and need. Users, like people with mental health problems and healthcare professionals, need to be involved in the planning process to make sure that smart technology meets their needs and is widely accepted and used.

- Data Privacy and Security: When using smart technology in mental healthcare, data privacy and security are very important things to think about. To keep patients' information private and secure, developers and healthcare workers need to use strong data protection measures like encryption, access controls, and regular checks.
- Integration With Existing Systems: Wearable technology should work with mental healthcare systems and processes that are already in place without any problems. Interoperability with telehealth systems, electronic health records, and other digital health tools used in mental healthcare are part of this. Integrating smart devices with current systems is important to make sure that doctors can quickly access and use the data they collect.
- Wearable technology should only be used in mental healthcare if it has been shown to work in other cases. People who make smart technology and people who work in healthcare should do a lot of study to see how well these gadgets help people with mental health problems. To find out how smart technology affects patient results, randomized controlled trials (RCTs) and other studies need to be done.
- Patient Empowerment and Engagement: Wearable technology should be used to give patients more power and get them involved in their own care. Giving people access to real-time information about their mental health can help them take charge of their situations and make things better. In mental healthcare, smart technology should be used to get patients more involved.
- Collaboration and Partnerships: For smart technology to work well in mental healthcare, makers, healthcare workers, academics, and patients must work together and form partnerships. Stakeholders can make sure that smart technology meets users' goals, is based on data, and works with current systems and processes by working together.

The successful use of smart technology in mental healthcare has taught us important lessons and best practices that we can use in the future. Developers and healthcare professionals can get the most out of smart technology and help people with mental health problems by following these lessons and best practices.

19.6 Future Directions and Challenges

19.6.1 Emerging Trends in Wearable Technology for Mental Health

Wearable technology for mental health is changing quickly. A number of new trends will shape the future of this area. These trends show that people are becoming more interested in using smart technology to help mental health, and they also show that there is room for more innovation in this area. A new trend is for smart gadgets to [23] include artificial intelligence (AI) and machine learning (ML) systems. Wearable technology can collect data that can be analyzed by AI and ML systems to find patterns and trends that could be signs of mental health problems. Wearable AI devices can help make mental health treatments more personalized and effective by giving doctors real-time information. This can lead to better results for people with mental health problems. The use of virtual reality (VR) and augmented reality (AR) technologies in mental health wearables is another new trend. Immersive experiences that mimic real-life situations can be made with VR and AR technologies. This lets people practice coping skills and handle their symptoms in a safe setting. Virtual reality and AR technologies can make treatment more effective and lead to better results by giving people a safe and helpful space to face their fears and problems. Also, people are becoming more interested in using smart technology to track and help the mental health of people who do not get enough help, like immigrants, soldiers, and people who live in places with few resources. Wearable technology can help these groups get mental healthcare that they might not be able to get otherwise, which can improve results and quality of life [24].

19.6.2 Challenges and Opportunities for Further Development

Wearable technology could be good for mental health, but there are some problems that need to be fixed before it can reach its full potential. These problems include technical, moral, and legal issues that need to be carefully thought through when making and using smart technology for mental health. One of the biggest problems is making sure that the data that smart devices receive is correct and reliable. Wearable devices gather data, but that data can be changed by things like human behavior, the surroundings, and the device's limits. To make sure that the data gathered is correct and dependable, especially when it is used to help make healthcare decisions, developers must carefully test and confirm their devices. Making sure that the data that smart devices receive is private and safe is another issue. Mental health information is very private and should not be shared or accessed by people who are not supposed to. To keep patients' information private and secure, developers and healthcare workers need to use strong data protection measures like encryption, access controls, and regular checks. Additionally, more study is required to find out how well smart technology can help with mental health. More and more proof supports using smart technology in mental healthcare, but more studies are needed to find out if it works, is safe, and is more cost-effective than traditional methods. The bottom line is that smart technology could completely change mental healthcare by giving people access to care, real-time data, and personalized treatments. Developers and healthcare professionals can get the most out of smart technology and help people with mental health issues by solving the problems and chances we talked about above.

19.7 Conclusion

Wearable technology has a huge potential to change how mental health is managed and tracked. Wearable gadgets are a new way to understand and treat mental health problems because they give constant, real-time data on bodily and behavioral factors. Psychiatric knowledge is very important for making sure that smart technology is used well in mental healthcare. One of the best things about smart technology is that it can help find signs early on, so that people can get help right away and avoid worse results. Personalization can also be helped by wearable technology, which lets treatment plans be made to fit each person's wants and tastes. This personalized method can lead to better results and more active patients, giving people the tools they need to take charge of their mental health. Wearable technology can also make it easier for patients and doctors to talk to each other and work together, which can lead to online tracking and support. This can make it easier for people to get care, especially those who are not getting enough of it. There are, however, problems that need to be fixed, such as the need for more study, data safety and security, and the correctness and reliability of the data. Going forward, it is important to keep improving and creating smart technology for mental healthcare, making sure it meets the greatest standards for privacy, safety, and efficiency. It will be very important for makers, healthcare workers, academics, and patients to work together to drive innovation and make sure that smart technology can fully change mental healthcare. As smart technology keeps getting better and more psychological insights are added to it, it could make the lives of people with mental health problems a lot better.

References

1. Xiong, J., Lipsitz, O., Nasri, F., Lui, L.M., Gill, H., Phan, L., Chen-Li, D., Iacobucci, M., Ho, R., Majeed, A., McIntyre, R.S., Impact of COVID-19 pandemic on mental health in the general population: A systematic review. *J. Affect. Disord.*, *277*, 55–64, 2020.
2. Rotenberg, S. and McGrath, J.J., Inter-relation between autonomic and HPA axis activity in children and adolescents. *Biol. Psychol.*, *117*, 16–25, 2016.
3. Gedam, S. and Paul, S., A review on mental stress detection using wearable sensors and machine learning techniques. *IEEE Access*, *9*, 84045–84066, 2021.
4. Moral-Garcia, J.E., Jiménez, A., Cabaco, A.S., Jiménez-Eguizabal, A., The role of physical activity and school physical education in enhancing school satisfaction and life satisfaction. *Int. J. Environ. Res. Public Health*, *18*, 4, 1689, 2021.
5. Shete, D. and Khobragade, P., An empirical analysis of different data visualization techniques from statistical perspective, in: *AIP Conference Proceedings*, vol. 2839, no. 1, AIP Publishing, Melville, New York, USA, 2023, September.
6. Pardamean, B., Soeparno, H., Budiarto, A., Mahesworo, B., Baurley, J., Quantified self-using consumer wearable device: Predicting physical and mental health. *Healthcare Inf. Res.*, *26*, 2, 83, 2020.
7. Liu, L., Stroulia, E., Nikolaidis, I., Miguel-Cruz, A., Rincon, A.R., Smart homes and home health monitoring technologies for older adults: A systematic review. *Int. J. Med. Inf.*, *91*, 44–59, 2016.
8. Kanchanachitra, C., Lindelow, M., Johnston, T., Hanvoravongchai, P., Lorenzo, F.M., Huong, N.L., Wilopo, S.A., Dela Rosa, J.F., Human resources for health in southeast Asia: shortages, distributional challenges, and international trade in health services. *Lancet*, *377*, 9767, 769–781, 2011.
9. Kaushik, A., Yndart, A., Jayant, R.D., Sagar, V., Atluri, V., Bhansali, S., Nair, M., Electrochemical sensing method for point-of-care cortisol detection in human immunodeficiency virus-infected patients. *Int. J. Nanomed.*, 10, 677–685, 2015.

10. Li, D., Wang, Z., Wang, C., Liu, S., Chi, W., Dong, E., Song, X., Gao, Q., Song, Y., The fusion of electroencephalography and facial expression for continuous emotion recognition. *IEEE Access*, *7*, 155724–155736, 2019.
11. Kumar, S.A., Kumar, A., Dutt, V., Agrawal, R., Multi Model Implementation on General Medicine Prediction with Quantum Neural Networks, in: *2021 Third International Conference on Intelligent Communication Technologies and Virtual Mobile Networks (ICICV)*, Tirunelveli, India, pp. 1391–1395, 2021, doi: 10.1109/ICICV50876.2021.9388575.
12. Raj, P., Dubey, A.K., Kumar, A., Rathore, P.S., Blockchain-based IoT architecture for software-defined networking, in: *Blockchain, Artificial Intelligence, and the Internet of Things*, Springer International Publishing, 2022.
13. Burri, S.R., Kumar, A., Baliyan, A., Kumar, T.A., Predictive Intelligence for Healthcare Outcomes: An AI Architecture Overview, in: *2023 2nd International Conference on Smart Technologies and Systems for Next Generation Computing (ICSTSN)*, Villupuram, India, pp. 1–6, 2023, doi: 10.1109/ICSTSN57873.2023.10151477.
14. Wani, S., Ahuja, S., Kumar, A., Application of Deep Neural Networks and Machine Learning algorithms for diagnosis of Brain tumour, in: *2023 International Conference on Computational Intelligence and Sustainable Engineering Solutions (CISES)*, Greater Noida, India, pp. 106–111, 2023, doi: 10.1109/CISES58720.2023.10183528.
15. Kour, S.P., Kumar, A., Ahuja, S., An Advance Approach for Diabetes Detection by Implementing Machine Learning Algorithms, in: *2023 IEEE World Conference on Applied Intelligence and Computing (AIC)*, Sonbhadra, India, pp. 136–141, 2023, doi: 10.1109/AIC57670.2023.10263919.
16. Raj, P., Kumar, A., Dubey, A.K., Bhatia, S., Oswalt, M.S., *Quantum Computing and Artificial Intelligence: Training Machine and Deep Learning Algorithms on Quantum Computers*, De Gruyter, Berlin, Boston, 2023, [Online]. Available: https://doi.org/10.1515/9783110791402.
17. Sasubilli, G. and Kumar, A., Machine Learning and Big Data Implementation on Health Care data, in: *2020 4th International Conference on Intelligent Computing and Control Systems (ICICCS)*, Madurai, India, pp. 859–864, 2020, doi: 10.1109/ICICCS48265.2020.9120906.
18. Swarna, S.R., Kumar, A., Dixit, P., Sairam, T.V.M., Parkinson's Disease Prediction using Adaptive Quantum Computing, in: *2021 Third International Conference on Intelligent Communication Technologies and Virtual Mobile Networks (ICICV)*, Tirunelveli, India, pp. 1396–1401, 2021, doi: 10.1109/ICICV50876.2021.9388628.
19. Burugadda, V.R., Pawar, P.S., Kumar, A., Bhati, N., Predicting Hospital Readmission Risk for Heart Failure Patients Using Machine Learning Techniques: A Comparative Study of Classification Algorithms, in: *2023 Second International Conference on Trends in Electrical, Electronics, and Computer Engineering (TEECCON)*, Bangalore, India, pp. 223–228, 2023, doi: 10.1109/TEECCON59234.2023.10335817.

20. Choi, J., Ahmed, B., Gutierrez-Osuna, R., Development and evaluation of an ambulatory stress monitor based on wearable sensors. *IEEE Trans. Inf. Technol. Biomed.*, *16*, 2, 279–286, 2011.
21. Northrup, C.M., Lantz, J., Hamlin, T., Wearable stress sensors for children with autism spectrum disorder with in situ alerts to caregivers via a mobile phone. *Iproceedings*, *2*, 1, e6119, 2016.
22. Ganguly, A., Rice, P., Lin, K.C., Muthukumar, S., Prasad, S., A combinatorial electrochemical biosensor for sweat biomarker benchmarking. *SLAS Technol.*, *25*, 1, 25–32, 2020.
23. Cho, B., Lee, K., Pyo, S., Kim, J., Fabrication and characterization of VOC sensor array based on SnO 2 and ZnO nanoparticles functionalized by metalloporphyrins. *Micro Nano Syst. Lett.*, 6, 1–6, 2018.
24. Zavyalova, E., Ambartsumyan, O., Zhdanov, G., Gribanyov, D., Gushchin, V., Tkachuk, A., Rudakova, E., Nikiforova, M., Kuznetsova, N., Popova, L., Verdiev, B., SERS-based aptasensor for rapid quantitative detection of SARS-CoV-2. *Nanomaterials*, *11*, 6, 1394, 2021.

20

Ethical Considerations in Mental Health Data Collection and Analysis: Ethical and Legal Aspects of Mental Health Data in Wearable Technology

V. M. Thorat[1]* and M. P. Ambali[2]

[1]*Department of Pharmacology, Krishna Institute of Medical Sciences, Krishna Vishwa Vidyapeeth "Deemed To Be University", Karad, Maharashtra, India*
[2]*Department of Anatomy, Krishna Institute of Medical Sciences, Krishna Vishwa Vidyapeeth "Deemed To Be University", Karad, Maharashtra, India*

Abstract
Wearable technology has changed the field of mental health by making it possible to collect data continuously and without being noticed. This data gives researchers useful information about people's mental health. Wearable technology in mental health, on the other hand, brings up a lot of social and legal questions about privacy, data gathering, and research. This essay looks at the moral and legal issues connected to mental health data in smart technology, focused on the values of liberty, beneficence, non-maleficence, and justice. People should be able to make their own choices about their health because autonomy is a basic moral value. People must be able to decide for themselves if they want to be a part of data collection and how that data is used when it comes to personal technology. This makes me wonder about informed consent, because people might not fully understand what it means to share their mental health information. Because of the principles of beneficence and non-maleficence, mental health smart technology should help people and cause them as little harm as possible. People who wear technology might be able to improve their mental health by showing early signs of mental health problems, but this also makes people worry about data protection and vulnerabilities. If mental health data is misused, then it could lead to shame and abuse against people who have mental health problems. For justice to be

**Corresponding author*: vmthoratkvv@outlook.com

Abhishek Kumar, Narayan Vyas, Pramod Singh Rathore, Abhineet Anand and Pooja Dixit (eds.)
Internet of Medicine for Smart Healthcare, (429–448) © 2025 Scrivener Publishing LLC

served, the pros and cons of smart technology for mental health should be evenly shared among all people. This makes me wonder about access to smart technology, because some people might not be able to afford or understand how to use these gadgets. Concerns have also been raised about the use of mental health data for business reasons, like focused ads, which could make inequality even worse.

***Keywords*:** Biomedical, confidentially requirements, informed consent, legal aspects, wearable technology

20.1 Introduction

Wearable technology has changed mental health by making it possible to collect data continuously and without being noticed. This data gives us useful information about people's mental health. But this progress brings up a lot of important moral and legal questions about privacy, data gathering, and research. This talk looks at the moral and legal issues of mental health data in smart technology, focused on the values of liberty, beneficence, non-maleficence, and justice. People have the right to make their own choices about their health, which is a basic social concept called autonomy. When talking about personal technology, liberty brings up questions about what it means to give informed consent. People must be able to decide for themselves if they want to be part of data collection and how that data is used. Of course, it can be hard to get informed consent when it comes to smart technology [1]. People might not fully understand what it means to share their mental health data, and getting real consent means being clear and honest about the risks and benefits of collecting and analyzing the data. Because of the principles of beneficence and non-maleficence, mental health smart technology should help people and cause them as little harm as possible. By giving early warning signs of mental health problems, wearable technology could help improve mental health results. Some examples of personal technology are heart rate monitors and sleep trackers, which can give you important information about a person's mental health. But the fact that mental health data is used in smart technology also makes people worry about data security and the chance of data breaches. If [2] mental health data is misused, then it could lead to shame and abuse against people who have mental health problems. For justice to be served, the pros and cons of smart technology for mental health should be evenly shared among all people. This makes me wonder how easy it is to get smart technology. Unfortunately, some people might not be able to afford or understand how to use these gadgets, which could make mental health care even less fair. Concerns have also been raised about the use of mental health data for business reasons, like tailored ads, which could make already marginalized groups even more so. A very important social issue to think about when using smart technology for mental health is getting informed permission. Researchers and practitioners need to make sure that people know why their data is being collected, how it will be used, and what the risks and benefits might be of taking part. To get informed consent, you should give people information that is easy to understand and access, let them opt out of data collection at any time, and make sure that data is only used for what it was collected for. Figure 20.1 gives an overview of ethical decision-making system.

When collecting and [3, 4] analyzing mental health data, data protection and privacy are also very important social issues to think about. Wearable devices collect private information about people's mental health, and this information needs to be kept safe from people who should not have access to it. Encrypting data while it is being sent and stored, setting up access controls to limit who can see the data, and regularly changing security measures to deal with new threats are all things that can be done to protect data and keep it private. Wearable technology could change the way mental health care is provided, but its use brings up a lot of social and legal issues. These worries need to be talked about by lawmakers, researchers, and practitioners to make sure that smart technology is used in a way that respects people's freedom, encourages good behavior, and follows fairness rules. By carefully thinking about these moral and legal issues, we can use

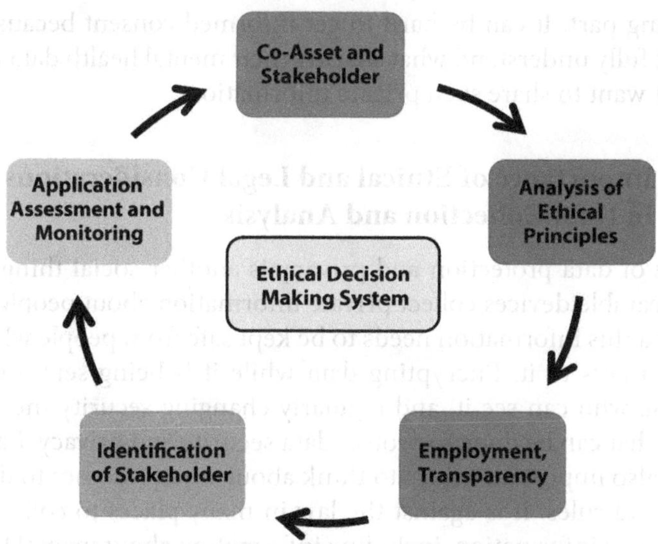

Figure 20.1 Overview of ethical decision-making system.

smart technology to help mental health while reducing harm and making sure everyone has equal access to care.

20.1.1 Overview of Wearable Technology in Mental Health

Wearable technology, like fitness [5] trackers, tablets, and other gadgets, has changed the field of mental health by making it possible to constantly monitor and record people's bodily and behavioral data. These gadgets can gather a lot of information, like your heart rate, how you sleep, how active you are, and even your mood. This information can tell us a lot about people's mental health and be used to look for signs of mental health problems like sadness, worry, and stress. It is especially important for mental health to use smart technology because mental illnesses tend to come and go, making them hard to identify and treat. Traditional ways of checking someone's mental health, like self-report surveys and in-person checks, might not show the whole picture of their mental health over time. Wearable technology lets you keep an eye on your mental health more continuously and in real time, which means problems can be found earlier and treatments can be more specifically tailored to each person [6].

But using smart technology for mental health brings up important social and legal questions, especially when it comes to gathering and analyzing data. The [7] question of educated permission is one of the most important social issues to think about. People need to know why their information is being collected, how it will be used, and what the risks and benefits might be of taking part. It can be hard to get informed consent because people might not fully understand what sharing their mental health data means or might not want to share such private information.

20.1.2 Importance of Ethical and Legal Considerations in Data Collection and Analysis

The value of data protection and privacy is another social thing to think about. Wearable devices collect private information about people's mental health, and this information needs to be kept safe from people who should not have access to it. Encrypting data while it is being sent and stored, controlling who can see it, and regularly changing security measures are all things that can be done to protect data security and privacy. Legally [8], there are also important things to think about when it comes to data security laws and rules. It is against the law in many places to collect, use, or store personal information, including information about mental health. To protect people's privacy rights, researchers and mental health professionals who use smart technology must make sure that they follow these laws and rules. Even with these problems, using smart technology in mental health has a lot of potential to make diagnosing and treating mental health problems better. Researchers and clinicians can use smart technology to improve mental health results and give more personalized and effective care by carefully considering the ethical and legal issues and putting in place the right protection.

20.2 Ethical Principles in Mental Health Data Collection and Analysis

When mental health data from smart technology is collected and analyzed, ethical standards are very important. These concepts help make sure that the rights and well-being of each person are respected at all times. In this case, liberty, beneficence, non-maleficence, and fairness are the four most important ethical concepts. Figure 20.2 shows the architecture of wearable technology in mental health.

20.2.1 Autonomy

Autonomy is the idea that each [9] person should be able to make their own choices about their health and well-being. Autonomy in mental health data gathering and research means that people should be able to decide for themselves if they want to be part of the data collection and how their data is used. It can be hard to respect liberty when it comes to personal technology. People might not fully understand what it means to share their mental health information, and it can be hard to get their informed permission.

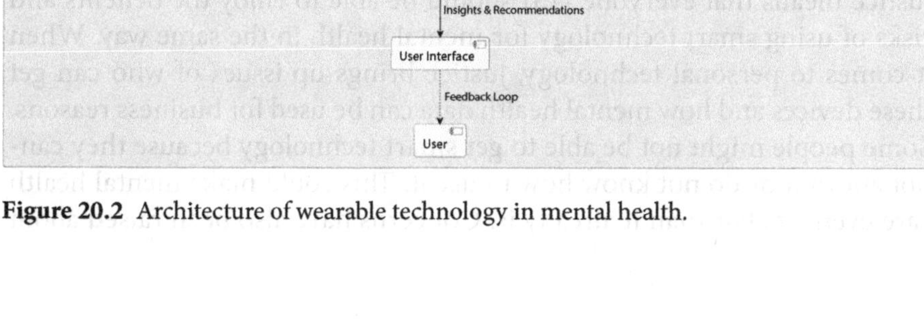

Figure 20.2 Architecture of wearable technology in mental health.

To deal with these issues, researchers and practitioners should be open and honest about why they are collecting data, how it will be used, and the risks and benefits of taking part. Also, they should make sure that people can ask questions and stop having their information collected at any time [10].

20.2.2 Beneficence

The idea that people should act in ways that help other people is grounded in the ethical principle of beneficence. When it comes to collecting and analyzing data on mental health, beneficence means that wearing technology should improve people's mental health. It is possible that wearable technology could help mental health by showing early signs of problems and making it easier to tailor treatments to each person. Some examples of personal technology are heart rate monitors and sleep trackers, which can give you important information about a person's mental health. For beneficence, researchers and practitioners should carefully think about the pros and cons of using smart technology in mental health and try to get the most good out of it while minimizing the bad [11].

20.2.3 Non-Maleficence

Non-maleficence is the idea that people should not do things that hurt other people. Non-maleficence means that academics and practitioners should take steps to make sure that the use of smart technology does not cause more harm than good when it comes to mental health data collection and analysis. One of the biggest worries about using smart technology in mental health is that data could be stolen or used in the wrong way [12]. If mental health data is misused, then it could lead to shame and abuse against people who have mental health problems. To make sure there is no harm, researchers and practitioners should take strict privacy and data security steps. For example, they should secure data while it is being sent and stored, control who can see it, and make sure that security methods are always up to date.

20.2.4 Justice

Justice means that everyone [13] should be able to enjoy the benefits and risks of using smart technology for mental health in the same way. When it comes to personal technology, justice brings up issues of who can get these devices and how mental health data can be used for business reasons. Some people might not be able to get smart technology because they cannot afford it or do not know how to use it. This could make mental health care even less fair than it already is. Concerns have also been raised about the use of mental health data for business reasons, like tailored ads, which could make already marginalized groups even more so. To promote fairness, researchers and practitioners should work to make sure that everyone has equal access to smart technology and should think carefully about what might happen if mental health data is used for business reasons.

20.3 Legal Frameworks for Mental Health Data in Wearable Technology

The laws that govern [14] mental health data in smart technology are complicated and are always changing. Many laws and rules have an impact on this area. These rules and laws are meant to protect people's right to privacy and make sure that their information is used correctly. Data security laws, permission standards, and privacy rules are some of the most important parts of the legal structure for mental health data in smart technology [15].

- Data Protection Laws: These laws spell out how to gather, use, and store personal data, which can include mental health data. These rules say that personal information about people must be gathered and used properly and legally, only for certain things, and kept safe. They apply to many places. The General Data Protection Regulation of the European Union, for instance, has strict rules about how to gather and use sensitive data, even mental health data.
- Consent Requirements: Giving permission is an important part of data security rules and is needed to gather and use personal data, such as mental health data. Consent must be made voluntarily, be clear, detailed, well-informed, and free of doubt. This means that people must be fully aware of why their information is being collected, how it will be used, and the risks and benefits of taking part. In addition, they should be able to change their minds at any time.
- Privacy Rules: Privacy rules are meant to protect people's right to privacy and make sure that their personal information is used correctly. These rules usually tell businesses they need to take technical and organizational steps to keep people's data safe from breaches and illegal access. As an example, in the US, the Health Insurance Portability and Accountability Act has strict rules about how to keep people's health information, including mental health information, safe.

20.4 Informed Consent in Wearable Technology

Informed permission [16] is a legal and moral requirement for collecting and using data in smart technology, especially when it comes to mental health. People give their informed consent when they fully understand the goal, risks, and benefits of data collection and can make an educated choice about whether to participate or not. When it comes to personal technology, there are a few important things to keep in mind in order to get informed permission. People must first be given clear information about why their data is being collected, how it will be used, and any risks or benefits that might come with it. People with different levels of health literacy should be able to understand this knowledge so that they can make an informed choice about whether or not to participate [17]. Second, people should be told that they have the right to stop having their information collected at any time and how to do that. This gives people power over their engagement and lets them quit if they do not like how the data is being collected or if they no longer want to take part. Third, permission should be freely given, without any pressure or unfair influence. People should not feel like they have to join or that skipping the event will get them in trouble. Researchers and practitioners should make sure that people can choose for themselves whether to take part in data collection. Lastly, permission should be constant and changeable, because the way data is collected and used in smart technology is always changing. People should be told about any changes to how their data will be used or how it is collected, and they should be able to give their permission again if they need to.

Due to the complexity of the technology and the sensitive nature of the data being received, getting informed permission for smart technology can be hard. Researchers and practitioners should make sure that people have all the information they need to make an informed choice about whether or not to participate. This could mean giving information that is easy to understand, letting people ask questions and get more information, and making sure that consent is given freely and not against their will [18].

20.4.1 Challenges in Obtaining Informed Consent

There are a lot of problems with getting informed consent for smart technology, especially when it comes to mental health. That the technology and data being gathered are so hard to understand is one of the main problems. Wearable technology can gather a lot of information, like bodily signals, trends of behavior, and information about where you are. It can be hard to explain the goal, risks, and benefits of data collection in a way that people with different levels of health literacy can easily understand.

The fact that [19] people might feel overwhelmed or scared by technology is another problem. A lot of wearable technology comes with high-tech sensors and software that can track and analyze data in real time. People may not want to take part in data collection if they think the technology is rude or annoying. To get informed consent, it is important to make sure that people are relaxed and have the power to decide if they want to participate. Another case where it can be hard to get informed consent is when someone is having mental health problems. Mental illnesses like schizophrenia, sadness, and anxiety can make it hard for people to understand and decide if they want to take part in data collection [20]. In these situations, researchers and practitioners might need to go the extra mile to make sure that people are fully informed and can make an informed choice about whether to participate.

20.4.2 Strategies for Ensuring Informed Consent

Even with these problems, there are a number of things that can be done to make sure that educated consent is properly gained when it comes to personal technology. One important tactic is to make sure that people can easily understand the reason for collecting data, as well as any risks and rewards that may come with it. This knowledge [21] should be given in a way that is easy for everyone to receive and understand, regardless of how much they know about health. Giving people chances to ask questions and get more information is another approach. The people should be able to ask questions about how the data is collected and get clear, honest replies. This can make people feel better about their choice to join and give them more confidence. It is also very important to make sure that permission is given freely and not because of pressure. No one should be forced or feel obligated to take part in data collection. Researchers and practitioners should stress that people can choose not to participate and can quit at any time without any consequences.

When people [22] are having mental health problems, researchers and practitioners may need to take extra steps to make sure that they give informed consent. This could mean giving people more help and knowledge, letting trusted providers or family members help them make decisions, and making sure that they can get to mental health services if they need to. As a conclusion, getting informed permission for smart technology is not always easy, especially when it comes to mental health.

Researchers and practitioners can help make sure that people are fully informed and can make an informed decision about taking part in data collection by giving them information that is easy to understand, letting them ask questions and get more information, and making sure that consent is given voluntarily. Researchers and mental health professionals can make sure that the use of smart technology in mental health is moral and upholds people's rights and liberty by tackling these problems and putting in place successful plans.

20.5 Data Security and Privacy in Mental Health Wearables

When using smart technology for mental health, data protection and safety are very important things to think about. Wearable technology collects private data, like bodily and behavioral details, that needs to be kept safe to protect people's privacy and stop people from getting to it without permission. A data theft is one of the biggest problems that comes up when trying to protect data security and privacy. Because wearable technology is linked to the internet, hackers and other online risks can get into them. To deal with this problem, experts and practitioners need to use strong security measures, like encryption, to keep data safe while it is being sent and stored. To protect data even more, only allowed users should be able to access it, and security checks should be done regularly to find and fix any problem areas.

Another problem is that info could be used in the wrong way. Wearable gadgets collect very private information about mental health that could be used for things other than what they were meant for. For instance, information could be used to show people more relevant ads or given to other people without their permission. To deal with this problem, researchers and practitioners need to make sure that data is only used for what it was collected for and that people's privacy rights are always protected. Besides these problems, there are also moral issues to think about when it comes to privacy and data security. Researchers and professionals need to think about how data hacks and misuse can affect people's mental health and well-being. They must also make sure that people understand the risks and rewards of collecting data and give their permission before any data is collected. The privacy and data protection are very important things to think about when using smart technology for mental health.

Table 20.1 Summary of privacy and safety of personal health information.

Measure	Description
Educate healthcare personnel	Provide training and education to healthcare personnel on the importance of data privacy and security, as well as best practices for protecting personal health data.
Conduct routine risk assessment	Regularly assess potential risks to personal health data, including vulnerabilities in systems and processes, and implement measures to mitigate these risks.
Secure data with a VPN	Use a Virtual Private Network (VPN) to encrypt data transmitted over networks, ensuring that personal health data remains secure and protected from unauthorized access.
Restrict access to data	Limit access to personal health data to authorized personnel only, ensuring that individuals who do not need access to the data cannot view or manipulate it.
Implement role-based access	Assign roles and permissions to healthcare personnel based on their job responsibilities, ensuring that individuals have access only to the data necessary for their role.
Two-factor authentication	Require two forms of verification (e.g., password and a unique code sent to a mobile device) to access personal health data, adding an extra layer of security against unauthorized access.
Encryption	Encrypt personal health data both at rest (stored data) and in transit (data being transmitted), ensuring that even if data is intercepted or accessed without authorization, it cannot be read without the decryption key.
Security awareness training	Provide ongoing training and awareness programs to healthcare personnel on the latest security threats and best practices for protecting personal health data.
AI for regular inspections	Use artificial intelligence (AI) to conduct regular inspections and audits of systems and processes to ensure compliance with regulations and identify potential security vulnerabilities.

Researchers and practitioners can help make sure that smart technology is used in the field of mental health in an ethical and responsible way by putting in place strong security measures, making sure that data is only used for its original purpose, and protecting people's personal rights. Table 20.1 summarise the privacy and safety of personal health information.

20.5.1 Security Risks in Data Collection and Transmission

When mental health tracking technology collects and sends data, there are a number of security issues that need to be dealt with to protect people's privacy and the accuracy of the data. Getting into private data without permission is one of the biggest security risks. Wearable technology gathers a lot of information, like changes in your body and trends in your behavior, which can be very sensitive. If someone gets access to this data without permission, then it could cause privacy breaches and even harm to people. Data capture while it is being sent is another security risk. Wearable technology often sends information over Wi-Fi networks, which bad people can steal. This could cause data leaks and give people access to private data without permission. To lower this risk, data should be protected while it is being sent so that it cannot be read by someone else.

When data is being sent or collected, data accuracy is another important security issue. Bad people may try to change or manipulate data while it is being sent, which could result in wrong or misleading information. To protect the accuracy of data, academics and practitioners should use tools like data validity and integrity checks to find and stop changes that were not allowed.

20.5.2 Privacy Protection Measures

Several steps can be taken to protect people's privacy when using smart technology for mental health. One important step is to make data anonymous. Anonymizing data takes out information that can be used to identify a person, like names and addresses. This protects people's privacy while still letting research be useful. Data reduction is another way to protect your privacy. Data reduction means only getting the data that is needed for the reason it was collected for. This lowers the risk of privacy breaches and illegal access. Researchers and practitioners should think carefully about the data they gather and make sure that it is needed for the research they want to do.

Encrypting data is also important for keeping your information safe when using smart technology. During encryption, data is changed into a safe code that can only be viewed with a decoding key. This keeps private data safe while it is being sent and stored. Strong security methods should be used by researchers and practitioners to keep data safe from people who should not have access to it. Along with these technology steps, privacy rules and practices are also important to keep people's privacy safe. Researchers and practitioners should make privacy rules that are clear and explain how data will be gathered, used, and kept safe. People should be told about these rules and given the chance to agree to the collection and use of their data. Finally, security issues must be fixed in order to protect people's privacy and the accuracy of data collected and sent by smart technology for mental health. Data protection, data anonymization, and data reduction are some of the steps that researchers and practitioners can take to make sure that smart technology is used in the field of mental health in an honest and responsible way.

20.6 Potential Misuse of Mental Health Data

Wearable technology that collects and analyzes mental health data has many benefits for both people and healthcare workers. There are, however, risks that come with the possible misuse of this data. People who are stigmatized or discriminated against because of their mental health data and the marketing of this private information are two major issues.

20.6.1 Stigmatization and Discrimination

One of the biggest worries about using mental health data in the wrong way is that people with mental health problems could be shamed and treated badly. Stigma is the negative thoughts and feelings that cause people with mental health problems to be treated badly. Stigmatization can lead to bad things, like being left out of social groups, losing your job, and having trouble getting medical care [23]. The collection of mental health data through smart technology could make shame worse by sharing private details about people's mental health. For instance, information gathered from smart technology could show trends of behavior or physical signs that are linked to certain mental health problems. If this information is shared or viewed without permission, then it could cause people with mental health problems to be shamed and treated badly because of it. To ease this worry, strong privacy protections must be put in place to make sure that mental health information stays private and safe. This includes securing data while it is being sent and stored, controlling who can see it, and getting people's permission before taking their data. Educating and advocating about mental health issues can also help fight bad attitudes and beliefs by making people more aware of them and lowering the shame surrounding them.

20.6.2 Commercialization of Mental Health Data

The sale of this private information for profit is another major worry about the wrong use of mental health data. There is a rising market for mental health data that can be used for focused ads, market research, and other business reasons as smart technology becomes more common. Mental health data may not always be used in these ways in a bad way, but there is a chance that it could lead to privacy breaches and the misuse of people's private information. When mental health data is sold, it brings up social concerns about turning personal health information into a commodity and the chance of taking advantage of weak groups. Concerns have also been raised about permission and control over personal data, because people may not fully understand how their data is being used or may not be able to agree to its business use. To ease these worries, it is important to set clear rules and guidelines for how mental health data can be used for business reasons. This includes making sure that people know exactly how their data will be used and that they have the choice to agree to or reject business uses of their data. There should also be strong rules in place to protect people's privacy and stop mental health data from being used illegally for business purposes. In collecting and analyzing mental health data through smart technology has many benefits, but there are also risks that this data could be used in the wrong way. To make sure that mental health data is used in an honest and appropriate way, it is important to set up strong privacy protections and clear rules and standards. By taking these worries into account, we can use smart technology to help people's mental health while still protecting their rights and privacy.

20.7 Ensuring Equity in Access to Mental Health Wearables

Wearable technology could change the way mental health care is provided by allowing for constant tracking and individualized treatments. Concerns have been raised, though, that not everyone may have equal access to these tools because of problems with technology and money. To keep health gaps from getting worse, it is important to make sure that everyone has equal access to mental health devices.

20.7.1 Addressing Technological Barriers

Technology hurdles are one of the main things that make it hard for everyone to get equal access to mental health devices. Some people might not have access to the gadgets or the technology equipment that they need to work. For instance, people who live in rural or remote places might not have access to a stable internet connection, which is needed to send data from trackers to healthcare doctors. To get around these technology problems, people should work to make it easier for people in poor areas to connect to the internet in a way that is both cheap and effective. This could mean building more broadband networks and giving low-income people grants or savings on their internet service. Wearable technology companies could also make products that are easier for people who are not very good with technology to use by giving them simple user interfaces and clear directions.

20.7.1.1 Addressing Financial Barriers

Financial hurdles are another big reason why not everyone can get mental health tools. Wearable technology can be pricey, and some people, especially those with low incomes, might not be able to buy it. Additionally, the price of internet plans and upkeep for smart technology can be too high for some people. To get around these money problems, smart technology should be made easier to get and more cheap. This could mean giving low-income people rebates or savings, letting people pay over time or with financial choices, and working with insurance companies to cover the cost of devices for people with mental health problems. Additionally, money should be set aside for study to help create smart tools that are cheap and available to people from all walks of life.

20.7.2 Promoting Inclusivity in Wearable Technology Design

Promoting inclusion in the creation of wearable technology is important to make sure that these gadgets can be used by and help a lot of different people, like disabled people and people from different cultures. In inclusive design, the wants and needs of all people are taken into account at all stages of the process, from coming up with an idea to trying and improving the final product. Making sure that gadgets can be used by people with disabilities is an important part of supporting equality in the design of smart technology. This includes making sure that devices work with help technologies like screen readers and other input devices and that best practices for usability are used when building interfaces. For instance, gadgets should offer different ways to connect with people who have trouble moving around, and they should have settings that can be changed for people who have trouble seeing or hearing. Designing in a way that is inclusive also means taking into account the different cultural backgrounds of people. As part of this, gadgets must be made that take into account national beliefs, values, and behaviors. Wearable technology should, for instance, let users change settings to fit their cultural tastes and should stay away from design choices that could be rude or inappropriate to some cultural groups. Promoting inclusion in the creation of wearable technology means not only taking into account the needs of people with disabilities and from different cultural backgrounds but also making sure that all users can easily understand and use the devices. This means making platforms that are easy to use, giving clear and brief directions, and helping and teaching people who may not be very good with technology. Overall, supporting inclusion in the design of wearable technology means taking the time to understand the different wants and needs of users and using this information during the design process. Designers can make products that are available, easy to use, and helpful for a wide range of people by putting inclusiveness first. This improves the general user experience and the usefulness of smart technology in supporting mental health and well-being.

20.8 Ethical Guidelines for Researchers and Practitioners

Wearable technology has the potential to greatly impact mental health care by providing valuable insights into individuals' mental well-being and enabling personalized interventions. However, the use of wearable technology in mental health raises important ethical considerations that researchers and practitioners must address to ensure that individuals' rights and well-being are protected. This section discusses ethical guidelines for researchers and practitioners in mental health wearables, focusing on best practices for data collection and analysis and ethical decision-making frameworks.

20.8.1 Best Practices for Data Collection and Analysis

- *Informed Consent*: Researchers and practitioners should obtain informed consent from individuals before collecting any data. This includes providing clear and understandable information about the purpose of data collection, how the data will be used, and any potential risks or benefits.

- *Privacy Protection*: Data collected through wearable technology should be kept confidential and secure. This includes encrypting data during transmission and storage, implementing access controls, and ensuring that data is used only for the intended purpose.
- *Data Minimization*: Researchers and practitioners should collect only the data that is necessary for the intended analysis. This helps reduce the risk of privacy breaches and unauthorized access.
- *Transparency*: Researchers and practitioners should be transparent about their data collection and analysis practices. This includes providing clear and understandable information about how data will be used and ensuring that individuals have the opportunity to ask questions and seek clarification.
- *Respect for Autonomy*: Researchers and practitioners should respect individuals' autonomy and right to make decisions about their own health care. This includes giving individuals the opportunity to withdraw from data collection at any time without penalty.

20.8.2 Ethical Decision-Making Frameworks

- *Principlism*: Principlism is an ethical framework that is based on four principles: autonomy, beneficence, non-maleficence, and justice. Researchers and practitioners can use these principles to guide their decision-making processes and ensure that they are acting ethically in their use of wearable technology in mental health.
- *Utilitarianism*: Utilitarianism is an ethical theory that states that the best course of action is the one that maximizes overall happiness or utility. Researchers and practitioners can use this framework to weigh the potential benefits and harms of using wearable technology in mental health and make decisions that maximize benefits while minimizing harms.
- *Virtue Ethics*: Virtue ethics is an ethical theory that emphasizes the importance of developing virtuous character traits, such as honesty, compassion, and integrity. Researchers and practitioners can use this framework to cultivate ethical virtues in their practice and ensure that they are acting in a morally good way.

20.9 Conclusion

It is very important to think about ethics when using smart technology to gather and analyze mental health data. Wearable technology has a lot of promise to make mental health care better, but it also brings up important legal and moral issues that need to be dealt with. To begin, it is very important to make sure that educated consent is given. People need to know why their information is being collected, how it will be used, and what the risks and rewards might be. In addition, they should be able to stop giving information at any time. Second, it is very important to protect privacy and secrecy. Mental health information is very private and needs to be kept safe to avoid misuse and access by people who are not supposed to have it. This means securing data while it is being sent and stored and putting in place strict controls on who can view it. Third, it is important to encourage diversity in design. Wearable technology should be easy for people with disabilities to use and should be aware of the different cultures of its users. This means making sure that all people can easily understand and use the gadgets. To make sure that their use of smart technology in mental health is moral and helpful, academics and practitioners should also use ethical decision-making models like utilitarianism and principlism. The use of these models can help people make decisions and make sure that researchers and practitioners live by ethical standards. Researchers and clinicians can make sure that the use of wearable technology in mental health is moral, responsible, and good for people's mental health by following these ethical guidelines and thinking about the moral and legal aspects of mental health data in wearable technology.

References

1. Morley, J., Machado, C.C., Burr, C., Cowls, J., Joshi, I., Taddeo, M., Floridi, L., The ethics of AI in health care: a mapping review. *Soc. Sci. Med.*, *260*, 113172, 2020.
2. Čartolovni, A., Tomičić, A., Mosler, E.L., Ethical, legal, and social considerations of AI-based medical decision-support tools: A scoping review. *Int. J. Med. Inf.*, *161*, 104738, 2022.
3. Lang, M., Knoppers, B.M., Zawati, M.N.H., International mHealth research: old tools and new challenges. *J. Law Med. Ethics*, *48*, 1_suppl, 178–186, 2020.
4. Oliva, A., Grassi, S., Vetrugno, G., Rossi, R., Della Morte, G., Pinchi, V., Caputo, M., Management of medico-legal risks in digital health era: a scoping review. *Front. Med.*, *8*, 821756, 2022.

5. Nittari, G., Khuman, R., Baldoni, S., Pallotta, G., Battineni, G., Sirignano, A., Amenta, F., Ricci, G., Telemedicine practice: review of the current ethical and legal challenges. *Telemed. e-Health*, *26*, 12, 1427–1437, 2020.
6. Monje, M.H., Foffani, G., Obeso, J., Sánchez-Ferro, Á., New sensor and wearable technologies to aid in the diagnosis and treatment monitoring of Parkinson's disease. *Annu. Rev. Biomed. Eng.*, *21*, 111–143, 2019.
7. Merola, A., Sturchio, A., Hacker, S., Serna, S., Vizcarra, J.A., Marsili, L., Fasano, A., Espay, A.J., Technology-based assessment of motor and nonmotor phenomena in Parkinson disease. *Expert Rev. Neurother.*, *18*, 11, 825–845, 2018.
8. Maetzler, W., Domingos, J., Srulijes, K., Ferreira, J.J., Bloem, B.R., Quantitative wearable sensors for objective assessment of Parkinson's disease. *Mov. Disord.*, *28*, 12, 1628–1637, 2013.
9. Silva de Lima, A.L., Smits, T., Darweesh, S.K., Valenti, G., Milosevic, M., Pijl, M., Baldus, H., de Vries, N.M., Meinders, M.J., Bloem, B.R., Home-based monitoring of falls using wearable sensors in Parkinson's disease. *Mov. Disord.*, *35*, 1, 109–115, 2020.
10. Demrozi, F., Bacchin, R., Tamburin, S., Cristani, M., and Pravadelli, G., Toward a wearable system for predicting freezing of gait in people affected by parkinson's disease. *IEEE J. Biomed. Health. Inf.*, *24*, 9, 2444–2451, 2019.
11. de Vries, N.M., Smilowska, K., Hummelink, J., Abramiuc, B., Van Gilst, M.M., Bloem, B.R., de With, P.H.N., Overeem, S., Exploring the Parkinson patients' perspective on home-based video recording for movement analysis: a qualitative study. *BMC Neurol.*, *19*, 1–6, 2019.
12. Jayatilleka, I. and Halgamuge, M.N., Internet of Things in healthcare: Smart devices, sensors, and systems related to diseases and health conditions, in: *Real-time data analytics for large scale sensor data*, pp. 1–35, Academic Press, San Diego, California, USA, 2020.
13. Karlawish, J., Cary, M., Moelter, S.T., Siderowf, A., Sullo, E., Xie, S., Weintraub, D., Cognitive impairment and PD patients' capacity to consent to research. *Neurology*, *81*, 9, 801–807, 2013.
14. Kumar, S.A., Kumar, A., Dutt, V., Agrawal, R., Multi Model Implementation on General Medicine Prediction with Quantum Neural Networks, in: *2021 Third International Conference on Intelligent Communication Technologies and Virtual Mobile Networks (ICICV)*, Tirunelveli, India, pp. 1391–1395, 2021, doi: 10.1109/ICICV50876.2021.9388575.
15. Raj, P., Dubey, A.K., Kumar, A., Rathore, P.S., Blockchain-based IoT architecture for software-defined networking, in: *Blockchain, Artificial Intelligence, and the Internet of Things*, Springer International Publishing, 2022.
16. Burri, S.R., Kumar, A., Baliyan, A., Kumar, T.A., Predictive Intelligence for Healthcare Outcomes: An AI Architecture Overview, in: *2023 2nd International Conference on Smart Technologies and Systems for Next Generation Computing (ICSTSN)*, Villupuram, India, pp. 1–6, 2023, doi: 10.1109/ICSTSN57873.2023.10151477.

17. Wani, S., Ahuja, S., Kumar, A., Application of Deep Neural Networks and Machine Learning algorithms for diagnosis of Brain tumour, in: *2023 International Conference on Computational Intelligence and Sustainable Engineering Solutions (CISES)*, Greater Noida, India, pp. 106–111, 2023, doi: 10.1109/CISES58720.2023.10183528.
18. Kour, S.P., Kumar, A., Ahuja, S., An Advance Approach for Diabetes Detection by Implementing Machine Learning Algorithms, in: *2023 IEEE World Conference on Applied Intelligence and Computing (AIC)*, Sonbhadra, India, pp. 136–141, 2023, doi: 10.1109/AIC57670.2023.10263919.
19. Raj, P., Kumar, A., Dubey, A.K., Bhatia, S., Oswalt, M.S., *Quantum Computing and Artificial Intelligence: Training Machine and Deep Learning Algorithms on Quantum Computers*, De Gruyter, Berlin, Boston, 2023, [Online]. Available: https://doi.org/10.1515/9783110791402.
20. Sasubilli, G. and Kumar, A., Machine Learning and Big Data Implementation on Health Care data, in: *2020 4th International Conference on Intelligent Computing and Control Systems (ICICCS)*, Madurai, India, pp. 859–864, 2020, doi: 10.1109/ICICCS48265.2020.9120906.
21. Swarna, S.R., Kumar, A., Dixit, P., Sairam, T.V.M., Parkinson's Disease Prediction using Adaptive Quantum Computing, in: *2021 Third International Conference on Intelligent Communication Technologies and Virtual Mobile Networks (ICICV)*, Tirunelveli, India, pp. 1396–1401, 2021, doi: 10.1109/ICICV50876.2021.9388628.
22. Burugadda, V.R., Pawar, P.S., Kumar, A., Bhati, N., Predicting Hospital Readmission Risk for Heart Failure Patients Using Machine Learning Techniques: A Comparative Study of Classification Algorithms, in: *2023 Second International Conference on Trends in Electrical, Electronics, and Computer Engineering (TEECCON)*, Bangalore, India, pp. 223–228, 2023, doi: 10.1109/TEECCON59234.2023.10335817.
23. Sui, A., Sui, W., Liu, S., Rhodes, R., Ethical considerations for the use of consumer wearables in health research. *Digital Health*, 9, 20552076231153740, 2023.

21

Ethical Challenges and Guidelines for AI Deployment in Healthcare: Urological and Gastroenterological Perspectives on Ethical AI Deployment

Sujata Raghunath Kanetkar[1]* and V. M. Thorat[2]

[1]Department of Pathology, Krishna Institute of Medical Sciences, Krishna Vishwa Vidyapeeth "Deemed To Be University", Karad, Maharashtra, India
[2]Department of Pharmacology, Krishna Institute of Medical Sciences, Krishna Vishwa Vidyapeeth "Deemed To Be University", Karad, Maharashtra, India

Abstract

Artificial intelligence (AI) technologies have the potential to completely change healthcare by making diagnoses more accurate, planning treatments better, and patient results better. But using AI in healthcare brings up big social issues that need to be dealt with to protect patients' safety, privacy, and liberty. This part talks about the ethical problems and rules for using AI in urology and gastroenterology. It focuses on important rules and methods for using AI in an ethical way. The first part of the chapter talks about basic moral concepts that should lead the creation and use of AI technologies in healthcare. These include beneficence, non-maleficence, liberty, and justice. The article then talks about specific problems that come up when AI is used in urology and gastroenterology. These problems include worries about data security, the fairness and bias of AI algorithms, and how to use AI in clinical practice. There are ethical guidelines for using AI in urology and gastroenterology. These include suggestions for managing and governing data, getting patients' permission and protecting their privacy, finding ways to make AI programs less biased, and testing and validating AI technologies in the real world. There are also case studies that show how AI can be used in urology to find prostate cancer early and in gastroenterology to figure out what is wrong with the digestive system. At the end of the chapter, suggestions are made for what should

**Corresponding author*: sujatakanetkarkvv@outlook.com

Abhishek Kumar, Narayan Vyas, Pramod Singh Rathore, Abhineet Anand and Pooja Dixit (eds.) Internet of Medicine for Smart Healthcare, (449–468) © 2025 Scrivener Publishing LLC

happen next. These include making progress in AI ethics and regulation, getting parties to work together for ethical AI adoption, and keeping an eye on and judging AI technologies all the time. By following ethical rules and principles, healthcare professionals can get the most out of AI technologies while reducing the risks. This will improve patient care in urology and gastroenterology in the long run.

***Keywords*:** AI, ethical challenges, healthcare, medical privacy

21.1 Introduction

Artificial intelligence (AI) has come out as a major force in healthcare, providing new ways to improve patient results, make better use of resources, and raise the general standard of care. More and more, AI-powered tools are being used in clinical practice in areas like urology and gastroenterology. This [1] is changing the way diseases are found, treated, and controlled. But along with AI's potential, there are also big social problems that need to be carefully thought through to make sure it is used in a responsible and ethical way. AI has a huge potential to make patient care better in both urology and gastroenterology. In the field of urology, AI-powered tools can help find and diagnose urological diseases like prostate cancer, kidney stones, and urinary tract infections early on. AI programs can look at imaging data like MRI and ultrasound scans faster and more accurately than human doctors. This lets diseases be found earlier and treatments be planned more precisely. In the same way, AI could change the way that stomach diseases are diagnosed and treated in gastroenterology. AI programs can look at endoscope pictures and lab slides, which can help find diseases like colon cancer, inflammatory bowel disease, and stomach ulcers early. AI can improve gastroenterologists make more accurate diagnoses and more personalized treatments for their patients by analyzing data in real time and helping them make decisions. Even though it might be helpful [2], using AI in urology and gastroenterology brings up a number of social issues that need to be dealt with. An important worry is that AI programs might be biased. AI systems can unintentionally reinforce biases and gaps in healthcare if they are not properly taught on diverse and relevant data sets. This can cause unfair results for some patient groups. The problem of openness and responsibility is another social problem. AI systems are often "black boxes," which means that doctors and patients cannot see how decisions are made. This lack of openness can make people less likely to believe AI [3] systems and make them wonder if they are reliable and fair. Concerns have also been raised about how AI will affect the bond between a patient and a therapist. There is a chance that AI could replace

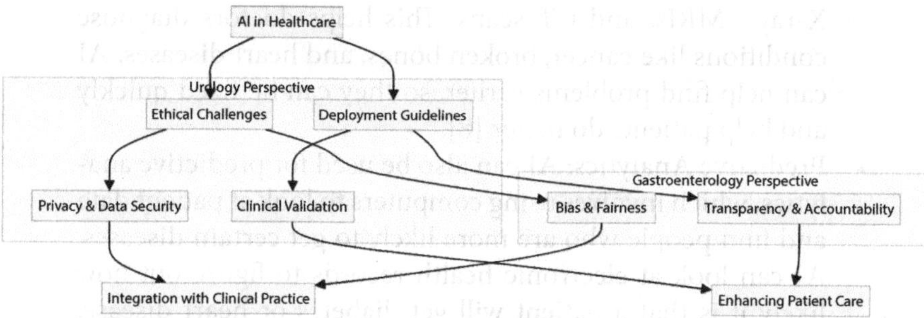

Figure 21.1 Overview of ethical challenges and guidelines for AI deployment in healthcare.

human judgment and make the relationship between a doctor and patient less important, even though it could help doctors make better decisions and patients do better. To make sure AI is used in a good way [4]. Figure 21.1 presents an overview of the ethical challenges and guidelines for AI deployment in healthcare.

Several ethics standards for the use of AI in healthcare have been put forward to deal with these problems. One important suggestion is to stress how important it is to be open and easy to understand. AI programs should be made in a way that lets doctors and patients know how decisions are made and, if necessary, question or appeal them. Another rule is how important it is to manage data and reduce bias. To [5] make sure that AI systems do not reinforce biases or unfair treatment in healthcare, they should be taught on large, representative sets of data that are varied. Also, when AI is used, it is important to put patient safety and agency first. Clinicians should always be in charge of making the most important healthcare decisions [6]. AI programs should only be used to help and improve their judgment. Also, patients should be told about how AI will be used in their care and be able to agree or disagree with it if they want to [7].

21.1.1 Overview of AI in Healthcare

AI is being used more and more in healthcare to find new ways to improve patient care, improve treatment results, and make operations run more smoothly. AI has many uses in healthcare, such as analyzing medical images, making predictions, personalizing medicine, and creating virtual health helpers.

- Medical Imaging Analysis: Medical imaging analysis is one of the most important ways that AI is used in healthcare. AI systems can very accurately look at medical pictures like

X-rays, MRIs, and CT scans. This helps doctors diagnose conditions like cancer, broken bones, and heart diseases. AI can help find problems earlier, so they can be fixed quickly and help patients do better [8].

- Predictive Analytics: AI can also be used for predictive analytics, which involves using computers to look at patient data and find people who are more likely to get certain diseases. AI can look at electronic health records to figure out how likely it is that a patient will get diabetes or heart disease, which lets doctors start treatment early and keep the disease from happening.
- Customized Medicine: AI is a key part of customized medicine, in which treatment plans are made specifically for each patient by looking at their genes, habits, and medical background. AI programs can look through huge amounts of data to find the best treatments for each patient. This [9] improves the results of treatments and lowers the risk of side effects.
- Virtual Health helpers: AI-powered virtual health helpers are becoming more and more popular. They give users personalized health tips, medicine alerts, and video consults. These virtual helpers can make it easier for people with long-term conditions to control their conditions, follow their treatment plans, and get to healthcare services [10].

21.1.2 Importance of Ethical Considerations in AI Deployment

AI brings up important social issues that need to be carefully considered. Some of the most important ethics issues to think about when using AI in healthcare are as follows:

- Concerns have been raised about the openness and comprehensibility of AI programs because they can be very complicated and hard to understand. AI systems are made in a way that lets doctors and patients know how choices are made and, if necessary, question or argue them.
- Bias and Fairness: AI systems can unintentionally reinforce biases that were present in the data that was used to teach them. This can cause results that are unfair or biased. To keep healthcare gaps from getting worse, it's crucial to implement rigorous bias detection and mitigation strategies

in AI development, ensure diverse and representative training datasets, and regularly audit AI systems for fairness and equity.

- Patient Safety and Autonomy: AI can help doctors make better decisions and help patients do better, but patient safety and autonomy must come first. In the end, professional choices should still be made by clinicians, with AI being used to help and improve their reasoning. Also, patients should be told about how AI will be used in their care and be able to agree or disagree with it if they want to.
- Data Privacy and Security: AI in healthcare needs a lot of data about patients, which makes people worry about data privacy and security. Strict rules and laws on data security must be followed to make sure that patient data is treated safely and privately.

21.2 Ethical Principles in AI Deployment

When AI tools are being built and used in healthcare, ethical concepts help guide the process. To make sure AI is used in a responsible and moral way, the four main principles—beneficence, non-maleficence, liberty, and justice—are very important.

21.2.1 Principles of Beneficence, Non-Maleficence, Autonomy, and Justice

As a matter of ethics, healthcare professionals should always try to do what is best for their patients and improve their health [11]. This is called beneficence. When AI is used in healthcare, beneficence means using AI systems to make things better for patients, raise the level of care, and learn more about medicine. For instance, AI systems can be used to find early signs of illness, suggest specific treatment plans, and help with surgeries. All of these uses add to the benefits of AI in healthcare. Non-maleficence is the moral concept that says doctors and nurses should not hurt their patients. When it comes to using AI, non-maleficence means making sure that systems are safe, accurate, and dependable so that people are at the least risk of getting hurt. This includes putting AI [12] systems through a lot of tests and making sure that they work right. It also includes regular checks and audits to find and fix any mistakes or biases that show up. When AI is used in healthcare, liberty means respecting patients' choices, values, and desires, even when AI systems are part of their care. This means making sure that patients know about how AI will be used in their care, giving them the chance to agree or disagree, and including them in the decision-making process [13].

The idea of justice stresses that healthcare resources and services should be shared fairly and equally. In terms of AI implementation, justice means making sure that all people can use AI systems, no matter their financial position, where they live, or other factors. This includes making sure that everyone has equal access [14] to AI technology and that AI algorithms are taught on varied and representative data sets so that biases and differences in healthcare do not get worse.

• Ethics to Think About When Using AI

These ideas are helpful for making sure that AI is used in healthcare in an ethical way, but they also bring up some important issues that need to be dealt with:

- Transparency and Explainability: AI systems can be hard to grab for patients and doctors because they are not always clear about how decisions are made. Making AI systems clear and easy to understand is important for gaining trust and making sure that patients and doctors can understand and question choices made by AI [17].
- Bias and Fairness: AI systems can unintentionally reinforce biases that were present in the data that was used to teach them. This can cause results that are unfair or biased. To make sure that everyone gets fair healthcare, it is important to reduce bias and make sure that AI systems are fair.
- Data Privacy and Security: AI in healthcare needs a lot of data about patients, which makes people worry about data privacy and security. To protect patient privacy and security, it is very important to make sure that strict data protection rules and guidelines are followed.

The concepts of justice, liberty, beneficence, and non-maleficence offer a useful moral framework for the use of AI in healthcare. We can make sure that AI is used in a responsible and ethical way that helps both patients and healthcare workers if we follow these rules and think about the ethical issues they bring up. Figure 21.2 represents the urological and gastroenterological perspectives on ethical AI deployment.

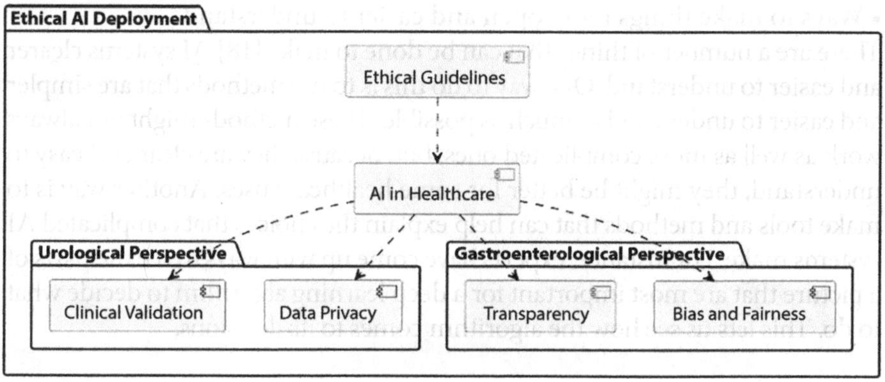

Figure 21.2 Representation of urological and gastroenterological perspectives on ethical AI deployment.

21.2.2 Transparency and Explainability in AI Algorithms

Being open and [15] able to be explained are important parts of using AI in a way that is responsible, especially in healthcare. Explainability is the ability to understand and make sense of the choices that AI algorithms make. Transparency is how open and clear AI algorithms are. Making AI systems clear and easy to understand is important for promoting trust, holding people accountable, and letting doctors and patients understand and trust choices made by AI.

• Why transparency and explainability are important
AI programs are used to [16] make important decisions in healthcare that can have a big effect on how well patients are cared for. AI programs can be used to do things like identify diseases, suggest treatment plans, or guess how well a patient will do in the future. It is very important for both doctors and patients to know how these choices are made and accept that they are based on good proof and thinking.

• Problems with being open and able to explain things
It can be hard to make AI algorithms clear and easy to understand, especially when the algorithms are complicated, like deep learning neural networks. A lot of the time, these programs work like "black boxes," which makes it hard to figure out how they make decisions. Also, because these algorithms are so complicated, it can be hard to explain their choices in a way that doctors and patients can understand.

• Ways to make things more open and easier to understand
There are a number of things that can be done to make [18] AI systems clearer and easier to understand. One way to do this is to use methods that are simpler and easier to understand as much as possible. These methods might not always work as well as more complicated ones, but, because they are clear and easy to understand, they might be better for some healthcare uses. Another way is to make tools and methods that can help explain the choices that complicated AI systems make. For instance, experts have come up with ways to see the parts of a picture that are most important for a deep learning algorithm to decide what to do. This lets us see how the algorithm comes to its decisions.

21.2.3 Accountability and Responsibility in AI Decision-Making

When AI makes decisions, accountability and responsibility are very important. This is especially true in healthcare, where AI programs' choices can have life-changing effects. Making sure that AI is accountable and responsible for its choices is important to make sure that they are made in an ethical, fair, and patient-centered way.

• Accountability in AI Decision-Making
People who build, run, or use AI systems need to be responsible for the choices those systems make. This is called "accountability in AI decision-making." This means being able to defend and explain these choices and taking responsibility for any harm they cause. Making sure that choices made by AI programs are open, fair, and answerable requires setting up clear lines of responsibility.

• Responsibility in AI Decision-Making
When it comes to AI decision-making, responsibility means that the people who build, run, and use AI systems have a social duty to make sure that they are planned, built, and used in a responsible way. This [21] includes making sure that AI systems are taught on a wide range of data sets that are representative of the whole population, are free of bias, and do not favor certain people or groups over others.

21.3 Challenges in AI Deployment in Urology and Gastroenterology

21.3.1 Data Privacy and Security Concerns

One of the focused challenges in the deployment of AI in urology and gastroenterology is data privacy and security concerns. However, this data is often sensitive and highly personal, raising concerns about patient privacy and the potential for data breaches. To address these concerns, healthcare organizations must ensure that patient data is secure and confidential. Additionally, clear policies and procedures should be in place to govern the collection, use, and sharing of patient data, ensuring that it is used only for its intended purpose and with the patient's consent.

21.3.2 Bias and Fairness in AI Algorithms

Another significant challenge in the deployment of AI in urology and gastroenterology is bias and fairness in AI algorithms. AI algorithms are trained on historical data, which may contain biases that can impact the accuracy and fairness of AI-driven decisions. To address bias and fairness in AI algorithms, developers must carefully curate and balance training data to ensure that it is diverse and representative of the patient population. Additionally, regular audits and monitoring of AI algorithms should be conducted to detect and correct biases that may arise over time. Finally, clinicians should be aware of the limitations of AI algorithms and exercise caution when interpreting their results, especially in cases where biases may be present.

21.3.3 Clinical Integration and Acceptance of AI Technologies

A key challenge in the deployment of AI in urology and gastroenterology is the alteration of AI technologies into health practice and the acceptance of these technologies by clinicians. While AI has the ability to improve diagnostic accuracy and patient outcomes, its adoption in clinical settings can be slow due to various factors, including lack of familiarity with AI technologies, concerns about job displacement, and skepticism about the reliability of AI-driven decisions [19]. To overcome these challenges, healthcare organizations must invest in training and education programs to familiarize clinicians with AI technologies and demonstrate their benefits. Additionally, clear protocols should be developed for the use of AI in clinical practice, outlining the roles and responsibilities of clinicians and ensuring that AI-driven decisions are integrated into existing workflows. Finally, ongoing monitoring and evaluation of AI technologies should be conducted to assess their impact on patient outcomes and adjust strategies as needed to ensure their effective and ethical deployment.

21.4 Guidelines for Ethical AI Deployment in Urology and Gastroenterology

As AI keeps getting better in urology and gastroenterology and used in a way that is appropriate to protect patient privacy, promote fairness, and improve patient results [20]. The following rules can help make sure that AI is used in urology and gastroenterology in a fair way:

1. *Explainability*: AI systems should be clear and easy to understand so that patients and doctors can know how decisions are made. This openness is very important for making sure that choices made by AI systems are moral and to build trust in them.
2. *Data Privacy and Security*: To protect patient data used by AI systems, healthcare organizations must put in place strong data privacy and security measures. To make sure that patient data is safe and private, this includes encryption, access rules, and regular checks.
3. *Bias and Fairness*: To make sure AI systems are free of flaws, developers should carefully choose and balance training data. To find and fix any biases that may appear over time, checks and tracking should be done on a regular basis.
4. *Informed Consent*: Patients should be told about how AI will be used in their care and gave the choice to agree or not agree if they want to. This lets people know how their information is being used so they can make smart choices about their care.
5. *Responsibility and Accountability*: People who build, run, and use AI systems should be responsible for the choices those systems make. This means being able to defend and explain these choices and taking responsibility for any harm they cause.
6. *Acceptance and Integration in Clinical Practice*: AI tools should be used in a way that helps clinicians make decisions, not takes their place. Clinicians should be taught how to use AI technologies well and should have a say in how these technologies are made and used.
7. *Constantly Checking and Evaluating*: AI algorithms should be checked and evaluated all the time to see how they affect patient results and make changes to strategies

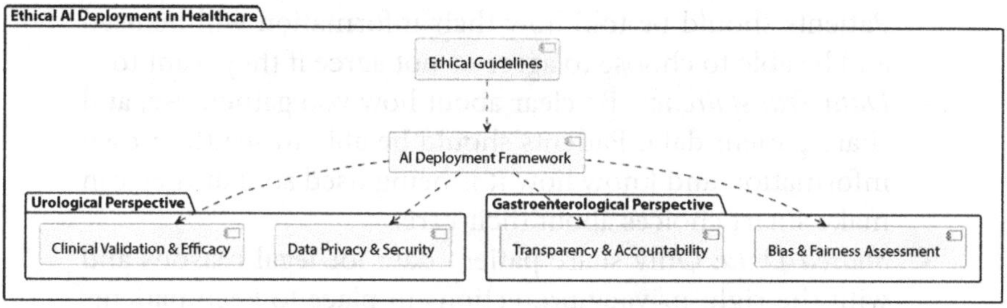

Figure 21.3 Overview of ethical AI deployment in urology and gastroenterology.

as needed to make sure that they are used in an effective and moral way.

8. *Patient-Centered Care*: AI should be used to improve patient-centered care, with the goal of making the experience and results of patients better. This includes making sure that choices made by AI are in line with what patients want and value.

Using AI in urology and gastroenterology in an ethical way means paying close attention to the principles of openness, privacy, bias, and fairness. By following these rules, healthcare companies can make sure that AI technologies are used in an honest and responsible way, which will eventually help people and make healthcare better. Figure 21.3 provides an overview of ethical AI deployment in urology and gastroenterology.

21.4.1 Data Governance and Management

Governance and control of data are important parts of using AI ethically in urology and gastroenterology. It also lowers the chance of data leaks, keeps patient information safe, and makes sure data quality stays high. When AI is used in urology and gastroenterology, the following rules can help with data control and management:

- *Quality and Integrity of Data*: Make sure that the data that is used to teach and test AI systems is correct, dependable, and up to date. To avoid bias and make sure that AI systems work well for all patient groups, data should come from a variety of sources that are representative of the whole community.
- *Privacy of Data*: Make sure that all privacy laws and rules are followed when collecting, using, and sharing medical data.

Patients should be told how their information will be used and be able to choose to agree or not agree if they want to.

- *Data Transparency*: Be clear about how you gather, use, and share patient data. Patients should be able to see their own information and know how it is being used so that they can make smart choices about their care.
- *Shared Data*: Only share patient data for legal reasons and with the right privacy protections in place to keep patients safe. Agreements for sharing data should spell out the rules for sharing data and include protections for data security and privacy.

21.4.2 Patient Consent and Privacy Protection

When AI is used in urology and gastroenterology, it is very important to get patient permission and protect their privacy. When AI is used, the following rules can help with patient agreement and data protection:

Before you collect, use, or share a patient's data for AI reasons, you should get their full permission. Patients should be told what kind of information is being gathered, how it will be used, and what risks and benefits might come with it.

- *Privacy Protection*: Encryption, access controls, and data anonymization are some of the steps that should be taken to protect patients' privacy. As much as possible, patient data should be de-identified so that it cannot be used to find out who the patient is again.
- Data minimization means that you should only collect the data that you need for the job and not too much or useless data. This lowers the chance of privacy breaches and makes sure that patient information is used in a good way. Being honest with people about how your data will be used and shared is important. Patients should be able to see their information, review it, and know how it is being used so that they can make smart choices about their care.
- *Accountability*: Make sure that healthcare organizations are responsible for keeping patient information private and following all privacy laws and rules. This includes putting in place privacy policies and procedures, figuring out how those policies and procedures affect privacy, and checking privacy practices on a regular basis.

Responsible use of AI in urology and gastroenterology requires careful management and control of data, as well as patient consent and personal protection. By following these rules, healthcare groups can make sure that patient data is gathered, used, and shared in a responsible way, which will help patients and make healthcare service better overall.

21.4.3 Bias Mitigation Strategies in AI Algorithms

When AI algorithms are biased, they can make decisions that are unfair or biased. This is especially true in healthcare, where choices based on these algorithms can have a big effect on how well patients are cared for. Because of this, reducing bias in AI systems is very important for making sure that they are used in a fair and responsible way. The following steps can help make AI programs used in urology and gastroenterology less biased:

- *Representative and Diverse Data*: To avoid bias, make sure that the training data is representative and diverse of the patient community. This includes getting information from a range of demographic groups and making sure the information is fair to show how common different diseases and traits are in the community as a whole.
- *Finding and fixing bias*: Use tools like statistical analysis and fairness metrics to regularly check and audit AI systems for bias. Check for bias and fix it if you find it. For example, train the program again with more varied data or change its settings.
- *Algorithm Transparency*: Make AI algorithms clear and easy to understand so that patients and doctors can know how decisions are made. Being open about how algorithms work can help find and fix biases in them and boost trust in their use.
- *Fairness measures*: To figure out how well AI systems work for different types of people, use fairness measures. This can help find and fix methods that are biased and make sure that they work the same way for all patients.
- *Bias Reporting*: Create a way for doctors and patients to report bias in AI systems so that developers can fix the problem.

21.4.4 Clinical Validation and Evaluation of AI Technologies

To make sure that AI technologies used in urology and gastroenterology are safe and successful, they need to be clinically validated and evaluated. In clinical validation, AI technologies are put to the test in real-life clinical situations to see how well they work and how they affect patient results. The following rules can help with the testing and approval of AI technologies in the real world:

- *Clinical Utility*: Make sure that AI technologies have shown that they are useful in the clinical setting by making patients' results or clinical processes better compared to standard care.
- *Safety and Effectiveness*: Make sure that AI technologies are safe and useful for professional practice by trying them thoroughly. This includes checking how well they work in real hospital situations and keeping an eye out for side effects.
- *Regulatory Compliance*: Make sure that AI technologies follow the rules set by regulators. For example, get approval from regulators before using them in clinical practice.
- *Interoperability*: Make sure that AI technologies can work with current healthcare systems and processes without any problems. This will keep things running smoothly and help patients more.
- *Long-Term Monitoring*: Set up ways to keep an eye on AI technologies over time to see how safe, effective, and positive they are for patients.
- *Collaboration with Clinicians*: Include clinicians in the creation, testing, and review of AI technologies to make sure that they meet the needs of clinical practice and work well with current processes.

The methods for reducing bias and clinical proof are important parts of using AI ethically in urology and gastroenterology. Healthcare organizations can make sure that AI is used in an ethical and responsible way by reducing bias in AI algorithms and making sure that AI technologies are clinically true. This will eventually help patients and make healthcare service better.

21.5 Case Studies

21.5.1 Use of AI in Urology for Early Detection of Prostate Cancer

Men get prostate cancer more than any other type of cancer, and finding it early is very important for a good treatment. Imaging data, like MRI and ultrasound scans, can be analyzed faster and more accurately by AI than by human doctors. This could help find prostate cancer earlier.

Case Study: AI Used to Find Prostate Cancer
Researchers at the University of California, Los Angeles (UCLA), did a study that shows how AI can be used in medicine to find prostate cancer early. The researchers made an AI program that looked at MRI pictures of the prostate to find spots that looked dangerous and could be signs of cancer. A lot of MRI pictures of people with and without prostate cancer were used to train the AI tool. After that, it was tried on a different set of data to see how well it could find dangerous tumors. The data showed that the AI system was better at finding dangerous spots than human doctors. It was more sensitive and specific.

Pros of Using AI to Find Prostate Cancer
There are several good things about using AI in urology to find prostate cancer early. First, AI systems can look at image data faster and more correctly than doctors. This lets diseases be found earlier and treatments be planned more precisely. This can help people have better results, with higher rates of life and lower rates of coming back.

In the second place, AI programs can help urologists and doctors do less work by automatically analyzing image data. This can give healthcare workers more time to work on other parts of taking care of patients.

Third, AI systems can help cut down on the number of tests that are not needed by correctly finding tumors that look dangerous and need more research. This can help patients feel less anxious and uncomfortable during treatments that are not necessary.

Problems and Things to Think About
Even though there might be benefits, using AI in urology to find prostate cancer comes with a number of problems and things to think about. One problem is that AI systems need a lot of different kinds of data to be trained well. So that AI systems do not have any bias, healthcare groups need to make sure that these files are representative of the whole patient

population. It is also hard because AI programs need to be tested and approved by regulators before they can be used in clinical practice. Before putting AI systems to use in healthcare, companies must make sure that they follow the rules and have been tested thoroughly.

21.5.2 Use of AI in Gastroenterology for Diagnosing Digestive Disorders

Gastroenterology is another area where AI has shown promise in making diagnoses more accurately and improving the health of patients. To help doctors figure out what is wrong with stomach problems like inflammatory bowel disease, colon cancer, and gastric ulcers, AI systems can look at endoscopy pictures and lab slides.

Case Study: How AI Can Help Diagnose Digestive Disorders
A study by experts at the Mayo Clinic shows how AI can be used in gastroenterology to help find stomach problems. The researchers created an AI system that looked at endoscope pictures of the gut to find problems that could be signs of colorectal cancer. It learned how to work with a lot of endoscope pictures of people with and without colon cancer. After that, it was tried on a different set of data to see how well it could find dangerous tumors. The results showed that the AI system was better at finding colon cancer than human endoscopists in terms of both sensitivity and specificity.

Why AI is Useful in Gastroenterology
Using AI in GI to find out what is wrong with gut systems has a lot of benefits. First, AI systems can look at endoscope photos and disease slides faster and more correctly than endoscopists. This lets problems be found earlier and treatments be planned more precisely. This can help people have better results, with higher rates of life and lower rates of coming back. The second way AI systems can help gastroenterologists do less work is by automatically analyzing scan data. This can give healthcare workers more time to work on other parts of taking care of patients. In the third place, AI systems can help make medical care better by giving doctors more accurate and trustworthy data. This can help cut down on missed treatments and processes that are not needed, which can improve the health of patients.

Problems and Things to Think About
There may be some benefits to using AI in gastroenterology to diagnose stomach issues, but there are also some problems and things to think about.

It can be hard because AI programs need to be tested and approved by regulators before they can be used in clinical practice. Before putting AI systems to use in healthcare, companies must make sure that they follow the rules and have been tested thoroughly. Another problem is that AI programs need to be added to healthcare processes that are already in place. To have the most effect on patient care, healthcare groups must make sure that AI programs can be easily added to current systems and processes.

21.6 Future Directions and Recommendations

21.6.1 Advancements in AI Ethics and Regulation

As AI keeps getting better at urology and gastroenterology, AI ethics and rules need to get better too to make sure that AI technologies are used in an honest and responsible way. For example, rules and guides should be made for the right way to use AI in healthcare, and rules and regulations should be put in place to control AI use in nursing. Building AI ethics rules that deal with the special ethical problems AI [21] brings up in healthcare, like the need for openness, responsibility, and fairness, is one area of progress. Healthcare workers, AI writers, lawmakers, and patients should all work together to make these recommendations so that they reflect a wide range of objectives and points of view. The creation of rules that control the use of AI in healthcare is another area that has made progress. Before they are used in clinical settings, these models should make sure that AI technologies meet strict rules for safety, effectiveness, and ethical use. This can help keep people safe and make sure that AI technologies really improve the way healthcare is provided.

21.6.2 Collaboration Between Stakeholders for Ethical AI Deployment

For AI to be used ethically in urology and gastroenterology, all parties involved must work together. People who work in healthcare, people who make policy, and patients all need to work together to make sure that AI technologies are created, used, and implemented in an honest, open, and responsible manner. Setting up multi-stakeholder agreements, which bring together people from different fields to create and apply ethical rules and legal policies for AI in healthcare, is one way to get people to work together. It is possible for these relationships to help make sure that everyone's needs and views are heard and that AI technologies are used in a way that helps people and society as a whole.

21.6.3 Continuous Monitoring and Evaluation of AI Technologies

AI technologies must be constantly checked and evaluated to make sure that they stay safe, useful, and moral throughout their entire lifetime. Healthcare groups should set up ways to keep an eye on how AI technologies are used in clinical settings and figure out how they affect patient results. Real-world data can be used to test AI technologies and see how well they work with different types of patients and in different healthcare situations. This can help find any problems or biases that may come up so that they can be fixed. Additionally, healthcare companies should regularly check and audit AI technologies to make sure they follow social standards and legal requirements. This can help find any possible risks or laws that are being broken and make sure that AI technologies are being used properly.

21.7 Conclusion

When AI is used in urology and gastroenterology, it brings up some special ethics issues that need to be dealt with to make sure that AI is used responsibly in healthcare. Concerns about data protection and security, bias and fairness in AI systems, and the use and acceptance of AI technologies in clinical practice are some of these problems. To deal with these problems, healthcare groups need to follow moral rules and standards that encourage openness, responsibility, and care that are focused on the patient. There should be rules about how to use AI ethically in urology and gastroenterology. These rules should cover things like data control and management, patient approval and privacy protection, ways to make AI models less biased, and clinical assessment and review of AI technologies. For AI to be used ethically in urology and gastroenterology, there needs to be progress in AI ethics and control, collaboration between parties, and ongoing tracking and assessment of AI technologies. Healthcare groups can make sure that AI technologies are created, applied, and used in a way that helps people and improves healthcare service by focusing on these areas. While using AI in urology and gastroenterology can be hard at times, it also has a lot of potential to make things better for patients and raise the level of care. While using AI in healthcare, companies should follow social guidelines and focus on patient-centered care. This way, AI technologies can be used to change the way healthcare is provided and make patients' lives better.

References

1. Lund, B.D., Wang, T., Mannuru, N.R., Nie, B., Shimray, S., Wang, Z., ChatGPT and a new academic reality: Artificial Intelligence-written research papers and the ethics of the large language models in scholarly publishing. *J. Assoc. Inf. Sci. Technol.*, *74*, 5, 570–581, 2023.
2. Wittmann, J., Science fact vs science fiction: a ChatGPT immunological review experiment gone awry. *Immunol. Lett.*, *256*, 42–47, 2023.
3. González, R., Classical AI linguistic understanding and the insoluble Cartesian problem. *AI Soc.*, *35*, 441–450, 2020.
4. Naber, N., Ambiguous insiders: An investigation of Arab American invisibility. *Ethn. Racial Stud.*, *23*, 1, 37–61, 2000.
5. Laird, J.E., Lebiere, C., Rosenbloom, P.S., A standard model of the mind: Toward a common computational framework across artificial intelligence, cognitive science, neuroscience, and robotics. *AI Mag.*, *38*, 4, 13–26, 2017.
6. Parrilla, J.M., ChatGPT use shows that the grant-application system is broken. *Nature*, *623*, 7986, 443–443, 2023.
7. Khan, S.H., AI at Doorstep: ChatGPT and Academia. *J. Coll. Physicians Surg. Pak.*, *33*, 1085–1086, 2023.
8. Jeyaraman, M., Ramasubramanian, S., Balaji, S., Jeyaraman, N., Nallakumarasamy, A., Sharma, S., ChatGPT in action: Harnessing artificial intelligence potential and addressing ethical challenges in medicine, education, and scientific research. *World J. Methodol.*, *13*, 4, 170, 2023.
9. Meyer, J.G., Urbanowicz, R.J., Martin, P.C., O'Connor, K., Li, R., Peng, P.C., Bright, T.J., Tatonetti, N., Won, K.J., Gonzalez-Hernandez, G., Moore, J.H., ChatGPT and large language models in academia: opportunities and challenges. *Biodata Min.*, *16*, 1, 20, 2023.
10. Kumar, S.A., Kumar, A., Dutt, V., Agrawal, R., Multi Model Implementation on General Medicine Prediction with Quantum Neural Networks, in: *2021 Third International Conference on Intelligent Communication Technologies and Virtual Mobile Networks (ICICV)*, Tirunelveli, India, pp. 1391–1395, 2021, doi: 10.1109/ICICV50876.2021.9388575.
11. Raj, P., Dubey, A.K., Kumar, A., Rathore, P.S., Blockchain-based iot architecture for software-defined networking, in: *Blockchain, Artificial Intelligence, and the Internet of Things*, Springer International Publishing, 2022.
12. Burri, S.R., Kumar, A., Baliyan, A., Kumar, T.A., Predictive Intelligence for Healthcare Outcomes: An AI Architecture Overview, in: *2023 2nd International Conference on Smart Technologies and Systems for Next*

Generation Computing (ICSTSN), Villupuram, India, pp. 1–6, 2023, doi: 10.1109/ICSTSN57873.2023.10151477.

13. Wani, S., Ahuja, S., Kumar, A., Application of Deep Neural Networks and Machine Learning algorithms for diagnosis of Brain tumour, in: *2023 International Conference on Computational Intelligence and Sustainable Engineering Solutions (CISES)*, Greater Noida, India, pp. 106–111, 2023, doi: 10.1109/CISES58720.2023.10183528.
14. Kour, S.P., Kumar, A., Ahuja, S., An Advance Approach for Diabetes Detection by Implementing Machine Learning Algorithms, in: *2023 IEEE World Conference on Applied Intelligence and Computing (AIC)*, Sonbhadra, India, pp. 136–141, 2023, doi: 10.1109/AIC57670.2023.10263919.
15. Raj, P., Kumar, A., Dubey, A.K., Bhatia, S., Oswalt, M.S., *Quantum Computing and Artificial Intelligence: Training Machine and Deep Learning Algorithms on Quantum Computers*, De Gruyter, Berlin, Boston, 2023, [Online]. Available: https://doi.org/10.1515/9783110791402.
16. Sasubilli, G. and Kumar, A., Machine Learning and Big Data Implementation on Health Care data, in: *2020 4th International Conference on Intelligent Computing and Control Systems (ICICCS)*, Madurai, India, pp. 859–864, 2020, doi: 10.1109/ICICCS48265.2020.9120906.
17. Swarna, S.R., Kumar, A., Dixit, P., Sairam, T.V.M., Parkinson's Disease Prediction using Adaptive Quantum Computing, in: *2021 Third International Conference on Intelligent Communication Technologies and Virtual Mobile Networks (ICICV)*, Tirunelveli, India, pp. 1396–1401, 2021, doi: 10.1109/ICICV50876.2021.9388628.
18. Burugadda, V.R., Pawar, P.S., Kumar, A., Bhati, N., Predicting Hospital Readmission Risk for Heart Failure Patients Using Machine Learning Techniques: A Comparative Study of Classification Algorithms, in: *2023 Second International Conference on Trends in Electrical, Electronics, and Computer Engineering (TEECCON)*, Bangalore, India, pp. 223–228, 2023, doi: 10.1109/TEECCON59234.2023.10335817.
19. Deulofeu, M., Kolářová, L., Salvadó, V., María Peña-Méndez, E., Almáši, M., Štork, M., Pour, L., Boadas-Vaello, P., Ševčíková, S., Havel, J., Vaňhara, P., Rapid discrimination of multiple myeloma patients by artificial neural networks coupled with mass spectrometry of peripheral blood plasma. *Sci. Rep.*, 9, 1, 7975, 2019.
20. Radakovich, N., Meggendorfer, M., Malcovati, L., Hilton, C.B., Sekeres, M.A., Shreve, J., Rouphail, Y., Walter, W., Hutter, S., Galli, A., Pozzi, S., A geno-clinical decision model for the diagnosis of myelodysplastic syndromes. *Blood Adv.*, 5, 21, 4361–4369, 2021.
21. Patel, S.S., Sekeres, M.A., Nazha, A., Prognostic models in predicting outcomes in myelodysplastic syndromes after hypomethylating agent failure. *Leuk. Lymphoma*, 58, 11, 2532–2539, 2017.

22

Future Directions and Opportunities in AI-Driven Healthcare: Family Medicine and Anesthesiological Future Directions in AI-Driven Healthcare

Vithal K. Dhulkhed[1]* and Shekhar M. Kumbhar[2]

[1]*Department of Anaesthesiology, Krishna Institute of Medical Sciences, Krishna Vishwa Vidyapeeth Deemed To Be University, Karad, Maharashtra, India*
[2]*Department of Community Medicine, Krishna Institute of Medical Sciences, Krishna Vishwa Vidyapeeth, Karad, Maharashtra, India*

Abstract

Artificial intelligence (AI) has become a major force in healthcare, providing new ways to improve patient results and make professional processes more efficient. This chapter looks at the future trends and chances of AI-powered healthcare, focused on how it can be used in general medicine and anesthesia. In family medicine, AI could change the way patients are cared for by using electronic health records to create personalized treatment plans, making patient screening and risk assessment more efficient, and using predictive analytics to better handle chronic diseases. Telemedicine systems and online tracking tools that are driven by AI can also make it easier for people to get care and get involved, especially in rural or neglected areas. In the same way, AI has the potential to improve perioperative care in anesthesia by helping with planning and assessing patients before surgery, watching patients during surgery and helping doctors make decisions in real time, and allowing for personalized care plans after surgery. AI programs can help anesthesiologists give anesthesia in a safer and more effective way, which can lead to better results for patients and fewer problems. Even with these improvements, problems like data protection, sharing, and following the rules need to be fixed before AI can fully be used in healthcare. It is believed that future advances in AI, such as better machine learning techniques and natural language processing, will make AI-driven healthcare systems even better.

**Corresponding author*: vkdhulkhedkvv@outlook.com

Abhishek Kumar, Narayan Vyas, Pramod Singh Rathore, Abhineet Anand and Pooja Dixit (eds.) Internet of Medicine for Smart Healthcare, (469–488) © 2025 Scrivener Publishing LLC

This paper looks at case studies and current trends in AI-driven healthcare to show how AI will be used in general medicine and anesthesia in the future. As AI keeps getting better, it could change the way healthcare is provided, make it more affordable, and improve patient results. This makes the field very interesting and full of chances for growth and new ideas.

***Keywords*:** AI, anesthesiologic perspectives, clinical applications, medicine, medical technology

22.1 Introduction

AI has changed the healthcare field by creating new ways to identify illnesses, tailor treatments to each patient, and make treatments more effective. AI has a huge potential to improve care, speed up processes, and, most importantly, save lives in the fields of general medicine and anesthesia. This essay looks at the future directions and chances for AI-powered healthcare, focused on how it can be used and improved in general medicine and anesthesia. Family medicine is an important part of basic care because it helps people of all ages with all of their health needs. The field of anesthesiology, on the other hand, deals with pain control and making sure that patients are safe during surgery. Adding AI technologies to both areas could be very helpful [1]. These technologies could make healthcare workers smarter, help people make better decisions, and speed up the care paths for patients. AI-powered healthcare in family medicine can help find and diagnose diseases earlier, make personalized treatment plans possible, and give people the tools they need to take charge of their own health. In anesthesiology, AI can help doctors keep a closer eye on patients during surgery, predict and stop problems before they happen, and find the best doses of anesthesia to get the best results. Anesthesiology and family medicine are not the only fields that face problems when they try to use AI. Concerns [2] about ethics, data protection, and the need for governmental control are all important problems that need to be dealt with. However, the possible benefits are much greater than the problems, so healthcare groups must use AI-based solutions. This paper will look at where AI is now in family medicine and anesthesiology, point out the best chances for future growth and development, and talk about the problems that need to be solved before AI-driven healthcare can reach its full potential in these areas. Family doctors and anesthesiologists can improve the level of care they give, assist patients better, and eventually change the healthcare system for the better by using AI technologies. Figure 22.1 provides an overview of family medicine and anesthesiology in AI-driven healthcare.

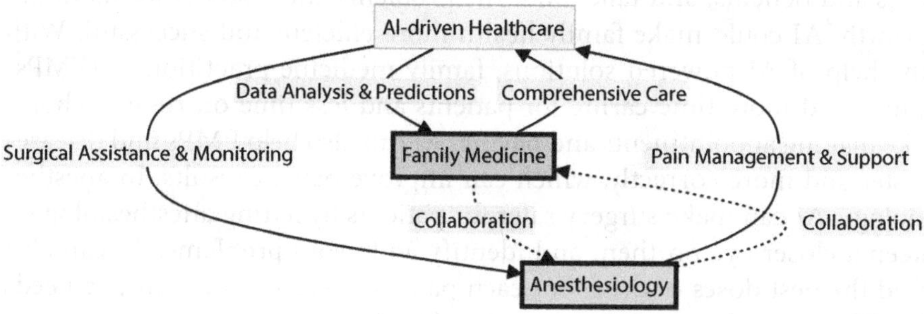

Figure 22.1 Overview of family medicine and anesthesiological in AI-driven healthcare.

22.1.1 Overview of AI in Healthcare

AI has become a major force in healthcare, offering new ways to solve problems that have been around for a long time in evaluation, treatment, and patient care. AI technologies like machine learning, natural language processing [3], and robots could completely change the healthcare industry by making clinical processes more efficient and accurate, making personalized medicine possible, and giving people more control over their health. In the past few years, artificial intelligence (AI) has been used more and more in healthcare systems around the world. It is used for everything from imaging for diagnosis and drug finding to managing electronic health records (EHRs) and keeping an eye on patients. In particular, machine learning algorithms are very good at looking at big datasets to find trends and make predictions. This helps doctors make more accurate evaluations and treatment suggestions. Natural language processing (NLP) has [4] also been very important in healthcare. It lets computers understand and analyze human language, which makes it easier for healthcare workers and patients to communicate, record, and find information. Robotics, on the other hand, has been used in surgery and therapy to make treatments more accurate and less invasive. On the whole, AI has the potential to change healthcare by making it better, easier to get, and cheaper. But problems like data protection, following the rules, and moral concerns need to be dealt with to make sure AI is used responsibly and effectively in healthcare.

22.1.2 Scope of the Chapter

This section will talk about where [5] AI-powered healthcare is going and what it can do in the future in general medicine and anesthesia. In particular, it will look at where AI is now in these areas, show its most important uses and benefits, and talk about the problems and chances for its future growth. AI could make family health more efficient and successful. With the help of AI-powered solutions, family medicine practitioners (FMPs) can spend more time caring for patients and less time on routine chores like making appointments and paying. AI can also help FMPs find diseases faster and more correctly, which can improve patient results. In anesthesiology, AI can make surgery safer for patients by letting anesthesiologists keep a closer eye on them and identify and avoid problems. AI can also find the best doses of drugs for each patient based on their unique needs [6]. This can help with pain control and healing.

22.2 AI Applications in Family Medicine

Artificial intelligence (AI) is changing family medicine by providing new ways to improve care for patients, make processes more efficient, and help doctors make better decisions. This part will talk about two important uses of AI in family medicine: managing EHRs and sorting patients into groups based on their risk.

22.2.1 Electronic Health Record (EHR) Management

Electronic health records (EHRs) are computer [7] copies of patients' paper charts that hold information about their medical history, illnesses, medicines, treatment plans, vaccine dates, allergies, x-rays, and lab test results. EHRs are necessary for giving good care to patients, but the huge amounts of data that they hold can make them hard for healthcare workers to handle. Natural language processing (NLP) and machine learning are two types of AI that can help healthcare workers better handle EHRs. NLP can be [8] used to take important information from unorganized text in EHRs, like release reports and progress notes, and turn it into structured data that is easy to find and analyze. Machine learning systems can look at EHR data and find patterns and trends that human workers might miss. For instance, machine learning can be used to figure out from a patient's EHR data which ones are most likely to get certain illnesses. This lets doctors act quickly and avoid bad results. Giving healthcare workers useful knowledge at the point of care is another way AI can help them make better treatment decisions. For instance, clinical decision support systems (CDSSs) driven by AI [9] can look at a patient's EHR data and suggest a diagnosis and treatment plan based on the most recent standards backed by proof. AI can make EHR handling in family medicine more efficient and effective by helping healthcare workers get useful information from EHR data and make better treatment decisions.

22.2.2 Patient Triage and Risk Stratification

Patient assessment is the process of figuring out which patients need [10] care the most based on how bad their health is. In family medicine, AI can help simplify and improve the patient screening process by looking at patient data and giving each patient a priority level based on their risk factors. Machine learning systems can look at a lot of information about a patient, like their traits, medical history, symptoms, and vital signs, to figure out which ones are most likely to have problems or need fast care. This data can help healthcare professionals figure out which people need help right away and make sure that they get it on time and correctly. AI can also help doctors divide people into groups based on how likely they are to get certain diseases. For instance, machine learning systems can look at EHR data to find people who are very likely to get diabetes or heart disease and suggest ways to keep them from getting those diseases, like making changes [11] to their lifestyle or taking medicine. AI can help FMPs better organize their time and resources so that patients get the right care at the right time by simplifying the processes of triaging patients and figuring out their risk. This could improve the health of patients, lower the cost of healthcare, and make the whole system work better.

22.2.3 Chronic Disease Management

Chronic diseases like diabetes [12], high blood pressure, and asthma cause a lot of sickness and death around the world. Taking care of chronic diseases requires constant tracking, managing medications, and making changes to one's lifestyle, which can be hard for both patients and healthcare workers. AI could make managing chronic diseases in family medicine better by giving more personalized, proactive, and effective care. Personalized treatment plans are a key way that AI is used to help people with chronic diseases. Machine learning programs can look at a person's medical background, genetic information, and living choices to make a treatment plan that is unique to them and meets their needs. For instance, AI can help doctors guess how a patient's diabetes will get worse over time and suggest changes to their lifestyle or medications that will help them better handle their condition [13].

AI can also help people with chronic diseases take their medications as prescribed. AI can find patients who are likely to not follow their treatment

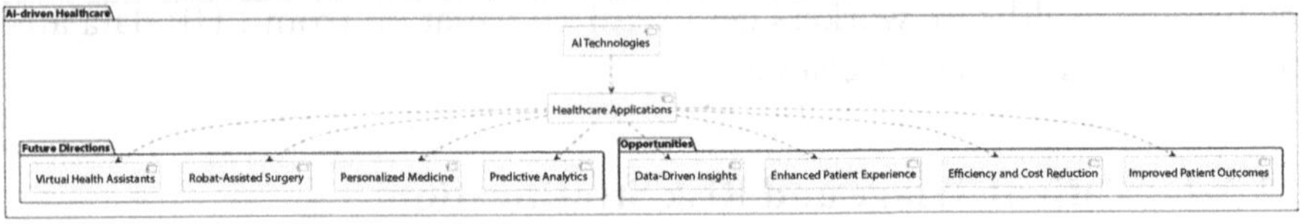

Figure 22.2 AI-driven healthcare system.

plans by looking at data from EHRs, medication records, and patient-reported results. It can then help these patients by reminding them [14], educating them, or giving them personalized support. AI can also make a big difference in keeping an eye on people with long-term illnesses from afar. Wearable technology and mobile apps with AI algorithms can keep an eye on patients' vital signs, exercise levels, and obedience to medicine in real time and let doctors know if there are any problems. This can help find problems early on and keep people from having to go to the hospital or have other bad things happen. Overall, AI has the ability to change how chronic diseases are managed in family medicine by making individualized treatment plans, making it easier for patients to take their medications as prescribed, and letting doctors keep an eye on them from afar. Family medicine practitioners (FMPs) can help people with chronic diseases get better care more quickly and effectively by using AI technologies. This will improve their quality of life and lower the cost of their care [15]. Figure 22.2 depicts an AI-driven healthcare system.

22.2.4 Telemedicine and Remote Monitoring

Because of the COVID-19 outbreak, telemedicine and online tracking are becoming more and more important in general medicine. AI can improve telemedicine and distant tracking by giving patients, no matter where they are, more personalized and effective care. Telemedicine systems that use AI can look at a patient's symptoms, medical background, and vital signs in real time to make better evaluations and treatment suggestions [16]. Patients can get care from the comfort of their own homes, cutting down on the need for in-person trips. AI systems built into remote tracking devices can also help doctors keep better track of their patients' health. For instance, AI can look at data from smart devices to find early signs of getting worse in people with chronic diseases and let doctors know so they can help before things get worse. Family medicine practitioners (FMPs) can give their patients more convenient and individualized care by using AI technologies. This can improve patients' health and make them happier.

22.2.5 Patient Engagement and Education

Getting patients involved and teaching them are important parts of managing chronic diseases well. By giving patients specific health information, messages, and support, AI can help get them more involved and educated. With the help of AI, robots and virtual helpers can give people specialized and engaging information about their health, medications, and lifestyle suggestions. This [17] can help people understand their health better and choose the best care for them. AI can also help patients be more involved by making things more like games and giving them rewards. Apps that use AI can, for example, thank people for meeting health goals like eating well or working out regularly. This can encourage them to be more involved in controlling their health.

22.3 AI Applications in Anesthesiology

The area of anesthesiology is changing because AI is making care safer, more efficient, and better for patients. AI technologies, like computer vision and machine learning, are being used to improve planning and assessment before surgery, as well as tracking and decision support during surgery. We will talk about these important uses of AI in anesthesiology in this part.

22.3.1 Preoperative Assessment and Planning

An important part of anesthesia care is the preoperative exam, which helps anesthesiologists figure out the best way to administer anesthesia for surgery based on the patient's health. AI can help with initial evaluation by looking at a patient's medical records, lab results, imaging studies, and other relevant data to find possible risks and make the best plans for anesthesia. Machine learning systems can look at a [18] lot of data to figure out how likely it is that a patient will have problems like sickness and vomiting after surgery, breathing problems, or unstable blood flow. This knowledge can help anesthesiologists make changes to their plans for anesthesia that will lower these risks and improve the results for their patients. AI can also help with planning before surgery by modeling different drug situations and guessing what will probably happen. For instance, AI programs can help doctors figure out the best amount of anesthesia drugs to give a patient based on their age, weight, and medical background. This way, doctors can get the level of anesthesia that they want while minimizing side effects [19].

Overall, AI can help with planning and assessing patients before surgery in anesthesiology by giving more personalized and accurate anesthesia care. This can improve results for surgery patients.

22.3.2 Monitoring During Surgery and Helping with Decisions

Anesthesiologists have to keep an eye on their patients' vital signs and change the amount of drugs they are given to make sure that they are safe and comfortable during surgery. AI can help anesthesiologists make decisions by studying real-time data from different sources, like anesthesia tools, patient monitors, and surgical equipment [20]. This can improve tracking during surgery. Patterns in the data can be used by machine learning algorithms to predict changes in a patient's state, like their blood pressure, heart rate, and oxygen levels, before they happen. Anesthesiologists can use this information to plan for and avoid problems like low blood pressure or low oxygen levels, which can improve the result for the patient. AI can also help doctors make decisions during treatment by giving them real-time advice based on the most up-to-date standards and best practices. For instance, AI programs can suggest the right amount of anesthetic drugs to use or steps to take to handle problems that arise during surgery. Overall, AI can help anesthesiologists make better choices and do better tracking during surgery by giving them fast and accurate information. This lets them make better decisions and provide better care for patients during surgery. AI is changing the field of anesthesia by making it easier to plan and measure before surgery, as well as to watch and make decisions during surgery. Anesthesiologists can give better, more specialized, and more efficient anesthesia care by using AI tools. This means that patients who are having surgery have better results [21].

22.3.3 Postoperative Care and Recovery

Postoperative care is an important part of anesthesia management because it includes keeping an eye on patients as they heal from surgery and taking care of any problems that come up afterward. AI can make a big difference in post-surgery care by using prediction analytics, personalized suggestions, and the ability to watch patients from afar. Machine learning algorithms can look at a patient's vital signs, lab results, and drug records after surgery to figure out how likely it is that they will have consequences like surgical site infections, breathing issues, or a thrombosis. This knowledge can help doctors and nurses act quickly to stop bad things from happening.

AI can also help make post-surgery care more personalized by looking at things like a patient's age, weight, and medical background to make sure their healing plans are just right for them. For instance, AI programs can suggest certain medicines, changes to a patient's food, or physical treatment routines based on the needs of each patient. Remote tracking devices with AI algorithms can also help doctors keep an eye on their patients' growth while they are not in the hospital. Wearable technology can keep an eye on patients' vital signs, exercise levels, and ability to take their medications as prescribed, and let healthcare professionals know if there are any problems. Overall, AI could make post-surgery care and healing better by offering prediction data, personalized suggestions, and the ability to watch from afar. Healthcare workers can improve the level of care they give to patients healing from surgery by using AI technologies. This can lead to better results and lower healthcare costs.

22.3.4 Anesthesia Drug Dosing and Management

Dosing and managing anesthesia drugs are important parts of anesthesia care because giving the right amount of drugs is key to keeping patients safe and comfortable during surgery. AI can help improve the dosing and

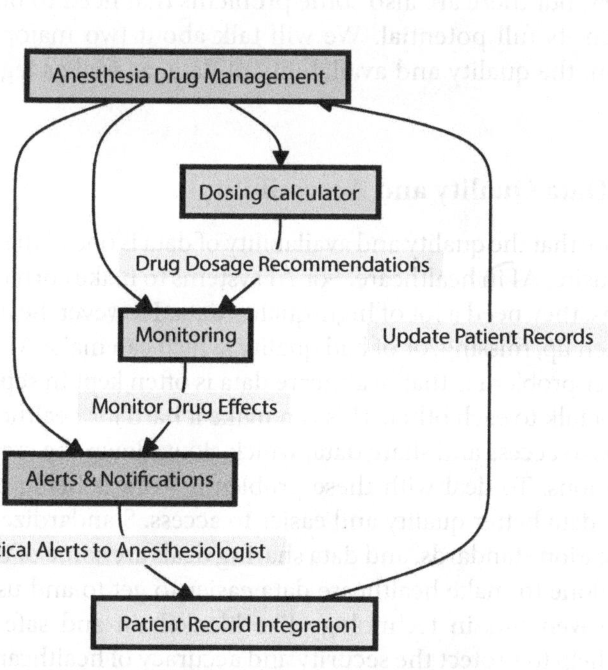

Figure 22.3 Overview of anesthesia drug dosing and management.

control of anesthetic drugs by giving anesthesiologists real-time tracking and decision support. Machine learning systems can look at bodily data about patients, like their heart rate, blood pressure, and oxygen levels, to figure out how much anesthesia drugs they should be given. This information can help anesthesiologists fine-tune the amount of anesthesia given, which lowers the risk of giving too little or too much. AI can also help with handling anesthesia drug combinations and side effects by looking at a patient's past medications and figuring out what risks might be there. For example, AI systems can let anesthesiologists know about possible allergic reactions or drug combinations, which helps them decide how to give medications. In general, AI could make dosing and managing anesthesia drugs better by giving anesthesiologists real-time tracking and decision help. Anesthesiologists can give sedation drugs more safely and effectively by using AI technologies. This means that patients who are having surgery have better results. Figure 22.3 provides an overview of anesthesia drug dosing and management.

22.4 Current Challenges and Limitations

There are many good things about AI that can be used in family medicine and surgery, but there are also some problems that need to be fixed before it can reach its full potential. We will talk about two major problems in this section: the quality and availability of data, as well as legal and moral issues.

22.4.1 Data Quality and Accessibility

Making sure that the quality and availability of data is one of the biggest problems with using AI in healthcare. For AI systems to make correct guesses and suggestions, they need a lot of high-quality data. However, healthcare data is often broken up, missing, or of bad quality, which can make AI apps less useful. Another problem is that healthcare data is often kept in separate systems that cannot talk to each other. This can make it hard for healthcare providers and groups to access and share data, which slows down the creation and use of AI solutions. To deal with these problems, work is being done to make healthcare data better quality and easier to access. Standardized data forms, communication standards, and data sharing deals are some of the things that are being done to make healthcare data easier to get to and use in AI apps. Also, improvements in technology like blockchain and safe data sharing platforms help to protect the security and accuracy of healthcare data, which makes it more suitable for use in AI apps.

22.4.2 Legal and Ethical Considerations

There are a lot of legal and moral issues that need to be carefully thought through when AI is used in healthcare. Data protection and security is one of the main issues. AI systems need to be able to access private patient data like medical records and x-rays, which needs to be kept safe to protect patient privacy. Another worry is that AI programs might be biased. AI programs learn from past data, which could show flaws or differences in how healthcare is provided. If these flaws are not fixed, then AI systems could make healthcare even less fair or even less fair than it already is. When AI is used to make healthcare decisions, there are also social issues to think about. Even though AI can give useful information and suggestions, healthcare workers are ultimately responsible for taking care of patients. It is very important that AI is used to help doctors make decisions, not to replace their expertise. To deal with these legal and moral issues, healthcare groups need to make clear rules and policies about how AI can be used in healthcare. This includes making sure that data security laws are followed, like the Health Insurance Portability and Accountability Act in the US, and putting in place ways to stop bias and make AI programs clear.

22.4.3 Integration with Existing Healthcare Systems

Adding AI to healthcare systems that are already in place is hard because healthcare infrastructure is complicated, systems do not always work well together, and people do not like change. Integration that works, on the other hand, can lead to better speed, accuracy, and patient results. One of the biggest problems is making sure that AI systems can work with other hospital IT systems. A lot of healthcare companies still use old methods that might not work well with AI. As a result, it can be hard to integrate data, talk to other systems, and make everything work together. Another problem is that healthcare workers do not like change. People may be skeptical or unwilling to change their habits, ways of doing things, or views in order to use AI technologies. Health care workers may be worried about losing their jobs or how it will affect the level of care they give to patients.

Healthcare groups should be smart about how they use AI to deal with these problems. To do this, you need to carefully look at the current systems and processes, find places where AI can be useful, and make a clear plan for how to apply it. When choosing AI options, healthcare businesses should also put connectivity and data sharing at the top of their lists. This includes making sure that AI systems can work well with other healthcare workers and systems and can easily connect with other IT systems. Overall, putting

AI into healthcare systems that are already in place needs IT experts, healthcare workers, and managers to work together to make sure that AI technologies are used correctly and help provide high-quality care.

22.4.4 Patient Privacy and Consent

When using AI in healthcare, it is important to protect patients' privacy and get their permission first. AI technologies often need to access private patient data like medical records, x-rays, and genetic information. This data needs to be kept safe to protect patient privacy. Making sure that patient data is used in an open and honest way is one of the biggest problems. A lot of data is needed for AI systems to make good guesses and suggestions, which can make people worry about how patient data is gathered, kept, and used. To deal with these problems, healthcare groups should set up strong policies and processes for protecting data. This includes getting patients' permission before using their data for AI purposes, making sure that data is protected and sanitized to protect patients' privacy, and setting clear rules for sharing and accessing data.

Also, healthcare groups should make it a priority to teach and raise knowledge among patients about the use of AI in healthcare. This includes telling people what will happen with their data, how it will be used, how their privacy will be protected, and how they can use their rights related to their data.

22.5 Future Directions and Opportunities

Artificial intelligence (AI) is about to change family medicine and anesthesia by giving doctors new ways to help patients, make processes more efficient, and make better decisions. We will talk about four main areas where AI could go and the chances it has to grow in family medicine and anesthesiology in the future: improvements in machine learning and deep learning, better CDSSs, personalized medicine and treatment planning, and AI-driven research and drug discovery.

22.5.1 Advancements in Machine Learning and Deep Learning

Machine learning and deep learning are areas of AI that are changing quickly and could have a big impact on healthcare. Advances in machine learning and deep learning can help doctors make more accurate evaluations, make more personalized treatment plans, and help patients do better. Medical imaging is one area where machine learning and deep learning can make a big difference. Medical pictures like x-rays, MRIs, and CT scans can be analyzed by AI systems to find problems and help doctors make assessments. For instance, deep learning systems have been shown to be very good at finding breast cancer in scans, with rates of accuracy that are the same as or even higher than those of human doctors.

In predicted analytics, machine learning and deep learning can be used in a different way. AI programs can look at patient data like EHRs, lab reports, and vital signs to figure out which patients are most likely to get certain illnesses or problems. This knowledge can help doctors and nurses act quickly to stop bad things from happening. Overall, progress in machine learning and deep learning shows a lot of promise for making evaluation and treatment more accurate and faster in general medicine and anesthesia. Health care professionals can give better, more personalized care to their patients by using these tools.

22.5.2 Enhanced Clinical Decision Support Systems

Medical professionals can use CDSS to help them make smart choices about how to care for their patients. AI can improve CDSS by making suggestions in real time, looking at large amounts of data, and making assessments and treatment plans more accurate. AI can improve CDSS by combining data from different sources, like EHRs, imaging studies, and genetic information, to give a fuller picture of the patient's health. This can help doctors and nurses make better choices about what to diagnose and how to treat people. AI can also make CDSS more accurate by looking at huge amounts of data to find patterns and trends that human providers might miss. For instance, AI systems can look at EHR data to figure out which patients are most likely to get sepsis. This lets doctors act quickly and avoid problems. Overall, AI could make CDSS better in general medicine and anesthesia by giving real-time advice, reviewing large amounts of data, and making evaluations and treatment plans more accurate. Healthcare workers can improve the level of care they give and patients' results by using these tools.

22.5.3 Personalized Medicine and Treatment Planning

Personalized medicine, which is also called precision medicine, is a way of providing health care that designs treatment plans for each person based on their unique genetics, surroundings, and way of life. AI can be very important in personalized medicine because it can look at patient data and make treatments fit the needs of each patient. AI can help make personalized medicine possible by looking at genetic information to find DNA traits that might affect how people react to certain drugs. This knowledge can help doctors choose the best medicines and doses for each patient, which lowers the risk of side effects and improves the result of treatment.

AI can also help make treatment plans more personalized by looking at information about each patient, like their medical background, symptoms, and habits, to find the best ways to help each one. AI programs can look at EHR data to figure out which patients are most likely to benefit from a certain treatment. They can then use this knowledge to make specific treatment plans for those patients. Overall, AI could change personalized medicine in family medicine and anesthesia by looking at patient data to make treatments fit the needs of each patient. With these tools, healthcare workers can improve the results of treatments, lower costs, and make patients happier.

22.5.4 AI-Driven Research and Drug Discovery

AI is also changing research and drug development by giving scientists new ways to find disease targets, make new drugs, and make the design of clinical trials better. Research that is based on AI can help doctors in family medicine and surgery come up with new treatments and solutions that can help patients do better and have a better quality of life. One area where AI is having a big effect is on finding new drugs. AI programs can look through huge databases of chemical molecules to find possible drug prospects and guess how they will interact with biological targets. This could help researchers find good drug options faster and more effectively than the old ways. AI can also make clinical trials better by looking at data on patients to find good candidates for trials and guess how patients will react to treatments. Researchers can use this knowledge to make better and more efficient clinical studies, which will speed up the approval process for new treatments and solutions. In general, AI-driven study and drug finding have a lot of potential to make family medicine and anesthesia better. Researchers and healthcare professionals can speed up the creation of new treatments and solutions by using these tools. This will improve patient results and quality of life.

22.6 Case Studies and Examples

22.6.1 Successful AI Implementations in Family Medicine

Family medicine has successfully used AI to improve care for patients, simplify processes, and make better treatment decisions. Several great uses of

AI in family medicine have shown that AI has the ability to change the way healthcare is provided. To give you some examples:

- *IBM Watson for Oncology*: IBM Watson for Oncology is a tool driven by AI that helps doctors give personalized treatment suggestions to cancer patients. Based on the most recent standards and clinical studies, the tool looks at patient data like medical records and genetic information to find the best treatment choices. It has been shown that IBM Watson for Oncology can make treatment suggestions more accurate and cut down on the time it takes for doctors to make treatment plans.
- *Streams by Google DeepMind*: Streams by Google DeepMind is an AI-powered mobile app that helps doctors keep an eye on patients with acute kidney injury (AKI). The app looks at information about patients, like blood test results and vital signs, to let doctors know when their health changes in a way that might need their help. Streams have been shown to speed up the time that it takes to find AKI and lower the risk of bad results for patients.
- *Ada Health*: Ada Health is a platform driven by AI that helps people figure out what their symptoms mean and get personalized health advice. The platform has a robot that asks patients about their symptoms and medical background. It then uses AI algorithms to come up with a list of possible findings and suggestions for what to do next. Ada Health has been shown to make it easier for patients to get health information and cut down on visits to doctors that are not necessary. What is Buoy Health? Buoy Health is an AI-powered tool that helps people figure out what is causing their complaints and get personalized health advice. The platform has a robot that asks patients about their symptoms and medical background. It then uses AI algorithms to come up with a list of possible findings and suggestions for what to do next. The use of Buoy Health has been shown to make patients happier and ease the workload of healthcare workers. Overall, these examples show how AI could change family medicine by making diagnosis and treatment more accurate and faster, getting patients more involved, and lowering the cost of healthcare. As AI keeps getting better, we can expect to see even more creative uses of it in family medicine that make care and benefits for patients even better.

22.6.2 New Ways That AI is Being Used in Anesthesiology

AI is being used in anesthesiology to make patients safer, improve clinical results, and make the control of anesthesia better. Several new AI uses in anesthesiology have shown potential in making care better while under anesthesia. The following are some examples:

- *Closed-Loop Anesthesia Delivery Systems*: These systems use AI algorithms to keep an eye on patients' vital signs all the time and change the amount of anesthesia that they are given in real time to make sure that they stay at the right level. It has been shown that these methods make it easier to give anesthesia correctly and lower the chance of problems that can happen because of anesthesia.
- *Predictive analytics for anesthesia problems*: AI systems can look at patient data like medical history, vital signs, and anesthesia doses to figure out which patients are most likely to have issues linked to anesthesia, like low blood pressure or low oxygen levels. This knowledge can help anesthesiologists step in early and stop bad things from happening.
- *Virtual Reality for Preoperative Anxiety*: Virtual reality (VR) is being used as a non-drug way to help people who are going to have surgery feel less anxious before the procedure. Virtual reality (VR) can make settings that are so real that they take patients' minds off of their worries and help them calm down before surgery. Studies have shown that VR can make patients happier and less anxious before surgery.
- *Machine Learning for Anesthetic Drug Dosage*: Based on a patient's age, weight, and medical background, machine learning algorithms can look at patient data and guess the best amount of anesthetic drugs to give them. This can help anesthesiologists make sure that the right amount of anesthesia is given to each patient, which lowers the risk of bad effects and improves the patient's result.

22.7 Conclusion

The future of AI-driven healthcare in family medicine and anesthesiology looks bright, with lots of chances to try new things and make patient care better. Improvements in machine learning and deep learning are making healthcare more personalized and efficient. AI can be used for a wide range of things, from better diagnosis and treatment plans to better patient involvement and tracking from afar. In family medicine, AI is changing the way doctors give care. AI-powered tools offer individualized treatment plans, the ability to watch patients from afar, and better CDSSs. These improvements are making it possible for doctors to give more exact and effective care, which is good for patients and makes them happier. AI is changing the field of anesthesiology by making it easier and more accurate to give anesthesia, as well as by better patient safety and clinical results. New technologies that are powered by AI are changing the way anesthesia care is given, making it safer and more effective. Examples include closed-loop anesthesia delivery systems and predictive analytics for anesthesia problems. The future of AI-driven healthcare in family medicine and anesthesiology will depend on how well AI technologies keep getting better and how well they are integrated into current healthcare systems and processes. Healthcare providers must stay alert as AI continues to change and deal with problems related to data quality and usability, as well as legal and moral issues. Overall, AI-driven healthcare in family medicine and anesthesia has a bright future ahead of it. It will help improve patient care, streamline processes, and make better clinical decisions. Healthcare workers can continue to give patients high-quality, personalized care by using AI technologies. This will improve patients' health and make the healthcare system run more smoothly.

References

1. Oren, O., Gersh, B.J., Bhatt, D.L., Artificial intelligence in medical imaging: switching from radiographic pathological data to clinically meaningful endpoints. *Lancet Digit. Health*, *2*, 9, e486–e488, 2020.
2. Baig, M.M., GholamHosseini, H., Moqeem, A.A., Mirza, F., Lindén, M., A systematic review of wearable patient monitoring systems–current challenges and opportunities for clinical adoption. *J. Med. Syst.*, *41*, 1–9, 2017.
3. Kim, J., Campbell, A.S., Wang, J., Wearable non-invasive epidermal glucose sensors: A review. *Talanta*, *177*, 163–170, 2018.
4. Monteriù, A., Prist, M.R., Frontoni, E., Longhi, S., Pietroni, F., Casaccia, S., Scalise, L., Cenci, A., Romeo, L., Berta, R., Pescosolido, L., A smart sensing architecture for domestic monitoring: Methodological approach and experimental validation. *Sensors*, *18*, 7, 2310, 2018.
5. Patel, D. and Tarakji, K.G., Smartwatch diagnosis of atrial fibrillation in patient with embolic stroke of unknown source: a case report. *Cardiovasc. Digit. Health J.*, *2*, 1, 84–87, 2021.

6. Sükei, E., Norbury, A., Perez-Rodriguez, M.M., Olmos, P.M., Artés, A., Predicting emotional states using behavioral markers derived from passively sensed data: data-driven machine learning approach. *JMIR Mhealth Uhealth*, 9, 3, e24465, 2021.
7. Kumar, S.A., Kumar, A., Dutt, V., Agrawal, R., Multi Model Implementation on General Medicine Prediction with Quantum Neural Networks, in: *2021 Third International Conference on Intelligent Communication Technologies and Virtual Mobile Networks (ICICV)*, Tirunelveli, India, pp. 1391–1395, 2021, doi: 10.1109/ICICV50876.2021.9388575.
8. Raj, P., Dubey, A.K., Kumar, A., Rathore, P.S., Blockchain-based iot architecture for software-defined networking, in: *Blockchain, Artificial Intelligence, and the Internet of Things*, Springer International Publishing, 2022.
9. Burri, S.R., Kumar, A., Baliyan, A., Kumar, T.A., Predictive Intelligence for Healthcare Outcomes: An AI Architecture Overview, in: *2023 2nd International Conference on Smart Technologies and Systems for Next Generation Computing (ICSTSN)*, Villupuram, India, pp. 1–6, 2023, doi: 10.1109/ICSTSN57873.2023.10151477.
10. Wani, S., Ahuja, S., Kumar, A., Application of Deep Neural Networks and Machine Learning algorithms for diagnosis of Brain tumour, in: *2023 International Conference on Computational Intelligence and Sustainable Engineering Solutions (CISES)*, Greater Noida, India, pp. 106–111, 2023, doi: 10.1109/CISES58720.2023.10183528.
11. Kour, S.P., Kumar, A., Ahuja, S., An Advance Approach for Diabetes Detection by Implementing Machine Learning Algorithms, in: *2023 IEEE World Conference on Applied Intelligence and Computing (AIC)*, Sonbhadra, India, pp. 136–141, 2023, doi: 10.1109/AIC57670.2023.10263919.
12. Raj, P., Kumar, A., Dubey, A.K., Bhatia, S., Oswalt, M.S., *Quantum Computing and Artificial Intelligence: Training Machine and Deep Learning Algorithms on Quantum Computers*, De Gruyter, Berlin, Boston, 2023, [Online], Available: https://doi.org/10.1515/9783110791402.
13. Sasubilli, G. and Kumar, A., Machine Learning and Big Data Implementation on Health Care data, in: *2020 4th International Conference on Intelligent Computing and Control Systems (ICICCS)*, Madurai, India, pp. 859–864, 2020, doi: 10.1109/ICICCS48265.2020.9120906.
14. Swarna, S.R., Kumar, A., Dixit, P., Sairam, T.V.M., Parkinson's Disease Prediction using Adaptive Quantum Computing, in: *2021 Third International Conference on Intelligent Communication Technologies and Virtual Mobile Networks (ICICV)*, Tirunelveli, India, pp. 1396–1401, 2021, doi: 10.1109/ICICV50876.2021.9388628.
15. Burugadda, V.R., Pawar, P.S., Kumar, A., Bhati, N., Predicting Hospital Readmission Risk for Heart Failure Patients Using Machine Learning Techniques: A Comparative Study of Classification Algorithms, in: *2023 Second International Conference on Trends in Electrical, Electronics, and*

Computer Engineering (TEECCON), Bangalore, India, pp. 223–228, 2023, doi: 10.1109/TEECCON59234.2023.10335817.

16. Chengoden, R., Victor, N., Huynh-The, T., Yenduri, G., Jhaveri, R.H., Alazab, M., Bhattacharya, S., Hegde, P., Maddikunta, P.K.R., Gadekallu, T.R., Metaverse for healthcare: a survey on potential applications, challenges and future directions. *IEEE Access*, 11, 12765–12795, 2023.
17. Shaik, T., Tao, X., Higgins, N., Li, L., Gururajan, R., Zhou, X., Acharya, U.R., Remote patient monitoring using artificial intelligence: Current state, applications, and challenges. *Wiley Interdiscip. Rev.: Data Min. Knowl. Discov.*, 13, 2, e1485, 2023.
18. Javaid, M., Haleem, A., Singh, R.P., ChatGPT for healthcare services: An emerging stage for an innovative perspective. *BenchCouncil Trans. Benchmarks Stand. Eval.*, 3, 1, 100105, 2023.
19. O'Mara-Eves, A., Thomas, J., McNaught, J., Miwa, M., Ananiadou, S., Using text mining for study identification in systematic reviews: a systematic review of current approaches. *Syst. Rev.*, 4, 1–22, 2015.
20. Weissler, E.H., Naumann, T., Andersson, T., Ranganath, R., Elemento, O., Luo, Y., Freitag, D.F., Benoit, J., Hughes, M.C., Khan, F., Slater, P., The role of machine learning in clinical research: transforming the future of evidence generation. *Trials*, 22, 1–15, 2021.
21. Suh, I., McKinney, T., Siu, K.C., Current perspective of metaverse application in medical education, research and patient care. *Virtual Worlds*, 2, 2, 115–128, 2023, April, MDPI.

About the Editors

Dr. Abhishek Kumar is currently working as an Assistant Director/ Associate professor in the Computer Science & Engineering Department at Chandigarh University, Punjab, India. He holds a Doctorate in computer science from the University of Madras. He is a Post-Doctoral Fellow in Ingenium Research Group Ingenium Research Group Lab, Universidad De Castilla-La Mancha, Ciudad Real, and Ciudad Real Spain. He has an MTech in Computer Science & Engineering, and a B.Tech in I.T. from Rajasthan Technical University, Kota, India. He has a total Academic teaching experience of more than 13 years, along with 2 years of teaching assistantship. He has more than 170 publications in reputed, peer-reviewed National and International Journals, books, & Conferences. He has guided more than 30 MTech Projects at national and international levels, and 4 PhD scholars completed their Degrees under his Guidance. His research areas include artificial intelligence, renewable energy image processing, computer vision, data mining, and machine learning. He has been session chair and keynote speaker at many international conferences and webinars in India and abroad. He has been a reviewer for IEEE and Inderscience Journal. He has authored/Co-Authored 7 books published internationally and edited 63 books (Published & ongoing with IET, Elsevier, Wiley, IGI GLOBAL Springer, Apple Academic Press, De Gruyter and CRC etc. He serves as Series Editor for four books series: Quantum Computing with De Gruyter, Germany, Intelligent Energy System with Elsevier, & Mathematical Methods in the Digital Age with De Gruyter, Germany, and AI for Environment Sustainability with De Gruyter, Germany.

Narayan Vyas is an Assistant Professor in the Department of Computer Science and Application at Vivekananda Global University, Jaipur, India, where he is actively involved in research and development in computer science. He qualified for the NTA UGC NET & JRF on his first attempt, showcasing his academic excellence. He has extensive knowledge of the Internet of Things and Mobile Application Development and has provided training to students worldwide. He has published numerous articles in reputed, peer-reviewed national and international Scopus-indexed conferences and journals. Additionally, he has served as a keynote speaker and resource person for several workshops and webinars conducted in India. His research areas include Remote Sensing, the Internet of Things, Machine Learning, Deep Learning, and Computer Vision. He is an IEEE member and an active member of various international and national societies, such as IEEE Young Professionals, the Indian Society of Remote Sensing (ISRS), the IEEE Geosciences and Remote Sensing Society (GRSS), the IEEE Sensors Council, ACM, and the International Society of Photogrammetry and Remote Sensing (ISPRS). He also received the International Distinguished Young Researcher Award from the ASET Journal of Management Science. He has edited more than 12 books with various reputable publishers, including Wiley, De Gruyter, Apple Academic Press, and IGI Global.

Dr. Pramod Singh Rathore is currently working as an Assistant professor of Department of Computer and Communication Engineering, Manipal University Jaipur. He is Doctorate in Computer Science & Engineering from University of Engineering and Management, Jaipur (UEM) and done M. Tech in Computer Sci. & Engineering from Government engineering college Ajmer, Rajasthan Technical University, Kota India. With over 12 years of academic teaching experience, he has published more than 85 papers in reputable, peer-reviewed national and international journals, books, and conferences, including Wiley, IGI GLOBAL, Taylor & Francis Springer, Elsevier Science Direct, Annals of Computer Science, Poland, and IEEE. He has co-authored and edited numerous books with well-known publishers such as Wiley, CRC Press, and USA. His research interests include NS2, computer networks, mining, and DBMS. He serves on the editorial and advisory committees of the Global Journal Group and is also a member of various national and international professional societies in the field of engineering and research, including the ACM, the International Association of Engineers (IAENG).

Dr. Abhineet Anand brings over 24 years of academic and administrative expertise to his role as Dean at Bahra University, Shimla Hills. His research spans key areas, including Cloud Computing, Cloud Security, Decision Trees, Nearest Neighbor Methods, Clustering, Rule Induction, Optical Fiber Switching in Wavelength Multiplexing, and Automata Theory. Research and Publications: Dr. Anand has a significant body of work, with 8 Book Editor roles, over 65 Scopus-indexed papers, 14 SCI-indexed papers, 16 papers in International Conferences, and 12 papers in International Journals. Academic Contributions: He has chaired or co-chaired multiple special sessions at international conferences and has been an active Technical Program Committee member for 20 conferences. His leadership and extensive research contribute to his reputation as a leading figure in the academic community.

Pooja Dixit is an Assistant Professor in the Department of Computer Science at Sophia Girls' College (Autonomous), Ajmer, India, and she is pursuing her Ph.D. in Computer Science at Manipal University Jaipur. With over seven years of academic teaching and two years of research experience, she has published 25+ research papers in reputed journals, books, and conferences. Her research interests include Artificial Intelligence, Machine Learning, and Data Mining. Pooja is a member of various professional societies, including IAENG, IRED, IAIP, ISRD, and ISOC, and serves on the editorial board of IOSRD. She has also edited a book published by Wiley. She holds an MCA and BCA from MDS University, Ajmer, India.

Index

Also of Interest

Check out these other related titles from Scrivener Publishing

Smart Hospitals: 5G, 6G, and Moving Beyond Connectivity, Edited by Arun Kumar, Manoj Gupta, Sanjeev Sharma, Er. Himanshu Sharma, and Khursheed Aurangzeb, ISBN: 9781394275441. Discover the potential of 5G, 6G, and smart hospitals beyond connectivity in Smart Hospitals: 5G, 6G, and Moving Beyond Connectivity and learn how these advancements are revolutionizing healthcare and the digital world.

Artificial Intelligence-Based System Models in Healthcare, Edited by A. Jose Anand, K. Kalaiselvi and Jyotir Moy Chatterjee, ISBN: 9781394242498. *Artificial Intelligence-Based System Models in Healthcare* provides a comprehensive and insightful guide to the transformative applications of AI in the healthcare system.

The Impact of Algorithmic Technologies on Healthcare, Edited by Parul Dubey, Mangala Madankar, Pushkar Dubey and Bui Thanh Hung, ISBN: 9781394305469.

Nanoengineered Materials for Medical and Healthcare Applications, Edited by Radhakrishnan E.K, Ashitha Jose and Visakh. P. M., ISBN: 978111979164.

3D Printing in Healthcare: Novel Applications, Edited by Rishabha Malviya and Rishav Sharma, ISBN: 9781394234202.

Artificial Intelligence-Enabled Digital Twin for Smart Manufacturing, Edited by Amit Kumar Tyagi, Shrikant Tiwari, Senthil Kumar Arumugam, and Avinash Kumar Sharma, ISBN: 9781394303571. An essential book on the applications of AI and digital twin technology in the smart manufacturing sector.

Quantum Computing and Artificial Intelligence: The Industry Use Cases, Edited by Pethuru Raj, B. Sundaravadivazhagan, Mariya Ouaissa, V. Kavitha and K. Shantha Kumari, ISBN: 9781394242368.

Artificial Intelligence Enabled Businesses: How to Develop Strategies for Innovation, Edited by Sweta Dixit, Mohit Maurya, Vishal Jain and Geetha Subramaniam, ISBN: 9781394233977.

INTEGRATED DEVICES FOR ARTIFICIAL INTELLIGENCE AND VLSI: VLSI Design, Simulation and Applications, Edited by Balwinder Raj, Suman Lata Tripathi, Tarun Chaudhary, K. Srinivasa Rao, and Mandeep Singh, ISBN: 9781394204359. With its in-depth exploration of the close connection between microelectronics, AI, and VLSI technology, this book offers valuable insights into the cutting-edge techniques and tools used in VLSI design automation, making it an essential resource for anyone seeking to stay ahead in the rapidly evolving field of VLSI design.

DECENTRALIZED SYSTEMS AND DISTRIBUTED COMPUTING, Edited by Sandhya Avasthi, Suman Lata Tripathi, Namrata Dhanda, and Satya Bhushan Verma, ISBN: 978139420436. This book provides a comprehensive exploration of next-generation internet, distributed systems, and distributed computing, offering valuable insights into their impact on society and the future of technology.

EXPLAINABLE MACHINE LEARNING MODELS AND ARCHITECTURES: Real-Time System Implementation, Edited by Suman Lata Tripathi and Mufti Mahmud, ISBN: 9781394185849. This cutting-edge new volume covers the hardware architecture implementation, the software implementation approach, and the efficient hardware of machine learning applications.

MACHINE LEARNING TECHNIQUES FOR VLSI CHIP DESIGN, Edited by Abhishek Kumar, Suman Lata Tripathi, and K. Srinivasa Rao, ISBN: 9781119910398. This cutting-edge new volume covers the hardware architecture implementation, the software implementation approach, and the efficient hardware of machine learning applications with FPGA or CMOS circuits, and many other aspects and applications of machine learning techniques for VLSI chip design.

The manufacturer's authorised representative in the EU for product safety is Oxford University Press España S.A. of El Parque Empresarial San Fernando de Henares, Avenida de Castilla, 2 – 28830 Madrid (www.oup.es/en or product.safety@oup.com). OUP España S.A. also acts as importer into Spain of products made by the manufacturer.

Printed in the USA/Agawam, MA
April 4, 2025

885451.001